PIMLICO

151

A HISTORY OF AUSTRALIA

Born in Sydney in 1915, Manning Clark was educated at the University of Melbourne and Balliol College, Oxford. He was Professor of History at the Australian National University and later became the first Professor of Australian History. In 1975 he was made a Companion of the Order of Australia, in recognition of his writing of the *History*, and was named Australian of the Year for 1980. He died in 1991.

Michael Cathcart was born in 1965. He was educated at Melbourne Grammar School, the University of Melbourne and the Australian National University. He is currently writing a history of water-dreaming in Australia.

A HISTORY
OF AUSTRALIA

MANNING CLARK

Abridged by Michael Cathcart

PIMLICO

P I M L I C O

An imprint of Random House
20 Vauxhall Bridge Road, London SW1V 2SA

Random House Australia (Pty) Ltd
20 Alfred Street, Milsons Point, Sydney
New South Wales 2061, Australia

Random House New Zealand Ltd
18 Poland Road, Glenfield
Auckland 10, New Zealand

Random House South Africa (Pty) Ltd
PO Box 337, Bergvlei, South Africa

Random House UK Ltd Reg. No. 954009

This abridgement first published by Chatto & Windus 1993
Pimlico edition 1995

1 3 5 7 9 10 8 6 4 2

Printed in England by Clays Ltd, St Ives plc

ISBN 0-7126-6205-7

Contents

Maps

Conversions

1d (penny)	0.83 cent
1s (shilling)	10 cents
£1 (pound)	$2
£1 1s (guinea)	$2.10
1 inch	2.54 centimetres
1 mile	1.60 kilometres
1 acre	0.40 hectare

Preface

The entry in my diary for 11 June 1991 reads 'Lunch with Manning Clark'. He thought an abridgement of *A History of Australia* was a good idea and wanted to look over this young man who reckoned he could make it work. Four days after that appointment was made, I woke up, switched on my radio and heard the news. Manning Clark was dead. It was an act of fate which Manning would have relished: he had lost his chance to vet me; I had lost my chance to meet the Great Historian.

It all began, let us say, in February 1956 when Charles Hope Manning Clark walked into the British Museum. At the age of 40, he had commenced research for his epic tragedy, a history which was to occupy him for the next thirty years. The first volume appeared in 1962. It was the passionate work of a still youthful and charismatic teacher, an intellectual who had attracted the attention of ASIO, a rebel who was taking a stand against both the simplicities of the Empire loyalists and the new orthodoxies of the young left-wing historians. When the final volume appeared in 1986, the author was a retired university professor: an august and prophetic public figure who was revered by many of his former students, fêted by the press but increasingly dismissed by younger historians as an anachronism. These historians mistrusted the reputation which *A History* had popularly acquired as the definitive Australian history, the authoritative version from which all others took their bearings.

Of course it was no such thing. As Clark's own carefully chosen title proclaimed, this was quite definitely *a* history of Australia, one of the many histories which might be imagined. But the physical appearance of the six famous volumes reinforced the popular misconception. They are large books, each bound in blue cloth, embossed in gold lettering and bearing the imprint of a university press. They look scholarly, authoritative and formidable. They had become cultural icons, reassuring Australians that they did indeed have a substantial national history. Few Australians appreciated how passionate and unconventional a world those books contained. The principal aim of this abridgement is to open Clark's rich and strange Australia to a wider public gaze.

Clark saw himself, not as a propounder of truths, but as an artist who posed those fundamental questions about the human condition which defy easy resolution. His purpose was both to enrich and to trouble a new society by giving voice to its tragedies, to tell his fellow Australians who they were, and what they might become. As a writer, he had much in common with T. S. Eliot. Though each man represented everything the other detested in politics, both believed that the twentieth century had become a wasteland, or, as Clark put it, a kingdom of nothingness, in which spiritual struggle had been abandoned for the vacuity of modern popular culture. Each saw himself as a Tiresias, a lone prophet in search of spiritual renewal— for himself and for the society to whom he spoke. Both believed that the Nietzschean view of tragedy, in which mighty opposites were held in tension, revealed great truths about the human condition; and both used vocal and literary fragments to create a literature which attempted to challenge the spiritual void.

Clark believed that in order to tell a story well, the historian needed to create what he called indirect narrators. He was constantly experimenting with the use of such voices to articulate historical points of view. Thus, when the Aborigines are spoken of as 'savages' or 'cannibals', it is because we are seeing them through the mind of a particular European. When we hear that Governor Darling's wife was a source of exquisite gladness to him, we are momentarily seeing her through Darling's eyes. Clark also used his *History* as a platform for his own passionate opinions. Over the years, as his preoccupations shifted and his political beliefs altered, his prose style underwent marked developments and changes.

By the start of Volume VI, Clark had added a new voice to his cast, a voice which he thought of as a Greek chorus, announcing arrivals and offering a demotic appraisal of public affairs. Astonishingly, it is a voice which always speaks in the present tense, sometimes interrupting halfway through a sentence. ('Frank Anstey has also decided to give up politics. Everything was sour in his mouth. He has decided the difference between Labor and the conservatives was the difference between Tweedledum and Tweedledee.') Some readers find these dislocations of tense unsettling, and it was suggested that the abridgement might be better without them. But they remain, for reasons which go to the heart of this project. This abridgement seeks to preserve Clark's core narrative, to develop his key characters, to dramatize his principal conflicts and to liberate Clark's prose at its best. It does not attempt to resolve disparities or to 'sanitize' views which have

become unpopular or to eliminate Clark's less fashionable manner-
isms. In short, this re-dramatisation seeks to remain true to the
shifting voices, spirit and concerns of Clark's original text.

But there are important differences between the original and its
abridgement. Clark was writing a vast, open-ended saga. His style
was often incantatory and repetitive; his examples were many; his
opportunities for diversion were unlimited. In order to re-stage
Clark's central drama in one-sixth of the original space, I have had
to intervene in his prose, adjusting its pace and rhythms as well as
editing its content. I have condensed, summarized, paraphrased
and inverted original sentences. I have written links, removed
adjectives, added clauses, shifted punctuation, excised events, cut
entire chapters and transposed key phrases from one passage to
another. Where the removal of a paragraph brought two remaining
sentences into an awkward juxtaposition, I altered a word or a
phrase to cover the join. I have done anything which seemed
necessary to translate Clark's *History* faithfully from one medium to
another, to transform a multi-volume epic into a book which functions as an organic work of literature. Oddly, the longer I spent on
this project, the less my own decisions seemed to matter. The more
engaged I became, the more strongly I felt that Clark's own prose
was re-creating itself, as though *A History* already had an abridgement embedded within it and my sole function was to lay it bare.

There is one other aspect of this book which requires explanation:
the fact that it opens with the First Fleet. Clark appreciated, much
earlier than did many other white historians, that the human
history of the continent began with the Aborigines. But the research
on which he relied for his discussion of Aboriginal history prior to
1788 is now largely out of date and of little interest to the general
reader, and I have decided to omit it. Those who wish to read this
earlier material have only to consult the original text.

My thanks to Dymphna and Sebastian Clark for their warmth
and encouragement, to John Hirst who suggested many improvements to the final draft, and to the University of Melbourne Library
for permission to reproduce the portrait sketch on page xvi. I owe
much to the members of the Geography Department at the University of Melbourne who gave me companionship, encouragement
and a place to work upon this most solitary of tasks. Venetia
Nelson's intelligent editing curtailed my excesses and improved
this edition in countless ways. As for the follies which remain, I can
only trust that the petty ones are my own and that the grand ones
belong to that landscape which is the vision splendid of Manning
Clark.

M.C.
University of Melbourne, June 1993

Kahan

Louis Kahan's portrait sketch of Manning Clark
Reproduced with permission from the University of Melbourne
Library

My hope then and now was that a history of Australia could have the same effect on the soul of its readers as did music on the soul of Saul. A story about the past, if well told, could take readers up into the high mountains from where they would see, as if were, all the kingdoms of the world, be aware of the field of the possible in human affairs, and might even catch a glimpse of the direction of the great river of life. I had read Aristotle on tragedy. I hoped that the story of the past in Australia would nourish in the reader the eye of pity. The story of the past should have the same effect as all great stories. It should increase wisdom and understanding. It should make the reader aware of what previously he had seen 'through a glass darkly'. It should turn the mind of the reader towards the things that matter. It must bring the reader to the frontier where music takes over from words. It must make the reader want to hear music even though words never can be music.

Manning Clark
A Historian's Apprenticeship, Melbourne University Press, 1992

BOOK ONE

From the First Fleet
to the
Age of Macquarie
1788–1823

Since Copernicus man rolls from the centre into X.

F. Nietzsche, The Will to Power

All the wealth of love lavished of old upon Him, who was immortal, would be turned upon the whole of nature, on the world, on men, on every blade of grass.

F. M. Dostoevsky, A Raw Youth

1

The Foundation

Civilization did not begin in Australia until the last quarter of the eighteenth century. Early on the golden morning of 13 May 1787, a fleet of eight ships, the *Sirius*, the *Supply*, the *Alexander*, the *Charlotte*, the *Scarborough*, the *Friendship*, the *Prince of Wales*, and the *Lady Penrhyn*, together with three store ships, weighed anchor in Portsmouth harbour, and sailed down the Channel for the high seas. In the town the shutters in the shops were still lowered, and one clergyman on shore went down on his knees to ask God's forgiveness on all of them. Otherwise no one noticed the departure. On board, in addition to over four hundred seamen, there were 750-odd convicts, 211 marines and officers, 27 officers' wives, 32 children as well as the Governor and his staff of nine—just over 1000 people. In London, the home of over a third of the convicts, the weather that day favoured the lovers of riding and walking. The parks presented a fine show of carriages, of smart beaux and nags. The weather favoured too the display of summer dresses, and as the tartan was all the fashion, nothing but highland laddies and lasses were to be seen in the parks. At Carlton House, the Prime Minister, Mr William Pitt, was closeted for three hours with the Prince of Wales, discussing the problems of the latter's debts, which had by then reached £161 000. On the movements of the Secretary of the Home Office, Lord Sydney, on 13 May history is silent. He had been a forceful advocate of the expedient of transporting British prisoners to New South Wales, but there is no reason to suppose that a man for whom votes were the stuff of life pondered what had happened at Portsmouth that morning. The *London Chronicle* contented itself with the simple statement that early on Sunday 13 May the transports and convict ships had sailed for Botany Bay.

Among the officers on board was Captain-Lieutenant Watkin Tench, a man who found it easy to like his fellow human beings, a man who wrote of their motives with an insight sweetened by charity, a man who delighted in the beauty of the world, who looked confidently to its improvement rather than brooded sombrely over any darkness in the hearts of men. According to him, the faces of the convicts indicated a high degree of satisfaction as the ships moved down the Channel, though in some the pangs of separation from their native land could not be wholly suppressed. Marks of distress were more perceptible among the men than among the women. One woman dropped some tears, but soon wiped them. After that, the accent of sorrow was no longer heard as more genial skies and a change of scene banished repining and discontent, and introduced in their stead cheerfulness and acquiescence in their lot, now not to be altered.

Tench and most of his fellow officers were men of talent and experience, men who had volunteered from motives of ambition, curiosity and a desire to serve, but they were not aware of those gigantic forces of good and evil which had driven their predecessors in the great south seas to glory and damnation. They belonged to a climate of opinion which encouraged restraint and moderation. Yet at least one of their number was passion's slave. He was Ralph Clark, a second officer of the marines, who shortly after the fleet weighed anchor began a diary in which he gushed out all the anguish and torment of his daily life:

> May the 13th, 1787. 5 O'clock in the morning, The Sirius made the signal for the whole fleet to get under way, O gracious God send that we may put in to Plymouth or Torbay on our way down Channel that I may see our dear and fond affectionate Alicia and our sweet son before I leave them for this long absence, O Almighty God heer my prayer and grant me this request . . . what makes me so happy this day is it because I am in hoppes the fleet will put into Plym Oh my fond heart lay still for you may be disappointed I trust in God you will not.

But the fleet did not put in to Plymouth; and on 14 May Clark wrote: 'Oh my God all my hoppes are over of seeing my beloved wife and son'.

The Reverend Richard Johnson was troubled too. He found the captain of his ship close, unsociable and ill-natured; and the ship's company very profane. On the second Sunday, after he preached to the convicts on the heinous evil of common swearing, he was pleased to note that for days afterwards no coarsenesses passed their lips. So he knelt down in his cabin and beseeched his God to convince them of the folly and wickedness of such conduct. On that same Sunday a design by some convicts on the *Scarborough* to mutiny and take possession of the ship was discovered, the two ringleaders being punished with two dozen lashes each. These things, however, did not trouble Johnson. He felt a warm desire of soul to pour out his sins and sorrows before the Lord.

As the fleet sailed to Teneriffe and then on to Rio de Janeiro, the convicts seemed incapable of experiencing that remorse and contrition which the pangs of exile were intended to rouse in their breasts, but displayed the depravity of their hearts. Some men used their ingenuity to gain admission to the apartment of the female convicts, while another coined quarter dollars out of old buckles, buttons and pewter spoons with such cunning and address that the surgeon, John White, wrote that he wished these qualities had been employed to more laudable purposes. The Reverend Johnson was torn between the temptation to blame their depravity and the temptation to blame his own poor powers for his failure to communicate his message of hope. Clark poured his guilt about drinking and gambling on to the pages of his diary, interspersed with words of tenderness for his fond Alicia and his darling son, and how very glad he was to see that when a corporal flogged one of the damned whores on board the ship he did not play with her but laid it home.

The mind of Captain Arthur Phillip, the commodore of the fleet, was on other things, sometimes on such mundane matters as adequate clothing for the women, and sometimes on the type of civilization they would create in New South Wales, the colony of which he was to become the first Governor-in-Chief. They arrived at Rio de Janeiro on 7 August 1787. Rum was laid in, and all such seeds and plants procured as were thought likely to flourish on the coast of New South Wales—coffee, cocoa, cotton, banana, orange, lemon, guava, tamarind, prickly pear, eugenia, and the ipeca-cuanha. On 4 September they sailed for the Cape of Good Hope.

When they arrived at Table Bay on 13 October 1787, some of the convicts were beginning to hope that the disgrace they had suffered in England would by good behaviour at Botany Bay be buried in oblivion; that removed from their wicked companions in London they would have no seducing opportunities to swerve them from the course of virtue; that in all probability they might be the founders of an empire greater than that from which they were banished. So the germ of the idea that the colony belonged to them and their posterity began to form in the anonymous minds of the convicts during the voyage of the First Fleet. At the same time Phillip and the officers purchased more plants and seeds and animals, so that as sailing day approached, the ships, having on board not less than 500 animals of different kinds, chiefly poultry, put on an appearance which suggested Noah's ark.

As the fleet sailed from Table Bay on 12 November, a melancholy reflection obtruded itself on the minds of a few. The land behind them was the abode of a civilized people; before them was the residence of savages. Refreshments and pleasures were to be exchanged for coarse fare and hard labour at New South Wales. All communication with families and friends was now cut off. To some this was an attractive challenge: this leaving behind civilization, this task of exploring a remote and barbarous land, and planting in it the arts of civilization. Others were so overwhelmed by their private anguish that their minds could not soar to such a theme. Whatever the feelings in their hearts, all were sailing ever closer to a country which at that moment belonged, as it had done for countless centuries, to the peoples the white man called 'Aborigines'.

By 20 January 1788 the whole fleet had cast anchor in Botany Bay, watched from the beach by a group of local people. In the next few days most of the officers were disappointed by what they saw. 'I cannot say from the appearance of the shore', wrote Clark, 'that I will like it'. Surgeon White looked in vain for the fine meadows which Captain Cook had seen in 1770 as commander of the first European vessel to touch upon that coastline. White concluded that that great navigator, notwithstanding his usual accuracy, was certainly too lavish in his praises of Botany Bay. King noted that the soil was nothing but sand. Only the irrepressible Tench detected joy sparkling in every countenance, and risked the prediction that from this great day, the foundation, not the fall, of an empire would be dated.

On 21 January Phillip embarked with three boats for Broken Bay, accompanied by Captain John Hunter, two other officers and sailors, hoping to discover a better harbour as well as a better country. Early that afternoon they had the satisfaction of finding, as Phillip put it, the finest harbour in the world, in which a thousand sail of the line might ride in the most perfect security. The next day Phillip examined the coves in the harbour, fixed on the one with the best spring of water, and honoured it with the name of Sydney before returning to Botany Bay in the evening of 23 January.

On 25 January he sailed again in the *Supply* from Botany Bay, the rest of the transports following next day. As the ships sailed up the harbour to Sydney Cove Mrs Whittle was delivered of a son. A group of Aborigines on the shore hollered 'Walla Walla Wha', or something to that effect, and brandished their spears as if vexed at the approach of the ships. In the afternoon, the officers and marines having landed, the flag was hoisted on shore, while four glasses of porter were drunk to the health of their Majesties and the Prince of Wales, with success to the colony. Then the marines fired a *feu de joie*. The whole group gave three cheers, which was returned by the men on the *Supply*. So, as one observer put it, the new town was 'crisned'.

On 27 and 28 January the male convicts and the rest of the marines landed. Some cleared ground for the different encampments; some pitched tents; some landed the stores; a party of convicts erected the portable house brought from England for the Governor on the east side of the cove. As the colony's first Judge Advocate, David Collins, put it, the spot which had so lately been the abode of silence and tranquillity was now changed to that of noise, clamour and confusion, though after a time order gradually prevailed.

On Sunday, 3 February, Johnson preached his first sermon under a great tree to a congregation of troops and convicts whose behaviour, according to one eye witness, was regular and attentive. But Johnson had begun to despair: a hopelessness, a sense of failure, now informed his language whenever he discussed the progress of his sacred mission—a sense of the impossibility of his task, and an even livelier one of the depravity of his charges.

At five o'clock on the morning of 6 February all things were in order for the landing of the women. All day the disembarkation went on, and about six in the evening at least one officer, Bowes, was enjoying the long wished for pleasure of seeing the last of them leave the ship. But what was one man's pleasure was as ever another man's pain, for one young seaman who impulsively swam ashore to visit the woman he had lived with on the ship caught a chill and died. The women, we are told, were in general dressed very clean, and some few among them could be said to be well dressed. That night the sailors asked for some rum to make merry with upon the women quitting the ships. Soon, as one observer put it, they began to be elevated, and all that night there were scenes of debauchery and riot which beggared description. To add to the confusion, a thunderstorm drenched the revellers.

The next morning the convicts and officers were gathered in a special clearing near Sydney Cove where the marines formed an outer circle. The Judge Advocate, David Collins, read the two commissions appointing Arthur Phillip Captain-General and Governor-in-Chief of the colony of New South Wales, the text of the Act of Parliament creating a court of civil jurisdiction, and the letters patent of 5 May constituting the vice-admiralty court. When the reading finished, the marines fired three volleys, while the band of the marines played the first bars of 'God Save the King' between each volley.

Then Phillip harangued the convicts. The accounts of those who listened to what he had to say differed somewhat as attention was bound to wander after the tedious reading, the activities of the previous night, and the hot, sticky day. All agreed that he addressed himself to the behaviour of the convicts, saying that he would ever be ready to show approbation and encouragement to those who proved themselves worthy by good conduct, while those who acted in opposition to propriety would meet with the punishment they deserved. The sentry, he warned them, had orders to fire with ball at any man seen in the women's camp in the evening, and all men practising promiscuous intercourse would be punished severely.

On 13 February, in the presence of the Judge Advocate, Phillip swore on the Bible: 'I, Arthur Phillip, do declare That I do believe that there is not any Transubstantiation in the Sacrament of the Lord's Supper or in the Elements of Bread and Wine at or after the Consecration thereof by any Person whatsoever.' After which he acknowledged George III to be the only lawful sovereign of the realm. With minds fortified by such a reminder of the Protestant ascendancy, they gathered again in the marquee of Lieutenant Ralph Clark on Sunday, 17 February, where Johnson celebrated the sacrament of the Lord's Supper, and Clark was so carried away by the solemn occasion that he vowed to keep the table as long as he lived, as it was the first table that ever the Lord's Supper was taken from in this country.

Transportation was, next to death, the most severe punishment known to the British criminal law, and in the years ahead the convicts who made camp on the shores of Sydney Cove that summer were to be joined by many others. Most of those who worked with them on the ships—the captains, the chaplains, the surgeons, the charity workers—have testified to their degradation and spiritual wretchedness. They denounced them as liars, as men driven to lying, as the weak from time immemorial have been driven to behaviour which provides the occasion and the pretext for the strong to torment them. They denounced them as treacherous.

For what the improvers did not detect in these convicts was the source of their future power and glory, the strength in their hands and their brains to create wealth, the drive to use that wealth to buy property, to acquire that degree of respectability which their society attached to property, to found families and so experience those nobler human emotions to which their pursuit of crime had left them a stranger.

They recorded their disgust with the drunkenness of the women, their coarse language and the brawls between these consorts of thieves, the women who hawked the body to supplement the takings from theft. But again the improvers missed the variety— that presence on the same ship of the alpha and omega of human behaviour—of the woman who died from a broken heart before the ship sailed; of Jewesses who masqueraded as Roman Catholics at Rio de Janeiro to increase their takings in the pursuit of one of the oldest professions known to mankind, while on the same boat there was a woman named Mary Bryant who, three years after her arrival in New South Wales, made a voyage in a small open boat from Sydney to Batavia.

Not all the men and the women, however, were recruited from the criminal classes. In the years to come, the ranks of the convicts would be swelled by convicted soldiers and sailors, such as William Redfern, transported for participating in the mutiny of the Nore in 1797. There would be middle-class men and women—lawyers, clergymen, teachers, journalists and clerks—who had been pushed by circumstance into the clutches of the law; there would be people convicted of political offences, such as joining in the Luddite riots or the Huddersfield rising; and a few idealists transported for propagating that monstrous doctrine of the rights of man.

The contribution of the Irish convicts lay not so much in their numbers, but in the transporting to New South Wales of the sense of their melancholy history, and Irish Catholicism. That history was reflected in the types transported; for whereas in England and Scotland the thieves predominated, of the 2086 transported from Ireland between 1791 and 1803, about 600 were convicted for riot and sedition.

They were a people whose holy faith and family affections lent a charm to and softened the harshness of their lives in their wretched cabins, and compensated them for their worldly privations. But the misery and idleness of their lives also encouraged drunkenness and feuds, and created the conditions in which loyalty to their own groups and treachery to their eternal enemies governed standards of conduct. They were a people who one hour were dignified with every kind and noble sentiment, only to be degraded the next by acts of the most brutal malevolence. They refused to believe in justice for Irish Catholics in British lawcourts: they despised British laws, defied British administration, and cursed all who collaborated with their oppressors.

The Protestant believed passionately that Protestantism represented the higher level or order—industry, intelligence, and civilization. The Protestant's madness was to believe that the Catholic Church was a gigantic conspiracy to enslave the mind of man, to upset the revolutionary settlement of 1688, to replace the British constitution by a continental despotism, to destroy the rights of conscience, and to reduce the material standard of their civilization to the level of the Irish or the Spanish peasant. To the

Protestant, the priests' claim to the exclusive possession of God's favour was proof in abundance that they were morally mad.

For the historian, the Protestants presented a bewildering variety of Christian persuasions—Anglicans, Presbyterians, Methodists, and the various dissenting sects. But the tone of the official religious life in the colony was set by chaplains and officers who preached and taught the principles of the evangelicals. Fortunately, like most groups who believed the Lord had singled them out as vessels of human salvation, they were not at all diffident in talking and writing about themselves.

The other faith with a vision of the future of mankind was the Enlightenment, which taught of the capacity of man to achieve happiness here on earth. Catholic and Protestant pointed to the Fall as the cause of evil. The Enlightenment taught that evil was the product of economic and material environment; that bad conditions, not innate depravity, were the cause of human vileness; that it was within man's power to create a society from which war, plague, famine, and all the other manifestations of human evil had disappeared. It taught that the end of the belief in immortality would develop in human beings a compassion and a tenderness for each other. Its champions were few, and their opportunities to gain converts negligible, but before the nineteenth century was out they had begun the struggle between belief and unbelief. In association with some of the Protestants they secularized the state, and created a society unique in the history of mankind, holding no firm beliefs on the existence of God or survival after death.

Finally there were the men and the women who were untouched by any one of these enthusiasms—the men of common sense. They accepted the Roman virtues of courage, stoicism, endurance; they disdained religion as a consolation for human suffering, and condemned its followers for their lack of strength and courage. They supported the established church, provided it effected subordination in society, and encouraged its clergymen to act as moral policemen. They approved of candour, benevolence and charity; they believed in the progress of the human race, but not its perfectibility; they believed with a quiet optimism that they were advancing towards a unique era in the history of mankind, in which improvements in science, liberal ideas in politics and religion, the abolition of the slave trade, and the genius of commerce would bring peace, plenty and freedom, and gradually spread European civilization over the whole world.

Such were the divers faiths of the convicts, their keepers and their betters. Such were the prejudices, the superstitions and the ideals which inspired and divided them as their axes broke the silence and they cleared a space for themselves in the dark and gloomy wood on Sydney Cove in the summer of 1788. But not one of these faiths—neither the Christian religion, the Enlightenment, nor the romantic notions about noble savages which some dreamers entertained—could restrain the rapacity and greed of the white man, nor afford him a workable explanation for the apparent backwardness and material weakness of the Aborigine. When Captain Cook and Joseph Banks sailed into Botany Bay in April 1770, the officers and crew of the strange vessel had been greeted by the horrifying howls of the Aboriginal women who lived in that place. That howl contained in it a prophecy of doom—that terrible sense of doom and disaster which pervaded the air whenever the European occupied the land of a primitive people.

2

Hunger

By the middle of February 1788 the task of housing, feeding, and preserving law and order had begun. In the beginning, all were housed in tents: Governor Phillip in a pre-cut canvas house constructed in London, the sick, the civil and military officers, the marines and the convicts in tents, and the stores under wretched covers of thatch. Some grumbled that a mere fold of canvas should be their sole check against the rays of the sun as they began the slow business of building first with canvas, then with wood, and finally with stone, but in all this the unexpected daunted them: the hard wood blunted and bent their tools; there was no suitable lime with which to mix cement; there were too few skilled workers. So they improvised, and made do with what they had.

It was the same with planting seed to grow crops and vegetables. The Governor established a government farm under the supervision of a member of his own staff, using the convicts to till the soil. He granted small plots of land to the civil and military officers, and assigned convicts to work the soil, supplying them with seed and tools to raise grain and vegetables. But the soil blunted the spades and the picks, and the men whose very aversion to labour had been the occasion of their pursuing the profession of crime had to be driven to labour. Until such time as they could master the problems of husbandry in their new environment, they were dependent on the flour, the meat, the pease and the butter brought from England and the Cape of Good Hope. These kept them alive, while exposing them to all those disorders to which men subsisting without green vegetables and fruits were liable. By May, the camp on the banks of Sydney Cove began to wear aspects of distress, as great numbers of scorbutic patients were daily seen creeping to and from the hospital tents. Some died, and the Reverend Johnson read over their shallow graves the solemn words 'Man that is born of woman hath but a short time to live'. By May, Tench had noted that fresh provisions

were becoming scarcer than in a blockaded town. The weather in
the late summer was oppressive, with much rain, thunder and
lightning. Flies which bred large maggots nauseated them; ants bit
them severely.

The behaviour of the convicts disgusted and appalled those who
came into contact with them. Some of the convicts had taken
advantage of the festivities on 7 February to steal food; for this some
were flogged, and one sent to a barren rock in the harbour to live on
bread and water. Thefts from the public stores continued. Such was
the depravity of human nature that neither lenient measures or
whippings, imprisonments nor degradations could apparently
operate upon their callous hearts to prevent theft. But so hardened
in wickedness and depravity were some of them that they seemed
insensible to the fear of death itself.

It was the same with the Aborigine. The white man came bearing
his civilization as his offering, expecting the Aborigine to perceive
the great benefits he would receive at its hand, including that of
being received into the Church of England, which was believed to
contain all that was necessary to salvation. Phillip had been
instructed to conciliate their affections, and to enjoin all subjects to
live 'in amity and kindness' with them. In the beginning Phillip
made all the traditional gestures of goodwill: he smiled with
compassion; he gave them presents of hatchets and other articles; he
ordered his men not to fire on them except when absolutely
necessary. For a season the Aborigines responded to Phillip with
affection, and even with veneration, as the white skin, the material
power, his status as leader, and a quite fortuitous gap in his front
teeth gave him some little merit in their opinion.

By the end of February, however, the Aborigines inferred from
the building that the white man intended to stay. At the end of that
month they stoned white men who attempted to land in one of the
coves of the harbour; they stole the white man's tools; they stole his
food; on 30 May they murdered two rush-cutters and mutilated
their bodies in a shocking manner. Such behaviour quickly changed
the white man from a delighted observer of the picturesque and the
quaint into a partisan defending his civilization. After six months,
one of them wrote of the Aborigine as a creature deformed by all
those passions which afflicted and degraded human nature,
unsoftened by the influence of religion, philosophy and legal
restriction. The behaviour of the white man was equally disgusting
to the Aborigine. To teach them the ways of the civilized, Phillip
instructed his men to gather as many Aborigines as possible to
witness a flogging. The few who watched manifested only symptoms of disgust and terror. In this way, the efforts to conciliate their

affections and to diffuse amity and kindness degenerated into theft and murder, as goodwill was pushed aside by the more primitive passions of an eye for an eye and a tooth for a tooth.

By June and July most of the officers began to despair. But when Phillip sat down in his canvas house to write a dispatch to his superior in London, Lord Sydney, in July 1788, the promise of better things prompted him to prophesy that the country would prove the most valuable acquisition Great Britain ever made. But remembering the thunderstorms, the flies, the ants, the blunted tools, the depravity and wickedness, and conscious too of the wound in his shoulder from the spear of an Aborigine, he added rather ruefully that no country offered less assistance to the first settlers than this did.

By July Phillip had conceived a policy for the future of the colony. To feed them until such time as the government farm and the plots of the officers produced enough food, he sent the *Sirius* to the Cape of Good Hope to purchase supplies. He also wrote to Lord Sydney for better axes, spades, and shovels. The difficulty was to find people interested in growing food, as all attempts to bully, cajole, flatter, or coax the convicts to work had failed. Phillip's solution was to encourage the migration of settlers who would be interested in the labour of the convicts, and in the cultivation of the country. As for the Aborigines, his faith in the fruits of treating them with kindness remained unshaken; he looked forward to the day when they were reconciled to living among the white men, to the day when the white men had taught them how to cultivate the land. The plans to grow food were still dogged with misfortune, however; very little of the English wheat germinated, while the barley rotted in the ground and the weevil destroyed the seed. By September Phillip was reporting the failure of the first crop.

Hope still ran high in Phillip, nevertheless, for in November he had established a second settlement at Rose Hill which, after 2 June 1791, was known by the Aboriginal word Parramatta (the head of the river or the place where eels lie down) where the top soil was free from the rocks and stones which littered it at Sydney Cove. The Aborigines, however, responded to all their advances with such violence that by October it was decided to compel them to keep at a greater distance from the settlement. The year drew to a close with food supplies and health causing grave anxiety, and the behaviour of the Aborigines a measure of irritation. The faint-hearted were tempted to despair, or to dismiss as a cruel mockery or a malicious irrelevance the Reverend Mr Johnson's message of peace on earth and goodwill towards men on the first Christmas Day. But Phillip, the one man who did not share the Christian hope, stood firm in his faith, that in time civilization would yet flourish in New South Wales without the labour of the most infamous of mankind.

On 14 July 1789 all was quiet and stupid at Sydney Cove. The inhabitants were suffering from boredom, or dreaming of being transported to happier climes. On that same day in Paris the crowd stormed the Bastille to begin a revolution to prove the capacity for and the rudiments of better things in man.

By August the conversation was on food, and the prospects of relief from London. In September 1789 the supply of butter was exhausted; in November the ration of every item of food was reduced to two-thirds, except for spirits. By February supplies of flour were low, and Phillip again sent the *Sirius* to the Cape of Good Hope for provisions. One officer described New South Wales in a letter to London as past all dispute a very wretched country and totally incapable of yielding to Great Britain a return for colonizing it.

On 5 April, to their unspeakable consternation, the colonists learned of the wreck of the *Sirius* at Norfolk Island. Divine service on the next day was held in one of the empty storehouses. People invited out to dine were instructed to bring their own bread. The lack of food so weakened the workers that the hours of compulsory labour were shortened. A convict caught stealing food was flogged with 300 lashes, chained for six months to two other criminals, and had his rations reduced for six months. Still the thieving of food continued. The convict men and women were short of clothing; the marines were so short of shoes that most did guard duty in bare feet. Phillip, from a motive that did him immortal honour, put his private food reserves into the common pool.

On the evening of 3 June 1790 they were preparing for a melancholy celebration of the King's Birthday. On that evening even Tench was musing on their fate in his tent, when he heard the joyful sound, 'The flag's up!'. He opened the door and saw several women with children in their arms running to and fro with distracted looks kissing their babies with the most extravagant marks of fondness. He ran down the hill, put a pocket glass to his eye—and saw the sign for which they had so desperately waited. A ship had entered the harbour. Tench was among those who climbed into a small boat and rowed out, through wind and rain, till at last they read the word 'London' on her stern—'Pull away, my lads! she's from old England!' they cried, 'a few strokes more and we shall be aboard! hurrah for a belly-ful, and news from our friends!'.

In a few minutes they had climbed on board the *Lady Juliana* transport to learn that she had been almost eleven months on her passage from Plymouth and carried 221 female convicts. They questioned the men on the *Lady Juliana,* asked a thousand questions on a breath; the men on the ship questioned them, but Tench and his party thought the right of being first answered lay on their side. 'Letters! Letters!' they cried. They were produced and torn open in trembling agitation. News burst upon them like meridian splendour on a blind man; they were overwhelmed by it, and many days elapsed before they were able to absorb it all. They read of the loss of the storeship *Guardian*, which had struck an iceberg off the Cape of Good Hope the previous Christmas Eve. They read of the liberal and enlarged plan for the future of the colony, of the stores soon to arrive on the ships of the Second Fleet which ended the threat of starvation, of the coming of free settlers, of the use of convicts to grow food on the land granted to officers, soldiers and settlers. They read of the outbreak of revolution in France.

In the last week of June, the landing on the west side of Sydney Cove afforded a truly distressing scene. More than thirty tents were pitched in front of the hospital, all of which were quickly filled with people suffering from scurvy, dysentery, or an infectious fever. These miserable wretches had been brought to the colony in the next three transport vessels to arrive, the *Scarborough*, the *Neptune* and the *Surprize*. Of the 1026 convicts who had started the voyage of this Second Fleet to New South Wales only 692 men and 67 women had survived; and 488 of these had arrived sick and unfit for work, victims of the cruelty and greed of the commanders of the ships. Naked, filthy, lousy wretches, many of them unable to stand, to creep, or even to stir hand or foot, were moved from the ships to the improvised hospital. The Reverend Mr Johnson spent so much time amongst them that he became quite ill.

Also on board were the officers and men of the newly formed New South Wales Corps. Among them was a quick-tempered and ambitious lieutenant named John Macarthur who was travelling with his wife Elizabeth. Travelling on the same ship as the Macarthurs was a tall, handsome and burly person by the name of D'Arcy Wentworth. On 12 December 1787 he had been tried at the Old Bailey for highway robbery, and was acquitted. His distant relatives, the Fitzwilliam family, arranged for him to serve as a surgeon at Sydney Cove. He had formed a liaison with a convict travelling on the same ship named Catherine Crowley, who had lived on the Fitzwilliam estates in Staffordshire. The landing of these four people passed unremarked among so many, for no one could know how profound was to be the influence of the Wentworths and the Macarthurs in the history of New South Wales or how entangled the two families would become.

The material fortunes of the colony improved quickly after the arrival of the Second Fleet. The climate exercised its beneficent influence on the sick; the old hours of compulsory labour were restored as food rations returned to normal; new buildings were planned; large tracts of land were cleared at Sydney and Parramatta; a pair of shoes was issued to each convict; some women began to make slops. Phillip was still trying to make men industrious who had passed their lives in vice and indolence and who dreaded punishment less than they feared labour. The more dissatisfied he became with their labour, the more disgusted with their vices and their appearance, the more he pinned his faith in the future of the colony on the coming of free settlers.

In the meantime reports and rumours circulating in London led to the whole future of the Botany Bay scheme coming up for public debate. In March 1789 it was rumoured in London that several people were committing robberies in order to be transported to Botany Bay. In April the London press reviewed cautiously Tench's *A Narrative of the Expedition to Botany Bay*, calling it a well-written, informing account, and drawing attention to Tench's view that as a receptacle for convicts it stood unequalled, but that when viewed in a commercial light he feared its insignificance would be very striking. Throughout 1789 and 1790 the newspapers occasionally published the gossip from the colony. But it was not till the beginning of 1791 that they published any account of the hardships of the struggle for survival endured by convict, marine and officer alike.

Back in the colony, the battle for survival may have been won, but the spirit of the place continued to depress. In April 1791 Tench gazed over the country near Richmond Hill: dreary wilds he found it, for as far as the eye could reach he could not detect a single gleam of change which could encourage hope or stimulate industry to attempt its culture. Few wanted to stay in the country. In July 1791 the expirees could choose between taking up land grants, working for wages, or returning to England. Most chose to return home. The officers and the marines were just as nostalgic. In November Phillip resigned on account of ill health, adding that every doubt respecting the colony's future independence as to the necessities of life was fully done away, and his wish to return to England in hopes of finding that relief from his pain which this country did not afford.

Phillip was as disgusted and dissatisfied as ever with the convicts even when they became settlers. As he saw it, very few of them were equipped for the life they must necessarily lead in the country where they were so entirely cut off from the gratifications in which most of them had always sought their happiness. He wanted neither a convict nor an ex-convict's colony, but a colony of free settlers using convict labour, a view which, by 1792, was being heeded in London.

In the meantime the convicts' way of life had already hardened into a pattern. They worked in the summer on the government farms, or on the plots of the officers, from five in the morning till eleven, and again from two till sunset, felling trees, digging up stumps, rooting up shrubs and grass and turning the ground with spades or hoes. The heat of the sun, the short allowance of food and the ill-treatment from their merciless overseers rendered their lives truly miserable. At night they were housed in huts which accommodated fourteen to eighteen, with one woman whose duty it was to keep the hut clean and provide food for the men at work. They were without the comforts of either beds or blankets. At mealtime they had neither bowl nor plate, and only such crude implements as they had fashioned out of the green wood of the country. In short, they were strangers to all the necessary conveniences of life. The women enjoyed a more comfortable life than the men. The fortunate were selected as wives to the officers and soldiers; others were made hut-keepers; the rest were set to work to make spirits, frocks and trousers, or to pick in the fields. The convicts did, however, enjoy the advantages of the laws as well as others: they could only be punished after trial; no person was allowed to strike them or ill-use them, and all complaints against or by convicts had to be referred to a magistrate.

The convicts, too, were beginning to develop a way of life of their own. They had transplanted with them the language in currency in the profession of crime, that flash or kiddy language which differed so sharply from standard English that an interpreter was frequently necessary in the lawcourts at Sydney Cove. The language irritated the officers, some of whom asserted that indulgence in such an infatuating cant was deeply associated with depravity and continuance in vice. There was only one who consistently tried to wean them from the ways of the ungodly, and his prescription never varied: read the Bible, he urged them each Sunday; observe and reverence the sabbath day; pray constantly and diligently to God; avoid profane swearing, an unclean and adulterous course of life, theft, dishonesty, villainy and idleness; pay due respect, submission and obedience to superiors. For the Reverend Mr Johnson looked to God to perform the miracle, not to man in his new environment.

Some, however, were finding things which delighted and pleased them. Elizabeth Macarthur had discovered how to pass the time cheerfully if not gaily, despite the oppressive heat in the summer and the absence of any female friend. She learned astronomy and botany from Mr Dawes, or chatted gaily with Captain Tench. Life indeed, as she put it, had become very amusing to her and she was abundantly content. In June 1791 her family moved to

Parramatta from where she spent pleasant days in boating parties
on the harbour, took refreshments and dined out under an awning
on some pleasant point of land, or in one of the coves in which the
waters of that harbour abounded. With the arrival of the Third Fleet
there were so many ladies in the regiment that she no longer felt the
want of female society. So by the end of 1792 some of the refinements of civilization, such as conversation, reading, music, and
delight in scenery, had thrown out their first tender shoots in a
society hitherto compelled by stern necessity to devote all its
energies simply to preserving life.

By the end of 1792, the European population of New South Wales
numbered slightly more than 3000 persons. About two-thirds were
convicts, and men outnumbered women by five to one. The settlement on Norfolk Island, which Phillip had established shortly after
the first landing in Sydney, numbered a little over 1115. By the end
of 1792 there were government farms at Sydney Cove, Parramatta
and Toongabbie; the colony traded with England, Ireland, Calcutta,
Batavia, Chinese ports, and the United States of America; whalers
and sealers had used Sydney Cove as a base from which to fish in
the south seas.

On December 1792 Phillip went on board the *Atlantic* transport to
sail for England. Voluntarily and cheerfully Bennilong and Yem-
merra-wan-nie, two natives who were much attached to his person,
boarded the ship with him. Some of those who were left behind
remembered him tenderly for his little acts of kindness. Others
paused to praise the zeal and perseverance which had enabled him
to surmount the obstacles which the country had thrown in his way.
All agreed that his role had been paramount if not decisive in
winning the battle for survival. Yet by one of those ironies in human
history, the other achievement of his term as Governor, the conversion of the British Government to policies which would transform
the gaol into a colony of free settlers using convict labour, sprang as
much from his prejudices and idiosyncrasies as from any vision he
entertained for the future of European civilization in New South
Wales. For within Phillip two men survived to the end. There was a
man who with grace, dignity, industry and great self-control had
won the battle for survival: there was also a man who had once
wanted to hand over murderers and sodomites to be eaten by
cannibals.

3

The Battles Begin

The battle for survival was followed by the traditional battles of societies with a European civilization. In the battle for economic and social power, the ownership of wealth was gradually concentrated in the hands of the few. In the collision of opinion, there was a never-ending debate between conflicting views of human nature and human destiny. There was all that hubbub and uproar of human intercourse which some have taken as evidence of the follies and passions of the human heart. By another of the ironies of history, the man at the centre of these momentous events was a man singularly lacking in distinction or any power to perceive the significance of his actions.

Major Francis Grose assumed the office of acting Governor when Phillip sailed for England. He had arrived in Sydney in February 1792 aged 36 and had found to his great surprise that the whole place wore the appearance of a garden in which fruit and vegetables of every description grew in the greatest luxuriance. He found a good house, a not unwholesome climate, plenty of fishing and good shooting. Major Grose was a man of little cultivation, a man who on his own confession spoke French indifferently and was not acquainted with any other foreign language, a man to whom the obscurity of second-in-command ministered both to his distaste for the burdens of command as well as to the complete absence of that power to command. Chance, however, presented him with a situation he had not coveted.

As Governor, he decided to increase the quantity of foods and goods available. To achieve this he allotted 100 acres of land to every officer who asked for it, because work on government farms proceeded slowly and never with that spirit and energy which were created by private interest. This policy affected the private fortunes of most of the officers in the settlement. John Macarthur received 100 acres of some of the best ground that had been discovered at

Parramatta, and the labour of ten convicts to clear and cultivate it. By 1794 he had a farm of nearly 250 acres at Parramatta, of which 100 were under cultivation. He had built a most excellent brick house consisting of four rooms, a large hall, closets, and cellar, with a kitchen, servants' apartments and other necessary offices adjoining. The house was surrounded by a vineyard, fruit trees and an excellent vegetable garden of about 3 acres.

In addition Grose granted land to non-commissioned officers, to privates, to emancipists and to expirees, the number of acres being decided by their station in society. All of them received supplies for two years from the public stores, and the services of convicts free of charge. The Reverend Thomas Fyshe Palmer was predicting it would soon be a region of plenty, and wanted only virtue and liberty to be another America. He prophesied that transportation might well become a blessing and heartily wished all the paupers of Great Britain would make efforts to be sent to New South Wales.

Grose also encouraged the military and civil officers to engage in trade, permitting them to negotiate directly with captains of ships for their cargo, believing that the incentive of material gain would hasten the transition to abundance. The officers very soon used their power to preserve a monopoly in trade for themselves. They allowed no one but themselves to board ships as they arrived. So long as masters of ships, settlers, and others dealt exclusively with the government store, the prices of goods had been high but not exorbitant. Now the officers were making profits of 100–200 per cent in the simple transaction of buying a cargo and reselling it. Rum, luxuries and necessaries: no import was immune. Many of the civil and military officers became dealers in spirituous liquors. Even a convict could go and purchase a pint of rum from an officer and a gentleman, while some employed their wash-women or others as saleswomen. Many were making their fortunes. The settlers groaned under this load of oppression; some were forced to sell their holdings and so became dependent on the government to victual themselves and their families, which in turn increased the expenses of government.

Grose had succeeded on one point where all Phillip's efforts had failed. He had found an incentive to induce the convicts to work on the farms of the officers by permitting the latter to pay the convicts in rum on those days or during those hours when they were not employed on government work. So the rum worked where kindness and the lash had failed.

While Grose and most of the officers seemed indifferent to the effects on behaviour of that mode of payment for such extra labour, the Reverend Richard Johnson grieved that in the evening the

convict camps became scenes of intoxication, riots and disturbances. He continued his efforts to persuade the convicts, the
ex-convicts and the soldiers to restrain the evil passions of their
hearts, telling them of the glory of God's mercy in the eternal
salvation of the elect, and of His justice in the damnation of the
wicked. But his message fell on debauched ears. Besides, to his
mortification and chagrin Grose openly displayed his contempt
for Johnson, whom he suspected was one of the people called
Methodists, which he probably equated with sedition.

In June 1793 Lord Dundas informed Grose of the appointment of
the Reverend Samuel Marsden as assistant chaplain to the colony.
A month later, the young priest and his wife Elizabeth sailed from
England for New South Wales. On Sunday, 2 March 1794, while
their ship was being buffeted by high seas off the east coast of Van
Diemen's Land, Elizabeth Marsden was brought to bed of a fine
girl. The child was no sooner born than a great wave washed
through the porthole, fell upon the little child and wet their linen,
which Marsden then dried by placing it between his shirt and his
skin. Having got the child dressed and their little place put to rights,
he knelt down to return God thanks for the great deliverance He
had brought to them.

They arrived at Sydney Cove in March 1794, where Marsden
quickly took up his duties as assistant chaplain, assuming responsibility for the parish of Parramatta. Like Johnson he was appalled by
the vice and depravity. He was shocked to find that the convicts
condemned to death were greatly alarmed, and had no idea of a
God of grace and mercy. He suffered acutely the pangs of exile; he
missed that happiness and conversation he had enjoyed in England
in the company of God's people. His faith strengthened him to
endure all these privations, and he decided to become a farmer, to
till the soil and breed sheep. It was a decision he felt called on to
justify: he had entered the country when it was in a state of nature,
and was obliged to plant and sow or starve. It was more than want,
however, which drove him to accumulate 1720 acres of land, 1200
sheep, as well as unspecified numbers of cattle, pigs and horses
within ten years of his arrival. This laying up of treasures on earth
was not calculated to win him that respect for the mission which
touched him most deeply—the salvation of the souls committed to
his charge.

Grose resigned in May 1794 and sailed for England the following
December, leaving Captain Paterson, an amiable procrastinator, to
direct the settlements of New South Wales until September 1795. In
that month a man of incorruptible integrity, unceasing zeal, and a
sound and impartial judgement assumed the office of Governor. He

was John Hunter, a captain in His Majesty's navy. Age and experience were on his side. It was Hunter who had first entered Port Jackson with Phillip in January 1788 and Hunter who had sailed for supplies to the Cape of Good Hope in October 1788. Throughout his naval career he had showed himself to be a man who combined physical toughness with some of the gifts of the artist, a man who looked to Providence as a prop and support, and who wrote and spoke of Christ as his saviour. He might have retired with honour, but chance and ambition pushed him at the age of 57 into the office of Captain-General and Governor-in-Chief of the colony of New South Wales.

He sailed on the *Reliance*, which dropped anchor in Sydney Cove on 7 September 1795. He had brought Bennilong back from London, to display to other Aborigines the benefits of civilization. On his first appearance, Bennilong conducted himself with the greatest propriety at the dining table, wore the clothes of his civilizers, and extended their courtesies to women. He presented his wife with a very fashionable rose-coloured petticoat and a jacket made of a coarse stuff to persuade her to put on the white man's clothes and abandon her lover. When she discarded the clothes and returned to her lover, Bennilong fought him, insisting on using fists instead of the weapons of his country. But soon Bennilong's absences from the Governor's house became more and more frequent, and when he went out he usually left his clothes behind.

Events in New South Wales simply did not correspond with Hunter's view of the world. Like Phillip, he had been instructed to conciliate the affections of the Aborigine, to live in 'amity and kindness' with them, and to prepare them for civilization. But the closer the Aborigines' contact with civilization, the more they were degraded. Bennilong became so fond of drinking that whenever he was invited to an officer's house he was eager to be intoxicated, and in that state was so savage and violent as to be capable of any mischief. Even as he disgusted his civilizers, he began to lose the respect of his own people, and so rushed headlong to his dissolution as a man, without the eye of pity from the former, or affection from the latter.

A harsher, angrier note began to appear in white descriptions of the Aborigines. During 1796 the parents of an Aboriginal girl were murdered by Europeans, who then adopted the girl, lavished on her their amity and kindness, and trained her in their ways. This angered the Aborigines, who lured her into the woods, murdered her, cut off her arms, and mutilated her body. The Europeans complained that the Aborigines repaid kind treatment with base ingratitude. In 1799, five white settlers on the Hawkesbury, angered by Aboriginal thefts, burnings and a murder, met in the home of the widow of the murdered man to exact revenge, captured two suspected Aboriginal boys, tied their hands behind their backs, marched them outside and shot them.

Hunter was horrified. He charged the five men with murder. In their defence the accused pleaded vengeance and justified murder of black men on the grounds that the Aborigines were treacherous, evil-minded and bloodthirsty. When the court returned a verdict of guilty, Hunter appealed to London for guidance. By the time the reply came he had left the colony, for by then the same professions of goodness had been tried and found wanting in an encounter with his fellow-Europeans. He had known the impotence of the good man before men of evil with malice in their hearts.

In the beginning of 1796 Macarthur made some suggestions for the administration of the government store at Parramatta. (The buying, selling and distribution of agricultural produce, seed and livestock were performed in the main by the store, which had branches in both Sydney and Parramatta. Until 1798, all the workers, the military and civil officers and their wives and families, were victualled from the government store, which also helped settlers with land grants to establish themselves.) It was advice which Hunter declined to accept. Shortly afterwards, someone whispered into Macarthur's ears words which he claimed to have heard Richard Atkins, a court official, use at the Governor's table, alleging that glaring partiality had been exercised by Macarthur in receiving maize into the store. Macarthur was so offended that Hunter had not rebuked Atkins there and then that he embarked on a savage campaign to destroy both men. He denounced Atkins as a man from whom public drunkenness, cheating and indecency were almost inseparable, and he wrote to the Duke of Portland charging Hunter with inept administration and extravagance in the expenditure of government money. He asserted that vice of every description was openly encouraged in the colony, while positions of trust were held by men whose characters were a disgrace to the British nation. His campaign against Hunter was unceasing. In his private rage and thirst for revenge Macarthur assumed the role of spokesman for the more opulent landholders. So wounded pride burgeoned into the higher purpose of cleansing the colony of its moral filth, and of protecting society from contamination.

Hunter was deeply hurt and deeply puzzled why he, a self-declared evangelist for goodness, for religion and morality, should be singled out for such an attack. He was astonished, too, that anyone, let alone an officer and a gentleman, should perpetrate such an impertinent interference in the duties of the Governor. All through 1797 he brooded over the paradox of this man Macarthur, who was drawing part of his income from the traffic in spirits, who was a member of the officers' ring and therefore in part responsible for such moral filth as existed in the colony, yet who dared to accuse him of encouraging wickedness. So deep became Hunter's conviction of his own righteousness that he cut himself off from the man with the mind and drive to shape the future of society in New South Wales.

While Hunter despaired at the evil in men's hearts, the Reverend Samuel Marsden was lost in wonder and astonishment at the various changes through which a kind Providence had led him. To his surprise, God had exalted him from his low station and rank to minister before Him in holy things. Now Hunter offered him the position of magistrate. Marsden, for his part, did not wish to offend the Governor; he was rather willing to cultivate his good opinion, as well as to convince the people under his charge that he wished to promote their temporal as well as their spiritual interests. In the meantime he would continue to preach repentance towards God and faith in our Lord Jesus Christ. So Marsden justified those decisions which were to cause him an infinity of anguish, and deprive him of the very respect he so desperately craved, the respect of his fellow-men.

In the late 1790s, Macarthur, Isaac Nichols and Marsden were experimenting in sheep-breeding. By crossing Bengal and Irish breeds Macarthur produced a mingled fleece of hair and wool, a result which suggested to him the idea of producing fine wool in New South Wales. In 1796 he imported four merino ewes and two rams from the Cape of Good Hope and continued his experiments till, by 1801, he had produced a merino with wool the equal of any Spanish wool and a cross-breed of considerable value.

Throughout the colony, economic life continued to develop rapidly. The demand for labour, either bond or free, exceeded the supply. This scarcity contributed to the high price of labour in the colony. The systems of payment for those ex-convicts who hired themselves out as labourers were both complex and diverse. On the large estates the settlers kept on hand large supplies of articles most needed by their workers, for shops there were none. The value of the articles purchased was then deducted from the wages. Most employers provided board and lodging for their workers, and either bartered goods such as sugar, tea and rum for their labour, and so provided them with both the necessaries and the luxuries, or paid them in coin. Rum was by no means the only form of such barter, despite the attempt of some contemporaries to delude posterity into believing that the whole of the working class of New

South Wales was debauched to placate the greed of the officers of the NSW Corps.

In March 1799 the Aborigines on the Hawkesbury warned the settlers of an impending flood but, not liking to be taught by untutored savages, the settlers treated their warnings with contempt. Soon a prodigious swelling of the waters began. The ground on which the settlers had erected their houses and farm buildings was soon inundated and their retreat cut off. Some climbed to the ridges of their dwellings; some took to boats; some improvised rafts. All that night nothing was to be heard but the firing of muskets and the cries of women and children, together with the noise of the torrent. In the morning the country appeared like an extensive sea, with here and there the top of a hill or the ridge of a house appearing above the surface; fragments of houses, swimming hogs, stacks of wheat, and dead poultry were seen driven before the torrent. Fortunately, only one man was lost.

The parsons, the moralizers, and all those in high places who had been touched by the evangelical view of the world, pointed to such disasters as a divine punishment for the beastly indulgences of the ex-convict settlers on the banks of the Hawkesbury. All misfortunes and privations were evidence of divine displeasure for the obliteration in the colony of all idea of a supreme being and that absence of respect for everything decent, moral and sacred. Or so Marsden warned Hunter, but by then his eyes were so misted by the evangelical view of the world that they could not see the economic developments, the signs of growth and development, which had convinced even *The Times* in London that the condition of the colony was most promising.

Prejudices and fears likewise stained the early relations between government and the Irish convicts with blood and tragedy. By October of 1800 there were 1207 of them in the colony. Hunter described them as a desperate set of villains, accused them of encouraging perjury in the lawcourts, and pleaded for fewer Irish convicts lest the colony be filled up wholly with the very worst of characters. The superstition of the Irish, which Hunter believed to be one of the many prices of their fatuous religious beliefs, exposed them to the wildest and the cruellest flights of fancy. They believed, for example, that there was a colony of white people 300 to 400 miles to the south-west of Sydney, where they could indulge in all the comforts of life without labouring for them; they cherished the delusion that it was possible to walk from Sydney Cove to China. They nourished these beliefs as comforts to make the world bearable.

In September 1800, having received information that certain seditious assemblies had been held by the Irish in different parts of the colony, Hunter decided to hold an inquiry. But the Irish, to the despair of their Protestant inquisitors, proved evasive, equivocal and jesuitical, and not prepared to inform on each other. Richard Atkins and Samuel Marsden ordered one of their number, Galvin, to be flogged until he revealed where the pikes of the conspirators were concealed. They flogged him on the back till he was raw; they flogged him on the bottom; they flogged him again on the back. When he still refused to inform, even Marsden admitted that Galvin would die rather than reveal anything. But Marsden as a magistrate had stooped to the temptation that the truth could be flogged out of a man, just as in other quarters he had stooped to the idea that souls could be flogged away from damnation. The man who wanted to be known as the dispenser of divine love became identified with one of the most savage punishments in the early history of the colony. To restore order and recall these deluded Irish to their senses, some were sentenced to 1000 lashes, some to 500, some to 200, and some to transportation to Norfolk Island. To the Irish the floggings were more evidence of that barbarity and savagery which the Anglo-Saxon was all too ready to use to maintain the Protestant ascendancy against Catholic tyranny and Jacobin anarchy. New South Wales had contributed its first page to that book on the melancholy history of the Irish.

Prejudices against the Irish, however, could not bring Hunter into disrepute in London. What damaged him there was his response to criticism. On 15 April 1800, Hunter opened a dispatch in which he found to his mortification that Portland had accepted the slanders of Macarthur and his fellow traducers; that he had sanctioned the officers engaging in a traffic which had disgraced His Majesty's service; and that Hunter should return by the first safe conveyance which offered itself after the arrival of Lieutenant-Governor King. King had served under Hunter on the First Fleet, and was twenty-one years his junior.

By 28 September 1800 all was in readiness. Hunter proceeded to the wharf along a road lined on each side by troops, to find a large number of the inhabitants of the colony who manifested by their deportment the sense they entertained of the regard he had ever paid to their interests, and the justice and humanity of his government. The civil and military officers gathered too to pay their tribute. The Aborigines called goodbye to their Be-an-na, or father.

He remained to the end of his days as he had seen himself in a moment of self discovery during those days of adversity in New South Wales, as a very plain man bred to the honourable and respectable profession of a seaman in His Majesty's navy, whose code of honour led him on to anguish and suffering, and in a measure to the derision of posterity, in a country which to the very end he loved passionately.

4

Rebellion

After 1800 the outlines of two societies began to take shape in the settlements of New South Wales. One drew its wealth from trade, the other from land and sheep. One laid the foundations of bourgeois society, the other created that class which aspired to being the ancient nobility of New South Wales. At the same time the Protestant ascendancy continued to dominate the civilization of the colony, despite some anguished protests from the Irish Catholics. The relations between Europeans and Aborigines rushed headlong towards tragedy. All these tendencies were strengthened when Philip Gidley King was Captain-General and Governor-in-Chief of the colony of New South Wales.

In February 1788, Phillip had appointed King commander of the settlement at Norfolk Island. In the beginning King's aspirations were high-minded. He wanted to dispense with corporal punishment; within six weeks he had a boy of 15 flogged with 100 lashes for stealing rum. He was appalled by the sexual promiscuity and the drunkenness; within two years he had fathered two illegitimate children, and had begun to drink heavily. Yet he never lost faith in the piety which had sustained him before his fall, urging his illegitimate children to say their prayers and not to forget their catechism. Gradually the flaws in his character converted the fresh open-faced young officer, who peered at the world with wonder and delight from the portrait of 1789, into the moody, maudlin, gout-ridden officer who took the oaths of office at Sydney Cove in September 1800. Soon after he arrived, stories of King's eccentric behaviour began to circulate in the colony, such as how in a moment of drunken buffoonery he had jumped into a basket of eggs. Such were the rages which cheated him of the respect and esteem to which his talents and achievements entitled him.

He saw himself late in 1800 as a man sent to clean up a mess. He immediately tackled the monopoly traffic in spirits. He reduced the quantity of spirits landed and encouraged the settlers not to mortgage their crops to buy necessaries and spirits from the officers. Meanwhile he introduced new procedures to render the labour of the convicts more productive. As the colony began to thrive, it looked as though the measures of a high-minded eccentric had succeeded where the goodness and the innocence of Hunter had proved ineffectual and impotent.

But something more than a difference in character, something more than a difference in type, contributed to King's success. Time played its part. So did luck, for King had the colossal good fortune to get rid of Macarthur. In July 1801, one Lieutenant Marshall was tried before the criminal court of Judge Advocate and six military officers for assaulting two superior officers, one of whom was John Macarthur. The court found Marshall guilty and sentenced him to a fine of £50 and one year's imprisonment. King upheld Marshall's complaints that the trial had been unfair, concluding that the six military officers who sat on the court had been motivated by vindictiveness and clannishness. Macarthur struck out against King, rousing the men under his command to such open disobedience and violence that King denounced Macarthur as a perturbator who had made a large fortune at the public expense and resolved to send him to London to face court martial.

When Macarthur sailed on 15 November 1801, there went with him all chance of destroying King as Governor of New South Wales. Macarthur's departure came just in time, for King was beginning to show signs of strain, beginning to call on the Deity as support for his integrity, as Hunter had done when too weak to fight such an opponent. Eighteen months later King had become the target of mockers and critics to such a degree that on 9 May 1803 he wrote to Lord Hobart, who had taken over the seals of office, and requested that he be permitted to submit the whole of his public and private conduct to a tribunal of civil, military and naval officers in London. Hobart agreed; King could return as soon as the important trust could be put in the hands of a person free from the spirit of party which had reached such an alarming height.

The feud with the officers, however, had borne some fruit. It forced King to question the composition of the courts and to insist on the legal rights of emancipated convicts, declaring that convicts who were the object of that mercy became as free as any free-born Briton in the territory. But King was not the man to entertain the wider vision. On other questions he did not break with the prejudices of his age. By 1805 less and less was heard of the early aspirations to civilize the Aborigines as a preparation for their becoming members of the mystical body of Christ's Church. King, like so many others, was losing faith in the official policy of kindness and amity. Experience was driving more and more settlers and officers to speak of the treachery, cruelty and inferiority of the Aborigines, and to explain the ineffectual results of all attempts to civilize them by their innate characteristics as a race. The whites were coming to believe that violence and reprisals were the only methods the Aborigines could understand. In a calmer moment King himself knew that the main cause of the trouble was that the white man had expropriated the original proprietors of the soil, but few contemplated the extinction of the Aborigine with remorse, guilt or regret. The European theft of the land, with the response of the Aborigine to such a theft, and European ideas on the nature of man and his destiny, rushed both groups into a clash which doomed the culture of the Aborigines, condemning them to destruction or degradation and the whites to peace, security and material success, at the price of a reputation in posterity for infamy.

This combination of material interest and an inherited ideology contributed also to the clash between the English Protestant and the Irish Catholic. On this issue King's mind mirrored the prejudices of his class and his country. The arrival of convicts sentenced to transportation for their part in the Irish rebellion of 1798 roused the fears and prejudices of the Protestants of New South Wales. Five hundred and sixty-five Irish convicts arrived between January 1800 and June 1802. King described them as ruthless, violent and turbulent characters with diabolical schemes for the destruction of all industry, public and private property, order and regularity. Cautiously, however, he began to move towards clemency, to grant conditional pardons to some because, somewhat to his surprise, the conduct of so many had been uniformly good and highly deserving.

He was not too happy about allowing them to practise their religion, but he thought that perhaps the Reverend Mr Dixon, who was by disposition a peace-loving man, and quite unequal to the task either to incite or to repress sedition or revolt, might be trusted to hold religious services. So, under regulations which provided that a certain number of police would be stationed at or near the places of worship during the service to ensure strict decorum, masses were first said in Sydney on 15 May 1803.

Such a concession did nothing to quell the restless spirit of Irish discontent. On 4 March 1804 William Johnston, an Irishman who had been transported for his part in the rebellion of 1798, moved from house to house on Castle Hill urging his compatriots to join him in a bid for liberty. By persuasion, charm, blarney and threat, Johnston gathered together a group of 333 men, armed them at Castle Hill with rifles, improvised pikes and cutlasses, and planned to raise another 300 at the Hawkesbury from where he proposed to march on Sydney and Parramatta using the catchcry of liberty.

At 11.30 on Sunday night, word reached Government House that the convicts at Castle Hill were in a state of insurrection. King issued a proclamation ordering them to surrender or face court martial, and in the early hours of Monday morning, he and a company of soldiers under Major Johnston set out for Parramatta to confront the rebels. Johnston rode on ahead accompanied by quartermaster Laycock and came up with the insurgents at 11.30 a.m. at Vinegar Hill, 7 miles out of Toongabbie. They advanced to within a pistol shot of the rebels and called on them to surrender and take advantage of the mercy offered them in the Governor's proclamation. When they refused, Johnston asked to talk to their leaders, who with that incredible folly which characterized the Irish in their dealings with the English, met Johnston and Laycock half-way. Johnston presented his pistol at Philip Cunningham's head and Laycock presented his at William Johnston's head. The men who had shouted for liberty offered no resistance.

In the meantime, Johnston's detachment of twenty-five soldiers had arrived on the scene. When Johnston ordered them to charge, they cut the insurgents to pieces. Within minutes nine lay dead, their leader, Cunningham, lay wounded, and the rest were in flight for the Hawkesbury. After Johnston caught up with them at 9 p.m., retribution began. After taking the opinion of the officers about him, he directed Cunningham to be hanged on the staircase of the public store, which he had earlier boasted that he was going to plunder. On 7 March King announced that the principal leaders had given themselves up; he appealed to the rest to surrender. The trials began next day. Only leaders were tried, because in the official pattern of thinking the rank and file were deluded and infatuated, but not wicked, men. Three hundred odd of the latter, who gave themselves up, were sent back to their work with a reprimand. With that zeal which he always used to serve the interests of the Protestant ascendancy, Marsden helped prepare the case for the prosecution. After a brief trial eight of the leaders were hanged and many others flogged. Thirty-four were sent to cut coal and cedar at Coal River, renamed Newcastle, which King decided to use as a penal settlement for the Irish.

The members of the Protestant ascendancy in New South Wales had tried to reduce the Irish to subordination by force. They never paused to sort out the muddle in their own minds on the origins of the revolt, blaming indiscriminately the Irish, the priests, the Church of Rome, the ideas of 1789. So in two of the major questions of the day, the relations between the Europeans and the Aborigines, and the relations between the Protestant ascendancy and Irish Catholicism, evil stalked in the land, and New South Wales added its drips to the never-ending tears of humanity.

5

Prosperity

Almost 130 years were to pass before any Europeans came to Van Diemen's Land after the Dutch navigator, Abel Tasman. The first was a French explorer, M. Marion, who sailed into Frederick Henry Bay on 3 March 1772. Next day some officers and soldiers landed to gather wood, when they met a group of Aborigines. The French tried to win them with small presents of mirrors, handkerchiefs and pieces of cloth, after which they showed them poultry and duck in an attempt to get them to understand that they wanted to buy such things. One of the Aborigines held out a bush as though inviting Marion to light it. Marion did so, only to find the act was a declaration of war. When the Aborigines withdrew swiftly to a little hill and hurled spears at the intruders, M. Marion and another officer were wounded. As the French retaliated by opening fire, the Aborigines followed them to the water's edge, uttering frightening yells, and hurling their spears. Again the French opened fire, wounding several Aborigines and killing one. In this way the first contact between the European and the Aborigine in Tasmania ended with death as the price of misunderstanding. Six days later the French sailed on to New Zealand.

On 24 January 1777 Captain Cook took on water at Adventure Bay in the *Resolution* on his way to explore the North Pacific. Between 1788 and 1793 William Bligh, Bruni D'Entrecasteaux and John Hayes each touched on the coast of Van Diemen's Land, but its relationship to the rest of the Australian continent was not established until 1799 when George Bass and Matthew Flinders completed their exploration of the coastline in the sloop *Norfolk* and established that Van Diemen's Land was separated from the mainland by a strait. Flinders was delighted by the country they discovered, by the fertile appearance of the soil, the good covering of herbage, and the strong grass of the valleys. He began to dream of the day when the white man would bring his civilization to the island which so resembled the parklands and meadows of England.

In May 1803 King proclaimed that it had become necessary to establish His Majesty's right to Van Diemen's Land. He declared that it was not only to prevent the French from gaining a footing on the east side of that island, but also to divide the convicts, to secure another place for procuring timber and other natural products, as well as to raise grain and to promote the seal industry. An initial settlement led by Lieutenant John Bowen was soon supplanted by David Collins, who arrived in the Derwent River on 15 February 1804 with two ships carrying 421 marines, convicts and settlers. Collins quickly decided that Bowen's site at Risdon Cove was not calculated for a town. He resolved to establish a new settlement on the south-west bank of the river, attracted by an extensive plain and a continual run of water from a lofty mountain. Collins named the place Hobart Town.

Where Phillip had set the highest standards of humanity and moral rectitude, Collins soon lapsed. When the convicts were flogged, he stood by the triangles and took snuff in handfuls. Soon he had taken a convict woman as his mistress. His chaplain, Robert Knopwood, drank wine, smoked a pipe, hunted, fished, and enjoyed the world hugely, without any of that disgust for the depravity of his charges or that concern for their salvation which had bothered the Reverend Richard Johnson during the pioneer days at Sydney Cove. But Collins, by his warm heart and amiable disposition, won the affection of those who thought of the Ten Commandments as an aspiration rather than a command.

As on the mainland of New South Wales, the Europeans began by attempting to conciliate the affections of the Aborigine. But when the Aborigines perceived that the newcomers had stolen their land, they began their raids. As on the mainland, the material interest of the settlers forced them more and more into deeds of hostility which belied all their protestations of goodwill.

While the settlers took up their farms in the upper reaches of the Derwent during 1804, the convicts began to till the soil on the government farm, and a plan for Hobart Town was drawn up. All that time food supplies continued to be so short that settlers, officers, soldiers and convicts lived off kangaroo and emu meat till well into 1806. The decision to establish a settlement on the north coast of the island at Port Dalrymple had been made in June of 1803, only a few months after the decision to establish a settlement on the Derwent. King appointed Lieutenant-Colonel Paterson as Lieutenant-Governor of the new settlement. He arrived there on 5 November with his wife, a captain, 2 subalterns, 4 sergeants, 2 drummers, 58 privates and 74 convicts.

This increase in the number of settlements reflected the changes in the economic situation of New South Wales. In the beginning the

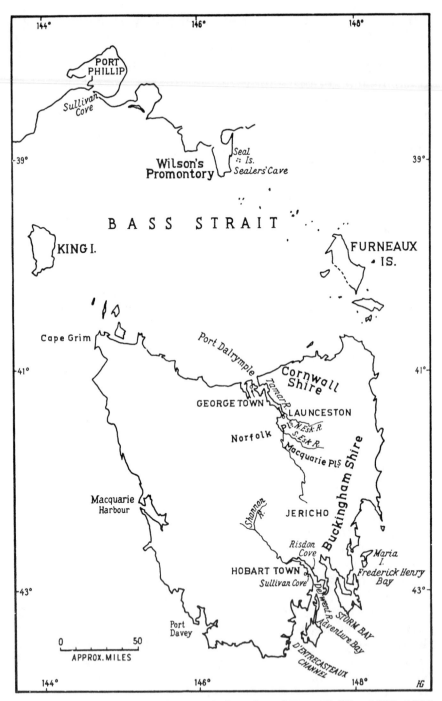

The settlements in Van Diemen's Land and Port Phillip, 1803–1820

problem had been to produce and import enough food to win the battle for survival, but now the problem was how to dispose of surplus grain. The area under crop continued to increase: from 7595 acres in 1800 to 11 254 acres at the end of 1806. Shipbuilding, coalmining and cedar-cutting were expanding. Trade with India, China, North America, the Pacific islands and Europe was increasing, as was the colony's involvement in sealing and whaling in the south seas. By 1803 King was discussing the possibility of allowing convict ships to go whaling or to trade with China after disembarking at Sydney. Prices began to fall; the monopoly of the officers withered away; the traffic in spirits assumed a less prominent place in the economy, and even in the weekly pronouncements from the pulpit. The proportion of people victualled from the government stores had decreased as the population increased. King saw all this as the effect of his stern measures, while others saw it as the effect of expanding economic activity.

Among those who accumulated wealth from the expansion of trade was Simeon Lord. Sentenced to transportation for seven years at Leeds in 1790 for stealing 200 yards of cloth, Lord had become an employer of labour by 1798. In 1801 he was trading in coal and between 1801 and 1806 he had entered the sealskin, whale oil and Pacific islands trade. Lord was the first of the emancipists to find in trade a career open to talent. He was one of those men, trained in the tough school of competition with American traders and Chinese and Indian merchants, who helped to establish a class to whom the distinction between bond and free, or even previous occupation, was less relevant than success in building up for themselves treasures on earth.

In the meantime, another group was beginning to contemplate quite a different future for New South Wales, when wool had created their wealth and the possession of the land conferred on them the distinction of forming 'the ancient nobility' of New South Wales. At the forefront of this emerging class was John Macarthur.

In December 1802 Macarthur arrived in England where he had been sent by Governor King, but he evaded court martial by resigning his commission in the army. By cunning, flattery and the use of his influence on the men in high places, he turned the situation to his own advancement. He impressed English manufacturers with specimens of fine New South Wales wool, and won the support of the Earl of Camden, the Secretary of State for the Colonies. Camden issued instructions to the Governor of New South Wales to grant 10 000 acres of land to John Macarthur in the vicinity of the Cow Pastures, to provide him with thirty convicts, and to give him every encouragement to grow fine wool. So Macarthur left London at the end of 1804 to return triumphantly to the New South Wales he had left in ignominy four years earlier.

When Macarthur arrived at Sydney Cove in June 1805 he found that King, who in 1802 had been prepared to warn all and sundry of the evil intent which lay behind that pair of basilisk eyes, was by then so debilitated by drink that when he saw Macarthur again he burst into tears and was unable to conduct business. After recovering his composure, King fussed over Macarthur, and granted him the 10 000 acres in the vicinity of the Cow Pastures, which Macarthur, in gratitude to the man who had set the seal of official approval on his plans, named Camden Park. He was to become a rich man.

In 1807 *The Times* sensed the possibility both of greatness and novelty in a country which had begun its history, like ancient Rome, as an asylum for fugitives and delinquents. It was the perception of the possibility of material advancement which caused Viscount Castlereagh, who had taken over the seals of office that same year, to encourage settlers of responsibility and capital to emigrate to New South Wales. The encouragement offered was a free passage, a large grant of land and convicts to work it on condition that the settler invested capital of up to £6000. The first permissions to settle under these terms were granted to Gregory and John Blaxland, two brothers who farmed in Kent and who were threatened by material misfortunes to lose their positions in society.

Such free settlers sought not only material advancement. Many also sought to become respectable, through education or through public religious piety. When Marsden preached at the opening of St John's, Parramatta, in April 1803, he adverted to the many solid advantages the colony must derive from a proper observance of the duties of Christianity. In describing the becoming silence that prevailed, the writer in the *Sydney Gazette* singled out for special mention the many ladies of the first respectability who were present. By a curious irony, Marsden, who courted the respect of the powerful with a desperation which exposed him to ridicule, adopted a cold and haughty tone in his relations with the emancipists. Marsden could see no reason why the hopes of the poor or those whose families had been stained by crime should be raised in this world, where such people did not increase in divine things but remained permanently depraved. So ineluctable was the tie between public religious piety and respectability that most affluent ex-convicts ignored these snubs.

Early in 1803 another source of opinion in the colony began to propagate the connection between the evangelicals and respectability. That was the *Sydney Gazette and New South Wales Advertiser* itself, which began publication on 5 March 1803 under the editor-ship of George Howe, who had been transported in 1800, probably for a political offence. The pages of his newspaper between 1803 and 1823 mirrored faithfully the values of the Protestant cast of mind which were to rise to power and ascendancy in the period of Macquarie.

It was a religion which rejoiced in the blessings that Divine Providence seemed so wantonly to lavish on the English race and which encouraged an insolent superiority to all other religious persuasions. It was typical of the *Sydney Gazette* that it should report how, one Thursday in March 1806, some Asiatic seamen marched in procession from the waterfront in Sydney Cove to a house at the lower end of Back Row East with torches, where they paraded round a fire, all the time uttering the most hideous howls. The paper reported how, after they had ranged themselves in front of a temple, they performed wild and incredible extravagances amidst the odoriferous fumigation of sandalwood and other perfumes, till two of them seemed to pierce the cheeks, tongues, and thighs with peculiarly constructed instruments, at the same time bellowing with pain, as three tambourines beat time for the vocal accompani-ment of the whole group. Howe, who each Sunday recited his belief in the communion of saints, the resurrection of the body, and the life of the world to come, dismissed their behaviour as very extrava-gant and bearing strong marks of unaccountable superstition.

Such Protestants were not concerned, however, with debating or inquiring into the meaning of life: they knew it. They believed life to be a preparation for eternity. They believed passionately that what happened to a man was his just desert; the righteous, they believed, were launched by death into paradise, the evil were launched into everlasting damnation. The supreme example of a just desert was death by hanging, an awful spectacle which, the *Sydney Gazette* hoped, might serve as a lasting warning against the prosecution of crime, and therefore effectually promote the ends of moral rectitude.

In April King read first in the London newspapers, and then in a dispatch, of His Majesty's entire approbation of his conduct as well as His Majesty's satisfaction at the great improvement of the colony under his superintendence. In the same dispatch he read that his successor had sailed for New South Wales. On 7 August William Bligh arrived at Sydney on the *Lady Sinclair*, and took the oaths as Captain-General and Governor-in-Chief of the colony of New South Wales and its dependencies on 13 August. The next day George Johnston, for the military, Richard Atkins, for the civil officers, and John Macarthur presented King with an address in which they

respectfully entreated him to accept their unfeigned wishes for his
health, happiness and prosperity as well as a hope that His Majesty
would duly appreciate his services. King was unaware that the
developments in trade and sheep-breeding to which his own contribution had not been negligible had laid the material foundations
of a civilization in both New South Wales and Van Diemen's Land.
His strength had been so undermined by the severe attacks of gout
which had wasted his powers since the days on Norfolk Island that
he died in England on 3 September 1808 before any official recognition of his nineteen years of service to New South Wales had been
made.

6

Mutiny

When William Bligh was welcomed ashore at Sydney Cove with great ceremony and rejoicing, he was almost 52 years old. In stature he was short. His form erred on the side of the corpulent, but not from over-indulgence in food or drink, for he was by nature temperate in all the passions of the flesh. In his soul, however, he harboured a deep and ungovernable rage which was to unleash a great upheaval among the men and women he had been sent to govern. For the man who stepped ashore at Sydney Cove that day was little changed from the Captain Bligh who, in November 1787, set out from Spithead for the South Seas in search of breadfruit and glory as captain of the *Bounty*. Near Tahiti in April 1789, a section of the *Bounty's* crew, led by John Adams and Fletcher Christian, found themselves so tormented by the rages and cruel discipline of Bligh that they seized him in his cabin and set him adrift in a long boat with his supporters, provisions and a compass. With the courage and determination he always displayed in the face of adversity, he sailed his long boat through treacherous waters to the safety of Timor. With the blindness which he was display to the end of his days, he gained no wisdom from his ordeal, but attributed the mutiny to the sensual appetites of those who had deposed him.

On 14 August 1806 the acting Judge Advocate, Richard Atkins, administered the oaths of office. A few weeks later Macarthur met Bligh and King at Government House, Parramatta, and moved the conversation round to sheep, whereupon Bligh exploded and asked him what he, Bligh, had to do with his sheep, sir, and what had he to do with his cattle, sir and was Macarthur to have such flocks of sheep and such herds of cattle as no man heard of before, and though Macarthur, sir, had 5000 acres of land in the finest situation in the country, by God sir, he would not keep it. King wept.

Bligh was appalled by the condition of the colony and by the customs and manners of its inhabitants. He soon adjudged Atkins so given over to inebriety that he had become the ridicule of the community. In a tour through the colony Bligh lamented that the most calamitous evils had been produced by the system of bartering in spirits, and on 14 February 1807 he issued orders to prohibit the exchange of liquor as payment in any circumstances. The penalties for a breach were severe. A prisoner, for example, was to receive 100 lashes and twelve months' hard labour. A free settler was to lose all indulgences granted by the Crown and pay a fine of £50, a portion of which was to be granted to the informer.

Bligh was convinced that the immediate economic future lay in the encouragement of agriculture rather than in the development of the wool trade or the Bass Strait and overseas trade, or in manufactures. He educated the farmers in methods of soil conservation; he taught them to sow rye and clover grass to improve their pastures and, to the delight and approval of the farmers on the Hawkesbury, and near Parramatta and Sydney, spoke and wrote of them as the backbone of society in New South Wales. Those with interests in wool, such as Macarthur, or trade, such as Simeon Lord, were understandably less enthusiastic.

Others started to complain about the new Governor's harsh administration. Some were angered when a row of houses occupied by emancipists was ordered to be demolished at the cost of what looked like the total ruin of the wretches who inhabited them. Some were disgusted by the vile and degrading language which Bligh used to the prisoners and other vagrants. Some were nauseated by the pleasure Bligh seemed to derive from signing a death warrant and by his singular lack of generosity in using the power to pardon. If anyone dared to object or remonstrate with him, he seemed to lose his senses: his features became distorted, he foamed at the mouth, stamped on the ground, shook his fist in the face of the person so presuming, and uttered a torrent of obscene abuse. His opponents began to call him Caligula. Early in 1807, Samuel Marsden warned Bligh that a great political storm was fast gathering in the colony. Bligh replied that he fully relied on the authority of His Majesty's commission to protect him, whereupon Marsden decided to gratify his desire to preach the gospel in New Zealand, and sailed away from trouble on 8 February 1807. Bligh still had powerful supporters in the colony, but before the year was out he had the singular folly to convince both Simeon Lord and John Macarthur that the comparison with Caligula was not inept.

Lord had written to Bligh seeking permission to transfer goods from one ship to another without first landing them. Bligh, suspicious of any attempt to evade the letter of the regulations, prosecuted Lord for presuming to make such a request. He was convicted, and

Atkins signed an order by which Lord had the mortifying experience of being imprisoned for one calendar month, and reduced once
again to the company of common criminals. By the end of the year
Macarthur had also been prosecuted, after the crew of a ship, in
which he allegedly held an interest, violated the regulations by
coming ashore to obtain rations. When the trial began on 25 January
1808, Macarthur asked that Atkins step down from the bench,
because a suit was pending between them. When Atkins refused to
budge, Macarthur told the court they had to decide whether law
and justice should finally prevail. He condemned the contrivances
of the convict attorney George Crossley, and declared that, in his
eyes, the reputable were on trial before the disreputable in some
low mockery of justice. At the end of his impassioned speech the
court broke up in confusion.

The following day was 26 January, the anniversary of the foundation of the colony, a day traditionally observed in drinking and
merriment. Early that morning the soldiers, whom in a moment of
great foolishness Bligh had described as wretches, paraded in their
barracks as usual. Almost at the same hour, Macarthur was arrested
and placed in Sydney gaol. At ten o'clock, the six military officers
who had sat with Atkins asked Bligh to restore Macarthur to bail,
and appoint an impartial person to replace Atkins. Bligh consulted
Atkins, who responded by accusing the six officers of inciting
rebellion and treason. Bligh then wrote to each of the officers,
requiring them to appear at Government House at nine on the
following morning to answer certain charges.

Macarthur was restored to bail, and went to Barrack Square
where he wrote to Major Johnston imploring him instantly to place
Governor Bligh under arrest and to assume the command of the
colony. The letter concluded, 'We pledge ourselves, at a moment of
less agitation, to come forward to support the measure with our
fortunes and our lives'. It was signed by more than 100 inhabitants
of all descriptions including John Macarthur, Gregory and John
Blaxland and Simeon Lord. That evening Major Johnston
announced that Bligh, Atkins and one Robert Campbell had been
arrested, and told the inhabitants of Sydney and Parramatta that in
future they were to obey him. All night the carousing, the cheering,
and the singing went on in Barrack Square, while no one so much
as lifted a finger to help Bligh, as he raged into the night, impotent
and alone except for the company of his faithful daughter and his
secretary. Atkins and the magistrates were replaced, and the trial of
Macarthur resumed. The court of six officers, with Charles Grimes
as acting Judge Advocate, unanimously acquitted him of all
charges.

By September both Johnston's and Bligh's accounts of the events had reached London. The man to whom their dispatches were addressed had a peculiar horror of mutiny. He was Robert Stewart, Viscount Castlereagh, a model of wit and discretion to his supporters, but reviled by others as an unfeeling tyrant. Byron called him an intellectual eunuch, a despot who deemed the chain the fit garb for man. To such a man Johnston had appealed, not knowing that no feeling dwelt in that ice when questions of law and order were involved.

In the meantime, Bligh's hopes ran high. By April 1808 the people who had deposed him were hopelessly divided, and beginning to reproach each other. The freeholders and cultivators of land in the County of Cumberland, Sydney Cove and its hinterland denounced Macarthur as a scourge of the colony, a fomenter of quarrels, and the creator of a system of monopoly and extortion. From Van Diemen's Land, Paterson and Collins expressed their highest indignation at the proceedings of the memorable twenty-sixth.

On 28 July, Lieutenant-Colonel Joseph Foveaux arrived at Sydney Cove on his way back to Norfolk Island from England. The convicts at Norfolk Island knew him as the man who laughed when they asked for mercy during a flogging, as a man who had ordered so many floggings for one man that his back was bare of flesh and his shoulder blades exposed like two polished ivory horns. He had also permitted young and attractive female convicts to be sold openly to free settlers and convicts. But people who mixed in Government House society in Sydney found him handsome, attentive and obliging. Bligh believed that Foveaux, who was senior to Johnston, had arrived in the colony with authority to reinstate him. But within a month Foveaux had placed Bligh under house arrest and had written to Castlereagh that Bligh had so violated private property, and so tyrannized over the colonists, that nothing but his removal from the government could have prevented an insurrection.

Foveaux was anxious to wash his hands of the mess he had inherited and in December gladly handed over authority when a reluctant Paterson arrived from Port Dalrymple to assume command. Any thought Paterson had of supporting Bligh vanished after Bligh vented his fury against him. Cut adrift by his colleagues and subordinates, and with few supporters, Bligh spent the next two months in impotent rage, sometimes as a prisoner in Government House with his spy glass still trained on the waters of Sydney Cove, looking desperately for the arrival of a ship which would confound his enemies, and sometimes scheming aboard his ship, the *Porpoise*. In March he fled to Hobart Town in a futile, blustering attempt to win support from Collins and his fellow officers there, during which time, in another of those incredible acts of madness and folly, he had the son of Lieutenant-Governor Collins tied up and flogged with two dozen lashes for insubordination.

He was still in Hobart Town when relief arrived from England and was not present to hear his successor tell the crowd assembled on Sydney Cove on 1 January 1810 of His Majesty's high displeasure at the mutinous and unwarrantable removal of his late representative, William Bligh.

When the *Porpoise* did arrive at Sydney Cove, however, on 17 January, Bligh was saluted by His Majesty's ships and from the battery at Dawes Point. When he landed the next day, the ships in the harbour again saluted him, while on shore he and his loyal daughter were received by the Governor-in-Chief and his lady with every possible mark of respect. But the new Governor soon found him a most disagreeable person, as he had no regard whatever for his promises or engagements however sacred, and his natural temper was uncommonly harsh and tyrannical in the extreme. He was heartily glad to get rid of him when, after a round of festive farewells, Bligh finally sailed out on to the high seas aboard the *Hindostan* on 12 May with only the madness of revenge to comfort him during his long journey across the ocean to England. There he would confront Johnston and Macarthur who had set sail several weeks earlier.

Eleven days before Bligh's departure, at eleven in the morning, Colonel William Paterson and his lady had boarded the *Dromedary* to a salute of guns. As the party passed the public landing wharf a numerous body of inhabitants burst into cheering, while crowded boats followed the colonel's pinnace to the ship. The cheering, the shouting, the displays of grief at parting, all the unmistakable signs that the crowds were saying farewell to a likeable and benevolent man, drifted over the waters to the *Hindostan*, to be heard by an unloved man who was probably comforting himself with dark and monstrous thoughts about his enemies rather than advancing in wisdom by examining the causes of his cruel fate. Fate, however, was more cruel than man to Paterson; he died on 20 June, during the passage around Cape Horn, and was buried in the great water of the south seas.

Fate also snatched away another actor in the drama before the judgement of the powers that be was proclaimed. Towards the end of 1809 an unwonted melancholy began to descend on David Collins at Hobart Town. Early in the new year he died, and his dignified funeral was attended by over 600 persons.

In the meantime Bligh, Johnston and Macarthur, with their supporters and their accomplices, prepared to face the judgment of man. On 7 May 1811, a general court martial began at the Royal

Hospital, Chelsea, at which Major Johnston was arraigned for beginning, exciting, causing and joining in a mutiny. After having duly and maturely weighed the evidence the court pronounced Johnston guilty of the act of mutiny and sentenced him to be cashiered. At the same time the Commander-in-Chief explained that in passing a sentence so inadequate to the enormity of the crime the court had apparently been actuated by a consideration of the mood and extraordinary circumstances which appeared to have existed during the administration of Governor Bligh, both as affecting the tranquillity of the colony and as calling for some immediate decision. Johnston was allowed to return to the colony as a settler in October 1812, when he took up land at Annandale and farmed quietly. He died on 3 January 1823 just when the War Office was getting round to giving sympathetic consideration to his appeals for compensation. Macarthur was not granted permission to return till the end of 1816. For a season, he wrestled with a fate which separated him from his beloved wife and his dear girls, for at that time he could see no hope that he would ever be permitted to reside in New South Wales exempt from danger and persecution.

So it seemed that Bligh's enemies were confounded, and he was rewarded, for on 31 July 1811 he was promoted to Rear Admiral. But when news of his death on 7 December 1817 at the age of 65 reached Sydney Cove, a generation which so frequently and so lavishly indulged in displays of public grief did not bestir itself. The clergy were silent, while the officers, both civil and military, were indifferent. By then, a new vision was taking hold of the colony, a vision in which the deeds of William Bligh had no place. Once again, chance and circumstance connived to ensure that in the history of human affairs the man who was angry without cause bequeathed no monument of achievement to posterity, and tasted deep damnation on earth as the fruit of his disquiet.

7

The Convict System in New South Wales in 1810

When Bligh's successor arrived in 1810, he was assuming responsibility for a society which contemporaries divided into six groups. First there were the military officers; second, the civil officers; third, the settlers, including both those from England and those who had taken grants of land after receiving their pardons. Emancipist settlers were treated by the military officers as socially inferior to the free settlers, but a convict past was not regarded by all the free settlers as a perpetual bar to a social future. Fourth, there were the landholders, men paying rent, a class which included some ticket-of-leave men; fifth, the free workers; and sixth, the ticket-of-leave workers and the convicts. At the base of the social pyramid were the men and women undergoing the punishment of exile and forced labour originally designed to punish, to reform, and to provide a work force for the colony. In practice, it was a system based on meeting the economic needs of the colony, a system of regulations and conventions which remained unaltered in its essentials from 1806 until the abolition of transportation to New South Wales in 1840.

After convicts came ashore, those with property were immediately granted tickets-of-leave, and women with husbands in the colony were assigned to them. The rest were divided between those who were to work for the government and those who were assigned to military and civil officers and settlers. Women were assigned for domestic service either in Sydney or one of the settlements, or sent to work in the Female Factory at Parramatta which opened in 1804 on the first floor of the new gaol there. Women might be employed in the manufacture of wool, or spinning, picking oakum, husking corn, picking weeds, sail-making, caring for orphans, hospital nursing, dairying, midwifery or in domestic service to the NSW Corps.

The male convicts in government service were divided into gangs: for every two or three gangs there was a superintendent, frequently chosen from among the convicts with a good-conduct record. The hours of labour were prescribed in the regulations governing convict discipline. Gunfire at daylight, followed by the tolling of a bell, marked the beginning of the day's work, which, with intervals for meals, continued for up to nine hours on week-days and five hours on Saturdays. Those on task work finished as soon as their task for the day was performed. On Sundays all labour was forbidden. After regulation labour the convicts could hire themselves out for wages, paid in money or kind or both. As skilled labour was short, there was ample opportunity for the skilled worker to earn good wages. There was a career in the colony for the skilled and the industrious, an economic advancement which had little if anything to do with moral behaviour.

The occupations of male convicts were as varied as the needs of the settlement. In Sydney in 1805, for example, the building labourers were building Fort Phillip, a wharf, a brick house for the Judge Advocate, a brick house for the main guard, a brick printing office, a repairing store, and houses; at Parramatta they were making alterations to the brewery, building a brick house for the Reverend Samuel Marsden, and repairing storehouses and officers' and soldiers' barracks; others were building a school house at the Hawkesbury. The boat and shipbuilders were fitting the *Investigator* for service and working on other ships, building rowing and longboats for the use of all the settlements, keeping the punts in repair, and squaring some 5 500 feet of ship timber. The wheel and millwrights were making and repairing carts, timber and gun carriages, ploughs and harrows, or repairing the mills. Those who worked on colonial ships helped to establish the new settlement of Port Dalrymple, or carried supplies between Sydney and Norfolk Island, Hobart Town or the Hawkesbury, or carried coal, cedar and salt from Newcastle. The town and gaol gangs built and repaired roads and loaded and unloaded boats, while those employed in manufacturing in hemp, flax, and wool made canvas, sacking, girthing, linen, blankets, flannel, coarse cloth and collar cloth.

The condition of the assigned servant varied from employer to employer. Broadly, the condition of convicts assigned to an opulent settler was superior. The convicts were not encouraged to wander from their master's farm, as by exertion they could accumulate wealth and obtain property. In any case, they were not to absent themselves without leave; nor were they to go from one settlement to another without a pass from a magistrate. By contrast the convicts assigned to the less opulent settlers perforce wandered in search of extra labour, and in such wanderings were exposed to temptations. They generally inhabited the same houses as their masters, and frequently the same apartments. But whether assigned to the opulent or to the poorer settler, few possessed habits of cleanliness and order.

This was an alienated working class, a class with no spiritual or material interest in the products of its work. It quickly developed that habit of defiance and that spirit of resentment which characterize people driven or terrorized into labour. The men sought escape from the squalor and wretchedness of their lives in drinking, violence, gambling and sexual licence. Contemporary critics attributed some of their vicious behaviour to the close association of so many depraved and desperate characters. Such treachery, however, was nourished by the atmosphere of terror, as the officials—the Governor, the military and civil officers, the chaplains, the magistrates, the superintendents and the overseers—believed one and all that physical terror was the one effective restraint.

A major incentive to industry and good conduct was the ticket-of-leave, which released the convict holding it from government work to engage in any lawful occupation for his own advantage. There were certain restrictions on his freedom of movement, however, and limits on his legal rights; he could not leave his police district without permission; he could not own though he could lease land. Tickets-of-leave were granted to newly arrived convicts who possessed property or social standing, or had been transported for an action not involving criminal turpitude. Up to 1810 observers praised them as an incentive. By 1820 men of a conservative cast of mind were beginning to wonder whether they had enabled men to climb not only to the rank in society they had forfeited but to much higher ranks, thereby subverting the traditional hierarchies in society.

The major incentive to reformation was the prospect of a pardon—absolute or conditional. An absolute pardon contained a declaration that the unexpired term of transportation was absolutely remitted. A conditional pardon contained a declaration that the unexpired term of the convict's sentence was remitted to him on condition that he continued to reside within the limits of New South Wales (including Van Diemen's Land) for the remainder of the original sentence. In practice, pardons were granted for displays of bravery, for performing essential work within a prescribed time, for convicts transported for political offences, for persons sentenced to transportation during a period of crisis such as 1798—the year of troubles in Ireland.

Emancipists and expirees who elected to stay in the colony were eligible for a land grant if, in the opinion of the Governor, they were deserving of favour. Others became hirelings for wages. By 1810 a few ex-convicts, by the exercise of industry and cultivation, had raised themselves to a state of affluence. Andrew Thompson, who had arrived in 1792 under sentence of transportation for theft, was pardoned in 1797, obtained a lease of land in 1799, put up a granary, bought ships for trade with King Island, Van Diemen's Land, New Zealand and the Pacific Islands, and built both a saltworks and a bridge across the Hawkesbury. James Larra was transported for stealing a silver tankard in 1790. By 1806 he was regarded as one of the wealthiest proprietors in New South Wales, while the regularity of his habits and the honesty of his character won for him genuine respect. But for most convicts, getting on in the world was no easier than for the camel to pass through the eye of the needle. Although there were abundant opportunities for skilled and unskilled to work in their leisure moments for high wages, the system provided as many opportunities for their dissipation. Environment worked hand in hand with innate disposition to ensure that few convicts in government service rose out of the working class.

Up to 1810 no emancipist or native-born talked of the colony as peculiarly his own, let alone of 26 January as a day of general significance in his life. The men with pretensions, the men of sentiment, and the men sensitive to family ties or the tug of 'the Old Dart', or indeed any haunt for which they felt strong affection, worked their passages back to England or Ireland, while the women prostituted themselves to the officers and sailors on ships sailing for England or Ireland.

Meanwhile, the inhabitants spent part of their time in ceremonies which reminded them of their homeland. On St Patrick's Day the Governor gave an entertainment for the government labourers and artificers, on which day, according to the *Sydney Gazette*, British hospitality displayed itself, and every heart was filled with sentiments of respect and gratitude. Each year the birthday of their most gracious sovereign was ushered in with the ringing of bells and display of flags. Flags flew from the mastheads of all the ships in the cove, while the royal standard waved conspicuously at Fort Phillip, and the Union Jack at Dawes Point. Such were the symbols which stirred their affections, for this was an isolated society in a state of siege, with human depravity in the attack, and force, terror, fear, spying, prying, rumour and meddling the weapons for its defence. But the plain fact was that the system worked, and a civilization had been planted by convict labour.

8

Macquarie

Shortly after midday on 1 January 1810, Lachlan Macquarie addressed his fellow citizens and fellow soldiers in a short and very animated speech on the parade ground at Sydney Cove. To many who listened as he pledged to exercise authority in the spirit of justice and impartiality, and expressed himself hopeful that all dissensions and jealousies would end, it appeared that the man to bring unity and purpose to the divided colony had that day taken office as their Captain-General and Governor-in-Chief and that Caligula had been succeeded by an improver. That night the town of Sydney and the ships in the harbour where brightly illuminated. The brilliant spectacle seemed pervaded by the sentiments of reconciliation, moral improvement, welfare and prosperity which Macquarie had declared to be both his ardent wish and his duty to promote.

Macquarie was born into a society which, by tempering the inhumanity of Calvinist teaching with some of the common sense of the Enlightenment, had put forward the upright man as the ideal of human behaviour. He was born in 1761 on the island of Mull, the son of a farmer. His mother imbued him with great gifts of industry and courage. He entered the army as an ensign in 1776 and served with distinction in North America, India, Egypt and Europe. All that he saw in foreign climes confirmed the principles he had imbibed in his homeland that the Protestant religion and British institutions were indispensable both for liberty and a high material civilization.

First he had to carry out his instructions for dealing with the rebels. On the day of his welcome, he posted a proclamation expressing the high displeasure of His Majesty on account of the late tumultuous and mutinous proceedings to depose Bligh. Three days later, he dismissed all the officers appointed by Johnston, Foveaux and Paterson, restored those who had been dismissed, and declared all trials and investigations held after the mutiny invalid, and all pardons, grants and leases of land null and void.

Within weeks he turned to improve the morals of the people, especially those of the lower orders. The very shameful and indecent profanation of the sabbath was prohibited. He reduced the number of licensed houses and placed an import duty on spirits in the hope that high prices would reduce drunkenness and idleness. He addressed a proclamation against the scandalous and pernicious custom of persons of different sexes living together unsanctioned by the legal ties of matrimony. To instruct the rising generation in those principles which, he believed, could alone render them dutiful and obedient to their parents and superiors, honest, faithful and useful members of society, and good Christians, he established more schools in Sydney and the outlying settlements. To improve the religious tendency and morals of all classes in the community he issued an order that convicts of all religious persuasions must attend divine worship on Sundays, conducted according to the rites of the Church of England.

On 16 November 1810, Macquarie and his wife set out from Parramatta on a tour of the outer settlements, visiting the Cow Pastures, George's River and the Hawkesbury. On the whole he was delighted with the natural fertility and beauty of the country, with the progress in clearing the land, the increase in the area under grain, and the industry of the settlers. He could not, however, forbear expressing his regret that they had not built adequate residences for themselves nor provided suitable houses for the reception of their grain and cattle. He regretted too their neglect of decent apparel, as well as their disregard for economy and temperance. To encourage such behaviour in future he proposed to grant land and other indulgences to those who could procure unquestionable vouchers to their honesty, industry and sobriety.

Motivated by a sense of high moral purpose, he began a vigorous programme of public works. The making of roads and bridges was, as he put it, one of the first steps towards improving a new country. He began work on new barracks, a grand new hospital, granaries and other public stores. He instituted a scheme for the ornament and regularity of the streets of Sydney, to secure the peace and tranquillity of the town as well as reduce the number of disorderly and ill-disposed persons. It was the plan by which the centre of Sydney received the layout and street names it has preserved to this day. Its grandeur was part and parcel of Macquarie's concern for order and morality. He announced plans to erect a township for each settlement—at Richmond, Windsor, Pitt Town, Wilberforce, Castlereagh and Liverpool—with a church, a school house, a gaol and a guardhouse in each as the outward and visible signs of what Macquarie understood by civilization.

Macquarie had noticed that some men who had originally been sent out as convicts had, by long habits of industry and total reformation of manners, not only become respectable but by many degrees the most useful members of society. Yet these persons had never been countenanced or received into society. With great caution and delicacy, he invited four emancipists to his table: Mr D'Arcy Wentworth, principal surgeon, Mr William Redfern, assistant surgeon, Mr Andrew Thompson, a wealthy farmer and landowner, and Mr Simeon Lord. He also appointed Andrew Thompson to be a justice of the peace and a magistrate at the Hawkesbury, and planned to confer the same marks of distinction on Lord and Wentworth when vacancies occurred.

In the *Sydney Gazette* on 31 March, Macquarie announced the appointment of Marsden, Simeon Lord and Andrew Thompson as trustees and commissioners for the turnpike road to be built between Sydney and the Hawkesbury. Marsden, who had only recently returned to the colony, informed Macquarie that he would not sully the reputation of his sacred office by serving in such a capacity with ex-convicts. Macquarie flew into a rage, shouting that it was just as well Marsden held a civil commission, or he would have had him tried for disobedience by court martial. When Andrew Thompson died seven months later, at the age of 37, Macquarie attended the funeral as chief mourner. The Governor who had dedicated himself to the destruction of faction in the colony had begun to identify himself ostentatiously with the cause of the emancipists.

By the end of 1812, both in England and in the colony, Macquarie was on the crest of the wave of success. Perhaps his reputation in England was even higher than in the colony. A committee of the House of Commons was set up to inquire into transportation. It found that the colony was entirely answering the ends proposed by its establishment. The committee made recommendations for reforming the court system and for introducing some kind of council to share administration with the Governor, but they were full of praise for Macquarie's achievements. They singled out for special mention his principle that good conduct should lead a man back to that rank in society which he had forfeited.

As more settlers arrived, and increasing numbers of officers and former convicts took up land, the settlement began to expand along the valley of the Hunter River and to the south-west towards Bringelly and the Cow Pastures. Expansion west of Penrith was blocked by the Blue Mountains, and all attempts to cross them had failed. By 1811 Gregory Blaxland believed it had become essential that more grasslands be found to support the colony's sheep and cattle. He set out with a party of three Europeans and two Aborigines, and came back convinced that it would be possible to cross the mountains by keeping to the crowning ridge. The drought of 1812–13 quickened his desire to find more grass. With William Charles Wentworth (the son of D'Arcy Wentworth and Catherine Crowley), William Lawson and four servants, five dogs, and four horses laden with provisions and ammunition, Blaxland set out from his farm at South Creek on 11 May 1813. By 31 May they were standing high on the western edge of the mountains, looking down on the plains beyond, at forest and grassland sufficient to support the stock of the colony for the next thirty years.

At the end of the year, Macquarie appointed G. W. Evans to lead a party of five over the mountains. They followed Blaxland's track and descended into the plains till they reached a river on which Evans conferred the name of Macquarie. As soon as Macquarie heard of this beautiful country, he decided to build a road across the mountains. It was begun in July 1814 and finished six months later. On 25 April Macquarie set out with his wife and a small party of public officials to see the new district. On Sunday 7 May, on the west bank of the Macquarie River, Macquarie fixed on a site for the erection of a town, to which he gave the name of Bathurst in honour of the Secretary of State for the Colonies. Here, as he saw it, was an opportunity for sober industrious men with small families from the middling class to receive from 50 to 100 acres of land, and where gentlemen of the upper class of settlers and great graziers might receive large grants of fine country. Here, indeed, was the opportunity, and the man with the imagination to dream the great dream.

In May 1815 Evans travelled over 100 miles through fine country to the west of Bathurst, where he discovered a river flowing to the south-west to which he gave the name of Lachlan. The country, he wrote to Macquarie, was good indeed. On 31 May Evans and his party came on an Aborigine who was quite terrified. The Aborigine ran up a tree in a moment, where he hollered and cried so much that he could have been heard a mile away: the more Evans spoke to him the more he cried. By a curious coincidence this cry of fear was uttered on the Bathurst Plains at a time when Macquarie was beginning to make his bid to conciliate the affections of the Aborigines and to civilize them, so as to render them industrious and useful to the government, as well as to improve their own condition.

To civilize the Aborigines Macquarie established a Native Institution at Parramatta under Mr William Shelley in which the native youth of both sexes were to be educated in habits of industry and decency, beginning with six boys and six girls. The institution was opened on 18 January 1815; but the parents immediately retrieved some of their children. As Macquarie noted with regret, the natives, timid and suspicious as they were by nature, had not sufficient confidence in Europeans to believe that the institution was solely intended for their advantage and improvement. He also allotted a piece of land on the shore of Port Jackson where adult natives could settle and cultivate the land, till they had learned to prefer the productive effects of their own labour and industry to the wild and precarious pursuits of the woods.

Throughout all this time, Macquarie remained a champion for the rights of the reformed convict and of the humble settler. It was a commitment which was to make powerful opponents, and which was destined to prove his undoing. On 13 June 1813, Phillip Connor and Archibald McNaughton, both officers of the 73rd Regiment and both much intoxicated, followed Elizabeth Winch down Pitt Street using indecent expressions to her. She took sanctuary in the house of Mr and Mrs Holness. The two officers forced their way inside, and a fight ensued in which Mr Holness was killed. In the trial which followed, the Judge Advocate's court found the officers not guilty of murder, but guilty of feloniously slaying and killing William Holness, fined them one shilling each, and sentenced them to imprisonment for six months. Macquarie was appalled by the verdict. Little justice, he wrote, could be expected towards the poor while the court consisted of brother officers of the prisoner at the bar. To him it was a melancholy and disgraceful occasion. But so virtuous a man might himself fall victim to his own high-mindedness. The exclusives—those who would exclude convicts and their kind from positions of rank and power—were becoming increasingly impatient with Macquarie's emancipist sympathies and had begun to say among themselves that the Governor was a threat to order, decency and prosperity.

Macquarie's strengths and weaknesses were revealed in his handling of the affairs of Van Diemen's Land and David Collins's successor, Lieutenant-Governor Thomas Davey. Davey arrived in Hobart Town in February 1813 to face problems which he had neither the capacity nor the inclination to handle. He was appalled with the magnitude of his task; the most deplorable chaos prevailed, the stores were pillaged of their contents, little regard was paid to religious worship, Government House resembled a barn, the troops lacked a barracks and the sick a hospital, the settlers were exposed to depredations by the convicts, and subordination was not observed. Within three years Davey had certainly improved the material conditions, but he was also venal and corrupt in his public life, as he was privy to and sanctioned the smuggling of spirits. Furthermore, he was winning notoriety for his eccentricities of behaviour. 'Mad Tom' or the 'Mad Governor' the locals called him. By day and by night he caroused at the Bird in Hand in Argyle Street, frequently with convicts as his drinking companions. He was unconventional in dress and manner of speaking, walking the streets in his shirt sleeves, calling all and sundry by their Christian names or even by their nicknames, dropping in at the first house he came to for a drink, and cohabiting openly and unashamedly with convict women.

Lord Bathurst endorsed a recommendation by Macquarie that Davey should be removed, and instructed him to appoint Colonel William Sorell in his place. Macquarie was to grant land to Davey in the neighbourhood of Port Jackson as that appeared the only way to afford relief to his wife and family. Davey died in England on 2 May 1823, bequeathing to his wife and daughter the land which had been intended to console them for all the humiliations and indignities they had suffered from his waywardness.

So far, Macquarie could sing with the psalmist that the ungodly were trapped in the work of their own hands, and the wicked turned into hell. But at the very pinnacle of his achievement Macquarie had begun to follow the road that would lead him to his private hell. His preoccupation with the righteousness of his own position was becoming so overpowering that it engulfed more and more of his time and energy. Such was the story of his worsening relations with Marsden. Despite the heat engendered by several disagreements over matters temporal and spiritual since 1810, Marsden had rejoiced to have so moral a man as Captain-General and Governor-in-Chief of the colony of New South Wales, for Marsden was not a man to challenge the Governor's authority, not only because he accepted without question the principle that the powers that be had been ordained by God, but because by temperament he was prepared to cringe before the temporal power.

But on 15 July 1815, Marsden addressed a memorandum to Macquarie on morals and crime at Parramatta. Macquarie replied promptly, thanking him for the information and suggestions, and telling him of the steps he proposed to take to reduce crime and immorality. On the surface it appeared a polite exchange, but appearances deceive, for unwittingly Marsden had sown in Macquarie's mind the idea that he held him responsible for the vices and miseries of these people. By then other events had planted in the Governor's mind the dark thought that Marsden's motives were unqualified opposition to him and his government. That emerged from his quarrel with the Bents.

Late in 1813 the Judge Advocate, Ellis Bent, argued with Macquarie over delays in building a new courthouse, losing his temper in what Macquarie called a passionate and unbecoming manner. The two men had once enjoyed a mutual cordiality, but from the day of their falling out Bent never again visited Government House except on official business, and rudely declined an invitation to dine there. From that time Macquarie detected slights to his person and his position in everything Bent did. In church, as a mark of respect, all the laity rose when the Governor entered, but now Bent remained in his seat in a quaint outburst of nonconformity in the service of human vanity.

Towards the emancipists Bent acted as though nothing could ever restore a man to his former rank in society, and heatedly opposed Macquarie's attempts to elevate them to such offices and stations in society as caused offence to the sensibilities of respectable people.

Macquarie was puzzled by Bent's antagonism. As he saw it, his best endeavours had been uniformly and strenuously exerted to produce the welfare and prosperity of all the inhabitants. He had served in the army for 38 years with honour and credit and Ellis Bent was the only officer with whom he had ever had any serious disagreement on points of public duty. Eventually Macquarie asked Bathurst to instruct and admonish Bent to behave with more respect and deference, and tell him plainly how far he was subject to Macquarie's orders.

This was what Bent at the same time was urging Bathurst not to do. He was groping his way towards a statement of a position which would separate the judicial and executive powers. The Governor, he wrote, considered the Judge Advocate as a subaltern officer, a cipher, a person sent out simply for his convenience, and merely to execute his commands as one of his staff. Macquarie, he said, saw the court as a species of court martial, assembled by a brigade order issued from headquarters.

On 7 February 1814 Ellis Bent's brother, Jeffery Hart Bent, was commissioned in London as the Judge of the newly constituted Supreme Court of New South Wales. A graduate of Trinity College, Cambridge, he was endowed by nature with a sensitive mind, a love of etiquette, and a horror of cruelty. When he arrived at Sydney Cove on 28 July, he was mortified to learn that Macquarie was reluctant to receive him with an appropriate salute of guns, lest such a ceremony might convey false ideas of importance.

The following February the new court building was at last ready for use, and the *Sydney Gazette* was writing with enthusiasm of the massive pillars of stone and wood, the commodious size and the air of solemnity. Jeffery Bent, however, was not prepared to be grateful let alone impressed, for by then his relations with Macquarie were strained to the point where anger and folly governed the behaviour of both of them. When Bent refused to summon the Supreme Court because no solicitor had arrived from England, Macquarie snorted at it as a frivolous reason. In April, Macquarie asked Bent to permit emancipist attorneys such as George Crossley and Edward Eagar to practise in the Civil Court, but Bent would not hear of it. When the Supreme Court met on 11 May, Crossley rose to petition the court. Bent immediately ordered him to stop. The emancipists protested, but Bent insisted that he would not allow the court to be addressed by convict attorneys who had been transported as felons and who had never been admitted to the society of gentlemen. He determined to adjourn the court until the opinion of His Majesty's Government could be obtained.

Macquarie detected a deeper significance in the brawl; the Bents, he believed, were attempting to raise a party against his government. He told Bathurst that he would resign if the Bents were not removed. While the dispute was still raging, Ellis Bent become mortally ill with a dropsy of the chest. He died on 11 November. A week later, those who had attended the funeral assembled again at St John's Parramatta to hear the Reverend Samuel Marsden preach a panegyric. Those in authority, said Marsden, should use that authority to promote virtue and religion. God, he went on, had used Bent for His purposes. Bent had relieved the oppressed, judged the fatherless, and pleaded for the widow; and just as God had removed an upright judge from the Israelites, so He had taken Bent to punish them for their sins. But though sorrow might continue for a night, joy would come in the morning. Rejoice therefore, in the Lord, he counselled them, O ye righteous, and again rejoice.

These grounds for rejoicing escaped Macquarie. He left the church not in love and fellowship with his neighbour, but aware that he had enemies in the land. He sent for Marsden and in the presence of the Reverend Mr Cowper and Major Antill lectured him severely on the content of the sermon, stating that it was blasphemous to speak so highly of any man. The man who had dreamed the dream of material and moral greatness on the bank of the Macquarie River at Bathurst in May 1815 now had a mind darkened with thoughts of treachery and had turned to the lonely defence of his honour and his reputation.

9

A Question of Virtues

On the morning of Thursday 17 January 1816, news of great moment reached Sydney Cove. Under the Duke of Wellington, the British army had won the sanguinary but decisive battle of Waterloo. That night a gay assemblage graced a room at the new general hospital for a ball and supper. Stars, insignia and mottoes ornamented the arches and pillars, while the royal arms appeared at the upper end of the room through an elegant transparency. It was a memorable moment not only in the history of British civilization in the Old World, but also in the New. For by then the colony of New South Wales had begun to face problems whose solution was to influence its history until the discovery of gold in the middle of the century.

Not the least of these was to explore the land beyond the Blue Mountains to provide for the increasing number anxious to become settlers. The incentive to explore was sharpened by hope and curiosity about the destination of the inland rivers, as well as Lord Bathurst's command that such exploration should continue. In 1817 Macquarie fitted out an expedition to follow up the discoveries by Evans to the west of the Blue Mountains. As leader he chose John Oxley, the Surveyor-General of lands, with Evans as second-in-command. They were accompanied by the botanist Allan Cunningham and a team of men, and furnished with five months' provisions, carried by thirteen strong packhorses. On 27 April they began their expedition down the Lachlan River, finding to their chagrin that it was constantly dissipating in lagoons and swamps. Their hopes of finding fertile river valleys in the inland, their fantasies of an inland sea, as well as of the river as a source of life for generations yet unborn, were dashed. They left the river on 14 May and travelled south-west but found only a barren and desolate country. On 18 June a new peril beset them as rain began to fall and transformed the valley along which they were travelling into a bog.

On 23 June they arrived back at the river, and decided to proceed further down it along the edge of extensive morasses covered with water, as the land to the south was a barren scrub. For seven days there was not the least appearance of natives; nor was bird or animal of any description seen during the day, except a solitary native dog. As Oxley put it, nothing could be more melancholy and irksome than travelling over wilds which nature seemed to have condemned to perpetual loneliness and desolation. With that certainty that despair nurses in the human heart, Oxley told Macquarie by letter that they had demonstrated, beyond shadow of doubt, that no river whatever could fall into the sea between Cape Otway and Spencer Gulf, and that the land thereabouts was uninhabitable, and useless for all purposes of civilized man. In time the European was to discover that the very river which inspired these words eventually ran into the sea between Spencer Gulf and Cape Otway. The European was in time to live in this country. It was, however, to take great courage, endurance, and heroism to solve that mystery of the inland which caused Oxley to call halt in anguish on the banks of the Lachlan. In 1644 Abel Tasman had written that he who might wish to know this country must first walk over it. The first man who had followed that advice had sent up a cry of despair.

The return journey had promised to be difficult and tedious, but on 19 August they came to the long-sought Macquarie River, the sight of which, Oxley wrote, amply repaid them for all their former disappointments. The banks of this river were low and grassy, the blue gums on its banks extremely fine, and it rendered fertile a great extent of country. They reached Bathurst between eight and nine o'clock in the evening of 29 August, where the hospitable reception from Mr Cox, the superintendent of Bathurst, caused them almost to forget in the hilarity of the moment that nineteen harassing weeks had elapsed since they had set out on their journey.

Still hoping that a communication with the ocean or interior navigable waters would be discovered by following the course of the Macquarie, Macquarie fitted out another expedition under the command of Oxley. In their attempt to trace the Macquarie to its mouth, however, they failed, for by early July that river, like the Lachlan, seemed to terminate in the morasses of a marshy inland sea, and again Oxley despaired of throwing light on the obscurity in which the interior of this vast country was still shrouded. For this reason they turned east towards the coast, and by August came into a beautiful and fertile country. They met Aborigines whose appearance was most miserable, whose features, to Oxley's eye, approached deformity, and whose persons he thought disgustingly

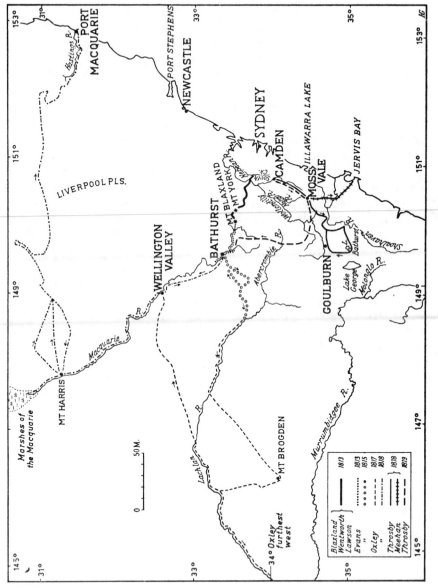

Land exploration

filthy. After crossing the mountains, the party descended to the plains where they came on a river, which Oxley named Hastings in honour of the Governor-General of India. They followed this river till the night of 4 October, when their ears heard the welcome murmurs of the ocean on the beach. They entered the bay, on which Oxley conferred the name of Port Macquarie, and then they turned their course homewards with all those feelings which that word can inspire in the wilds of Australia.

By the middle of 1819 prospects of expansion to the south-west were opened up by the fifteen-day journey of Charles Throsby from the Cow Pastures to Bathurst. He set out on 25 April accompanied by John Rowley, two servants, and two Aboriginal guides, Cookoogong and Dual. They found rich, fertile country, abounding in fine runs of water. Macquarie was delighted. New South Wales promised to be a land of opportunity for free settlers, offering an economy and a way of life clean different from a convict farm.

At the same time, a sudden increase in the number of convicts arriving also contributed to this change in the material setting. In May 1818, for example, five convict ships arrived at Sydney within one month and five days, bringing no fewer than 1046 male convicts into the colony in that short time. The settlers could not employ them all as they were suffering from the preceding year's scarcity, and the government had to employ and feed as many as it could. So Macquarie caused a great number and variety of public works to be begun. To give grace and distinction to some of the buildings the convicts built, Macquarie had the extraordinary good fortune to have the services of Francis Howard Greenway as civil architect. Greenway had practised as an architect of some eminence in Bristol and Bath where in 1812 he was charged with forging part of a building contract, and sentenced to death, a sentence which was commuted to fourteen years' transportation. So, by an act of folly, regency Bath was transported to parts of Sydney and its settlements, while churches were built to the greater glory of God which evoked that majesty and simplicity appropriate to Protestant Christianity which abhorred all intercessors and images between man and God.

A new convict barracks was built in Sydney, intended by Macquarie as a commodious spacious building for 500 to 600 convicts. On the King's Birthday, 4 June 1819, in company with the Lieutenant-Governor, the Judge Advocate, the Judge of the Supreme Court, and his own wife and son, Macquarie dined at the barracks with 600 convicts, who were enjoying material comforts before unknown. Over and above what it would contribute to their health and happiness Macquarie believed the barracks would gradually improve their morals and prevent nocturnal robberies, thefts, and various depredations. But the convicts' material and moral well-being were being achieved at the price of regimentation. Macquarie simply could not perceive that their previous life of filth, squalor and licentiousness carried with it the great boon of independence. Nor did he pause to consider that their labour could be used to develop the wealth of the older districts and the new country discovered by Oxley and Throsby. Such a vision was not vouchsafed to Macquarie because by then he was so engrossed in answering criticism, so consumed by his own righteousness in punishing the wicked.

Under the strain of opposition, Macquarie's attitude to the aspirations of the trading classes became disdainful (he described one Mr Ingle as 'a Low Vulgar Man Who has Accumulated a Considerable Property by Carrying on Trade'), and his attitudes to the weak became more and more censorious. In April 1816, his concern for the moral well-being of others led him to actions which his enemies construed as evidence of his arbitrary disposition. The shrubbery on the government Domain in Sydney was, he knew, much frequented by both men and women for 'improper purposes', and so in 1816 he issued a proclamation threatening to punish future trespassers. On Thursday18 April Daniel Read walked across the Domain on his way to work, and William Blake had also slipped into the Domain. On the following morning, for an undisclosed reason, William Henshall also crossed the Domain over the broken-down wall. They were arrested and Macquarie summarily ordered all three to receive twenty-five lashes. Bent properly took statements from all three and sent them to Bathurst as evidence of Macquarie's authoritarian excesses.

Once again Macquarie believed he was cleaving to that which was good, and abhorring that which was evil. But his enemies moved against him. They listed his arbitrary actions in a petition to be conveyed to the House of Commons by the Reverend Mr Vale. Macquarie had influenced the decisions of a jury at an inquest in which his coachman was interested; he had personally given orders for corporal punishments without any previous magisterial inquiry; he had sold pardons to convicts; he had prohibited banns of marriage; he had arbitrarily pulled down houses; he had seized lands which were presumably private property; he had influenced the courts of justice.

Macquarie was also facing opposition from the officers of the regiment. The hostility began after the arrival of the 46th Regiment in 1815. The officers soon made it clear that they resented their posting to a prison colony. They scoffed at the actions of the civil government and ridiculed Macquarie's lenient policies towards convicts and emancipists. In July 1816, Ensign Bullivant drew on the wall of the guardroom in Sydney a caricature of Macquarie in a position of ignominy with indecent scurrilous labels under it. At the same time the officers began to decline invitations to dine at Government House.

It was becoming clearer that Macquarie confounded all criticism and opposition with insubordination. On 6 February 1817, Bathurst censured Macquarie for attempting to courtmartial the Reverend Mr Vale, who had presented the 1816 petition to the House of Commons. Military chaplains, he pointed out, could only be court-martialled for absence from duty, drunkenness, or scandalous and vicious behaviour. There was worse to follow, for on 22 April 1817 Bathurst wrote instructing Macquarie to reinstate a longtime opponent, W. H. Moore, as a solicitor.

This expression of displeasure and censure had truly mortified Macquarie. He tendered his resignation as Governor-in-Chief on 1 December 1817. He had hoped, he wrote, to hold office for two or three years more, to see the matured effects of his system of government for the reformation of the inhabitants, and for their improvement and their prosperity. All his hopes had been dashed by the harsh tenor of his lordship's late letters. This utterly unmerited change was achieved by those with the rank of gentle–men, those deep designing men whose delight it was to sow the seeds of discord and insubordination.

Early in 1818 Macquarie's falling out with Marsden became increasingly bitter as each accused the other of misconduct in the treatment of prisoners. Macquarie openly accused Marsden of insolence and insubordination and of being the head of a seditious, low cabal which was seeking to bring him down. Neither man gave ground, and as the dispute worsened, Macquarie turned on Marsden by announcing in the *Sydney Gazette* that he was pleased to dispense with his services as a magistrate. Thus ended Marsden's career on the bench, that service to Caesar which he had first assumed in 1796 when he saw himself as a man not born of noble birth, nor heir to any great inheritance, but as a man whom God had highly exalted.

In the meantime Macquarie continued his efforts to civilize the Aborigines. At the end of 1816 he invited them to a friendly meeting at Parramatta, assuring them they would be kindly received, and plentifully furnished with refreshments of meat and drink. At ten o'clock on the morning of Saturday 28 December, the natives formed a circle in the marketplace at Parramatta, with the men whom the whites believed to be chiefs placed on chairs, and the rest on the ground. In the centre of the circle, several large tables groaned under the weight of roast beef and potatoes, bream, and a large cask of grog, which, as the *Sydney Gazette* saw it, lent its exhilarating aid to promote the general festivity and good humour which so conspicuously shone through the sable visages of this delighted congress. Macquarie arrived at 10.30, with all the members of the Native Institution, and several of the magistrates and gentlemen of the district. After he had met the 'chiefs', he conferred badges of distinction on them. Then came Mrs Macquarie and after her the fifteen Aboriginal children of the Institution, who were reported to look very clean, well clothed and happy. There followed an oral examination in which the children displayed their progress in learning and civilized habits of life, while the chiefs clapped the children on the head, and one turned to Macquarie with extraordinary emotion and exclaimed: 'Governor,—that will make good Settler—that's my Pickaninny'. Some of the Aboriginal women shed tears. The *Sydney Gazette* believed they were weeping to see the infant and helpless offspring of their deceased friends so happily sheltered and protected by British benevolence.

When they met again on an intensely warm day, exactly two years later, the numbers had almost doubled to nearly 300. They included Aborigines from the country west of the Blue Mountains, who were distinguishable from the rest by the feathers decorating their hair, and the teeth of wild animals suspended over their foreheads, their bodies and faces being painted with a red and white ochre. They had a degree of confidence in their manner which at least one observer interpreted as indicating a consciousness of security in the protection of European friendship.

In April 1819, prizes were distributed to the European and Aboriginal schoolchildren who had excelled in the early rudiments of moral and religious education. The *Sydney Gazette* stated it was pleasing to remark that a black girl of 14 who had been in the school for three or four years had won the first prize. Any doubt of the natives' capacity and of the quality of their intellect must now wear off. Or so the *Gazette* argued. Such might have been the grain of mustard seed. But the fruits of everyday experience were producing a climate of opinion quite unfavourable to the aspirations of the high-minded. In the country settlements, whites became convinced that their only protection lay in driving the Aborigines away by force.

The conflict between Aborigines and Europeans was being also played out in Van Diemen's Land. Macquarie's new Lieutenant-Governor, William Sorell, arrived at Hobart Town on 8 April 1817. But his attempts to carry out official policy of amity and kindness bore little fruit. The Aborigines avoided the settlements, and they destroyed livestock, as their hatred for the white man appeared to be fixed and ineradicable. The musket and the sword remained the only weapons the Europeans believed the natives could understand. Terror was the instrument of policy, and no man on the island yet dreamed such dreams as had sustained the few on the mainland.

One outsider noted Aboriginal resistance to the white man's civilization. According to the testimony of Captain Bellingshausen, a Russian officer who visited Sydney Cove and Hobart Town in 1820 on a voyage of exploration in the Pacific, the natives of Van Diemen's Land lived in a state of perpetual hostility against the Europeans. They destroyed flocks of sheep not for food but to inflict material damage upon their enemies. They hated all Europeans because of what Bellingshausen called the inexcusable behaviour of the first English settlers at the Derwent. On the day after the Russians arrived at Sydney Cove, an Aboriginal named Boongaree clambered on board the *Discovery* and, pointing to the country, told Bellingshausen: 'This is my Land.'

Bellingshausen saw that contact with European civilization had been disastrous to the natives. They had borrowed all the bad language habits of the Europeans, their oaths and curses, and had learnt to lie, to steal, to smoke, and to drink alcohol. They had gained no material possessions. They had made no progress in education in thirty-three years, and had not even the elementary notions of Christianity. All that was left to them was a memory of their former independence, and a spark of vengeance smouldering in their hearts.

At the same time, Macquarie entertained high hopes for the improvement in the material and moral well-being of the European inhabitants of Van Diemen's Land. On 14 April 1817, Sorell issued his first proclamation against bushrangers, and established a system of passes for people wishing to proceed to the country districts. By then the situation was desperate. For some of the bushrangers vengeance against society was stiffened by the concept of a higher purpose, of bushranging as a calling in which the Irish could punish the Anglo-Saxon for the wrongs of Ireland. Sorell pursued his campaign with success. On 21 October 1818, a soldier of the 48th Regiment shot Michael Howe, said to be the last of the bushrangers, at a place near the Shannon River. But this was only a lull before the storms to come, for no man could have removed the causes driving such men to the bush.

Nevertheless, in high places, zeal and enterprise had replaced the sloth and the indulgence of the Davey period. In 1818 Port Davey and Macquarie Harbour were discovered. Lieutenant-Governor Sorell proposed to form a small settlement at Macquarie Harbour to supply the other settlements with the region's abundant coal and Huon pine, and as a place of banishment and security for the worst description of offenders.

The curious thing was the response from Macquarie to all these advances. By the last quarter of 1817 he had been so wounded by opposition to his policies, and so hurt by censure when he needed approval and co-operation, that much of his enthusiasm began to drain out of his official comments on the colony. Macquarie's desire to confound his enemies engulfed him at a time when the dispatches from England should have soothed his injured pride. Early in 1819 he had received a dispatch from Bathurst approving his dismissal of Moore for affixing a signature to a petition without the signatory's consent. In March Macquarie read of the considerable satisfaction the Prince Regent had derived from his assurances of the peace, tranquillity and progressive improvements of the colony placed under his administration. He read too that the barracks for the convicts, the factory and the churches had Bathurst's entire approbation. A few months later he should have read a private dispatch in which Bathurst disavowed any imputation upon his character or the uprightness of his intentions and discounted the attacks to which in common with other public men Macquarie had been exposed. By some extraordinary mischance Macquarie did not read this dispatch till he returned to England. In any case, the initiative in the colony was passing to other hands, while Macquarie's dark thoughts were encouraged by the announcement that a commissioner had been appointed to inquire into the conditions of the colony of New South Wales.

In January 1819 Macquarie gave permission to the gentlemen, clergy, merchants, settlers and other free subjects to convene a meeting at the courtroom in the new general hospital, to prepare a petition to the throne. The petition urged the British government to lift British import tariffs and to repeal regulations which prevented smaller vessels from trading between the colony and the mother country. In addition, they respectfully requested reform of the military-dominated courts and the introduction of trial by jury. They concluded by touching upon the problem of free discussion, an inalienable right in the mother country, but here only a boon conferred by the grace of the Governor. All this was written in the respectful but common-sense language of money-changers and tillers of the soil—men who saw the future of the colony in the expansion of its trade, and who perceived vaguely that there was a connection between trade and the rights of Englishmen. It was

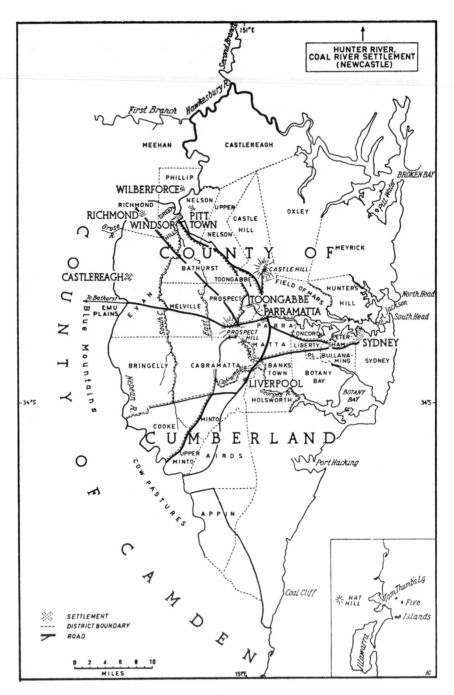

The settlements in New South Wales, *c.* 1820

signed by 1260 persons who represented, in Macquarie's words, all the men of wealth, rank or intelligence throughout the colony.

Many were Protestant, most were proud to call themselves British, and almost all aspired to material improvement and social respectability. In the society they were creating, there were signs that some of the graces of civilization were taking root. For over and above the concerts, the dances, the horse-racing, the yachting, the picnics, and the hunts of the kangaroo, other activities were beginning. In January 1818, T. Florance announced his intention to open a boarding school for young gentlemen at 74 Pitt Street where they would be instructed in English, Latin, Greek, Reading, Writing, Arithmetic, Book-keeping, Geography, Geometry, Algebra, Surveying, Navigation, and Nautical Astronomy for a fee of £40 a year with extra charges for French, Italian, Fencing, Dancing, Music, and Drawing. The next year Mrs Hickey opened a boarding and day school for young ladies at Bent Street to instruct them in English Grammar, Writing, Geography and the French Language, promising speedy improvement in pupils at £20 a year. On 16 October 1819, the first number of a literary magazine appeared which was called appropriately the *Australian Magazine,* and contained agricultural and commercial reports, original essays, British intelligence, domestic occurrences and philosophical, moral and poetical essays.

In the same year a volume of verse by Barron Field was published in Sydney with the title *First Fruits of Australian Poetry.* Whatever its quality as verse, the significant thing was that Field was writing about Australia, and seeing its harsh country, and its curious animals, through the eyes of an exile from civilization:

> Kangaroo, Kangaroo!
> Thou Spirit of Australia,
> That redeems from utter failure,
> From perfect desolation,
> And warrants the creation
> Of this fifth part of the Earth,
> Which would seem an after-birth,
> Not conceiv'd in the Beginning
> (For GOD bless'd His work at first,
> And saw that it was good),
> But merg'd at the first sinning,
> When the ground was therefore curst;—
> And hence this barren wood!

At the same time the native-born were becoming aware of themselves as Australians. In speech they had taken over the flash

language of their parents, and were developing their own distinctive pronunciation. Most of the older ones regarded the colony as
their future home. Some of them believed the colony belonged to
themselves and their descendants. For many years it had been
customary to celebrate the anniversary of the foundation of the
colony with a dinner. On Monday, 27 January 1817, for example, a
party of about forty sat down to dinner at 5 p.m. in the house of
Isaac Nichols, a respectable emancipist who held the licence of a
successful inn in George Street. At the dinner a Mr Jenkins sang
some verses of his own composition to the tune of 'Rule Britannia',
in which he sang not only of the day when Australia first rose to
fame, and seamen brave explored her shore, but of one difference
between Europe and Australia, for here was a country free from the
Old World scourge of war. So the early sentiments of Australian
patriotism, even the use of that name, were expressed at gatherings
of ex-convicts.

By 1820 these early sentiments of belonging to the country went
hand in hand with ideas of exclusive ownership: their passion of
patriotism was fed by xenophobia. For Australian xenophobia has
had a long history, and its origins might be traced to the passions
and aspirations of the convicts. From the idea that the colony
belonged to the convicts and their descendants stemmed both the
notion that the Australians could create a society free from the evils
of the Old World and that the enjoyment of such an achievement
should be reserved for the native-born.

In 1817 Macquarie, sensitive as ever to the emancipist mind,
recommended that Australia should be the name given to the
country instead of the very erroneous and misapplied name of New
Holland which, properly speaking, only applied to a part of the
immense continent. By 1820 Australia was looking undeniably
prosperous. The bulk of the wool grown in New South Wales was
shipped direct by the growers to England, and there was broad
acceptance for the principle that the settlers should use their great
natural advantages of grass and climate to grow food and wool and
should import the other goods they needed. Between 1810 and 1820
the numbers of sheep trebled, and some settlers were finding
it profitable to sell the fleeces rather than the carcasses. They
imported manufactured goods from England; sugar, spirits, soap
and cotton goods from Bengal; sugar candy, silks and wearing
apparel from China. They exported sandalwood, pearl shells and
bêche de mer to China and Java. With the islands in the Pacific they
exchanged coarse cottons and ironware for coconut and salt pork.

In the British Isles, reports that rich new territories had been
discovered began to appear in the press. The idea of New South

Wales as a land of opportunity began to take root. At the same time the feuds and brawls in the colony drifted over the seas to be metamorphosed into rumours of convict insubordination, caused by the mild and amicable manners of Governor Macquarie. Into this little world, in October 1819, walked John Thomas Bigge, appointed by Bathurst as a commissioner to inquire into conditions in the colony, and into the effectiveness of transportation as a form of punishment.

10

Macquarie and Mr Commissioner Bigge

Early in October 1819, in the great saloon of Government House in Sydney and before a large assemblage, Macquarie welcomed Commissioner Bigge to New South Wales and assured him of every aid and assistance in conducting an investigation into the affairs of the colony over which he had so long had the honour to preside. John Thomas Bigge had been educated at Westminster School and Christ Church, Oxford, and had served for a time as Chief Justice of Trinidad. He was no stranger to such occasions. In reply he adopted the tone and manner of the man who did not wear his heart on his sleeve. He assured his distinguished audience that the strictest impartiality to all, facility of access to all, and the attainment of truth would be his principal objects. Nothing, he added, would be gained from concealing the truth for private purposes, or from the gratification of malignant feelings and personal resentment. Such were the undertakings which the leading colonists heard from Thomas Bigge, the man whom the men with ideas in their minds as well as the men with madness in their hearts wanted to bend to their purposes.

Macquarie's vision for the future of the colony was fading fast as his mind fed more and more on schemes to confound his enemies and to win recognition from the people in high places in London. To achieve this, Macquarie had first of all to win the approval of Bigge. Matters began to go wrong on 30 October, when Bigge let Macquarie know that he objected to the appointment of the emancipist William Redfern as a magistrate. Bigge warned Macquarie that the appointment would not be approved at home, that it would give great offence, and might be annulled. Macquarie respectfully declared that experience had convinced him that some of the most meritorious men in the colony had been convicts. They were the men who had tilled the land, built the houses and the shops, and made wonderful efforts in agriculture, maritime speculations and manufactures. He appealed to Bigge to let these souls, as well as millions yet unborn, bless the day on which John Thomas Bigge landed on their shores and gave them what he himself so much admired—freedom.

But Bigge insisted that the appointment of a former convict to the magistracy was a measure replete with danger to the community. If Macquarie insisted on appointing Redfern he must solemnly protest against being forced in the course of his duties into any public association with him. Macquarie did insist, at the same time enjoining Redfern not to attend any bench of magistrates where there might be the least chance of meeting with Bigge.

In the meantime Bigge had begun to collect his evidence and sort out his ideas on the colony. He travelled to Bathurst and to Van Diemen's Land. He made notes and he received the views of colonists and officers, all the time gathering material for the reports which Macquarie hoped would win him the acknowledgement he craved.

Bigge came to appreciate the concern of those in high places in Sydney with the problems created by the sudden increase in the number of convicts. Between 24 August 1819 and 28 January 1820, fifteen convict ships arrived at Sydney bringing a further 2559 male and female convicts from England and Ireland, all of whom arrived in good health and without complaints about their treatment on their respective ships. The influx added greatly to the expense of the colony. It also raised again the problem of how to employ them. As Macquarie believed the settlers required very few of them, he sent as many to Van Diemen's Land as were needed there. The rest he employed on the public buildings and streets in Sydney, on building roads and bridges in the interior, and the residue on the government farm at Emu Plains.

As Bigge soon realised, Macquarie's policies were not without their critics. He himself was shocked by the extravagance of the government building programme. He read letters in which Samuel Marsden laid out his own visions of the moral reform and sobriety for the convicts, explained his plans for a female orphan institution built at Parramatta which would operate as a house of industry, and complained about the many unmerited kicks he had received from those in authority. Bigge heard what both Marsden and Macarthur had to say about the future importance of the wool industry, and listened as they praised the economic benefits and moral virtues of the assignment system. So Macquarie's decision to employ surplus convict labour on public works was made at a time when the settlers were developing the argument that an assigned convict could be reformed, and contribute to the wealth of the colony without costing government a penny. But Macquarie had lost touch, if not with the creative forces in society, then certainly with the powerful forces in that society. Events were beginning to pass him by.

While Bigge was travelling about the settlements collecting information and formulating his views, two Catholic priests, John Joseph Therry and Phillip Conolly, arrived in Sydney. On 7 May 1820, Father Conolly celebrated the mass in a temporary chapel in a house in Pitt Row, and on 8 May Father Therry offered holy mass for the glory of God and St Michael, from which day the belief spread among priests and laity that he had found that the sacred particles of the host he brought with him, consecrated by his predecessor, Father O'Flynn, had remained free from corruption. The Catholic community hailed this as a miracle. For the Catholic population of Sydney, the arrival of the priests was the day of mercy they had yearned for, and an answer to prayers that God would not allow them to be for ever shut out from the blessings of His Holy Church. For them, too, it meant at least the temporary supremacy of that priest-ridden, puritanical, superstitious, credulous Irish Catholicism in which priesthood and laity had united in an unbreakable alliance to avenge an ancient wrong. It meant, too, a Catholicism in which charity, compassion, the love of God and the preservation of the faith were entangled with the worldly aspirations of the Irish people.

Though in time the Protestants sneered at such beliefs as evidence of an attachment to a disgusting superstition, the arrival of Therry and Conolly in 1820 provoked neither anxiety nor dismay. The younger Macquarie had seen himself as a man if not sent by God, then sent at least by the British to protect the higher civilization against the corrupting influence of popish superstition and Irish squalor. Now, however, Macquarie confined himself to reporting to Bathurst that Roman Catholic chaplains had, with the permission of government, come out as passengers in the *Janus*. For the rest, the Protestant community seemed disposed to assist rather than frustrate the work of the Catholic chaplains. A Protestant, John Piper, helped them to find board and lodging. At a public meeting held on 30 June at the courthouse, Protestants agreed to unite with Catholics to raise funds to build a church. So the Catholic clergy began their pastoral work in what was to prove to be, in Australia, one of those rare calms between sectarian storms.

On 6 June 1820, Macquarie informed Conolly and Therry of the restrictions on their freedom in New South Wales. They could celebrate mass; they could marry two Catholics, but not a Catholic and a Protestant; they could baptize the children of Catholic parents; they were not to endeavour to win converts; they were not to interfere with the religious education of orphans in the government charitable institutions of the colony, who were to be instructed in the faith and doctrine of the Church of England.

There was much in what Macquarie prescribed for them which, according to the teaching of their church, contravened the laws of God. There was much, too, in the laws and practices of the colony which contravened the teaching of the Roman Catholic Church. Some of these the Roman Catholic community touched on in a petition to Bigge on 30 August 1820. The tenets of their faith, they pointed out, would not admit them to be governed in their religious offices by the ministers of any other religion or sect. In the colony there were ten public schools, in which the Protestant chaplains were zealously initiating the children of Catholics in the ceremonies of the Established Church. This system of taking advantage of the unwary debarred numerous Catholics from being educated, as it was contrary to their religious principles. They therefore petitioned Bigge to excite the compassion of their prince and ministers to look with sympathy on the dejected religious state of His Majesty's Catholic subjects, to sanction three Roman Catholic clergymen to come out to this colony, to sanction the free exercise of their sacerdotal functions, to build houses of worship, and to open seminaries for the education of their children.

In the meantime Father Conolly had left for Van Diemen's Land, where he soon created a reputation for indolence and self-indulgence. Therry remained on the mainland, and dedicated himself to the work of ministering to the religious needs of the faithful, saying mass every Sunday at Parramatta and Liverpool and twice at Sydney, giving public instruction in the mysteries of his faith, visiting the sick, and attending all persons professing the Catholic religion who might be in danger of dying within a circuit of 200 miles. Once word was brought to Father Therry that a convict sentenced to death wanted to see him for confession. After a long ride Therry came to a river in flood, and shouted to a man on the opposite bank to give help in the name of God and a departing soul. The man threw over a rope which Therry tied round his waist and plunged into the river to be hauled across to the other side, where without pausing for a rest or a change of clothing he mounted another horse and arrived in time to bring the consolation of religion to the convict before he was launched into eternity. By such acts of heroism and devotion and a boundless charity Therry demonstrated that the image of Christ lived in the sons of the Church.

While Therry and Conolly were beginning their ministry to the faithful, a political storm was brewing in the colony. Early in 1820 in the courtroom at Parramatta, Judge Barron Field held, in two cases before him, that an act of pardon did not restore the right to sue in a court of law. Furthermore, he laid down in the broadest terms the principle that persons holding absolute or conditional pardons were not thereby restored to any civil rights of free subjects, nor put in the capacity to acquire, hold or convey property, to sue or give evidence in a court of justice, unless and until their names should be inserted in some general pardon under the great seal of England. In short, an emancipated convict was not a free man. This decision forced the emancipists to appeal to the Crown, and both Houses of Parliament. Promoted by Simeon Lord and eight emancipist house-holders, a meeting was held on 23 January 1821, just as Bigge was concluding his investigations. The *Sydney Gazette* had never witnessed a more numerous, orderly and well-conducted gathering. After William Redfern was unanimously called to the chair, those present proceeded to pass a series of resolutions concerning the rights of emancipists.

On 26 January, with Redfern as president and Simeon Lord as vice-president, and eight well-known emancipists such as Samuel Terry and James Meehan as stewards, the emancipists held their anniversary dinner at Gandell's Rooms, Hyde Park, to celebrate the foundation of what they had come to call *their* colony at a time when the lawyers, the scribes and the pharisees among the officials and the free emigrants as far as they could see were threatening to take it from them. Their claims and clamour were not lost on Bigge. Redfern, whom Bigge had described as guilty of the foulest crime known to man, and Simeon Lord, whom he had disdainfully described as a man who sold things, were presiding over a group who in the heat and passion of the moment were drinking toasts proclaiming that the colony belonged to them and their posterity. It was in the main a patriotism of convenience, of men driven by the hope of material gain, and not by any lofty conviction that the man who lost connection with his country lost his gods and walked into the night. While Bigge prepared for his departure, the emancipists began drafting a petition to be sent to London. This was the group who had shouted from the housetops their debt to Macquarie. Yet Macquarie remained not so much untouched by their expressions of gratitude but strangely remote, no longer showing his heart like Samson and no longer writing those passionate dispatches to Bathurst in defence of the cause he had espoused. For by then his mind was on other things.

Impatience to vindicate his name and honour had become the ruling passion of his life. All that remained of the old Macquarie was the upright man who could not conceal his contempt for the lazy, the dissipated, the turbulent and the discontented. Such were his preoccupations when, in the last week of January 1821, he attended a dinner given in Bigge's honour at the house of Sir John Jamison in the presence of a large party of officers, civil and military. It was an occasion for much speech-making and many assurances of goodwill. As Bigge left the shores of New Holland behind him in February 1831, his thoughts were taken up with the challenge of establishing a prosperous British colony and of raising a civilization in the wilds. He had with him enough material to write both a survey of the colony and its history from its foundation to the end of 1820. He did not foresee that the white man's civilization and religion would doom the Aborigine; indeed, the Aborigines were not even mentioned in the commission he had received.

In October 1821 Macquarie recommended the emancipists' petition to Bathurst, assuring him that there was nothing improper or in the smallest degree disrespectful in it. The petition pointed out that by the labour of the emancipists the colony of New South Wales had been converted from a barren wilderness of woods into a thriving British colony; and urged that the recent court decision should be overruled and the emancipists restored to all the civil rights and privileges of free subjects. The petitioners submitted that unless this disability was removed, party animosities and diversions would be introduced and perpetuated in the colony; that the colony would also revert to that state of immorality, poverty, and distress which had prevailed during the early period of its establishment. It was signed by 1367 persons including all the principal emancipists of New South Wales. On 25 October 1821 Redfern and Edward Eagar sailed with the petition for London.

Macquarie himself was about to return to England. In March 1821 he was gratified to learn that Bathurst had at last accepted his resignation and named his successor. From that day until his departure he toured the settlements and was received with praise and affection by officials and settlers wherever he went. In Sydney there were fireworks and outpourings of joy for a man who had sought to bring order and dignity to the lives of those who lived there.

On Wednesday 12 February 1822 the shores of Sydney Cove were lined with innumerable spectators on whose countenances, as the Sydney Gazette put it, there was an indication of feeling too big and too sincere for utterance. As Macquarie and his family left Government House for the last time to pass down to the landing barge, he noted with obvious satisfaction the immense numbers who were manifesting by melancholy looks a sincere and undisguised regret at their departure. So Australia, as the Gazette put it, saw her benefactor treading 'her once uncivilized unsocial shores' for the last time. As the *Surry* moved down the harbour, boats loaded with respectability and opulence farewelled the man whose chief principal aim and happiness had been the good of the colonists. The *Surry* sailed out on to 'that very vast sea', with Macquarie still wanting that something more, that something he could never have while he was alive—the vindication of his name and honour as well as the recognition, from those whom he had served, that what had happened to him was unjust.

When Macquarie arrived in London in July 1822 he believed the time was at hand when he and his friends would taste the wages of their virtue, and all his foes the cup of their deservings. Consuming his energy on what was unattainable, not only for Macquarie, but for any man, he rushed on to his destruction. As soon as he arrived in England he became one of the many trying to influence the mind of Earl Bathurst. Among them was Jeffery Hart Bent who, ever since he had returned to London, had been using every opportunity to poison Bathurst's mind against Macquarie. Macquarie certainly had his supporters in London; there were Eagar and Redfern, who had arrived in 1821 to plead for the legal rights of emancipists. But both were vulnerable men, for Eagar was haunted by that most terrible fear that his mask of piety might be stripped off and the worldliness of his motives exposed, while Redfern's irritability of temper did not ingratiate him with the men who held the fate of the emancipists in their hands.

By this time it was a commonplace of English opinion that the colony of New South Wales had ceased to be exclusively a gaol for the punishment and reformation of British criminals. As early as 1819 *The Times* was reminding its readers that the inhabitants were producing all the necessaries of life and had begun to export their surplus produce. In the next year they were advising people thinking of emigrating that they would be well directed to the settlements in New South Wales. In April 1822 the *Quarterly Review* informed its readers that the government no longer considered New South Wales and Van Diemen's Land as the mere resort of felons, and that, with the removal of such a stigma, not only had the reluctance felt by many to emigrate there disappeared, but an influx of a better description of people to both of them had begun. Letter-writers in the press, speakers in Parliament and pamphleteers were busy discussing the type of constitution suitable for a society exploiting convict labour.

Bigge presented his report in three parts, which were published between June 1822 and July 1823. He wrote with insight on the character and work of the individuals in that remote society. He understood the points of view and motives of both Macquarie and Marsden. But Macquarie wanted something more than understanding: he wanted personal vindication. He wanted also vindication of his policy, but Bigge had little to say for that. He recommended the abolition of the main features of the convict system Macquarie had administered. Where Macquarie believed in leniency, Bigge recommended a maintenance of that degree of severity and vigour by which alone, in his view, the punishment of transportation might be made a subject of dread even to the worst offenders. He recommended the abolition of land grants for emancipists and a restriction of the privileges of ticket-of-leave holders, since both groups, he believed, had been allowed to climb dangerously beyond their proper station. Macquarie believed in the distribution of convicts to government work. But Bigge had heeded other counsel. He recommended that the employment of convicts in the management of sheep might be made highly conducive to their improvement and reform, and that hardened criminals should be employed in new penal settlements at Moreton Bay, Port Curtis and Port Bowen to effect their entire separation from the mass of the population.

Macquarie had encouraged Simeon Lord in the manufacture of coarse cloths, stockings, blankets and hats; Bigge recommended that this should be discouraged because Lord was engaging in the manufacture of goods in competition with goods which could be exported from the mother country. Macquarie believed in introducing trial by jury; Bigge believed it would be highly inexpedient and dangerous. He also rejected the arguments of the emancipists for the introduction of a legislative council. He did, however, accept their arguments for the restitution of their legal rights as free men. He also recommended some changes to the judicial system and the introduction of separate courts to Van Diemen's Land.

On 22 November 1822 when the *Eliza* arrived in Sydney bringing copies of Bigge's first report, Macarthur was at Camden entertaining Macquarie's successor, Thomas Brisbane, to sheep-shearing. Within a few days Macarthur was reading how the Bigge report had been productive of much pleasure to his sons in England, and of much land to himself. As for Marsden, he rejoiced that his long, laborious and praiseworthy exertions on behalf of religion and morality had at last received some recognition, while he comforted himself for the aspersions on his severity as a magistrate with the text, 'All that will live godly in Christ Jesus shall suffer persecution'. Lying and slander and all manner of evil speaking he believed he must submit to, but the day was coming when the Judge of all the earth would do right.

In London one man was deeply hurt. That was Macquarie. He sought an audience with the King; he saw friends with influence in high places. On 10 October 1823 he wrote to Bathurst 42 folio pages in defence of his administration. But a year earlier Bathurst had already assured Macquarie that the colony's great increases in agriculture, trade and wealth could not but be highly creditable to his administration. There was nothing else to be said. Carried away as Macquarie was by a passion for true recognition of his achievement, he nowhere showed any awareness that he and Bigge had really differed in their conception of what the colony should be, and that, in this sense, he was fighting not so much his traducers as the trend of events, for which he was entitled to understanding, even to sympathy and pity, but not to approval and support. Macquarie withdrew to Mull for the winter of 1823–24.

He returned to London in April of 1824, and on 26 April, with his usual candour and enthusiasm for his successes in high society, he listed the people he had visited that day: HRH the Duke of York, Earl of Harrington, HRH the Duke of Clarence, Sir Henry Torrens, HRH Prince Leopold, Colonel Macdougal, and Earl Bathurst.

Bathurst was flattering, kind and friendly. On succeeding days Macquarie dined at the club, attended royal levees, and spent the evenings pleasantly in the salons of London. He applied for a pension, and was awarded £1000 a year. There was only one terrible darkness amidst the gaiety, and the pleasure: that vile and insidious Bigge report was everywhere, and in the hands of everyone, and had gone all over the world. He asked for a title as a mark of his sovereign's approval, and a means to clear his name. He heard on 25 May that such was not to be. Then a greater darkness descended, as his physical powers wasted away in a mortal illness, ending in the silence of death on 1 July. His face expressed both exhaustion and resignation at the end.

The news reached the colony late in October 1824. In the *Australian* a correspondent proposed mourning for six months by the friends of the late esteemed Governor, and a subscription to erect a monument to his memory. To his friends and supporters the whole colony was a monument to his work and he the father of Australia. To his friends he was the man with the benevolent heart and the sagacious head, who counteracted distress and misery, who gave employment to the convicts, improved the streets, erected buildings of the highest utility and ornament, built the roads, befriended popular freedom, sowed the seeds for the reformation of the convicts and the civilization of the Aborigine. They saw him as a man not without faults, indeed, as a man who had committed arbitrary acts, which, his friends said, were the fault not of the man but of the system. They saw him as a man subjected to obloquy, misrepresentation, and incessant vituperation, who passed through that fiery ordeal unscorched. They viewed his passing with grief and detected neither what came up from inside the man to lead him on to his destruction nor the tragedy of a man whose very creation swept him aside. Those who eulogized his work or execrated his memory as a tyrant were all unaware that his errors were those of the understanding rather than of the heart; they lacked that eye of pity with which a historian should contemplate those who are powerless to avoid the anguish in their last days.

BOOK TWO

New South Wales and Van Diemen's Land 1822–1838

Some men, like bats or owls, have better eyes for the darkness than for the light.

Charles Dickens: *Pickwick Papers*

The land, boys, we live in.

Anniversary Dinner, Sydney, 26 January 1825
W. C. Wentworth, President

1

Darkness

Some who came to man's estate in the cities and country districts of the British Isles in the decade between 1820 and 1830 who knew the defeat of good, the success of evil, the physical pain and the mental anguish considered that the human race was out of joint with the purpose of its creator. From the East End of the great city of London right to the outskirts of Westminster, unwashed, unshaven, squalid and dirty men constantly raced to and fro ankle deep in the filth and mire. In that mass of dirt, gloom and misery drunken tramps jostled with the rich and the titled. Men and women craving for booty, their bellies filled with beer and gin, committed crimes for which they were hanged by the neck until they were dead after which their bodies were cut down and given to their friends.

In Vauxhall Gardens, orgies of lust and drunkenness prevented the industrious in the neighbourhood from sleeping, and the dying from departing in peace. In the streets, ragged and half-starved Flemish boys importuned females, and thrust forth from under their coats disgusting monkeys to terrify the women. In the court-yard at the Old Bailey men were publicly whipped. Women gave birth to children in public places, because of their extreme misery and degradation. Multitudes of Irish loitered in the vicinity of St James's Palace from dawn till dusk in the infatuated delusion that the royal family would assist them, only to learn in the lawcourts the consequences of pestering people in high places. Virtuous young girls, deceived by the fair promises of men and then betrayed by their paramours, swallowed poison, and died bewailing their cruel fate and the callousness of their destroyers.

Bishops, priests, and deacons laboured to explain to all and sundry that the filth, the violence, the savagery, and the cruelty were the consequences of human depravity. As punishment for that offence in the Garden of Eden all creatures great and small were condemned to live in a vale of tears for the term of their natural lives. Men who dreamed dreams of the life of man without God, or of the happiness, the joy, the pleasure and the enrichment to be achieved by dropping that jealous Jehovah and his savage laws were hounded by the gaolers of mankind as common criminals. In June 1823 a young man of 19, his heart hot within him for the moral improvement of mankind, published Thomas Paine's *Age of Reason*. For publishing such libellous and blasphemous passages, as well as for exceeding the bounds of common decency during the proceedings in the court, he was sentenced to three years in Newgate Gaol, after which he was to enter into a bond of £100 to be of good behaviour for life.

The courts of criminal law were a stage designed to incite terror, but not pity, in the breasts of all the players in the drama of life. The great consolation was held out to the dying thieves and murderers that God pitied and loved them. On the evening of their last day on earth, in all the gaols of the United Kingdom, prison chaplains preached in the chapels in which the coffins destined to contain the bodies of those set down for execution were visible from the pew reserved for those about to die.

Surrounded by darkness, brutality, filth and squalor in their daily lives, some turned to that jealous God who had promised that he could still the madness of the people, and sang of their hope that in the chaos and confusion, the terror, the brutality, and in all the changing scenes of life the God of Jacob would be their refuge. Some, later, setting aside the explanations of the parsons and priests as an opiate exploited by the oppressors to distract men from the true cause of their misery, asked whether the darkness, the savagery and the brutality were but the symptoms of a change in the relations of productive forces, which were in turn the result of changes in the methods of production. By reducing the workers' needs to the barest and most miserable level of physical existence men had been deprived of the need for both activity and enjoyment. The workers were gradually being converted into insensible beings who only wanted to work to earn enough to meet the needs of a savage. Man was being alienated from tenderness and pity just as he was being alienated from the fruits of his labour. Industrial society was ushering in a new age of barbarism in which some men, like bats or owls, had better eyes for the darkness than for the light.

In Scotland it was the same. Glasgow and Edinburgh were cities where half-naked savages drew knives and daggers against each other, or threw vitriol in each other's eyes, like the citizens of an Italian state. By day and night the unwary were exposed to the begging of half-starved, ill-clad savages. In the villages, while the preachers thumped the pulpit boxes and thundered that God would punish dancers, drinkers, fornicators and all unclean livers with hell-fire, in taverns nearby, to the music of the bagpipe, men and women, lightly clad, the breasts of the women shaking in the general merriment, sang, danced and shouted in drunken sprees. So some were full of love divine, and some were full of brandy.

In Ireland the same savagery and brutality darkened the land. Haunted by their own melancholy history, and preserving in their folksongs and ballads the memory of an ancient wrong committed against their people, some blamed their misfortunes on the English who had trampled on their ancient laws, had confiscated every acre in Ireland, destroyed the political institutions of the country, and then stripped the altars and melted the chalices and sacred utensils of her venerable church, but could not destroy their ancient and holy faith. Then in the decades after the Napoleonic Wars another darkness began to descend on that stricken people. The population began to increase alarmingly. At the same time tenant farmers were being evicted into a world of unemployment and begging. Poverty became one of the wrongs of Ireland.

Uproar and outrage broke out through the length and breadth of the country. Rural Ireland began to furnish a fearful catalogue of deeds of terror, intimidation and violence. The English Parliament responded with its own brand of terror, punishing outrages with whippings, transportation or death. At Mallow, near Cork, in the autumn of 1823 a crowd assembled to hear one victim of the criminal law urge his erstwhile companions to take an example from his awful fate, and turn from their evil ways of terror and outrage, and fear God. As the lad dropped into the silence people screamed and wailed, and hurried off to their rude cabins, nursing in their hearts not that advice about their own folly, but an implacable hatred of those enemies of their people who had brought a comely youth to an untimely and cruel death.

Some of the men and women who were driven to transgress the laws of God or man were transported to New South Wales and Van Diemen's Land. Between 1821 and 1830, 21 780 convicts were transported to New South Wales, and 10 000 to Van Diemen's Land. Men outnumbered women by around seven to one.

At their trials, some mocked their judges. Some wept; some laughed; others bragged, and strutted in their dock. Some were the victims of a dark side of the human heart. In September 1828 one Anne M'Gee, driven not by want or need, but by some demon within her with an insatiable appetite for the subterranean satisfaction, enticed a girl from her house, and stripped her of her clothing. For this she received a sermon from the judge on her infamy, and transportation beyond the seas for the term of her natural life. At Lewes, in Sussex, a man who had extorted money from another man by threatening to denounce him as a sodomite was transported for life. For giving his wife 'what cheer' with such violence that she died from his beatings, James Clegg was called on to expiate his offence by forced labour for the term of his natural life.

Some, driven to desperation by poverty and suffering, pinched some trifle, for which they were sent over the oceans for their transgression of the divine command: thou shalt not steal. Mary Corbett, with one son dead, two children at home starving, and no husband to act as provider, stole two books, and found herself in a convict ship with women who had sold their bodies for mere tots of gin, and the opportunity to pick the pockets of the lecherous.

Some belonged to families who depended for their livelihood on crime. When Sarah Stanhope was found guilty at the Hull Sessions early in 1828 of stealing, the Recorder informed the court that she was a relation of the notorious Snowden Dunhill Bounders. Several of her relations had already been gaoled or transported for their crimes. Her own father had been twice transported. One of her sons had been executed in Hobart Town.

Some had no connection with the criminal classes. In 1831, 464 men, farm labourers, reapers, mowers, milkmen, herdsmen, shepherds and stable boys, the men whose legs were calfless from half-starvation and whose shoulders were sloping from hard labour, were transported. In the severe winter of 1830–31 a bad harvest and high prices drove them to demand higher wages from their local landlords, who refused. Some then burnt haystacks, broke threshing machines, and set fire to houses. They were a threat to the security of the kingdom. The judges lost no opportunity to remind the men of the enormity of their offence: 'You will leave the country all of you', Mr Justice Alderson said to three young machine-breakers, 'you will see your friends and relations no more ... the land which you have disgraced will see you no more: the friends with whom you are connected will be parted from you forever in the world'. Before leaving for the colonies they were forced to stand at the scaffold and witness the agonies of another man's execution. For some this was their last picture of a life at the heart of which there seemed to be a great darkness.

In the meantime the men in high places in London had decided to encourage the migration of free settlers to the colonies of New South Wales and Van Diemen's Land. Staggered by the enormous burden of running the colony of New South Wales, which in the year 1822 had cost the British taxpayer £450 000, swayed by rumours trickling back to London of the moral evils of building a society from the dregs of mankind, and influenced too by rumours that transportation had ceased to arouse anything like the appropriate degree of apprehension and terror in the minds of the criminal classes, they decided to encourage settlers to proceed to the colony where, in return for employing convicts, they would receive a grant of land in proportion to their capital. The rumour ran through London Town and all over the British Isles that the adventurous, the needy, the failures and the misfits could start afresh in New South Wales or Van Diemen's Land. The wife of Thomas Davey, one-time Lieutenant-Governor of Van Diemen's Land, because of her many privations and her husband's claim to be the first European to land at Port Jackson on that 26 January 1788, wrote for permission to proceed to New South Wales or Van Diemen's Land, only to be told in the best prayer-book prose of the Colonial Office that those who had no capital beyond their head and their hands could expect no grant of land. On the other hand, those who had funds sufficient to cultivate a large portion of land, as well as testimonials to their respectability, promptly had their letters marked 'Grant'. Unto those that had, it was given.

Some, too, apprehensive lest developments in England should deprive them of their expectations, turned their minds towards the prospects of New South Wales. James Henty, merchant and manager of a family bank in Worthing, Sussex, and a member of a family which had belonged for centuries to the class of gentlemen farmers in those majestic Sussex downs, had come to the conclusion that New South Wales would do more for his family than England ever would. They would not only be wealthier in New South Wales; they would be placed in the first rank in society—and thus avoid the humiliation of the second rung of the ladder, which would be their eternal fate in England.

There were the wives and children who made the long journey over the oceans to be reunited with husbands and fathers. There was Johanna Casey of Garryfine in Ireland who reached Cork one day hoping to see her husband once again before the convict ship sailed only to find that he had gone. Months later when she received a letter from him from far away New South Wales, she burst into tears. The poor children were at her every day to take them to their father and she replied to her husband:

> Be assured that unless I perish in the attempt that neither water, fire, or tempest will prevent me of going to you, O that I cannot fly to you, it's then I would not sigh for you, your Children would not cry for you, and we would all cease to moan . . . sending you my Blessing and the blessing of God may attend you and remain your ever loving Consort, Johanna Casey.

So Johanna Casey and other wives and their families, having satisfied the Colonial Office that nothing could be said against their characters, and that their appearances were extremely decent, set out on their long journey to join the men and women who were beginning to see New South Wales and Van Diemen's Land not as English parkland where the gentry could build their manors with cheap convict labour, but as a land which belonged to them and their remotest posterity. They were beginning to see it as a land where the darkness of the Old World might one day give way to light.

2

The Setting in New South Wales

One day in August 1822 the Reverend Samuel Marsden sat down in his study at Parramatta to write to two of his brothers in Christ in London. He had cause, he believed, to be thankful for many striking interpositions of Divine Providence in his favour. God had highly exalted him from the lowly station of son of a blacksmith and small farmer to minister before Him in holy things as the principal chaplain of the colony of New South Wales. He, the blacksmith's son, now owned 4 500 acres of land at Parramatta and many cattle, sheep, pigs and horses. God, too, had blessed him with a beloved wife and a quiver full of children.

He had just turned 50 and was beginning to approach that time of life when honour, the respect of his fellow-men, and recognition of his achievement should have been his. Instead he was aware of those curses, not loud but deep, which his past had kindled in the hearts of his enemies. For the Reverend Samuel Marsden had never gained the goodwill or the affection of those with whom he had had to deal. Twenty-seven years in the colony of New South Wales had brought him to the melancholy conclusion that those convicts who had not received the precious gift of God's saving grace could only be rescued from their wickedness by severity of punishment. Twenty-seven years had convinced him that anyone who urged mankind to turn from their wickedness could only earn their undying hatred and contempt.

He was hoping for much from the new Governor. This time he was determined not to give offence, believing that at long last God had delivered him from the hands of his enemies. But it was too late. Face and gesture were beginning to mirror the outrage, humiliation and insult he had endured as God's instrument to impart the means of grace and improve the morals of the inhabitants of the colony of New South Wales and its dependent territories. The great bulbous eyes were more and more startled by memories of terrible moments in the past, which came up from inside him to mock his days so that he cried in anguish to his Lord: 'O spare me a little . . . before I go hence and be no more seen'. The lips were more and more often seen to move, though no intelligible sound was heard by those near to him. The pious believed they were moving in silent prayer, but those with an eye of pity knew these mumbles were but one of the many signs of an increasing uproar in his soul. The Reverend Samuel Marsden was beginning to walk into the night.

At Parramatta, John Macarthur was also approaching the season of the sere, the yellow leaf. He turned 55 on 3 September 1822. When he had arrived back from London in September of 1817 he had written to his dearest best beloved wife that her sons, James and William, would hasten to her the moment they could procure a conveyance, while he would follow at a slower pace. For those passions which had driven him both to glory and damnation with his own kind were calming down. He waited till the heat of the day was over, and then set out in his carriage for Parramatta. His ideas for the promotion of his private interests and the welfare of the colony of New South Wales were still in the grand manner. By 1821 his ideas on New South Wales and Van Diemen's Land as colonies for the growth of fine wool were gaining a wide currency in London among those who were unhappy about the dependence of the British manufacturer on the fine wools of Spain, Saxony and Austria. No serious disease had been prevalent among his own sheep. The whole emphasis was on improvement. He had planted olive trees for oil to rub on the fleece to improve its quality.

In the autumn glow of his life he began to unfold his vision of the role of his family in New South Wales. He spoke of erecting a manor at Camden which would be worthy of their position as the doyens of the new nobility of New South Wales. He spoke of how, for his part, he would prefer chaste and simple lines, no baroque splendours, or extravagances, but a building cut from stone, something to stand against wind and rain, earth and sky, as an austere symbol both of his worldly grandeur and of his claim to distinction for his person and his class. He wanted the landed proprietors to become powerful as an aristocracy, a development which, he knew, would excite the envy and even the hatred of the multitude, as a pernicious democratic feeling had taken deep root in the colony in consequence of the absurd and mischievous policy pursued by Macquarie.

He had visions of a race of sober, industrious, and moral agricultural labourers growing up in the country districts of New South Wales under the paternal and kindly eye of titled proprietors of the soil. He was proud of his own record of humanity, proud that only two convicts had ever been punished on his estates, proud that no convict had ever petitioned to be released from his service, nor caused any commotion which indicated that he had employed cruelty or unnecessary rigour on his convict servants.

Life, as he saw it, was a dance, and a fearful lottery. In the world a few artful knaves led a multitude of fools. He had decided to turn his back on the world, to retire to his estate where he could enjoy the pursuits of a country gentleman, sowing wheat, lambing, growing corn, tending the ewes, buying and selling stock, and growing grapes for wine. He could bask in the love and affection of his family, and savour those passages in Shakespeare, Milton, Byron, Scott, Crabbe, and *Hudibras* which he quoted to them with such skill and passion.

But there were dark moments. By 1822 he was beginning to spend more and more of his time in bed, a victim of gout, and of an obscure melancholy, during which strange visions and queer thoughts came up from inside him. The past was beginning to haunt him, reminding him of how he had crushed all who had stood in his way. Here he was, the pioneer breeder of fine wool in New South Wales, the man with a vision to see how a sordid gaol would be metamorphosed into a plantation society, the man who under the new Governor must surely receive some public recognition for his achievement, haunted and hunted by his past—throwing, as his dearest love put it rather delicately, an accumulated gloom round the family.

For Elizabeth Macarthur had anxieties over her husband's health, over the hostility to which the family, and possibly all the gentry, had been exposed by the violence of his passions, and the consequent lack of sympathy to which it would expose all of them in the coming days when her dearest love, her own darling John, walked into a night where she could no longer comfort or relieve him. The society she had known in the old days was fast changing, as numbers of strangers began to arrive. Things would be all right, she believed, if people were contented with bread, milk, meat, vegetables and fruit, but, alas, in New South Wales, even the servants had begun to demand tea, and sugar, and other imported luxuries, which many of them, she was sure, had never been accustomed to in their former lives. Happily she knew that she and all mankind were under the superintendence of an Almighty Ruler. The Lord was her shepherd: therefore she could lack nothing.

Besides she found much to delight her in the trivial round and the common task. She loved the occasions when hundreds of Aborigines gathered for a corroboree near Parramatta. They painted their bodies and decked themselves with green boughs and performed dances while others sat apart and chanted a wild song. They always held corroborees on bright moonlit nights when the small fires gave brilliance and mystery to the surrounding woods and lit up the faces of the blacks. So what did it matter if the white man's social gatherings left much to be desired: what did it matter if nothing like the splendour and gaiety of a ball in England could be exhibited in New South Wales for many years to come? With God in His heaven, what did it matter who was Governor of New South Wales: what did it matter who was in, and who was out in that coterie of little men who shouted and fretted on the stage of little Sydney?

In November 1821, chance brought to the high office of Captain-General and Governor-in-Chief of New South Wales a man who was indifferent to the worldly hopes of the men and women who lived there. Thomas Brisbane was born in 1773, the year Captain James Cook dropped anchor in Adventure Bay in Van Diemen's Land. He was educated by tutors and at the University of Edinburgh, where he developed a lasting interest in mathematics and astronomy: he entered the army as a profession where in 1812 in the Peninsula Wars he formed a firm and lasting friendship with Arthur Wellesley, later Duke of Wellington. In November of 1819, he was united by marriage to Anna Maria Makdougall, a gracious and intelligent lady who became a source of exquisite gladness to him.

From the earliest days, Brisbane had lifted up his eyes away from the world towards the heavens in more senses than one: he was an enthusiastic astronomer. Those who judged by appearances, and what a man gave out about himself, took him as a Christian, a scholar and a gentleman. The discerning few shook their heads. For Brisbane's mind was set on the heavenly prize, for that peace which the world could neither give nor take away. For him an immortal soul was the unspeakable object of value in human life.

He arrived to be greeted with warmth and cheer. Hopes were running high. When divine service was celebrated for the first time in St James's Church on 6 January of the following year, the Reverend Samuel Marsden, sensitive as ever to the whims and vanities of the rulers of this world, chose an appropriate text for his sermon: 'Arise, shine; for thy light is come, and the glory of the Lord is risen upon thee'.

Marsden had his own private reasons for delight that day. Brisbane had offered to restore him to the high office of a magistrate at Parramatta. Once again he took his seat on the bench, knowing at that moment only the satisfaction of vindicating himself before the public against the malicious attacks of Macquarie. It was music in his ears to hear Brisbane say he was back again on the bench because he, Brisbane, was anxious to get the bench of magistrates as respectable as possible.

Five months later, the magistrates were occupied with a case which kindled the faction fires of their world. A convict girl, Ann Rumsby, had alledged that her employer, Dr Douglass, had lifted her petticoat and attempted to seduce her. Ever since Douglass arrived in the colony in May of 1821 he had irritated and provoked the exclusive coterie, centred as they were in Parramatta, by openly fraternizing with the convict party in New South Wales. Douglass was a man of liberal and independent principles. A distinguished doctor, he was a member by birth of the Protestant ascendancy in Dublin. But he had had the audacity to treat lags, old hands, and currency lads and lasses on a footing of equality with the members of the ancient nobility of New South Wales. He, too, was a magistrate.

Marsden and the exclusives of Parramatta snatched greedily at the opportunity to show the public that men such as Dr Douglass who were loose in their politics were also lax in their morals. But when the matter came to trial, Ann Rumsby denied the charges against her employer. The sitting magistrates believed she was now telling lies and announced that from that day they would neither associate with or act with Dr Douglass. The court further declared that Ann Rumsby had been guilty of wilful and corrupt perjury, and sentenced her to be imprisoned until such time as she could be sent to Port Macquarie.

Then Brisbane took action. Impressed by the integrity of Douglass, and irritated by the posturings of Marsden, and the animus of the exclusives, he informed the bench of magistrates that if they persevered in their resolution not to act with Dr Douglass, they might adopt the alternative of transmitting their resignation. To the acclaim of their brother magistrates, Marsden and his colleagues stood their ground. But Brisbane stood firm. The bench of magistrates at Parramatta was dismissed, and the punishment of Ann Rumsby remitted. So, once again, that service of Caesar ended in public humiliation for Marsden.

While the vulgar, the profane, and the men without the eye of pity mocked Marsden as an unctuous hypocrite, one Thomas Hassall, who had arrived as a babe in arms in Tahiti in the mission ship *Duff* in February 1797 with his parents, and then moved with them to New South Wales, wrote to ask for the hand of his daughter Ann in marriage. Marsden replied with a dignity and tenderness strangely lacking in his public life:

Dear Thomas,

I received your Letter in which you solicit my permission to pay your Addresses to my daughter Ann. In reply, I need only say you have my Approbation to do so as she is at Liberty to please herself in a matter in which her own future Happiness is so Nearly interested.

I am, Yours Truly, S. Marsden.

But that was not his subject, for marriage as a coming together of true minds, or as an example of how two people made in the image of God could tear at each other like wild beasts, touched him not at all. His one all-consuming, self-destroying passion was female morals. Tell him a story of seduction, a story of men behaving like insects to whom God had given sensual lust, and he became like a man possessed. So when James Hall began spreading stories that the Colonial Secretary, Goulburn, wishing to reduce the amount of sodomy among the convicts on government farms, had sent women convicts to the Emu Plains establishment, and solemnly drawn up a timetable prescribing the maximum number of men they could take on in an hour, once again the huge bulbous eyes of the stern champion of female morals began to dance with a wild glee (which reminded the discerning in that little world that there was madness in men's hearts while they lived).

Through all this sound and fury Brisbane remained deeply pleased with himself. He knew he was surrounded with foes, but he could, he believed, exultingly state at the end of that year in the face of the colony, and of the world at large, that no human being could accuse him of an unjust, illegal, cruel, harsh, or even an improper act. His scientific pursuits had been no less crowned with success. He had observed a great variety of eclipses and occultations, which would form the basis of his catalogue of all the stars of the hemisphere. Of any favouritism or improper act during that year his internal monitor fully acquitted him.

Among those who sailed into Brisbane's little world was the Reverend John Dunmore Lang, who arrived in Sydney on 23 May 1823. Fashioned by Glasgow and Calvinism, he became the preacher of an avenging Jehovah—a harsh faith for a harsh society. The potter had so fashioned his clay that it was pleasing to him to smite sinners and humiliate the proud.

Another wild boar had strayed into the vineyards of the Lord in New South Wales. In the first weeks Lang told his congregation of the mortification at having to share the schoolroom with Catholics, in which their incense stank in his nostrils, and the ringing of the sanctuary bells offended his ears. He decided to appeal to government for funds to build a church. But the Colonial Secretary, acting on instructions from Brisbane, refused to grant such assistance because he was not convinced that Presbyterians wanted to keep the unity of the spirit in the bond of peace. Relations between Lang and Government House became so acrimonious that Lang, with that daring and energy which sustained him to the end of his days, announced that he would return to London to defeat the eternal enemies of his church and his people. Brisbane wrote off to a friend in England, to say he knew the Presbyterian faction was very angry with him, but, dammit man, if he gave in to the kirk party he would soon have the Jews down upon him for a synagogue!

Heaven knows, for Sir Thomas, it was bad enough to have to stomach giving assistance to the Catholics. Ever since his arrival in the colony the Catholic chaplain, Father Therry, had been trying to interest him in his dream to build a church. Public donations had already been collected, but an unfinished church stood as a reproach to Therry's incompetence with the money-changers. Eventually Brisbane was persuaded to assist. He saw it as a problem of law and order, rather than the correct way to salvation. Since his arrival in the colony he had found that every murder or diabolical crime had been committed by Roman Catholics, who were so bereft of every advantage that could adorn the mind of man that soon there would be nothing but the shade of their skin to distinguish them from the Aborigines. He had hoped they would dwindle away or become ingrafted with the Protestants, but as they seemed to cherish their faith as dearly as their lives, and as their priest counselled obedience and subordination with the same zeal as the Protestant chaplains, he had agreed reluctantly to contribute to the building of a church for them. To his disgust Therry had proceeded to draw up plans which included the tinsel and show appropriate for a rich and populous city rather than the dregs of Irish slums and bogs. So while Therry dreamed of the greater glory of God, Brisbane shook his head over these craven slaves to a vulgar superstition. That was how Brisbane explained matters to Bathurst in October 1824.

While Father Therry laboured to win souls for heaven, the Wesleyan missionary, the Reverend W. Walker, was labouring to tell the Aborigines the glad tidings that there was a home for little children above the bright blue sky. He had promised his God to convert the Aborigines to Christianity. After he had arrived in Sydney in 1821 he had found much that had caused him pain. Duty had compelled him to attend the corroborees, but he had been a most uneasy spectator at scenes which were too shocking, too unseemly and too disgraceful to describe. 'To a sensible and sus-ceptible mind', he had told his missionary brothers in London in

November of 1821, 'it is sufficient to say, they were naked. For the sustenance of the indelicate I have no descriptive food'. To his disgust he had seen with his own eyes an Englishwoman enjoying one of these obscene assemblies. What was worse, he had seen the Catholic priest, Father Therry, gabble Latin prayers to gaping black children, sprinkle them with holy water, and then have the effront- ery to claim them as members of Christ's church.

For the men who believed the Aborigines were heirs to the same eternity as all other men, there was much to ponder over. In the bays and harbours along the coast where the sealers and whalers called for water and timber, ex-convicts and absconders used Aboriginal women as their mistresses, and peggers-out of their skins. In drunken rages, brought on by disappointments in the chase, or at times by some darkness in themselves, they tied these women up and flogged them in the most cruel manner, for God had given men other hungers than the hunger for food.

In the country districts terrible scenes of degradation occurred. The convict workers, the ticket-of-leave men, lags and old hands bartered with the Aborigines for the use of their women, and when the Aborigines took offence, or retaliated for some breach of their way of life, of which the white remained blandly ill-informed, the white men hit back. So the Aborigines speared the sheep and cattle of the invaders of their land, the robbers of their hunting fields and violators of their women. As atrocity followed atrocity more and more settlers lost patience with the official policy of amity and kindness, and demanded that troops be sent to pacify the country and terrify the Aborigines into submission. The Aborigines began to despair: 'Black man die fast since white man came', one of them told the Reverend Mr Mansfield at the end of 1821: 'Old black men nigh all gone. Soon no blackman, all whitemen'. The Reverend Mr Walker, in grief and shame, wondered whether his society in London should not also send missionaries to the white man.

While the Reverend Mr Walker was musing on his mission station near Parramatta on why God's creatures should drink iniquity like water, far away in London my lord Bathurst decided to accept most of Commissioner Bigge's recommendations on the future of the colony of New South Wales. In May 1823 he instructed Brisbane to remove the convicts capable of being reformed from the towns and assign them to settlers in the country districts where they would be free from contagion. In this way the cost to government would be reduced. He told Brisbane that settlers with capital were to be encouraged to migrate to New South Wales and Van Diemen's Land in return for employing corrigible convicts. So settlement was to spread—and the Aborigine to be doomed. The incorrigible were to be sent to penal settlements at Port Macquarie and Moreton Bay.

All those elements in the old convict system which had aggravated ill feeling between the emancipists and the exclusives during the era of Macquarie were to be dropped. Land grants to ex-convicts were abolished. Brisbane was instructed not to appoint an emancipist as a magistrate until that man had proved himself by the meritorious discharge of other civil employment, and until such time as he had been able to form a full estimate of his private character. The Simeon Lords and the Samuel Terrys could store up for themselves treasures on earth, but they must not expect to break bread at the Governor's table or hold high office in the colony of New South Wales.

3

The Return of the Native Son

William Charles Wentworth was 34 years old when he stepped ashore from the *Alfred* in July1824. The native son had returned to the land of his birth. There was about him the air of one of the gods who was mixing with mortals. His head was leonine, his language had a brilliance befitting a scion of the Whig aristocracy, and his ambitions a grandeur to match the promise of his appearance and his words. The man seemed likely to fulfil his great hope not to be outstripped by any competitor. Appearances were perhaps deceptive. For those who looked more closely there were blemishes: there was the slight cast in the eye, the walk was clumsy, the features coarse. This scion of the Whig aristocracy lapsed at times into the language of a coarse brat. This man who hoped to take his place at the top of society had a long record of savaging the very people who alone could confer that distinction on him.

There was enough in his past to explain these contradictions. His father's connections with one of the great Whig families in the English aristocracy qualified the boy for the exclusives with their hopes of a plantation society headed by a colonial aristocracy; his mother's arrival in the colony as a prisoner qualified him to join the convict party in New South Wales, with their egalitarianism and their levelling. Then there were the five and a half years he spent as a young child with his parents—D'Arcy an officer, Catherine and her children classed as convicts—at Norfolk Island. It was a place where nature was lavish in her bounty and her beauty but men behaved so vilely to each other that an earthly paradise became the hell of the Pacific. This early experience possibly turned William Charles Wentworth into a wild man, who raised his hand against every man because deep down he feared every man's hand was raised against him. There was also the early death of his mother in 1800, four years after the family had moved to Parramatta. There she was buried by Marsden, who was not to know that the child of this woman would one day write all manner of evil things against him.

Finally, there was the shock of discovering when he came to man's estate that his father had not taken that place in colonial society to which his birth entitled him. To prepare his two sons, William Charles and D'Arcy junior, to mix in the top ranks of society, D'Arcy had sent them to England to receive the education appropriate for gentlemen. William returned in 1810 to find his father excluded from the drawing rooms of the self-styled gentry of New South Wales. Rumour had it that the circumstances of his private life were the cause of this affront to his father's pretensions. William Charles retaliated by savaging in words the very families whose regard and esteem he was coveting. He circulated a lampoon round Sydney in which he mocked the Macarthurs as a family of corset-makers risen above their station.

Three years later in 1814, still flaunting his solidarity with social outcasts, he acted as witness to the marriage of the wealthy emancipist, Simeon Lord. Two years after that he again took up his pen to ridicule the opponents of the pro-emancipist policy of Governor Macquarie.

But there was more to the man than this superb use of vulgar spite against the competitors who threatened to outstrip him. When in company with Blaxland and Lawson he had found a way across the Blue Mountains in 1813, he alone of the three had an eye for the majesty of the occasion. For him it was like one of those moments when

> a meteor shoots athwart the night,
> The boundless champaign burst upon our sight,
> Till nearer seen the beauteous landscape grew,
> Op'ning like Canaan on rapt Israel's view.

Three years later in March of 1816, being then 26 years old, he set sail for England to study law, actuated, as he put it, by a desire of better qualifying himself to perform the sacred duties his birth had imposed. By acquainting himself with all the excellence of the British constitution he hoped to advocate at some future period the right of his native land to a participation in its advantages. He entertained, too, the proud hope that, by the very excellence of his services in the law, he would be considered not unworthy of the name of Fitzwilliam. The man who had poured scorn on souls attached to filthy pelf had begun to conceive of his own destiny on a grand scale.

When he enrolled at the Middle Temple on 5 February 1817, he had dreams of marrying a daughter of John Macarthur. For a brief season he wrote as though without her his universe would turn to a mighty stranger. He wondered whether a man of ardent character, rebel wits and wild passion, driven as he knew himself to be with a sacred fervour for his country's cause, with a Byronic scorn of tyrants and a love of equal laws, could know anything but wounded pride in his relations with women. Besides, the union would contribute to the respectability and grandeur of his family. Happily, too, John Macarthur senior, one of the objects of his witty lampoons, who was about to return to the colony, had given his blessing to the union, and his son John had urged him to write a work on the colony of New South Wales.

In the flowering time in his life he began to conceive for himself a destiny and a mission to match the splendour of his worldly ambition. He had no intention of abandoning the country that gave him birth: he was conscious of the sacred claims it had upon him. That year he began to roister by night with other bosom cronies who were reading law at the Middle Temple, and to read the poetry of Lord Byron, and go each Sunday against his will to that church in the Middle Temple. As he sat and listened to dreary prayers and sermons, he never believed that either God or man could come between him and the fulfilment of his great dream.

In 1817 he moved to Paris to acquire a language so generally known that it was a reflection on a gentleman to be ignorant of it. There, too, he pushed on with writing a book about New South Wales. It revealed his vision of how his native land, which had hitherto been considered more in the light of a prison, might be rendered one of the most useful and valuable appendages of the Empire by diverting from the United States of America some of the vast tide of emigration then flowing thither from all parts of Europe.

His remedy was simple: grant the colonists the enjoyment of those rights and privileges from which they ought never to have been debarred; remove the unmerited and absurd restrictions on their trade; replace the present arbitrary system with a free government, or else the colony would degenerate into what he called a 'vast stye of abomination and depravity'. It was a vision of what Australia might become once it was freed from the oppressor and the 'convicts' clanking chains', a vision of men living in the colony as though they were in Arcady, of gay innocents who had not been tainted by power or the pursuit of filthy material gain.

In the early months of 1819 in London, his world seemed to be crumbling around him. Stories of his father's past were circulating: unkind souls were saying that D'Arcy Wentworth had once been arraigned at the English bar of justice on a criminal charge. Someone must be punished for his humiliation and pain. He told his father it was all the doing of 'that dark villain Samuel Marsden'. In the middle of all the hurry to get out his book he heard from Sydney that John Macarthur senior would not grant him permission to marry his daughter. Again Wentworth snatched at the idea of vengeance: `as soon as I get over the hurry of my work, I will pay him off in his own coin', he told his father. Of all the dreams he had entertained in 1817, that hope of making great and powerful connections, that happy union of heart and pocket in marrying into the Macarthur family, only the ambition remained. `You may rely', he told his father that August of 1819, `that I will not suffer myself to be outstripped by any competitor and I will finally create for myself a reputation which shall reflect a splendour on all who are related to me'. Eminence was now the master-mistress of his passion.

Yet even though one part of him cast hungry eyes towards the great Whig houses, circumstances had driven him again into association with the pro-convict party in New South Wales. In his report Commissioner Bigge dropped some measured words on the stormy career of William Charles as a writer of lampoons. Wentworth immediately accused him of wilful misrepresentation of evidence, and of misrepresenting his father. He demanded satisfaction by ten the next morning. Not being a man for death with honour, Bigge promptly expressed his concern for attributing authorship of the pipe to Wentworth.

Wentworth wanted darker satisfaction. In collaboration with Edward Eagar, the ex-convict who was then in London to present a petition praying for the restitution of the legal rights of emancipists, he arranged to publish a third edition of his book on New South Wales, in which he exposed the unctuous hypocrisy of the Mahomet of Botany Bay, Samuel Marsden, and ended with a passionate call for British institutions in the land of his birth. John Macarthur, who had not been happy about the first edition, finding it highly mischievous, was not surprised to hear from his son that Wentworth was bound to offend grossly.

Early in the new year Wentworth entered Peterhouse, Cambridge, the college which had received copious benefactions from the Fitzwilliam family. Shortly afterwards he had a chance to distinguish himself in a way which would minister to his delight. He could submit a poem for the Chancellor's Medal and, if he won, he would distinguish himself more in a month than John Macarthur junior could contrive to do during his four years there. The subject that year was Australasia. He had to accept the mortification of gaining second place.

In the poem he had risen to the occasion magnificently. On the title page he called himself an Australasian. In the preface he wrote of his fervent prayer that Macquarie might receive his due recognition from those who had 'Australasian hearts'. The poem was a song in praise of Australia. He loved it all, from the rich pastures where the wild herds strayed, to the desolate, stunted woods where eagles brooded and torrents roared. He loved the people: he loved especially the women. For that tempest lived in him, too, and that wonder of a man with a maid had already brought him great pleasure, and great anguish to those who ministered to his delight.

He sang of a future when, freed from the convict taint, the native-born Australians dedicated themselves to science. For him the Greeks and the Romans were the fountains of human wisdom: celestial poesy was his spiritual food. He looked to the day when an Austral Shakespeare, Milton, or Pindar would soar like an eagle in the sky—as though men could and should steal fire from heaven. His theme was man's glory, and pride and honour—not God's. He looked forward to that day when Australasia would

> float, with flag unfurl'd,
> A new Britannia in another world.

No wonder the *Sydney Gazette*, the currency lads and lasses, and the supporters of the convict party welcomed him with pride and pleasure when he stepped ashore in July 1824. Yet from the start the man behaved in ways which bewildered his companions and angered his enemies. There were all the contradictions in his behaviour, for at one moment he gave out a drunken boast that he would scotch that yellow snake, John Macarthur, or expose that dark villain, Samuel Marsden, and at the next he was bragging about his great connections. Soon the tongues of the gossips were wagging. It was said there were great drunken carousals in a house in Castlereagh Street, and much bawdy conversation. The *Sydney Gazette*, which had welcomed him as a hero, began to drop hints that Australia's native son was a prodigal and a wanton.

Happily, during his absence in England, his beloved father had waxed fat in the land to which he had been banished. From grants of land in the Parramatta district, from the profits made from his trade in rum and the business partnership with Simeon Lord for trade in the Pacific, D'Arcy had become very rich, and William Charles knew, and so did some of the gossip-mongers of Sydney, that most of this wealth would pass to his son.

In September he was admitted to practice in the Supreme Court where he spoke for two hours, impressing the *Sydney Gazette* with his ardour and talent. The following month, in partnership with

Robert Wardell, his old boon companion from his student days at the Middle Temple, Wentworth published the first edition of a newspaper for which he used the name of the country he loved best in all the world: he called it the *Australian*. When he and Wardell announced their intention to publish the paper Brisbane decided to try the experiment of the full latitude of freedom of the press. Robert Howe then successfully applied for removal of all government restraint on the *Sydney Gazette*. A free press, Wentworth and Wardell told the readers of the first issue of 14 October, was the most legitimate, and at the same time the most powerful weapon that could be employed to annihilate the influence of individuals, frustrate the designs of tyranny, and restrain the arm of oppression. The joint owners introduced a note of gaiety and gusto in their paper. They told their readers they liked fairs because they promoted good fellowship and brought the lads and lasses together. The sin, the smut, and gloom of the parsons were to be spirited away on gales of laughter and ridicule.

A week later lists of the persons eligible to sit as jurors in civil cases were nailed to the doors of the churches and other places of worship in Sydney. The name of every person who had not come free to the colony had been omitted. Wentworth, sensing the influence of his implacable enemies, the Macarthurs, in this decision, denounced it as a sweeping act of exclusion. If trial by jury was to be modified in this way, he wrote in the *Australian*, then instead of becoming a bond between two discordant and heterogeneous classes, it would keep them more aloof, and apply to those fatal feuds which had already sprung up and threatened one day or other to cleave the society to its centre. The native son, it seemed, had donned the mantle of a tribune of the people. The opposition to the exclusives had acquired a leader.

The native-born were beginning to sense that they too could steal that fire from heaven, and increase and replenish the earth of their native land and subdue it. When Brisbane wanted to ascertain whether any large and navigable rivers flowed over the territory to the south of the Goulburn Plains to the oceans on the east or south coasts of New South Wales, Hamilton Hume volunteered to lead the expedition, 'presuming myself '(altho' an Australian) capable from experience of understanding such an expedition'. An Englishman, W. H. Hovell, also volunteered to take part in the expedition. A venture designed to increase man's knowledge of a harsh and elemental land soon developed into a trial of strength between a currency lad and a bloody immigrant.

They set out from Appin near Sydney with their six packhorses, a tent of Parramatta cloth, two tarpaulins, and three convict servants each, for Lake George, which they reached on 13 October 1824. Soon after, the trial of strength between the dinkum Aussie and the Jimmy began when they reached the banks of the Murrumbidgee River near Yass. To the mingled scorn and delight of Hume and Thomas Boyd, a convict member of the party, Hovell, the Englishman, became faint of heart and despaired of ever crossing the river. The Australian-born knew no such temptation. With magnificent cheek and effrontery Hume taunted Hovell on the banks of the Murrumbidgee in that south country where courage and resource meant all: 'If you think you can't, you may go back, for I mean to go on'. Hovell, bewildered by the role his companion had thrust on him as the representative of the civilization of the Old World, could only register his surprise that such vulgar and groundless feeling of envy should have awakened in the mind of a man whom he preferred to think of as his companion in adventure.

On 29 October they crossed the Tumut River, after which Hume, once again claiming for himself the sagacity of the native-born to find his way in the Australian bush, insisted they should strike south-west towards the rolling plain country, and so avoid the passage of mountains. Following this course on 16 November, they came upon a noble stream to which Hume gave his own surname in memory of his father, but in this fate cheated the native-born of his attempt to bequeath the name of his family to posterity. Five years later Charles Sturt, an Englishman, a man of vision and faith and a stranger to the passions swirling in Hume's heart, reached the same river lower down and called it the Murray after His Majesty's principal Secretary of State in the Colonial Office.

After crossing this river they pushed south over dreary plans which induced such a state of depression in the men that the leaders promised to turn back if they did not soon sight the sea. Then on 13 December Hume, impatient as ever, having pushed on ahead, came to the top of a big hill, where he cheered so long and loud that the other men rushed towards him, Mr Hovell being among them. In one of the rare moments of companionship on that long journey, the Australian and the Englishman looked down from the top of that hill over a plain where in time men would attempt to plant British civilization in that alien soil. Within three days they were camping on the shores of Corio Bay on the edge of the country where the gentry would raise their mansions of stone as supports of civilization and refinement in a great sea of barbarism.

No such vision was vouchsafed to either Hume or Hovell on that day. On 18 December they set out on their return journey, vying with each other to be first in Sydney with the news. Hovell broke camp at Gunning to steal a march on his precocious companion but

Hume, not to be outdone, caught up with him at Berrima, and they entered Sydney together late in January. Hume, brash and boastful as ever, quickly laid claim to the success of the expedition. The *Australian*, possibly influenced by Wentworth, sensing the significance of the occasion for posterity, hailed the achievement with a characteristic piece of rhetoric. Hume and Hovell, they wrote, had rescued a large part of Australia from the stigma of Oxley, who had branded the inland as uninhabitable and useless for all the purposes of civilized man. Soon a tide of settlement would move into the new lands.

By the year 1824 Brisbane's detachment reflected not just the mind of a man for whom star-gazing and personal salvation enjoyed pride of place over such mundane subjects as the government of men, but also the mind of a man who had turned away from the human scene in disgust. He had come to the melancholy conclusion that such a society as New South Wales had not existed since the introduction of Christianity into the world. By contrast the currency lads and the emancipists were turning, noisily, exuberantly and boisterously, to embrace the world they knew. On the night of 26 January 1825 a party of them, with Wentworth as president, and Redfern as vice-president, met at Hill's hotel to celebrate the thirty-seventh anniversary of the colony. They drank toasts to many things—to the King, to the memory of Governor Phillip, and of Macquarie, to Sir Thomas Brisbane who believed that all human striving was vain, to trial by jury, to a house of assembly, to freedom of the press, to commerce and agriculture, and to the currency lasses, for Wentworth was a man. There was much merriment, and much shouting when Robinson, an effective writer of doggerel verse for such occasions, called on them to drink the toast: 'The land, boys, we live in'.

A few months later copies arrived of the third edition of Wentworth's book on the colony of New South Wales. The emancipists hailed him as their historian and their advocate, a worthy native son of 'the land, boys, we live in'. John Macarthur was not greatly alarmed. The rodomontade and the savage invective only confirmed what he had been telling himself for a long time about Wentworth—namely, that the man would offend grossly. But Marsden was deeply hurt. Wentworth and his collaborator, Edward Eagar, had held him up to public ridicule as a turbulent and ambitious priest, who had set his face against every philanthropic project. They had taunted him as an unctuous hypocrite whose reverence for the Lord's day was not such as to permit a windmill of his, which stood in full view of the very sanctuary where he officiated, suspending its profitable gyrations even during church time.

When Brisbane was recalled to London, the opponents of the exclusives farewelled him as their hero. The *Australian* wrote on 20 October that the days when the Nimrods of the colony dominated convicts, emancipists, and free men alike, and trampled on men's rights, and used the cat-o'-nine-tails to cow people into obedience were drawing to a close. Now, thanks to Brisbane, New South Wales was no longer a penal settlement: a British public inhabited the territory, and enjoyed a free press.

They were not to know that the men in high places in the Colonial Office had decided in future only to transport those convicts who were capable of labour, and certainly not those who would swell the number of republicans, or the amount of immorality in the towns. They were not to know either, as they called out over the water their fond farewells to Brisbane, that by their own folly they would push his successor into the arms of the gentry of New South Wales.

4

The Native Son Offends Grossly

The agent of the Australian Agricultural Company, R. Dawson, arrived in Sydney on 27 November 1825 with sheep, cattle, choice plants and servants to select land for the company. Under the terms of a charter issued by Bathurst, the company was to receive large areas of land in New South Wales, in return for its investment of £1 000 000. It was planned that the company would farm this land using convict labour. Several prominent citizens bought shares in this vast enterprise, including John and Hannibal Macarthur, Samuel Marsden, the Tory churchman Archdeacon Thomas Hobbes Scott, and the newly arrived Chief Justice, Francis Forbes. The *Australian* cast a disapproving eye over the whole venture. The company, they said, would raise up a monopoly. They opened up on the Macarthur interest in the company. It was, they said, a case of 'my son, my son-in-law, or my nephew's brother-in-law . . . so snug a corner in which to form family contacts'. It would enable the Macarthurs, they said, to bring their sheep to a very good market.

Wentworth, sensing an opportunity to use the affair in his own vendetta against the Macarthurs, reminded a meeting of the native born that the free immigrants were getting their 'filthy paws' on all the good land in the colony. The solution to this state of affairs was obvious, he told them. They must put down the faction which was keeping them in a state of vassalage. Nothing short of a legislative assembly and unlimited trial by jury would satisfy the wants of the colonists.

John Macarthur, meanwhile, had cloistered himself away on his estate where he spent more and more time planning great journeys abroad, and brooding over schemes to destroy his enemies, chattering away like a wayward child. With that courage she always displayed in the face of adversity, his wife turned more and more to the Mighty Ruler of the universe to give her strength to endure the last days. Nevertheless, there were lucid moments between the mad fantasies, when Macarthur cast a cold eye on the unprincipled, profligate characters who roistered every night in the rooms of Mr Wentworth. He had reason to be confident that the society of which he had dreamed his great dream was beginning to take shape. There was a new Governor in New South Wales, Lieutenant-General Ralph Darling. From far away England, John Macarthur junior had written to his father to warn him that Darling's manners were so cold that it would be difficult to become intimate. But, he wrote, he had a great merit: he would entertain great jealousy towards the convict party. Now, Macarthur noted with satisfaction, the convict party was no longer being heeded at Govenment House. Darling had moved rapidly to reduce the number of convicts in government service. The Legislative Council had removed 500 convicts from the penal settlement at Port Macquarie for assignment to settlers. The newly established Executive Council had rejected any suggestion that emancipists be permitted to serve on juries in the Supreme Court.

A year earlier, fearful lest the system of granting land might contribute to an age of barbarism in New South Wales, my lord Bathurst in January 1825 had told Brisbane of the injury to society when land remained in a barren state from either the lack of capital or a disinclination to employ it. The settlements of the richer or more enterprising colonists became separated from each other by intervening tracts of the original wilderness. It must be remembered, said Bathurst, that it was anomalous for ex-convicts to become landowners. What was needed were settlers with access to capital.

The Surveyor-General, John Oxley, prepared a report on how the land should be divided up for the purposes of such sale. Acting on Oxley's advice and after consulting the Executive Council, in September 1826 Darling published new regulations for the granting and purchasing of land. Applicants who satisfied the Governor of their character and respectability would receive grants at the rate of one square mile for £500, the maximum grant to be 2 560 acres. Persons wishing to obtain more could purchase up to 9 900 acres by tender. Such settlement was to be confined within an area convenient for administrative and financial purposes. With an unerring eye for the drift of events, the *Australian* groaned at the ineptitude and folly of their rulers in London, who, they argued, had taken one further step to prevent a class of small proprietors from coming into existence, and would favour the rich land monopolists.

Such criticisms drew Darling's attention to the conduct of those newspapers which, he believed, were promoting civil unrest, particularly among the Irish. The seditious tendencies of the press showed in the reporting of the court martial of Joseph Sudds, who had committed a brazen theft, in the belief that a convict's life would be easier than a soldier's. Darling, determined to make an example of Sudds and his accomplice, Patrick Thompson, had their trial transferred to a military court which sentenced them to be drummed out of their regiment and worked in chains. At a military parade their uniforms were stripped from the two men, the yellow clothing of convicts was substituted, irons were placed on their legs, and iron collars locked round their necks, after which the two culprits were drummed off the parade ground to the tune of the Rogue's March. The *Australian* said that this was carrying severity too far, as the men could not even lie down to sleep when yoked with such monstrous collars.

When Sudds died in irons on 27 November the popular press set up a great howl. A man who was a mass of tumour from head to foot, and who was approaching his last mortal struggle, had had his neck and heels enclosed in iron shackles. A dying man had been tortured by the believers in severity. Darling, unmoved as ever, cast a cold eye over the affair. It could hardly be supposed, he wrote, that a man who could deliberately commit such an act with so base an interest could possess any sense of shame or really feel the degradation to which he had wantonly and wilfully subjected himself.

How different for Wentworth. The death of Sudds, he said, would have softened any heart not made of stone. The use of irons on a dying man was proof, strong as Holy Writ, of the existence in Darling of a most wicked, depraved and malignant spirit. On 15 December he wrote to Bathurst of the universal feelings of horror prevailing in Sydney, adding that he would write at greater length as soon as he had decided whether Darling should be charged with murder or a high misdemeanour. After collecting the required twenty-four signatures, he asked his staunch ally the Sheriff, John Mackaness, to call a public meeting at the Court House on Anniversary Day, 26 January.

There before all the landholders of wealth in the colony, with only a few notable exceptions, Wentworth presented a petition to the King and the two Houses of Parliament for trial by jury and a house of assembly. Why, he asked, should they not have those safeguards which would shelter them from oppression—those bulwarks of the constitution—trial by jury and a house of assembly? Was not New South Wales in the same situation as America in 1776? Might it not be forced to shake off the yoke? The landholders roared their approval, and accepted the petition unanimously after some observations from Sir John Jamison, Mr Gregory Blaxland, Mr D'Arcy Wentworth, Dr Wardell and Mr Hall.

This wild talk of shaking off the yoke alarmed Darling. The extravagant behaviour of Wentworth during the Sudds affair had convinced him that he was a vulgar, ill-bred fellow, utterly unconscious of the civilities due from one gentleman to another. Now he wondered whether Wentworth would become a 'man of the people', join hands with Hall, Father Therry and the Reverend William Walker to incite the lower orders to sedition. Archdeacon Scott, that great sleeve-plucker in the corridors of Government House, kept whispering in his ear that the press would continue to sow the seeds of discord and sedition so long as it was allowed to be licentious, for was it not notorious that Hall, the editor of the *Monitor*, mingled freely with the convict classes in Sydney?

For months past Darling had been wondering whether the time had not come to take up Bathurst's suggestion that government should issue licences to newspapers, to be forfeited if the proprietor or publisher were found guilty of a blasphemous or seditious libel. On 11 April 1827 he introduced two bills into the Legislative Council to control the press. At the end of that month and all though May, the Council debated the issue. John Macarthur turned up regularly as evidence of his conviction that Darling was right: delay was pregnant with danger. So did Scott, McLeay, Robert Campbell and Charles Throsby, all supporters, not only of press censorship, but also of exclusion of the low-born from society in New South Wales.

Then Francis Forbes intervened. Forbes was a man born with great intellectual and imaginative gifts, and a keen eye for his own advancement. Three years earlier he had been received into the life of Sydney with great pomp as the first Chief Justice of the newly established Supreme Court. Under a provision enacted in London in 1823, which Forbes himself had recommended, a bill of the Legislative Council could not pass into law until the Chief Justice had issued a certificate affirming that the bill was not 'repugnant to the laws of England'. Anxious not to damage his own career, Forbes had tried to stand aloof from the quarrel. But on 1 May, he set out in dignified and measured language his reasons for not granting the certificate. The bill (he meant the second of the two bills) was repugnant to freedom of the press, as by law established, as every man had an undoubted right to lay what sentiments he pleased before the public. In the proposed bill this right had been confined to such persons only as the Governor should deem proper. To vest such a discretionary power in the head of the executive was repugnant to the principles and practice of English law. The press might be licentious, but that did not, and indeed could not, justify the proposed restraints on the freedom of the press. The law of England provided adequate remedies against such licentiousness, and if the law should be found inadequate, the remedy was to change the law of England.

Darling, with that eye of the soldier for the coward in the civilian, concluded that Forbes was just too pusillanimous to risk his popularity. The *Monitor* and the *Australian* hailed Forbes as the champion of freedom, and their ally in the coming struggle for the extension of trial by jury and the creation of a house of assembly, unaware that their popular idol had feet of clay. How were they to know that the Francis Forbes who had refused to bow the knee to a coterie of alarmists and fuss-pots in Sydney town would stoop before his masters in London? How did they ever come to think that a Tory government in England would lend a sympathetic ear to a group tainted with republicanism, a group of free-thinkers and radicals? The men in high places in London had already taken decisions calculated to promote the interests of those exclusives who had already got their filthy paws on all the good land in the colony.

Just as the controversy over the press was warming up, Darling ordered convicts assigned in Sydney to be sent to persons up-country so that they might be placed out of reach of those pleasures which corrupted their souls in the towns. At the same time he announced his intention to enforce a more strict discipline at the penal settlements. Darling's cold authority began to chill the ardour of his opponents.

By the time the bells rang out that Christmas of 1827 their promise of peace and goodwill on earth the tumult and the shouting had dropped to a whisper. It was known in Sydney Town that Darling had already dismissed Sheriff Mackaness because of his association and intercourse with certain factious individuals, who in the most open and wanton manner had endeavoured to degrade the government in the eyes of the public, and to create discord between it and the people. It was known too that Douglass had been suspended because he had been carousing with the emancipists. Now, on the eve of the season of goodwill, the rumour flew around Sydney that Darling had written a peremptory note to Foster, the Solicitor-General, to ask him whether he had ever spent a night in Wentworth's house.

Immediately the timid and the cautious, the career men, and all those dependent on the patronage of the Governor for either land or assigned servants, or just for a good word dropped in the right place in London, took fright. When the patriots, the men with Australian hearts, gathered for the dinner to commemorate the foundation of the colony on 26 January of the new year, 1828, Mackaness, bound by deep ties of conviction to what he thought Wentworth stood for, proposed a toast to their absent friend the

'Australian Counsellor'. An uneasy silence descended on the gathering. The men kept their places. There was one, an Australian by birth, who, despising the conduct of the elders, stood up alone, and drank to his fellow-countryman's health, and then left the company. While the patriots were displaying their political prudence when untouched by the brilliant oratory of Wentworth, Darling was putting down on paper his ideas on the future constitution of New South Wales.

5

Towards a Colonial Gentry

At Westminster on 18 April 1828, Sir James Mackintosh presented the petition, drafted by Wentworth and signed by some of the gentry, the merchants, landholders, yeomen, traders, and other free inhabitants of the colony of New South Wales, praying that the members of the House of Commons would bestow on all His Majesty's loving subjects those inherent birthrights of the British constitution of trial by jury and an elected assembly. But it was too late. The Tories, encouraged in their views by John Macarthur junior and Governor Darling's brother-law, Henry Dumaresq, had already made up their minds. They replied to such suggestions using the argument with which conservatives have resisted change down the ages—namely, that the time was not ripe.

Some alterations were necessary; on that every one was agreed. But the constitutional changes introduced by the government's Act for the better adminstration of justice in New South Wales and Van Diemen's Land were not calculated to meet the demands of a rabble of ex-convicts, publicans and shopkeepers, led by that gross and notorious father of bastards, William Charles Wentworth.

On 1 April 1828 Mr Secretary Huskisson had explained in a brief speech to the House of Commons that because of the peculiar situation in which the population of New South Wales was placed, about two-thirds of the population having forfeited their civil rights, His Majesty's government had decided to continue the existing system of administration, provide a system of justice suited to the nature of the population, and provide for the introduction of British institutions as soon as circumstances permitted. Because of the peculiar composition of their society, New South Wales was not ready for a legislative assembly.

The Act increased membership of the Legislative Council to a maximum of fifteen appointed members. The Council was empowered to draft all details respecting the introduction of juries.

Following Forbes's own recommendation, the repugnancy power of the Chief Justice was revoked; in future, all new laws passed by the Council would be reviewed by the Supreme Court. If the court and the Council were unable to agree on the supposed repugnancy of a new law, that Act would take effect until such time as the royal pleasure should be known. The power of the Governor to pass laws in opposition to the advice of the members of the Legislative Council was withdrawn. The government had not been prepared to include a clause for the restraint of the press, because, as the Secretary of State put it to Darling in his covering letter, they would not fetter a privilege which, in its legitimate exercise, was so highly conducive to the welfare of society. On two matters at least, the exclusives had won an important victory.

While John Macarthur, Robert Campbell and the other members of the Legislative Council were drafting laws and regulations to convert New South Wales into a sheep-walk for the profit and pleasure of the gentry, one man at long last had acquired the wisdom and the grace to turn from wickedness and live. That was the Reverend Samuel Marsden. He was happy to say he had lived in great peace and quietness since General Darling's arrival, which, he added ruefully, was a new thing for him. As the man within had calmed down, he had heeded more and more that last appeal by the holy voice on that green hill without a city wall—'Father, forgive them; for they know not what they do'. The man who in his early days in the colony had thanked his God he was not as other men, had in July 1827 committed to the grave the body of D'Arcy Wentworth, and had shaken hands with William Charles Wentworth on whom in his darker moments he had plotted to seek vengeance in the lawcourts of New South Wales. Forbes said publicly that he respected Marsden as an old and zealous minister of religion. For the first time, men gave him their regard. With pride, and some surprising tenderness for his fellow-man, he wrote to London that the publishing of his most recent pamphlet had produced a very extraordinary effect in the colony in his favour, among all ranks. An air of dignity and tragic grandeur began to descend on him as he went about God's business—comforting and relieving the sick, giving patience in their sufferings to the dying, preaching God's holy word, freed at long last from the meshes of the world's great net, just at that moment when desire began to fail.

Towards the end of that long trying summer in Sydney, that season of storms and southerlies, Wentworth did as he had long threatened: he sent off 30 000 words to the Right Honourable Sir George Murray, KCB, His Majesty's principal Secretary of State for the Colonies, about Darling's act of atrocity against Sudds. He likened Darling to the greatest monsters of antiquity: he accused him of a series of fraud, tyranny and corruption such as had never occurred before in the history of colonial government: he wrote of him as a man guilty of a system of misdemeanours, of which murder itself glared at the centre: and ended by asking whether it was fitting, whether it was decent, whether it would not in fine be an outrage on the feelings and opinions of all His Majesty's loyal subjects in the colony to suffer anyone who stood thus guilty and degraded in their estimation, to fill any longer the dignified office of His Most Gracious Majesty's representative among them.

By contrast, when E. S. Hall wrote to Murray, he raised a great question. The root of the matter, as he saw it, was that the good land of New South Wales had been picked and occupied by twenty-nine persons only, and a large portion of it by four families, the Macarthurs, the Macleays, the Berrys, and the Throsbys, who were closely allied to the executive. Great families by being magistrates and civil officers thus formed a strong chain of political power in the colony. As he saw it, the faint distant cry of the poor people seeking land, if it should happen to penetrate to Government House in Sydney (which was not very probable) would have to break through the clamour and misrepresentations of a host of wealthy, interested and greedy men. These men, Hall continued, were on terms of friendship with the members of the closed Legislative Council, who were the makers of those laws by which the poor of New South Wales were now being every day sacrificed to the rich.

Murray wrote to Darling on the evils of the mutual jealousy and ill will which had been permitted to take possession of the minds of the colony's principal officers, and warned him that should such dissensions continue he would feel himself called upon to recall the judges, and to relieve him of his command. Darling had the mind of the server; he received the dispatch with feelings of infinite pain and disappointment, but both he and Forbes promptly proceeded to compose their differences.

Only Wentworth held out against this pressure from London for conciliation and harmony. He was fighting, not for those hopes for better things for mankind proclaimed in the declaration of the rights of man, or for that divine promise of the day when men should neither hurt nor destroy, but rather for revenge against Darling. Happily, as he saw it, there was still in Sydney a torrent of public indignation which would denounce Darling as the man who had tortured and murdered Sudds.

As the bitterness between the social classes in Sydney continued to fester, a party of men was struggling heroically to return to Sydney after a journey in which they had uncovered part of the mystery of that harsh land over which men were wrangling in the centres of civilization. The leader of this expedition was Captain Charles Sturt. He had been born in India in 1795, the son of a judge in the East India Company, educated privately and at Harrow, and had entered the army. In May 1827 he arrived in Sydney with a detachment of his regiment. He was a man on whom the gods seemed to have smiled as he was both monstrous handsome and lovable. A simple faith sustained him through all the changing scenes of life: by one way only was peace to be found, and that was by prayer. In many a scene of danger, of difficulty, and of sorrow he had risen from his knees calm and confident. His was a faith for a man to whom much had been given.

In an earlier expedition, in 1828, Sturt had travelled with Hamilton Hume and a party of eleven other men on an expedition which traversed a large sun-blasted plain and found the river which Sturt named the Darling. He had returned home to report that it was a matter of mystery whether the Darling made its way to the south coast, or ultimately exhausted itself in feeding a succession of swamps, or fell into a large reservoir in the centre of the continent. He came back, too, to tell those settlers who were hungry for new farmlands what they already feared, namely that no beneficial consequences would immediately follow from what he had seen, which had only confirmed Oxley's cry of anguish on first seeing the dreary, inhospitable country to west of Bathurst.

There was one gleam of sunshine over that extensive melancholy landscape. There was still the veil of mystery over the channel of the Darling. Did those waters flow into a country where an Englishman's green and pleasant parkland delighted the eyes, rather than those dreary plains where even the vegetation disappeared off the face of a wind-cracked and sun-scarred earth? To answer this question, in November 1829 General Darling sent Sturt on another expedition to the Murrumbidgee to see whether that river flowed into the Darling, or emptied itself into the sea on the southern coast of the colony. This time he took with him George Macleay. All told, fourteen travelled in his party.

They came to the Murrumbidgee near Jugiong in countryside of surpassing beauty where Sturt lifted up his eyes unto the hills and praised his God that He had done such wondrous things. And they followed the course of the river through fertile land until they came to a country where it was impossible to describe the dreariness of the view. The plains were still open to the horizon, but here and there a stunted gum tree, or a gloomy casuarina, seemed placed by nature as mourners over the surrounding desolation. Neither beast nor bird inhabited these lonely and inhospitable regions, over which the silence of the grave seemed to reign. Sturt's native boy deserted him: the natives who visited their camp came to pilfer. But Sturt did not despair. Concluding that the horses and the drays could make but slow progress through the swamps, he decided on the bold and desperate measure of building a whale-boat and sending home the drays. Then in January 1830, as the morning mists blew over their heads, and the sun funnelled through, Sturt and his party of seven men embarked on the bosom of the Murrumbidgee, and made rapid progress between its gloomy banks till the afternoon of 13 January when they saw that they were approaching a junction, and in less than a minute afterwards they were hurried into a broad and noble river. Sturt named it the Murray.

They proceeded down this river till 22 January when they came upon a river entering their own from the north, which Sturt rightly determined to be the Darling. The natives, who had evinced hostile intentions, changed miraculously from anger to curiosity, for as soon as the white men landed their wrangling ceased, and they swam towards Sturt's boat like a party of seals. For Sturt this was yet another example of the merciful superintendence of that benevolent providence to which they had humbly committed themselves. In pride at his achievement, Sturt directed the Union Jack to be hoisted and they all stood up in the boat and gave three cheers. It was, Sturt thought, an English feeling, an ebullition, an overflow which their circumstances and situation alone could excuse—but very pleasing. The eye of every native had been fixed upon that noble flag, to Sturt at all times a beautiful object, and to them all there in the heart of a desert.

In the succeeding days of January and February they continued their journey downstream searching for the outlet where this great river emptied itself into the southern ocean. They travelled through dreary plains until they entered upon a more promising country at a bend in the river where it began to run away to the south. The traces of kangaroos were numerous. They began to see signs that the sea was not far away from them: seagulls flew over their heads, and one of the party raised his gun to fire at them, but Captain Sturt prevented him. The gulls, he said, should be hailed as messengers of glad tidings, and not be greeted with death. They began to pull the boat against the heavy swell that rolled up the river from the south seas, stroking the oars with the elation of men for whom the tang of the sea in their nostrils, the gulls wheeling overhead, the sandhills and the stiff breeze blowing all conveyed the promise of their impending victory.

When it came, it was not quite that for which their captain was prepared. On 9 February their whale-boat shot into the waters of a beautiful lake, a fitting reservoir for the noble stream that had led them to it, and now ruffled by the sea breeze that swept over it. Sturt wondered whether the lake had any practicable communication with the sea. It was not a harbour which man could use, but a lake surrounded by a sandy and sterile country. His hopes began to be damped, but the following day the sound of the sea came gratefully to their ears, and they promised themselves a view of the ocean on the morrow. On that day the captain stood on the shores of Encounter Bay, as the thunder of the heavy surf shook the ground beneath him. The voices of the Aborigines echoed through the bush, as the men enjoyed the cockles they had boiled.

Their return was a journey of unmeasured hardship. The exhausted and hungry men pulled their oars against the current of the mighty river, Sturt ever trustful that a benign Providence watched over them. By 12 May they were at Yass Plains, and reached Sydney by easy stages on 25 May 1830. The word soon passed round Sydney that the captain had laid open a boundless extent of excellent well-watered country to the south of the colony: that he had found districts to which the tide of migration could flow, and a noble river whose banks would one day be studded with settlements. Southward, the womb of the country was neither dry nor sterile.

Even as new lands were being discovered in the name of the Crown, the method of disposal of such lands had been a subject for discussion in London. In a dispatch of 9 January 1831 Viscount Goderich had told Darling he had come to the melancholy conclusion that the existing regulations for the disposal of land had failed. They had not prevented large tracts of land being appropriated by persons unable to improve and cultivate them. At a time when large landholders were complaining of a shortage of labour, the existing regulations had also encouraged acquiring land, which prevented the growth of a class of labourers for hire. To remedy these evils Goderich proposed the simple measure of declaring that in future no land whatever would be disposed of other than by auction at a minimum price, say of 5s an acre. The money raised would be used to fund immigration.

In the beginning the response in the colony to these changes was enthusiastic: 'Our readers', wrote the *Sydney Gazette* in July, 'will rejoice to hear, that the British government is concerting measures for the promotion of pauper emigration to these colonies, which will be the means of supplying us with abundance of cheap, honest, and industrious labourers'. Some mocked at the absurd suggestion that anyone would want to buy Crown land in New South Wales. By September the grumbles, groans and apprehensions of the landowners had swollen into a roar of anxiety, and a clamour for public meetings at which they could draw up petitions against such absurd, impractical schemes.

Then one day in October Wentworth met James Macarthur in the streets of Sydney, and found that as a landowner he had much in common with him, and agreed to put his name down together with Macarthur's on a list of those requesting a meeting to discuss the propriety of the new regulations for collecting quitrents. Divided as ever, it was not given to Wentworth to see that the power of the man against whom he had directed his most brilliant attacks had been reduced by the London decision to withdraw the Governor's patronage over the disposal of land. Besides, as he talked then to Macarthur, one part of him was taken up with the plans of his cronies for the vilification and discomfiture of Darling when he left the colony.

For Darling had been recalled. On first receiving the news he had been dejected, haunted as always by fear of failure in his relations with men. Now, at last in October he had been cheered a little to receive His Majesty's approbation for the zeal he had manifested, and was pleased a little by the praise both from the members of the Legislative Council and one section of the press for the uprightness and utility of his administration.

On 22 October 1831, the *Monitor* printed in large capitals the expression of their joy that a disquieting and oppressive administration was at last ending:

HE'S OFF!
THE REIGN OF TERROR ENDED

None of them could know that the occasion would be remembered in time as that day when they also said farewell to Wentworth as the leader of the radical party in New South Wales, for from that day he began to uncover in public the great master-mistress of his passion, that aim to take the top place.

6

A High-Minded Governor in Van Diemen's Land

Early in 1824 James Stephen of the Colonial Office told the Lieutenant-Governor elect of Van Diemen's Land, Lieutenant-Colonel George Arthur, that he had an opportunity to make that dependency of New South Wales one branch of a great and powerful nation, which must exercise a mighty influence for good or evil over a vast region of the earth. He told him of the importance of his mission to establish a Christian, virtuous and enlightened state in the centre of the eastern hemisphere.

Arthur seemed to be the man to undertake such a mission. Born in Plymouth in June of 1784, he had joined the army as an ensign in 1804, and had seen active service. After promotion to the rank of major he had accepted the position of superintendent in Honduras in 1814, where he remained for eight years. In 1814 he married Eliza Orde Usher, the daughter of a Lieutenant-General in the British army. Then while reading the scriptures he had begun to be weighed down with guilt and the knowledge that the heart of every man was desperately wicked. Happily for him in the midst of this abasement, it had pleased God to convey to his soul the most cheering reflections. In Honduras he had read of the all sufficient atonement by Christ, and had become perfectly tranquil, perfectly cheerful and perfectly happy. Through the free grace of God he had come to believe he would one day enter into eternal life.

From that day he had prayed fervently to be weaned away from the amusements of this world so that he might prepare for a better. Dances, concerts, or cards were not innocent amusements: they were the work of the devil, the way of Mammon. By his life he hoped to testify to his fellow-creatures that he was walking in the Gospel light, and so assist others in the way to heaven.

When he and his family arrived on the ship *Adrian* on 11 May 1824, Arthur surveyed the colony with the pious eye of a soldier of God, taking guard against the assault of Satan. The appearance of the man reflected the faith by which he lived. He wore black clothes. He walked with a stoop, as though his shoulders were weighed down with the burden of human evil. Arthur was a Tory who was always looking for a system of discipline which could curb depravity in man without degrading him. For man was made in the image of God, and must always appear worthy of his most Holy Maker. For the rest he affected a vast indifference to what went on in the world. Yet he never ceased to sigh for worldly honours, and never ceased to lay up for himself treasures on earth as well as in heaven.

To the Aborigine he stood both as a protector and evangelist. The need for protection had become urgent. The Aboriginal population of Van Diemen's Land had shrunk to less than 500. In June of 1824 just one month after his arrival Arthur issued a proclamation warning those settlers and others who were in the habit of maliciously and wantonly firing at, injuring, and destroying the defenceless Aborigines that they would be prosecuted. All magistrates and peace officers were to enjoin the inhabitants of their districts, especially stock-keepers, not only to avoid all aggression, but to exercise great forbearance towards the Aborigines, treating them on all occasions with the utmost kindness and compassion.

It was the same with the convicts. Of the 12 643 white people in Van Diemen's Land in the year of his arrival, 5938 were convicts. Of these 5467 were men, and 471 were women. The convicts were there both for their punishment and reformation, and to provide labour for the settlers. But the penal discipline of convicts and the application of their services to the settlers were in a continual state of collision in the new colony. Arthur had found to his mortification that instead of improving the character and behaviour of their servants the settlers universally encouraged their dissipated propensities, partly out of dread and partly from a desire to prevail on them to work.

There were stories of escaped convicts resorting to cannibalism to keep themselves alive. There were stories of ex-convicts purchasing women from the Aborigines for the carcase of a seal or a kangaroo. If these women were not pleasing to the men, or the men came back from the hunt with great darkness in their hearts, they tied the women up and flogged them in the most cruel manner. These men lived on animal food and birds, and were scarcely a remove from the savage.

Arthur looked to the pious settlers for the moral improvement and discipline of the convicts, which he took to be a main point in the administration of the colony. There, alas, was the source of misunderstanding, anger and bitterness between him and the settlers. They had come, and were coming, to exploit the labour of convicts, not to save their souls. They came to cut away all that stood between them and their goal—the primeval forest, the beasts of prey, and the people they thought of as savages—only to find the Lieutenant-Governor of Van Diemen's Land lecturing them on their solemn duty to God to treat the Aborigines on all occasions with kindness and compassion. These settlers had learned the hard way how to survive in a harsh land, and some soon began to express doubts about whether a man like Arthur, who was fanatically concerned with the moral improvement and discipline of the convicts, could at the same time minister to their needs.

In the Cat and Fiddle, and in the Bird in the Hand, where Arthur's predecessor Davey had sat in his shirt-sleeves swapping stories with the locals, the mention of Arthur's name that summer was greeted with howls of anger or ridicule. When members of the Turf Club asked Arthur to become a patron of their club, Arthur replied that he disapproved of horse-racing and thought it an amusement highly injurious to a convict colony. In the pothouses of Hobart Town, in the coffee rooms, drawing rooms and salons, men and women took up the cry that there was a spoilsport, a killjoy, a bloody saint presiding over the affairs of Van Diemen's Land.

As the rude jokes began to circulate, the *Hobart Town Gazette* came out on 8 October 1824 with an editorial in which it described Arthur as a 'Gibeonite of Tyranny'. No one in Hobart Town was quite sure what the editor meant, except that he must have meant an especially bad form of tyranny. But Arthur knew about the Gibeonites—they hanged their enemies on the hill before the Lord—and he began to alarmed about the effect of the editor's words on the convict population.

The owner of the *Hobart Town Gazette*, Andrew Bent, an ex-convict, represented the forces Arthur saw as trying to divide him from his vocation as a vessel of God's saving grace. The paper's criticisms convinced Arthur that all the privileges so happily enjoyed in England, however gratifying to British subjects, were quite inconsistent and unsafe in penal colonies. There was, he believed, no stopping half-way. So began his great struggle to control the dissident press, a struggle which was to see men gaoled, papers closed, and his own legislation rejected in London as being repugnant to the laws of England.

The conflicts of the parties were put to one side when the independence of the colony was proclaimed on 3 December 1825. All Hobart Town celebrated with expressions of generosity and optimism. The Governor even called for a second bottle of port after dinner at Government House that evening and one man went home and noted in his diary that Colonel Arthur had a heart. Such unity and goodwill were not to last. That May, Arthur had other things of great moment to occupy his mind. Edward Curr had arrived with instructions that he be permitted to select 250 000 acres in the north-west corner of the colony for the Van Diemen's Land Company, for which he had been appointed chief agent at a salary of £800 a year.

Arthur had been giving much thought to the whole problem of the disposal of land in Van Diemen's Land and had commissioned Edward Dumaresq, Peter Murdoch and Roderic O'Connor to make a survey of all the lands within the island. From their journals Arthur found much to confirm his own pessimistic view of the human situation. The commissioners wrote of a wicked and debauched society in which the powerful preyed on the weak and vast acres of land lay idle. They wrote of how Arthur's one-time Attorney-General, Joseph Tice Gellibrand, had used great cunning to buy and sell land at an enormous profit, and of how a few ex-convicts and their children had acquired vast properties. Of the lower orders of rural society they had an equally depressing story to tell, a story of idleness, beggary and sheep-stealing. To Arthur this was that human society where on the side of the oppressors there was power, where there was much evil work done under the sun, where if a man fell, he had not another to hold him up. Here indeed a man could say in his heart concerning the sons of men that they were beasts. The free inhabitants might argue politics and talk of the rights of man, but Arthur was concerned with that much deeper battle in the heart of a man between damnation and impassioned clay. The changes he longed for could be wrought, not by legislative assemblies, but by God's saving grace.

In any case, he had other matters on his mind. By the second half of 1826 Arthur had come to the melancholy conclusion that the Aborigine had acquired an implacable hatred for the white man. The least of the little ones whom Arthur had hoped in 1824 to lead into the bonds of love and ways of peace were stealing property, butchering white men, and crying out during their raids: 'Fire, you white bastards'.

Appalled by the report of the murder of seven Europeans in the vicinity of Penny-Royal Creek and the Macquarie River, and anxious of what those soldiers of God in Downing Street would think of him allowing Englishmen to be slaughtered by 'sooty savages', Arthur issued a proclamation in November of 1826 in which he declared that, on numerous occasions, the Aborigines had met the kindness of the settlers with wanton barbarity. In order to prevent the repetition of these treacherous and sanguinary acts, Arthur announced a new policy: if it should be apparent that there was a determination on the part of one or more of the native tribes to attack, rob, or murder the white inhabitants generally, any person might arm, and, joining themselves to the military, drive them by force to a safe distance, treating them as open enemies.

This was a declaration of war. But war, as a policy of protection, proved no more effective than compassion and forbearance. A year later Arthur announced further measures to put an end to the acts of barbarity of the Aborigines against the settlers. Sufficient troops would be placed at the disposal of the magistrates and constables in every district for the common defence and protection of the community. All to no avail, for each week the press of Hobart Town and Launceston carried stories of outrages committed by the blacks. In the following October at Green Ponds, as a warning of impending danger, the dogs began to bark outside the hut of a settler. With the men away working in the bush, a mother grabbed her son and daughter and fled. The press described how the savages, eager for both plunder and blood, pilfered the hut, then shrieking their blood-curdling yells, gave chase, killed the son and wounded the daughter, the mother saving her own and her daughter's life by feigning death. Again the press in both towns demanded that some check be put to this horrible havoc on human life. Surely, it was argued, something must be done quickly with these people.

The question was: what? Some clamoured for extermination: shoot the black bastards, and have done with it, and cut the mawkish and sentimental cackle. The *Colonial Advocate* put the case quite simply in May of 1828: 'Let them be removed, or they will be exterminated'. In 1826 and 1827, the *Colonial Times* had kept telling its readers that, as the settlers and stock-keepers were determined to annihilate every black who might prove hostile, the more merciful way to proceed would be to transfer them to King Island in Bass Strait to prevent the bloodshed which would otherwise inevitably ensue.

Despite all the clamours and urgent appeals for harsh measures Arthur could not divest his mind of the consideration that all aggression originated with the white inhabitants, and that therefore much ought to be endured in return before the blacks were treated as an open and despised enemy by the government. In one part of him, he had never given up the idea, or rather the hope, that the Aborigines would be brought to know God's grace. So, while some settlers were swearing over their pots of ale, their brandy and water, or their rum toddies, that they would shoot all the black bastards, Arthur appointed G. A. Robinson as guardian to the Aborigines on Bruny Island.

Robinson, like Arthur, was devoutly religious, a member of the Auxiliary Bible Society of Van Diemen's Land, and a foundation member of the Van Diemen's Land Mechanics' Institute. Before leaving for Bruny he told Arthur that he proposed to instruct the Aborigines in the arts of civilization, and to adore that Supreme Being by whom all things were made. Arthur, who believed there was a special providence in the fall of a sparrow, wanted desperately to believe that God, through Robinson, was about to work a great miracle.

On Bruny, where he had landed on 31 March 1829, Robinson learned the language of the Aborigines, talked hunting with them and gradually gained their confidence. The Aborigines were delighted to learn how to use the white man's gun; they were prepared to use the white man's medicines to cure sickness. But when Robinson told them that the roar of falling waters, the sombre vegetation, the mournful cry of the birds, and the strange eerie silence by night reminded him of the utter precariousness of man's mortal pilgrimage, and his future appearance before an all-wise and omnipotent tribunal, the Aborigines looked at this kind man who had taught them such useful things with puzzlement—for that was not their experience of life.

What he saw and heard over the following year filled him with compassion. The children had witnessed the massacre of their parents and relations, and then been carried away by those merciless invaders who had taken their country from them and slaughtered their source of subsistence. Was it any wonder, Robinson asked, that they bore such hatred to the white man, and such a flame of righteous sentiment? British benevolence must prevent the race being entirely annihilated.

It was too late. Four days earlier on 9 September Arthur had published a fatal proclamation. He called on every settler to volunteer cheerfully with the police and the soldiers for one cordial and determined effort which would afford a good prospect of either capturing the whole of the hostile tribes or of permanently upsetting them from the settled districts. His plan was to round up the natives of Van Diemen's Land into the county of Buckingham, and progressively drive them into Tasman Peninsula, from where there would be no escape. Press and public were jubilant. Doubts of the legality of shooting blacks or qualms of consciousness were silenced sharply by atrocity stories. At a public meeting Gellibrand deprecated the shooting of blacks: Mr Horne shouted him down with the case of a woman and her twin babes who had been butchered recently at the Regent Plains.

After the meeting some began to be tormented with doubt. Dr Turnbull, Arthur's secretary, wondered why no one had cried shame upon a group of men who could reason on the cold-blooded extermination of a whole nation. Was Van Diemen's Land to rival

Mexico in scenes of carnage and unrelenting butchery? But Dr Ross in the *Hobart Town Courier* urged the military to use dogs. The pack was beginning to form: the hunt was on.

On Sunday 5 October in all the churches of Van Diemen's Land men and women prayed fervently to the great Author of all, the creator and guardian of the blacks as well as the whites, that success might be the result of all their efforts. In St David's Church in Hobart Town those erstwhile implacable enemies, Arthur and Gellibrand, asked their God that this time the battle might be to the strong. Pray on, Gellibrand, for chance has in store for you a terrible fate at the hands of those savages about whom you were praying that day to the God of Battles.

On 7 October the great movement began. Three thousand took to the field, including 550 from the Launceston district, and about 1600 from Hobart Town and the Derwent Valley. The whole island appeared in commotion, as bugles, muskets and the cries of the chase echoed and died away in the sombre bush. Hope was in the air men breathed that spring. By the end of the month reports began to come back to Hobart of fatigue and difficulty of the expedition. There were reports that between 50 and 100 natives of the Big River and Oyster Bay tribes had been encircled. At night as the men settled down round the camp-fire, being careful not to make any noise, the note of optimism gave way to one of doubt and even despair. The blacks were eluding them.

By the end of October the volunteer force had occupied a line from Prosser's Bay on the east coast to Sorell, believing the natives were trapped between that line and the coast. Five scouting parties were then sent into the neck of the Tasman Peninsula to count the number of natives in the white man's cage. After scouring the whole peninsula the scouting party came back to the white man's line to tell the score: two natives had been shot and two had been captured. The great campaign had failed. It was as though the white man, like the fox, knew many things, while the land and the black man, like the hedgehog, knew that one big thing which was forever beyond the white man's reach.

7

The World of Betsey Bandicoot and Bold Jack Donahoe

In 1828 a Devonshire farmer, who had migrated to New South Wales a few years earlier, reflected wistfully on his new way of life in a country where no holy bells knolled him to church on Sunday, where the village church evoked no serious or tender reflections in his mind, where the churchyard contained no inscription on the tombs of his family or his friends to remind him of man's great hope during his journey through life. He shook his head, and summed up his despair and his nostalgia in his own way: 'It b'ant like home', he said, 'It b'ant like home'. It was not just the absence of all the outward and visible signs of civilization, of buildings such as the venerable pile of St Paul's, or the sprawl of the Abbey, or the great houses of the gentry in town and country, or that sense of continuity and permanence which was part of the air men breathed in older civilizations. Here the very climate and environment seemed alien or indifferent to all human endeavour. Here there was no long summer day, no long winter night, no fall of leaves, no sudden exuberance of the flowers in the spring, no birdsong, no continuing twilight, and no season of absolute gloom. Here there was none of that fierce contrast which in Europe had excited the imagination to man's eternal glory, but only a dull, plain level of uniformity. Where were the roots that would clutch in that barren land? Who would ever turn such a flint-stone into a springing well?

The members of the social set of Sydney and Hobart Town were not bothered by such questions. It was said in Sydney that the parties there were as gay as in Montagu Square in London, and that burgundy and champagne were in abundance. In choosing the days for celebration and rejoicing they followed the calendar of the London season. In the streets, dandies, imitating their counterparts in the Mall in London, dressed in the very extreme of puppyism, stalked along, silly, inconsequential beings, who measured their importance by the quantity of proud cloth in their trousers, by the width of their coat collars, by the position of the curl on the side of the head, by the strut and air of their walk, or by their very English dandy fal-lal-la way of replying to the most common question.

But while the gentry, the civil and military officers, and the clergy of the Church of England were attempting to reproduce the fashions and gaieties of the London season, out on the streets, in the taprooms, pothouses, bush huts, amidst all the uproar, commotion, the lust, the thirst and hunger, the world of Betsey Bandicoot and Bold Jack Donahoe was being fashioned. In the streets of Sydney nests of drunken, brawling women cursed each other in such coarse and obscene language that a decent woman could not venture through the streets without having her modesty shocked.

While Sydney, Newcastle, and Parramatta, Hobart Town and Launceston were disturbed from time to time by drunken brawls between soldiers and civilians, the lower orders provided their own distraction by indulging in a behaviour which provided amusement, entertainment or cause for indignation to the men and women in higher places. In the wretched hovels at the Rocks in Sydney terrible scenes of infamy occurred. The press often reported stories of women dying of drink. Margaret O'Brien was brought up before the magistrate in Sydney in April of 1826 by Father Therry for the highly reprehensible conduct of being in a public street in a state of great drunkenness. In the course of the inquiry it came out that the wretched woman had encouraged her daughter, aged 13, in her course of prostitution.

Of the 36 598 white persons living in the colony of New South Wales when the first census was taken in the year 1828, 20 930 were classified as free, and 15 668 as convict. But such figures counted the expirees, the emancipists, and the children of the convicts as free, a category to which they belonged by definition, though not necessarily by loyalty, tradition or conviction. In both New South Wales and Van Diemen's Land, males outnumbered females by more than three to one. The men in the lower orders, driven on by that first law of nature, practised prostitution, or the vices of the cities of Sodom and Gomorrah. The men in higher places kept concubines. From the time of Macquarie in New South Wales and Arthur in Van Diemen's Land, the government had repeatedly declared they would not overlook the practice. Men keeping concubines were not invited to Government House, or recommended for promotion.

Despite the cry against existing abominations, the encouragement of marriage led to offences against God and man being committed with tenfold enormity. That stern defender of morals, the Reverend Samuel Marsden, reminded his congregation that not a week passed without the majesty of heaven being insulted by members of the prisoner population. Husbands, he thundered, forsook their wives, who, finding themselves in want, became desperate, and gave themselves up to drunkenness, prostitution and theft. Parents abandoned their children, who were taken into the Female Factory where they became a charge on the government. According to the parsons, the priests, and all the self-appointed guardians of public morals, a more wicked, abandoned, and irreligious set of people had never been brought together in any other part of the world.

Yet by the year 1822 in New South Wales, if not in Van Diemen's Land, a group of men and women were growing up who were angered by any attempts to confound them with those persons in the convict community who were said to be incurable addicts of profligacy and vice. They were the local-born, the colonial-born, the native-born; the currency lads and lasses—all those who in the words of William Charles Wentworth had 'Australasian hearts'. By 1828 there were just over 3500 native-born persons in New South Wales over the age of 12— one quarter of the population.

Observers began to notice both their appearance and their demeanour as early as 1822. Even Mr Commissioner Bigge, who cast a cold, judicial eye on all human strivings, and was no friend to the mass of men not conceived in the beds of the gentry, had a warm word for the native-born. He remarked that they were generally tall in person, and slender in their limbs, of fair complexion and small features. They were capable of undergoing more fatigue, and were less exhausted by labour than native Europeans; they were quick in their habits but remarkably awkward in their movements. In their tempers they were quick and irascible, but not vindictive. He could, he said, only repeat the testimony of persons who had had many opportunities of observing them, namely, that they inherited neither the vices nor the feelings of their parents.

Aware that they were called on to endure injuries and injustice from the mere chance of being born in the colony rather than in the British Isles, the native-born began to clamour for their rights. Immigrants, they said, had been well treated on their arrival. Large tracts of land had been granted to them, and other indulgences bestowed on them. The Australians were not unreasonable, they were not envious. But the land was their birthright, their legitimate inheritance. Why should they be reduced to the status of the helots of Rome, sowers of the soil from which the immigrants would reap a rich harvest? Why were the native-born excluded from possession of the land?

With the passions of men cheated of their expectations, and wounded by gratuitous insults to their capacity and their morals, the native youth began to brag about their powers. They boasted of how much they could eat: some bragged of their capacity to use their fists: they were proud that a one-time convict, Samuel Terry, excelled all others in wealth.

Four years earlier in October 1823 one Fanny Flirt had written some rather disparaging remarks about Australia and Australians to the *Sydney Gazette*—saying, among other things, that riding through rows of gum trees was not to her taste, and, as for colonial conversation, why, nothing could be so sheepish. As for music, well, as Fanny Flirt put it, you only had to ask for a song in Sydney town, and young 'wholesale' would promptly chant to you, over an invoice, of course, 'Money is your friend, is it not?'. This was too much for those with Australasian hearts. Two weeks later Betsey Bandicoot replied, with that magnificent, vulgar, cheeky confidence of those who loved the land they lived in:

MISTER EDITOR,

. . . every one knows their own liking; she [Fanny Flirt] might prefar the soft-singing notes of her Italian in his gondola (all the same as a boat, the dictionnary says) to the loud coo-hee of a currency lad riding over the blue mountains. But our Bill can play the flute, hunt the wild cattle, and shoot and swim with the best in the Colony.

It would do your heart good, Mister Editor, to see how Bill tucks in, when I've fried him a pan-ful of pork, swimming in fat, and a smoaking hot cake from the ashes . . . But ma'aps this woud'nt be to the liking of Miss Flirt; as she is so dainty as not to be fond 'of riding through rows of gum-trees;' but, la! she should see me galloping without a saddle, a'ter Bill, when he has a mind for a bit of a frisk; and as for shoes, I never thinks of putting them on, only when I goes a shopping to Sydney, at Mother Marr's or Joe Inch's for a bonnet; or a Little or Big Cooper's for a frying-pan; and I beg a wager, I could swim further and faster than Miss Fanny, and carry my clothes on my head into the bargain, without wetting so much as my comb, which cousin Bill paid for in 'tatoes at Josephson's last Christmas hollidays . . .

I remain, dear Mister Editor,
your unworthy humble servant,
BETSEY BANDICOOT

Except for this confidence that they knew what's what, and a belief in sticking up for currency lads and lasses in things both great and small, they were not committed to any political or social creed. Their public speeches were not distinguished by high-minded talk of all men being created equal, let alone that all men were endowed by their creator with certain inalienable rights. They came together as men determined simply to have a share in the fruits of their land.

In press, pulpit, pamphlet and schoolroom all through the decade the battle went on for the hearts and minds of the people of New South Wales and Van Diemen's Land. From the day of its first publication on 14 October 1824, under the proprietorship of W. C. Wentworth and R. Wardell, the *Australian* praised all human activities which brought lads and lasses together: they loved all gay and lively intercourse. Not for them the black looks, the pursed lips, the tut-tuts of the parsons and the *Sydney Gazette* when they surveyed the human scene. They wrote up the behaviour of the convict community, their whoring, drinking, fisticuffs and brawls, as a huge joke. For them drunkenness was not the occasion for talk about hell-fire from a lugubrious parson, but just part of the human comedy. They wrote as the true sons of the Enlightenment—as men who were called to lay low those breast-beating sinners who begged a jealous Jehovah for his favour in the life of the world to come. The parsons were held up to ridicule as pompous asses, men puffed up with vanity and pride, and receivers of absurdly high salaries.

The pride and confidence of the native-born permeated the poetry of the period. Where Wentworth dreamed only of a 'new Britannia', other poets proclaimed the slogan 'Advance Australia!' The venerated poet, Michael Robinson, an ex-convict, won admiration and praise among emancipists and native-born for his songs of an Australia whose watchword was 'Freedom for Ever!' Some said Robinson's verse would outlive that of Barron Field who had insulted Australia as a land of perversities.

By an odd irony it was neither an emancipist, nor a native son, but an immigrant and a parson who wrote of Australia as a land of hope. He was John Dunmore Lang, that fiery particle whom the members of his church associated with some lively images from the pulpit each Sunday on the torments of the damned. In 1826 he published his book of verse, *Aurora Australis; or Specimens of Sacred Poetry, for the Colonists of Australia*, in which he invoked

> Australia! land of hope!
>   . . .
> From Superstition's snare
>   And Slavery's chain,
> To set the wretched free;
> 'Till Christian liberty,
> Wide o'er the Southern Sea,
>   Triumphant reign!

Sydney and Hobart Town were Protestant cities in which the public buildings, the churches, and the schools were outward and visible signs of the Protestant concept of God and man. Yet to the dismay of the parsons, the seed they sowed fell on the stony ground of a generation who had never known any belief. They were tempted to attribute the indifference to God to human depravity. The greater the indifference, the more savagely the parsons denounced from their pulpits the behaviour of a wicked and adulterous generation.

Amid all this babble of tongues, with the *Australian* cheekily proclaiming that heaven and hell were priest's inventions, and Betsey Bandicoot saying that for her part she proposed to stick up for currency lads and lasses, a new voice was heard in the land. On 1 September 1830 Jack Donahoe, 23 years of age, low in stature, but remarkably well made, was shot dead at Bringelly. Donahoe, who had been tried in Dublin in April 1823, arrived in Sydney on the *Ann and Amelia* as a convict in January 1825. He was tried again before the Supreme Court in Sydney in January 1828, after which he took to the bush, murdered a man with whom he had lived, and burnt his body to a cinder. After Donahoe was shot in 1830 the *Sydney Gazette* and all the respectable people in the colony rejoiced that they were rid of him.

But soon, in the taverns, pothouses and bush shanties, some men, using an old Irish melody, began to sing a song about a wild colonial boy, Jack Dowling [Donahoe] was his name, of poor but honest parents, a heart that knew no danger, no stranger for to fear, who had been sent across the main for seven long years to wear a convict's chain. There scorning to live in slavery bound down by iron chains, he had uttered his great cry of defiance:

> I'd rather roam these hills and dales, like wolf or kangaroo,
> Than work one hour for Government!' cried bold Jack Donahoe.

The song had such an evil influence that its singing was prohibited in any public house on pain of the loss of the licence. The song lived on. Bold Jack Donahoe had become part of the popular imagination of Australia.

Wherever convicts, their relatives, and sympathizers came together during the decade, they sang the story of Jim Jones. This, too, was a shaking of the fist not at God, or their society, but at their floggers and tormentors:

> For night and day the irons clang, like poor galley slaves
> We toil, and toil, and when we die must fill dishonoured graves.
> But by and by I'll break my chains: into the bush I'll go,
> And join the brave bushrangers there—Jack Donohoe and Co.;

And some dark night when everything is silent in the town
I'll kill the tyrants, one and all, and shoot the floggers down:
I'll give the Law a little shock: remember what I say,
They'll yet regret they sent Jim Jones in chains to Botany Bay.

Over the waters in Van Diemen's Land, the convicts and their sympathizers had begun to find words to express their cruel fate:

The first day that we landed here upon the fatal shore,
The settlers came around us, some twenty score or more;
They ranked us up like horses and they sold us out of hand,
And they yoked us up to ploughing-frames to plough Van
     Diemen's Land.

On 26 January 1828, the day of the anniversary of the founding of the colony, the bells of St Philip's Church kept ringing their merry peals, aided and abetted by the sonorous tonal bell of the Presbyterian Church, for Lang was not a man to allow the Anglicans to outdo him in anything. That night forty to fifty ex-convicts and native-born sat down to a most sumptuous dinner at Cumming's New Hotel in Macquarie Place. Mr Samuel Terry, a winder by trade, who had once been whipped for stealing poultry, but now one of the wealthiest men in the country, was in the chair. Thomas Cooper, who had been transported as a fence, and had made a fortune by manufacturing gin, which the colonists lovingly knew as 'Cooper's Best', was also there. He sat down at the same table with Mr Haynes, another ex-convict, who was now a proprietor of a whole fleet of whaling ships. They all joined together in toasting the King, other members of the royal family, governors past and present, Mrs Darling and the ladies of the colony, prosperity, trial by jury and so on into the night. At the end of the evening, after the wine had flowed freely, they rose to their feet to drink to their one big thing—to the currency lads and lasses, adding with pride 'The land, boys, we live in'.

8

A Whig Governor amidst High Tory Counsellors

Early in October 1831 James Macarthur communicated to his old rival, William Charles Wentworth, his opinion on the recent regulations for the disposal of land in New South Wales, in which sale at auction had been substituted for free grants. Wentworth was then aged 41. Six years had passed since he had shouted in a moment of drunken anger that he would remove the fangs of the Macarthurs. Time had not mellowed him. Chance and circumstance had brought him nearer to that other ambition so close to his heart, that dream of regaining for himself that access to the salons and drawing rooms of the gentry which his father had forfeited by some deeds of folly in his past. With the death of his father in July 1827 he had inherited a fortune. He had not only traded successfully in bulls and horseflesh, but had become one of the largest landowners in New South Wales. He had begun to collect at Vaucluse those outward and visible signs of worldly grandeur. In October 1829 he had given his hand in marriage to Sarah Cox just before she was brought to bed with his child. Just over a year later, on 4 November 1830, Jemima Eagar, the wife of the Edward Eagar who had helped him with the third edition of his book, had borne him a son. A year after that he had handed out free grog at Vaucluse to all who were prepared to mock and deride General Darling on the eve of his departure from New South Wales. Yet he was still striving to win the regard and esteem of the members of high society, without being endowed with the power to resist that madness in the blood which caused the very people he was courting to shun, despise and fear him.

Like Wentworth, James Macarthur was native-born. But whereas Wentworth consumed so much of his energy proudly defying retribution for the sins of the fathers, Macarthur knew of a family struggle of quite a different kind. He was born at Parramatta in 1798, the fourth son of Captain John and Mrs Elizabeth Macarthur.

Like Wentworth, James Macarthur became in childhood and adolescence more like his mother than his father, acquiring her graciousness and charm. He was, as Henry Parkes wrote, 'the English gentleman Australian-born'.

Overshadowed in his youth by the reputation of his father for ruthlessness and reckless folly as well as the odium of supporting the extreme exclusive position, he had also inherited his father's convictions and aspirations, the dream of establishing a plantation society in Australia, led by large landholders who derived their wealth from growing wool by cheap convict labour. But the old man had begun to fall prey to delusions that his family were taking things from him. Chance was about to bestow on James a role he had never coveted, the role of leader of the Macarthur family in New South Wales. So on that day in October two victims of the sins of the fathers, two inheritors of what others had sown—the one kind and gentle in his disposition with a manner which at once inspired confidence and respect, the other coarse-grained, a prey, so his enemies said, to vulgar ambition and sensual lust—confronted each other.

On one question only could they see eye to eye. That was the new regulations for the disposal of land in the Australian colonies. They were two of the largest landowners in New South Wales. They agreed that a public meeting of landholders and others should be held at Parramatta to consider petitioning the King on the subject of the land regulations. At the meeting on 6 October 1831 those present resolved that the regulations would produce ruinous consequences for the agricultural interests and the community at large, as they were injurious to the production of revenue and the progress of immigration. They appointed a committee to draft a petition. So exclusive and emancipist, immigrant and native-born, conservative and liberal, men such as Marsden and Wentworth who had once vowed implacable hostility to each other, were drawn together by a common interest in the laws affecting the ownership of land. The gentry and colonial bourgeoisie discovered a common interest against the policy of a British government.

In December 1831 a forceful and generous man stepped into the midst of this impassioned opposition. He was the new Governor, Richard Bourke. A liberal in religion and supporter of reform in politics, he was a soldier who displayed a natural gentleness and charity and a reverence for all men. Within a month he announced an extension of three years for those indebted to the Crown for the purchase of land. That temporarily appeased the opponents of the British Government's land policy, but the land question was to disrupt colonial politics for decades to come.

On other matters of popular concern, Whigs, liberals, emancipists and currency lads were delighted by the new Governor, Richard Bourke. By the end of his first year in office there was a promise in the air that Bourke, ably aided by the liberal Chief Justice, Francis Forbes, and prodded by Wentworth, would achieve in New South Wales a part of that liberal dream of material progress, equality before the law, and the establishment of free institutions. Juries were introduced for civil trials in the Supreme Court, the introduction of assisted passages for female immigrants was announced in England, the post office and the roads were improved. By mid-1832 the *Sydney Herald* was hailing Bourke as the friend of Australia and telling him it was his great good fortune to confer a lasting benefit on the colony by convincing their masters in London that the people of New South Wales were now fit for British institutions.

These advances were being achieved despite opposition from the Tory-dominated Legislative Council and despite the dire forebodings of the exclusives, who believed that no property could be safe, no industry could be pursued in security until the accursed radicals were suppressed. To the simmering anger of those advocates of severity, Bourke introduced changes to the system of assignment to protect convicts from the more brutal and arbitrary treatments meted out by harsh employers. Bourke's popularity with the native-born gave new lustre to Wentworth's reputation with the people. By the end of that summer, as the humid weather changed from time to time into a blistering westerly blowing over the hot interior, or a southerly buster swept in to refresh jaded nerves, it looked as though the future lay with Wentworth and his magnificent oratory on the birthrights of Englishmen. Under his leadership, the voices calling for the introduction of self-government were increasing in number and confidence, but a perceptive observer would have noted that the tribune of the people had ceased to use the language of the leveller. More and more he was finding it right and proper that he should be known as a Whig. Those who stamped and clapped him were not to know that it was the gold lace and the salons of the Government House group which Wentworth secretly craved just as passionately as those birthrights of Englishmen.

At Camden one other voice, which had always spoken up when radicals, levellers, and Botany Bay worthies were working great mischief, was now still for ever. Two years earlier John Macarthur had begun to rave round the house at Parramatta with pistols and swords in his hands. By the middle of 1833 his wife had tried to place him under restraint at Parramatta, but to her great grief and shame he slipped out from time to time and chatted inanely in the streets with those who came to mock and those who came to mourn. One day in May, as he shouted madly in those streets in which he had stormed and raged and dreamed a great dream to his everlasting glory, in the days when his heart was hot within him, they bustled him into a carriage and hurried him off to the seclusion of Camden. There he died on 11 April 1834 and was buried at Camden Park on a spot selected by himself.

In spite of the lonely madness of the last year, which brought such anguish to his wife, the achievement lived on. He had built his plantation; he had pioneered the life of the gentry in New South Wales; he, with others, had pioneered the growth of fine wool from sheep grazing on the grasses of New South Wales; he had risen from comparative obscurity to an eminence of tragic grandeur in a country which had rewarded all his dreams and ambitions with unending mockery. His son James became the squire of Camden.

In the meantime the number of free immigrants arriving each year was beginning gradually to change the composition of the population. In 1833, 8000 people had arrived, of whom 2500 were free. The *Sydney Herald* began to write of a distinguished era in the annals of the colony, in the not too distant future, when the disparity in numbers between the free and the bond would disappear. They foresaw the emergence of a bourgeois liberal type of society in which the bourgeoisie were free to worship their gods of wealth and respectability, and the lower orders were sober and industrious, and content with their humble station in life.

The bourgeoisie were beginning to see that if immigration, land laws and education were to be administered in their interests, they must take over the government and run it as a committee controlling their affairs. But they had first to resolve the most divisive question of all, the future of transportation. Outrages committed by undisciplined convicts and stories of convict idleness inflamed the newspaper editors, the guardians of public morals and the likes of 'Major' Mudie, a large landholder at Patrick's Plains. Mudie's voice was heard loudly among those of the Tories who called for greater severity in the treatment of prisoners so that their labour could be more profitably exploited, and the security of life and property be more nearly guaranteed. Others retorted that severity was no solution. The *Sydney Herald* declared that the convicts were so tainted by their levelling and egalitarian tendencies as to debauch the manners of all with whom they came into contact. On 13 February 1834 the *Herald* demanded that the penal farce be quickly brought to an end. The demoralizing system of transportation should cease.

As the dispute raged, news reached Sydney of the fate of a group of men who had mounted their own opposition to the convict system's most brutal institutions. Thirteen men who had taken part in a mutiny at the penal colony on Norfolk Island the preceding January had been launched into eternity after remarkable displays of penitence. On the morning of 15 January 1834 thirty convicts of the worst character had made a rush on the guard, as another group who had feigned sickness overpowered the attendants at the hospital. In the meantime another party of convicts from Longridge had broken into the tool-house, and were rushing to join their confederates. But, thanks to the energetic measures taken by Foster Fyans, the captain of the guard, the soldiers soon had the situation in hand. All told 162 convicts had joined in the mutiny. Of these two were killed, and seven died later from their wounds. Thirteen were executed on 22 and 23 September in the presence of the convicts and two chaplains, the Reverend H. T. Stiles and the Reverend W. B. Ullathorne, who stood at Gallow's Gate, from where the condemned men could take their last look at that very vast sea, and then followed them on the last journey to that beautiful spot where they were given back the earth from which they had come. Ullathorne, unable to stop being haunted by the terrible experience of seeing comely young men nipped by death's untimely frost, of seeing God's creatures acquire the heart of a beast in that hell of the Pacific, was never quiet again until he found the words in which to express his horror. He told his fellow-men that they had been doing an ungracious and an ungodly thing: that they had taken a portion of God's earth and had made it a cesspool, and that the removal of such a plague concerned the whole human race.

As though to confirm these fears of what convictism was doing to humanity in New South Wales, Robert Wardell left his house astride a white horse one day in September, and came upon two prisoners of the Crown, John Jenkins, a runaway from the iron gang, and Thomas Tattersdale, an assigned servant, whom he questioned, not knowing that Jenkins was seeking revenge for floggings he had received at Wardell's instigation. Wardell asked superciliously 'Who are you?' to which Jenkins replied: 'I am a man', and then shot him dead. Wardell was then 41. By the splendour of his talents the lamented gentleman had, in the course of his professional career, amassed the handsome fortune of £30 000. He had about him that air of distinction and achievement which excited the envy of the convicts. Wentworth, overwhelmed with grief at the loss of a man with whom he had shared not just the pleasures of the bottle but a vision of life, a man to whom he had given his heart, announced with a becoming dignity that the funeral procession would leave from Wardell's home.

Two months later John Jenkins and Thomas Tattersdale were convicted of murder by the Chief Justice and a jury of civil inhabitants. Just before Forbes passed the awful sentence, Jenkins knocked out Tattersdale, and looked for a moment as though he would kill Forbes had he not been deterred by the sword of the officer standing by his side. Two days later Jenkins spoke from the scaffold: 'Goodbye, my lads', he said, for he too had his bonds in life, 'I shot the Doctor not for gain, but because he was a Tyrant . . . If any of you take to the bush shoot every tyrant you come across . . . I have not time to say any more lads, but I hope you will all pray for me'. He refused to shake hands with Tattersdale: 'Let every villain', he shouted as the hangman let him drop, 'Let every villain shake hands with himself'.

From such episodes Tories drew the somewhat hysterical conclusion that the spirit of the convicts threatened the annihilation of every decent person. On the solution to this threat Tory opinion was divided, but they were agreed that so long as those infatuated Whigs, Bourke and Forbes, continued their policies of leniency to convicts and liberality to emancipists, then life, property and morality were in peril.

Not everyone was tempted to give way to despair, or throw up their hands in disgust. Just as one order of society was dying, giving off its own smell of decay, and impressing some minds with the impotence of men in the face of human evil, others were responding to a promise of better things from the spread of Enlightenment. On Christmas Day of 1834, one Henry Carmichael announced his intention to begin a normal school in Sydney for the education of teachers. In that school no one would be taught religious opinions: no attempt would be made to pledge a man to any creed. On the contrary every encouragement would be given to the pupils to form opinions of their own. They would be taught the duties of morality, amiability and rectitude of intercourse with each other. For Carmichael believed that Enlightenment would free men from gross and grovelling appetites, and give everyone a passport to the society of honourable men.

9

Botany Bay Whigs and
Botany Bay Tories

By 1835 Bourke was drawing closer to Wentworth. Unlike the
rapport which had developed between Bourke and Forbes this was
not that coming together of two men who held identical opinions on
the world of politics and the life of the world to come. To Bourke's
Christian hope of meeting in a better world those whom he had lost
in this, Wentworth was a stranger. But in the here and now they
seemed to have much in common. They were both Protestant Irish
and both, on their own confession, Whigs by political conviction.
That alone prepared the way to an understanding. There was even
more to it than a vague agreement on political principle. Wentworth belonged by birth to the Fitzwilliam family, who had been
patrons of Edmund Burke, to whom Richard Bourke was not only
distantly related, but with whom he felt such a bond that he was
using his leisure moments in Sydney to put down on paper notes
for a life of that statesman. Chance, too, had drawn Bourke and
Wentworth closer together in the politics of the colony. By the
beginning of 1835 Bourke had become quite exasperated by the
opposition from Alexander McLeay, the Tory Colonial Secretary, to
the extension of trial by jury—optional criminal juries had been
introduced in 1833—and to the proposed introduction of a house of
assembly. Wentworth had already savaged McLeay as a bloated
pensioner and a defender of a dying order of society. Bourke
deplored the intemperate language, but he had much sympathy
with the political convictions which had induced the attack.

The *Sydney Herald* spoke for the Tories. It had campaigned
against the new system of trial by jury in criminal cases in which, as
they put it, cattle-stealers tried their comrades, and the receivers of
stolen goods tried the thieves, and consequently acquitted them. It
also rebuked Bourke for associating with a man who they mis-
takenly believed was the spokesman for the pro-convict group in
New South Wales and who, they inferred, had the politics of the

rabble, and the morals of all those who had been tainted by associating with ex-convicts. In the Council, there was growing support
for the view that the price of the convict systems was too high:
violence, lawlessness, theft and the moral odium of having to live
in a society of prisoners were beginning to take their toll.

All through the long hot summer of 1835 the *Sydney Herald*
thundered on the cost of the convict system to the settlers, on the
lawlessness of the convicts, and on some mob of ex-convicts in
Sydney who were aping the worst actions of a Westminster mob.
Now there were rumours that the colony would be required to pay
for the keep of convicts, to fund the police and pay for the gaols. To
the dismay of the large landholders, Bourke confirmed that the
rumours were true. Up in the Hunter and down in the Limestone
Plains, on the Monaro, and at Camden, where that English gentleman Australian-born, James Macarthur, resided, these Botany Bay
Tories were faced with two questions. Were convicts any longer
an economic advantage? and how were the Tory landholders to
transfer power over land and immigration from the Governor in a
nominated council to their own group without increasing the
power of the bourgeoisie, the Botany Bay Whigs, and their sinister
supporters among the emancipists and mobs of Sydney? So when
the *Sydney Herald* went on to argue that New South Wales was a
gaol-yard, that their Governor and Council were but a standing
committee to regulate a prison, that all the habitants were prisoners,
and that the early answer to their situation was to abolish penal
servitude and establish a free system of labour, some of the large
landowners shouted a loud 'Amen'.

The doubt was whether they could obtain an adequate supply
of free labour which would have some of the advantages of the
bond—cheapness, and obedience. To resolve that doubt the Legislative Council appointed in June a select committee under the
chairmanship of Forbes. After hearing evidence from the Colonial
Secretary, the Treasurer, the Reverend J. D. Lang, unofficial members of the Legislative Council, landowners and other employers of
labour, Forbes reported that a great number of the migrants, particularly the females, who had arrived recently were quite unsuited
to the wants of the colonists. The problem, as he saw it, was a simple
one. The colony had been made the receptacle for the outcasts of the
United Kingdom, and was consequently loaded with a vast dispro-
portion of immoral people, who could only be counteracted by an
extensive introduction of free and virtuous inhabitants. Bourke
announced in October that he proposed to accept some of the
recommendations of the committee to promote the introduction of
men and women of good moral character and industrious habits.

He proposed to send an agent or agents to the British Isles to pick up such migrants. He also proposed to offer to those settlers who had the means and would prefer to engage mechanics or agricultural labourers by their own agents, a bounty equal or nearly equal to the expense of such persons, being married couples under the age of 30 years, and single men between the ages of 18 and 25. This would be another means of supplying the deficiency of labour in New South Wales.

In the meantime, outside the Legislative Council the landholders and bourgeoisie who were excluded from that select circle had already demanded a more sweeping solution to their problems. They wanted self-government for New South Wales. Seventy-five magistrates, gentlemen and other respectable householders of the colony gathered at a public meeting at the Court House on 29 May 1835. In a rather lukewarm atmosphere, John Stephen read aloud a letter from Henry Lytton Bulwer, an author and member of the House of Commons with an eccentric passion for colonial affairs, in which he offered to act as parliamentary advocate for the colony. Bulwer suggested the colonists should form a permanent committee which, he believed, would give them weight with the minister and the English press. At the moment in England, he warned them, no one cared about New South Wales.

Wentworth told the meeting that he for one warmly supported the creation of a committee, as the forerunner of that house of assembly on which he had set his heart. The question was who would have the right to elect such a committee. Wentworth suggested all those who contributed £5 a year. Richard Hipkiss, a believer in self-help and self-improvement through co-operation, was known in the colony among the Botany Bay Tories as a leveller and a Chartist. He thought £5 was too high, as it would tend to represent property alone. Intelligence also should be represented. Then Wentworth rose to his feet, and in a brief speech revealed at last where he stood on the question of who should exercise political power in New South Wales. He poured scorn on the suggestion of Hipkiss. As he saw it, the important measures which they had under consideration were more likely to be forwarded by the talent and intelligence which property naturally combined with itself than by adopting a measure which would leave their council open to an undue proportion of colonists of humble talent and pretension. He was now using in public the language of the Whigs, and dissociating himself from radicals and those pro-convict groups who wanted to reduce the whole of society to one level.

A provisional committee of 60 was appointed. They called themselves the Australian Patriotic Association. Throughout their history they were bedevilled by that same conflict between the Whig view of political power as reflecting the interests of property, and the liberal view that political power should reflect intelligence and population. By December when the members had got round to drafting a constitution for New South Wales they were so divided on the qualification of electors that they were tempted to leave that space blank, and ask the British Parliament to fill it in. Wentworth, sensing a groundswell among his erstwhile supporters against his Whiggish principles, astutely suggested they should rely on the liberality of the members of the British Parliament, knowing full well that in that excellent club for the gentry and Mr Money-Bags, the interests of the men of property would not lack effective advocates.

By that time Wentworth had moved further away from that section of the Australian Patriotic Association which was sympathetic to liberal principles and emancipist interests. In September, when one of his convict servants whom he had charged with insolence to members of his family was sentenced to twenty-five lashes, Wentworth shouted at the Sydney bench of magistrates that this was but a mockery of punishment. In the following month, when five of his convict servants at Vaucluse and some others had stolen his ketch and attempted to escape, he had told the bench he had no doubt the ringleader had planned to poison him as an act of revenge as six weeks earlier he had had the man flogged for drunkenness and intolerable insolence. When the *Herald* wound up the year of 1835 by asking their readers to say whether England was justified in persisting to deluge the colony with her criminals, the squire of Vaucluse said not a word.

In October 1835 a judge of the Supreme Court started a great commotion. Mr Justice Burton had addressed a jury on the degraded state of the colony. Masters of convicts were not sufficiently attentive to the morals of their men: overseers were careless: the men in road parties lived by plunder: improper persons held licences for public houses. The grand cause of all this profligacy and crime was an overwhelming defect of religious principle. So lamentable a circumstance must seriously retard the establishing of those free institutions which were the pride and the boast of the parent country.

The *Herald* used the judge's remarks as proof that the policy of leniency had deluged New South Wales with crime, and held Bourke up to public contempt as the leader of the 'court and convict faction'. Hall published the judge's charge in full in the *Monitor* on 21 November. Political gossips detected the hands of McLeay and that hard-hearted landowner, Major James Mudie, behind these reports. Bourke, never a man to waver when the Tories rocked his little world, commissioned his ally, William Wentworth, as a justice of the peace. The new commission contained more than a friendly bow towards the master of Vaucluse. It contained a stern rebuke to all those magistrates who had actively opposed Bourke's administration. Riddell was suspended from the Executive Council, the leading Tory magistrates were dropped from the list, Bulwer was representing the Patriots in London, and Wentworth had the ear of Bourke. The Tories of Botany Bay needed to act quickly if they were to have any say in drafting the future constitution of New South Wales.

By 1836, the various camps took steps to press their cause in London. Petitions were drawn up to support their cases. Wentworth's voice rang out in defence of the Whig proposals. He would have nothing to do with the suggestion that the Legislative Council should be nominated in Downing Street. At a public meeting in April 1836 he spoke passionately in defence of Bourke as the head of a government which had invaded no man's property, violated no man's liberty, and wantonly sacrificed no man's life. Then he let slip his pride in Bourke—'We've now got a Whig governor', he shouted, 'and being myself a Whig', he went on, 'I am well pleased'. 'Show Whitehall', he cried, left hand on hip, and with that characteristic sweep of the right hand, as though he were defying the world, and with the eye no longer of the angry man but rather of the man who had began to view the human comedy with disdain, if not with contempt—'show Whitehall', he shouted, 'that you know the difference between a Titus and a Nero'. In his moment of triumph he was making it plain for all who had ears to hear that if he were to draft the constitution of New South Wales, then it would be a constitution based on the Whig principle that political power should be exercised by those with some stake in the country. He went on to move the adoption of a petition which humbly prayed that the honourable House of Commons would be pleased to address His Majesty for a representative assembly upon a wide and liberal basis.

It was a time of a great exodus of colonists to London. James Mudie sailed in March to present Stephen and Glenelg at the Colonial Office with his extravagant denunciations of that wicked and adulterous generation in New South Wales. The gentle James Macarthur sailed in July. He was a gentleman who built an absolute trust in other men; he was both blessed and cursed with the innocent man's unwillingness to believe that some men's imaginations were evil from the start.

Among the passengers who boarded the *Abel Gower* with James Macarthur was the Reverend J. D. Lang, believing that the welfare of the Presbyterian Church required him to take another voyage to England, but with one eye firmly fixed on Whitehall and the impending inquiry into the future of transportation. On 1 January 1835 he had begun to publish the *Colonist*. There was no hint in his newspaper of the spirit of his divine master. Week in, week out, Lang had savaged his rivals in the convict-dominated *Sydney Gazette* as levellers and men who wanted an early escape from the convict taint. Then in June William Bernard Ullathorne, after a trip to Van Diemen's Land which only served to convince him that more men were required to tend Christ's vineyard in Australia, and still haunted by that ghastly experience in Norfolk Island, boarded the *Eldon* in Hobart Town and sailed for London. He was looking for priests, but wanting too to say his big thing about that nation of crime where men stole, murdered, committed adultery, and swore falsely. The zeal and energy displayed by Mr Broughton as Anglican archdeacon also caused him to make the journey to London. On Bourke's suggestion, Broughton attended a lavish ceremony at Lambeth Palace chapel on 14 February 1836 and was ordained and consecrated Bishop of Australia. Broughton vowed that day that he would show himself gentle and be merciful for Christ's sake to poor and needy people, and to all strangers destitute of help.

On his return, Bishop Broughton soon became entangled in one of the great debates which divided colonists one against the other—the debate over the establishment and funding of schools, and the role of the various churches in education. On 25 July Bourke moved in the Legislative Council that a sum of £3000 be appropriated towards establishing national schools. He believed that in a new country in which there were persons of all religious persuasions it was impossible to establish a dominant church without provoking much hostility. Believing that the inclination of the colonists was decidedly adverse to such an institution, he suggested government should create national schools for the general education of colonial youth after the manner of the Irish schools established in 1831. In such schools the children would have their religion in textbooks which were Christian in context but free of dogma.

The *Sydney Herald* would have none of it. 'Being Englishmen', they wrote on 4 July 1836, 'we do not like the name Irish system of education . . . [We] also have an objection to theoretic governors, and lawless Irish convicts'. Then they let slip their real objection. The children of the respectable, they thundered, should not have to associate at school with those who would corrupt and destroy their morals.

Broughton, too, took fright, fearful that the bill would prevent the education of Anglicans in the principles of their distinct polity. He began to fear that the whole Protestant position was in danger. On 3 August 1836 he addressed a meeting summoned by a committee of Protestants to protest against the national schools. To roars of applause from those Baptists, Presbyterians, Methodists, Congregationalists and Jews whom in calmer moments he had denounced as wreckers of order and stability, Broughton shouted that Protestantism rested upon the principle that Holy Scripture contained all things necessary to salvation; that the use of it should be free to every man who had a soul to be saved; that if they yielded to an interdict upon the use of the scriptures in one place, the same power might one day prohibit the free use of them at any time and in all places. The Roman Catholics supported Bourke's education bill: the Protestants opposed it.

Bourke came to the melancholy conclusion that Broughton was not only cursed with the vice of intolerance but was also, alas, an exclusive in politics, a collaborator for the defence of the old order in society with McLeay and all the other high Tory counsellors with whom he was plagued. It had become clearer that behind this sectarian brawl there lay the much more fundamental question of who was to exercise power in New South Wales. Why, asked the *Sydney Herald*, should the immigrant Protestants (they meant the wealthy and the respectable ones) be plundered for the support of convict papists, under the guise of general education? This, it thundered, was the wish of Botany Bay Whigs and convict papists. It was an argument which was to blaze for many years to come.

As the various parties carried their struggles, their vituperations and their rising prosperity into the year 1837, labour continued to be in short supply. Some colonists were suggesting that Asians might be employed to relieve the shortage. In May 1837 Bourke received a memorandum from John Mackay urging the introduction of Indian labourers who, Mackay hold him, ate little rice, but many snakes, lizards, rats and mice. They were clothed in a simple and scanty way, were unacquainted with the luxury of a bed, and had the patient disposition and tractable habits which should make them excellent shepherds. Wentworth said he could not approve of the introduction of Indians, because it would be impossible to prevent an intermixture of races, which, he believed, it would be highly desirable to avoid. He looked to the United Kingdom for a future supply, and of those he preferred Irish labourers to any other, because a good word went a long way with an Irishman. Hannibal Macarthur also preferred Europeans to Asians. Sir John Jamison, Alexander Berry and James Bowman were prepared to take the Indian hill-coolies, partly because the need was desperate, and partly because they could not see how any immigration scheme could get them the 10 000 labourers they needed from the United Kingdom.

But these questions no longer concerned Governor Bourke. Glenelg had accepted his resignation. The great questions which confronted the colony—the future of the convict system, the encouragement of free immigration, the establishment of a legislative assembly, the reconciling of religious differences and education—these great debates would carry on without him. As His Excellency left Government House on 5 December to embark on the *Samuel Winter* one continual cheer followed him all the way to the water's edge. But it was said that those were not the cheers of the higher and respectable classes, but rather the cheers of that felon mob whose popularity Bourke had courted. The shirtless and shoeless waved their hats and gave off shouts that rent the sky; they followed him till at long last the sea delivered him from their filthy adulation. Swept on by that great gust of popular passion they were all contributing to the Tory thesis that convictism, both as a corrupter and leveller of mankind, had rendered New South Wales unfit for the institutions of the free.

10

The Saint of Hobart Town

At the beginning of the year 1831 the Lieutenant-Governor of Van Diemen's Land continued as great an enigma as ever to all the observers of the human comedy in that harsh land. There was about Arthur that air of bloodless majesty, that air of mingled awe and bewilderment which surrounds those who believe they have been allotted a chosen place in the divine plan for the salvation of man but consume their energies fighting a losing battle against the tendencies of their age. Knowing that the hearts of the sons of man were filled with evil, Arthur began the year determined to shield the surviving Aborigines of Van Diemen's Land from human wickedness. He had accepted the suggestion of that great booby, that fool in Christ, G. A. Robinson, that those whom the white man could catch as well as those whom the white man could talk into accepting civilization should be moved to an island in Bass Strait. Like Arthur, Robinson saw the Aborigines as another manifestation, if a rather surprising one, of the glory of God, who might be converted from barbarism to civilization. But if they could not or would not be converted, then at least on an island in Bass Strait they could inflict no further harm. Even if they were to rot and pine away on a lonely, windswept island, it was better that they should meet their death in that way, while every act of kindness was being shown towards them, than that they should fall sacrifice to the inevitable consequences of their continued acts of outrage upon the white inhabitants.

In February 34 Aborigines were uprooted from the land of their birth and transported to an island where they were taught things they did not wish to learn by a man who saw himself as the instrument of divine providence to bring them the message of salvation. Not being endowed with the gift of tongues, and lacking even the crudest means to hand on to posterity memorials of their grief and rage, they pined away their time, while Robinson spent his days either instructing this band of survivors or trying to persuade others to accept the white man's plan of conciliation for that wretched people. When the Aborigines from the wild, inaccessible country on the west coast put to death two white men with peculiar cruelty, again the settlers clamoured for protection and revenge, shouting their own piece of savagery, that ancient cry of an eye for an eye and a tooth for a tooth, and dismissing with anger and contempt the policy of the Saint of Hobart Town with his mealy-mouthed words of forbearance and compassion.

Arthur turned for a solution to the men of this world, who advised him to appoint a committee of the Legislative Council to look into the matter. These men believed the kindness and forbearance of the previous year's great round-up had more than atoned for the injuries sustained by the natives in the earlier period of British occupation. They held the Aborigines to be the treacherous ones, the wanton aggressors and thirsters after plunder, whose path was marked by fire, rapine and the most dreadful atrocities. They urged Arthur, in the name of God, to protect the white man from such savages. The solution as they saw it was to speed up the removal of the remaining Aborigines to an island in Bass Strait.

In the very month in which Arthur meditated upon these matters Edward Broughton, a prisoner of the Crown at Macquarie Harbour, felled a tree on top of a constable for no other reason than because he was a constable, and the unwilling or passive instrument of flogging the men. In company with four other convicts, including one Macavoy, Broughton absconded into the bush, where, driven to desperation by hunger, four of them agreed to kill the luckless fifth and ate heartily of his flesh. Hunger drove Broughton and Macavoy to kill and eat the other two. But then with the folly of men who had given way to such madness, or maybe driven to seek expiation for their crimes, as though their guilt were stronger than their hunger, they gave themselves up, were tried for their horrid crimes, and sentenced to be hanged at Hobart in August.

For Arthur the sovereign remedy for all human depravity was to encourage the spread of religious feeling. He proposed to build schools and churches: he proposed to bring out more persons to teach the convicts of the great battle raging in the human heart between Jehovah and Beelzebub. The drunkenness and other vicious habits of these men which it would defile his pen to name, would then decrease. He never looked forward to that time when the convict system had withered away. As he saw it Van Diemen's Land was a gaol for the punishment and reformation of British criminals: his task was to make it an efficient instrument for that purpose.

His role as an improver of mankind exposed him to the undying hatred of some of the convicts and to the wrath of those settlers for whom the presence of convicts was simply a temporary expedient for their own aggrandisement. As long ago as March of 1827 the gap between the settlers and Arthur had first appeared. Some of them had prepared a petition to the King and both Houses of Parliament for trial by jury and legislation by representation. Convictism, they said, exposed the free population to frightful indignities and terror—both from convicts and from the police. They demanded greater representation on the bench of magistrates, and they sought secure legal title to their lands. For his part, Arthur was not convinced that their support for free institutions was other than lukewarm. Like Dr Ross of the *Hobart Town Courier*, he had yet to hear a full-throated colonial roar of approval for these proposed changes from the respectable members of the society of Hobart Town.

When it was announced in Hobart Town on 11 June 1831 that in future all land in Van Diemen's Land was to be disposed of not by grant but by sale at a minimum upset price of 5s an acre, and that the proceeds from such sales would be used to pay passages of female migrants, again a gap yawned between the response of the Governor and that of the settlers. For his part Arthur heartily rejoiced that as Governor he had been relieved from the duty of making grants of land which though sometimes gratifying was often exceedingly distressing. By contrast, the settlers greeted the new regulations with a roar of disapproval. They had come to the colony expecting a land grant and convict labour in return for their investment of capital. Now government was not honouring an essential part of the contract.

But their disappointment did not touch Arthur deeply. He had other subjects to ponder much more important than the material well-being of the free settlers of Van Diemen's Land. When Robinson triumphantly entered Hobart one Saturday early in January of 1832 with a party of some forty blacks from the Oyster Bay and Big River tribes, Arthur and the inhabitants received them with the most lively curiosity and delight. The *Hobart Town Courier* reported how the band struck up a merry tune outside Government House and the natives evinced once again the susceptibility of the savage breast to the white man's music. Excited by the music into a mood of great good humour and a desire to make themselves agreeable, they displayed feats of wonderful dexterity on the lawns of Government House. Then, still laughing and joking and gambolling down the street like little children, they boarded the boat in which they were to proceed to Great Island in the Furneaux Group. Swept on by the white man's benevolence and compassion, and their own fatal love of fun and games, and the promise of better things to come, some forty more left the land on which their people had lived since time immemorial. They left, according to the *Courier*, not in grief and rage but in high good humour. The Lieutenant-Governor rendered up his thanks to Almighty God that the colony had been delivered from the black man's bloody vengeance, and asked the divine blessing on his scheme to treat them with kindness in their asylum on Great Island.

While he was still singing praises to his God a dispatch arrived from London with instructions that all public works should be done by contract, that the convicts in government employment should be distributed among the free settlers. In this way the cost to government of transportation would be reduced. Never a man to be swayed by ledger sheet arguments, Arthur looked in detail at what he was interested in—whether the suggested change would promote the moral reform of the convicts.

The simple fact was that the situation of the convict was greatly improved by being removed from a state of destitution in England to a country where labour was scarce, and the labourer consequently in great demand. What disturbed Arthur was not the effect on the dread of transportation of such a high standard of life, for he was a sensitive and indeed a most compassionate man. What disturbed him was that any indulgence might encourage the tendency of the convict to depravity. Arthur was convinced that convicts were not deterred from crime by the fear of punishment, but rather by the removal of every opportunity for moral laxity. He thought it unreasonable that assigned convicts were enabled to indulge in debauchery out of their surplus wages while innocent men lived and starved in their native country. What he liked about the system for convicts employed in government service was that they had few opportunities of making money. Male convicts were locked up at night, and so deterred from the opportunity of indulging in excess, or gratifying their implacable desire to be mischievous. It was the same with the women. Their riotous and disorderly conduct when confined in the House of Correction in Hobart made it absolutely necessary that another yard should be added with cells for separating the women. To confine 100 women together tended to destroy all subordination, he had found. So once again he displayed concern for their reformation, so that they might prepare themselves to face their judge on the resurrection morning with confidence. In his evangelical zeal, it never occurred to him that he was depriving the convicts of the few pleasures they could enjoy in Van Diemen's Land, and stirring up in their hearts an implacable anger against a soldier of Christ.

Landholders too were beginning to grumble and groan. Their grievance was Arthur's insistence that they should pay to government the arrears of quitrent. Quitrents had been imposed first in November 1823 in the time of Sorell. All persons receiving grants of land were to be free of quitrent for the first seven years. After that time a quitrent of 5 per cent per annum was to be paid upon the estimated value of the land, with a small discount for those landholders who had saved the government money by employing and maintaining convicts. When Arthur informed the landholders of Van Diemen's Land that government proposed to collect arrears of quitrent, they responded in that extravagant language of the man on the land when asked to pay tribute to Caesar. They had not broken their backs in order to fill the government coffers. At meetings at Hamilton, Bothwell and Swan Port in 1832 they drew up petitions which thundered against the tax as unequal, unjust, intolerable. In grief and rage they began to speak of Arthur as a man who was so puffed up with compassion for the murderous, plundering savages of Van Diemen's Land or so preoccupied with the reformation of their wretched convict servants that he could not spare a thought for the long-suffering landholders. The voice of the bourgeoisie, shouting the gospel of work, was beginning to be heard in a land which hitherto had heard only the monotonous chants and the laughter of the Aborigine, or the swish of the flagellator's lash and the howls of its victims.

On the night of 24 August, in thick and hazy weather with a great gale blowing up from the South Pole, news reached Hobart Town that the *Princess Royal*, with the first assisted unmarried female migrants on board, had run aground in the estuary of the Derwent. Arthur was in a quandary. He wondered how he could save their lives without endangering their virtue. He doubted whether there was any able-bodied civil officer whom he could trust in the company of unmarried women. In desperation, deciding that at least he and the Chief Police Magistrate could be trusted, he set off with him in a small boat, and rode the waves with a single-minded concern for the morals of those women, and supervised their conveyance in small vessels to Hobart Town, where they were lodged in the Female Orphan School. In the weeks that followed it became clear that a great many of the females were too abandoned to allow them to live with reputable families. So Arthur sat down and wrote to London and urged them to send women who could marry tradesmen or who could be domestic servants, but for God's sake to send no more of that most abandoned class which had recently disgraced the streets of Hobart Town. They wanted, as the *Colonial Times* put it, good, useful and virtuous females who would marry industrious ticket-of-leave men, expirees and pardoned men, build them comfortable homes, and so restrain them from following evil propensities. They wanted women who could tame the old Adam, not Magdalenes. The bourgeoisie were beginning to sketch their ideal of a society of order and decorum; they dreamed of a little England where the virtuous and the respectable reaped their rewards, and the ungodly were left struggling on the slippery slope to damnation.

So matters stood when the news reached Hobart Town that in future the expenses for the penal settlement at Port Arthur were to be paid out of the colony's funds instead of being defrayed by the mother country. The opposition press was incensed. This dipping the hands *ad libitum* into their pockets for purposes over which they had no control was, they argued, an additional reason for a legislative assembly chosen by themselves. If the prisoners had been set to the roads, so as to enable farmers to bring their produce to market, there would be some reason for it. But no, their money was to be used to put to hard labour a number of strong, able-bodied fellows who would be driven to perform heavy and laborious work of no benefit to the colony as a punishment and a means of reforming their morals. This, indeed, was a wild-goose scheme—for which the industrious, thriving settlers of Van Diemen's Land had to pay. The *Colonial Times* went on to tell its readers that anyone who saw the wretched outcasts dragged from ships would be left in no doubt that transportation was slavery.

This was a conclusion which Arthur was never prepared to accept. He believed passionately that transportation should be neither a boon to evildoers nor the cause of their greater degradation or slavery, whether the convict was assigned to a settler or employed by the government on public work. Nowhere was this problem of a severity of punishment for the incorrigible which would not degrade or cause despair more apparent than in the penal settlements. In October 1832, having been instructed to reduce the number confined in such settlements, and to assign the corrigible to more productive labour, Arthur had closed down the settlements at Maria Island and Macquarie Harbour and housed all the convicts sentenced to penal settlements at Port Arthur, which he hoped to make into a model settlement where the convicts would experience both severity and certainty of punishment. There were 475 convicts there at the beginning of 1833.

The indulgence of a ticket-of-leave could be obtained by a convict conducting himself in such manner as to convince the authorities that he was so far reclaimed from his evil course that it became no longer dangerous to society to entrust him partially with his liberty, as he was bidding fair to make an atonement for his former misdeeds. The slightest lapse returned him to that state of bondage from which the ticket had relieved him. The Saint of Hobart Town was concerned to make men virtuous rather than happy. It never occurred to him to ask whether he was receiving some dark subterranean satisfaction from such behaviour. It never bothered him that when he visited one of the convict gangs of Van Diemen's Land he was greeted with neither affection nor enthusiasm. He was never hailed as their saviour, their protector or their friend.

Elinor Brady was sentenced in Dublin to transportation for seven years and arrived in Van Diemen's Land in 1817. By the end of the year she was up before a magistrate for disobeying the orders of Arthur's predecessor and confined in a solitary cell on bread and water for a week. One week later she was again charged with disobeying orders and confined in the same way for 14 days. Early in 1818 she was charged with being drunk and disorderly and sentenced to one week's hard labour in gaol. On 7 December 1818 she was again charged with being drunk and disorderly, for which she forfeited her ticket-of-leave and endured hard labour in gaol until assigned. On 24 April 1819 she was charged with being drunk and disorderly and sentenced to three months' hard labour in gaol. On 9 March 1820 she was charged with being drunk and disorderly and disguising herself in man's clothes, and was sentenced to hard labour in gaol. But at that point her convict record ceased: she dropped back into anonymity, and left no lasting memorial, except possibly in the collective consciousness of those who came after her.

What she felt about the Saint who so rigorously committed himself and the free settlers of Van Diemen's Land to her salvation, history is unable to say. But the pages of the newspapers of Van Diemen's Land bear witness to the tide of discontent and anger which was mounting against the Governor. More and more the free settlers were calling for a legislative assembly and for trial by jury. They were not divided as Sydney had been, between Whig and Tory, liberal and conservative; they were driven on by something quite elemental. They were driven by a sense of threat to their possessions, to their pockets as well as their pride, to ask the fundamental question: by whom are we governed? As Mr Horne shouted at one empassioned meeting, when a man realized that the answer to that question was: not even by the King, but by a Secretary of State 16 000 miles distant, then, he said, he felt warm, and his words ran hot.

On the question of what they should do about the convicts, they were divided. The editor of the *Colonist* suggested that all assigned convicts should be returned to the government. If the settlers ceased to be dependent on the government for their servants, then the terrible power of the Governor over all their lives would be broken. Gilbert Robertson took over the paper and republished it as the *True Colonist* on 5 August 1834. He told his readers that the abolitionist view was too absurd to admit of argument. Gellibrand, never a man to take lightly any sacrifice of income, condemned the convict system as degrading, and added that, anyway, free men would always work harder than bond. Whatever side they took in this issue, they were alike in one respect. They were not concerned with the effect of transportation on crime in the United Kingdom. Their concern was with 'the land we live in'.

While the white players were thumping tables in the name of their rights, the surviving Aborigines on Flinders Island were setting up a wail of lamentation for the land they had lost. On 4 December Mannalargenna, a celebrated native of Van Diemen's Land, became numbered with the dead. On the following day more than 100 Aborigines followed the body to the grave. G. A. Robinson, loving and tender as ever to a people whom he saw as victims of some purpose which God would undoubtedly uncover in His own good time, preached to them on the meaning of that death. He told them to rejoice for without the mercy of God they might have been born of heathen parents. Before the white man, the black man had been guided solely by the light of creation. Now he had the knowledge of salvation. When a good white man or a good black man died, God told his angel spirits to take them to heaven where they never would be sick any more, never be hungry any more, never be cold any more, but they would be happy forever. There was no music like heavenly music. If they did everything according to God's word, they would certainly know that bliss.

In the meantime the drift against Arthur gathered momentum in the minds of the free. There was a persistent rumour that he was about to be appointed Governor of New South Wales, and the catty were beginning to whisper to each other 'the sooner the better'. Week in week out, a section of the press reminded their readers of all the abominations and disgraceful cruelties which had occurred at Hobart Town under his administration. In January 1836 a public meeting called on the Crown to remove him. Gilbert Robertson told the meeting that Arthur had acted as if it had been his object to destroy agriculture and bring the colony under the grasp of the money-lenders and Indian adventurers—that the object nearest His Excellency's heart was filching money from the people. Another

speaker said that after all they were Britons, although Arthur
tried to misrepresent them in London as a factious and dis-
affected people.

On 25 May Arthur opened a dispatch from London. Within an
hour the news was all over the town that Arthur had been recalled.
That night the news seemed to diffuse a general joy. On Tower Hill
Mr Kermode lit a huge pile to celebrate the event. George Meredith
spoke with glee to his friends of their approaching emancipation.
The timid Mr Boyes, for whom the streets of Hobart Town had
become a nightmare where the respectable were insulted and
attacked, rejoiced that they were about to be delivered from their
frightful position. Colonel Arthur stood guilty: he had taken the
part of butchers who excited bulldogs to madness and set them on
to tear each other to pieces. He was the cause, the sole, distinct cause
of all the mischief.

It was some comfort to Arthur to read the words of praise from
his masters in London for his long career of distinguished public
service. It was some comfort to him to know that he had not disquieted himself as a soldier of God in vain, as he had earned
the gratitude of the colonists at large. It was some comfort to read
the words of praise of Dr Ross in the *Hobart Town Courier*, who
called him the father of his people. But in private there were many
who rejoiced that they had been delivered from the clutches of
a tyrant.

In the few moments of leisure he allowed himself from his
labours before his departure in October, Arthur sat for his portrait
by Benjamin Duterrau, an artist of French descent who had
migrated to Van Diemen's Land in the early 1830s to take up a
position as art master in a school. Probably at about the same time
the same artist painted Truganini, daughter of the chief of Bruny
Island, and one of the last Aboriginal women of Van Diemen's
Land. Duterrau thus had a chance to put on canvas the faces of two
representatives of a doomed way of life: Arthur, an apologist for a
religious view of the world, who wanted Van Diemen's Land to be
a terror to evildoers for the next quarter of a century; and Truganini,
who was attempting to preserve on Flinders Island the way of life
of the Aborigines. But Duterrau did not risk a guess at what was
going on behind those masks which they both presented to the
outside world. Arthur looked at Duterrau with that inner calm of a
man who believed one day he would render his account in a higher
place. Truganini looked at him not with grief or anger, but with
that expressionless, timeless face with which the physically weak
confront their conquerors.

As the time for his departure approached Arthur began to survey the scene with a becoming pride. But the historians did not treat him kindly: the man who had lived for the day when he would appear before the throne of grace became sport for the fault-finders. A man with a forgiving spirit and a deep compassion had paid that terrible price men exact from those who seem to resist the march of humanity from the darkness towards the light.

BOOK THREE

The Beginning of an Australian Civilization 1824–1851

The mighty Bush with iron rails
Is tethered to the world.

Henry Lawson, 'The Roaring Days'

. . . it's not only the things that we've inherited from our fathers and mothers that live on in us, but all sorts of old dead ideas and old dead beliefs . . . there must be ghosts all over the country— as countless as grains of sand. And we are, all of us, so pitifully afraid of the light.

Mrs Alving in Henrik Ibsen, *Ghosts*, Act 2

1

Another Province for Britain's Gentry

On 1 June 1829 wind and rain were lashing the south-western coast of New Holland. Husbands and wives huddled together on the beach among pianos, chairs, beds and stores and wondered where the promised Garden of Eden could be. As the storm raged about them, bewildered children asked why the trees of Western Australia grew in snow. Their parents explained that it was not snow they were seeing but sand, and wondered when the rain would cease and they would enjoy the promised light of the sun.

Almost three weeks later James Stirling, the leader of their expedition from the mother country, proclaimed the formation of a settlement within the territory of Western Australia. As their Lieutenant-Governor, he requested them duly to regulate their conduct as good and loyal subjects and to obey all legal commands and regulations. He went on to warn them that any person who behaved in a fraudulent, cruel or felonious manner towards the Aborigines would be tried for that offence as though the same had been committed against any other of His Majesty's subjects. All men between the ages of 15 and 50 were to enter themselves on the muster roll for military service in the event of the territory being invaded or attacked by hostile tribes. All persons who wished to take up land were to apply at the office of the Colonial Secretary. All persons intending to leave the settlement must seek permission to do so. The white man had come to Western Australia.

Stirling had first visited this part of the Australian coast two years earlier, in January 1827, and had been convinced that a naval, military and commercial station could be advantageously situated in the vicinity of Swan River. He returned to London and persuaded His Majesty's Government that a huge area of New Holland which had previously been dismissed as barren could become a new province for Britain's gentry. The men in black in Whitehall showed some interest, but jibbed at the expense. So Stirling asked whether there would be any objection to the employment of private capital to finance his proposed settlement. He was given sufficient encouragement to set about the task of promoting his scheme to ambitious men and women in London.

By the end of the year he had attracted partners for the venture and convinced enough people of adequate means that they would make their names and their fortunes in this unclaimed corner of the New World. The Colonial Office granted its blessing to the project. It appointed Stirling as Lieutenant-Governor and gave him permission to select 100 000 acres for himself.

Anxious to forestall French ambitions, the British Government dispatched a ship from the Cape of Good Hope to claim the western third of the continent—that part of the landmass not already included in New South Wales. On 2 May 1829, Captain Charles Howe Fremantle arrived at the mouth of the Swan River and took possession of New Holland. He had been instructed to ask the Aborigines whether they consented to this act of possession. After he had satisfied himself that he had fulfilled these instructions there was not so much as an inch of Australia left for the French, Spaniards, Dutch, Russians, Americans, or the Aborigines of New Holland.

The first party of would-be settlers arrived in the midst of that storm four weeks later. Stirling was not appalled despite problems 'enough to appal the stoutest hearts', nor was he overwhelmed with the difficulty of making a success with men whose habits had been formed in other modes of life 'as wide from this as Earth from Heaven'. At the mouth of the Swan he built a port, which he named Fremantle. He took a party up-river to a basin which had delighted him when he had first visited the place in 1827 and decided that it would be the site for his capital. On 12 August he assembled a party at the basin of the Swan, where a Mrs Dance gave one blow to a large tree with an axe, chivalrously guided by Captain Stirling, and christened the site Perth in honour of the native town of the Secretary of State for the Colonies.

After the arrival of three more ships there were 200 settlers, 35 horses, 17 cows, 3 bulls, 25 draught oxen, 10 calves, 200 sheep, 100 pigs and hogs, a large stock of poultry, and some garden ground which was already producing vegetables. The officers of the *Sulphur* and the other ships had begun to amuse themselves with dinners, dancing, music, cards and drinking. On 1 October Stirling declared the land on the banks of the Swan open for settlement. A month later he declared land open for selection between the coast and the Darling Ranges to the east. But the demands for land exceeded what was available and those who had searched spread gloomy rumours that apart from the river banks the land was not what they had been led to expect.

Soon prospective settlers hanging round the shanty towns of Fremantle and Perth were grumbling at the Government for gobbling the best land or granting it to their 'cronies' in the 'men-of-war'. Gentlemen's sons were standing behind improvised counters selling tea and sugar to kill time, while women, still tent-dwellers rather than mistresses of manor houses in the Australian bush, gossiped outside their tents. Had they come all that way to be roasted by the sun and tormented at night by the shouts and laughter of drunken soldiers and the mosquitoes and fleas which infested their tents? Had they come to a land where a fierce sun turned the green shoots of their crops into the sickly dry yellow of death? What manner of men would survive and prosper in such a land?

On 12 October 1829 James Henty and his party reached Fremantle on the *Caroline*. Like the other members of the gentry migrating to Swan River, he hoped that he and his family could plant an English village in the Australian wilderness, complete with squire, parson, tenant farmers and agricultural labourers. He had left England because he and his family were threatened with a descent of many steps in the social ladder, which their 'feeling could ill stand'. At first he had planned to go to New South Wales, but Captain Stirling persuaded the Henty family that they could have all their hearts' desires—the social standing, the amusements and the huge income—at the intended Swan River colony.

So James Henty chartered the *Caroline* and signed on four personal servants and twenty-nine indentured servants. He also loaded the ship with bloodstock, seed, trees, farm utensils, a telescope, a bugle, 10 pounds of shaving soap, 30 silver spoons, pens, ink, paper and 100 books. The rest of the family were to follow later. On arrival in Perth he joined the army of settlers searching for suitable land, but found nothing on which to risk his seed and stock. He found only heat, flies, fleas, mosquitoes, and that plague of every settler—the clamour of the indentured servants for houses, food and clothing, and higher wages. He drew little comfort from the claim that society on the Swan was above reproach simply because it was free of those vulgar upstarts, the successful ex-convicts who set the social tone in Sydney. In January 1832 he decided to try his fortunes in Van Diemen's Land.

They were not the only ones to know the bitterness of disappointed hopes. Elizabeth and William Shaw arrived at the settlement on 14 February 1830. Shortly afterwards, Elizabeth wrote home saying that Swan River was a province where gentlemen had been reduced to the way of life of gypsies. Ladies, gentlemen, children and working people, many without shoes or stockings, went about their lives of gardening, carting water, cooking, washing or nursing their babies. The Governor sometimes received guests without his shoes or stockings on, and was to be seen wearing a dressing-gown *en plein jour*. Mrs Stirling was sometimes to be seen at the bathtub. The man-servants were drunken, the women dirty, idle, saucy and sluttish. Stockbrokers and Jews got the good land while gentlemen who once rode in carriages were now soiling their hands weighing out tea and sugar. Both she and her husband pined for Old England, for there the world belonged to men of good family, but here the world was beginning to belong to the strong—men with the faces of vulgar louts who had neither opinions nor ideas and were proud of it.

At the same time others, fashioned of sterner clay, went about their daily business. One of these was George Fletcher Moore. Born in Country Tyrone, Ireland, in 1798, a member of the minor gentry, he had studied law at Trinity College, Dublin, and had hoped to obtain a position in the new administration at Swan River. He had arrived in 1830 with sufficient property and indentured servants to give him a right to choose 12 000 acres of land. Luck was with him from the start. He was able to obtain land on the Swan above Guildford where the pastures were lush and the soil fertile. He loved sowing beds of carrots, turnips, cabbages, radishes and peas. He loved the climate. He loved joining with those of like mind and heart every Sunday in a hymn of praise to the author and giver of such good things. He was not altogether happy about his servants, who were too often idle or drunk. But he knew also the divine command 'Judge not', so he did not let his heart be troubled.

True, the Aborigines were stirring up 'anxious throbbings' in his 'emigrant's heart'. No one knew how many there were. No one was quite certain how in fact white men could hold the land if the blackfellows learnt how to use firearms. But for himself he was inclined to think they were not such a despicable race as was at first supposed. He looked forward to the day when the natives became the bottle-washers, kitchen boys, stable hands and plough-boys of the white man's civilization, for he liked to believe that a day would come when the Aborigine, too, looked as though he had been made in the image of God.

Others, enraged by the sight of Aborigines murdering white men or disgusted by the sight of black men beating black women, decided they were not human beings but monkeys on two legs. Had not these 'black barbarians' resisted all exertions to teach them habits of industry, and did they not refuse to cover their nakedness?

As they entertained no system of religion they must belong to the animal rather than the human kingdom. One son of a gentleman deeply shocked another man of genteel birth by saying that he had been out hunting all one morning and had only shot one black. The lower orders, too, were said to hold the life of a native of no value.

In September 1831 Stirling and his wife gave a ball in Government House for the members of those eighty or ninety families, the civil and military officers and their wives, who had survived the great ordeal of the first two years without loss of self-respect. There were quadrilles, Spanish dances, gallopades and waltzes for those familiar with the latest dancing fashions in London, while for plain country gentry the master of ceremonies called for sets. During the evening that handsome popular couple Governor Stirling and his wife danced a special waltz to show they were as competent on the dance floor as in the labours of the pioneer. Champagne flowed. Toasts were drunk to the ladies. G. F. Moore by special request sang his song 'Western Australia for me'. In a rough stone house some 200 white men and women were showing that 'home', the 'throne' and 'gentility' could live on in their hearts in the wilds of Australia.

All along the coast between Perth and Cape Leeuwin by the end of 1831 there were tiny settlements of gentlemen, their families and their servants. On Christmas Day 1826 a military garrison and a party of convicts had established a settlement of fewer than fifty persons at King George Sound. After a miserable four years they withdrew and a handful of settlers quickly descended on the Sound to build a nest of gentlefolk in that unpromising-looking place.

Poor land, hot climate and the uncooperativeness of the Aborigines began to take their toll. Settlers who had been lured to the colony with promises of gentility and wealth were finding themselves burdened with toil and debt. Responsible men in Perth were predicting that they might soon preside at the death of all the white man's settlements in Western Australia and hand back the land to the Aborigines. The labouring classes for want of steady employment were already becoming, like the Aborigines, vagabonds and scavengers on the face of the earth. The settlers were suffering from scarcity of labour, and absence of roads and public transport with which to bring their goods to markets. In 1832 an angry and anxious babble of voices began to be heard on the Swan, at York and down at the Vasse, Augusta and Albany. Stirling decided to seek aid in England. He turned up at the Colonial Office early in 1833 only to find the men at the top speaking a language to which he was a stranger. Instead of promises of relief or assistance he was lectured on the folly of unsystematic colonization and making huge grants of land to capitalists.

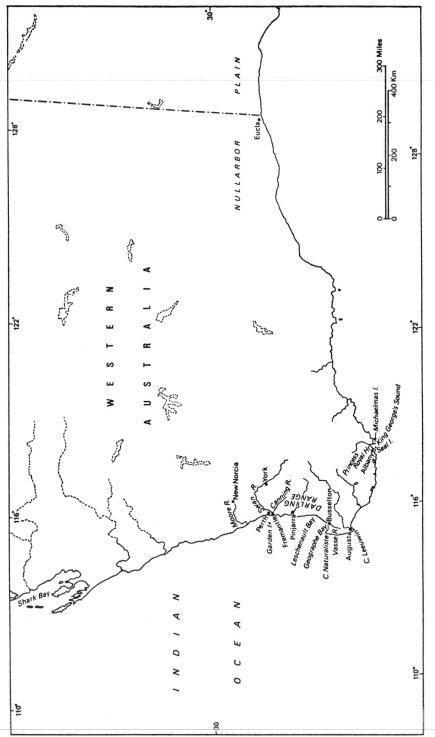

The main settlements in Western Australia

In the meantime in Perth some in high places began to behave like men who were looking for scapegoats. In April 1833 the cry went up for vengeance against the Aborigines for disturbing the public peace in Fremantle. On instructions from the Executive Council the police seized an Aboriginal leader, paraded him in front of Perth Gaol and then shot him dead. Overwhelmed with remorse for what they had done, they captured the victim's son and offered him the gift of being a member of the white man's society, only to find to their mortification that the boy spurned such a gift from his father's murderer. Stirling returned in June 1834, apparently as optimistic as ever about the prospects of the colony, despite his fruitless visit to London. But he found to his dismay that a great change had come over the white people in their attitudes to the Aborigines. The Aborigines, it was being said, were very revengeful and never forgave an injury. Alarmists were even prophesying that such a warlike people would exterminate the white man if ever the white man was foolish enough to give him the means to do so. At the same time some Aborigines had come to the conclusion that the white man would in time reduce all the Aboriginal women to harlots and helots and kill all the men who tried to resist the invasion of their tribal lands.

When Stirling heard in October 1834 that a tribe of natives in the Murray district had grown so bold, after murdering four or five white people, that they were threatening to spear all the inhabitants in that area, he decided to deal effectually with the guilty tribe. Mustering a party of twenty-five, consisting of some senior civil officers, Captain Ellis, five mounted police and nine soldiers, he set out from Perth to scour the countryside round the estuary of the Murray in search of natives. At Pinjarra they opened fire on a group, killing fifteen to twenty at the expense of the life of Captain Ellis. Stirling hoped the punishment, distressing though it was to the private feelings of individuals, would stop the career of mischief by Aborigines. Lord Glenelg rebuked him and instructed him to remind the settlers that government was determined to punish any act of injustice or violence to the natives with the utmost severity. But by then Stirling believed that if at any time the natives overcame their material weakness and their chronic inability to combine they would exterminate the invader. The one way for 2000 white people in those scattered settlements to prevent 50 000 Aborigines waging a bloody war of attrition with their primitive weapons was for the white man to display and make use of his superior fire-power until such time as he outnumbered the Aborigines.

In colonial language, that was the whole bloody trouble! The population of the white man did not increase. When Stirling left for

London in 1832 there were 1497 people in the settlement. In June 1837 there were only 2032 whites, of whom 590 were in Perth, 387 in Fremantle, 524 in the Swan River district, 41 on the Canning, 65 at York, 170 at Plantagenet, 17 on the Murray, 32 at Augusta, 21 at the Vasse, and 185 members of the military community.

It was said that by 1836 scarcely a property was free from mortgage. The settlers' methods of farming were said to have the slovenly character of men who had lost hope. Deeply wedded to the old established English or Scottish farming methods, they were reluctant to make any changes to suit the climate or soil. With ruin staring them in the face, their property mortgaged and themselves without a sixpence, they went on giving dinner parties, buying the finest clothes that came to the colony, and living in general as though they were well off. The cause of their financial difficulties was the high price of labour, and the high price of the necessaries of life. Those who used the laws of political economy to explain the distribution of prizes in the human lottery pointed out that they were all the victims of the 5s minimum upset price for Crown land introduced in 1832. No settler would pay 5s an acre to settle in a colony where labour was dear when for 5s he could obtain land and cheap convict labour in the penal colonies of New South Wales and Van Diemen's Land. But that 5s minimum upset price was but a symptom of one of those great upheavals in Europe, the effects of which were felt even at the Antipodes. Western Australia had been started by men whose grand conception of an aristocratic society, fresh from a victory over its mighty opposite, was becoming an unreality. Within a year of the foundation of Western Australia in 1829 men took over the seals of office in London who were looking for a solution to the problem of the redundant population of the British Isles rather than for spoils for the heroes of the Peninsular Campaign. Those men of high courage and a capacity for breaking bounds, such as Sir James Stirling, Thomas Peel, Sir Richard Spencer and Captain Molloy, touched as they were by some of the daring of a Byron, were about to be swept off the stage of human history and replaced by the men of the middle class. The British Isles which had housed men with 'largeness of vision' were about to come under the sway of the 'straighteners'.

The 2000-odd victims of that turn of fortune's wheel in Western Australia snarled at each other like wild dogs. Men who had admired Stirling in the early days began to whisper that his energies were erratic and that not the least reliance was to be placed on his word since he was notorious for changing his mind at least ten times a day. The Stirling dream of Swan River as a province for some of Britain's gentry was fading away. Stirling tendered his resignation in October 1837 and waited patiently till almost the end of 1838 to hear of its acceptance. On the eve of his departure in January 1839 the settlers, artisans and mechanics thanked him for his contribution to the foundation of a 'scion of the best and greatest nation upon earth'. Stirling spoke of his pride in having annexed so vast a region to the British Empire with so small a body of adventurers. And off he sailed on 5 January 1839 for London to serve again the Empire he adored.

If anyone doubted that the days of the 'enlargers' were numbered and the days of the 'straiteners' about to begin, Stirling's successor soon stripped away the remnants of that delusion with which they had sustained themselves for the first ten years. John Hutt belonged to the great English middle class. He was of an austere turn of mind which seemed to cause the kindlier feelings to shrivel up in him, one of those 'calculators', those 'economists', who believed systematic colonization was a solution to the problem of redundant population in the British Isles. Within ten days of his arrival he announced that all land grants that had not met the improvement conditions prescribed in the regulation of 1829 must be surrendered forthwith. On 22 April he announced that Her Majesty's Government had conferred on him the responsibility of deciding whether the minimum upset price of Crown land should be raised from 5s to 12s an acre.

By an odd irony of fate, the day before Hutt let the settlers see that what mattered most to them could never be, a miserable object of a man walked into a hut in the northern outskirts of Perth and told the inhabitants about the land beyond the limits of settlement. His name was George Grey. In 1830 while a young ensign in Ireland he shrank in horror from the cruelty practised by the English to preserve their domination, and began to turn his eyes towards the New World as a place where the absence of such ancient wrongs might prevent the defilement of mankind. He submitted to Glenelg a plan for the exploration of the north-west coast of New Holland. On 2 December 1837 he and his party of eleven reached Hanover Bay.

After landing they made their way south to the Glenelg River, where Grey had the satisfaction of seeing a stretch of country as verdant and fertile as the eye of man ever rested on. He wondered why so fair a land should only be the abode of savages and thought it was anomalous that savages should roam over unused riches. Surely a British population, rich in civilization, would soon follow in his steps. He had other things on his mind. He was prostrated by the great heat. He was racked with pain from a wound inflicted on his hip by an Aborigine who resented the white man's invasion of his hunting ground. But the religion he had learned on his mother's knee taught him that all men were made in the image of God, and he came to the conclusion that under proper treatment the Aborigines might easily be raised very considerably in the scale of civilization.

A second journey in the Shark Bay district between February and April 1839 strengthened Grey's conviction that the Aborigines of New Holland were in a depressed condition because they were the victims of the white man's prejudice. He came back to Perth believing that it was their laws, rather than any lack of intelligence, which prevented the Aborigines from rising above barbarism. His remedy was to make them subject forthwith to the elevating influence of British law. The other main causes retarding the civilization of the Aborigine were the uncertain demand for their labour and the white man's practice of only employing them in the lowest order of manual labour, which was so badly paid as to offer no inducement to abandon a nomadic bush life. He suggested that the way to overcome this was to reward each settler who civilized an Aborigine with money or a grant of land. He suggested that natives who could produce a marriage certificate should receive a small reward as should natives who registered the birth of a child. In these ways the work of the civilization of the Aborigines would at once start on a great scale.

After being appointed Resident Commissioner at King George Sound in August 1839, Grey pushed on with his study of the Aborigines with such zeal that within four months he was ready to publish his *Vocabulary of the Dialects Spoken by the Aboriginal Races of S. W. Australia*. In the late spring of that year he fell in love with 'a very fascinating girl'—Eliza Lucy Spencer—and married her in November and was very happy for a while. He was not to know that a day would soon come when his idea of heaven was to be a place where he could no longer hear his wife talking, and she would know that terrible moment when she discovered that this gifted, high-minded, handsome young army captain only had room in his heart for his career and his mother.

After he returned to London in September 1840 he met in Downing Street men who wanted to hear how the natives of New Holland could be saved from being wiped off the face of the earth by the expansion of the white man's society. He communed with James Stephen, Permanent Under-Secretary in the Colonial Office, who shared his view that prayer and meditation on God's holy word, rather than railways, steam-engines and spinning jennys, were the 'inexhaustible unfathomable source of all pure consolation and spiritual strength'. Now it happened that Stephen and other senior men in the Colonial Office believed they saw in Grey the man to take over the government of yet another province in Australia which was having trouble. For those who pray together are apt to be weak at reading the mind's construction in the face of each other. So Captain George Grey and his wife Eliza, big with his child, were 'bound for South Australia' where the 'straiteners' of mankind were in the ascendancy. In the meantime the would-be 'enlargers' in Western Australia were surrounded with the wrecks and remnants of their hopes.

2

The Moral Improvers Arrive in South Australia

By 1835 two methods of planting European civilization in Australia had been tried and both had been found wanting. The problem was to find a method of transplanting civilization to a wilderness without the moral evils of using slave labour or causing civilized people to fall back into a primitive way of life. Late in 1829 the *Morning Chronicle* in London began to publish a series of letters by an anonymous writer who claimed to have the answer to the problem.

The author argued that colonies went to utter ruin either because an extreme facility in acquiring land caused dispersion of settlement or because of the evils of using slave or semi-slave labour. With dispersion of settlement the people of Australia would lapse into barbarism; with slave labour they would become rotten before they were ripe. They could avoid either fate by a simple remedy. Instead of land being granted to capitalists, the waste lands of the Australian colonies should be sold at a 'sufficient price', by which he meant a price sufficiently high to prevent labourers from becoming landowners too soon, and sufficiently low to attract men to invest capital. The money raised from the sale of such lands should be used to pay the passages of migrants who should be selected in equal numbers from both sexes to put a stop to the era of the 'roaring lions' in the Australian colonies. The transportation of convicts should be abolished and free institutions introduced. The author wanted colonization to be conducted 'systematically', for he had the gift of dropping the memorable word. He also wanted men to enjoy the sun in Sydney, for running through all the letters was this note of a prophet of political economy who wanted men to live life more abundantly.

At the end of 1829 the twelve letters were published as a pamphlet, *A Letter from Sydney, the Principal Town of Australia*. The author was Edward Gibbon Wakefield. There were at least two persons inside him. There was a man filled with compassion for the victims of human savagery. There was also that 'coarse, sinister, clever fellow', that man of evil intentions and brutish impulses, that 'child-stealer' who had been imprisoned in 1827 in Newgate Goal for abducting a ward in chancery. When news reached London in the summer of 1831 of the fertile land the gallant Captain Sturt had seen between the mouth of the Murray River and Gulf St Vincent, Wakefield, just as quick in stealing ideas as in stealing a child-wife, came up with the idea that the struggle for civilization could be won on the southern coast of Australia. Soon others were making similar suggestions. In 1833 Robert Gouger proposed that all the people interested in establishing a province on the southern coast should form a South Australian Association.

The promoters of the scheme spoke as men with a vision of a new, moral society. They would implement Wakefield's idea of using the sale of Crown land at a fixed price to regulate the expansion of the settlement and to fund immigration. They told a public meeting of their dreams of a sober, hardworking, God-fearing community where there was no aristocracy and men were rewarded by the fruits of their labour. Men like George Fife Angas recorded their hope of performing an act of mercy for the natives of southern Australia by bringing them the gift of their great civilization and their holy faith. They declared their hope of rescuing the worker from his life of brutality and stupefaction in the United Kingdom and of providing a refuge for the pious Dissenters of Great Britain.

While settlers were recruited for the venture and funds raised, Colonel William Light was sent out with an advance party to select a site for the capital city. On 21 November 1836 he found on the east coast of Gulf St Vincent one of the loveliest spots a man could behold. The harbour, the river, the fine, rich-looking country and the delightful hills reminded him of the Mediterranean where men freed at last from the sense of those 'guilty stains' could pursue a life of pleasure. For William Light was a man of Byronic temperament, an enlarger of the human spirit. Already boatloads of men, women and children had begun to arrive at Kangaroo Island. That July and August they landed and were swept into a frenzy of drunkenness when relieved from the terrors and tedia of a four months' journey. After that evil spirit left them, in fits of remorse and shame they turned to their God for comfort and strength and swore they would try by His help not to sin again. These men, women and children were prospective tenants and artisans of the South Australian Company, a company which had decided to 'have no connections with any persons of dissolute habits or immoral principles or whose former actions could not undergo a strict examination'. Between the conception and the creation fell the shadow of human nature.

Six months later the settlement was well established at the place Light had chosen, and which was now called 'Adelaide'. As men and women set about the task of planting a God-fearing and prosperous civilization in the soil of the ancient continent, faction-fighting began to divide the tiny community. The British Government had appointed Captain John Hindmarsh, a Tory who was said to be neither particularly clever nor of even temper, as first Governor. Hindmarsh was involved in constant disputes over the division of authority between himself and James Hurtle Fisher, a wily, pedantic lawyer, who had the title Resident Commissioner. He represented the interests of the colonization commissioners, based in London, who were responsible for the administration of the programme of settlement. Hindmarsh railed against the supporters of the Resident Commissioner as 'the dirty Fisher faction'. Not to be outdone, Fisher countered by describing Hindmarsh as 'a man with a vulgar mind'. By August, Hindmarsh came to the conclusion that four senior officers—Mann, Fisher, Gouger and Brown—were such promoters of sedition that he wrote off—yet again—to London an account of his efforts to vindicate the authority of His Majesty in a remote province of the British Empire against these social upstarts. Nor were relations between the senior officers any more cordial. Gillies, when heated by strong drink, threatened to blow a hole in Gouger's 'b—— carcase'. Newspapers began to appear which promoted one or other of the rival factions.

The pattern of relations with the Aborigines already experienced in the other colonies began to repeat itself. Influenced by the humanitarian sentiments of the intellectual climate of London in the 1830s, the colonization commissioners had expressed their hopes of the blessings the coming of civilization would confer on the Aborigines. At the outset the settlers and officials had expressed their serious intention to treat the Aborigines with justice, kindness and forbearance. By the end of 1847 some were calling for acts of retaliation against the Aborigines while the high-minded were still beseeching their fellow colonists to base their conduct towards the Aborigines on the will of God and not on the standard of utility. At year's end a native woman surprised the proud bearer of the gift of civilization with the retort, 'You go to England, that your country; this our country'.

By year's end, too, there were ominous signs that they were not going to be any more successful than any other colony in planting civilization in an extensive and uninhabited country without disasters during the colony's infancy. It had been calculated that a minimum upset price of 12s an acre for waste lands was sufficient to prevent labourers becoming landowners too soon, and to thereby ensure both an adequate labour supply and the proper subordination of servant to master. But by year's end there was a labour shortage and complaints of the subversion of good order between master and servant.

The rumours of failure came as no surprise to James Stephen. He had always thought the *éminence grise* Edward Gibbon Wakefield to be coarse and sinister; he had always thought the ideas of the systematic colonizers to be impractical. As for the division of authority between Governor and Resident Commissioner, that was quite fatuous. So with the colonization commissioners, the directors of the South Australian Company, and prominent investors in the city clamouring for action, he recommended that the colonization commissioners and the Colonial Office should exchange minds on the future of South Australia.

While the men in London deliberated, the most interesting and important event since the formation of the colony occurred in Adelaide. On 4 April 1838 a man in the bushman's garb of blue shirt, soiled cabbage-tree hat with broad black ribbon, booted and spurred, with a stockwhip in the hand, and a clay pipe in the mouth walked out of the bush and into the streets of Adelaide. He was Joseph Hawdon who had spent the previous ten weeks overlanding sheep and cattle from New South Wales. He was the forerunner of those adventurers who would bring to South Australia the elements of the sheep-walk society of New South Wales that the political economists and systematic colonizers were so anxious to avoid. In July, another overlander, Edward John Eyre, was telling people in Adelaide that by far the richest land he had ever seen in New Holland lay between that town and the eastern boundaries of the province.

The significance of Hawdon's journey was not fully appreciated in Adelaide, where idealists still believed that it was the moral improvers, rather than the systematic colonizers or sheep-walk men, who were to shape the destinies of mankind in South Australia. Decisions had been made in London: Hindmarsh would have to go, and the functions of the Resident Commissioner would be taken over by Hindmarsh's successor. James Stephen and the colonization commissioners agreed that that 'godly man' Lieutenant-Colonel George Gawler was a happy choice. A 43-year-old one-time hero of Waterloo, Gawler arrived in South Australia in October 1838 with his wife Maria, who was said to be as devout and earnest a Christian as Gawler himself, and that, according to the mockers, was saying quite a bit. G. F. Angas rejoiced that a pious man had been chosen to make South Australia into that 'happy land' promised in Holy Scripture to all God's faithful children.

Before departure, Gawler's attention had been drawn to the worldly concerns of the colony. He was told of the decision of Her Majesty's Government to combine the offices of Governor and Resident Commissioner in his person. He was solemnly reminded by the Colonial Office that the colony must attempt to support itself and that except in cases of pressing emergency no public works nor any extraordinary expenditure were to be undertaken without prior authority from London. As the public debt then stood at £20 000 he was to exercise every possible economy to reduce that sum.

The forces of the moral improvers were greatly strengthened by the creation of two settlements of German colonists. Seeking the religious freedom they had been denied in Prussia, 537 German Lutherans had arrived at Holdfast Bay by January 1839. Half of the newcomers arranged to lease land from the company at a site on the north bank of the Torrens River, which they called Klemzig after their native town in Prussia. In January 1839, the others were approached by one W. H. Dutton, an overlander, who helped them to establish a settlement which they named Hahndorf on part of the 4000 acres he and his partners had acquired in the neighbourhood of Mount Barker.

By this time, the country districts of South Australia were being occupied by large landed proprietors like Dutton, who were leasing land to frugal, industrious and virtuous tenant farmers. In the verdant district of Mount Barker respectable families on their leases of 40- to 80-acre blocks soon created all those creature comforts with which men were familiar in the Old World. They put up their stone houses, sowed crops of wheat, barley and oats, planted potatoes and maize, bred dairy cows, sheep and pigs, and cultivated luxuriant gardens and orchards. The large landed proprietor rather than the systematic colonizer was about to show that it was possible to found a society in the New World without using slave labour or lapsing back to barbarism.

Just as the overlanders, capitalists, clergymen and schoolteachers were winning the battle against barbarism, Edward John Eyre came back from the interior of their colony to tell them of the seas of desolation to the north and the west. He and three other Europeans, two Aborigines, sundry drays, horses, dogs and supplies for two months had left Adelaide in May 1839. Until they reached Clare they travelled through familiar country, but then they turned towards the Flinders Ranges, where Eyre had his first sight of the salt-glazed bed of a lake, which was surrounded by such a vast and sterile desert that he turned east. He made for the great bend in the Murray, and then back to Adelaide where his companion, James Baxter, remained drunk for a week while Eyre wondered why a benevolent Providence had made the womb of their country so dry and barren. On a second journey into the hinterland he again passed the bed of the great salt lake, which he named in honour of Colonel Torrens. This time he reported that he had not crossed a single creek, river, or chain of ponds, or seen any permanent water anywhere.

This dryness of the interior and the taking up of the usable land by capitalists such as the Dutton brothers, J. Finniss, J. Morphett and the directors of the South Australian Company provided the setting both for a crisis in relations with the Aborigines and in the financial stability of the government of South Australia. In July 1840 David McLaren on behalf of the South Australian Company, and several other owners or would-be owners, complained to Charles Sturt, as Assistant Commissioner, that areas of desirable country had been withdrawn from public choice in favour of the Aborigines. They asked Sturt not to confirm the choices of land made by the Protector of Aborigines until after they had made their selections. Sturt was instructed by Governor Gawler to inform them that the Aborigines had the prior claim by virtue of their 'natural indefeasible rights', which were vested in them as their birthright, and confirmed by the royal instructions to the Governor, which commanded him to protect the Aborigines in the free enjoyment of their possessions and not to disturb them in possession of those lands over which they might have proprietary rights and of which they were not disposed to make a voluntary transfer. If the claims of the natives were not void before all, they were preliminary to all. They could not occupy a middle station.

At the same time the settlers were gradually pushing the Aborigines out into areas where their chances of survival from hunting and fishing diminished. On the frontiers of settlement there were bloody encounters. After the brigantine *Maria* was wrecked at Encounter Bay in July 1840, the Aborigines butchered the survivors and strewed human legs, arms and mutilated bodies all over the sands. Gawler, believing that to allow this band of 'most ferocious, insidious, unprovoked, and inveterate murderers and robbers' to go unpunished would defeat the ends of justice and humanity, summoned the Executive Council which recommended the execution of summary justice by 'temperate means'. He then dispatched the Commissioner of Police and a party of armed men to overawe the Aborigines of Encounter Bay. On 25 August they captured two Aborigines, took them to the spot where the white men had been butchered, charged them with murder, hanged them and left the bodies dangling there so that their fellow-Aborigines might learn what happened to murderers. Back in Adelaide there was talk of treating the Milmenrura natives of Encounter Bay as a foreign enemy. But Gawler pinned his faith to reports that the temporary resort to terror had caused the Milmenrura savages to vacate the district. He was not to know that for months they met around the decaying bodies of their fellow countrymen and vowed to kill every white man they saw and any member of their people who was friendly to white men.

By then the bourgeoisie of Adelaide and the settlers in the country districts were disturbed by the drift of events in the public life of the colony and discontent was mounting against Gawler's administration. There were complaints of intolerable delays in the Survey Department, and malicious stories that Sturt was so blind he could not even see the files in his department, let alone read what was inside them. Government revenue from the sale of land had dropped alarmingly, partly because settlement had reached the frontiers of dryness and partly because immigrants were leasing land from the South Australian Company or the lucky holders of special surveys, rather than buying and so contributing to government revenue. There was discontent, too, among the representatives of the commercial, agricultural, pastoral and general interests who were complaining that they were not represented on the Legislative Council.

By April 1840 settlers with property had won the right to be represented on an Adelaide municipal council, but Gawler was determined to resist any further devolution of power to men who had already displayed their liberal leanings in public meetings. While Gawler was comforting himself with the delusion that at least in Downing Street there was 'a shire of men who understand', the men in the Colonial Office were puzzled by the reports from South Australia and wondered what to do. The colony was drifting further into debt and Gawler had been signing bills on the treasury in London in excess of his authority. By December the financial state of the province had become such a source of dismay in London that the Colonial Secretary of State, Lord John Russell, at last wrote to Gawler relieving him of his post and appointing Captain George Grey as his successor. Gawler left the colony amid great displays of affection and gratitude and found a cordial welcome awaiting him in London. Till his death on 7 May 1869 he never realized that he— a man who professed to love all mankind and to have compassion for 'the least of the little ones' because of the love of Christ—lived in a dream world.

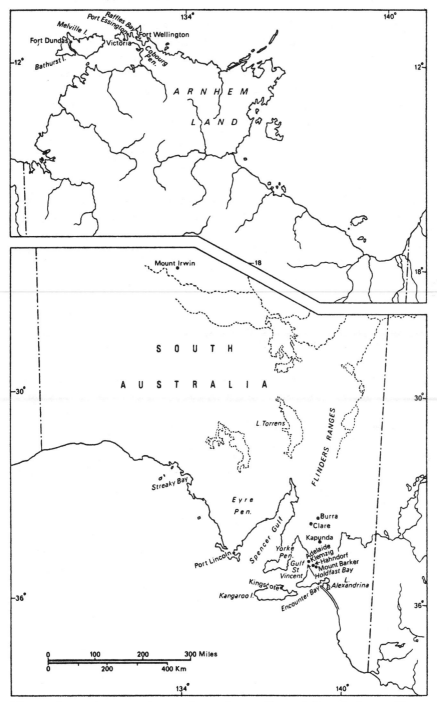

The main settlements in northern Australia and South Australia

Grey was full of plans for making economies and cutting government spending. He had both the gifts and the luck to preside over the colony while government proved it could be self-supporting and society at large proved it was possible to plant a colony without establishing some sort of slavery or experiencing the disasters that usually befell new colonies planted in an extensive country. George Grey looked very much the part when he arrived in May 1841. He was tall and upright in figure, his face wore a pleasing, amiable expression, and his manners were gentle, polished and agreeable. He was then only 29. His wife, who was a mere 20, was a remarkably pretty woman with beautiful dark eyes and hair and the presence of a graceful hostess. She waited at Holdfast Bay until the time came to put her child in the baby basket, the head resting on a pillow inscribed 'Welcome, little stranger'. But the child died, giving the Governor's lady a moment of insight into the heart of her husband, for he was foolish enough to let her see that to him her agony meant little and his triumph on the stage of public life everything. While she waited in vain for one word of sympathy and understanding from her husband, he was ingratiating himself with all the respectable people of Adelaide.

He moved quickly to reduce government expenditure. Positions were retrenched; salaries were slashed. The members of the Legislative Council were delighted. No one could accuse Captain Grey of softness of heart. When the number of people dependent on government relief reached 1240, that is, one in every twelve of the population of the province was living on public charity, he offered them reduced payments out of government funds, or assistance to find work with the settlers up-country. When the unemployed sent a deputation in October to protest against the hardships they suffered from such economies, he docked them a day's payment.

While Grey was presiding over the transition from extravagance to moderation in government expenditure, others were keeping alive the high-minded aspiration of the founders of the province to spread civilization over the wilderness of South Australia. On 18 June 1840 a party of men gathered at Government House for the reading of prayers and the presentation by Captain Sturt to Edward Eyre of a Union Jack, woven in silk by the ladies of Adelaide, which Sturt urged Eyre to carry to the centre of the continent and leave there as a sign to the savage that the footstep of civilized man had penetrated so far. That day Eyre, John Baxter, E. B. Scott, two Aborigines, thirteen horses and forty sheep, plus stores for a three months' journey set out to discover the interior of Australia. Driven back once again by the arid country around Lake Torrens, Eyre took his party west to Streaky Bay, from where he made yet another futile attempt to strike north. Undaunted he set out from Streaky Bay with Baxter, the Aborigine Wylie and two other Aborigines to walk the length of the Great Australian Bight to King George's Sound, which he and Wylie reached on 7 July. When Eyre got back to Adelaide by ship a year later he had a sorry story to tell of the murder of Baxter at Eucla by two treacherous Aborigines. He also told them how he had passed over a barren and desolate region which was almost destitute of grass, timber and water, and covered in places with an impenetrable useless scrub. Optimistic as ever, the colonists hailed Eyre as a hero who would one day plant the emblem of civilization, the Union Jack, in the centre of their mysterious province.

By then Grey was anxious to use Eyre for the other 'laudable purpose' for which the white man had come to South Australia—to prevent that 'lamentable thing': the 'progress and prosperity of one race conducing to the downfall and decay of another'. Eyre, like Sturt, was known to cherish a special kindness towards the Aborigines and to feel some sympathy with them. When he came back to Adelaide the overlanders of stock, who had followed in Hawdon's tracks from New South Wales, were reported to be having trouble with the Aborigines at the big bend of the Murray. In April and May 1841 pitched battles were fought between parties of ten or eleven overlanders and 300 to 400 natives. Extremists asked Grey to declare war on the Aborigines as a hostile foreign power. Grey decided to follow a middle course. At the end of May, he dispatched the Commissioner of Police, T. O'Halloran, to ensure a safe passage for the overlanders and their stock. This display of force so pacified the district that Grey was ready to ask Eyre in July to take on the role of Resident Magistrate and Protector of the Aborigines at Moorundie, and try what kindness could do to replace fear with respect.

As evidence of friendship Eyre mustered the Aborigines at every full moon and handed out blankets and flour. He began to teach them the rudiments of bartering and to show them the benefits of working for wages in the hope that their adoption of civilized ways would end those physical clashes with the white man which could only end in their total annihilation. Looking upon the white men as their foes, the Aborigines soon renewed attacks on overlanding parties. Eyre could do nothing to put an end to their habit of avenging wrongs against their people. Once again the overlanders shot down the would-be avengers, and the wails of Aboriginal women and children mourning for their dead men could be heard along the high banks of the Murray from Moorundie to the Rufus.

As these stories of bloody revenge and retribution reached Adelaide, opinion hardened in favour of using bullets to deter the wildness in the black man's heart. In 1846, when no signs from earth or heaven testified to any lasting good being accomplished, Eyre set off to take up the position of Lieutenant-Governor of New Zealand, where he squabbled incessantly, showed a strange preoccupation with gold braid and ceremonial and a sanctimonious preoccupation with sabbath observance. He then went as Governor to Jamaica, where his brutality in putting down a negro insurrection in 1865 caused Karl Marx to liken the beastliness of the 'true Englishmen' to the Russians, and John Stuart Mill to accuse him of murder. The hero of the Nullarbor Plain and the 'gentle spirit' of Moorundie was metamorphosed in time into a murderer in a 'nigger insurrection'. He lived in seclusion in Devon for thirty-six more years, a kindly old man of few words, looking more like the man who had had compassion on the original tenants of the desert of Australia than the hangman of Jamaica, and doing his duty, as he saw it, in that state of life in which it had pleased God to call him. His life was one of those riddles God sets the sons of men to unravel as best they can. He died on 30 November 1901.

Grey was pleased, that June of 1842, with the world as it was. Nothing any longer disturbed the quiet of Adelaide. The debt of the government to the South Australian Company had been paid off; the number of able-bodied labourers receiving government assistance had been reduced by seventy-one. Grey dismissed the increasingly loud demands of the colonists for elected representation in the Legislative Council with offhand disdain.

Just as the press began to turn against him, news reached Adelaide of fundamental changes in the constitution of the colony and the disposal of its waste lands. In London, the government had abolished the humbug of the colonization commissioners, and created a Legislative Council of at least seven members nominated by the Governor. More importantly, the government indicated its willingness to approve the creation of a general assembly elected by the freeholders of the colony, once the colony had become self-supporting. It reaffirmed that no convict was to be transported to any place within the province. Since evidence before the Colonial Office suggested that the price of 12s an acre had not been high enough to prevent the excessive appropriation of land, the price was increased to £1 an acre.

The foundations of civilization had been laid without the use of slaves or convicts. In their population, which reached almost 15 000 in 1842, the balance of the sexes was nearly even and the number of Catholics so low that the society could give off the air of the Protestant stamp of mind: industry, frugality, sobriety, and that concern for liberty which was said to distinguish such men of heroic ingredients, men with such a stake in the country that they were not likely to allow their society to be convulsed by those upheavals which threatened to engulf the Old World.

The convicts of New South Wales and their families and to a lesser extent those of Van Diemen's Land were quick to shed their ties with their mother country and look on Australia as a country which belonged to them. But the South Australians were free immigrants: they had accepted the complex fate of living at the Antipodes while their minds were stuffed with the sentiments of the Old World. In South Australia each Christmas migrants became nostalgic for an English, an Irish or a Scottish Christmas. At Easter they were nostalgic for that renewal of nature which was so appropriate to and congruous with the Christian looking for the resurrection of the dead. Unlike the convict colonies the tone of South Australian society came from those very zealous supervisors of morals, the clergy and the laity—those supporters of Sunday as a day on which men should neither labour nor rejoice, and even abstain from idly gazing out of windows because that exposed them to the risk of 'beholding vanities abroad'.

There was the sameness and the dryness of the land, but hope was rekindled at year's end when news reached Adelaide of the discovery of a new rich country stretching along the western banks of the Glenelg River, admirably suited for grazing or agriculture. When the Governor and his lady, the civil and military officers, the clergy and most of the respectable inhabitants of Adelaide and the country districts gathered at Government House on the night of 28 December 1842 to mark the sixth anniversary of the foundation of the colony, they were brimful with joy. Gaiety prevailed as couples danced the mazurka, a traditional Polish dance which had only been introduced into the ballrooms of London twelve years previously. It was a dance for those who took pride in their bearing, a dance, too, which had its moments of wild ecstasy. It was as though they were dancing towards those 'better things' which they believed they could fashion out of the wilds of Australia, not sensing then in the pleasure of the dance what would happen to them when they retained their morality after they had lost their faith, or that those 'better things' were to come not from any theories of colonization but from human ingenuity, and the mineral wealth in those arid places about which they preferred not to think.

3

Overstraiters, Overlanders and Others Descend on Port Phillip

The gentle Matthew Flinders had been so awestruck in 1798 by the huge seas rolling through Bass Strait, pounding the south coast of New Holland and the north coast of Van Diemen's Land, that he had chosen a symbolical name for the north-west promontory of the latter: he had called it Cape Grim. The few Europeans who visited the coast had damned it as a place of savagery: a place of wild seas, of dry and hostile land. At Sealers Cove on Wilson's Promontory, at Cape Woolamai on Phillip Island, at Port Fairy and at Portland Bay sealers and whalers pursued a way of life as savage and elemental as the never-ending roar of that sea, the gales that blew in the winter, and the storms that rolled over the land in the summer.

The intrusion of civilization on such a land was to prove just as relentless as the seas pounding the coast. In 1824 Hamilton Hume and William Hovell rescued this southern part of New Holland from the stigma of being barren and inhospitable. The press in Sydney and Hobart Town began to prophesy that the tide of civilization was about to sweep over those rich plains where the Aborigines of New Holland had floundered since time immemorial in a sea of barbarism. By 1832 settlers were pushing south from Jugiong and Gundagai to Wagga Wagga, the place of the crows, and Mullengandra. It was only a matter of time before they reached the Murray and crossed that noble stream near those majestic river gums and lush meadows.

Those settlers in the north of Van Diemen's Land who aspired to a way of life such as was enjoyed by James Cox at Clarendon or Joseph Archer at Panshanger or Edward Dumaresq at Mount Ireh knew that they must find fresh land on which to plant their manors. At the same time, thousands of miles away in the United Kingdom, young men of good family were anxiously surveying the press, pamphlets and printed books for an account of a country that

promised that one thing denied them in the land of their birth—
membership in the landed gentry. There were others, too, anxious
simply for that bellyful which the Old World denied them and their
families. They were waiting to be shown where they could have
their bellyful without loss of virtue or respectability. They were a
freak tide backing up, waiting to flood any land suitable for its
own purposes.

In 1833 the tide began to flow. In that year Thomas Henty, who
had concluded that neither New South Wales, nor Western
Australia, nor Van Diemen's Land would place the members of his
family in that 'first rank in society' to which he believed he and they
were entitled, sought to acquire 25 000 acres for himself at 5s an acre
and 25 000 acres for each of his sons of beautiful and picturesque
land in the neighbourhood of Portland Bay. Not waiting for a reply,
in October 1834 his son Edward set out from Launceston in the
Thistle, loaded with sheep, bullocks, cows, calves, heifers, dogs,
seed and plants. For two years his men watched the sheep, thatched
a roof, coopered a barrel, cooked their food, enticed Aboriginal
women to share their beds and turned the dogs on Aborigines who
pilfered their supplies. Their only excitements were those days
when 'Dutton got a whale' (William Dutton had been whaling in
the bay since 1829) and the days on which a ship arrived from
Launceston. Just when they were ready to take that step forward
from the crude improvisations of the pioneer into the splendours of
squatterdom, news trickled down to the bay that other overstraiters
were starting a settlement at Port Phillip. By yet another cruel turn
of fortune's wheel, Thomas Henty and his sons were condemned to
a life on the frontier of a new society rather than given that central
position, that 'first rank in society', which had driven them to make
the long journey across the oceans of the world.

To add almost a note of comic irony to the news of Port Phillip,
the prime mover for the settlement, John Batman, belonged by birth
to that convict society in New South Wales whose vulgar rise to
wealth and prominence had been one of the reasons deterring
Thomas Henty from trying his luck in the mother colony of
Australia. Batman's father was a convict; his mother was a convict.
He himself was one of those native-born members of the convict
class who made no secret of their belief that all the land of Australia,
including Van Diemen's Land, belonged to them and their descendants. He was born in Sydney on 21 January 1801 and moved to
Hobart in 1821 where he lived with a convict woman, Eliza
Thompson, whom he married in 1828, after he took up land grants
in Kingston near Launceston. Inside Batman was a man who
allowed no restraint to come between him and the satisfaction of his

desires. He had about him the air of a man prepared to steal fire from heaven and defy the gods to punish him for his excesses. When drunk he terrified those near him so much that one brave man said he would gladly give away all the fleeces of New Holland rather than expose himself again to the cruelties of a drunken Batman. His appetite for women was just as huge as his thirst for drunken oblivion. Though on paper he was as much a broad-acres man as Thomas Archer, Joseph Archer, or James Cox, those three lived in their manors in lush countryside while Batman and his family lived in a stone-and-mud hut in scruffy country at Kingston, hemmed in by the surrounding hills, and, besides, had to endure the malice and insolence of the free-born towards convicts and their descendants. Port Phillip offered a kingdom where a man, he believed, had a chance to be freed from such ghosts of his past.

In 1835 he joined with John Helder Wedge, Charles Swanston, James Simpson, T. J. Gellibrand and nine others to form an association which became known as the Port Phillip Association, by which they committed themselves to a plan of sending John Batman to Port Phillip to negotiate with the chiefs of the Aborigines for the purchase of their land by the association.

The members of the association knew that the British Government still stood by its instruction to Captain Cook that no European nation had a right to occupy any part of a country or settle in it without the voluntary assent of the original inhabitants. Privately some of their number proposed that they should drive the blacks out by force. As for Batman, there was a great difference between Batman drunk and Batman sober. Drunk, he loathed all men, especially wives and 'black bastards' and anyone to whom he was responsible. Sober, he entertained quite a different vision of the world. He wrote to Arthur about his hopes to civilize a large portion of the Aborigines of New Holland. At the same time he told all the scoffers at brotherly love for blackfellows that he was only putting it this way because that was what 'Little George' (he meant Arthur) liked to hear.

At the end of May, Batman, his party of seven Aborigines and three European servants set out from Launceston on the *Rebecca* and proceeded to Indented Head near the western entrance to Port Phillip Bay. There in a moment of ecstasy Batman fingered the 10-inch-high grass on which his beasts would fatten. He then continued to the head of the bay where he found a site where ships could ride in safety at the mouth of a river which the Aborigines called Yarra Yarra, or flowing water. The following day he met the chiefs of the Aborigines at a place where a creek, which they called Merri, joined the Yarra Yarra.

Through his interpreters Batman explained to the chiefs that he had come to settle among them on friendly terms, adding that although he was a white man he was 'a countryman of theirs' and would protect them. That day he gave the men blankets, tomahawks, knives, scissors, and looking-glasses and hung around the necks of each woman and child a necklace. They appeared highly gratified and excited. The next day he explained to the chiefs that the object of his visit was to purchase a tract of their country, since he intended to settle among them with his wife, his seven daughters, his sheep and his cattle. He proposed, he said, to employ the people of their tribe, clothe and feed them, and pay them an annual tribute in necessaries as a compensation for the enjoyment of the land. The chiefs, he told Arthur, seemed fully to comprehend his proposals, and much delighted with the prospect of having him live among them. On the following day, 6 June, after the deed of purchase was read out and carefully explained, the chiefs of the Dutigallar tribe in the district of Iransnoo and Geelong granted to John Batman 100 000 acres in exchange for 20 pairs of scissors, 50 handkerchiefs, 12 red shirts, 4 flannel jackets, 4 suits of clothes, 50 pounds of flour, and a yearly rent or tribute of 50 pairs of blankets, 50 knives, 50 tomahawks, 50 pairs of scissors, 50 looking-glasses, 20 suits of clothing and 2 tons of flour. By a similar deed of purchase he took possession of 500 000 acres in the vicinity of the Yarra Yarra. In return for a few knives, tomahawks, scissors and looking-glasses, and enough grog to put them in a mood to say 'yes' to anything and laugh about it, a few local Aborigines had made John Batman and the other members of the association among the largest landed proprietors in the world. In the mood of a man feeling like a king he wrote down in his diary a few days later, 'this will be the place for the future village'. Then on 14 June he left for Launceston.

Some days after his return to Launceston, with an air of quiet confidence, he wrote to Arthur an account of his expedition. He assured Arthur that his object had not been possession and expulsion or, what is worse, extermination, but the civilization of a benighted but intelligent people. He told him of his plans to graze 20 000 stock. He assured Arthur that he need not fear yet another convict Sodom and Gomorrah, because the members of his association proposed to use only married men of good character as overseers or servants. That surely should 'gull Little George'. Little George was no fool. He was not deceived by all these protestations of brotherly love for black men. He wrote to Richard Bourke, Governor of New South Wales, early in July that Batman's pretensions were quite absurd. Two months later Bourke proclaimed to all and sundry that any such treaty made with the natives for possession of vacant land was void and of no effect against the rights of the Crown. All persons found in possession of any such lands without the licence or authority of His Majesty's Government would be considered trespassers.

In the meantime, with an astonishing insensitivity to the way the wind was blowing in high places in Hobart Town and Sydney, John Helder Wedge resigned from his job in the Survey Department so that he and Henry Batman (John Batman's brother) and his family could return to Port Phillip as an advance party for the men, sheep and cattle that were to follow. When they landed at Indented Head on 7 August, Wedge found to his surprise a wild white man, William Buckley, a most amazing sight since he was clad the same as the natives. He stood almost 6 feet 7 inches in his socks, this native of Cheshire and one-time convict, with his dark brown beard, his bushy eyebrows, an erect military gait, and tattoos on his arm. He had escaped in 1803 during an aborted attempt to settle Port Phillip and had found sanctuary among the local Aboriginal people. As the months passed, Buckley had forgotten his mother tongue as he acquired their language and lost all the habits of the white man except the white man's God, whom he thanked fervently for preserving him. Within a few days of Wedge's arrival, Buckley had gone over to the service of the white men and accepted their suggestion that he should try to keep alive good understanding between the two races. To promote this end, Arthur granted him a pardon.

After inspecting a site on the Barwon River in the Geelong district in company with Buckley, Wedge set out for the Yarra Yarra where he found to his dismay another party of white men camped. When he told their leader that they would have to go since they were intruders on the land the association had purchased from the Aborigines, he was told to 'take the treaty with him when next he had occasion for the use of waste paper'. On the banks of the Yarra Yarra the dream of the meticulous fusspot John Wedge and the Byronic John Batman, and those greedy bankers and merchants of Hobart Town, began to vanish into the mists of time. For Wedge was not to know then that just five days before, the Governor of New South Wales had branded all of them—the members of the association as well as this intruder he had met on the banks of the Yarra—as illegal trespassers.

The man behind that second party of white men on the banks of the Yarra, John Pascoe Fawkner, was also a member of convict society in Van Diemen's Land. He was born at Cripplegate in London on 20 October 1792. In 1801 his father was sentenced to transportation for fourteen years for receiving stolen goods.

Perhaps that was where the habit of lying about the facts of his life started, for who knows why the truth is in some men and not in others and why the great liars are often consumed with an inner loathing for their fellow-men. Who knows why the mysterious powers in charge of the universe should condemn Byronic figures such as John Batman to an early death and leave the Fawkners of this world to live on as gadflies to the stern-faced men who were destined to print their mark on the settlement.

It was not long before the tiny settlement which had assembled on the banks of the Yarra Yarra learnt what manner of man this John Pascoe Fawkner was. Within a few days of his arrival at Port Phillip he told that little world that John Batman was an illiterate drunkard who was claiming half a million acres of land in exchange for a few toys. He denounced him as a cheat and ridiculed him as 'King John the First of Port Phillip'. He accused Batman of bribing the natives to split open Fawkner's own head with a tomahawk so that 'King John' could once again become the lord of all he surveyed. Yet despite these private hells in his heart he managed to save £20 000 during his first four years at Port Phillip by following the trade in which he had first prospered in Launceston—hotel-keeping.

Soon after the arrival of Fawkner, the affairs of the members of the Port Phillip Association began to decline. After John Batman's eighth child—a son—was drowned, he seemed to lose all faith in himself as a man and to wander around the settlement of Bearbrass on the Yarra Yarra like a man who knew his days were numbered. Gellibrand lost heavily when many of his sheep were suffocated in the hold of his ship or died of thirst. Wedge only lost 50 out of his flock of 800 sheep, but he had other sources of disquietude. He was beginning to fear that Port Phillip might be Van Diemen's Land all over again, with the extermination of the Aborigines as the inevitable consequence of the spread of European settlement.

By then these seekers after the life of the free at Port Phillip began to think more kindly of the virtues of civil government. As soon as the stockmen stopped handing out presents to the Aborigines a 'day of collisions' began. The Aborigines speared their sheep; the packs of dogs that followed the natives also harassed their sheep; Vandemonian convicts were practising riot and uproar in their tiny settlement of 170 people. On 1 June 1836 the victims of such anarchy petitioned the Governor of New South Wales, who lost no time in establishing civil authority in the district for the protection of the Aborigines and the due administration of the laws: Captain William Lonsdale arrived at Port Phillip on 29 September 1836 to take up the position of police magistrate for the district of Port Phillip.

After a visit by Governor Bourke in March 1837 during which the settlement had been given the Whig name of Melbourne, the surveyor Robert Hoddle and his assistant Robert Russell were left behind to draw up a site plan for the town. A man with geometry in his soul, Hoddle began to design a city like a rectangular grid with the streets so straight that there was nothing to stop the north wind converting the town into a fiery furnace in the summer, or the south wind making it shivery and sodden in winter.

The coming of law and order to Port Phillip began to attract more settlers in search of pasture, wealth and respectability. In the meantime the news was spreading that the Surveyor-General of New South Wales, Major Thomas Mitchell, had walked over flowery plains and green hills to the south of the Murray River. By one of those odd ironies in the history of the country, he was a man who loathed Australia, the white men, the Whig Governor, the bishop, the clergy, the judges, the usurers, the Jews, the Aborigines and above all the appearance of the country. He had returned to Sydney in November 1836 with news that he had at long last seen in New Holland a patch of country worthy of being 'English for thousands of years'. He was then 44 years old. A veteran of the Peninsular Campaign, he had migrated to New South Wales in 1827 to take up the position of Deputy Surveyor under John Oxley at a time when promotion in the army was far too slow for a man of his restless temperament and ambition. Much given to denouncing his fellow-men for their folly and their stupidity, he was partial to a conversation with the ladies, for the beauty of women was one of the few pleasures he ever knew in New South Wales. It was his fate or his cross to belong to that long list of gifted and courageous Englishmen for whom Australia was a land that was cursed and its inhabitants as barren and empty as the land that surrounded them.

In March 1836 he was off again with a party of twenty-five to explore the Darling, Murrumbidgee and Murray river country. Again he raged against a 'vile scrub' country where a series of waterholes purported to be a river. But he was to enter a country of surpassing loveliness. Travelling south-west from Cohuna he climbed to the top of a hill, which he named Pyramid Hill, from where he could see pleasing grasslands instead of that dried-up salt-bush country out on the Darling. There was better to come. On 11 August, he reached the junction of two rivers, the Wannon and the Glenelg. There, near the present town of Casterton, he was refreshed, in the midst of such rich pasture, by what he foresaw as 'one of the finest regions upon earth'. From there Mitchell and his party set out for Portland Bay, where on 29 August he found to his surprise that there were Englishmen living there. The Henty brothers told him they were importing sheep and cattle as fast as vessels could be found to bring them over from Launceston. He told them of the beauty of the country at the junction of the Wannon and the Glenelg.

Leaving Portland early in September, Mitchell travelled north-east towards the Murray. By 21 September east of Mount Abrupt (east of the present city of Hamilton) he travelled over a country quite open, slightly undulating and well covered with grass. Here at long last in New Holland he found a land favourable for colonization. Flocks might be turned out upon its hills, or the plough at once set to work in the plains. The land, as he saw it, was open and available in its present state for all the purposes of civilized man. Having traversed in two directions the flowing plains and green hills fanned by the breezes of early spring, he decided to name the region 'Australia Felix', the better to distinguish it from the parched deserts of the interior. He hoped and believed his fellow countrymen would establish there 'a lasting monument of British power and colonization, thus to engraft a new and flourishing state, on a region now so desolate and unproductive . . . by such means as England alone can supply'.

In 1837 Edward Henty and his party threw up their hats with a cheer when they saw the country over which Mitchell had enthused and put their horses to the gallop for the site of a station in those rich plains at Muntham. They were followed by others: settlers who dreamed of the day when they would be surrounded by liveried servants; settlers inflamed with Mitchell's idea of the region being open and available for all the purposes of civilized man.

The Aborigines could do nothing to impede the spread of the white man over the plains of Australia Felix. The Russells, the Blacks, the Mollisons, the Learmonths, the Armitages, the Austins, the Hentys, the Faithfuls and others were making their takeover bid to plant a society that would be 'English for thousands of years', whatever other intimations men might get from that sea rolling forever through Bass Strait, or that spirit of the place which seemed to suggest a vast indifference to all human endeavour.

4

England's Echo in the Antipodes

In 1837 a committee of the House of Commons on Aborigines in British settlements overseas had come to the melancholy conclusion that intercourse with Europeans had cast over the Aborigines of New Holland a deeper shade of wretchedness than the debasement in which they had lived before the arrival of the white man. The effects had been dreadful: the Aborigines appeared to be vanishing from the face of the earth.

Acting on a principal recommendation of the Committee, Glenelg informed Sir George Gipps, the Governor of New South Wales, that Her Majesty's Government had decided to appoint G. A. Robinson as Chief Protector of Aborigines. He would fix his principal station at Port Phillip, and would be aided by four assistant protectors who were to divide Port Phillip into four districts. Each assistant protector should attach himself closely and constantly to the Aboriginal tribes in his district and accompany them in their movements until they could be induced to assume more settled habits of life. He was to endeavour to conciliate their respect and confidence and to make them feel he was their friend. He must watch over the rights and interests of the natives, protect them from any encroachment on their property and from acts of cruelty, oppression or injustice, and faithfully represent their wants, wishes or grievances through the Chief Protector to the government of the colony. For that purpose each assistant protector was to be commissioned as a magistrate. If the natives could be induced to locate themselves in a particular place, each assistant protector should teach and encourage them to engage in the cultivation of the grounds, building suitable habitations for themselves, and whatever else that might conduce to their civilization and social improvement. The education of the children was to be regarded as a matter of primary importance. Each assistant protector was to promote the moral and religious improvement of the natives by instructing them in the elements of the Christian religion. He was to learn the language of the natives so as to be able freely and familiarly to converse with them and was to obtain as accurate information as possible of the number of natives within his district, and of all important particulars with regard to them.

At the time of his new appointment, Robinson was in charge of the Aboriginal establishment on Flinders Island. He had striven mightily to do God's work among the Aborigines he had removed to the island in the hope of protecting them from further murderous conflict with the settlers in Van Diemen's Land. His Christian faith remained unshaken, but a great sadness was beginning to show in his face. Despite all Robinson and his catechist and the convict workers had done to make the Aborigines comfortable by providing stone houses, a chapel, agricultural implements and clothing, the Aborigines spent much of their time sitting on top of the hill which overlooked the settlement, from where they gazed with tears in their eyes at their homeland which the white man had forced them to leave. Robinson had written in his diary the melancholy truth that he must leave this place of sickness before all the black men were dead. When the call came to take up his new position in Port Phillip he tried to persuade the Governor to allow him to take the remaining Tasmanian Aborigines with him. After sounding out opinion in Sydney, Gipps permitted him to take a handful of the Vandemonians. By then Robinson was once again a man inspired by a great vision, but had no clear idea of how to carry it into effect.

For the most part the four assistant protectors worked diligently, as dilgently as the various missionaries who, at the same time, were attempting to settle Aborigines in villages and teach them western ways and western faith. But the pattern was so often repeated: early optimism gave way to despair. At first the missionary, or the protector, found the Aborigines to be intelligent and energetic, but once they were confined to the mission or settlement their communities were ruined by melancholy, violence and drink.

Meanwhile settlers were saying openly that a few pleasant rounds of musketry would settle the problem of the Aborigines far better than the 'nostrums of exaggerated philanthropy'. These settlers knew the Aborigines as wild animals who broke the legs of their sheep and then danced a corroboree round them as they writhed in agony on the ground, after which they left their dogs to finish off the work they had begun. The country districts of Port Phillip were reproducing the same rude and licentious form of society as the interior of New South Wales, a society of sly-grog shops, marauding bushrangers and murderous savages who so terrorized country districts that men were being compelled to give up their establishments and sell off their stock: only one in twenty, it was said, could be persuaded to stay on a sheep station. When the settlers asked for adequate protection they received lectures from city philanthropists about the rights of the Aborigines.

The odd irony was that all those high and mighty men in London who felt such pity for this 'helpless race of beings' and such a desire to prepare them to receive the doctrines of Christianity and all the other advantages of civilization, had themselves sanctioned a waste lands policy which contributed to the dispersion of settlement in Port Phillip and elsewhere and proved so fatal to the Aborigine. In 1839 the minimum upset price of Crown land was raised to 12s an acre and in 1840 to £1. The men of moderate or slender capital who flocked into Port Phillip between 1839 and 1842 to purchase land in response to those reports about a 'champagne country' were obliged to go beyond the limits of location, outside the boundaries of the counties of Bourke, Grant and Normanby, where they could depasture the stock purchased by their capital on a run for which they paid a licence fee of £10 a year, and where further conflict with Aboriginal people for the possession of land, water and food was inevitable.

As settlement spread, life was fading fast from John Batman. Reduced to being wheeled around the town in a rushwork perambulator, his face rendered hideous by nasal syphilis, he was a shadow of that man who four years earlier had had his moment of ecstasy on the banks of the Yarra Yarra. In his last months he had raged against his wife and had taken mad revenge against her by leaving her only £5 in his will, and the rest to his beloved daughters. On 6 May Batman breathed his last, being then 38 years old, just as the men of moral rectitude began to set the tone of public life in Melbourne.

Five months later, with the rain pouring down in torrents, the new superintendent of Port Phillip, Charles La Trobe, told the inhabitants of Melbourne it was not by the possession of numerous flocks and herds that a people secured enduring prosperity and happiness but by the acquisition and maintenance of sound religious and moral institutions without which no country could become truly great. La Trobe was a man of such elegance and the possessor of such an effeminate giggle that local barmen summed him up as a man with the tastes and morals more suitable for looking after blackfellows than governing civilized colonials. Born in London on 30 March 1801, in the twenties he had travelled extensively in Mexico and North America, and had returned to Europe with the reputation of 'a man of a thousand occupations'— a botanist, a geologist, a hunter of beetles and butterflies, an amateur musician, a sketcher of no mean pretensions—a busy and a cheerful man. After marrying the daughter of a Swiss councillor in 1835 he had won a reputation in the Colonial Office by his reports on the measures necessary to fit the emancipated slaves in the West Indies for their freedom.

Glenelg and his advisers decided that La Trobe was the man to preside over the civilization of the natives of Port Phillip. The man himself was a bundle of contradictions. Publicly he spoke of the noble task of elevating the Aborigines from barbarism to civilization; privately he saw himself as an exile in a country where nature was in its swaddling clothes, the natives wild animals, the white man's society in its infancy, and the arts and sciences unborn. In the year of his arrival the inhabitants of Melbourne either wallowed in mud or choked on dust. Some of the houses were brick, some of weatherboard, but most were wattle-and-daub huts roofed with sheets of bark or coarse shingle. The sight of a woman in the streets was rare. The most conspicuous white people were the squatters down from the country to sell their wool or buy stores—heavily bearded men in serge shirts, cabbage-tree hats, moleskin trousers, boots and spurs, and ample tobacco pouches buttoned to their belts amidriffs. La Trobe was so disgusted that black people wandered about the streets half-naked that he asked the Chief Protector to do his best to get them out of earshot and sight of the white men. The streets resounded to their cooees, the barking of their mangy dogs, the shouts and curses of the bullock drivers, and the groans of drunks in the gutters.

For spectator sports there were the fights between the Aborigines. On 15 April 1840 Niel Black, a Scottish farmer's son who had established himself on a fine run on the luxuriant plains of Australia Felix, was in Melbourne to pick up supplies. That afternoon, hearing yells coming from the bank of the Yarra, he followed the crowd running towards the source of the noise where he saw black men, under the influence of a most fearful excitement, hurling spears at each other. The white spectators cheered and urged them to greater deeds of violence till suddenly the spear-throwing stopped and a great cackling noise replaced the previous savage roars as a lubra rushed into the middle of the ring and shook her whole body in a wild frenzy while the anger of participants and spectators simmered down. To Black's horror he heard black and white people gloating over the prospect of further sport of a similar kind within a day or two.

Some were shocked to find that in Melbourne in its raw days even the country gentry cared so little for their appearance that the shopkeepers and workers lost all respect for them. Tradesmen and labourers were in the habit of abusing anyone who was obnoxious to them. Even the members of the Melbourne Club, which had been founded in November 1838 by a collection of squatters, looked rough and uncouth. One in particular disregarded attention to personal appearance so much that he actually walked about with 'such a rent in his trowsers as displayed to the wondering gaze of the multitude the ample fullness of his brawny buttocks'.

While some wallowed in the mud, others were working feverishly to lay the foundations of the bourgeois way of life. In 1839 James Conway Bourke opened an overland mail route from Yass to Melbourne, and banks and insurance companies opened for business. In May 1840 the Melbourne Water Works Company was formed to supply water to the town. In July G. W. Cole started business as a general merchant, and owner of a fleet of paddle-steamers which plied on the Yarra and Port Phillip. In the same month the first directors of a Port Phillip Steam Navigation Company were elected as talks took place to form a Joint Stock Company to build a bridge across the Yarra. By the end of the year there were nearly 10 250 white people in the district.

While traders and merchants preached the gospel of industrial progress, priests and clergy held out to their congregations the prospect of prizes in this world to the straitlaced, and the richer prize of eternal salvation in the life of the world to come. By Christmas of 1840 the publicists for the repression of those poisonous passions of revelry, riot and debauchery were pleased to note that Melbourne was already presenting those features of repose and order which distinguished the best of the English towns. Instead of the brawling and drunken revelry of previous years the working classes were now displaying a sober demeanour and a very proper distaste for the tippler's life. Improving lectures, concerts featuring sacred music, and the decorous dancing of a quadrille or a waltz were replacing the swinish pleasures of the days when John Batman and other wild men reeled drunkenly around on the banks of the Yarra.

But life in the bush was still rough and sometimes brutal. There were no schools or churches, and most landholders were content to erect rude dwellings so long as they were only squatters on government land and liable at any time to be removed from it if a purchaser made his appearance. Such terrible stories were reaching Melbourne of the degradation and savagery practised by blacks and whites upon each other that La Trobe feared the squatters were reaching the limits of endurance. He knew the Protector and his assistants had not achieved any moral influence over the behaviour of the Aborigines. All men with eyes to see knew that the Aborigines were oppressed by famine because the game on which they relied for food had been driven into the interior by the rapidly increasing flocks and herds of the settlers. For that reason alone the Aborigines were 'jealous of the intruders'. All men of goodwill knew that 'blood-thirsty and villainous atrocities' were also committed by men whose skins were white.

But those who spoke for enterprise and industry were unmoved. He who would exploit the wealth of the country, they argued, must steel his breast to the wrongs he must commit against the Aborigines, for all such wrongs were unanswerable. For them, the question of questions was not the rights of naked Aborigines, but the shortage of labour. Down at Glenormiston in the very heart of Australia Felix, Niel Black wanted at least five times the workers he could get. For himself he was not very keen on hired labour. He found Vandemonians great bouncers, men who believed they had no equal even though they were only paltry shopkeepers' boys. He wondered whether the solution was to import coolie labour from India or China. At his new station at Muntham, Edward Henty refused to allow the 'convict polluters' on his estate.

By the middle of 1839, the merchants, landholders, stockholders and other residents of the newly settled province were calling for the separation of Australia Felix from New South Wales. They complained that revenue derived from the sale of Crown lands in the province was being spent elsewhere while the needs of the rapidly growing settlement and its chief town went unmet; their police force was inefficient; a town of 4000 had scarcely any public resources; the streets were impassible in wet weather; the harbour lacked a lighthouse and there was insufficient labour about to develop the ample resources of the region. The more the Melburnians convinced themselves that they were wallowing in mud or choking in dust because of those 'old women' in the Legislative Council in Sydney, the more they protested that they were the true sons of Britain. In their whole history they were to be cursed by this quest for the unattainable, this insistence that they had not changed their inner selves by that long journey across the seas, and cursed, too, by the conviction of the moral superiority of a society of new chums over the descendants of the thief colony at Botany Bay.

In September 1842 Lord Stanley agreed to the right of Melbourne and the right of the Port Phillip District to elect members to the Legislative Council, but did not agree to their erection into a separate province. At the same time Samuel Pratt Winter at Murndall, Edward Henty and his brothers and all their wives at Muntham, George Russell at Golf Hill, Niel Black at Glenormiston, Thomas Learmonth at Ballarat, and most of the other eighty-odd run-holders in the Port Phillip District struggled to erect that society of country squires and landed gentry who were tied by the nexus of the market and by sentiment to English things, not knowing that in the country that had put such a picture in their hearts the railway, the steamship, the factory, and the electric cable were dealing a death-blow to country gentry, and not foreseeing that the wool they shipped directly to Liverpool was speeding up the development of industrial civilization. For they were both the creators and grave-diggers of their own type of society. In their eyes the rolling country from Coleraine to Casterton was the Sussex Downs of the Anti-podes, and the land round Koroit like those parts of Ireland in which the Protestant ascendancy had enriched English landlords. They did not sense that that huge sea, over which Batman had ridden to his damnation, and Edward Henty to his glory, and the spirit of the place were indifferent alike to both winners and losers in the human lottery, indifferent, too, to the success of the white man in putting his mark on the land, and to the terrible price the Aborigines paid for their failure to resist the invader.

5

Governor Gipps and the Massacre at Myall Creek

In 1838 the people of New South Wales, both black and white, knew the terrible experience of drought. It was such a dry year that from Australia Felix to the Riverina, the Monaro, the Bathurst Plains, Patrick's Plains and the Liverpool Plains the growth of vegetation had almost completely stopped. Up at Inverell whenever stockmen gathered for a yarn over a quart-pot of tea or something stronger there was talk of the need to wipe out the 'black bastards'. On 9 June, led by a 'cleanskin' named John Fleming, the son of a local squatter, eleven of the 'felonry' of New South Wales arrived at the Myall Creek bush hut on Henry Dangar's squatting run and told the shepherd George Anderson, an assigned convict, that they were going to rope together any Aborigines they caught, take them over the hill and frighten the daylights out of them. A few minutes later Anderson heard shots. Two days later, after an unsuccessful search for more Aborigines, the party of white men piled together the bodies of the men, women and children they had slaughtered and set them alight.

Some days later when William Hobbs, Dangar's manager on the Myall Creek run, returned to the hut and saw the charred remains of twenty-eight bodies of men, women and children, he saw it as his duty to report the crime. So off he went on the 250-mile journey on horseback over the Liverpool Plains to Quirindi and Muswellbrook where he reported what he had seen to Captain Edward Denny Day, a magistrate of wisdom, justice and mercy. He decided to pass on what he had heard from Hobbs to the Colonial Secretary, Edward Deas Thomson, who in turn asked the new Governor, Sir George Gipps, whether twelve white men should be charged with the wilful murder of twenty-eight Aborigines.

Sir George had been welcomed to Sydney only four months earlier, in February when the summer heat was at its most unforgiving. A sensitive, vulnerable man who took refuge in prayer and hard work, he had come to preside over a society enslaved to vulgar passions, to extravagance, violence and barbarism. For days after he heard the report of the massacre, he went through terrible anguish of heart and mind. Sir George was a paragon of obedience to those in authority. He knew the importance the Colonial Office attached to the life of a native. The problem was that if he obeyed his superiors in London he might antagonize the landed proprietors of New South Wales. Two months earlier he had drafted a Government Notice which referred to the Aborigines as 'the original possessors of the soil', and proclaimed the principle that British law protected blacks and whites equally from crimes of violence. To treat Aborigines 'as aliens, with whom a war can exist', he wrote, was 'at variance with the dictates of justice and humanity'.

That was in April. By July Gipps was still refraining from publishing the notice. By then the settlers outside the boundaries were talking of a war against the blacks. But Gipps's trusted Attorney-General, the liberal John Hubert Plunkett, convinced the Governor that the law should be upheld, and Gipps ordered Captain Day to proceed to Myall Creek with a party of mounted police to inquire into what had happened and to collect evidence in order to bring the offenders to justice. After an absence of some 53 days Day reported that he had captured eleven of the twelve persons known to have taken part in the massacre, that these eleven had all arrived in the colony as convicts and that the free man, John Fleming, a native of the colony, had escaped. The squatter's son lived on; the eleven members of the convict community faced the possibility of death. The Attorney-General formally charged the eleven on four counts with the murder of an Aboriginal black named 'Daddy', and on five counts for the murder of an Aboriginal black name unknown. The landholders and stockmen of New South Wales were incensed. Up on Patrick's Plains they formed a Black Association to raise money to buy the best legal brains for the defence of the white men.

The trial opened on 15 November before the Chief Justice, James Dowling, and a jury of twelve. George Anderson, the assigned servant hut-keeper for Mr Dangar at Myall Creek, told the court what had happened on that day in June when the twelve white men roped the Aborigines together. He told the court that the blacks cried for assistance, that there were children who could not walk, and that Daddy and another old man named Joey were crying. He told how he had heard two shots, how later Edward Foley, son of one of the accused, showed him a sword which was covered with blood, and how on the day after the slaughter three of them took fire-sticks out of the hut. After hearing other evidence, the Chief

Justice solemnly told the jury it was quite clear that a most grievous offence had been committed; their duty was to decide whether the accused were the men who had committed that offence. He charged them to remember in their deliberations that in the eye of the law the life of a black man was as precious and valuable as that of the highest noble in the land. The gentlemen of the jury took twenty minutes to decide the accused were not guilty. The spectators in the court cheered. Within a week one member of the jury was telling his friends, 'I look on the blacks as a set of monkeys, and I think the earlier they are exterminated the better. I know well they are guilty of murder, but I, for one, would never consent to see a white man suffer for shooting a black one!'. The *Sydney Herald* raved on about the prevalence of cannibals in the land, and sets of monkeys, while the *Australian* and the *Colonist* urged their readers to take a more magnanimous stand.

Plunkett asked for the prisoners to be remanded so that they could be charged with murdering the women and children. He decided to lay the information of murdering an Aboriginal child named Charley against seven of the prisoners (Kilmaister, Hawkins, Johnston, Foley, Oates, Parry and Russell) and give the other four (Palliser, Lamb, Toulouse and Blake) an opportunity to give evidence on behalf of the seven accused should they wish to do so. On 29 November, with the *Sydney Herald* spluttering angrily that the court should not allow white men to be put in peril of their lives for every jaw-bone, thigh-bone, finger or toe the scouts of the Attorney-General might ferret out, the seven men were tried before Judge Burton and a jury of twelve. The trial lasted till 2 a.m. the following morning when the prisoners were found guilty of murdering the child. On 5 December, Judge Burton sentenced seven frightened men to death.

On 7 December the Executive Council unanimously agreed that the sentence of the law should take effect. The *Sydney Herald* went on vilifying the Aborigines as that most degenerate, despicable and brutal race of beings who stood to shame the whole human race. On the morning of 18 December the four Anglicans were escorted by their two chaplains and the three Catholics by their chaplain to the scaffold, where that unfortunate hot-hearted man Kilmaister seemed deeply dejected. All shook hands with the gaoler and kissed each other, resigned themselves and 'were speedily launched into eternity'.

The terror of black against white, and white against black, redoubled in fury. Some said Gipps and Plunkett had planted in the minds of Aborigines the idea that in their deeds of retaliation they were acting with the sanction of public authorities. Down at Portland Bay a black man caught red-handed carving up a bullock saucily told a white man, 'If you touch me, the Gubbna will hang you'. The execution of seven white men only served to make the blacks so outrageous that great numbers of them fell victims in 1839 to the vindictive spirit kindled in the hearts of white men. As the wilder blacks were incited into more and more deeds of violence to the property of settlers, shepherds, hut-keepers and stockmen shot them with no more compunction than they shot a dog. The more ruffianly and ferocious among the whites got rid of troublesome Aborigines by poison. Again the settlers raised their old cry: give us protection or there will be a bloody war of extermination; send men with guns, because that is the only way to bring the Aborigines into submission. The missionaries redoubled their efforts to win these 'mischievously bent . . . sable creatures' for Christ and civilization, but nothing they could do could efface from the mind of the Aborigine the simple fact that the white man had deprived him of his land. Why should he adopt the religion or the way of life of a people who had done him such evil?

Inch by inch the Aborigines were losing their country. What once was theirs was now called Crown land. The white man's government had begun to sell that land, at a fixed price, and was using the proceeds to promote a new wave of white settlers. Free immigrants, working people of 'good character' were being lured to the Australian colonies to provide labour in return for the promise that, in time, they too might become the respectable owners of land.

6

But Colonials Do Not Make
Their Own History

The problem in the transition from a convict to a free working class was to subordinate the free servant to his master without the aid of a penal code whose savage punishments were designed to enforce obedience by terror. The foundations of authority in the Old World were absent in rural society in New South Wales. In England, Scotland and Ireland the local Justice of the Peace lived in an imposing mansion; in New South Wales he often lived in a sod hut. In England, Scotland and Ireland the local Justice was distinguished by dress, speech and deportment from those to whom he dispensed justice; in New South Wales, bush life stripped away most of these external differences between man and man. In England, Scotland and Ireland the labour pool was a cornerstone in the building of hierarchy and authority; in New South Wales the labour shortage eroded the authority of the master and strengthened the power of the servant. In New South Wales convict servants, ticket-of-leave holders, and emancipists and their slave-masters had stripped away all the ideological mumbo-jumbo with which in the Old World the exploitation of man by man was softened and concealed. This left terror as the nexus between master and servant.

The problem for the master was to find a sanction over the free as effective as the lash and other punishments had been for the bond. The masters of New South Wales had been so corrupted by the power the law conferred on them to exploit the labour of convict servants that they understandably looked to the law to provide a satisfactory foundation for their authority over the free. In 1828 the Legislative Council of New South Wales imposed a maximum penalty of six months' gaol for servants absenting themselves from their employment, or refusing or neglecting to work without the consent of their employer. Despite this law, all through the 1830s the masters grumbled as much about the indiscipline of the free as about the incompetence and the degradation of the bond. While Sydney mechanics called for three groans for Hannibal Macarthur, the avowed enemy of the working classes, and sections of the press deplored the landed classes of New South Wales using the government for the oppression of their servants, the Council passed on 20 October 1840 an Act to ensure the fulfilment of engagements and to provide for the adjustment of disputes between masters and servants in New South Wales and its dependencies. This was on the very day that Sir George Gipps solemnly told the members of Council a momentous piece of news. Transportation to New South Wales was to end.

While the landowners of New South Wales had been debating whether or not convicts were an efficient form of labour, the decision-makers in London had been asking whether transportation was an effective means of punishment and reform, and whether assignment amounted to a form of slavery. In 1837–38 a committee of the House of Commons, chaired by Sir William Molesworth, heard many hours of evidence from colonists and others, and came to the conclusion that assignment should be discontinued. Thus it had fallen to Gipps to announce that the assignment of male convicts in Sydney and other towns of the colony would cease on 1 January 1839. A year later Gipps was announcing the end of transportation to the eastern mainland, though convicts would still be sent to Van Diemen's Land.

The leaders of the Patriotic Association attempted to have these decisions reversed. As early as February 1839 they summoned a public meeting at which Wentworth, Jamison and Bland had no difficulty in persuading those present to accept the view which prevailed within the Legislative Council, namely, that the material and moral well-being of New South Wales depended on the continuance of transportation. But the Patriots and their supporters had the air of men who were no longer moving with the river of life. A great change that was taking place in eastern Australia. The use of convict labour to exploit the material resources and to plant the rudiments of civilization over a vast area was coming to an end. Another invasion of the ancient, barbaric land was beginning—the invasion of British migrants who, like their counterparts in South Australia and Port Phillip, were strangers to all those loves and longings, and hatreds and resentments seething away in the hearts of native-born Australians.

For a season people carried on unaware of the change. The members of 'high' society, the government officers and their wives, the members of the 'ancient nobility' of New South Wales, and the colonial landed gentry continued not to know merchants;

merchants with 'stores' continued not to know merchants who kept 'shops', and shopkeepers had their own idea of the distances to be observed between drapers and haberdashers, butchers and pastry-cooks; citizens who drove in carriages did not choose to mingle with tradespeople who only had gigs. In fashionable circles etiquette was studied more closely than in London itself. Cards were ceremoniously left by ladies and gentlemen who made 'calls'. If a lady made a 'call' she must not repeat it until it had been returned on pain of being voted ignorant of due form. The whole convict community—those in servitude, those set free from servitude, their wives, their children, and their children's children—continued to be poisoned by a silent, deep-rooted hostility to the free settlers and the 'bloody immigrants'.

It was difficult to imagine a New South Wales in which squatter-dom and convictism were not long-term features. The 'Cabbage Tree Boys' greeted immigrant women with coarse jokes and lewd gestures as they clambered down the rope-ladder from their ships. The 'larkers' bumped deliberately into men and women of some distinction in dress and deportment and mocked them with the words 'all round my hat'. Convictism had bred a race of levellers, who were only happy when they were laughing cruelly at the misfortunes of others or getting a rise out of the pretentious, and sneering at all the mighty men of renown. Convictism had also bred a race of men who were indifferent to the great creations of the human spirit. In Sydney the vaudeville theatres were crowded each week-night, but when Conrad Knowles, a native-born Australian, celebrated his return from London in 1839 by putting on a performance of *Hamlet*, the attendance was so beggarly on the second night that Knowles had to take it off and give the locals the melodrama they craved as a mirror of the wild unbridled passions they took to be part of the fate of being a man in Australia.

Changes in the material setting had already prepared the way for a new life. Mr Bourke in Sussex Street, Sydney, manufactured a steam-engine by copying an American model. In January 1839 two shops were brilliantly lit by gaslight, a promise that the time was not far distant when the streets of Sydney, like London, Paris, New York and Vienna, were lit up by gaslight. That May, gaslight was also installed in the Independent Chapel in Sydney; a colonial wit added that preparations were happily in hand for Dr Lang's Scots Church to be similarly enlightened. In June, steam communication was established between Sydney, Melbourne, Launceston, Hobart and Adelaide. Some prophesied that the time was not far off when steamships would connect Swan River with the rest of Australia, and Australia with the ports of the United Kingdom.

The one-time prison settlement was changing rapidly. The quantity of wool exported increased sevenfold between 1831 and 1840, earning a total of £566 112 in 1840. Between 1836 and 1841 the population increased from 77 096 to 130 856. There was an even more radical change in the composition of the population. In 1821 there was one convict to every free person in the colony. When the indeterminate numbers of ex-convicts, their families and their descendants were added to the numbers of the bond, they comprised over 80 per cent of the population of New South Wales. By 1841 it was being said that with the end of transportation to New South Wales, the swelling numbers of free immigrants and the high birth-rate in immigrant families, the bond and their descendants would soon become an insignificant proportion of the population of New South Wales.

The immigrants brought with them new ideas and hopes of a better life in the New World. Among them was a young man named Henry Parkes. Early in 1839 this man with a Dionysian frenzy in his heart boarded the *Strathfieldsaye* with his wife Clarinda, the two of them hoping to find prosperity in a strange land. Their first year was spent living roughly in the country, but by 1841 Henry's heart was filled with confidence. He had found steady work in Sydney and was reading widely. In Australia he found purpose: he predicted that he and his fellow exiles would liberate Australia from the convicts' clanking chains and allow freedom's voice to be heard across her ransomed plains.

To the alarm of some Protestants, the proportion of Catholics in the colony was increasing. By 1841 they comprised 27.72 per cent of the population. In April the Reverend J. D. Lang warned Protestants that their future civilization was in danger of being transformed into a 'Province of Popedom'. The *Sydney Herald* warned that if they became a majority they might even destroy the institutions of the free and establish arbitrary power and a priest-ridden society. The Anglican bishop of Australia, William Grant Broughton, and his fellow members of the Immigration Committee of 1841 felt the same way. They wanted their new country to be a place where the English race would spread from sea to sea without being tainted by mixing with the people of a lower race or caste.

In 1842, as immigrants continued to arrive in search of a land of plenty, the press was warning that monetary and commercial affairs were in such a depressed state that even the richest merchants were beginning to tremble. In the first half of the year, several Melbourne businesses closed their doors. The bourgeoisie of Melbourne felt increasingly powerless to take control of their own affairs, and they increased their agitation for separation from

Sydney. Sydney Town itself was beginning to look as dull and disconsolate as an Irish clergyman on a tithing day. Insolvency petitions were becoming more and more frequent. In February 1842 the brewer J. Wright and the gentleman J. Roberts filed their petitions in bankruptcy court. There were rumours of a catastrophic decline in British investment, and prophecies of dire consequences such as more insolvencies, the end of land sales, the end of immigration, and increases in unemployment. The commercial state of Sydney was so gloomy that some said there was scarcely a mercantile house in Sydney which was not now undermined by threat of bankruptcy. Despite widespread unemployment both in town and country, employers still wanted to inundate the colony with workers because, accustomed to having the convict's toil for nothing, they could not bring themselves to pay for a free man.

As men and women in all stations of life speculated about the future of the colonies, the 'sheep-walk for ever' men were quite determined that the institutions of the free should never come under the control of Chartists, radicals and levellers. As the debate over the future constitution of New South Wales became more pressing, the men of property elected a constitution drafting committee composed of patriarchal men such as James Macarthur, large landowners such as Henry O'Brien of Yass, 'Old Iron Bark' Lawson of Blue Mountains fame, Dr Nicholson, T. Icely and J. R. Holden, those two spokesmen for the Patriotic Association, W. C. Wentworth and Dr Bland, and William àBeckett. This group, composed of exclusivists and emancipists, anti-transportationists and pro-transportationists, survivors from and inheritors of old family feuds, united in their determination not to allow the lower middle-class men of Sydney to use the institutions of the free either to destroy the sheep-walk of New South Wales or to create a Yankee-style democratic, egalitarian republic.

Macarthur and Wentworth persuaded their fellow members that no such thing as a universal franchise could exist in their society, because like all other proposals to level out differences in society it would produce not equality but inequality. Whenever the principle of property came into collision with the equality principle the former must prevail. Wentworth told them he was now a firm believer in a Legislative Council that was part nominated and part elected on a high property qualification. The man who had written in his youth of an elected assembly as the birthright of the creators of a new Britannia became an advocate for Colonial Office ideas on the institutions of New South Wales. The *Australian* —the paper Wentworth himself had co-founded—denounced this headlong descent from the sublime heights of patriotism to the woeful depths of Whiggism. Wentworth's day, they said, had ended. The man who had first taught the native-born what liberty was had betrayed them and lost their confidence.

While the flock-masters of the country districts were applauding the Macarthur–Wentworth scheme for confining political power to the men of landed property, crowds lined the shores of Sydney Harbour in July 1842 to watch the arrival of the adventurer and cloud-topper Ben Boyd on the yacht *Wanderer*. A banker and large investor, he had a financial interest in the future of the steamship, and dreamt of building a kingdom for himself in New South Wales by exploiting cheap convict labour. But the days of the 'half a million acres' men were numbered, cheap convict labour was no longer available in New South Wales, and society was in the grip of a commercial depression in which prices for wool, sheep and, cattle were falling every day. Besides, the bourgeoisie of Sydney, shop-keepers, tradesmen and mechanics saw the steamship and not the plantation planter as the symbol of the future of their society.

On 20 July the bourgeoisie of Sydney Town had their first sniff of future power. At long last the Legislative Council had passed an Act to declare the town of Sydney to be a city and to incorporate the inhabitants thereof. The Act conferred the right to vote on every male person of the full age of 21 years who for one year had occupied a house, warehouse, countinghouse or ship of the annual value of £25.

As election day approached the conservatives openly feared that the men of good sense and reputability were about to be over-mastered by the illiterate and the vulgar. Thousands of pounds were spent by candidates in the distribution of drink. At one polling booth an infuriated drunken mob drove a police magistrate who was endeavouring to preserve order into an enclosure surrounded with high palings and pelted him with bricks, stones and large pieces of paling. After polling day on 1 November, the Tories and Whigs of Sydney took fright at the number of emancipists, carcass butchers, tanners, wine and spirit merchants, builders, publicans and bankers who were to wear the rich robes of office in the corporation of Sydney. Because of the low property franchise ex-convicts and Chartists and levellers such as Edward Flood and Henry Macdermott were among the first councillors. There was worse to come. On 9 November the councillors elected John Hosking, an Australian by birth and a merchant by profession, to be the first mayor of the city of Sydney. Hosking was the son of a Wesleyan missionary. After his rise to wealth, he had joined the Church of England and taken up a run among the gentry on the Limestone Plains. But marriage with Martha Foxlowe Terry, the daughter of Samuel Terry, the wealthiest ex-convict in Sydney, barred his entry into the drawing rooms of the country gentry.

On the evening of 10 November 1842 Hosking entered the diningroom of the Royal Hotel in Sydney wearing a purple gown edged with ermine while the band played 'Oh the Roast Beef of Old England' and then a special number for his wife, the Robert Burns song 'John Anderson My Joe'. To words expressing the democratic and egalitarian sentiments sweeping the cities of the civilized world, the daughter of a convict took her bow as the first lady of the city of Sydney. Once again the sentimental attachment to Britain lived side by side in their hearts with the hope of creating in the New World a society free from the blemishes of the Old. Radicals who were disappointed in Hosking for copying the dress which promoted rank in society accused him of starting a new aristocracy which would forge fetters for their children to wear.

In the following month the property-owners of Melbourne took part in the election of their first municipal council. The campaigns were no less rowdy than they had been in Sydney, and the class of person elected to office was equally distressing to gentlemen of quality. The highly cultivated La Trobe was so shocked to have no 'infusion of people of the higher order' as councillors that he believed the auguries for popular government were unfavourable.

The triumph of grocerdom in the corporation of Sydney caused the conservatives to look to London for a possible saviour. Edward Stanley, the eldest son of the thirteenth Earl of Derby, seemed the answer of Divine Providence to the conservatives' prayer. He had whiled away those early days in his career lolling in the House of Commons, but by 1842 he had left behind the giddy days of his youth and faced up to the central question for his class—how to preserve their privileges and their power against the flood of industrial civilization and egalitarianism. When reports reached London in the middle of 1842 that the colony of New South Wales was threatened with a deluge of levellers, Chartists, Jacobins and emancipists, Stanley was quick to see that the heart of the problem was the absence in the colony of a class similar to the landed grandees of the Mother Country who could keep afloat the ark of liberty, order and hierarchy.

The problem was to devise political institutions to ward off the days of 'wreck and desolation'. Ever since April 1838 James Macarthur had been urging the Colonial Office to create for New South Wales a Legislative Council composed in part of nominated members who would be as strong as those oaks of Old England, the landed aristocracy, which no revolutionary wind had uprooted, and in part of elected members, it being understood that the qualification for voting would be a high property qualification. How could this be done in New South Wales where the men who owned the sheep and cattle were grazing their beasts on land in which they had no security of tenure? The very precariousness of their rights to the land had put into their mouths the slogans of would-be revolutionaries rather than supporters of conservatism.

By 1842 Stanley and his advisers had had the advantage of studying the ideas of Alexis de Tocqueville, whose *De la Démocratie en Amérique* had been recently published. Tocqueville had suggested that man needed a new political science for a new world. As he saw it the gradual development of equality of conditions was the principal characteristic of his age. It was not wise to believe that such a movement could be stopped. It was not wise to believe that, having destroyed feudalism, democracy would recoil before the bourgeoisie. He had written his volumes under a sort of religious terror produced in him by the sight of this irresistible revolution striding over the centuries and knocking down all obstacles in its way. The future belonged to this equality. The question was, was it possible to instruct this democracy, to revive its beliefs, purify its customs, and control its movements, and gradually to replace inexperience and its blind instincts with the knowledge of affairs, and the knowledge of its true interests? For that, man must find a means of preserving liberty in a world in which the overwhelming majority had a depraved taste for equality, and a willingness to place themselves under the tyranny of the majority, or some plebiscitary dictator, provided they themselves could gratify their own passions for material well-being. The remedies Tocqueville prescribed were: indirect election to increase the number of conservatives in the central house of assembly; local government to give men practice in and induce a taste for participation in public life; a federal constitution, because it combined the advantages of a powerful central government with protection of liberty by the division of legislative and executive powers, and the rights of property by in-built constitutional checks on radicalism; religious education so that citizens might know what was 'good and just'.

In the Colonial Office there were men who quickly became converts to the Tocqueville view. When the news reached London that Sydney radicals such as Edward Flood and Henry Macdermott had spoken of the rights of man at a public meeting, and that Chartists such as Henry Parkes were already in the wings waiting for the call to testify to the day when all men would live in dignity, Stanley steered through the British Parliament an Act for the Government of New South Wales and Van Diemen's Land which combined the ideas of the Macarthurs and the teachings of de Tocqueville. The Legislative Council was to consist of 36 members, 24 of whom were to be elected and 12 nominated. It enacted that the District of Port Phillip was to elect 5 members, the town of Melbourne one, and the town of Sydney two. So the two towns which contained 27 per cent of the population were to elect three members, and the country districts twenty-one. The right to vote was given to all persons who possessed lands and tenements of the clear annual value of £200, or a householder occupying a dwelling house of the clear annual value of £20 at least. No man could be elected a member of the Legislative Council unless he possessed an estate of freehold of the yearly value of £100 or of the value of £2000, above all charges and incumbrances affecting the same. By omission the holders of licences to depasture stock outside the boundaries were ineligible to vote or stand for election. Members were to be elected for a period of five years. The Governor was empowered to assent, withhold assent, or reserve bills for the signification of Her Majesty's pleasure.

This looked like a sharing of power between the property-holders of New South Wales—both landed and mercantile—and the Imperial Parliament, which had delegated part of its sovereignty, but not surrendered any of it. It looked like a constitution which the 'son of Britain' men and the 'birthright of Englishmen' supporters could applaud, as well as all those who looked for the victory of conservatism in the politics of New South Wales. These groups at first welcomed the Act, while the radicals, Chartists and levellers called it a 'mockery of self-government' and a mockery of all those who were looking to 'a considerable extension of popular rights'.

But the opposing sides were agreed in their opposition when the government announced that a new minimum price for Crown land had been set at 20s an acre. News of so high a price was enough to spread panic around Sydney and the country districts, for if it meant anything, some said, it meant that no land whatsoever would be sold, and hence there would be no money to pay for the passages of immigrants. Immigration would cease and the sheep-walks of New South Wales would relapse to the natural state of lands wandered over by kangaroos, possums and Aborigines. In any case, only half the revenue raised by land sales was to be spent on immigration. Why, people were asking, should such matters be determined in London? Bourgeois, gentry, squatter and working man, Tory, Whig, liberal, radical and Chartist, the Protestant and the Catholic joined hands to demand self-government for New South Wales.

The tide was turning, but the renewed surge for change had not yet reached the island of Van Diemen's Land. In the settled districts of the Derwent River, in the Midlands around Campbelltown and in the northern districts around Longford, bounteous countryside provided the grasses and the soil for a concentration of settlement, and a community of farmers in a countryside not unlike the country districts around Cork in Ireland or Dorchester in England. Outwardly things seemed propitious. Observers described the agricultural countryside as 'smiling', and added that the faces of those living in the country were both 'smiling' and 'prosperous'. The convict servants were 'well fed' and 'well dressed'. The gardens in the town houses were filled with geraniums in bloom and sweet English flowers; the children looked happy and healthy, stout and rosy like children in the English countryside.

Under Arthur's successor, that good and tragic man Sir John Franklin, the voices against the continuation of transportation were as few as ever. The large number of convicts and their descendants in Van Diemen's Land were simply angered by those who argued that convicts were a contamination of decent society. At the same time, settlers and large employers were reluctant to dispense with convict labour or with the £500 000 the British Government spent each year in the colony on convict administration. This expenditure, they said, flowed like a luxuriant current through the colony, enriching and irrigating it. The whole of society was tied to the convict system—the senior government officers, the military officers, the chaplains, the schoolteachers and the employers of labour. But the surge of opinion in Whitehall was running against them. The liberal consensus in London was that the assignment of convicts was a form of slavery. It was that time in the history of a society when the swan's down feather stood upon the swell at full tide and was neither way inclined.

7

Self-Government

As the 1840s drew to a close, the Australian colonies, especially those founded as prison colonies, were changing, and the need to reform the institutions of law and government was being widely discussed. There was still no agreement on what form the new constitutional arrangements should take. The squatters remained passionate in their opposition to talk of popularly elected governments. As they saw it, what the colonies needed was not government controlled by the democratic ruck but a government which was able to remedy the shortage of cheap, compliant labour. Some enterprising squatters managed to secure 'coolie' labour from China and India. Ben Boyd sent his own ship to Polynesia to recruit islanders to work on his run near Deniliquin. Most of all, the squatters wanted a resumption of transported labour, but the mass of opinion in the colonies, and within the new liberal government of Lord John Russell in England, was opposed to any resumption of transportation and preferred to encourage free immigrants.

There was no doubt that migration was the answer to the evils of both the Old World and the New. In the Old World it would help to cure pauperism, and provide an invaluable market for British manufactures, and a happy British alternative to radicalism, Chartism, socialism and all the other 'isms' that threatened the very foundations of society. In the New World it would alleviate the chronic shortage of labour and provide a 'moral and industrious' working class as a substitute for the 'convict polluters'. In all the Australian colonies except Van Diemen's Land, labour was in intense demand, wages were high, and there was comfort, abundance and happiness for the workers.

Between 1841 and 1846, a pious Englishwoman in her thirties named Caroline Chisholm won herself a saintly reputation for her labours among the newly-arrived immigrants. She led parties on excursions into the bush to find work for them on outlying properties. She provided sanctuary for young unmarried women and found them respectable spouses. Hundreds of bachelors made applications to her for wives. By 1846 hundreds of men were writing letters of gratitude to her for 'suiting' them. That year she returned to England where she continued to work as an advocate of immigration, as a proclaimer of the virtues of kindness, sobriety and prayer, and a champion of the role of women as 'God's police'.

In the 1840s North America was a far more popular destination for British migrants than Australia, not least because it was closer and fares were cheaper. Neither the introduction of free immigration, nor the enforcement of moral standards and improved conditions on the ships made any difference. In 1850, nearly 30 000 migrated to British North America, just over 223 000 to the United States and just over 16 000 to the Australian colonies and new Zealand. But in England a new mythology about Australia was beginning to take hold, a mythology about the place which would become known in time as 'the workingman's paradise'. In the eyes of the recent migrants the Australian colonies were places where no person was starving, where the dogs destroyed each year more beef and bread than all the poor in Ireland could eat and where the poor man could eat beef and mutton just like a rich man.

Letters took back to the United Kingdom words of gratitude from men and women who saw themselves as having said farewell to want, crime and sorrow, and having found the secret of human happiness in a bellyful. 'Dear mother and father I ham very happy and comfortable, and should be more so if you was all with use', wrote one migrant, 'I never was happy before I came in this beautifule country as I ham now.' Migrants also liked the chance of rising out of the working classes. 'Come, men, women, and children, for you can do well here', wrote another migrant, 'I am getting good wages . . . plenty here to eat and drink, and plenty of money. Next year I do intend, if please God spare my life, to go on my own hands.'

The migrants arrived in a country where there were now four principal groups inhabiting the bush. The first were the Aborigines, whose suffering continued under the care of well-intentioned missionaries and at the hands of murderous thugs. Second were the country gentry who had built up comfortable and productive properties in the more closely settled areas of southern and south-eastern Australia. The third were the bush barbarians who continued to live in squalor and degradation beyond the limits of location. The fourth were the squatters who presided in grandeur over vast tracts of land for which they paid minimal rent, jealous of their privileges and ever fearful that a change of policy in London would see their rent increased, their land sold, their domination of the legislature undermined or their access to cheap labour further eroded.

In 1843 the first elections were held for seats in the New South Wales Legislative Council under a system which ensured the squatters would continue their domination of the legislature: a property qualification had to be met by voters and candidates, and the country electorates far outnumbered the city ones. Just over 47 000 townsmen were represented by six members, while 66 500 countrymen were represented by eighteen. In Parliament, at least, the squatters were secure.

In the early 1840s a severe depression threatened livelihoods in all the colonies except South Australia and many squatters resorted to slaughtering their sheep and boiling them down for tallow. But their faith in the future of Australia as a sheep-walk remained unshaken. In New South Wales, squatters were enthusiastic about a scheme to introduce steam communication from Port Essington in the north-western corner of the continent to carry produce to London via India. Attempts to open up an inland route from New South Wales to the north western coast continued—and with it came continued speculation about what lay at the heart of the continent. Some said any exploring party in search of such a route would confirm John Oxley's prophecy that the interior was impassable. Others prophesied that they would find an inland river emptying into a inland sea which would be used to convert that vast and mournful wilderness into a smiling seat of industry.

In 1843 Charles Sturt volunteered to roll back those 'mists of uncertainty'. His final foray into the inland was to shatter his stubborn faith that Providence had marked him out to discover Australia's 'mediterranean'. When he rose to his feet to address a dinner in his honour held in Adelaide on 20 February 1846 after his return, he broke down and wept at the memory of the 'fearful desert' which he had endured and where one of his companions had lost his life.

In 1848 the inland claimed another explorer. Ludwig Leichhardt was a man who had begun a mystical communion with the Australian bush four years earlier when he had led an expedition, again financed by squatters, from Moreton Bay to Port Essington. In April 1848 he set out from Cogoon with seven others to cross to the west coast of the continent. As ever, he was full of hope that his Mighty Protector would bring his darling scheme to a successful termination. The party was never heard of again. No one was to know whether Leichhardt welcomed the 'great doom's image' with dignity or with terror. No one was to know whether he and his party were slaughtered by Aborigines, died of thirst, were swept away by floods, sank into quicksand or butchered each other. He was to live on in the poetry and prose of those who were aware that in 1848 somewhere on that vast continent there was a great going of a mighty spirit.

If the colonists could not finally measure or rule the ancient continent in which they found themselves, how much more difficult it was for the men in London to govern the colonies and make sensible laws for the management and disposal of their lands. The campaigns for self-government went on, not least because the colonists wanted to manage land policy for themselves. The issue of transportation remained bitter and unresolved. When transportation to New South Wales was abolished in 1840, Lord Russell had planned to reduce the numbers transported to Van Diemen's Land, but a change of government in England upset these plans. Van Diemen's Land was swamped with convicts. At the same time assignment was abolished, with no adequate plans being made for the government to house or employ the increased number of prisoners. The convicts were now a burden on the economy of the little island, and the tide of opinion in Van Diemen's Land, among all classes, turned against transportation.

Wentworth led the squatters in their invitation to the British Government to renew transportation to New South Wales, but a brief resumption in 1849 provoked large and militant demonstrations on Circular Quay and in Port Phillip. In London, Grey was not convinced by the opposition. FitzRoy had assured him that the anti-transportationists were a disloyal rabble. Real public opinion, as Grey put it, using one of his favourite elitist phrases, was not always gathered from the clamour and the newspaper press. But the opposition forces in New South Wales were now irresistible and there was a real threat of social disorder if the government did not pay heed. On 1 October 1850 the Legislative Council of New South Wales called on the British Government to end transportation once and for all. Wentworth left the chamber without saying a word, convinced that the world he dreamed of was about to be inundated by the levelling flood of bourgeois civilization.

At the same time, the colonists of Western Australia had found that their plans for a paradise of the gentry had stalled for lack of labour and arable land. They petitioned the British Government to send them convicts at exactly the moment the opposition in the east was becoming irresistible. Between 1850 and 1869 the colony received 10 000 convicts. Their labour helped rescue the colony from its torpor, but here, as in the east, it was to be the discovery of gold which would finally propel it into prosperity.

On 3 October, just two days after the Legislative Council of New South Wales had settled the great and important question of transportation, there was glorious news to gladden the heart of every friend of British freedom and the British connection. Under the Australian Colonies Government Act of 1850 the elective franchise had been granted to the £10 householder. The aristocratic legislator Parliament had realized in the nick of time that the only safeguard against 'democratic' turbulence and 'red republicanism' was to be found in the admission of the populous masses to a fair and well-regulated share in making the laws. Once again a 'prolific source' of revolution had been dried up by the English genius for compromise, or the policy of the embrace of moderates and the isolation of revolutionaries by the established order.

Grey explained to FitzRoy that Her Majesty's Government had had no other object in view but that of establishing in the Australian colonies a system of government founded on those British principles of well-regulated freedom under which the British Empire had risen to so high a pitch of greatness and power. Under this Act the District of Port Phillip should be separated from the New South Wales and erected into separate colony, to be known as the 'Colony of Victoria'. Part-elected, part-nominated legislative councils were to be established in Victoria, South Australia and Van Diemen's Land. A legislative council might be established in Western Australia as soon as they were able to sustain the expense of their own civil government by means of local revenue. Throughout the colonies there was celebration and delight. The opponents of transportation confronted the squatters with renewed determination.

Out in the Never Never things seemed as though they would never change. The great dryness, the dearth of inland water transport and the precarious, slow means of land transport by coach over the few made roads, on horseback, or by bullock-dray forcing its way through mud and dust over trackless wastes and miles of solitude, had imposed a never-changing pattern of life. At distances of 40 to 60 miles from each other, small numbers of people clustered in towns: in Gundagai there were 234 men and 163 women in 1851, in Albury 263 men and 179 women, in Yass 370 men and 283 women, in Ipswich 530 men and 402 women, and in Braidwood 116 men and 96 women. Not even Christmas brought relief from the monotony of these dull country towns. In the hilarious season the only relief men found from the heat, the flies and drudgery was in the local temples dedicated to Bacchus. People in towns like Mudgee, Bathurst or Albury had to wait at least fourteen days for a reply to any correspondence they might have about the things that matter in life—love, money or physic.

In those towns the convicts had practically disappeared. Ipswich had thirty convicts, Gundagai one and Braidwood two. Each town had its own flour mill, its school, its courthouse and gaol and its churches. For by mid-century in the Australian bush two buildings in a tiny hamlet testified to the memory of that day over 300 years earlier when the single monk led astray by private judgement had set himself against a body which had been held as the repository of absolute truth for a thousand years and more. The very names in common usage symbolized the way of life. Albury was known as 'Sleepy Hollow'; Gundagai was known as the town of 'Lazy Harrys'. In these country towns those weighed down by the curse of earning their living with the labour of their hands amused themselves on holidays with games such as climbing the greasy pole, horse-racing and chasing the pig.

Already there were signs that a great change was coming. In March 1850 Sir Charles FitzRoy made a flying visit to an iron foundry at Mittagong. At Berrima and other centres people were talking about how they would be able to market their goods once a railway was built. On 3 July 10 000 people gathered at Redfern in Sydney to watch Mrs Keith Stewart, the daughter of Sir Charles FitzRoy, cut the first turf for that first railway in Australia with a spade manufactured from materials indigenous to Australia. Charles Cowper, the chairman of the Sydney Railway Company, spoke briefly on the influence of the railway on the social and moral advancement of the colony. The English ensign was hoisted at the spot where the turf was turned. After the ceremony John Lamb, one of the few merchants in Sydney's Squatting Club, the Legislative Council of New South Wales, proposed the loyal toast to the Queen, and spoke of the effect the electric telegraph would soon have on isolation and distance. Cowper spoke again some affectionate words about Prince Albert and how, if he had his way, a railway would girdle the earth. Sir Charles FitzRoy cheered them by pre- dicting that the railway would be especially beneficial to a country that was wholly destitute of internal water communication and in which a scattered population prevented the formation of good roads. Over first-rate viands and wines, those present were given a vision of an Australia in which bush barbarism, material backward- ness, isolation, alienation and solitude would gradually disappear.

In August 1852 the first steamship arrived in Sydney from England. On 12 September 1854 the electric telegraph was first used in Sydney. Between 1851 and 1861 the number of white men increased from 437 665 to 1 168 149. As British philistinism and industrial civilization began to leave their mark on the ancient barbaric land, another voice was added to the immemorial cry of the crow and the melancholy chant of the Aborigine. After 1788 the men in black taught that the hearts of men were filled with evil, and that madness was in their hearts while they lived. The bush barbarians added their sardonic comment that Australians were certain to be down on their luck. But as industrial civilization provided the machines with which to subdue the mighty bush, some Australians began to dream a great dream: that they could banish the Old World errors and wrongs and lies, that heaven and hell were priests' inventions and that they could build a paradise in the land that belonged to them.

Edward Hargraves left Guyong near Bathurst on 12 February 1851 with a companion and moved down the course of the Lewes Pond Creek searching for gold. He scratched the gravel, filled a pan with the earth, and washed the dirt away till he saw that speck he was looking for. 'There it is!' he exclaimed. 'This is a memorable day in the history of New South Wales. I shall be a baronet, you will be knighted, and my old horse will be stuffed, and put into a glass-case, and sent to the British Museum.' That did not happen to Hargraves, or his man, or his horse, for they were not destined to gain prizes in the great lottery of life. But something was about to happen to the land about which men of renown in China, India, Indonesia, Catholic Christendom, Protestant England, and Europe of the Enlightenment had dreamed their own great dreams. An iron rail was about to tether the mighty bush to the world of British industrial civilization.

BOOK FOUR

The Earth Abideth For Ever
1851–1888

In many respects it is an age of ruins.

Cardinal Moran, 18 September 1890

Creed and Caste are Hell's inventions
Trust the brotherhood of man.

'Prometheus' in *Bulletin*, 8 November 1890

1

The Possessed

At dawn on 6 February 1851 in the district of Port Phillip the sky threatened a day of great heat. By ten in the morning at Kilmore, 36 miles north of Melbourne, a hot north wind blew clouds of suffocating dust over the town, leaving the sun a bluish red above the swirling particles. By noon grass fires, started in the stubble, dry as tinder after the long hot summer, sent tongues of flame and red-hot balls of burning grass floating over the town. Down at Portland, where the thermometer registered 112°F by noon, particles of fire whirled down the streets and over the tops of the houses. The stench of burning goats, sheep and cattle wafted into the town, as men and women and children trembled in the streets. In the Cape Otway ranges flames of fire fanned by a savage wind roared and crackled in the gum trees. A total darkness overspread the whole of Gippsland, changing day into night. One man said that in unsaddling his horse he could not see it though he was standing right next to it. The Aborigines wagged their heads sagely and declared 'bright fellow [i.e. the sun] had got the blight in his eye'. In Melbourne, where the thermometer rose to 117°F by noon, palls of smoke swirled over the roof-tops, and ashes were blown all over the streets. The brassy yellow of the summer sun changed to a fiery red, rimmed by a menacing purple, as news of destruction, devastation and ruin in the countryside spread terror among the people. In the evening the cool breeze from 'the sweet south' blew away the heat, the smells and the dust. A gentle rain relieved the parched earth.

For days afterwards people read stories in the Melbourne news-papers of the toll of destruction. In the bush round the Dandenongs only one house remained standing; around Western Port many hard-working settlers had been brought to the verge of ruin; on the Plenty at least 100 families were homeless; in the Barrabool Hills houses, barns and stables were smouldering in ruins; over the plains of Australia Felix huge mobs of horses had galloped away from the fire. From that day the people of Melbourne knew the sixth day of February 1851 as 'Black Thursday'.

On the same day strange goings-on in the sky frightened the people on the north coast of Van Diemen's Land. Huge black clouds rolling over the Strait darkened the sky: the sun turned to a blood-red mass; birds squawked, dogs howled; men and women whispered to each other; hysterical men asked whether the end of the world was at hand, hysterical women went down on their knees to implore God to save them.

Nature in Australia was so powerful that it often set aside all man's attempts to assert his supremacy over the earth. Sixty-three years' experience of planting a European civilization in an uncouth land had imprinted in the minds of the white men a sense of their impotence and insignificance. A harsh environment had fashioned animals like the kangaroo, which had the appearance of being left unfinished by the creator. In Australia nature, not man, was the 'Lord of Creation'. The land itself seemed the victim of some primeval calamity, bearing on its surface the marks of being cursed by a malevolent being. The savageries of the convict past and the abominations of the bush barbarians seemed to be the behaviour appropriate to such an inhospitable soil.

In the Old World the flag of progress was flaming in the van. When half a million people gathered in London on 1 May 1851 to hear Queen Victoria open the Great Exhibition, William Makepeace Thackeray found the sound of the machines a 'wondrous song'. Charles Dickens told his readers that Chinese civilization had come to a full stop; by contrast, thanks to the machine, British society was on the march forward to material well-being, happiness and the brotherhood of man.

In Australia one man was confident that his adopted country was about to enjoy 'a great feast'. Within a week after Edward Hargraves found his gold speck, he set off for Sydney to tell the Colonial Secretary, Edward Deas Thomson, that there was gold in the colony and to ask for £500 as a compensation for his labours. They confronted each other one wet day in Sydney. Hargraves, a mountain of flesh, was the quintessence of the vulgarity, brashness and coarseness of the men of the New World. Thomson was a fine representative of that drawing-room society of Sydney, Parramatta, Cobbity, Penrith and Camden, which hoped to win the victory for elegance and refinement against the barbarians of the New World. Fearing that the world he treasured would cease to be, that shepherds would desert their flocks and farm labourers their crops, that policemen and civil servants would abandon their duties, and that society would descend into anarchy, riot and disorder, Thomson played for time. Sound civil servant that he was, he asked Hargraves to put his request in writing.

It was too late. The men of the drawing room could not dam up the levelling flood. When Hargraves got back to Bathurst in April, he heard of the discovery of another rich field by John Lister and William Tom at Yorky's Corner. Hargraves was a greedy man: he hungered not only for riches but also for fame. He wanted to be hailed as the discoverer of gold. It was the elixir of life for him to be told, 'Everyone is talking about you'. On 6 May he visited the Lewis Ponds Creek field with the Tom brothers and Lister. This time he named the place 'Ophir' after the biblical city to which Jehoshaphat sent ships for gold, for Hargraves was driven to endow everything he touched with grandeur. At a meeting two days later, he showed the gentlemen of Bathurst samples of fine gold. The *Bathurst Free Press* prophesied that the discovery would lead to a 'complete social revolution' in Australia. There would be much immediate social confusion, they said, as the temperate and sober pleasures of domestic life were sacrificed for 'the dreamy and intoxicating but illusive expectations of a golden future'. A great madness was about to begin.

On 15 May 1851 the *Sydney Morning Herald* announced the discovery of an extensive goldfield in the Wellington district of New South Wales. Immediately a great excitement unhinged the minds of all classes of the community. Crowds milled round the offices of the Bathurst mail-coach to book a seat. Within twenty-four hours 200 persons set out for the diggings, some of them on foot, with their tin pots and stocks of provisions slung across their backs. The conversation of Sydneysiders centred round the question, 'Are you going to the diggings?' or 'Have you seen the lump of gold?' or 'Have your servants run yet?' or 'Is your coachman off?' or 'Have you seen a magnificent specimen of virgin gold in the jeweller's window in George Street?'. Within a week the decline in the street population of Sydney was very visible. One coach-maker lost ten of his workmen; a tailor lost seven. An assistant to a veterinary surgeon gave his employer the option of raising his pay, or he would be off on a trip to the diggings. Employees were continually flashing the threat of bolting in the face of their employers. Gold, it was feared, was about to lift some men 'above their natural sphere'.

Rumours of similar excitement and the dissolution of social order up-country flew round the city. Shepherds, it was said, were deserting their stations and making for the diggings as fast as their legs or their horses could carry them. Sydney itself began to take on an entirely new appearance as shop fronts put on new faces. Articles for gold-digging replaced the traditional wares: blue and red serge shirts, Californian hats, leather belts, diggers' boots and huge blankets hung outside the shops; the pavements were cluttered with picks, pans and pots. One sign of the times was a street sign for 'Gold shovels' swaying in the wind outside a diggers' outfitter in George Street, and another was the appearance of the Virginia cradle, or gold-working machine, an indispensable tool for those whose appetites had been whetted by the 'unholy hunger'. Such a mania seized the whole community that in all other matters, including church matters, a state of terrible quiet descended. In Melbourne the excitement exceeded even that of Sydney, many hundred workmen of different descriptions throwing up their employments and shouting drunkenly, 'Hurrah for Australia the golden'.

By 24 May, over 1000 men had gathered on the diggings around Ophir. Tents provided shelter for some, while the only protection others enjoyed against the wind and the rain were gunyahs of boughs and bark thrown together 'after the fashion of a black fellow's camp'. Several stores had been opened and were doing a roaring trade, and some women were already doing a profitable trade at the washtub. The farmers and stationhands in the locality were also profiteering by selling mutton and flour at high prices to the diggers. The cold and the wet and the hard work converted the diggers into ravenous and roaring lions.

The capriciousness of the rewards surprised observers. Stout, willing men, with what was called 'a capital rig', slaved from dew to sunny eve, and did but moderately well. Others, equipped only with a two-pronged pitchfork and a superannuated fire-shovel, were doing a raking business. As a letter-writer put it in the *Bathurst Free Press*, one little shrimp of a fellow, an 'insignificant little varmint' with no earthly equipment but a two-forked stick, was minting money to the tune of £5 a day, while strapping fellows were earning practically nothing.

By the end of May men were working so close to each other they were as thick as mushrooms after a brisk shower. Merchants, cabmen, sailors, magistrates, convicts, amateur gentlemen, cooks, lawyers, doctors of medicine, doctors of music, an ADC from Government House and a real live lord, were all rockers of the cradle and pick-swingers. All were levelled by this common occupation: all had the same dress and all had the same appearance. There was 'a pure democracy'—a society which acknowledged no distinction between man and man. The barriers of exclusiveness which had previously kept the different classes of society apart were being broken down on the goldfield. Once broken, they would never be rebuilt in the same way.

Those who believed society should be like a regiment in the army, a community in which rank was outwardly and visibly recognized, took fright. James Macarthur, susceptible as ever to a rush of blood to the head wherever the word democracy was mentioned, thought the colony was in a perilous position, because of the 'gold-seeking excitement'. On 29 May he told Deas Thomson that he had been watching its effect upon decent men of the working classes, who thought there was no time to be lost in clutching the golden spoil and filling their pockets. He urged government, for God's sake, to do two things quickly: to forbid any further digging until surveys were made, and to enforce this by declaring martial law in the Bathurst and adjacent districts. The Reverend W. B. Clarke too, on weekdays a geologist and on Sundays a man of God, reminded the members of his congregation that gold fed the sinful lusts of the flesh and held out to giddy mortal men the promise of enjoying to the full the pomps and vanities of this wicked world.

Down in Van Diemen's Land, too, all the respectable members of society wrote and spoke of gold as a corrupter of mankind. Sir William Denison feared gold might speed up what convictism had begun, spread equality over the whole of society, and place a low estimate on everything that distinguished one man from his fellows. Gold would stick to the fingers of the merchants, shop-keepers and tavern-keepers, while those who actually did the work would be sent empty away. Over in South Australia, a province where men went down to the temple to pray on Sundays to thank their God they were not as other men, sinners, drunkards, fornicators and liars, the opinion-makers warned against the 'dangerous and maddening pursuit of gold-digging'. Gold was only 'a delusion and a snare'. The best chance for a man was to remain where he was, plough the fields of South Australia, and sell the grain he grew in the sweat of his brow to the diggers on the goldfields.

Deas Thomson was fearful lest a digger democracy should barbarize society. Something had to be done. Sydney was going stark, staring mad. The gold mania had thrown the whole population into a fearful commotion. Governor Charles FitzRoy, despairing of the chances of the government to stop the flood, decided to contain and control it. 'Your Lordship', he told Earl Grey, 'will readily conceive the excitement which prevails throughout the community'. Much misery and much disorder, he believed, would accrue. But he insisted, 'to have prevented persons from proceeding thither and digging for the gold would have been quite impossible'.

He decided to try a deterrent. On 22 May FitzRoy proclaimed that gold in its natural places of deposit belonged to the Crown, and no person should dig for it or disturb the soil until he had been duly authorized by Her Majesty's government. The following day he proclaimed that after the first day of June no person would be permitted to dig, search for, or remove gold without first obtaining a licence, the cost of which would be fixed at £1 10s a month. His Excellency was also pleased to appoint John Richard Hardy, a justice of the peace, to be a commissioner of Crown lands and to carry out the regulations for the issue of licences. On 3 June John Hardy, supported by ten armed men, set up his tent at Ophir, where human greed had converted a wilderness into the appearance of a blackfellows' camp in fourteen days.

Change was in the air. Gold, some said, had put the last nail in the coffin of convict transportation. It would be a little too much, said Henry Parkes in the *Empire* on 16 May 1851, even for Downing Street philosophy to transport a burglar or a highwayman to the gold-mines, or to give a free trip to the criminals of England to enable them to career 'over the waves in prison ships to be bandit chiefs in the gold regions of New South Wales, and eventually Australian revolutionists'. On this question the Chartist and friend of humanity Henry Parkes saw eye to eye with William Charles Wentworth, the Whig, who was known to his political opponents as 'the bullying, bellowing champion of the few'.

The peoples of the colonies would no longer consent, Wentworth said to the electors of Sydney on 29 July 1851, to be 'the receptacles of the criminals of the British empire, even if the minister were insane enough to have a try'. His subject was the great dream of his life—the greatness of Australia. 'A new and unexpected era', he declared, 'has at length dawned upon us—an era which, however, must in a very few years precipitate us from a colony into a nation'. The radicals and republicans of Sydney agreed. The goldfields, in the words of the *People's Advocate* on 9 August 1851, contained 'the elements of all the future greatness—the elements of future nationality, and of coming independence . . . Yes! we shall be a NATION; not a dependency of a far off country . . . [Our country] must ere long become what God and nature designed it should be—"First flower of the earth, first gem of the sea".' A few months later in October the Reverend J. Dunmore Lang told the diggers on the Turon River that God had vouchsafed a 'brilliant and glorious future for Australia . . . He who sits in the Heavens and laughs at the impotent combinations of unprincipled men' had disclosed an extensive goldfield. Australia would cease to be a despised colony; the relationship between Australia and the Colonial Office would now cease and be replaced by a relationship between Australia and England; the bush barbarians would be civilized.

In June 1851, fossickers found gold dust sprinkled along the bed of the Turon in the ranges east of Ophir 'as regular as wheat in a sown field'. When Goldfields Commissioner Hardy visited the field, he was surrounded by an excited crowd of diggers thrusting pound notes in his face and pestering him to issue the licence quick smart so that they could get down to business. For, despite a good deal of passive resistance and schemes to shirk payment, including scampering into the bush, the diggers at that time thought of a man who did not earn enough to pay as a 'crawler'.

In July, gold was found on the property of Dr W. J. Kerr near Bathurst by an Aboriginal man known as Kerr Tommy. When the news reached Sydney on 18 July, men foamed at the mouth and rushed about with that demented look in the eyes of those who have surrendered to a great frenzy. The migration of adventurers to the goldfields recommenced. By the end of July 1500 to 2000 arrived by sea from the other colonies to try their fortune with the pick, the shovel and the cradle; numbers were coming overland from the new colony of Victoria. By that time 1750 diggers held licences on the Turon, and £28 110 7s 6d worth of gold had been exported from New South Wales. On 17 June 1851 the Executive Council accepted FitzRoy's recommendation that government undertake the convey-ance of gold from the diggings to Sydney as it did the conveyance of letters, without however being responsible in case of loss. A suitable carriage was to be provided for the purpose, which was to be under the protection of a special guard. Government was to levy a charge of 2 per cent on the value of the gold. In this way the escort of gold by armed guard from the diggings to the vaults of the Sydney banks began.

At the same time the diggers' way of life seemed to threaten the values of the society their gold was enriching. At the Turon that August many of the diggers were said to have lost all respect for the sacredness of the Sabbath. The parsons and the moralizers raved on about 'disgraceful scenes', 'abominable nuisances' and the rebirth of barbarism in the Australian bush. Send the clergy to the fields, they pleaded, for they were the nation's 'chiefest police': when divine and moral duties were not preached, lawlessness reigned, as without religion there was always anarchy and crime.

One golden dawn in August 1851 just as first light was spreading over the sombre bush by the Turon, William Grant Broughton, the Anglican bishop of Sydney, summoned the members of his persua-sion to join him in prayer. In the evening of his life, he was still not free from that chill in the heart he had felt when he first saw Australia in 1829. Now with the zeal he always displayed in the battle for Christian civilization over bush barbarism, he seized a pickaxe and dug with his usual wild frenzy the first hole to lay the foundations of the first bush church on the goldfields of Australia. Three days later when the building was finished he put on the gorgeous robes of a bishop and dedicated the building to the greater glory of God. That day he told the diggers of a prize far richer than the one with which they were infatuated.

In Melbourne, the self-appointed guardians of morals were helpless to prevent the spread of gold fever south of the Murray River. William Campbell announced on 8 July the discovery of gold at Clunes. In the same month, Louis Michel, a Melbourne hotel proprietor, found gold near Warrandyte. On 8 August a blacksmith, Thomas Hiscock, saw flakes of the precious metal in the creek at the foot of Mount Buninyong. In September John Dunlop, 75 years of age, walked beside a dray from Geelong to Buninyong and found gold in abundance under the wattle trees at Ballarat. When news reached Melbourne and Geelong in September of gold the size of 'nuggets' being picked up in the creek beds in the Buninyong district, the strong and the weak poured out of Melbourne, driven like men in a delirium. Gentlemen foamed at the mouth; women fainted; children somersaulted. Another great madness had begun.

Charles Joseph La Trobe, Lieutenant-Governor of the newly independent colony of Victoria, had many anxious discussions with Charles Perry, the Bishop of Melbourne, and others of like mind. Believing like FitzRoy that a licence fee might keep down numbers as well as make a welcome addition to government revenue, La Trobe announced on 16 August 1851 that on and after 1 September no person would be permitted to dig, search for or remove gold without first taking out a licence at a cost of 30s a month.

When the news reached Buninyong, the diggers were incensed. They talked together of their 'Victorian Czar', of a 'juggernaut tax to crush the poor'. The plain fact was, they said, that the diggers could not afford to pay it. Some even said that diggers should collect firearms so that they could resist that effeminate fop who wore the hat with the ridiculous white feathers. On the night of 26 August a huge fire lit up the faces of the forty or fifty diggers who responded to the call for a 'roll-up' to ponder on the act of government in imposing the 'bloody licence tax'. There under the canopy of heaven, in the dead silence of the Australian bush, these cabbage-tree men of the gold decade condemned the licence as impolitic and illiberal, and threatened that if government persisted, they would vacate their present ground and proceed at once to Bathurst. The *Argus* correspondent wrote that he had never been 'more struck with a scene' in his life. Something whispered to him that it was a 'solemn protest of labour against oppression—an outburst of light, reason and right, against the infliction of an effete objectionable royal claim'. Government, he said, was playing with fire: it was trampling on the principle of British politics of no taxation without representation. The 'hat and feathers', and the 'fat pigs' of Melbourne had indulged in a 'hun-like assault on the industry of Victoria's children'. They would be stopped.

By contrast when the diggers gathered at Sofala in New South Wales on 8 November 1851 to discuss the licence grievance, there was no violent language. They argued that the licence system was unjust and exorbitant and the method of collection unnecessarily vexatious. But all observers expected the diggers on the New South Wales fields to continue their 'steady perseverance in a loyal, peaceable and virtuous course'. As Commissioner Hardy put it, 'there is no storm on the horizon'.

That September of 1851, men flocked in their thousands to the diggings at Ballarat, the new name for Buninyong. They came in drays, in carts, on foot, in wheelbarrows. Bank clerks, captains of ships, aldermen, councillors, lawyers and doctors, every grade of human being down to the man who humped his swag poured into Ballarat. Picks, shovels and crowbars scarred the earth in feverish searches for the coveted glint. By November, 1855 licences had been issued at Ballarat, and 4678 at Mount Alexander.

Every man became his own architect. In their haste to get at the 'yellow stuff', men made do with tents and bark huts of the most primitive construction. Two poles, stick athwart, with calico stretched over the top for protection against the wind and rain, provided sleeping quarters. There, to a chorus of frogs, the snarl of the possum and the drunken shouts of other diggers, men slept and dreamed of gold. Shaving was dispensed with, because, while soaping up, a man might miss out on a nugget. So beards luxuriated, as did moustaches. 'Everyone', as the *Argus* correspondent put it, was 'transmogrified'. The scene whirled on as though it were a dream or a fantasy.

Another 'hot fit of the auriferous fever' took possession of the men in Melbourne and Geelong. As in *Macbeth*, men stood not on their social rank in going, but went at once. Painters put on a first coat, and then vanished; plasterers mixed their mortar, then threw away their trowels; bricklayers on scaffolding turned giddy with the thought of gold; carpenters shook with the fever till they flung their tools away and bolted for the fields; attendants at the lunatic asylum in Melbourne rushed off; teachers at the denominational schools dropped all pretence about their higher calling and made for the fields; capitalists saddled up horses and joined the army of prospective diggers on the road.

A mad rage for emigration to Australia seized all classes in the British Isles. Seamen deserted their ships to get on board any boat bound for Australia; respectable women jostled with tarts to attract the eye of the shipping agents; runners, thimble-and-pea men and confidence men preyed on the unwary and the gullible in that great human uproar on the docks of English, Irish and Scottish ports as the passions of men, women and children were raised to fever pitch by these stories of gold lying on the ground just waiting to be picked up.

In Collins Street in the centre of Melbourne, mobs of unwashed, unshaven diggers, togged up in the broadcloth of gentlemen, poked their noses against the shop windows behind which rapacious and cunning jewellers displayed showy, trashy trinkets. Huge rings sparkled on grubby clay-stained fingers. Women recruited from the whorehouses of Melbourne were decked out in gaudy silks and satins for a romp round the streets of Melbourne. One digger bought up the entire stock of champagne in a hotel, poured it into a horse trough, and asked the passers-by to take a swill; another ordered the publican to wash the counter of the bar with claret; another lined up all the glasses in a hotel on the bar, smashed them to smithereens with a stockwhip and then offered to pay for the damage.

A barber who had soaped and lathered faces in the good old easygoing times before the discovery of gold, and cursed his fate as the proprietor of a plot of 'ungrateful soil', found himself transported from lather and bristles into £4000 a year. A butcher whose soul was said to be encased in fat in the boiling-down days suddenly found his line of business one of the best paying in the colony and became 'great in purse'. He became part of the 'furor in money-getting', part of the vulgarization of the wealthy classes in society. Riches became the test of a man's position. As one observer put it, 'it is not what you were, but what you are that is the criterion . . . your father might have been my Lord-of-England-all-over, it goes for nothing in this equalising colony of gold and beef and mutton'. A story was being told in the drawing rooms of Melbourne of a squatter, 'a true blue gentleman', who had offered a digger a shilling to lift a bag of sugar off a dray. The digger looked at him a moment and then, putting his foot on a stump, said, 'There, tie my shoe, and I'll give you five shillings'. Plebeianism of the rankest kind was growing stronger every day.

'Things are come to a pretty pass indeed!', the *Argus* declared on 7 April 1852. Day by day, they continued, Victoria was wading deeper into crime, lawlessness and insecurity. The day before, highway robbers had pirated £25 000 worth of gold dust, the day before that there was a murder in Bourke Street, and the day before that a murder in Geelong. 'Shooting in the streets, bushranging upon the roads . . . robbery, insult, outrage of every sort, shape and degree' so astounded them that they wondered whether Victoria was 'rushing upon an abyss'. They were getting worse and worse, day by day, sinking into a nation of cut-throats.

2

One Step Forward for the White Man

During the night of 29 July 1852 the Peninsular and Oriental Steam Navigation company's ship *Chusan* steamed into Port Phillip Bay. The long-promised and much deferred steam communication with England was now an established fact. The keystone, it was said, had now been placed in that bridge which united Victorians to the mother country. After the *Chusan* entered Sydney Harbour, on 3 August, Deas Thomson gave a ball on 21 August to celebrate the event. The *Sydney Morning Herald* wrote with enthusiasm of 'this mighty improvement', which had reduced the distance between them and old England. Henceforth the journey would take seventy days.

On 3 March 1854 telegraphic communication was opened between Melbourne and Williamstown, a distance of 10 ½ miles. On 12 September in the same year the first railway ran between Melbourne and Sandridge (Port Melbourne). As the *Argus* put it, though it was only a 'day of small things, it was pregnant with interest as the initiatory step in that grand career of material progress which has become the distinguishing characteristic of modern civilization'. That first scream of the steam whistle heralded a new era in the history of Australia: the iron horse had started on its mission to tether the mighty bush to the world. In the words of the *Argus*, the train would flash past the gunyah of the native black. The black would listen with a vague terror to the 'first scream' of that whistle. 'Yes,' continued the *Argus*,

> listen, dusky fellow-subject, for there comes Christian England; the great, the powerful, the intelligent, the good! There comes Christian England, who, if you were strong enough to demand a price for your land, would buy it from you; but who, as you are few and weak, and timorous, generously condescends to steal it! There comes Christian England, to absorb your hunting-grounds, destroy your game, innoculate you with her vices, and shew her Christian spirit by

dooming you to 'extirpation'! There comes Christian England, who carries many hundreds of tons of your gold without setting apart one ounce for you; who hands you over to be contaminated by the worst and lowest of her own people, to be taught their crimes, to be impregnated with their diseases; and who, while rapidly destroying you, cants in her churches and her religious meetings about doing to others as she would be done by! Rejoice, you dark-skinned savage, at the advent of your kind, magnanimous, and most Christian brother!

The march of progress was promoting the material well-being of the white man at the expense of the way of life and possibly the very existence of the black man. In Sydney, on the eve of the discovery of gold, the sole surviving Aborigine from the Botany Bay tribe who had greeted Lieutenant James Cook with a 'dart' and had hollered 'Walla Walla Wha' and brandished their spears at Captain Phillip and his party on 25 January 1788, was Mahroot. In 1849 he had told an English visitor, 'Well Mister . . . all black fellow gone! All this my country . . . Only one left now'. At Oyster Cove some 20 miles from Hobart Town the fifty-five members of a people which had once occupied the entire island lived in a miserable collection of huts and outbuildings. They were profoundly dirty, they swarmed with fleas. The roofs of their huts were not waterproof, the windows broken, bedsteads the merest apologies, and the blankets had all gone. The Aboriginal women attributed that to the white man: 'Bad white fellow—him steal 'em all.' The superintendent had a different explanation: men and the women, he said, sold blankets and clothing to the 'low population' in the district in return for liquor.

The outrages by the Aborigines continued. Near Grafton on 13 August 1853 a party of blacks entered a shepherd's hut and dragged a white woman outside. While two threatened her with nulla-nullas, a third used 'the poor helpless woman as he thought proper'. After this act of cruel and wanton sensuality they plundered the hut of all its tea, sugar, flour and blankets. Then they returned with their loot to their roving life as savages of the Australian bush.

Over in South Australia the serious-minded were deeply troubled by the condition of the Aborigines. Men in high places contended that civilized nations who took possession of territory previously occupied by nomadic and uncivilized tribes must accept responsibility for the consequence of such dispossession. As they saw it, the one remaining chance for the Aborigines was to isolate them from the white man. At Poonindie Archdeacon Hale had opened an institution in which the natives were instructed in moral and religious subjects and trained in steady industrious habits. The tough-minded complained that the value of the labour of black-fellows did not exceed the cost of administration. The sheepmen grumbled about setting aside land which blackfellows had neither the capacity nor the taste to turn to profit.

In the meantime among the men in Whitehall there was much discussion on the future of the Australian colonies. The discovery of gold had rendered the debate on the future of the convict system obsolete. No British government was prepared to pay for criminals to become bandit chiefs on the goldfields of Australia, or swell the numbers of that convict rabble which had already threatened to destroy law and order. In February 1853 a dispatch left Whitehall informing the Lieutenant-Governor of Van Diemen's Land, Sir William Denison, that the era of transportation was ended.

When this news reached Van Diemen's Land, the anti-transportationists lit bonfires all over the island on 10 August 1853 to celebrate the end of the 'birth-stain'. In Hobart the children received a slice of commemorative cake, a medal, and much moral-izing from supporters of the Australasian League on the victory of respectability over human cupidity. On 16 August the elite of the youth and beauty of Hobart Town gathered for the jubilee ball at which the band struck up 'Tasmania is Free', which the company caught up with a shout. All night the greatest enthusiasm prevailed.

No phoenix was to rise from the ashes of those fires. The pro-convict press branded the celebrations as a 'sanctimonious jollification'. Those two heroes of the Australasian League, John West and Henry Dowling, were 'missionary firebrands' who 'under the cloak of the most pharisaical virtue' had insulted four-fifths of the population of their island. Transportation was dead; convictism lived on. It had left the colonists of Van Diemen's Land a stricken people who would hand on the curse of convictism to the third and fourth generation of those who came after them.

Gold provided the occasion for the abolition of transportation but not the means of production with which to allay the ghost of convictism. The workers who had 'ploughed Van Diemen's Land' rushed off to the Victorian goldfields in droves. The advantage of cheap convict labour had disappeared, without any corresponding increase in free labour. The Athens of the South was to lapse into a long torpor.

As evidence of their new standing in the world the colonists had been invited by the Secretary of State to draft their own political institutions. On 15 December 1852 the Secretary of State for the Colonies informed the Governor of New South Wales, the Lieutenant-Governors of Victoria and Van Diemen's Land, and the Governor of South Australia that 'considerations arising from these extraordinary discoveries of Gold' had imparted such 'new and unforeseen features to their political and social condition that it had become more urgently necessary than heretofore to place full powers of self-government in the hands of a people thus advanced in wealth and prosperity'. He was therefore inviting the Legislative Councils of those colonies to draft new constitutions and transmit them to the Imperial Parliament for their approval or rejection. On 20 May 1853, the Legislative Council of New South Wales asked Wentworth to chair a select committee to draft a new constitution for the colony.

Wentworth turned 63 that year. Outwardly he had some of the appearance of an English drover. He wore a heavy, loose-fitting coat, and a wide-brimmed colonial hat to cover a mass of grizzled hair. His step had become faltering as the dissipations of the earlier years wrought havoc to the flesh which encased the mighty spirit of William Charles Wentworth. There was about him in the winter of 1853 that air of what one observer called a 'commanding ruin'. Those with eyes to see now saw him as a man who had known greater days. In their eyes, what survived was but 'the scattered fragments' of grandeur in a man who possessed no common soul.

By May 1853 it was not only the step that was faltering. Wentworth was beginning to wonder whether there was any future for a Whig in colonial society. He had begun to fear that the price of attempting to preserve the old plantation society might be a social revolution in which not only the private ownership of land would be threatened with destruction but the institution of private property might be replaced by common ownership. Then, he believed, Australia would lapse back into that barbarism of the period before the coming of the white man. Goths and Vandals in the guise of Sydney radicals and socialists would destroy the foundations of civilized life in Australia. The country would be left as a desert over which sheep and Aborigines roamed at will. He could see no way to protect the landed gentry against the middle classes, with their principle of equality of opportunity. He could see no way to protect civilization against the working classes, who wanted to drag everyone down to their own level.

The other members of the constitution committee lacked his great vision. James Macarthur was not a man to dream a great dream; he was a fusspot who squeaked in public in his 'penny trumpet voice' about the evils of democracy while Wentworth roared. None of them could match Wentworth's single-minded authority. His was the committee's dominating voice, and he was determined to 'take no model from foreign schemes of revolutionary rebellion'. He was still determined to raise a New Britannia in another world, to sow the seeds of a constitution and a civilization similar to the one from which they had all sprung, with similar forms of monarchy and aristocracy. He had persuaded the committee to accept two aims: to have 'a form of Government based on the analogies of the British Constitution', and not 'to sow the seeds of a future democracy'.

To achieve that end he recommended the creation of hereditary titles, leaving it to the option of the Crown to annex to the title a seat for life in the Legislative Council. Such hereditary titles would lay the foundations of an aristocracy, and the formation of an upper house modelled, as far as circumstances would admit, upon the analogies of the British constitution. He also recommended the extension of the elective franchise for the lower house to include all persons having a salary of £100 a year, all occupants of any room or lodging paying £40 a year for their board and lodging or £10 a year for their lodging only. This was, as he put it, 'a very close approximation to universal suffrage'. He was aiming at that balance of interests which existed in the British constitution. He also recommended the establishment of a general assembly of the colonies of the Australian group, to make laws in relation to inter-colonial questions such as tariffs, railways, roads, canals, postage, and a general court of appeal from the courts of the colonies.

Outside the walls of the Legislative Council howls of anger and moral indignation greeted the proposals. In the *Empire* Henry Parkes charged Wentworth with presenting a 'wretched patch work of political absurdities', whose tendencies were all oligarchical, a constitution which, while it kept them slaves, would make them the laughing-stock of every civilized nation. The poet Charles Harpur was cheeky and irreverent. What, he asked, would be the criterion for being a lord? Would it be drunkenness, or money, or the posses-sion of 'a thumping great nose'? The Wentworth upper house would be one more cobweb, he said, which the broom of the future revolution would sweep utterly away.

The people were on the march. On 15 August 1853, 2500 crowded the stage, the pit, and the first and second tiers of the Victoria Theatre in Sydney for a meeting to resist this flagrant attack upon public liberty. Wentworth again heard the dreaded sound of the tocsin, and the threat of what he called the 'insane rabble'. But the speakers on that day spoke like good respectable bourgeois rather than advocates of mob rule. J. B. Darvall, himself a member of the Legislative Council, an MA of Cambridge University, a pastoralist and a director of at least two banks, and Henry Parkes, the one-time Chartist, who had begun to use the bourgeois talk about equality of opportunity, urged them to oppose Wentworth's undemocratic constitution.

Dan Deniehy, a saint and a larrikin, held them spellbound as he unfolded his dream for Australia: 'there is', he told them in his gentle, angelic voice, 'an aristocracy worthy of our ambition. Wherever man's skill is eminent, wherever genius merits its elevation, there is an aristocracy. That is an aristocracy that will grow and expand under free institutions'.

Wentworth was not impressed. He saw his opponents not as men of standing in the community but as red republican rabble, dirty libellers and paltry ruffians, whose names he did not wish to know. He wanted a British, not a Yankee, constitution, because the latter was contaminated by the degrading influences of democracy. He wanted to stem the democratic current and erect some bulwarks to keep erect the grand fabric their fathers had built.

The voices of bourgeois democracy grew impatient with his thunderings and denunciations. The Sydney and country press, the *Sydney Morning Herald* alone excepted, rebuked him for his 'coarse anger' and likened him to a 'spent volcano'. By December 1853 all agreed that there should be two Houses of Parliament. All agreed that the lower house should be wholly elective. The one contentious issue was still the composition and powers of the upper house. By then Wentworth was prepared to drop the proposal for a hereditary order of colonial nobility, provided the upper house was nominated by the Governor. That and a requirement of a two-thirds majority of both houses to amend the constitution were the 'without which not' of his great aim to 'sow the seeds of good constitutional principles', to make this 'a British community and not a democratic community'. Having won that part of the battle for conservative principles Wentworth and Deas Thomson were chosen to act as watchdogs in London when the bill was introduced into the Imperial Parliament. While they were packing their bags Henry Parkes was telling the readers of the *Empire* that they must persuade Whitehall not to perpetuate squatting because that was the prime cause of barbarism in the Australian bush.

In the other colonies all agreed that the constitution should provide checks against hasty legislation. All agreed that there was an advantage in balancing the aristocratic and democratic elements in society, but no one was able to say quite what that meant. In Victoria, the model colony, no one wanted to have anything to do with Wentworth's proposal for a hereditary nobility. In the end, the Victorians settled on a similiar system to that adopted in New South Wales. Power was to be divided between the people, property, and intelligence. The Assembly was to be the house of the people; the Council was to be the house of property and intelligence. The bourgeoisie and the landed classes were each given a share. The constitution of Victoria was to be both a voice for 'democracy', and a voice for 'honour and distinctions'.

In South Australia the proportion of men with a stake in the country was so high, and the working classes were so wedded to the aim of becoming themselves owners of property, that the men of property were prepared to introduce manhood suffrage for elections to the lower house. So, it was argued, a very democratic form of government could be introduced with greater safety than in almost any other of the British colonies. It was therefore possible to introduce manhood suffrage and still have, in the eyes of the conservatives, 'a safe form of government', for men with a stake in the country would not be seduced by the 'flattery of vulgar demagogues'. In South Australia it was possible for the conservatives to 'trust the people'. By contrast in Van Diemen's Land the antagonism of the ex-convict working class for the men of property, the bitterness and resentments inherited from the convict era, made manhood suffrage a weapon of revenge which no man of property was prepared to hand over to the working classes. As in Victoria and South Australia, the upper house, the Legislative Council, was to represent the men of property and the men of intelligence. In Western Australia the presence of convicts was accepted to be incompatible with self-government. There the men of property put profit before participation in government.

In the meantime Wentworth and Deas Thomson pushed on with their preparations to leave for England. Parkes sneered at Wentworth's hope of receiving a baronetcy and the governorship of New South Wales as the reward for all his public services and achievements. Parkes was not to know that by then Wentworth was beginning to be concerned with other things than the blanks and prizes in the human lottery. The one-time Don Giovanni of Botany Bay was becoming a bit of a metaphysician. While Parkes was jeering at Wentworth as the author of a feudal constitution for New South Wales, Wentworth was thanking his daughter Timmy, the one he loved best in all the world, for her concern for his future destiny in those countless ages which lay before them all. He was telling her that a belief in the life of the world to come was both desirable and comfortable, as well as a source of hope and consolation at the latest hour. So far, try as he would, he could not believe. One day he hoped to remove all his doubts, because what mattered to him was that he had an affectionate child who was 'praying for the salvation of her Father, with a Simple and ardent Sincerity'. So he took his leave of her: 'and now my first born, dearest child adieu . . . And if forever still forever fare thee well. So says your ever affectionate W. C. Wentworth'.

Three days later on 20 March tears rolled down his furrowed cheeks as he farewelled the friends who had gathered at Circular Quay to wish godspeed. Some ruffians hooted and yelled but soon their voices were hushed in the majesty of the moment as onlookers sensed that the 'greatest son of Australian soil' might be leaving their shores forever. 'But whatever may be my destiny', he said as the tears rolled down his cheeks, and his body shook, 'believe me that my latest prayer shall be for the happiness and prosperity of the people of Australia, and for its rapid expansion into a nation, which shall rule supreme in this southern world'. Then the barge took him to the steamship *Chusan*, that symbol of the dawn of a new era in the history of his country, where he joined his fellow passenger John Bede Polding, the Catholic Bishop of Sydney, whose face and sweetness of disposition conveyed intimations of that other prize to which his beloved daughter Timmy was leading him. In London the ghosts of the past haunted him. The gossips of Whitehall and London society let him know they were talking behind his back about whether he looked like other ticket-of-leave men. The sins of the fathers were coming between him and that baronetcy he coveted. By then the war in the Crimea was the one talking point in London. The shops of London were filled with Balaclava pants, Inkerman ties, Crimean coats and suits, Raglan redingotes, Sevastopol shirt collars and the like. As Wentworth and Thomson stayed on, waiting for the spring session of Parliament in 1855, stories of terrible carnage began to circulate in London, stories of hardship during that savage Russian winter, of gross incompetence and huge waste. The flower of the British army had been slain and thousands of families made mourners by aristocratic incompetence. What was worse, 50 000 men had been chilled, drenched, famished, and marched off to their graves while the English governing classes, the cause of their destruction, had the colossal effrontery to go on as usual with all the fashionable fun of the London season; they hunted foxes and shot pheasants for pleasure.

Wentworth, the advocate of conferring privileges on the landed gentry in the colonies, had arrived in London at a time when his political opponents were exposing the class privileges of the British landed gentry as the cause of all the disasters in the Crimea. Robert Lowe, his old rival in Sydney, and now a member of the House of Commons, was urging government to replace the aristocratic principle of awarding office according to birth with the bourgeois principle of the career open to talent, which would confer high office only on men of merit.

Sensing the direction of the political wind, Lord Russell included in the constitution bill a section which conferred on the colonial

Parliament the general power of constitutional amendment. When the second reading of the bill took place in the House of Commons on 17 May 1855 Wentworth sat morose and silent in the visitors' gallery, while Robert Lowe in that high-pitched voice of the man who was all head and no heart described the Wentworth proposal as the 'iniquitous device' of an 'oligarchical clique', and a conspiracy by the large landholders of New South Wales to preserve the sacred rights of landed property and prevent the sowing of 'democratic seed' in the Australian colonies. Wentworth was watching his world slipping away. Humanity was once more on the march: even in Ballarat, where three years earlier only sheep, shepherds and Aborigines disturbed the silence, the tocsin of rebellion was being heard.

3

Who Would Want to be a Digger?

By the middle of 1852 gold was subverting the old social order of rank and degree. At the diggings it was already being said, 'Jack is as good as his master'. All was confusion. Respect for worth, talent and education had also been subverted. In the cities it was a master-stroke of diplomacy to induce a man with a horse and cart at his disposal to convey luggage to a hotel. Gentlemen and their good ladies were giving up servants and doing everything for them-selves. Governor La Trobe had to groom his own horse and feed it. Captain Sturt had already sent his eldest son to Rugby School to have him educated as a gentleman. By the end of 1852 he was so exasperated by the lack of servants to help his wife, and so mortified by his failure ever to do anything that was pleasing in her sight, that he decided to take his family away from the democratic vulgarians in Australia and put them in an elegant English environ-ment such as Cheltenham where birth and blood and breeding still counted for something. On 19 March 1853 he and his family fled on the *Henry Tanner* from the land of democracy.

Melbourne was in a ferment; no one knew what it would be like when the excitement died down. The streets were full of swindlers, vagabonds, runaway convicts and murderers. As a sign of the mania of the times, more people were going insane than in any other city of the civilized world. It was said to be almost as un-healthy as Calcutta. Every day there were thirty funerals. Bugs multiplied in the timbers of the houses; fleas were everywhere; flies swarmed in every house, settled on the faces and backs of people in the streets and crawled into their eyes; snakes infested the outskirts of the city.

Out on the track to the goldfields there was both excitement and material hardship standing between the diggers and the fulfilment of their mad dreams. The horses sank in the black loam trampled to deep mud by so many feet, and no human persuasion or terror could move them. Travellers to the fields often came on children screaming their hearts out in bedding piled high on a wagon, while a frightened horse, the whites of its eyes showing and saliva pouring from its mouth, strained at the bit, as Dad and Mum, often bogged up to the knees, pushed and heaved at the rear. Men, women and children, drenched to the skin in winter and roasted by the sun in summer, struggled over the 80- to 90-mile journey. The appearance of the country horrified those accustomed to England's green and pleasant land, or the green of the Emerald Isle, or the majestic highlands of Scotland. It was burnt up, barren and brown; the sky, like God, was out of hearing.

Their excitement was not allowed to flag for one instant. They heard stories of fabulous finds and of murders in the forests around Ballarat and Bendigo. They heard wild and contradictory rumours of diggers picking the yellow stuff off the surface of God's earth. They heard of meetings of angry diggers addressed by men in swallow-tails, who blathered about the rights of man till diggers who were feeling the pinch shouted at the speakers to cut the cackle and get on to that 'bloody licence tax'. They heard stories of diggers being chained to trees and left there in the boiling sun all day because they had been offensive to 'traps' and 'joeys', those brutal hirelings of the gold-laced bastards who were fashioning an Asiatic-style despotism over diggers. Sometimes they heard stories on the road which were calculated to plant terror in the heart of the most placid of men. At the end of May 1853 a man was brought into Ballarat after wandering nine days and nights in the bush without shelter or food; he had roamed round in a circle, puzzled and bewildered as were most 'new chums' by the everlasting sameness of the bush. It was feared he would lose both his legs as the exposure had already brought on decomposition.

The population of the goldfields was in a state of perpetual motion as men descended on a field, robbed it, and fled. In July 1853 there was a flourishing field at McIvor Creek in Victoria. In August rumour reached the field of a lucky strike on the Goulburn River near Seymour. Men, women, children, horses, bullocks, goats, tubs, cradles, picks, tools and stores were all off for the Goulburn, leaving the shepherds to return to their ancient solitude on the lovely banks of the McIvor. In their haste to be off, some left their tents standing, with bed, bedding and cooking utensils strewn over the ground. So the shepherds again took up residence in their huts among the mullock heaps, where pieces of torn calico still flapped in the wind to remind posterity that the robbers and the fleers had once been there.

On the fields themselves the bird's-eye view was both picturesque and appealing. At Ballarat in 1852 the newcomer first saw bullock-drays and tents pitched under the old gnarled gum trees in the foreground, the diggers busy washing their pay-dirt in the distance, and the whole surrounded by a rich green valley and the primeval forest, with its eerie silence and its air of vast indifference to all this feverish animation. The human scene also had its attractions for those with an eye for the bizarre. Rough-looking men with bushy beards, clay-stained hats and every variety of clothing swung picks while native policemen in the picturesque dress of a red shirt, a dark-green jacket and trousers stood by, or patrolled the fields in their role of guardians of law and order. All nationalities and classes seemed to be represented: there were Englishmen, Scots, Irishmen, Frenchmen and Italians; there were Yankees with their blatherskite about California, Sikhs with turbans, Muslims with their skull-caps, Hindus in their dhotis, Chinese with pigtails, and Maoris from New Zealand. There, as one observer put it, professors of the law and the lancet together with renegade ministers of religion were hunting their fortunes in pits of clay alongside carnal and ignorant creatures. The highly educated Oxonian was neighbour to the illiterate farm labourer from Wiltshire or Somerset or the poverty-stricken, superstition-ridden Irish peasant.

These were the early days on the fields, the halcyon, romantic days before the overcrowding and the decline in the income of the diggers wiped the laugh off their faces and put rifles rather than picks and shovels on their shoulders. Only those with the gift of prophecy sensed the shape of things to come. Friedrich Engels predicted as early as September 1851 that the Australian goldfields would turn the world upside-down: in California the blackguards were lynched; in Australia the blackguards would lynch the *honnêtes gens*; Carlyle would see his aristocracy of rogues established in full glory.

In Australia the men in high places were confident that they had the situation well in hand. In New South Wales the Attorney-General, John Hubert Plunkett, and Governor FitzRoy both paid visits to the goldfields in mid-1852 and were delighted to find the diggers both law-abiding and enthusiastic in their expressions of loyalty. From Victoria, Charles Joseph La Trobe kept telling London how pleasantly surprised he was by the small amount of crime and disorder on the fields. Lord Robert Cecil, who visited the goldfields of Victoria in March and April of 1852, was equally enthusiastic: these rough, unshaven, coarse-mouthed diggers were able to recognize a gentleman and defer to him. As he saw it, the setting should have predisposed men to crime, save for one all-important fact: here, unlike California, 'the government was of the Queen and not of the mob; from above, not from below, holding from a supposed right . . . and not from the people'.

The diggers lived in a constant state of excitement which found outlets in all kinds of emotional extravaganzas. In their professions of loyalty to Her Majesty they were profuse; in their account of their feelings for each other they were excessive; in their account of their feelings for their enemies they were bloody, murderous and extreme. When a strike was made, the fields rang with enthusiastic huzzas. The eager cry went up, 'There's a speck'. A gleam of wild delight shone in the eyes of the successful; a terrible look of despair darkened the eyes of the men who had missed out. The sudden transitions from gloomy despondency to joyous success often proved too much for those who were pitifully equipped to ride the storms assailing the human heart. Many went mad. One man at Bathurst in 1852 threw himself from a rock and fractured his skull, another took to the woods and was seen no more. All day violent quarrels, thefts and even murders occurred at those spots on the fields where the gold was handed in for assaying. At the store-keeper's tent where every article of food, clothing or digging equipment could be bought for money or gold there was indescrib-able confusion, din and medley. Children bawled, men swore and shook their fists at each other, and women's tongues wagged at nineteen to the dozen. When the gold dust was handed over for measurement, shopkeeper and digger practised all the tricks of the trade such as using false beam-balances, long finger-nails, magnets, and a greasy pan. The violators and robbers of the soil slid naturally into violating and robbing each other.

Men who lived at fever pitch were not satisfied with merely putting on black looks when their neighbour behaved in ways that were displeasing to them. At Mount Alexander in July 1853 a digger named Goldsmith was put in a sack and thrown into a shallow hole. At the Golden Gully, Bendigo, in 1853 the diggers caught a man plundering a tent. In fury they seized him, tore off his clothes and began to argue about what to do with him while women shrieked, men yelled and the dogs, sensitive as ever to the emotions of their masters, barked in that tone which drove them on to desperate deeds. Some were for drowning him, some for throwing him off a height, and some for hanging him from a tree. One man had the courage to tell them death was a savage punishment for stealing. The cry for blood was dropped and the mob settled for a 'tight lashing'. The man was stripped, tied to a tree and whaled on the bare back with a rope. When he was let go, he could hardly walk to his refuge in the bush where he joined those other outcasts—the white transgressors and the uncultivated savages.

The black bottle also stirred men to dark deeds. Grog sold on the sly intensified the law evasion, quarrelling and fighting. Some sly-grog sellers operated in tents, where thirsty men and greedy women gathered for a 'heels up' indulgence in what the Book of Common Prayer called 'all the sinful lusts of the flesh'. Women dressed in the most exaggerated dresses, designed to make prominent all those areas which drove men out of their wits and to conceal those signs of excess with which nature punished them for their gluttony, offered themselves as 'wives' for such modest charges as 1s 6d a week. When the commissioner heard of such goings-on, he sent mounted police to confiscate the grog, pile dry wood in the middle of the tent and set a light to the whole lot. As lurid flames shot skywards drunken men and women muttered that one day they would take a terrible revenge against those bastards, the 'traps', for coming between them and their fun.

Itinerant musicians, acrobats and strolling players moved from field to field in Victoria and New South Wales to provide entertainment. Some provided music at dancing saloons where forty or fifty couples of men, dressed in muddy clothes and clay-stained heavy boots, danced the mazurka. They ate with equal gusto. At Ballarat and Bendigo enterprising 'restaurateurs' filled their tables at mealtimes with huge quantities of food. At these tables all distinctions of class were levelled as men with coarse, sunburnt faces, their hands nobbled and calloused with toil, and their clothes grimy, sat down with the sensitive flowers. The hero of the table was generally a 'stalwart son of toil' who flaunted so many shining nuggets that his fellow-diners deferred to him despite his unfavourable outward appearance.

By the beginning of 1854 on all the Victorian goldfields more and more diggers believed they were not getting their true deserts for all their striving. There had been a prodigious increase in wealth. Population in Victoria had increased from 75 000 in 1850 to 283 942 in 1854. Bank deposits increased from £822 254 in 1851 to £4 334 241 in 1852; the number of ships arriving increased from 555 in 1850 to 1657 in 1852; the exports rose from £1 041 796 in 1850 to £7 451 549 in 1852; the amount of gold exported increased from 145 138 oz in 1851 to 2 497 723 oz in 1853. Yet it was becoming clear that this wealth was not ending up in the pockets of the alluvial diggers.

In the beginning there was wild talk that gold had subverted the conventions governing the drawing of prizes in the human lottery. Nature had so strewn gold on the surface of the earth that it was within the reach of the poorest man who possessed active hands and sharp eyes. Now, at long last in the history of mankind, the race would be to the swift, and the battle to the strong: the strongest, the hardiest, the men of brawn and muscle were about to come into their own. Successful diggers indulged in reckless extravagance:

they drove about four-in-hand in Melbourne spending their money in the most riotous manner, their rough hands bedecked with rings, their behaviour characterized by every vice that can degrade the human race.

By the end of 1853 a retribution for succumbing to the 'unholy hunger' was beginning. On the Turon every business, trade and calling from top to bottom, from the gold-digger to the sharper, was as stagnant as a dirty stream. The income of the alluvial digger was said to be on the decline. The labour to extract a living under great hardship in rain and mud, in frail and badly supported tunnels, was already inciting some diggers to look for a scapegoat. Gentlemen's sons who had seen themselves as saviours of the landed gentry of England were now slinking off the fields grateful to hold such lowly positions as hut-keepers, stockmen, horse-keepers or cowboys. Diggers who had dreamed of becoming rich were now carrying hods of bricks for some parvenu builder who had got rich quickly meeting the demand to house the ever-increasing population of Melbourne or Sydney.

Week after week the gold escorts arrived in Melbourne, Sydney and Adelaide with unheard-of quantities of gold. But statistics made it plain that if that wealth were divided by the number of diggers, each individual digger would not be left with as much as 30s a week. The would-be owner of property in land or in business was earning a worker's wage by the most arduous labour and without most of the creature comforts available to other members of the working class in industrial societies. Some said the lazy and the dissipated were failing while the industrious and the steady were gaining enough to make profitable investments.

The problem was how to increase the yield. Up to the middle of 1853 the digger had proved to be a man of resource, an improviser, but not an inventor. As a writer to the *Empire* put it in August 1853, the diggers had only dug holes. They remained after two years what they had been at the beginning, 'shifting, irresolute and ignorant diggers'. Colonial peoples not only did not make their own history: their very status, their dependence on Mr Mother Country, drained away their creative energies. By the end of 1853 every party was still digging its own hole without any reference to the doings of others. The pick and shovel and cradle still constituted the principal machinery of Australian goldmining. Their proudest boast that they were British, that they had inherited the British constitution and the birthrights of Englishmen condemned them to dependence, to that state of pupillage and infancy out of which neither prophets nor inventors could grow. They had borrowed all the steps forward—the railway, the steamship, the electric telegraph, political institutions and law from Britain, and the road coach from America.

The demand for more gold was met not by the inventive genius of the digger or by an increase in his working hours, but by the use of machinery imported from Britain and from America. Gold contained in quartz was extracted by crushing machinery. Gold-mining began to replace gold-digging on the larger fields. Some of the diggers ceased to be workers on their own account and became hirelings for wages. In the eyes of the digger, companies, capital and machinery, in their colossal proportions, threatened the 'whole cherished vocation of individual mining', and his freedom of action. Those who continued to wield the pick and the shovel became like men who had been superseded by the march of human progress. They became lost, bewildered and frightened, just as wild in their fears as they had been previously in their hopes. They replaced the extravagances of success with the extravagances of men who no longer had a role to play in the history of mankind except as protesters. Henceforth they looked for a scapegoat on which to explode that anger of men who had asked for bread and been offered a stone. At the same time as they feared the loss of their economic freedom, they became afraid that those men in high places were plotting to deprive them of another freedom—their freedom as men.

4

That Bloody Licence Tax

At Mudgee, New South Wales, in May 1852 some Scotsmen celebrated the end of the week's work down the hole. Bagpipes played.
The mountain Dew, that magic potion which makes men think that
they do not always face each other alone, or even that a day might
come when men's dirty slate is wiped clean, was much in evidence.
The songs of Robert Burns were sung with great gusto. Drunken
men looked at each other with the eye of affection as they roared the
line 'Comin' thro' the Rye'. Everything was joyous and happy.
Suddenly the police arrived. They chained one man to a tree,
smashed the bottles containing the precious fluid, and ordered the
Scotsmen to retire to their tents. Before falling asleep the Scotsmen
asked each other ruefully whether perhaps there had been some
mistake: was not this supposed to be a free country?

On 11 February 1853, 1000 diggers gathered at the future site
of Beechworth on the Ovens River in Victoria to discuss their
grievances. Dr John Downes Owens, one of those advocates for
popular rights who took such little thought for the morrow that the
world never gave him his due reward, took the chair. He told the
diggers the time had come for them to resist insult and indig-
nity from whatever quarter it might proceed. He had taken up
their cause when he found it impossible to have justice done to a
policeman who had shot a digger. He told them they must have a
government which was strong in the affections of the people. He
told them of the behaviour of a Mr Mackay, the head of the police,
who went out at night after a glass too much and annoyed and
insulted diggers by poking bayonets into closed tents. He told them
about Sergeant Worsley who had kept hundreds of diggers waiting
for their licences, while he privately obtained licences for those who
had bribed him. The diggers shouted, 'Yes, the wretch, shoot him',
and 'Put a rope round his neck'. He ended by urging all of them to
conduct themselves in an orderly manner and to petition for the

redress of their grievances in a constitutional way. They agreed to ask the Governor to inquire into the conduct of the officials and the illegal impounding of horses by the neighbouring squatters.

A stone had started to roll; no one knew where it would end. Over in Bendigo that June 1853, placards on a gum tree announced the 'startling news' that 400 000 people were about to be thrown on the colony and that a Captain Brown would address them on what could be done about it. On 25 June 600 or 700 diggers resolved that in their opinion the prospective increase of population demanded some energetic steps by government to 'prevent an extensive pauperisation among the diggers'. They also resolved that because of the squatters' land monopoly, the chief field for the development of labour was the diggings. For that reason reduction of the licence fee was imperative. As it was desirable to secure the cooperation and fraternization of the other diggers at the various goldfields of the colony, they suggested the formation of an Anti-Gold Licence Association.

On 2 July 2500 diggers gathered to hear Dr D. G. Jones state his reasons for opposing the licence tax. He denounced it first because it was excessive and bore alike on the fortunate and the unfortunate digger; second because it required the armed power of the government to collect it. Some of the commissioners appointed to administer the laws of the goldfields had on various occasions chained unlicensed diggers to trees or logs, and condemned them to hard labour on the public roads of the colony, under the surveillance of armed men. This proceeding, Dr Jones maintained, was contrary to the spirit of British law, which did not recognize the principle of the subject being a criminal because he was indebted to the state. Before the meeting closed, a Mr Goobie (sic), a German gentleman, mounted the platform and told the multitude he and his hundred fellow-Germans were ready with the rifle or the sword to assist their English friends to obtain their rights. He concluded, to loud cheers, by taking the liberty of reminding their friends the English that if they submitted to the poll-tax, they were not worthy of that glorious English nation which ruled the destinies of the world.

By then the fields were alive with agitation. Lampoons and cartoons were nailed to gum trees on the fields at Bendigo and Ballarat. Placards bore the slogan 'No chains for free Englishmen'. On 21 July many thousands gathered at View Point and resolved to send a delegation to Melbourne to register their grievances.

When the delegates met Lieutenant-Governor La Trobe in Melbourne they told him how one of his police officers had placed a double-barrelled gun on the counter of a storekeeper in Bendigo and demanded to see the licence. They also told him that after the storekeeper had exclaimed 'It was a bloody shame', the magistrate had mulcted him of £10 for using that word to a police officer. Nice, kind Charles La Trobe did not want to believe that was the way justice was administered at Bendigo. Nor could he believe foreigners, Yankees, Germans and mad Irishmen were discriminated against. People just did not behave like that in a British society. But when they asked him to suspend the 'bloody licence tax' again, he took refuge in the law. 'You ask me', he said, 'to do the impossible. I cannot destroy the law . . . while the licence tax is a law it must be obeyed'. To which the diggers replied, 'Then, sir, give the diggers representation'. La Trobe became impatient, making it plain by the frown on his face and the line on his lips that having a voice in government was nothing appertaining to diggers. He rebuked them for their 'loose and intemperate discussion of questions of importance', and indicated that he would not be a party to any victory for the disorderly in the community.

When the delegates reported this exchange to a meeting at the Protestant Hall in Melbourne on 4 August 1853, loud disapprobation and showers of hisses greeted the words of La Trobe. The ball had started to roll. La Trobe, the Colonial Secretary John Foster and the Attorney-General William Stawell had not seen what was before their eyes. The leaders of the diggers believed they could control the roll of the ball by moral suasion, but at a meeting at View Point on 12 August 10 000 to 12 000 diggers turned up wearing a red ribbon around their hats. The old cabbage-tree hat of the Sydney radicals and republicans was now decorated with the red of revolution. In alarm George Thompson, one of the delegates who had been sent to Melbourne, called three cheers for the good old Union Jack and asked them to remember that they were pledged to what he called 'necessary reform, not revolution'. William Dexter, waving the diggers' flag, roared to them about the evils of 'English Tyranny' and the virtues of 'Republicanism'. Dr Schulzen rebuked 'that stupid blockhead' La Trobe for insulting that old and noble nation, the German people. They agreed to meet again on 27 August to debate the proposals that all those in favour of the diggers' demands should wear on their hats tufts of red cloth or ribbon, that in consequence of the diminished yield of gold the sum of 10s be offered as a licence fee, and that should this be refused the diggers were determined to pay no more.

That Saturday 27 August, as rain descended in torrents, 15 000 gathered again to discuss the 'bloody licence tax'. Diggers discharged pistols into the air as they passed the officers' camp. The 'boy' officers taunted the diggers with what they would do to them with four troopers armed with whips. Danger was in the air. The diggers unanimously resolved that the licence fee ought to be abolished, that they should have full and fair share of representation in the elective assembly of the colony. They talked of raising 'volunteers'. They resolved too that if the licence fee were not abolished they would not pay it. Every man then left wet to the skin.

The senior assistant commissioner in charge of the Bendigo goldfields, Joseph Anderson Panton, believed the time for compromise had arrived. Panton was another of the boy commissioners. He had just turned 21 when he took up his appointment at Bendigo. Panton informed La Trobe that as Bendigo was in a state of revolution, if the licence fee were not reduced or if an attempt to enforce it were made, it would end in bloodshed. The reduction of the licence fee, if not its abolition, was essential. Ever a timid man, La Trobe proposed to the Legislative Council on 30 August that the licence fee be abolished. That fine body of men, encouraged by the squatters, thought that was going a bit too far and appointed a committee of inquiry. Impulsive as ever, La Trobe signed a proclamation which waived the collection of the licence fee as from the end of September, and dispatched an express rider to Bendigo with the news.

In true British fashion at the banquet to celebrate the victory on 3 October, redcoats and diggers who had been eyeing each other with fear and loathing now toasted each other and vowed eternal friendship. While the diggers were getting on with the drinking and what one observer called 'other fun', a Captain Harrison was telling the more serious-minded that their next task was to unlock the land and enfranchise the diggers. That afternoon the diggers believed they were toasting the death of the old order on the fields. Over the door of the office of the Anti-Gold Licence Association mock ribbons of mourning for the licence swayed in the wind. The words of triumph 'Old Licence U Dead' were written on the placards and banners. In a mood of optimism the diggers resolved to replace the Anti-Gold Licence Association with the Gold Diggers' Union for the promotion and protection of their social and political rights. That month Charles Thatcher the balladist composed a song of triumph for the diggers:

> Hurrah for Australia the golden,
> Where men of all nations now toil,
> To none will we e'er be beholden
> Whilst we've strength to turn up the soil;
> There's no poverty here to distress us,
> 'Tis the country of true liberty,
> No proud lords can ever oppress us,
> But here we're untrammelled and free.

Within a week of that feast of good fellowship, La Trobe turned another somersault. The licence was restored in a new form. A licence for one month was to cost £1, for three months £2, for six months £4, and for twelve months £8. He of the hat and feathers had done it again. Boy commissioners, redcoats and traps were back in business. Within six weeks the diggers at Ballarat were rolling up to monster meetings. On 21 November, to the traditional background of music and flags, a huge number gathered at Eureka on the Ballarat field to hear Dr Carr tell them that the new regulations for the government of the goldfields would lead to armed rebellion. That day J. B. Humffray, already favourably known on the field as a 'new chum' Chartist, ridiculed the officials on the fields as discarded or younger members of the aristocracy. Speakers drew angry comparisons between the privileges of the squatters and the burdens of the diggers; again speakers dwelt on the need for digger representation in the Legislative Council.

The government took another action that convinced the diggers they had no sympathy for the little man: all storekeepers were to pay a licence fee of £50 a month. This, it was said, would have the effect of crushing the small stores by creating a monopoly of the large storekeepers.

At year's end on 17 December 1853 all the speakers at a meeting at Ballarat warned La Trobe and his minions that if they continued to go against the spirit of the age, they would precipitate the country into civil war, in which the liberties of the people would be swallowed up in one universal conflagration. The bone, the sinew and the indomitable energy of the diggers had put Victoria where she was; they had raised her from a little-heard-of place in the South to the proud position she now occupied on the face of the earth; they had raised Melbourne from an insignificant village to the palaced streets that now adorned it; they had poured wealth into the coffers of the squatters. In return for these contributions the diggers should receive their rights, or throats would be cut.

On 5 May 1854 the man who had tried to adorn their coarse life with some of the refinements of civilization boarded a ship for England and passed off the stage of their public life. La Trobe by his very nature was disposed to bend before a great wind. The man chosen to take his place had none of the gifts needed to effect reconciliation or compromise. Sir Charles Hotham came into their midst with the 'sorrowful heart' of a man who had wanted to achieve glory in the British navy in the Crimea but, to his chagrin, had been bullied into accepting a colonial governorship at the end of the world. Observers suspected him of emotional unsteadiness.

When opposed, his rage became so violent that some feared he would one day die of apoplexy.

In August Sir Charles and Lady Hotham visited Ballarat to find out 'the real feelings of diggers towards the Government'. He was delighted when the diggers burst forth into shouts of loyalty and cries of attachment to the Old Country such as could hardly be imagined, after which they formed into a procession to accompany Lady Hotham and himself a full mile and a half to their quarters. Diggers, he concluded, provided they were kindly treated, would be 'found in the path of loyalty and duty'.

Soon after his return to Melbourne he decided to put the finances of the government of Victoria in order. The increase in population had increased the costs of government. The problem was how to raise the revenue without imposing taxation that would cripple initiative. The answer, as he saw it, was to enforce the gold licence. He ordered that the police conduct licence searches on the gold-fields twice a week. At Bendigo and Ballarat that October of 1854 the traps again asked the offensive question, 'Got your licence, mate?'. All over Ballarat, Bendigo and the Ovens the cry 'Traps! Traps! Joe! Joe!' was once again heard almost daily.

Many diggers already believed that only base slaves paid for a licence. By contrast the commissioner and his offsiders regarded digger-hunting as a source of delightful recreation, in which those lousy impertinent diggers could be marched off in triumph to the commissioner's camp and displayed handcuffed like felons until such time as Mr Commissioner or one of the magistrates was ready for his sport—verbally tormenting a digger on trial for some offence against the goldfields regulations. 'Man-hunting' to discover the unlicensed diggers was carried out in the style of an English fox-hunt. Once again traps chained unlicensed diggers to trees; once again those with money paid their bail; the penniless and the friendless, the clumsy fellows with great beards, shaggy hair and rough hands stood before a fine gentleman on the bench with hands of shiny whiteness who fined them £5. All the behaviour of the officials seemed calculated to impress on the digger the idea that the commissioner and his fellow officers believed they would be degraded by contact with him. At the camp a wooden rail barred the digger from coming too close to the commissioner's tent.

Just as the hot winds began to blow over the fields, human behaviour took a nasty turn. On the night of 6–7 October 1854 James Scobie and a man named Martin, two diggers who had reached that point in a night's drinking when the only question was where the next drink was coming from, knocked at the door of the Eureka Hotel. The proprietor of the hotel, J. F. Bentley, told Scobie and

Martin to P.O.Q. Their need being great, they knocked again. The door opened. A scuffle ensued during which Scobie was kicked with such brutality that he died. A court of inquiry decided by two to one that there was no prima-facie case to charge Bentley and his associates with murder or manslaughter. Scobie's digger mates, smelling corruption and convinced in particular that one of the pro-Bentley men on the court of inquiry, J. D'Ewes, was a notorious receiver of bribes from Bentley, set up a great howl of indignation.

Robert Rede, commissioner of the goldfields at Ballarat since May 1854, belonged by birth to an ancient county family. He was so puffed up with a sense of his own social importance that he made no attempt to conceal his contempt for the diggers. He was always talking of giving the diggers 'a fearful lesson . . .'. It was the language of the English public school.

Convinced that the government camp was a hotbed of corruption, that bribery of officials was common and that the magistrates were bound in an 'unholy compact' with unsavoury publicans such as Bentley, a crowd of angry diggers gathered near the Eureka Hotel on 17 October to discuss the affair. A hot north wind, which had been blowing for two days, had already frayed the diggers' nerves. Copious swigs at the black bottle had put them into a reckless mood. Under the influence of the moderates and the believers in moral suasion, the diggers resolved unanimously to use every lawful means to have the case brought before other and more competent authorities. No sooner had most of the peaceful and the moderate dispersed than Henry Westerby, well known as a fomenter of riot and disorder, uttering the war-whoop of a drunken man, turned to his mates and said, 'We'll have the bugger Bentley out'. They replied, 'We'll smoke the bugger out'. Commissioner Rede chose that moment of all moments to teach the diggers one of his 'fearful lessons': he paraded a detachment of soldiers on the outskirts of the mob. Aided and abetted by Andrew McIntyre and Thomas Fletcher, well known to the camp as a man who knocked about sly-grog shops, Henry Westerby carried an armful of paper and rags to the windward of the hotel and lit them. Within two hours nothing was left of Bentley's den of infamy but glowing embers and fire-stained chimneys. While some diggers roared out, 'We want Bentley, We want Bentley!', drunken revellers ransacked the ashes in search of bottles of rum and other ardent spirits, while Westerby lay on his back in drunken oblivion. The great roar of the mob rolled over to the camp as a herald of a future day of reckoning. The following morning a very frightened Bentley staggered into the camp and begged for protection.

When the news reached Melbourne, respectable burghers spat out the words of horror, 'a disgraceful outrage'. Hotham, exercising that discipline he had learnt in the navy to conceal the storms of the man within, declared firmly that there was no occasion for panic. He ordered that Bentley and his accomplices be put on trial and that the ringleaders of the diggers be charged with riot and tumult. Bentley, who had been on the run all his life from the laws of man, once more had to face the men he could not handle. In obedience to Hotham's command Rede arrested Henry Westerby, whose memory of events on the night of 17 October was far from clear, Thomas Fletcher, the sly-grog shop frequenter, and Andrew McIntyre. Hotham also announced his intention to appoint a commission of inquiry into the management of the goldfields.

On 30 October placards were posted all over the Ballarat field calling on diggers to air the facts of injustice at a meeting on 1 November. At Bakery Hill, a brass band played rousing music and a large emblematic diggers' banner waved; with occasional sips at the big black bottle a crowd of 8000 to 10 000 discussed what to do about Westerby, Fletcher and McIntyre. The moderates pleaded with the diggers not to use physical force, because that was un-British. The militants used much stronger language. Tom Kennedy, an angry man from Scotland, reminded them that they were dealing with the 'very rags and tatters of a British Government', and that the diggers might well remember the good old Scottish couplet,

> That mere persuasion is all humbug.
> Nothing convinces like a 'lick in the lug'.

George Black, the editor of the *Gold Diggers Advocate*, reminded them how America had pleaded in vain until they took up the sword. He hoped the diggers would win their rights without a stain of blood. So did J. B. Humffray, the Welsh 'moral force' man, who felt the one-time chapelman's recoil from the taking of human life. Friedrich Vern, a Prussian whose head was stuffed with all those Schilleresque sentiments about the day when all men became brothers, raved for an inordinate time about 'red republicanism'. The diggers elected two 'moral suasion' men, J. B. Humffray and G. Black, and one 'lick in the lug' man, T. Kennedy, to be members of a deputation to Hotham to demand the release of Westerby, Fletcher and McIntyre.

The tumult and the shouting did not die down. When Bentley and two others were sentenced to three years' hard labour on the roads for the manslaughter of James Scobie, the diggers cheered that news. From that time Bentley kept himself going with huge draughts of brandy and laudanum until he destroyed himself with an overdose in April 1873. When news reached Ballarat in the last week of November that Westerby, Fletcher and McIntyre had been sentenced respectively to six, four and three months in prison, the tempers of the diggers again flared. The diggers had ears for only one item of news from Melbourne: the judge had taken the opportunity to drop some harsh words about the composition of the digger community, about their morals and their inferiority to other members of the community. At the same time rumours ran like wildfire that Commissioner Rede and Governor Hotham had entered into a secret agreement to use the first chance to give the diggers 'a fearful lesson'. Blood was about to soak the earth of Australia.

Angry diggers gathered again on 11 November for a meeting to discuss the negotiations with Hotham. Convinced that the people were the origin of all just power, they resolved that it was the inalienable right of every citizen to have a voice in making the laws he was called upon to obey. They resolved that taxation without representation was tyranny. In an unblushing and unacknowledged borrowing from their illustrious predecessors the Americans, they went on to declare it the duty of the people to remove an unjust power which was tyrannizing over them.

While the cheers of the diggers for the proposition that all power rested in the people were reverberating round Ballarat, Sir Charles 'Quarter Deck' Hotham, that Tory 'Alphabetical' John Leslie Fitzgerald Vesey Foster, and that enemy of the people William Stawell were whispering to each other in the corridors of power that the time had come to introduce 'Government by artillery' on the goldfields. The time had come 'to put them down'. In the meantime, unaware of the fearful lesson to which they were about to be subjected, the diggers promenaded over the vast goldfields the following Sunday in their best costumes, their wives and children walking beside them in their best frocks, all observing the greatest possible order and sobriety, all as calm and as becoming as in the best towns of Christian England. 'How delightful would it not be', mused the correspondent of the Melbourne *Argus*, 'to rule such men well!'

It was too late. When the delegates from the diggers, Black, Humffray and Kennedy met the Governor Sir Charles Hotham, the Colonial Secretary John Foster, and the Attorney-General William Stawell in Melbourne on 27 November, they were dismissed with off-handed disdain.

During the afternoon of the preceding day a detachment of the 40th Regiment had marched into Ballarat from Geelong. This wrought in the diggers a high pitch of excitement. They greeted the troops with ridicule and abuse, knocked down the driver of one of the baggage carts and kicked him so brutally that fears were entertained for his life. A digger shot a drummer boy in the thigh. Some said that was a warning to Hotham and Co., showing to what lengths an indignant population could go. At ten that night as a squadron of mounted police proceeded towards the camp they were greeted with angry cries of 'Joe! Joe! Joe!' and attacked with sticks and stones. The excitement lasted all through the night as diggers discharged revolvers and rifles into the air. Weary soldiers hurled threats of revenge at prowling diggers. Weary diggers taunted the soldiers with rude remarks about the quality of the perfume used by lords of creation who swilled champagne while diggers sweated their guts out in the bowels of the earth.

This threat of government by artillery played havoc with the minds of men already disturbed by that underlying fear for their future because of the decline in the income earned by alluvial diggers. No one had introduced machinery to assist in the working of the deep sinkings at Ballarat. Diggers who were down to 160 feet were still not using horse-gins to draw up their earth and their water. They were still using a windlass turned by two or three men. Companies might have introduced steam-engines, but the diggers were just as implacably opposed to companies as they were to the 'bloody licence tax'. They preferred to struggle on without such combinations, each independent of the other. By contrast, at Bendigo, much machinery had been introduced: quartz-crushing had started. Bendigo offered a future for men working for wages. Ballarat offered working on one's own account at the price of earning less than subsistence money. Men who believed their very existence was threatened were summoned to meet on 29 November 1854 to hear whether the men in high places in Melbourne had any idea at all of what it was like to be asked to climb up out of one of those 160-foot holes to show a licence to 'a bloody trap'.

At noon on 29 November the diggers gathered for another monster meeting on Bakery Hill. To the disquiet of the moderates on that afternoon the Australian flag, the Southern Cross, was the only flag hoisted over the platform. Friedrich Vern asked those present to take immediate steps to burn all their licences. If any party was arrested for having no licence, the united people would under all circumstances defend and protect them. The Reverend Mr Downing implored the diggers for the love of Christ not to do it, but he was heard in sullen silence. A digger tried to remind them that as all were British, they should use constitutional means to redress their grievances. He was shoved off the platform and only saved by the chairman from being torn to pieces.

A rather good-looking young Irishman who went by the name of Peter Lalor called on all present to unite for the redress of their grievances. He saw himself as an ordinary man who had been forced into action by the terrible necessities of the time and the feelings that rose out of them. He made it plain that by democracy he did not mean 'Chartism, or Communism, or Republicanism'. As he put it, 'if a democrat means opposition to a tyrannical press, a tyrannical people, or a tyrannical government, then I have been, I am still, and will ever remain a democrat'. As a boy in Ireland he had learnt from his father about those Englishmen who 'fattened on hunger, raggedness, and destitution' in Ireland. Now, it seemed to him, those same monsters in human shape, this time strutting round the goldfields of Ballarat as boy commissioners, were fattening on the labour of the diggers. To put an end to that he was prepared to do what his ancestors had done in Ireland: forge a pike to pierce the hearts of these Anglo-Saxon tyrants. And so an Irish gentleman, a bit of a conservative in politics, no believer in all the palaver and ballyhoo about the rights of man, stood there on the platform with radicals such as Vern and Kennedy.

All through the speeches on that very hot November day, when the sun threatened to melt all of them, a sly-grog seller plied the black bottle. So by the time the chairman, Timothy Hayes, asked them, 'Are you ready to die?' they cried out in a great drunken frenzy, 'Yes, Yes! Hurrah!'. A volley of revolver shots and rifle shots swelled that chorus. One man lit his licence. Soon a blazing fire consumed the licences, the ashes of which were still blowing over the fields as the diggers withdrew to their tents.

Robert Rede was not a man to treat insubordination lightly. He responded to this challenge by holding a council of war with Captain Charles Pasley and Captain J. W. Thomas. The officials must not give way to popular clamour. They must take steps to prevent a popular rebellion. They must teach the diggers a lesson. The three decided on a licence hunt on the following day.

At ten on the morning of 30 November Commissioner Rede, supported by a troop of mounted and foot police, their swords drawn and their bayonets fixed, declared to the diggers that he was determined to inspect their licences. When a junior officer threatened to apprehend all who had not got their licences, one universal cry went up from the diggers: 'To the camp, boys, to the camp'. Suddenly another shout was raised: 'Not to the camp, boys, not to the camp, but to our own ground on Bakery Hill'. The diggers fell into line two abreast behind Captain Ross from Toronto, who proudly bore the flag of the Southern Cross; the diggers chanted slogans against paying the licence fees and in favour of winning their rights. As the column moved towards the place known as Eureka, Peter Lalor pressed Raffaello Carboni, an Italian radical, by the hand and asked him to make sure that if foreigners could not provide themselves with fire-arms, they would attach pieces of steel with a sharp point to a pike with which to pierce the tyrants' hearts. Over at the camp the officer in charge of the police was telling his men that if a digger raised his hand to strike or throw a stone, they were to shoot him on the spot. It looked as though the time for reconciliation and composing of differences had passed.

By five in the evening 500 excited men gathered at Eureka. Irishmen with memories of English callousness during the potato famine of 1846-47 and of English brutality to the leaders of Young Ireland were there because those hateful members of the Protestant ascendancy in Ireland, men like Foster and Stawell, were at it again in Melbourne. Timothy Hayes, an Irishman with the airs of a high-born country gentleman, and Peter Lalor, both foes to the Anglo-Saxon tyrant, neither of them a friend of democracy or the rights of the people, rubbed shoulders with enthusiasts for that day when all men would be brothers. Men who were swept along by the excitement and the uproar, men who did not know what it was all about, and men who were still suffering so acutely from the excesses of the previous night that they were most of all concerned to know where their next drink was coming from found themselves in the same company as humourless 'future of humanity' men. Some were there because it was one way of ensuring that they would no longer hear their wives talking; some were there because they were told, 'Be in it, mate'; some were there because they were terrified that if they were not, their mates would never speak to them again.

After his election as leader, Peter Lalor made a manly speech. Then they knelt down on the earth of their adopted country on one of those radiant summer evenings in Australia after a cool change had refreshed man and beast and earth. The diggers declared in solemn measured tone, 'We swear by the Southern Cross to stand truly by each other, and fight to defend our rights and liberties'. A Vandemonian drunkard, spiritual brother to those drunken sots who had set Bentley's pub alight, almost smudged the epiphany of the moment by urging them to burn the bloody camp down straight away and roast the bastards inside it. Carboni silenced him with a 'respectable kick in his less respectable region' with a most 'respectable boot'. The ugly Australian was not to mar that day when the faces of simple men were transfigured. On Friday and Saturday, 1 and 2 December, the diggers feverishly constructed a stockade out of slabs of wood which had previously done service as pit-props in their holes, and armed themselves with rifles. Those without rifles sharpened pikes. A government corrupt to the core was about to fall.

Over in the camp, officers and men were showing by all sorts of gestures and attitudes and intemperate words their eagerness to give the diggers a taste of 'steel and lead'. Captain Pasley was more convinced than ever, as he had put it first on the night of 30 November, that 'very strong measures are necessary in this gold field, and that sedition must be put down by force'. To risk the camp was to risk the colony. At a council of war on the night of 2 December he and his fellow officers decided to destroy the stockade and sweep the whole goldfield with shot on the following day.

By then the windlasses were silent; manual labour, buying and selling and even tippling had stopped. Everyone was excited and confused. On one side of the field the scarlet-shirted and white-capped men of the cavalry, the infantry and the police stood at the ready. Across the valley on the other side the 'bone and sinew' of the colony, armed with the Irish pike of yesteryear, the latest American revolver, the 'Djerid' of the Arab and the cutlass of 'Jack tar', the ploughshare and the reaping hook were also at the ready. By Saturday night the numbers had fallen from 2000 to 150 as men, for motives as diverse as the motives that brought them to that fever pitch of the night of 30 November when they swore allegiance on bended knee to the Southern Cross, drifted back to their tents. Some of the 150 who remained spent the night carousing till they lost consciousness. They slept there under the canopy of that very vast sky, not knowing that this time men with hangovers and alcoholic remorse were to be changed by smoke and shot into folk heroes.

As first light spread over the valley, Captain Thomas was telling his troops the time had come to save the colony by destroying the stockade. To achieve that the troops and the mounted police would proceed at once to the place where the revolutionary flag was flying. When the troops were within 150 yards of the stockade, they were received by a rather sharp and well-directed fire from the rebels. Captain Thomas then ordered the bugler to sound the 'commence firing!'. Captain Wise, the cheerful man whom every-one loved, fell, shot in the knee, gaily telling his comrades his dancing was now spoiled forever. As he spurred on his men he was shot again and was carried from the field just as the troops climbed over the slabs into the stockade. John King, a native of Mayo in Ireland, climbed the flagstaff, pulled down the rebel flag and tore it to shreds, to the cheers of his fellow soldiers. In the madness of the moment the soldiers threatened to murder every one of the 150 rebel bastards inside the stockade. Captain Pasley shouted above the uproar that any soldier who murdered a prisoner would be shot on the spot. Captain Thomas then ordered the firing to cease, the bugle sounded the retreat, and the whole force, together with their large contingent of prisoners, retired to the camp. It was all over in fifteen minutes.

As the bugle call to retreat echoed round the valleys the mounted police burned down tents, laid waste sly-grog shops and chased terror-struck diggers back into their holes. In one tent two diggers who had been seeking a happy issue out of all this danger in drunkenness were too far gone to move. Their bodies were consumed in the flames. Peter Lalor, who had been shot in the arm, was hidden from the troopers who were hunting for him. Friedrich Vern and Tom Kennedy also eluded their captors. John Humffray had not been seen at the stockade, he not being a man to be surrounded by smoke and blood and shot. As Raffaello Carboni bolted towards his tent a trooper fired at him and blew his cabbage-tree hat off his head. Father Smyth found the men who were dying and prepared them as best he could for the life of the world to come.

On the field of battle five soldiers lay dead with bullet holes in their bodies, and twelve were wounded, including one policeman; twenty-four diggers lay dead with their eyes now glazed and staring with stony fixedness. Probably twenty were wounded. Women moaned over dead husbands and brothers and sweethearts. A dog refused to leave his dead master. Back in the camp Captain Wise had intimations that that body of his which had brought him so much pleasure was about to go back to the dust from whence it came. The shopkeepers were wondering when buying and selling would start again; the tipplers were wondering how long they must wait before they could get a drink. No one on the field or in the camp detected any majesty in the moment or prophesied that the diggers would one day be heroes of the people and hailed as the founders of democracy in Australia. Law and order had been restored. The shutters on the shops could now be removed and the flaps on the sly-grog tent tied back.

Governor Hotham, rash as ever, thanked Her Majesty's faithful subjects for ending the anarchy and confusion sown by 'strangers in their midst'. Driven by that fatal tendency to overreact to every situation, he also issued instructions that the 114 Ballarat rebels taken prisoner by Captain Thomas should be charged with insurrection and substantial rewards paid for the apprehension of those leaders such as Vern, Lalor and Black who had unlawfully, rebelliously and traitorously levied and arrayed armed men with the view of making war against their Sovereign Lady the Queen.

By contrast, as early as 5 December the storekeepers were so keen on the resumption of buying and selling that they resolved at a public meeting to use every constitutional means to restore tranquillity and good feeling. They appointed delegates to talk things over with Hotham in a spirit of conciliation and Christian forbearance. At the same time in the *Ballarat Times* the editor, Henry Seekamp, called on his fellow countrymen, on nature and on Heaven itself for a 'vengeance deep and terrible' for 'the foul massacre' of human beings. Again Hotham overreacted. He ordered his officers to arrest Seekamp and Humffray, both gentle spirits with faith in man's capacity for better things, and to charge them with insurrection. Hotham wanted to put visionaries behind iron bars.

In Melbourne, too, a terror-struck bourgeoisie rallied round those forces of law and order which alone gave promise of preserving buying and selling and that social calm which for them was the heart of the matter. All day on 3 December the city had been in a fearful commotion as rumours swept through town that 500 well-armed diggers were marching to Melbourne where, with the help of the criminals, the madmen and the drunkards, they proposed to ravage and lay waste the city that had become the citadel of rectitude, godliness and respectability in the Australian colonies. When news of the fighting at Ballarat reached the city, feelings of grief, horror, shame and indignation agitated all hearts. Some called for revenge against the foreigners who perpetrated such an outrage and brought disgrace to the British name.

On 5 December over 3000 gathered in front of the City Court House in Swanston Street to call for law and order, and denounce those who would descend to the methods adopted by the excited multitude in France. The population of Melbourne was just as sharply divided as the population on the goldfields. Law-and-order men deplored the behaviour of the diggers; the people shouted 'Down with Foster', 'Three cheers for the diggers' and called the members of Hotham's government 'a set of wholesale butchers'.

On the following day 6000 gathered in the open space adjoining St Paul's Church to hear Henry Langlands, one of those shop-keepers who had been alarmed by the events at Ballarat, vow that from henceforth the people of Melbourne would seek reform peaceably, constitutionally and by moral force alone. That was the Christian way; that was the British way; that was the effective way. The *Age* was delighted: the people of Melbourne, in its view, had regained their nobility. The bourgeoisie were beginning to win the victory over digger riot and disorder.

In the *Empire* Henry Parkes wrote of events at Eureka as an 'un-British error' which had probably been instigated by reckless foreigners; it was not the British way to yield to the threat of physical violence. Such bourgeois sentiments resounded through the other colonies. On the one hand, bourgeois opinion wanted a system of government which promoted talent rather than privilege; on the other, they denounced the forces of anarchy and mob rule.

In London Karl Marx, prophet of the doom of bourgeois civilization, explained why it was that in an Australian colonial society the grievances of the diggers would be redressed, but the revolutionary movement would be weakened, because of the absence of any class on which to build such a movement. Marx detected the interest of the bureaucracy and the bourgeois monopolists in the stability of government in the colony. For the year in which he was writing, 1855, the government of Victoria had allocated over £1.5 million to such public works as roads, docks, wharves, barracks, government buildings, custom sheds, botanical gardens, government sheds, etc. Here was a fat cow for Mr Money Bags to milk, while taking care not to provoke the people into riot by that incompetence and insolence the bourgeoisie now realized to be inseparable from government by 'gentlemen'.

Early in the New Year Sir Charles Hotham decided to charge thirteen of the state prisoners from the riot at Eureka with high treason. When the trials came on in February and March, the *Age* pointed out to its readers that the accused belonged to the very class who could save Victoria from the crises and disasters into which it had been plunged by Hotham and his class. By 22 March the *Age* was ready to sum it all up: the heart of the people was sound; the heart of the government was rotten.

The task of the colonial bourgeoisie was twofold: to discredit the revolutionaries, the 'lick on the lug' men in the digger movement, and isolate them from the moderates, the 'moral suasion' men, the men who believed in the British way of redressing grievances by constitutional means; and to capture political power in the colonial parliaments. On the latter they faltered because as a colonial bourgeoisie they were too timid or too cowardly to become masters in their own house and too dependent both on the goodwill of the squatter in their own country and on the capitalist in Britain to take up the cry of freedom and independence for the Australian colonies, far less the cultivation of an Australian national sentiment. This dependence of the colonial bourgeoisie on London, and their success in educating the working class in their own values laid the firm foundations for conservatism in Australia.

As so often in the history of the country, an artist and a drunkard perceived the direction in which the river of life was flowing. Samuel Thomas Gill, who was already known in the colony at large for his watercolours and black-and-white drawings, was pondering the question of who had drawn the prizes and who the blanks in the lottery of life on the goldfields. He had the insight of the drunkard into what was happening in society at large. When he painted the Ballarat Subscription Ball at the end of 1854, he put on his canvas the unsteady men, the men, like himself, whom women would brand as untrustworthy and unreliable. He also showed the men with the values of Mr Money Bags, the shopkeepers and the bankers, who had come to the top of that mass of human beings which had swarmed over the goldfields. The bourgeoisie were the victors in the battle for wealth on the fields: the Humffray, Seekamp, Carboni, Vern and Kennedy dream of a glorious future for humanity had fallen on stony ground.

5

A Colonial Bourgeoisie

In February 1855 the press published the story of the melancholy charge of the Light Brigade on 25 October 1854 in the Crimea. Out of 600 who rode into that valley of death only a few had survived. By then the Australian press was beginning to single out the English governing classes as the cause of these disasters and abominations. The *Sydney Morning Herald* was suggesting that the root of the trouble lay in the English system which subjected the distribution of offices to the 'etiquette of the drawing room'. Aristocratic government was associated with senility and lack of purpose. The middle classes, the bourgeoisie, were promoting themselves as the regenerating spirit of the nation. In Australia, the bourgeoisie had long tired of aristocratic Englishmen. More than ever, they were determined to take over the management of the state from the landed gentry, the colonial bureaucrats and the Imperial Parliament. The difficulty was that they had interests in London which condemned them to the role of a colonial rather than a national bourgeoisie. When J. D. Lang raised his voice in 1852 for Freedom and Independence for the Golden Lands of Australia, they rebuked him. For the British provided the capital for all those enterprises—railway-building, roads, public buildings, schools, universities, churches—which brought profit to the colonial bourgeoisie. Both the colonies and the mother country were contributing to that spread of British commerce over the whole globe, that industrialization of the world which would bring in its train to all the world that peace of the bourgeoisie which passed all understanding.

The colonial bourgeoisie believed it was possible to achieve material progress, promote equality of opportunity and abolish the privileges of birth while remaining loyal subjects of Her Majesty. Suburban house-building in the wake of the gold discoveries was the outward and visible evidence of their faith. In both Melbourne and Sydney surburbia flowered. The successful erected mansions, piles of grey and turreted masonry, imitations of the 'classic' or 'gothic' styles which were in vogue. Colonials were the beneficiaries of an imported civilization rather than the creators of their own. The park-like grounds were copied from England. The grasses, the ornamental trees and the shrubs were imported from England. They grew in splendour side by side with the gaunt gum or the sombre mimosa as further evidence of that dual loyalty and attachment which permeated their lives.

As evidence of the special colonial twist to the principle of equality of opportunity, a worker might end up the owner of the mansion he had once worked on as a builder's labourer, or the lord of the drawing room in which he had once worked as a plasterer. In preparation for that rise, he had a 'gothic', or 'classic' villa, like his master's but with fewer rooms and a much smaller garden both back and front. The house was often decorated as was his master's with iron-lace edging, plaster urns flanking the front steps, and narrow stained-glass windows to either side of the entrance door. As domestic servants were in short supply, labour-saving devices for the preparation of the food and for domestic cleaning appeared in the kitchens of the affluent, while in the kitchens of the rest 'Mum' or some young girl was reduced to domestic slavery. The houses of both the masters and their men were generally sheltered by a verandah which afforded some protection from the glare and heat of a summer's sun. The climate and the spirit of the place often dictated variations on the English theme for which their hearts were not as yet prepared. They belonged both to the land of their adoption and the home of their ancestors. That was their complex fate.

Their schools also wore the scars of their past. The bourgeoisie professed a belief in minimal education. Part of the price of not breaking with their past in the United Kingdom was that they were obliged to accept a compromise on the education question. For the education argument was still bogged in the mire of sectarianism. Bitter hostility between the leaders of the Catholic and Protestant churches continued to stifle all attempts to introduce universal education. Solons of Spring Street or Macquarie Street either had to grasp the sectarian nettle or leave well alone. They chose the cowardly course: they left well alone. The debate on education in all the colonies was characterized by the way in which public men called down the wrath of God on their opponents for presuming to 'inoculate school-children with the virus of sectarianism', the colonial bourgeoisie thereby revealing their powerlessness to wrestle with the demons of sectarian discord.

The other reason why they shied off the education question was that they had schools of their own in which their sons and some of their daughters were being educated. In the period before the discovery of gold the King's School at Parramatta, St Peter's College at Adelaide, and Launceston Grammar School had been opened. In the 1840s the sons of the squatters and the bourgeoisie were first introduced to the civilizing influence of Greek and Roman literature and the Christian view of the nature of God and man, both of which planted in their minds values that collided with the tendencies of their generation. The Greeks, the Romans and the Christians taught an elitism, a stoicism, a pessimism about the fruits of human endeavour, and a scepticism about the possibilities of human happiness clean different from that taste for equality, that belief in material well-being, and that pursuit of happiness which characterized the temper of the times. Gold increased the number of such institutions in Australia. In Melbourne, the Melbourne Academy, the forerunner of Scotch College, enrolled boys who were taught in the classroom by Robert Lawson, a great wielder of the cane, and looked after in the dormitory and the dining room by his wife, a childless woman who was said to enjoy lording it over small boys. The Anglican Bishop of Melbourne, Charles Perry, had plans for similar grammar schools for Anglicans in Melbourne and Geelong.

At the ceremony for laying the foundation stone of Geelong Grammar School on 24 June 1857 the proceedings began with the band playing 'Rule Britannia'. The bourgeoisie accepted without demur the notion that the minds of their sons should be steeped in the history and literature of an ancient civilization and the Old World rather than their own. Their sons were to receive that 'sound learning' and 'religious education' which would preserve them as British Australians, prepare them to take the senior positions in church, state and the professions of the colony as distinct from a nation.

At the universities of Sydney and Melbourne, the heads of the governing bodies and the professors were exiles from the Old World. They introduced their students to the science and culture of Europe, never thinking to encourage them to be pathfinders of a new civilization in their adopted country. In April 1853 the council of the University of Melbourne elected the 'Cheery, Cultured, Courteous' Mr Justice Redmond Barry to be its first chancellor. Barry was a fine flower of that British culture kept alive in the Australian colonies by the immigrant-dominated community. By birth and education he belonged to the Protestant ascendancy in Dublin. He was born at Ballyclogh, County Cork, on 7 June 1813, the son of a major-general in the British army of occupation; he was educated at Trinity College, Dublin, and did terms at Lincoln's Inn in London, only to find himself at the age of 25 a man of talents but no prospects. Melbourne provided the ideal setting for his success. He arrived there in 1839. By 1852 he was a judge of the Supreme Court, and the following year became chancellor of the university, an advocate for a public library, and patron of benevolent societies, philharmonic societies and mechanics' institutes, and indeed of every activity that spread sweetness and light in the cultural deserts of Australia.

He was a man of huge appetites, swallowing oysters and champagne in such quantities that not even the ample robes of a judge could conceal the effects of such gluttony on his figure. Nor was he ever able to prevent the sight of a pretty woman from stirring the fire in the blood. His love for Mrs Louisa Barrow was a tempestuous passion unaffected by the passage of time, yet he refused ever to live with her, refused to have anything to do with marriage. She was there to minister to his delights—like reading Gibbon, or drinking a vintage wine, or the subterranean satisfactions of tormenting a witness in the lawcourts, or making men of imagination confess that the truth was not in them. Barry believed in education as a contributor to pleasure, and a bastion of that way of life in which he moved. For him civilization meant the Melbourne Club, the best seats at the theatre, the bowings and scrapings in the lawcourts, and brass bands on Sunday to give the people pleasure.

Barry's histrionic gifts and Irish love of verbal and emotional extravaganza made him a superb figurehead for an institution created to be 'the glory of the South and the civilizer of the East'. At the commencement ceremony on 13 April 1855 he told an audience of all the respectable people in Melbourne that the university would promote 'wisdom, learning and virtue'. It would also be 'the nursing mother and generous instructress of a race of distinguished scholars'. What he did not foresee was the consequence of those scholars reproducing in Australia a faint echo of the scholarship of the Old World.

While institutions were being erected to promote a future meritocracy, bourgeois publicists continued to occupy themselves with the moral well-being of the working class, preaching the doctrines which would lead them to redemption. True joy and true pleasure were to be found in work. The workers should avoid the haunts of riot and vice as they would the dens of savage beasts, for they were the dens of monsters of vice, poverty and disease. The working men should study, they should practise cleanliness, they should never take a meal without washing the hands, particularly around the

fingernails, they should be provident, frugal, temperate, and antici-
pate want of employment, old age and infirmity by saving. Idleness
and vice robbed them of their dignity and that place they ought to
hold in society, that place which was the reward of work, temperance, providence, and the pursuit of the Christian Dionysius rather
than the pagan Bacchus. The virtuous worker would be rewarded
with membership of one of those leagues of universal brotherhood,
and brotherly fellowship. The brotherhood of mankind was just as
much one of the rights of man in the bourgeois creed as liberty,
equality, or the pursuit of happiness.

This itch to improve the morals and souls of the working classes
was echoed by the leaders of that class. When the members of the
Early Closing Association met in Melbourne in November 1855 to
discuss the reduction in the hours of work, one of their leaders after
paraphrasing the words of their Saviour that man should not live by
bread alone, went on to remind his listeners that men were not
animals who were driven to toil without doing some good to
themselves. They needed time for recreation and self-instruction so
that they might improve themselves. The leaders and teachers of
the working classes were not sustained by any vision of a better
society or by any conviction that the cause of all the moral infamy
and degradation of mankind lay in the private ownership of
property or the profit motive, but rather by the hope that the use of
machines for the production of goods and commodities would
create the material well-being and leisure that would enable them
to fulfil that promise made to them by their Saviour, that men might
have life and have it more abundantly. Their first task was to win
more time for leisure; the one way to achieve that was to reduce the
hours of work.

On 26 March 1856 a mass meeting in Melbourne of workers and
employers, inspired by speeches by James Stephens and James
Gilvray Galloway, both Chartists, both recent immigrants, both
believers in working on their own account, both members of the
recently reformed Operative Stonemasons Society, resolved that an
eight-hour day must be introduced. On 11 April 700 members of the
mechanical trades crowded into the Queen's Theatre in Melbourne
to discuss the expediency and practicability of abridging the hours
of labour to eight hours. Dr Thomas Embling, one of those doctors
who wanted human beings to be kinder to one another, gave them
the slogan 'Eight hours labour, eight hours recreation, eight hours
rest'. He told them to improve themselves so that they might be
worthy of being electors and of being elected. All the speakers were
obsessed with the morals of the workers. It was made known that
this was no trade union combination to raise the rate of wages; the

workers would find that they could have all the wise and good men to help them.

Not all the employers were prepared to go hand in hand with the tradesmen. When the contractor for the building of Parliament House in Melbourne refused to cut the hours of labour to eight per day on 21 April 1856, the stonemasons on the university building downed tools and marched to Parliament House. There, having been joined by other tradesmen, they resolved not to work for employers who did not accept the eight-hour day. The contractor capitulated. To celebrate this victory a few thousand operatives with their wives and children gathered at the Cremorne Gardens in Melbourne on 12 May for a dinner of the good old English fare of roast beef and plum pudding followed by dancing to the strains of a band, a display of fireworks, and a mock bombardment of Sevastopol. The whole proceedings were conducted with that order and decorum appropriate to a class that had been granted extra leisure so that it might behave like men made in the image of God, and not like the first working class in Australia, who were accused by their masters of wallowing in a sensual sty.

A new society was taking shape, a society in which the bourgeoisie and the workers were determined to win political reform. Although the governments of the Australian colonies still courted the favouring smiles of the squatters, some said the days of squatterdom's domination were numbered. A Commission of Inquiry was held into the goldfields. On its recommendation the 'bloody gold licence' was replaced by the miner's right, £1 per year, introduced in June 1855. Also on the commission's recommendation, wardens, efficient, utilitarian, and free from the gentleman's sniff, replaced the gold-laced commissioners. The diggers had also won the right to elect representatives to the Legislative Councils of Victoria and New South Wales. Under the Victorian Electoral Act of 22 May 1855 the number of the members of the Legislative Council was increased by twelve to sixty-six, of whom four were to be appointed by Her Majesty and eight elected by the new electorates of Castlemaine, Sandhurst, Ballaarat (sic), Avoca and the Ovens. It was not quite what the diggers had demanded. They had asked for electorates in which diggers alone would elect diggers to the Council: under the Act they had to share their electoral right with storekeepers, professional men, pastoralists and farmers of the district.

In May of the following year the news of that senseless carnage in the Crimea led the *Age* in Melbourne to wonder whether the time had come for the Australians to press for independence: 'Fellow colonists', they wrote in May 1855, 'You see how your interests are trifled with in England: don't you think THE TIME HAS COME WHEN WE SHOULD PREPARE TO TAKE THE BUSINESS ENTIRELY INTO OUR OWN HANDS?'. By the end of the year J. D. Lang wanted the Victorians to go further and declare their independence, to assert their natural, inherent and indefeasible right to entire political freedom and National Independence, and to defend that independence by force of arms if necessary.

Again the bourgeoisie of the Australian colonies preferred to remain colonial and provincial rather than sail over those uncharted waters of independence, partly because of the influence of the immigrants and partly because independence was tainted with radicalism and socialism. Even Van Diemen's Land was becoming respectable. On 11 August 1853 it had celebrated the end of 'convict pollution'. To mark this transformation, the British Government had agreed that from the first day of January 1856 the colony should be known as Tasmania.

When the news reached Sydney in December 1855 that Her Majesty had at long last given her assent to an act to confer a new constitution on the colony of New South Wales, Henry Parkes predicted that the days of gentry government were numbered, as were those of the snobs who were prepared to fall at the feet of imported titled gentlemen, like Sir Charles FitzRoy in Sydney and Sir Charles Hotham in Melbourne, and lick their boots. In Melbourne Hotham got so excited when he heard the news that he became ill and died on 31 December 1855.

All was not lost, however, for the colonial landed gentry, the clerical aristocracy and their patrician supporters in the towns. The privilege and influence they had worked so hard to achieve and to defend were now challenged by the forces of vulgarity and disorder. In each of the colonies, earnest gentlemen gathered in panelled rooms and wondered how they were to keep the levellers, the Chartists and the low Irish mob out of power. In the cities it looked as though the innings of the people, as distinct from government by gentlemen, was about to begin. In the elections to the newly created legislative assemblies of New South Wales, Victoria, Tasmania and South Australia, which were held on various dates throughout 1856, the supporters of government by gentlemen behaved like tired old men who had lost touch with the creative forces of their society. They were alarmed by the conduct of the campaigns. In Hobart, Sydney, Melbourne and Adelaide rowdyism and mob rule prevailed in the streets while candidates plied voters with free drinks. But the bourgeoisie had no reason to fear the consequences of 'rowdyism'. In every colony the candidates of the gentry won a victory over the candidates of the people. The constitutions of the colonies had produced the political results they were designed to achieve: the gentry's ideal of the representation of 'interests' as distinct from the bourgeois principle of the representation of population. Plural voting, the property qualifications for voters and members, and weighting of electorates had provided the opportunity for the pastoral, clerical and urban aristocracy 'interest' to obtain a bare majority in the legislative assemblies and a vast superiority in the legislative councils. Similar constitutional arrangements came into force in Queensland when the state separated from New South Wales four years later, but representative government did not arrive in Western Australia until 1890.

As the members of the colonial legislative assemblies took their places following those turbulent elections of 1856, the men on the Opposition benches waiting to take their turn in the saddle were almost indistinguishable from the ministers and their supporters. But there were some differences. In New South Wales the opposition leader was Charles Cowper, a country squire, a supporter of the clerical aristocracy, with liberal ideas on land and constitutional reform. He was supported by Henry Parkes, who was driven in contrary directions by vanity, ambition, the ideas from his Chartist past, his role as the leader of liberal sentiment in Sydney, and his pride that he, a poor bloody immigrant, was now invited to dine in the houses of the most respectable people in Sydney.

Strong British feeling characterized most of the new men on the stage of public life in Victoria. But Charles Gavan Duffy had come to Melbourne in 1856 with the reputation of being that prominent member of the Young Ireland movement in Dublin who had ended up in the House of Commons in London while his fellow patriots Smith O'Brien, Thomas Meagher and John Mitchel were suffering the agonies of convict life in Van Diemen's Land. The great passion of his life, ever since he walked into public life in Dublin, was to 'strike a blow in the hereditary contest' of his people against the English. Soon after he arrived in Melbourne he told his admirers he was 'still an Irish rebel to the backbone and to the spinal marrow'. Modesty was not one of his virtues. Privately he told his friends in Melbourne that in colonial society he felt himself to be a whale among minnows. Publicly no one quite knew what he stood for. He called himself a 'radical reformer', who was no more a 'Red Republican', as some alleged, than a 'Red Indian'. That year it looked as though there was a role for the radical reformer in public life, because the popular element which Gavan Duffy professed to serve was on the march.

He joined the chorus calling for manhood suffrage and representation on the basis of population. At the same time, in both

Melbourne and Sydney petition after petition demanded that the Crown lands be thrown open to settlement. But so long as the 'Club and Squatting Party' commanded their majority in the Legislative Council no bill for land reform could become the law of the land. There was a great babble of voices, and a great confusion of ideas. The people were now upon the right scent and had only to hunt down their game.

As popular agitation for electoral reform became increasingly vocal, Cowper and his followers in Sydney, and Duffy and his followers in Melbourne, came up with proposals for manhood suffrage, abolition of property qualifications for members, and more equal electoral districts which were compromises between representation of interests and representation of population. It seemed something must be done quickly, as in the month of July news reached Melbourne and Sydney of yet another riot on the Australian goldfields. On 4 July at the Buckland River in north-eastern Victoria the yell of the people had again been heard, as a mob of demented white men drove those 'yellow bastards', the Chinese, off an Australian goldfield.

6

The Barbarians of Lambing Flat

By the middle of 1854 there were 4000 Chinese on the Australian goldfields, and all who were interested in the welfare of the Australian colonies were giving their grave consideration to what should be done about Chinese immigration. Public men were prophesying that serious evils would one day arise from the presence of these strangers. The peculiarities of their language, dress and habits of life were enough to arouse suspicion. On the goldfields meetings were being held at which proposals to drive them out of the country were gravely discussed. In Melbourne working men were heard muttering their fears and their displeasure that these men had come here to lower wages and threaten their own material well-being.

In July 1854 Henry Parkes argued in the Legislative Council that ways needed to be found for preventing the degrading consequences of the introduction of a coloured or an inferior race. In June of 1855 the Legislative Council of Victoria passed an Act under which the master of a ship had to pay a poll-tax of £10 for every Chinese immigrant on his ship. The masters of ships sailing from the ports of Kwangtung, the province in China where most of the immigrants originated, discovered that the way round that Act was to land their passengers in South Australia. From there they made their way overland to the Victorian goldfields. In 1857 nearly 11 000 Chinese overlanded from Robe to the Victorian goldfields. By 1857 there were 23 623 Chinese on the goldfields of Victoria, and a total of 25 424 in the colony at large. The Aborigines of the south-east now had to cope with another invader of their land.

Some of the diggers on the fields were intrigued by the quaint customs and food of the Chinese rather than angered by their morals or fearful of their competition. Some diggers were also applying to the Chinese that great Australian compliment, which was a mixture of arrogance and condescension and a limited affection, 'They're harmless enough'. At the festival to mark the Chinese New Year on the Ovens in January 1857 crowds of Europeans mingled with the Celestials. Europeans tasted the roast sucking-pig, stewed duck, jellies, rice and macaroni with delight. The sight of human beings reclining in every stage of intoxication from opium tickled the fancy of the Europeans. The high-minded spoke of the obligations of Europeans as Christians to think kindly of all manner of men God had placed on the earth. Caroline Chisholm reminded her contemporaries that there would be no rest until man was recognized as man, without distinction of 'colour or clime'.

But there was madness in the blood of the diggers. Many were disgusted by the orientals, or resentful of them. The worst of the goldfield riots occurred at Lambing Flat in New South Wales where in the last months of 1860 500 Chinese and 1200 Europeans were burrowing away furiously along the creekbeds. On 13 November the white diggers stuck notices to quit on the trunks of the gumtrees near the Chinese holes, and burnt their tents. The storekeepers were alarmed, wondering as they did who would buy the huge quantities of rice they had brought up from Sydney.

By the beginning of January 1861 there was much discontent among the Europeans about the presence of large numbers of 'filthy, immoral treacherous and quarrelsome heathen' Celestials. All the traditional objections were raised: they wasted water, stole gold, ruined good digging ground, spread leprosy, and practised secret vices on the bodies of white women and white boys. On 27 January 1500 European diggers gathered to discuss whether Burrangong was a European goldfield or a Chinese territory. One speaker called on them to proclaim before God and man that as 'free-born Britons' they would not allow themselves to be 'trampled to the dust like dogs'. To immense cheering and waving of flags they agreed to give those Chinese bastards two days in which to quit the field. When the Chinese ignored the ultimatum, 1000 diggers marched into the Chinese district at Garibaldi Gully to expel the 'Plague of the country', like chaff before the wind, and escorted them off the diggings.

Hearing of armed digger agitation on Lambing Flat to expel the Chinese, the Premier of New South Wales, Charles Cowper, decided to set out to meet the miners in person and encourage them to talk to him about their grievances. Nothing he had to say, however principled, could win their support. Amid talk of riot and rebellion, Cowper returned to Sydney and dispatched troops to Lambing Flat. Their function, he said, was to assert the supremacy of the law and to prevent any occurrence of bloodshed. For Cowper was a liberal, a believer in sweet reason, and deep down was revolted by the idea that human society could be improved by the shedding of human blood.

The absence of merriment among the diggers on the night of Saturday 29 June betokened the coming storm. Early on the Sunday morning they began to assemble from all parts of the field. By the middle of the morning 2000 to 3000 had gathered. English, Irish, and American flags floated in the breeze. So did another flag with a blue cross in the centre of a ground of white, surrounded by the stars of the Southern Cross. On it, cleverly done in scroll-work, were the words 'No Chinese! Roll up! Roll up!'. To the music of a brass band, the waving of the flags, and the cheering of the members of the procession, they moved into Lambing Flat. As the band played Rule Britannia and the Marseillaise, the men moved into the Chinese area. Before the Chinese could take any effective measures to protect their property or their persons, tents were pulled down, their goods seized and placed on a huge pile which was set alight. Yelling white men slashed at the pigtails of the Chinese, who were crying pitifully for mercy. They also struck them with spades, which made them shriek in terror, to the enormous satisfaction of their attackers. As at the Buckland River in July 1857, in the heat of the moment, civilized men were converted into brutes. Men, or rather monsters, on horseback, armed with bludgeons and whips, tore at the Chinese with a fiendlike fury. One Chinese boy went down upon his knees and, with tears running down his cheeks, pleaded for mercy; a ruffian felled him with one blow. A cripple crawled towards the shelter and safety of the bush, bearing his blanket; it was grabbed from him and thrown on to the fire. Another Chinese was propped up against a tree, his forehead laid open and blood running down his face. The monsters had no eye of pity for him. They were busy throwing clothing, carpets, boots and shoes, food, gold scales, books and writing-paper on to a fire for a grand act of vengeance.

When all the Chinese property they could lay their hands on had gone up in flames, the band again played a march, and the diggers marched off, again 'irrepressibly thirsty', but this time triumphant and exalted. As they drank to the day when there would be no more Chinamen in New South Wales, other members of the digger community who detested the Chinese and wanted them sent back to the place whence they came were shocked that the reputation of the goldfields had been irretrievably harmed by such wanton cruelty. The *Sydney Morning Herald* made the point that Englishmen redressed grievances by constitutional means, adding that in a country in which universal suffrage had given to the poorest a right equal to the most intelligent there was no excuse and there could be no toleration for violence or disorder, or attacks upon property and life. Radicalism and colonial nationalism were indelibly stained with racial intolerance and ruffianism.

When the police attempted to arrest the ringleaders of the barbarous assault on the Chinese, they only managed to catch three of them. On Sunday 14 July 1861, a traditional day on the diggings for the airing of grievances and the settling of scores, there was another 'Roll up' to demand the release of the prisoners. The police refused. The diggers attacked the camp to rescue them by force. In the course of two hours' fighting one of the rioters was killed. The following day when 3000 diggers moved towards the camp, the commissioner, the troopers and the police abandoned the site and set out for Yass, taking their wounded and their prisoners with them. Everything was in a state of disorder: the prison doors were opened and the inmates escaped. Just as everything was verging towards chaos, the diggers formed their own vigilance committees for the protection of the law and the preservation of property from thieves and vagabonds. Digger justice proved to be no less severe on idle and vicious characters than the commissioner and the police. At the burial of the digger killed in the riot on 16 July, the funeral orator named the police as his murderers.

The cry of 'Out with the moon-faced barbarians' was giving way to 'Down with government' and even 'Down with all governments'. When this news reached Sydney, Cowper sent a detachment of 100 troops to Lambing Flat, for the electric telegraph and the new rifle gave governments weapons against revolutionaries not available to their predecessors. Soon after the arrival of the troops on 31 July the diggings returned to normal. The Chinese reappeared at Back Creek: shopkeepers, bankers, hotel-keepers and brothel-keepers reopened for business. That 'harmonious shout' the diggers had hoped would echo all over Australia had ceased to be; the revolutionaries of Lambing Flat returned to their role as workers on their own account. Once again in the history of Australia the workers, after a few days of revolutionary enthusiasm, had remained loyal to those petty-bourgeois aspirations of men of property. The dream of the digger was the ownership of property, rather than the creation of a new society.

Two years after the riots, Lambing Flat as a goldfield was on its last legs. The diggers moved on to other fields. Some moved across the Weddin Mountain to Grenfell in 1866. There in the following June 1867 a child was born in a tent. Within a year his family joined the rush to Pipeclay (Eurunderee) near Gulgong. There as he lay in his bunk in the dark he heard his father and mother tormenting each other; he heard drunken diggers singing lustily that chorus which had been composed during the days of uproar at Lambing Flat:

> Rule Britannia! Britannia rules the waves!
> No more Chinamen will enter Noo South Wales!

The child became the apostle of Australian mateship; the mother became a leader of the movement for that elevation of women designed to end their role as madonnas of the bush and slaves of the kitchen sink. Her name was Louisa; the boy was Henry Lawson.

7

Glory, Folly and Chance

Between November 1859 and January 1860 a committee of the Philosophical Institute of Victoria (later the Royal Society) inquired into the practicability of fitting out an expedition for traversing the unknown interior of the Australian continent. As they saw it, Victoria's duty as the wealthiest and the leading member of the Australian colonies was to succeed where New South Wales and South Australia had failed in removing the mantle of mystery which lay over the centre of the continent. They could not feel indifferent to the advantage of leading the path of civilization into a part of the interior which although politically belonging to New South Wales might commercially be regarded as an enlargement of Victorian territory. Victoria was about to incite the ardour of Australian youth in the cause of science and Australian progress: she would add fresh laurels to the fame of their adopted country and respond nobly to the claims of science, of humanity and of Australian settlement. The bright star of Australian progress was in the ascendant.

They were a committee of gentlemen. Their chairman was Sir William Stawell, the Chief Justice of Victoria. He accepted the Australian tradition that the leaders and officers of exploring expeditions should be gentlemen, and that their men should be drawn from the lower orders of society. Aborigines should be used as guides to the wealth of Australia, always provided care was taken to prevent them becoming maddened and infuriated under the influence of that 'potion' they craved but could not contain.

There were also men of science. John Macadam, the secretary to the committee, was an analytical chemist. Ferdinand von Mueller, a PhD in botany of the University of Kiel, had won a reputation for his knowledge of the flora of the inland of Australia. He wanted to lay the foundations of science: works of art, statues and the adornments of civilization would come after man had established his dominion over the earth. All the members of the committee had a supreme confidence that the progress in communication, in transport, in hunting equipment, in direction-finders, food preservation and water-divining would protect men from all the perils of the Australian desert. The time was ripe for man to establish his mastery over the earth in Australia.

The South Australians also saw themselves as singled out by God to be a great people and builders of one of the finest agricultural countries in the world. John McDouall Stuart was one of those gentlemen officers in the Survey Department. He was a Dionysian figure of a man, who was sustained at times by that vision of glory which had lived in Sturt and who had the fierce pride of the man who stood apart from his fellows. He was an extravagant man, an exaggerator, whose face was said to light up with hope whenever he got within 500 miles of a public house. He also had the strength to endure to the end his cruel fate of walking through life with such a flaw in his clay. On 4 November 1859 he had set out on yet another attempt to reach the centre, but was forced to turn back. On 2 March 1860 he set out again, and reached the centre of Australia, where, two days later, he performed the ceremony Charles Sturt had dreamed of performing: he raised the British flag on a hill he called Central Mount Sturt, a name which was later changed to Central Mount Stuart. After travelling a further 150 miles to the north-west, the scurvy, and his craving, drove him back to Adelaide. He and his party tried again on 29 November 1860 to cross the continent, but again without success. By then it looked as though it would be only a short time before Stuart reached the Gulf of Carpentaria. The Victorians had to hurry if they were to stay out in front.

First they had to raise money, and raise it quickly. By September 1858 an anonymous benefactor had offered £1000 on condition that the exploration committee raised £2000 by subscription. Subscriptions had poured in: the squatters on the route had given generously in expectation that by so doing they were laying up for themselves treasures on earth.

The exploration committee early in 1860 turned to the important duty of selecting a leader for the expedition. After much anxious enquiry and careful deliberation they selected Robert O'Hara Burke, esquire, Superintendent of Police in the Castlemaine district, who had once been a cavalry officer in the Austrian service. Chance or the gods had planted in him an insatiable hunger for glory and public acclaim but had mocked him by also planting in his clay forces which always cheated him of what he coveted. He had much to commend him to Sir William Stawell and his fellow-gentlemen on the committee. He was a man of 'fair fame' and a 'gallant leader'. He was born in a country gentleman's manor house at St Clerans, near Galway, in 1821. He had the appearance and habits of a gentleman; he was a member of the most exclusive club in Melbourne, the Melbourne Club. He was in the tradition of the gentlemen explorers of the Australian wilderness.

He was kind, generous and brave with those who agreed with him, but if anything happened out of the ordinary, he became confused, then so excited that he lost all his composure, and his judgement fell to pieces. He also had one curious failing for a man who was to lead an expedition across unknown country: he had no 'bump for locality' and was continually losing his way on his short trips about Beechworth during his years as a police officer. As a child of his age he believed Providence had chosen the British to go out into the wilderness and subdue it and exercise dominion over every living thing. It never occurred to him that any of those 'living things', least of all the original tenants of the deserts he was to traverse, could teach him how to live off the land. The white man was coming as a conqueror, a bearer of human mastery, not as a conservator or an accepter.

Trusting his own very fallible judgement, Burke chose George James Landells as his second-in-command, not sensing then that that greedy man would stir the madness in his own blood. Deciding rather hastily that success might lie in the camel, Burke dispatched Landells to India to buy twenty or so camels. After buying twenty-four in the markets at Peshawar and Afghanistan he returned to Karachi where he met a young English soldier, John King, who was still recovering from the shock of seeing the abominations the English had committed against Indians who had participated in the mutiny against Her Most Britannic Majesty. Landells offered King a job as camel-tender to the Victorian expedition. In this way George James Landells, a man who could not bear to be told what to do, and John King, a simple-minded, God-fearing man, who looked up without envy or malice to those placed in authority over him, found their way to Melbourne, in June of 1860, to be tried in a fiery furnace. Landells was found wanting, and King had the one thing needful.

As surveyor and astronomer Burke appointed William John Wills, a young English migrant from Totnes, who had just turned 26. He was another young man who had dreamed of finding glory in the interior of the mysterious continent, and yet was as different from Burke as a measurer from a man of feeling. Ever since he had arrived in Victoria in 1853 he talked of his 'longing desire to explore the interior of Australia'. In 1856 he had walked 90 miles in the hope of joining such an expedition. For Wills was methodical, meticulous, not given to rash, impulsive decisions. The gale of life blew high through Robert O'Hara Burke, but not through William John Wills. Wills was the scientist, a man with neither the need nor the desire to ask any God to forgive him for his great folly. Yet to their great delight, though ultimately to their great harm, Mr Burke and Wills adored each other. Mr Burke called every other member of the expedition by his surname; he called Wills affectionately 'Wil'. Neither of them was to know when they first met and liked each other and felt that bond between men to which women must be forever strangers, that Wills's adoration of Mr Burke was to contribute to their undoing. Burke also chose Hermann Beckler as their medical officer and botanist, Ludwig Becker as their artist and naturalist, and Charles D. Ferguson, an American, as foreman—three men who did not take kindly to the lordly and overbearing. He also appointed nine assistants, including William Brahe, a German or Scandinavian who could trace his family back into the mists of antiquity, and John King, that one-time soldier, only 18 years of age. He was now about to see another 'ghastly country' and learn more about the madness in men's hearts.

No dark thoughts troubled the members of the expedition as they prepared for their departure. Science and human ingenuity had given man dominion over madness and folly. Science had discovered how to bake a special expedition biscuit, composed of pulverized meat mixed with an equal quantity of wheat flour, so no one would ever go hungry. Science had produced the pocket charcoal filter to purify the most putrid waters, so no one would ever go thirsty. Science had invented the breech-loading rifle, so every man would have dominion over the fowls of the air and every living thing that moved over the earth, both the four-legged and the two-legged creatures, if ever the latter should be so foolish as to resist the onward march of a great civilization into the Australian bush. Science had invented the rocket, the blue light and the gong, the sounds of which would echo for miles around. So no one would ever be lost. Science had given man dominion over the deserts of Australia.

When the expedition assembled in the park adjacent to the Melbourne General Cemetery on 20 August, an air of supreme confidence pervaded the whole gathering. Everyone who was anyone in Melbourne was there to wish them godspeed. The men were attired in the clothes of gentlemen, the women resplendent in the fashions of the drawing rooms of the day. Those from the humble stations in life bowed to those in high places. Mr Burke, wearing the tall hat of a gentleman rather than the wide-awake of a man about to move into the outback, his eye single and his whole body full of light, looked quite transfigured on his grey charger Billy. The band struck up 'Cheer boys, cheer', as the cavalcade slowly moved out of the park and along the road to Essendon where they camped for the first night.

The next day they set out for Swan Hill, which they reached on 6 September. There as Burke charmed and entertained the ladies in the squatter's parlour at Murray Downs Station, the assistants became disgustingly drunk on beer, and the camels indulged in sexual play before the eyes of the ladies of the town to the disgust of Burke's prudish Irish heart. A letter arrived from the exploration committee in Melbourne urging him to curb his extravagance. Burke, never a man to practise moderation in anything, put his party on a spartan diet. Ferguson, the baggage man, resigned in protest. The one bushman in the party, the one man with a 'bump for locality', was on his way back to Melbourne. Mr Burke was also much taken by a man everyone called Charley Gray, and Mr Burke, reckless as ever, offered Gray a billet. Burke heard to his alarm that that wild ass of a man, John McDouall Stuart, was again assembling a party in Adelaide to make a dash for the Gulf of Carpentaria. It was to be a race across the continent from the south to the northern shore, a race between camel teams, a race between two flawed gentlemen.

Believing his own honour as well as the honour of Victoria to be in his hands, Burke struck camp promptly on 11 September. As the huge cavalcade rolled over the bridge at Swan Hill and made for Menindie on the Darling River, they were moving away from civilization into the great silence. By the time they reached Menindie in October, Burke had fallen out with both Becker and Landells, and they too were on their way back to Melbourne— Landells with stories that cast grave doubts on Burke's sanity. Burke appointed Wills his second-in-command.

On 19 October 1860 the party set out from Menindie for Cooper's Creek, taking with them William Wright, a local odd-job man who knew the back-country through which they were to travel. One hundred miles along the track they reached Mootwingee, where, since time began, the Aborigines had gathered to sing to each other their vision of life and to share the wisdom of their ancestors on how to survive in a dry country. Burke decided to press on, after reminding Brahe once again to take care that their camping place at night was fortified against any surprise attacks by the natives. In his eyes the natives were a menace, not a source of wisdom. They did not pause to look at the carvings on the rocks with their intimation of a kingdom quite different from what was eating at the heart of

Burke. They saw the gaunt gidgee trees, the wattles which emitted an unbearable stink before rain, the fragile, sombre mulga, the tussocks of grass, the rock pools, the flat, uninviting bare earth, and the apostle birds. They shuddered and went on their way to the Cooper.

Rarely a man to commit his thoughts to paper—anyhow that 'capital fellow Wil' was scribbling it all down every night in his diary—Burke was chewing over the problem of how to get to the gulf. His instruction from the exploration committee had ordered him to proceed to the Cooper, establish a means of keeping up communication with Melbourne, and mark the trees on their route, so that, if disaster struck, they could be quickly rescued. The instructions left the rest to him. He came up with the idea of sending Wright back to Menindie bearing messages for the committee and instructions to return as soon as possible with fresh supplies of food to the depot they would establish at the Cooper. Wright would also take back the two black trackers, because those Stone Age men, in Burke's mind, had nothing to offer to the men with the tent, the beasts of burden, the compass, the theodolite, field-glasses, the axe, the rifle and the safety match on how to cross those plains of desolation. After selecting a site for the depot on the Cooper, Burke proposed to take a small party with him to the gulf and leave Brahe in charge of the depot at the Cooper. He had promoted Brahe to the rank of officer, because those, like Brahe, who traced their ancestry back to the remotest antiquity were always pleasing in his eyes.

By then they were in that area where the gallant Captain Sturt had written on the rude structure of stones that overlooks the lonely grave of his brave companion Poole that it would stand for ages as 'a record of all we suffered in the dreary region'. By contrast all that Burke left as a sign to posterity was the carving of his initials on the trunk of one of those tough trees: 'R.O.B.'. Underneath he cut the number of the camp and the date. Burke was a stranger to the metaphysical anguish of the gallant Captain, who saw the hand of Providence in everything but never wondered why a benevolent being should have created those gibber-plains or allowed that sun to scorch every living thing by day.

On 11 November 1860 the party pitched camp on the banks of a waterhole of Cooper's Creek. There—where the yellow-belly fish were an easy catch for the white man's hook and the blackfellow's net, where in a good year the bush was teeming with game, where some of the grasses could be eaten, where the Aborigines had learnt to find the fish in mud-holes in a dry year and to dry pelican flesh for tucker when the birds had migrated—Burke commanded

William Brahe to put his assistants to work to build a stockade for protection against the wild blacks and to wait there for at least three months, as Wright would be back by then from Menindie with the fresh stores.

On 16 December 1860 Burke, Wills, John King and poor Charley Gray set out in the direction of the Gulf of Carpentaria. Mr Burke was making for the gulf on a journey that in his eyes would cause posterity to number him with the mighty men of renown. As they proceeded up the bed of the Diamantina to the site of the present settlement of Birdsville, they were delighted to find that the country improved with every step they took, that in a green year the teeming bush gave them no hint of any 'horrors to come'. Near the banks of the Diamantina they found a most welcome oasis in the desert, where the blacks gave them fish. In return Burke gave the blacks beads and matches. For a brief season Burke became god-like, a lord of creation.

He still spoke of those consummate food-gatherers as men who might try to 'bully or bounce them', men who ought to be repulsed. He sprinkled English and Irish names, redolent of the country gentry, all over a land which the hand of European man had scarcely touched, let alone refined. On 20 January 1861, with the wet season threatening to start at any moment, just to the west of the present site of Cloncurry, Burke became again danger-ously excited. An attack of the 'sillies' swept through him. He became impatient to get to the gulf. Before him stood the Selwyn Ranges, to the east and then to the north the flat country leading to the gulf. He decided to take the camels and the men straight over the ranges.

By the time they pitched their tents at Camp 119 near the east bank of the Little Bynoe, the wet season had begun and the whole country had been converted from dry land into a sea of mud in which men and beasts floundered. They were tasting the bitter fruit of Mr Burke's act of foolishness. In the dry season, all they would have had between them and the sight of the sea was a walk down the Bynoe River to the gulf west of the present town of Karumba. In the wet the beasts of burden sank to their knees in the mud, the men were exhausted by the sticky heat and pestered by the insects which swarmed around them by day and night. Finding that the camels could scarcely be got along, Mr Burke decided to leave them at Camp 119 and to proceed with his horse Billy, and Wills on foot, leaving John King and Charley Gray at the camp. The two set out on Sunday 17 February to walk to the gulf, floundering along knee-deep in water, till they reached a channel through which the sea water entered.

There they halted. They could not obtain a view of the open ocean, although they made every endeavour to do so. For their long-awaited moment of glory the rain poured down incessantly, till the ground became so boggy than no animal could move over it. They were not far from the sites where Dutch seamen had once cried out in horror and despair on seeing the land and the people of New Holland. Neither man could see or hear the sea. Their only satisfaction was to taste the salt water which swept over that boggy ground at high tide.

To add to their misery, the weather turned so oppressively hot and sultry that the slightest exertion made them feel as though they were being suffocated, and left them both with a helpless feeling of lassitude. That silence between men fearful of having missed out, men who had been given a vision of emptiness where they had expected to know glory, descended on them as they turned back to Camp 119 to pick up King and Gray for the long walk back to the Cooper. For two weeks after they left the camp on 13 February 1861, the state of suffocation continued, as they plodded doggedly on, with the rain seldom easing, humid mist rising off the hot earth, and thunder rumbling round the horizon. Burke began to feel very unwell and so giddy that sometimes he could not keep his seat either on his horse Billy or on a camel. By 6 March they had travelled far enough south for the dryness of the atmosphere to have a beneficial effect on them. Burke seemed a little better, and Charley Gray again looked comparatively well. One of the camels was so done up that he could not come on with them. The rain kept following them, making the ground boggy and sapping their strength. As evidence of what they were going through, Wills called three camps running 'Humid Camp', 'Muddy Camp', and 'Mosquito Camp'.

On 25 March just after they left Native Dog Camp, Wills found Gray wolfing down the flour. Gray excused himself for pinching more than his ration of flour because he was suffering from dysentery. Wills reported him to Mr Burke who gave him a good thrashing. The other three were in good spirits. Fourteen days later on 8 April as poor Charley Gray struggled along fifteen minutes behind the others, Wills believed he was 'gammoning'. Gray did not speak a word distinctly again. At sunrise on 17 April, near the eastern shores of Lake Massacre, Charley Gray died. Burke, tormented by guilt, taught as he had been from childhood in Ireland to display compassion to all those who had ended the one journey all mankind share, ordered King and Wills, weakened though they were by their great ordeal, to hack away at the stubborn earth till they had cut a hole befitting the last resting place of their companion. In their weakened condition that took them one whole day.

The following day, 18 April, they set out for Camp 65 on the Cooper. They were followed by the natives, who seemed desirous of their company, but as they preferred camping alone they took measures to get away from them. They were now almost within cooee of 'Fort Wills' on the Cooper, which had been designed to keep blackfellows from doing any mischief. At the depot they anticipated a feast on all the food Wright had brought up from Menindie. There would be jerked meat, vegetables and sugar. There would be other human beings to whom they could describe those well-grassed pebbly plains they had seen on which thousands of cattle could graze. They were about to become members of the 'congregation of the mighty'. All had not been in vain.

Although they were by then so done up that they could scarcely crawl over the desert, they struggled on till the evening of 21 April 1861. As a cold wind drew weird shapes out of the shadows cast by the moonlight, Mr Burke called out 'Brahe, Patton, McDonough, Dost Mahomet'. There was no reply. Frantically he cooeed again, but no human sound broke the eerie silence, except the echo of his own voice. When they reached the campsite, they found the warm ashes of a recent fire. Carved on the trunk of a coolibah tree were the words 'Dig. 3 ft.N.W. Apr. 21 1861'. Burke swooned and fell to the ground. Wills and King dug as instructed and found rations of meat, rice, flour, sugar, and a bottle enclosed in which was a letter from Brahe which explained that as Patton had been unable to walk for eighteen days and as no person had been up from the Darling he, Brahe, had left the camp that day to return to the Darling. Chance had made its first alliance with Burke's acts of folly, to bring them to the edge of destruction. From that day they were fighting for their lives rather than their reputations in the portals of renown.

In their exhausted state after four months of travelling and severe privations, their legs being almost paralysed, they could barely walk a few yards. Nature so abounded with fish, game, nutritious seeds and water that within two days their strength returned, and with it their hopes that all would soon be well. Brahe must surely return as soon as he got Patton to safety and found out what Wright was up to. Then Mr Burke, his judgement always aberrant in difficult situations, decided that they must leave the depot on the Cooper. As he became more and more excited working out what they should do, a wild idea took possession of him. Instead of making for Menindie along the track they had followed the previous October and November, he decided that they should make their way down the Cooper and then down the bed of the Strzelecki till they came to the settled areas of South Australia at a station which

Edward Eyre had named Mount Hopeless. Wills was astounded, but the great bond he felt for Burke soon silenced his doubts. John King had never found any reason to question Burke. In his eyes 'Mr Burke was the leading man of the party'. Besides it was outside his range of vision to question the decision of a gentleman. The habits of a lifetime did not suddenly disappear in the Australian wilderness. Mr Burke also had one other strange notion. He decided that they must not leave any signs that they had been there, otherwise the blacks would be after them. They therefore carefully restored the ground where Brahe had placed the bottle and the provisions to the condition it was in when they arrived. They made their camp-fire look like a black man's, not a white man's camp-fire. Then on 23 April after only two days of rest, having gathered together enough provisions to get them to Mount Hopeless, they abandoned much of that scientific equipment which had held out the promise of dominion over the wilds of Australia, and set out to walk down the south bank of the Cooper.

After moving down the Cooper and the Strzelecki at a rate of 4–5 miles a day, their strength draining away, their optimism giving way to despair, they decided to make their way back to the Cooper. A few days before they returned within striking distance of the Dig Tree at Camp 65, Brahe, who had encountered Wright on his way down to Menindie, had returned to the Dig Tree site on 8 May. Seeing the cache undisturbed and the fire much as he had left it, he decided Burke had not been there and rode off again towards the Darling to raise the alarm. On that day Burke, Wills and King were back on the Cooper in a district known to the blacks as Innamincka, or place of ill omen. They were resting beside a waterhole in the Cooper, to which the blacks of the Yantruwanta tribe gave the name of 'bidi', or hole in the earth. The blacks thought of it as the hole of life. No such thoughts crossed the minds of the three white men. 'The present state of things', Wills wrote in his journal early in May, 'is not calculated to raise our spirits much'. Their rations were diminishing, their clothing, especially the boots, were going to pieces. All he had left was his watch, his prism compass, his pocket compass, and one thermometer. 'I suppose', he added, 'this will end with our having to live like the blacks for a few months'.

For their part the blacks were delighted to show white men how to find the seed of the nardoo plant, how to grind it into a flour and cook it. The yellow-belly still rose to the bait; birds were still shot. Nature was generous to them in that year in which the blacks taught them how to remain alive. On 27 May Wills decided to walk to Camp 65 at the Dig Tree to deposit his journals and leave a record of where they were, leaving Burke and King in the care of the blacks. When he reached the depot on 30 May he found no sign that

Brahe or anyone else had been there. He deposited the journals and a notice of their present condition before setting off again to rejoin Burke and King.

Soon after he got back, the blacks decamped. In another moment of great folly Mr Burke, to satisfy some subterranean desire, had knocked the fish-nets out of the hands of the blacks, fearing, he told King, that if they were too friendly the blacks would be always hanging around. Now they had to support themselves. By then both Burke and Wills were growing weaker. The nardoo was having an extraordinary effect on their constitution: it was causing them to pass huge stools, for which the effort required left them even weaker. By 20 June Wills was completely reduced by the effects of the cold and their inadequate nutriment. Burke was getting weak in the legs; King was holding out best as the food seemed to agree with him pretty well. The following day Wills was so weak he could scarcely crawl out of the mia-mia on the south bank of the Cooper. That day, accepting death as inevitable, he wrote in his journal that it was a great consolation to know that they had done all they could, and that their deaths would rather be due to the mismanagement of others than to any rash acts of their own. He sat there growing weaker every day, his tattered clothing now the only remnant of that proud civilization to which he belonged, while all around him the bush and the waterholes of the Cooper teemed with a life he was too weak to use.

On 27 June Burke and King set out to search for the blacks as their last hope of survival. Wills, his legs and arms nearly skin and bone, was too weak to follow them. In the presence of death he grew in stature. 'I can only look out, like Mr Micawber,' he wrote in his journal on 26 June, 'for something to turn up'. Starvation on nardoo was by no means very unpleasant, except for the weakness he felt and the utter inability to move. As far as appetite was concerned, nardoo gave him the 'greatest satisfaction'. That day he found the strength to write a letter of farewell to his father:

> Cooper's Creek, June 27,1861.
> My Dear Father,—These are probably the last lines you will ever get from me. We are on the point of starvation, not so much from the want of food, but from the want of nutriment in what we can get.

He went on to give a clear summary of their achievement in walking from Cooper's Creek to the gulf and back, and then continued:

> I find I must close this that it may be planted, but I will write some more, although it has not so good a chance of reaching you as this. You have great claim on the committee for their neglect. I leave you

in sole charge of what is coming to me. The whole of my money I desire to leave to my sisters; other matters I will leave for the present. Adieu, my dear father. Love to Tom [his brother in Melbourne]
   W. J. Wills.
I think to live about four or five days. My religious views are not the least changed, and I have not the slightest fear of their being so. My spirits are excellent.

Within a day or so of writing those words he died.

In the meantime Burke and King struggled over sandy patches on the south bank of the Cooper in search of the blacks. It was the time of year when wild flowers were blooming and the air had that majestic radiance of the winter months in the inland. By then they were blind to all the beauty in the world. After travelling 9 or 10 miles Burke became too weak to go any further. King left him at his own request, unburied, and with his pistol in hand, clothed still in a manner befitting a gentleman. As so he died, his huge eyes still staring at sandy wastes, and his back facing the bidi, the great source of life in Cooper's Creek.

King then joined the Aborigines who treated him with great tenderness when he made them understand that the other two white fellows had died. When he showed them the mortal remains of Burke, they wept bitterly and led him to a place by the river where he would come to no harm. They brought him nardoo and fish, and King, who also had his pride, explained to them that before two moons had passed the white men would come for him. The children of nature succoured the child-man in the party.

In the meantime people in Melbourne began to ask questions about the fate of the expedition. As early as 17 April 1861 the *Argus* urged the exploration committee to take vigorous steps to find out 'where on the map of Australia we are to look for him'. In June the exploration committee appointed Alfred William Howitt to lead a search party. On 15 September they found King. He presented a melancholy appearance, wasted as he was to a shadow, indeed barely to be distinguished as a civilized being except by the remnants of clothes he was wearing to cover his emaciated body. He seemed exceedingly weak and found it occasionally difficult to follow what Howitt said. The natives were just as gratified and delighted for King's sake as they had been compassionate and tearful before. Howitt, King and the other members of the party then set out to perform the melancholy duty of finding and burying the remains of both Burke and Wills.

On a Saturday, 2 November 1861, the manager of a theatre in Melbourne interrupted the evening performance to tell the audience that Burke and Wills had perished. The following day grown men wept in the streets of Melbourne, women wrung their hands in agony and sobbed and moaned. Little children, who could not understand the nature of the calamity, imitated their parents and walked round the streets bathed in tears. By Monday the men in high places took up the point which in their minds was what the expedition was all about—the greatness of Victoria, and her ascendancy in the Australian colonies. They lamented the untimely fate of those gallant men, Gray, Wills and Burke. They boasted of the achievement: they were the first to cross the continent from sea to sea; they had given their lives to the cause of Victorian exploration; their names would never be forgotten.

Within a few weeks of the return of Howitt to Melbourne the public split into two groups in their response to the tragedy. One, composed of the members of the exploration committee, the Government House circle, the Melbourne Club, high society, indeed almost everyone who thought of himself as anyone, kept up a hymn of praise for Burke and Wills. They suggested the erection of an imposing memorial in Melbourne to keep them 'greenly in our memories'. They suggested that Howitt be sent back to the Cooper to retrieve the remains of Burke and Wills, but not Gray, and bring them to Melbourne for a funeral which should be worthy of their great achievement. They vilified the non-gentlemen, such as Landells and Wright, as cowardly, ignorant and lazy men who had contributed to the death of two men with the courage and the capacity to solve the problem of the nature of the centre of Australia.

The other group was composed of the radical fringe of Melbourne society, the men who had been exasperated and angered by the fruits of aristocratic imbecility and irresponsibility during the Crimean War, the insufferable arrogance of the 'boy commissioners' on the goldfields, and the presence of cast-offs from the English aristocracy in so many key positions in the Australian colonies. This group raised the class question. In their eyes those gentlemen on the exploration committee were a party of old women who, thanks to the way Victoria was run, had charge of the destiny of gallant fellows. They pitched into the exploration committee as the evil party in the story. They wanted the bones of 'poor Charley Gray' brought back, because holding a lower position in life did not mean he was not of equal significance with those two gentlemen, Burke and Wills.

The gentlemen of the exploration committee and their supporters had their way. On 6 November 1861 they sent Howitt off again to bring back the bones of Burke and Wills, but not of Gray. But that other voice, the voice of the people, was not silenced. When John King, still enfeebled by his great ordeal, arrived at North Melbourne station on 25 November, some hailed him as the man of the people, a hero who had had the strength to endure to the end when the two gentlemen in the party cracked up. By contrast the Governor, Sir Henry Barkly, and the gentlemen of the exploration committee welcomed him with that air of condescension, a pose of effortless superiority, which indicated to a man such as John King and the rowdy and unruly mob who were crowding round him that he and they were condemned by birth to live their lives as inferiors to men of breeding. The *Argus* explained why King should be spared 'a preposterous glorification': there was, they said, a broad distinction to be drawn between 'moral heroism' and 'physical endurance'. King seemed to have owed his preservation to that tenacity of life which characterized some constitutions and which was not a moral quality but a physical accident. Gentlemen such as Burke and Wills had that moral quality which was outside the reach of a man of the people.

Early in December 1862 Howitt brought the bleached bones of Burke and Wills from the Cooper down to Adelaide. Thousands thronged the streets to gaze on all that was left of Mr Burke, as a brass band solemnly played 'The Dead March in Saul'.

The same week a horseman galloped into Clare, an agricultural settlement 80 miles north of Adelaide, with the news that that Ishmael of a man, John McDouall Stuart, was about to enter their town after successfully crossing the continent from the south to the north. By then everything near Stuart had the smell of decaying mortality. But he had survived. Although his body was reduced to that of a living skeleton, and he felt himself to be a 'sad, sad wreck of former days', he wanted to think 'the Almighty Giver of all Good, that He, in His infinite goodness and mercy, gave me strength and courage to overcome the grim and hoary-headed king of terrors', and allowed him to live a little longer in this world. Stuart had come back with ideas of the track to be followed by a telegraph line linking Australia with the world. Burke's journey had been as barren as that fig tree which had roused Christ's wrath. In the race of life the victory had not gone to the swift, nor the battle to the strong. The people of a city dedicated to sobriety, godliness and quiet living went mad with excitement to welcome a drunkard and a profligate. The crowd drew Stuart's carriage along North Terrace. That paragon of an old English gentleman, James Hurtle Fisher, one of the founders of the province, his face ravaged by the savageries of those early days, the passion now nearly all spent, hailed the Dionysian Stuart as one of Australia's great sons, while those bones of the sober and prudish Mr Burke and his faithful 'Wil' were being carried over the water to Melbourne. Life is immense.

The story of Burke and Wills—and young John King—became the sport of the myth-makers. The conservatives used it as an example of the heroic exploits of Anglo-Irish gentlemen in the Antipodes; the radicals used it as further evidence of the imbecility of gentlemen, a prelude to that innings by the people in Australia which was about to begin.

8

The Bush Barbarians

At Weetangera near Canberra in 1861 a small farmer named Samuel Shumack had much on his mind. He had just bought a grand mare of the Suffolk Punch breed and was planning to buy another mare and a plough and a harrow from the proceeds of the harvest for that year. God was fulfilling the promise of the Psalmist to fill the garners and afford all manner of store to those who sang hymns of praise unto Him and walked in His ways. There was one dark cloud on the horizon. That year the whole of New South Wales was agitated from one end to the other by the Free Selection Act. Samuel Shumack's neighbour, Mr Davis the squatter, kept telling him that if it was passed, it would ruin most of the squatters.

Vast areas of eastern Australia were 'locked up' in leases held by the squatters, many of whom had grown wealthy while rural workers lived in poverty. By the start of the 1860s there was wide support for the idea that the stranglehold of the squatters should be broken, that much of the land should be subdivided and made available to 'selectors', farming families who would settle the land more closely and enjoy some of the prosperity of which immigrants dreamed. In Sydney William Charles Wentworth was afraid the world in which he could fulfil his own dream of Australia as a land for English country gentlemen was about to be shattered. Gentlemen in Australia, he feared, were 'like the last roses of summer'. He left for England on 22 October 1862 to take up residence as a country gentleman at Wimborne in Dorset, not far from that village of Bockhampton where the young Thomas Hardy first observed the disruption of rural England by industrial civilization. Once again the knighthood that Wentworth had coveted was denied him. He lost interest in the world of affairs, in all the prizes for those who strove after the power and the glory. He turned his mind to the problem of salvation, hoping that there was some rest in the shades for those whose hearts had been so hot within them that they had not been spared in this world.

Also taking refuge in England were James Macarthur, the English gentleman who happened to have been born in Australia; Stuart Donaldson, the head of the first government of gentlemen in New South Wales, the prospective saviour of drawing-room society in Australia; and Charles Sturt who had taken up residence at 19 Clarence Square, Cheltenham, in one of those graceful Regency houses. There, when his wife was out of the room, he had many edifying conversations with that fat little lady Lady Eliza Darling about the life of the world to come.

In New South Wales and Victoria the conservatives prophesied that the masses were about to use universal suffrage to create a 'dictatorial tyranny' and destroy the social and political influence of the landed gentry. The selection acts would so stunt the growth of the gentry, they said, that they would be unable to compete at the ballot-box with the gold-digger, the political adventurer and the publican. The much-vaunted path of material progress would become a descent into hell, in which the people would dance among the ruins of the civilization they had destroyed. The 'unwashed' were about to build their ugly huts within a mile of the big homesteads and end the squatters' dreams of perfect solitude and happiness on their parklike lands.

After the New South Wales Selection Act was proclaimed in Sydney early in 1862, the reactions of all classes were just as varied as had been the pronouncements by the prophets. Samuel Shumack, the selector who had been spun a tale of woes to come by the squatter in his district, had his eyes opened. None of the predicted calamities took place. Even though he was only a selector farmer, he shared new machinery, ideas, workers, and swapped yarns with Mr Campbell at Duntroon and Mr Davis at Gundaroo. They all helped each other when untimely frosts nipped their seedlings, or a summer hailstorm laid waste a crop, or the Molonglo flooded the low-lying land. Each Sunday Samuel Shumack trembled in the presence of that Lord of his who was now filling his barns with golden grain.

In many parts of the colonies of New South Wales, Victoria and Queensland the most noteworthy matter that came to light was 'the class contest for the land', which covered most of those colonies. In this class contest the selectors were sandwiched between Capital and Labour, the selector either rising into the ranks of the capitalist or being pushed down into the class the acts were designed to help him out of—the class of hirelings for wages on the land. This class war raged all over the countryside. It was fought in the colonial parliaments, where both sides used bribery, persuasion, blackmail—any method either inside or outside the law—to control the lands owned or coveted.

The war between classes was fought also in the various land offices throughout the colony. When the Land Office was opened in Hamilton in Victoria in September 1862 hundreds joined the crush to receive applications for selections under the Selection Act introduced into the Victorian Legislative Assembly by Charles Gavan Duffy. Under the Duffy Act, 10 million acres of land were to be proclaimed as agricultural areas on which a person might select a surveyed block of not more than 640 acres. The selector might buy the whole allotment, or buy part and rent the rest. If there was more than one applicant for one block, selection was to be by lot. Payment was £1 an acre, with a rental of 2s 6d per acre per year for eight years for the balance. There were safeguards to ensure that the reform benefited the genuine small selector. No man was to select more than one allotment within twelve months. No infant or married woman whose marriage was still valid was to become a selector. The selector was either to cultivate one acre in ten or erect a habitable dwelling or enclose his selection with a substantial fence. One-quarter of the money in the land fund was to be used for immigration. The vain Charles Gavan Duffy assured the Solons of Spring Street that all the loopholes for the land sharks, the rogues and the villains had been skilfully plugged in the Victorian Act.

When two areas were proclaimed open for selection in September 1862 near Hamilton in the heart of the richest grazing district of Victoria, all hell was let loose. The hotels were gorged with people, billiard rooms were turned into dormitories, every available space was used to accommodate the strangers. There were squatters who were frightened that the lands on which their stock was grazing might pass out of their hands. There were burly fustian-clad farmers, who were looking for a chance to buy more land at bargain rates. There were also smart young men sent down from Collins Street in Melbourne with orders to buy up land so that their employers might enjoy that rise in the social scale conferred by the possession of 640 acres in the heart of Australia Felix. Land agents, sinister-looking men, blackmailed purchasers into paying a commission of 1s an acre to buy them off, and threatened victimization if the purchaser did not pay. Other mysterious persons, owners of faces the like of which had never been seen in the district before, whispered over brandy and water to prospective purchasers that they had the ear of the minister in Melbourne or, for a consideration, might be able to persuade the local member to use his influence with the minister to ensure that lands held by Mr Broad Acres were never declared open for selection.

When land was declared open for selection in the Inglewood district of Victoria in July 1865, the squatters in the district trained men to act as 'dummy' selectors, and paid them £1 a day for their expenses. Officers in the Department of Lands in both Melbourne and Sydney received tips for ignoring the practice. Local members of Parliament had their palms greased. The selection acts, it was said, were re-festering that old sore of bush barbarism. For their part the selectors complained that they were obliged by their lack of adequate financial resources to throw themselves on the mercy of the local storekeeper, to pay their annual rent and supply them with essentials in return for the right to foreclose on the debt in the event of non-payment. These storekeepers were sucking the life-blood out of them, waxing fat and moving up in the social scale.

The selectors who did well were able 'to keep all straight as they went on'. They used horses to assist them with their labour. They lived in homesteads in which their women provided a way of life, a domestic economy of home cooking, home sewing, home boot-making, home jams, home honey, home decoration, and home gardening which approached the idyll of the English yeoman, or the Baucis in Goethe's *Faust*. They aimed at and acquired independence. Others attained only beggary. While the squatters grumbled that beef from their cattle was smoking on the tables of 'white trash' cattle-duffers of New South Wales, Victoria and Queensland, others were saying that some of the selectors were so 'lamentably and unmistakably poor', with such large families of small children dependent upon them, that the squatters should look on them with the eye of pity.

For poor selectors, life, it was said, was 'certainly not worth the conventional farthing dip'. Bands of young Australians of 6 to 7 years of age were frequently to be seen driving horses for the chaff cutter, or doing other work of a useful character. On the dairy farms the mothers and daughters got up between two and four in the morning to milk the cows. Fathers and sons at the same time got ready to transport the milk to the nearby town. The men fought the land, the changes in the weather, that never-ending cycle of drought and flood, rust in the wheat, scab and fluke in their sheep, the money-lenders and the storekeepers. The women were enslaved to the kitchen and the backyard. The kitchen range was their altar, on which they enacted their daily sacrifices. They kept a dull glow on its black surface by polishing it regularly with black lead, bluestone, turpentine and methylated spirits. They churned the milk into butter, baked bread, made soap with salt-free fat, caustic soda and resin, which was then placed in flat boxes lined with cloth. They cut it into cakes of soap with a fine wire. In the backyard they tanned and dyed sheepskins, cattle hides, kangaroo skins, rabbit skins and possum skins, and used them for floor covering, winter clothing, bedding and for decorating the house. They made candles from fat and beeswax. The more successful selectors and farmers bought the new mineral oil lamp at the local store, a lamp which provided as much light as six candles at a cost of one halfpenny an hour. To wash the clothes the successful selector's wife had a wash tub, wringer, mangler and a flat-iron, the amount of decoration on whose handle informed the neighbours of the rank and wealth of the mistress of the kitchen.

Some women were tormented with doubt and savage indignation at all the drudgery and humiliations they had to endure. Others took everything in their stride, put up with the bashings from their menfolk, collected them when they were lying dead drunk outside some rum shanty and drove them back to the selection in a jinker or buggy. A wife knew full well that when the man recovered he might give her 'two lovely black eyes' for her trouble, but she shrugged off that pain and humiliation with some philosophical remark such as 'He's like that', or 'Life's like that'.

Selection was introduced into Queensland in 1868. Within a decade the same cry of anguish and despair went up into the sky over south-eastern Queensland as had been uttered in New South Wales and Victoria. Despite the pluck, perseverance and back-breaking labour of the pioneers, the wallabies, cockatoos, land agents, storekeepers, the dry hard soil and their lack of money and equipment mocked all their striving, their agony and their hopes. This was the childhood world of Arthur Hoey Davis whose father had taken up 160 acres at Emu Creek near the half-way mark on the road between Warwick and Toowoomba in 1870. The boy grew up to be a writer, using the experiences of his childhood at Emu Creek for his masterpiece, *On Our Selection*. He called himself Steele Rudd.

In the beginning the Rudd family endured great hardships: they cleared 4 acres with the labour of their hands; they planted seed only to see most of it gobbled by the cockatoos, and the young shoots eaten by the kangaroos; the storekeeper kept £9 out of the £12 Dad received for his first harvest. Mum and Dad Rudd endured poverty, sickness, bureaucrats, drought and flood. Things more often went wrong than right. But Dad had his faith. He believed in the benevolent intentions of the 'Great Architect of the Universe' towards those who did no wickedness and walked in His ways. He was not sure about whether God heeded the petitions the parson used. There was that occasion when the parson had no sooner asked the 'Great Architect' to 'lead us not into temptation' than the kangaroo dog grabbed all the fresh meat on the table. As for that remark 'as ye sow, so shall ye reap', he was not quite sure about that either. One year he sowed a paddock with barley and reaped rye.

Dad was Australia's Everyman—not a Prince Hamlet, or a Mr Pickwick, or a Sam Weller, or a Huckleberry Finn, or an Evgeny Onegin, or a Faust, but Dad Rudd, the man who slaved his guts out to win the status of a landowner, got dead drunk and was carried home from the local pub, and did his block, and shouted and raved, and sometimes bawled like a bull, but at other times was tender with man and beast. He did not know why the material reward was not commensurate with all their striving, all their suffering; he did not whine, or blame others, or shake his fist at the 'Architect of the Universe'. He did not cry out that he did not accept God's world, and wanted to 'hand Him back his ticket'. He had no metaphysical anguish: he was an Australian.

By 1880 all over eastern Australia, in parts of South Australia, and in that red sand-plain country on the coast of Western Australia from Northampton to Carnarvon, a broken-down chimneystack here, the shell of a house, a woody rosebush and lichened fruit trees there, the stone walls of what had been a church, the frame of a general store with faded lettering over the lintel, proclaiming the name of the owner and the goods he retailed—these were all that remained of the work of those who set out in the 1860s to plant a society of small farmers, a group of petty-bourgeois property-owners, between the 'swell coves' in the big houses and the bush workers. One generation came, another went: the earth of Australia abided for ever.

By contrast South Australia witnessed for a brief season the victory of human endeavour; Providence seemed to be smiling on the land. There new fields for human enterprise had been opened up to the north in the area around Clare, and in the south-east in the Naracoorte–Mount Gambier district. Crop failures in the wheat lands of the Ukraine and Russia meant a huge sale of American wheat to Russia, which left a great market for South Australian wheat in dear old England. The South Australian farmers were thankful to Providence for such 'bounteous blessings'.

South Australia already had a successful class of wheat farmers long before the selection acts brought the class war to the bush in eastern Australia. The country gentry had established estates like the seats of the fine old country gentlemen in England. George Charles Hawker had established his seat at Bungaree near Clare: Francis Stacker Dutton had established his seat at Anlaby. Both were renowned for that generosity and kindliness which were said to be the distinguishing characteristics of the English country gentleman. Both were friends to the farmers. Both started the tradition of selling portions of their estates to those workers who had displayed character, ability and enterprise, for South Australia, unlike eastern Australia, where class distinctions were cemented into caste by the land laws, was founded on the principle of a mobile society, not a New World aristocratic society.

In the 1870s South Australians were using the new stump-jump plough, a five-furrow plough which was constructed to allow each plough to work independently of the others so that in uneven or stony ground the blade of the particular plough would rise or fall over obstacles such as mallee roots. By May 1871 the South Australian government gave way to popular pressure by throwing open to selection more and better areas in the Mount Gambier and Clare districts. Soon the press in those areas was filled with unqualified optimism and enthusiasm. Between 1869 and 1884 nearly 2 million acres of land came under cultivation. In 1884 the wheat harvest was almost 15 million bushels. Wheat had surpassed wool and copper. Up at Clare in December 1874 the cry was the same cry with which the old hands welcomed new chums to the goldfields in Victoria, 'And still they come'. Scarcely a day passed but wagons loaded with furniture and women and children were seen travelling to the northern areas, as the fine land up north attracted farmers from every quarter of the province.

By the 1870s the pioneer settlers of the colony of Western Australia had long since abandoned their hope that a Garden of Eden might be built on the banks of the Swan River. A land of sand, scrub and forest, deficient in herbage and distinguished by a number of poisonous plants, it seemed like a country cursed by nature, a country only half created. The climate was harsh and water was in short supply. The Aborigines who lived in the areas overrun by the whites had been brutalized by the white man's civilization, not least because the way of life of white bush workers was itself so harsh. For ever since 1850 the settlers in the country and the employers in the towns had drawn their labour from convicts and their descendants. On 1 May 1849 an Order in Council had nominated Western Australia as a colony to which convicts might be transported in response to requests by the settlers to make Western Australia into a penal colony on a large scale. Those in servitude were to be housed in the gaol in Fremantle and employed in essential public works. Ticket-of-leave holders could work for settlers in return for wages. Between 1850 and 1868 forty-three convict ships transported 9669 convicts to Western Australia. Within three years of the introduction of convicts, Governor

Fitzgerald was telling the Duke of Newcastle that convicts had made a major contribution to the advancement of Western Australia 'from a most lamentable state of stagnation and despair to one of rapidly increasing prosperity', both by their labour and by the demand they created for products.

By 1868 the convicts and their descendants made up nearly half of the 22 000 white settlers in the colony. By then a deep gulf had developed between the free and the bond. Western Australia was in danger of dividing into two nations. As in the eastern convict colonies, the bond were accused of living without any regard for the observances of religion; drunkenness was universal among them, and most of them were strangers to the refining influences of female society. Bush barbarism, it was said, was spreading over the red sandy deserts of the inland; the moral sewage of Great Britain had once more been let loose in the Australian wilderness, corrupting and still further degrading the Aborigine, and making life in white society hideous. The eastern colonies clamoured for abolition, and in deference to the eastern alarms Her Majesty's Government decided in 1867 to end the transportation of convicts to Western Australia.

Meanwhile, some exploration of the disappointing hinterland of Western Australia continued. Between 1869 and 1874 John Forrest led three expeditions of the inland and of the territory between Perth and Adelaide. He returned to Perth in December 1874 convinced that he had shown that the only way civilization could subdue the desert was by the use of such inventions as the telegraph and the railway.

By then William Ernest Powell Giles had come to the melancholy conclusion that the deserts of Australia had been designed by Providence for purposes which had nothing to do with the aspirations of civilized human beings. Giles was one of that legion of men on whom the gods or chance had played a cruel joke. He had both the strength to traverse the deserts of Australia, and the weakness rarely to put the cork back in a bottle once it was opened. In 1861 he almost won immortal fame by rescuing Burke, Wills and King on the Cooper, but chance cheated him of that sort of glory. He had to win it, if at all, the hard way. There at Mootwingee he carved the letter 'G' on a rock as evidence to posterity that he had been there. At Mootwingee Giles had seen for the first time the cave paintings of the Aborigines. He was not impressed. He wrote of them later as 'the weak endeavours of these benighted beings to give form and semblance to the symbolisms of the dread superstitions, that, haunting the chambers of their darkened minds, pass amongst them in the place of either philosophy or religion'.

In 1872 von Mueller chose Giles to lead an expedition to explore the country west from the overland telegraph line to the coast of Western Australia. So Giles, who had once entertained the hope of being hailed as a beneficiary of his adopted country, assumed in his own words the role of 'chronicler of her poorer regions'. After following the Finke River to the Missionary Plain south of the MacDonnell Ranges, he was driven back by lack of water. Everywhere he looked he had 'the most gloomy and desolate view imaginable; one almost enough to daunt the explorer from penetrating farther into such a dreadful region'. He found the natives even more hostile and forbidding than the landscape. They greeted his party with 'demoniacal yells' such as he never wished to hear again. He found them 'indignant and infuriated creatures' who made uncouth sounds to indicate to the white men that they were not wanted. He returned to Adelaide in January 1873.

Taking up renewed offers by von Mueller of financial assistance and joined by his young friend William Harry Tietkens, he assembled a small team which departed from Adelaide in March 1873 to essay again the crossing of the continent from the telegraph line to the coast of Western Australia. Again misfortune dogged his path. William Christie Gosse and Colonel Peter Egerton Warburton stole the limelight from him; they had government backing, while Giles had to rely on private subscription. No man interested in a return on capital was likely to give generously to explore the wastes of central Australia. Gosse got to Mount Olga first. Giles saw in the centre a huge rock of a terracotta colour, 1100 feet in height. He found to his chagrin that he was neither its discoverer nor its namer, Gosse having discovered it in the previous year and named it Ayers Rock after the Premier of South Australia.

Giles had lived through terrible privations. He had lost Alfred Gibson in that 'worst desert upon the face of the earth' in such painful circumstances that he named the area the Gibson Desert as a reminder to posterity of what they had been through. He suffered so acutely from hunger that when he escaped from 'the jaws of that howling wilderness' he drank and drank water from a creek and saw a small baby wallaby, young enough to be scarcely furnished with fur, and pounced upon it, and 'ate it, living, raw . . . —fur, skin, bones, skull, and all'. 'The delicious taste of that creature', he wrote, 'I shall never forget'.

Giles wanted to know why we were all here, and what it was all for. He despaired of ever finding the answer to the question of the original production of life and matter. That was beyond the powers of man to discover. But he was certain that 'having passed through the portals of the valley of death' men (i.e. all human beings) enjoyed life after life 'in new body after new body, passing through new spheres, arriving nearer and nearer to the fountain-head of all perfection, the divinely great Almighty source of light and life, of hope and love'. Once again life in a 'ghastly country' turned the mind of a man of sensibility to the eternal questions. The desert had spawned another prophet.

When he and his band of heroes arrived in Perth in November 1875, they rushed on down to Fremantle to dip their bodies in the warm waters of the Indian Ocean, there always being this sacramental note in the behaviour of Giles. Then, to the astonishment of those who did their business in that city on the edge of the great emptiness, Giles announced his intention to repeat the journey from west to east. In November 1875 he repaired to Geraldton, from where he set out on his camels to cross the deserts again. He did not know then that those men in black in Adelaide would fob him off with 2000 square miles of land in the Northern Territory as a reward for all his disquiet, and reject all his applications for official positions because he 'gambled' and his habits were 'not always strictly sober'. The man who had triumphed over the deserts of Australia was crushed by the bourgeois philistines. He died in obscurity at Coolgardie on 13 November 1897.

While Giles was fighting against the 'dreadful regions' of Australia, uproar had started again in the Australian bush. The selection acts, which were designed in part to reduce barbarism there, had whipped up a wave of crimes against property and the person. The selection acts had not borne Henry Parkes's 'fruit of the choicest kind'. They had stirred up the rarest vagabonds Australia could produce. Once again as in the old convict period some were tilling the soil and others had taken to the road. All over the bush of Australia an air of terror prevailed. Robberies were being committed 'right and left'. In June 1864 the *Port Denison Times* was reporting on the doings of a Rockhampton gang in central Queensland who, in bold defiance of the police sent out after them, were still outwitting the police with the greatest of ease. No one seemed to know how to put an end to their outrages against humanity. Even the pious folk of South Australia were not spared. In the next three years eleven policemen were shot dead by bushrangers in New South Wales and sixteen were wounded while attempting to capture bushrangers. By June 1867 three bushrangers had been executed, two were then under sentence of death, seven had been shot dead, one was supposed to have been murdered by his fellow-bushrangers, and eight were undergoing long sentences of imprisonment. One bushranger had a tally of forty-five offences, another a tally of twenty-eight.

Some said the cause of the trouble was that the bushrangers had become a 'race of heroes' for the country people, that so long as they were seen as being more than a match for the whole of the British cavalry, a 'race of imitators' would foster the spirit of bushrangers in the Australian bush. Some said the root of the trouble was the inadequate and incompetent police force in the country districts. Some accused the local police of basely participating in the spoils of the bushrangers, of enjoying both the bushrangers' rum and the bushrangers' women. The bushrangers, it was said, used part of their spoils to corrupt a whole neighbour-hood and terrorize those whom they could not corrupt. Some said the police would never be able to strike terror into the hearts of the bushrangers until they had won a victory in the heart of the country people.

The truth was that in the country districts there was much sym-pathy with crime and criminals among large numbers of people. Some said the root of the whole trouble was the system of free selection, which had isolated from the old settlements of all the colonies, except Western Australia, a class of people who were peculiarly exposed to the temptation to commit crime. Having failed in their attempt to secure a livelihood by lawful means, they were now driven into unlawful acts. The selection acts in all the colonies had strengthened those tendencies in the bush which had begun during the old convict period, the creation of the germ of a nation most thoroughly depraved in its vicious propensities. Convictism had bred bush barbarism; convictism had bred undying hostility towards the police: the selection acts had compounded the evils and ghosts of the past.

All these strands were woven into the character and behaviour of Ben Hall. Between 1863 and 1865 the respectable members of society in the districts of Wheogo, Binda, Yass, Crookwell, Collector and Canowindra were reduced to a fearful state of terror by his army of bandits who pillaged that beautiful country and drove a pathway of fire and destruction through it. During that period Hall was accessory to two murders and committed sixty-four robberies under arms. In twenty-nine weeks between October 1864 and 18 April 1865 he robbed the mail-coach many times in the Gundagai–Jugiong district, plundered the stations of the squatters, stuck up carriers on the great south road, robbed country stores, attacked gold escorts near Araluen, stole racehorses and robbed the Nubriggan Inn, compelling Mr Brazier the landlord, the travellers and servants all to drink and sing for many hours. Hall had a private hell in his heart against society in general and the police in particular. The son of ex-convicts, he became a stockman, leased a run in partnership with another Irishman with convict ancestors, married an Irish lassie, went on a spree at the local picnic races, and came back at the end of a week to find the local policeman had moved in with his wife. Again chance was conspiring with the traditions of his people and the failure of his own attempts to earn his daily bread to drive him into the ways of the highwayman and the robber. He nursed in his heart that viper of undying hostility to all 'traps' and 'swell coves', especially those effeminate Englishmen from whom officers were recruited for the police force in the country districts of New South Wales.

His associates were Frank Gardiner, who had spent five years in gaol for horse-stealing, and John Gilbert, a Canadian who had lived it up with petty thieves, drunkards, brothel-keepers and sly-grog sellers on the goldfields of eastern Australia. All three encouraged the picture of themselves as heroes of the people, as avengers of the poor and robbers of the rich, as men who were going to take down the mighty from their seat, send the rich empty away and hold the police up to public ridicule.

Their generosity towards and sympathy with the poor was already a legend in their lifetime. At Robinson's Hotel in Carcoar in October 1863 John Gilbert gave the poor people free drinks and threw bundles of cigars on the tables, and a huge pile of sweet-meats. But the forces of law and order were not idle. Gilbert was shot dead near Binalong on 13 May 1865.

On 29 April 1865 the subinspector of police, James Davidson, left Forbes with five men and two black trackers to capture Ben Hall. On the night of Thursday 4 May one of the trackers, Billy Dargan, saw Hall scraping the ground as though, like some wild animal, he was making a place for a bed in a hole, having nowhere else to lay his head. At daybreak the following morning the police and the trackers followed Hall from his resting place to his camp, challenged him to stop, and fired when he ran for dear life. Hall ran to a cluster of timber, grabbed a sapling and said, 'I'm wounded; I am dying'. He then fell, riddled with bullets.

When Ben Hall was buried in Forbes Cemetery on 7 May 1865, a crowd of over 100 sympathizers, including 40 or 50 women, gathered at the graveside to hear the Reverend Father James Montgomery recite the words, 'Man that is born of woman hath but a short time to live; he is cut down, like the flowers of the field.' Over the grave his friends and sympathizers erected a stone on which were cut the simple words 'In Memory of Ben Hall. Shot 5th May 1865. Aged 27 years'. Within a few years of his death the man whom the bourgeois press had vilified as a wild beast was apotheo-sized into a hero of the bush people of Australia:

Come all Australian sons with me
For a hero has been slain
And cowardly butchered in his sleep
Upon the Lachlan Plain.

Pray do not stay your seemly grief
But let a teardrop fall
For many hearts shall always mourn
The fate of bold Ben Hall.

Flowers on his grave, renewed and refreshed by loving hands, and that song lived on as proof that between some of the bush people and the bourgeoisie of the towns there was a great gulf fixed.

There were others, like Daniel Morgan, of whom it was said that killing a human being was his great sensual satisfaction, but who was befriended by the ex-convicts, stockmen and shepherds of that wild country around Tumbarumba, Corryong, Beechworth and Holbrook. There were the Clarke brothers, Thomas and John, who struck terror into the hearts of settlers in the wild mountainous country between Michelago and Araluen. Respectable people cried out in horror and indignation at the trail of plunder and murder left by the Clarkes, but many bush people refused to collaborate with the police. They professed to see little difference between the legal robbers, who had fattened on their fellows by their schemes and devices to put money in their purses as landowners or storekeepers or stock and station agents, and those like the Clarke brothers who presumed to prey on the rich with pistol and rifle in hand. The root of the trouble, it was said, was intimately connected with the squatting system. 'The end of the present system of land monopoly', wrote the *Empire* on 11 February 1867, 'will involve the end of bushranging. Whenever the interior wilderness is thrown fully open to the industrious cultivator of the soil—when families are allowed to make permanent homes —then and not till then will the bushranging brood be extirpated'. Cattle-duffers, gully-rakers, all those men who were not yet fully fledged bushrangers, would no longer curse the country with their crimes.

By 1860 there were few who still believed in their hearts that it was possible to win the Aborigines over to the white man's civilization or to win their souls for Christ. There was a large audience for the view that the Aborigines were filthy, thievish, lazy gluttons. Nevertheless, during this decade of the 1860s some white men thought of the Aborigines not as a menace or an enemy, but as friends, who could be taught by patience and kindness to perform useful services for white men. On many stations in the settled districts of New South Wales, Queensland, Victoria, South Australia and Western Australia women from the blacks' camp came to the white man's house to scrub the kitchen and the verandah floors, never presuming to enter any of the inner sanctuaries, such as the bedroom or the living room. The men worked at odd jobs on the station to earn a few pence for their baccy and their booze. Both sides often treated each other with every mark of affection. A 'Black Harry' and a 'Black Maggie' became part of the scenery on the stations of Australia. Sometimes, on the stations and in country towns such as Clare in South Australia, or Yass in New South Wales, or Warwick in Queensland, the Aborigines from the camps enlivened and entertained white folk with their corroborees.

One shadow which sometimes fell across this grandeur of the white man was the 'sin of the bush'—sexual intercourse with a black woman. The practice was said to be attended with serious consequences to the health and happiness of both parties. The black women often contracted the white man's disease of syphilis and some were punished by being ostracized from their own people.

White men often treated fallen women among the Aborigines with a brutality and callousness out of keeping with the amity and kindness professed by those in high places. In March 1877 a young black girl of 15 who had been disowned by her own people for granting her favours liberally to the white men in return for food, tobacco and alcohol, wandered round the streets of Echuca, quite unprotected and friendless. A white man befriended her and took her to the police station, hoping the sergeant would be moved with compassion. The sergeant took the stern line that she had worked her way to Echuca and would be able to get back 'by her own line of business'. In the eyes of the few who viewed such events with pity, another young life was wrecked.

The beauty of young white women faded as quickly as the beauty of the spring flowers as their price for obeying the unwritten commandment that no white woman must commit the 'sin of the bush'. The young white men who had not taken the vows of holy matrimony were under no such prohibition. Their problem was what to do with their lubra after they had gone down on their knees in some Christian church and vowed before Almighty God that from that day forward they would forsake all others and cleave to one white woman until death did them part. Some found that a quick blow with the stirrup iron, followed by a shove of the body into the river, solved all problems. Some were tortured by conscience, because they were not able to fulfil their promise to God: they went on lusting after the black girl and, when she succumbed, lacerated themselves again for their swinishness and treachery. One man was so tormented by his failure to stop and so hungry for that forgiveness neither God nor man seemed to want to bestow on him that he hanged himself with a bridle. All over eastern Australia and in the West, families who were proud of their ancient lineage, or proud of their elevation to a rank in society comparable with that of the landed gentry in the mother country, acquired a skeleton in the cupboard when the son and heir became the father of a half-caste child. Of love between white man and black woman, as distinct from lust or what Australians called 'doing something about it', there was never so much as a whisper.

On all the frontiers of settlement, settlers treated the Aborigines as vermin which had to be destroyed. In the settled districts they were called the blacks; in the frontier districts they were called the savages. In the settled districts they were held to have a role to play in the white man's world; in the frontier districts they were reviled as cannibals and barbarians. Reports came down from central and northern Queensland of abominations committed by savages against white settlers. There were reports of women, children and clergymen being massacred with the most revolting cruelty by savages whose ringleaders had been employed by a family in various menial occupations. In attacks on the pastoral stations Aborigines spared the lives of the Chinese shepherds on the ground that they too were being oppressed and degraded by the white man. By 1860 some white men believed that the savages had resolved to drive the Europeans out of their tribal territory.

The white man responded by terrorizing the savages who were spearing their cattle, setting fire to their grass, murdering shepherds and settlers and plundering stations and outstations. The government of Queensland used the native police, squads of black men serving as policemen under white officers. By 1861 these native police were practising indiscriminate slaughter of the native population. Government had instructed the inspectors of the native police to 'Keep the roads clear of the natives'. Few, if any, questions were ever asked about the methods they used. They had a new weapon, the carbine, a rapid-firing rifle, which enabled them to convert a punitive expedition into a slaughter. In Maryborough, Rockhampton, Townsville, Cairns and Cooktown, massacres of Aborigines occurred rather similar to the massacres of the Indians in California, ending in those spectacles which revolted and shocked the eyes of the civilized. Old women lay weltering in blood, their brains dashed out; the bodies of infants were ghastly with wounds. The native police often stupefied the black men they arrested with alcohol, bound their hands behind their backs as though they were trussing a fowl, and tossed them on to a dray or dragged them to the lock-up. When prisoners refused to obey any commands, they shot them dead like wild dogs.

Down in Hobart, Truganini, said to be the last of the Tasmanian Aborigines, had intimations that her end was near. In the early 1830s when she had roamed as free as a bird in the forests of Tasmania a haunting beauty had suffused her face. Forty years of living off the white man's 'hand-outs' had left her a ruin. In Hobart, where she was looked after by Mrs Dandridge at Lalla Rookh in Macquarie Street, she got through the day by stupefying herself with the odd glass of beer and the whiffs of tobacco. She got through the night with sips at a glass of hot ale spiced with ginger and sugar. On the night of 3 May 1876 she hollered to Mrs Dandridge to get rid of the Devil, who was sitting on her hand, but when none of the shooings and 'get away with yous' of that good lady had the slightest effect she lapsed into unconsciousness. She died on 9 May. On Flinders Island some descendants of unions between white men, Tasmanian Aborigines and other visitors to the Furneaux group lived on. In the south-east of South Australia other descendants of the wild days hung round the settlements along the coast, testimony for those with eyes to see that terrible things had happened long ago.

The land itself was still totting up its own victims—victims of the vast indifference of the country to all human dreams. By 1880 it looked as though the ancient, uncouth continent would destroy all human endeavours to create a class of small property-owners between the big men and their employees. Once again, as in the convict period, the bush had barbarized its would-be robbers and destroyers just as it had condemned the Aborigines to a perpetual state of barbarism in the countless centuries before the coming of the white man. In the cities belief in progress had not been diminished by the survival of barbarism in the Australian bush. There men, liberated from that religious creed which had pressed the point about man's powerlessness to change the nature of things, believed they had acquired three things with which to establish man's dominion over the whole continent—the railway, the telegraph, and education. The mind of man, they believed, was mightier than that land which threatened to reduce all its invaders to nomads, eccentrics, and seekers after false comforters.

9

The Calm-Down Begins

By the end of the gold decade, Melbourne had grown into a town where drunken blaspheming diggers, rushing from taphouse to taphouse, were flinging money around like dust, and running riot in the streets, sometimes accompanied by bedizened Jezebels who fleeced them of their money and anything else they had to offer. The hotels and drinking houses were places of riot and disorder.

In society at large the same confusion prevailed. The owners of many of the largest houses and some of the most expensive equipages to be seen on the streets of Melbourne were men from the lowest class who had made fortunes on the diggings, while scions of noble families in England, men who had won high honours at the ancient universities, were driving the cabs in which the nouveaux riches lolled or displayed their wealth in some incredibly vulgar manner. But in the middle of this great confusion of classes, the bourgeoisie were slowly imposing their great calm-down on the way of life of the people. The cities of bedizened Jezebels were about to give place to cities of merchants, bankers, shopkeepers, and a tame, calmed-down working class which had adopted the petty-bourgeois values of frugality, industry, private property and the family.

Population increased rapidly. There were 77 345 people in Victoria in March 1851, 729 654 in April 1871. New South Wales had 197 265 in 1851, and 503 981 by 1871. South Australia had 66 538 in 1851, and 188 644 by 1871. Queensland had 34 367 in 1861, and 121 743 by 1871. Only Tasmania and Western Australia missed out on the great burgeoning. In the former the population of 69 187 in 1851 had increased to 101 900 by 1871, and in the latter from 7186 in 1851 to 25 447 in 1871. Neither the shedding of convict labour in Tasmania nor the eager use of it in Western Australia seemed to affect their destiny as stricken peoples condemned to the role of billabongs while the river of life passed them by. By contrast, the number of Aborigines had shrunk sharply. In Tasmania, in 1871 less than 10 survived. In Victoria, the 1871 census revealed there were probably only 859.

In Melbourne a proud, confident bourgeois class saw their city as 'a little Paris' and wanted their city to be worthy of its position as the 'metropolis of the Australian colonies'. It should be and was already becoming conspicuous for the beauty of its architecture, the 'cleanliness, coolness and umbrageousness' of its leading thorough-fares, the embellishments of its parks and gardens, the elegance of its theatres and concert rooms, and the number of its libraries and galleries. This concern with superiority began during the gold decade. In 1853 the government of Victoria invited architects to submit designs for a parliament house which would be worthy of Melbourne's position 'in the vanguard of humanity'. In an age which confounded greatness with size and ornamentation, the architects S. G. Knight and P. Kerr submitted a design which brought together in one massive pile the 'pick of the whole world', a mixture of Roman arches, Greek columns, Venetian and Florentine interior decorations, Italianate floor tiles, and a front to the whole building which breathed the spirit of the British bulldog. Their concern was to echo the Old World of Europe rather than capture the spirit of the New.

It was the same when they came to design their banks, churches, cathedrals and other public buildings. The Melbourne Public Library was designed by John Reed, a provincial of the Old World who found it fatally easy to adopt the style of a colonial in the New World. The building materials were local: Victorian bluestone for the walls and Tasmanian freestone for the facings. The style was borrowed from Europe. The dome was an imitation of the one over the reading room in the British Museum; the external columns were Corinthian; the statues gracing the interior represented the gods, goddesses and muses of the Ancient World. The books on the shelves, selected with the utmost skill and judgement by the librarian, Augustus Tulk, another exile from the Old World, were spiritual food for transplanted Britons rather than material for the enlightenment of the Betsy Bandicoots of Australia. Encouraged by the approval of the chairman of the library board, Redmond Barry, another man who saw nothing incongruous in this slavish imitation of the Old World, Tulk filled the shelves with those books which for him were synonymous with civilization—with the literature of the ancient world and the literature of England.

When the building of the Great Hall of the University of Sydney was finished in July 1859, the *Sydney Morning Herald* told its readers it had been designed after the fashion of, and indeed partly in imitation of, Westminster Hall in London, hastening to add that anyone who had the good fortune to see this 'chef d'oeuvre of taste, science and constructive art' would immediately perceive the 'superiority of this antipodean creation'. The interior decoration reminded all who frequented the building that New South Wales was a society of transplanted Britons. On one wall were the rose of England, the thistle of Scotland and the shamrock of Ireland. On another wall each stained-glass window illustrated a figure such as Shakespeare or Samuel Johnson and others who had been prominent in the literature and art of Great Britain. There was an Oxford window, a Cambridge window, and one large window filled with the sovereigns of the British Isles from the earliest times until the reign of their present illustrious sovereign Queen Victoria. The only references to the local scene were a window for James Cook and a marble statue of William Charles Wentworth.

Such elegance dwelt cheek by jowl with filth and degradation. Sydney and Melbourne were never free from the smell of human excreta. Their streets were choked with dust in summer and covered with mud in the winter. Carts sank to their axles in wet seasons. Any horse rider who had business with the Bank of Australasia in Melbourne in the winter might, as his horse sank to its chest in the mud, see with his eye the fluted columns on the facade of that building, the ornamented cornices and the statues of the graces.

The poor were still the 'pariahs of the streets' in Sydney, Melbourne and Adelaide. They floated about the streets like fish in a pond. Their dwelling places were said to be unfit for human habitation: the rain leaked in through the roof, and filth of all kinds washed in through the front door. All contrivances for domestic comfort such as indoor sinks, pantries, indoor stoves and clothes closets were absent from the houses of the unskilled workers and the poor. In Europe high-minded men like John Ruskin, John Henry Newman and Karl Marx had prophesied a terrible retribution for a society which tolerated such moral infamy in its midst. By contrast, in the Australian colonies a complacency pervaded the debate about the future of society. Here, as the *Argus* wrote in December 1882, there was not the squalor and wretchedness to be met with in such great cities as London, Liverpool or Glasgow. The bourgeoisie in Australia had their own special kind of terror: the yell of the ruffian had already been heard outside the door of Parliament House in Melbourne. Hordes of 'lazy Lazzarini' had already sensed that the bourgeoisie were not standing on 'entrenched ground', that behind the regal power and glory which they presented to the world there existed not that kingdom against which the gates of hell would not prevail but the kingdom of nothingness. This was one of the many fears which tormented Marcus Andrew Hislop Clarke. He was a young man in whom nature had planted the power to interest the world in the truth about the human situation by telling a story. He had the imaginative gift to see Julius Caesar in a Collingwood bus-driver, and Cleopatra in a barmaid in a Bourke Street hotel.

The son of Anglo-Irish gentry fallen on hard times, Clarke emigrated to Australia in 1863. In Victoria he tried to join the world of the sheepmen on two sheep stations near Glenorchy belonging to his uncle Andrew Clarke, one of the 'kid-glove swells' of the Government House set in Melbourne. There he sensed the spirit of place in Australia. He concluded that the utilitarian civilization which fashioned him in England shrank into insignificance beside 'the contemptuous grandeur of forests and ranges'. In Australia alone, he wrote later, was to be found the 'Grotesque, the Weird— the strange scribblings of Nature learning how to write'. For him it was a 'fantastic land of monstrosities', of trees without shade, flowers without perfume, birds which could not fly and beasts which had not yet learnt to walk on all fours. In the Australian bush a man learnt that there was beauty in loneliness, in the barren and the uncouth. He learned to see a beauty in 'haggard gum trees blown into odd shapes' or 'distorted with fierce hot winds'.

The experience left him a stranger, afraid in a world he now found no God had made. The loss of his religious faith left him like a man bereaved. When in 1868 he went down to the great city again, he found in the streets of Melbourne a reflection of all the uproar in his own soul. It was 'as vicious a city as any in the southern hemisphere'. His subject was Bohemia and low life, for he was a Bohemian at heart and a secret sharer of those who lived in the lower depths. By night Melbourne was teeming with such life. In the music halls girls served with lightning speed 'brandies hot', a 'glass of ale', 'nobblers for five', 'whiskies hot', and 'sherry and bitters' which expectorating crowds of men and boys called for on all sides. In Bourke Street at night sewing girls and milliners' apprentices, driven by one of the great hungers of mankind, gaped at a group of up-country men who were in town to 'go on the bust' but had no eye for these girls from the lower orders. Drunken sailors staggered down the street. A preacher harangued a small crowd, while little boys picked the pockets of those who were hearing of God's plan for the salvation of mankind. Late at night vaudeville shows vomited forth a crew of drunken soldiers, prostitutes and thieves on to the street while a brass band played 'The Last Rose of Summer'. Cabmen helped prostitutes to 'inveigle a pigeon' into the houses of ill fame. Thieves, 'Jew Boys' and seedy characters sneaked up behind intoxicated sailors and befuddled old men, hoping to slip a quid or two off them after they fell into the gutter.

In pockets of Melbourne, such as Little Bourke Street, some men behaved as though they had been made in the image of the beast rather than in the likeness of God. Such types frequented the Chinese gambling houses and opium dens. In such opium dens brown and withered figures, with unstrung muscles, leaden eyes and corpse-like faces, reclined on benches puffing away at their pipes, hoping to induce visions of extraordinary beauty or to revel in those sensuous delights the Mussulman expected to enjoy in Paradise. Marcus Clarke sensed an emptiness behind the feverish search for pleasure, and a vulgar equation of happiness with a never-ending titillation of the senses. 'Woe unto you, ye bourgeois of Melbourne, and you, ye squatters of Australia Felix', he cried, because their grave-diggers were growing up in the cities they had erected.

It was also a society in which questions were being asked about the proper role of women. The great excess of males over females in the early convict days had created in Australia a male-dominated society in which power and prestige belonged to the human beings with the most masculine qualities. On the other hand the unsteadiness of the men in that society, their periodic bouts of erratic behaviour, had conferred a moral authority on the women. In time two of the major writers of imaginative literature in Australia— Henry Lawson and 'Henry Handel Richardson' (Ethel Florence Robertson)—would write works about gifted but wayward men married to gifted and reliable women.

In a society where the majority in the various colonial parliaments were committed to the extension of equality before the law to all adult members of society, that majority did not feel called on to explain why such equality should not be extended either to women or to Aborigines. The law excluded women from the institutions of higher learning, from all the learned professions, and from the right to vote for members of the legislative assemblies and councils. The Victorian Act to extend the right of voting gave the vote to every 'male person of the full age of twenty one years'; by 1859 all the other colonies except Western Australia had introduced similar provisions. Such discrimination was the rule rather than the exception in legislation touching on the rights of the two sexes. From July 1861 a man might petition for separation or divorce from his wife on the grounds of a single act of adultery; by contrast the woman had to prove her husband guilty of either incestuous adultery, or rape, or sodomy, or bestiality, or adultery coupled with cruelty. Similar discrimination was written into the first divorce acts of the other colonies. In the lawcourts of the various colonies the laws relating to the rights and liabilities of married women prescribed that the wages and earnings of a wife were deemed to be for the use of the husband. In the latter case the postmaster made the payment to whichever of the two he deemed proper. In this way a society in which a majority had opted for equality of conditions and boasted of success in breaking with Old World conventions, accepted in fact and in law the inferiority of women.

The law drew similar distinctions in the right to employment. The Coal Mines Regulation Act of 1862 in New South Wales enacted that 'no female shall be employed in or about a mine'. The factory acts of the various colonies distinguished the conditions applicable to men from the conditions applicable to women. In all the acts defining who could or could not work, the superiority of the male in physical strength and other intangible qualities was acknowledged, and the inferiority of the female tacitly accepted as the grounds for her exclusion from employment. Women in the middle classes were restricted to positions as governesses where, as an advertisement put it in October 1860, they would be expected to impart a thorough English education with French, music and dancing, or act as companions to genteel ladies. Women in the working classes had to choose between the near slavery of domestic service and being hirelings for wages in a factory.

As the inferiors of the men, employers expected women to work longer hours for less pay. In Melbourne in July 1882 a tailoress received 2s for making a coat, a man 14s. A woman received 1s for making vests and trousers, a man 6s. Meetings were held that year in Melbourne to discuss ways to rectify the matter. Those attending agreed the time had arrived for the tailoresses of Melbourne and the suburbs to form themselves into an association for mutual assistance and support, to secure a reduction of the present long and heavy hours of labour, and to draw up a time log for payments at a fixed rate per hour. It was a monstrous thing, it was said, that any human being should work for such long hours for such a trifling payment. No one at those meetings raised the question of discrimination between the sexes, or probed the deeper causes of oppression, exploitation and enslavement.

A few campaigners argued that the subjection of woman to man was the product of human endeavour, that what man had created, he could reform. Men in general affected to be uneasy at the prospect of such a change. They wanted women as they were, as God and nature had decreed they should be. In Melbourne the *Age* maintained in October 1874 that maternal duties 'must be the first consideration of every wife'. As they saw it, if the refinements and elegancies of civilized life were to be retained and increased, it would be by keeping woman as the queen of the family and the social circle. What woman wanted, they argued, was not legislation to make her free, but education to fit her to become more perfectly the companion and helpmate of man.

In the meantime changes in communication were contributing to the calm-down the bourgeois deemed essential both for their material profit and their spiritual well-being. Material progress was calming down the passions and enabling the bourgeois to win a great victory over the Goths and Vandals and larrikins of the cities just as the iron rail and the telegraph were wiping the bush barbarians and the surviving savages off the face of the earth. At the end of 1863 Niel Black heard from his partner in the United Kingdom that cable communication between London and Calcutta would soon take only five hours. He also heard that in France they were busy with flying machines and that if these experiments were successful the journey from Europe to Australia would be reduced to a few days. His partner added somewhat ruefully, 'But this will hardly be in our time'.

The journeys of John McDouall Stuart from Adelaide to the north coast in 1859–62 had proved it would be practicable to erect an overland telegraph line from south to north and connect Australia with the outside world at Java. *Bell's Life in Victoria* predicted in April 1864 that as soon as cable communication was established with England the names of the winners of the Derby and the Oaks would be posted outside the telegraph office forty-eight hours after each event. The line was built, and was opened on 27 October 1872. On that day, as the postmaster-general of South Australia put it, the 'Australian colonies were connected with the grand electric chain which united all the nations of the earth'.

At a banquet to celebrate the event in Sydney old Jack Robertson said the colony was now made habitable for civilized man. Henry Parkes predictably spoke of the 'magical work of uniting us hand in hand with the mother country'. Old John Dunmore Lang recalled that on the day in 1823 when he had landed in Sydney the streets were crowded with the stumps of trees. Now a copper wire had united them with the whole world. In Adelaide the *Register* rejoiced that inebriates had not marred the celebration, believing as they did that material progress was the handmaiden of moral progress.

Some prophesied that the overseas cable would end the other great cause of Australian backwardness—her isolation. Australians would now cease to be concerned with petty local affairs and turn their attention to the affairs of the world at large. Marcus Clarke prophesied that the oppression of the poor by the rich, and of the many by the few, would be rendered more difficult by each message that flashed along the wires. Now, north, south, east and west, men would realize that they belonged to 'one kindred blood'. The steam-engine, the railway, the telegraph, gaslight, the omnibus and the factory were achieving what no other society or ideology or religion had been able to achieve—the end of all differences between human beings, and the approach of that day when all men were brothers. In the consummation of that dream, democracy was the handmaiden of material progress.

10

Colonial Democrats

Colonials did not govern themselves entirely: defence and foreign affairs belonged to the Imperial Government. Colonials had the same prerogatives as the harlot: they had power but not responsibility. That was one reason why colonial politics had degenerated into a sordid struggle for power. Politicians contended not over great questions of principle, or matters of great moment, but rather over how to win 'the scramble for office'. Men formed groups in politics not from identity of political conviction but out of some belief that one leader was more likely to win office than another. Melbourne political life had some of the features Chekhov detected in Russian provincial life in the last quarter of the nineteenth century: it was difficult to find 'one honest man in the town'.

In November 1864 the Victorian Government announced that it intended to reform the land laws, adjust the tariff, and reduce the property qualification for members of the Legislative Council. It was a direct challenge to the gentry. David Syme's liberal newspaper, the *Age*, was warm in its praise: a tariff on imports would aid the development of an industrial civilization in Victoria, laying the basis for a 'moral and enlightened community'. The small businessmen who dominated the Legislative Assembly greeted the measure with enthusiasm. But the wealthy importers and the squatters who held sway in the Legislative Council were determined to block the introduction of such a tariff, and they refused to pass the annual Appropriation Bill in which the measure was contained. The lower house resolved not to amend the bill until their right to control taxation and supply had been acknowledged by the Council.

The two chambers were deadlocked. On 28 July the Treasurer proclaimed in the *Government Gazette* that as the amount of money legally available to pay the salaries and wages of public servants was inadequate, payment must be delayed until the necessary authority was obtained. The Governor, Sir Charles Darling, rescued the government by approving a loan from the London Chartered Bank. The conservative press was outraged, and Darling was recalled to England. The respectable and kind-hearted Chief Secretary, James McCulloch, fearing that further opposition by the Council might incite the people to revolution, backed down.

In the *Age* Syme thundered the word 'betrayal'; the scurrilous whispered that the Assembly had been bought. The *Argus* proclaimed in March 1866 that colonial democracy was only another form of tyranny. Society had transferred its allegiance from one despot to another. This must have been very mortifying to those who had set their eyes on democracy as the great redresser of wrongs and the final destiny of the human race. Society now had the tyranny of the majority. The question was whether the monster could be restrained. The bourgeois in the Legislative Assembly and the woolmen and aristocratic merchants in the Legislative Council thanked their God that colonial democrats had once again been rescued by the English governing classes from riots and rule by ruffians.

Within a year these colonial democrats were grovelling at the feet of a royal prince. When the Prince Alfred, second son of Her Gracious Majesty the beloved Queen Victoria, landed at Glenelg in South Australia on 31 October 1867, he was greeted by a large massed choir, the women dressed in white as a symbol of that mystical purity appropriate for a royal family which had made a fetish of virtue and respectability, and the men in an appropriate sober black. They sang lustily 'God Save the Queen', including a special verse about the Prince, followed by 'The Song of Australia', beginning with those banal words 'There is a land where southern skies are gleaming with a thousand eyes'. On all public occasions the colonials provided such evidence that they were both British and Australian, men not of a divided but of a double, harmonious loyalty. Women and children pelted the carriage with flowers, public dignitaries presented the Prince with declarations of loyalty, veneration and affection for the Queen and her Empire. Then the Prince was driven in an open carriage through the streets of Adelaide, which were decorated with huge portraits of him, portraits which caused him to whisper to the man next to him, 'I do not think Mother would recognize me in some of these illustrations'.

In the eyes of colonials the Prince resembled a god who could not err. When he declined to attend divine service on his first Sunday on Australian soil, all the grovellers at the throne of grace found his absence perfectly understandable, especially as he had so graciously complimented them on creating a city conspicuous for the absence 'of the poor and rowdy class'. They lapped that up.

When the Prince and his party went for moonlight shoots, leaving the ground over which they had walked littered with the blood and the bodies of possums, they praised him for his skill with the gun and his possession in abundance of manly qualities. When the Prince displayed his agility on the boards as a dancer, where he made no attempt to conceal his preference for buxom young girls rather than stately North Adelaide matrons, the ladies of riper age simpered behind their fans how very human he was, in fact just like one of them. When one of the organizers suggested that some Aboriginal women might dance naked before the Prince, just as the women of Jerusalem had danced naked before King David, the Aborigines themselves put a stop to any speculation about the Prince as a 'voyeur' by asking with some indignation, 'What for we do it, more than white women?'.

In the meantime Melbourne and the provincial centres of Victoria were feverishly preparing to show the Prince that the brightest of his memories must be associated with the colony that bore his mother's name. Men discovered things in themselves they had never suspected were there. The young Bohemian, Marcus Clarke, found himself cheering, shouting and screaming a welcome to His Highness, climbing on to the top of verandahs to catch a glimpse of the royal personage. He wondered what was in a man that permitted him to be overwhelmed by such strange passions. Borough councillors went wild; country men who spent their lives with sheep shook the hands of the royal visitor with a mad fire in their eyes and poured out to a bewildered young man what they felt in their hearts for his dear mother, their Queen, God bless her.

On the very night the press had urged the people of Melbourne to distinguish themselves by displaying that 'lusty gratification which should warm the hearts of benevolent souls', 3000 Irishmen gathered outside the Protestant Hall and began to sing that inflammatory song 'O Paddy dear, an' did you hear the news that's go-in' round? The shamrock is forbid by law to grow in Irish ground.' They threw stones at the Protestant mob which gathered quickly to display their strength. Shots were fired; an Irish Catholic dropped dead; the police arrested an Orangeman, as the Protestants called out 'Shame' and words too vile to be printed by the press of the day. The Catholics retaliated with similar abuse about the 'Prots' and all the evil they had perpetrated against Mother Ireland.

The next day, 28 November, was the occasion when the people met their Prince at a free banquet to be held on the bank of the Yarra River. It was one of those hot, north wind Melbourne days in late November, when the dust and the heat of midday frayed the nerves. When thirsty members in the crowd called for drink, the brazen broached a tub of wine and began to hand out goblets to their friends. Inflamed by drink, a hungry mob rushed the tables on which the food was laid out. A saturnalia began. Men and women rolled about in the grass and the dust on the river bank fumbling with each other's bodies, while mothers frantically urged their children to look the other way. Some men and women rushed across the fields with bottles of wine, legs of lamb, and loaves of bread tucked under their arms or held in their hands. Others lay on the grass dead to all the world, with their mouths open, their clothes stained by the wine, while flies crawled over their faces. Next day the *Argus* declared that a more 'miserable day' had 'never been witnessed in Victoria'; the *Age* regretted that those in power had permitted ruffians to convert a 'wild revelry' into a 'drunken debauch'; *Punch* contemptuously said this would teach people not to put their trust in princes and free banquets. Apart from that side-swipe, the Prince escaped without one rebuke. Loyal Victorians were still raving about the Prince and all his works as the bow of his ship, the *Galatea*, cut its way through that huge sea which rolls through Bass Strait.

In Sydney on 12 March, on one of those majestic days when the sun was reflected in thousands of golden fireballs dancing on the deep blue sea, the Prince graciously attended a picnic at Clontarf to raise funds for the Sailors' Home. Everybody who was anybody was there. After lunch Sir William Manning, a member of the Legislative Council, asked the Prince if he would be interested to see the display the Aborigines were about to put on for the white man. Before he could reply, a man of fair complexion, whose eyes wore the signs of a man who had suffered much, stole up to within 6 feet of the Prince, pulled out a revolver, and fired at his back. The Prince was wounded, but not mortally. The man then tried to shoot Manning, but missed. Then before he could fire again a Mr Vial pinioned his arm, so that the bullet entered the foot of George Thorne, who was carried away by Mr Hassall.

Alexander Stuart, a pillar of the Presbyterian Church, seized a carving knife and attempted to stab the assassin. Respectable lawyers and politicians called on the mob to hang the wretch there and then; hysterical voices were heard shouting 'hang him', 'lynch him', 'string him up'. Excited men tore the clothes off the back of the assassin and blackened his eyes and bruised his lips, as women screeched and yelled out, 'Cut him to pieces with scissors'. The police shielded him as best they could and carried him slowly to the wharf where he was put on board the police launch for Circular Quay.

The would-be assassin was Henry James O'Farrell, a deranged, sorry victim of brooding over the wrongs of Ireland, a God-botherer and a bout drinker, one of those men in whom nature had planted the mighty opposites of spiritual aspirations and a behaviour distinguished by coarse sensuality. He told his gaolers that he had acted on the instructions of the Melbourne branch of the Fenians, an Irish revolutionary brotherhood pledged to drive the English out of Ireland. The leaders of the Catholic community promptly denied the accusation. The *Freeman's Journal* pointed out it was absurd to believe there could be a Fenian circle in a society singularly free of any cause that might excite men to subvert the existing order of things.

Archbishop John Bede Polding, always a man to sense the imminence of disaster, even in the actions of a madman, was alarmed. He had lived for over thirty years in a community poisoned by sectarian bitterness. Now once again all the signs were ominous. The Governor of New South Wales had withdrawn his patronage from the St Patrick's Day regatta; the old Protestant establishment was again ostracizing the devotees of the Church. This time he used a phrase which was to be taken up and serve other purposes than those which inspired Christ's faithful servant: 'Australians we should all be', he said, ' . . . And I say, Australia for the Australians'.

At a great indignation meeting in Hyde Park, Sydney, on 13 March 1868 20 000 people greeted the leaders of the Protestant community with wild enthusiasm. When Charles Cowper, a devoted Anglican, addressed them on the errors and 'satanic delusion' of the Church of Rome, they cheered loudly and cried out the Australian words of approval, 'God bless you Charley'. Irishmen, Englishmen, and Scotchmen, Protestants and Catholics alike professed their horror, their indignation and their attachment to the person of the Prince. A large number of Catholic priests mingled with the crowd and gave hearty 'hear, hears' to every reference to unity. W. B. Dalley, a prominent Catholic layman, a son of Irish convict parents, pointed out that O'Farrell was not a man of the people, 'not of us, not a citizen of this country'. Father John McEncroe, now in the autumn of his life, wept for joy as the crowd cheered again and again for the Queen and her son and Old England. Sir William Manning was very pleased with himself on that day. God and the people were on his side. God had chosen him as the instrument by which this great blessing was vouchsafed. Now the people at large gave him a hero's welcome.

This popular fervour presented Henry Parkes with a great temptation. He had always been deeply attached to the Protestant religion, which for him was identical with material progress and universal liberty. He had flirted all his life with the idea that the priests of the Catholic Church were purveyors of a degrading superstition. In recent years his public standing had fallen as he had lapsed into demagoguery. Believing there was some political advantage to be gained in the heat of the moment by a whack on the drum of sectarian sentiment, Parkes decided to exploit the hysteria stirred up by the attempted assassination and the arrival of Fenian convicts in Western Australia. He wrote to the Chief Secretary of Victoria, James McCulloch, to tell him his government was in possession of information which left no doubt of the fact that the man O'Farrell was one of a band organized for the diabolical purpose of taking the life of the Prince, and that he had accomplices in Victoria and probably in Ireland. A few days later news reached Sydney that sixty Fenians had landed in Perth. Judging the time ripe for a 'man of the hour' to appear as the saviour of the people, Parkes rushed through both Houses of Parliament a bill for 'the better suppression and punishment of seditious practices and attempts'. He was supported by Manning, who still believed that in the eyes of Irish Catholics the end justified the means, and that anything was lawful if it helped to get rid of the oppressor. The *Sydney Morning Herald*, deploring the Irish tendency to look on traitors as patriots, and murderers as martyrs, applauded him for taking steps to protect the government and the nation against the daggers, the brand and the pirates. Parkes was once again 'the man of the hour'.

When a committee of inquiry cast doubt on his allegations, he swept their report aside and carried the Protestant ascendancy with him. He was fighting the great battle of the century, 'the battle of Protestantism and Progress against Roman Catholic Usurpation and Retrogression'. He told his audiences in his low soft squeaky tones that God had selected him to perform special work in New South Wales. God and the people, he believed, had chosen him to teach mankind to use democracy for the creation of an enlightened people in Australia. That was the Parkes who played the lofty role in public. In private, commercial difficulties and the love of office were forcing him to take steps to reassure Irish Catholics that he had their best interests at heart. He had about him both the air of greatness and all the pettiness, spite and failings of the little man.

When Wentworth died at Wimborne in Dorset on 20 March 1872, Parkes, instead of seeing the event as marking the disappearance of the most formidable opponent of what he had once longed for, saw it as a lesson about greatness in a human being. He readily agreed to the request of Wentworth's widow that the last wish of Australia's greatest native son should be honoured: his body should be brought back to be buried in the land of his birth.

For Wentworth things had not been well. He had been quite shocked when he received word of the death of James Macarthur in the summer of 1867. 'Poor fellow', he wrote in his letter of condolence to James's brother William, 'I little thought when I last saw him that we were to meet no more in this world'—so letting slip the drift of his mind on one of the questions that matter in life. His son D'Arcy was unhappily married and behaving in an odd and cruel way to his wife, accusing her of being a woman of the streets. From Australia there were unpleasant rumours about the behaviour of his son-in-law Fisher—rumours about living with a black girl, and the punishments he inflicted on himself for his swinishness. The evidence he had hoped for of the marriage of his father to Catherine Crowley had still not been found and the search for a pedigree of his father's family was running into all sorts of difficulties. The knighthood he had expected for his years of distinguished service had still not come his way. Charles Sturt got his posthumously in 1869; Wentworth had again been passed over.

In the winter of 1871–72 he received an intimation that death was near. He began to behave like a child. The man who had made the house at Wimborne cheerful stopped talking. After asking his wife to arrange for his remains to be deposited in his native land, he lost all interest in worldly affairs. He became even more gentle and childlike, until he fell asleep forever on 20 March 1872. His face looked so peaceful after death that his wife entertained the hope that he was safe at last and that Christ would ask him into His kingdom. She was left with the empty chair, a sense of desolation and irreparable loss.

Thanks primarily to Parkes, on 6 May 1873 the first state funeral in the history of the colony was accorded to Wentworth. The government proclaimed a public holiday; shops and business houses closed down for the day; thousands thronged the streets to see or take part in the ceremony. For the memorial service in St Andrew's Cathedral admission was strictly by ticket: only men were admitted. The clergy were there in their gorgeous robes, the consuls of foreign powers, the military and the judges were attired in their brilliant uniforms and colours. After the service the pageant, headed by a sarcophagus of a size and design similar to that deemed appropriate for the Duke of Wellington and Burke and Wills, proceeded to Vaucluse. There the police moved the people away from the vault where the sarcophagus was to rest. The choir sang mournfully the words

> My fathers were but strangers here,
> And as they were, am I.

But no one took those words that day as a stern reminder that the white men gathered there beside the waters of Sydney Harbour were but sojourners in this uncouth continent: that between what they stood for and the spirit of the place there never could be harmony or a sense of belonging.

11

The Kingdom of Nothingness

By 1860 the high-minded in Australia believed the most wonderful of all revolutions in the condition of mankind was about to take place. All boys and girls between the ages of 6 and 13 were about to learn how to read, write, add, subtract, multiply and divide. Parents were about to have the opportunity of endowing their offspring with the most enduring and most profitable of all worldly gifts, a sound secular and moral education.

The need was great. In the cities the men with education were conscious, as Dan Deniehy put it in July 1862, that here in Australia everything was 'anti-podean'. In Europe there was enlightenment; here there was semi-barbarism. In Europe and North America there were expensive schemes for the education of all children; here the wealthy alone could enjoy the higher branches of knowledge. In Europe and North America many countries had already introduced free education for all; here narrow-minded class legislation and sectarian animosity thwarted all such attempts.

Bedevilled by sectarian suspicion and bitterness, and despairing of Protestants and Catholics ever reaching agreement on a general system of education, the colonies of New South Wales, Victoria and Queensland had introduced a dual system of national schools and denominational schools. These systems were soon found to be attended with grave weaknesses. The sites chosen for denominational schools were often unhealthy. In Sydney in 1856 a Roman Catholic school and a Wesleyan school were held in dark, damp and unventilated cellars beneath chapels. In the same city many of the schools were also in bad repair, in some instances the children and the teachers being entirely unprotected from wind and rain. In all the colonies all parents except paupers were called on to pay fees to keep their children at school, the average being 6d a week.

The central weakness in the system remained the opposition of the parents to sending their children to school. Some parents, it was said, were not able to advance a definite reason for keeping their children away from school. Some said it was because of the fee, small though that was; some said it was because the parents could not afford to lose the wages otherwise paid to children, or the value of the children's services in their own enterprises both in the city and in the country. In farming districts children were kept at home during harvest, ploughing and seed-planting. Less important occupations such as tending cattle, sheep, pigs and poultry and scaring birds and kangaroos from the corn also kept them from school from time to time. Whatever the causes, in Sydney not more than half the children of the lower classes attended school in 1860. There the quays, the wharves and the public thoroughfares were crowded each day with idle children, who were learning from other street people to use bad language, to steal and to practise all those indecencies which scandalized the respectable virtue-mongers amongst the bourgeoisie.

The lack of proper books and apparatus was extreme. The method of instruction was so bad that the attainment of the scholars in such rudimentary subjects as reading and arithmetic was lamentable. In one school in New South Wales only half the children could read words of one syllable or recite the alphabet. Only a quarter were able to read aloud an easy passage of narrative prose, and only a tiny number could manage to read a poem. What disturbed men in high places was the failure of the teachers to correct what was called 'vicious pronunciation or improper modulations of voice', as this inattention to correct English pronunciation had a tendency to 'foster an Australian dialect' which threatened to surpass the American in disagreeableness. The teachers themselves were untrained and therefore, no matter how industrious, not properly prepared to discharge their duties. The condition of the schools as regards religious instruction was equally deplorable. The children in the Catholic, Protestant and national schools exhibited an amount of ignorance that disgraced a Christian country.

All those who were familiar with these weaknesses believed there should be one system of education, controlled and administered by one managing body. They advocated a system of national schools financed and administered by the state, which would provide a general education to prepare children for citizenship. Most proposals envisaged that some time would be given to religious instruction of a general kind. Once again sectarian suspicions and bitterness were the stumbling block to such a solution. The Anglicans and Presbyterians were divided: some supported the move towards secular education, others regarded it as a betrayal of their faith. The Catholic Church stood firmly against the proposals.

Catholic bishops such as Polding insisted that the true faith should be the basis of a Catholic's education. What was more, the bishops objected to the use of taxes for the establishment of a national system of education which Catholics could not, in all conscience, make use of. Catholic taxes would be being used to subsidize humanist error.

The reformers were determined. The Victorian government in 1872 was the first colonial government to introduce legislation which provided a system of education which was free, compulsory and secular. South Australia followed in 1875 with an act which allowed for fifteen minutes of Bible reading before the start of the school day. Queensland introduced free and compulsory education the same year. In Henry Parkes's Public Education Act of 1880 all aid from the consolidated revenue was withdrawn from denominational schools in New South Wales. Education at public schools was made free for those subjects in which secular instruction was given. Provision was made for the children of a denomination to be taught by their own religious teacher for one hour weekly. Parkes's original proposal for the introduction of secondary schools was dropped; so was his plan to provide textbook histories of England and Australia. But New South Wales, like Victoria and South Australia, was now committed to free, compulsory and secular education. Queensland introduced it in 1875 and Tasmania in 1885; Western Australia excluded sectarian teaching in the national schools in 1871 and abolished aid to denominational schools in 1895.

In the cities on weekdays those waifs and strays who had wandered round the streets alarming and scandalizing the bourgeois gradually disappeared from sight. Within a decade of the introduction of compulsory education observers were complaining that the ignorant larrikin who prowled the streets by night during the week, and by day too on Saturdays and Sundays, was being replaced by the educated larrikin. In the country districts farmers and the families of itinerant workers for whom the labour of their children was vital in their never-ending struggle for survival were forced to use this labour before sending them to school. Teachers who were supposed to be spreading enlightenment in the Australian bush often began their day by allowing the heads of the children of the cocky farmers to rest on their desks while they slept off the effects of an early-morning encounter with the teats of a cow.

The reforms entrenched the sectarian divisions they were designed to overcome, not least because the Catholic Church withdrew its children from the public system. The question of whether or not the government should subsidize denominational schools remained a bitter source of conflict into the following century. Nor were the Public Education Acts of 1866 and 1880 in New South Wales, of 1872 in Victoria, and of 1875 in South Australia any more successful than their predecessors in effecting that 'reconciliation of classes' so dear to the heart of the bourgeoisie. The children of the rich and the children of the poor did not meet on common ground either in the classrooms or the playgrounds of the Australian colonies. In some schools a room was set aside for the children of the rich. If no such room was available, a portion of the school was curtained off so that the rich boys might be spared contamination by the poor. Where possible the daughters of the wealthy were allotted or seized a portion of the playground for their exclusive use, where they played their hopscotch and 'skippy', while their brothers for their part carefully excluded all the little vulgarians from their own manly sports. In this way the parents of the gentry and the upper ranks of the bourgeoisie ensured that the fine edge of gentility should not be dulled by familiar intercourse with common children, until the time came to attend a private school such as Melbourne Grammar School or the Presbyterian Ladies' College where the prejudices they had inherited from their parents were consolidated into the habits of a lifetime.

On the surface the instruction in the Catholic schools differed sharply from instruction in the national schools. In the national schools the children were taught to venerate Her Majesty Queen Victoria; in the Catholic schools the children learned to venerate 'he Holy Father, and to adore the Holy Mother of God. In the national schools the children learned of the glories of British arms, and the spread of a beneficent British civilization over the whole world, British civilization and Bible-based Christianity being represented as that 'sea of glory' which, as the hymn put it, was one day to 'stretch from pole to pole'; in the Catholic schools Ireland was presented as the centre of the universe, and England as a place from which had come the men who had reduced the loveliest island on God's earth to a land of skulls. In the national schools the day sometimes began with a ceremony designed to plant a dual patriotism in the minds of the children by asking them to repeat together a profession of their love both for their country and for the Queen of the country from which their ancestors had come; in the Catholic schools the day began with a recitation of the Hail Mary. In the national schools the classroom walls were decorated with likenesses of Queen Victoria and of civil and military heroes of English history; in the Catholic schools classroom walls were decorated with prints of the Sacred Heart of Jesus, the Virgin and the Pope. Yet they had much in common. Both school systems enforced a strict segregation of the sexes; both urged their pupils to mortify the flesh; both taught a morality pleasing to the ears of the men who held the purse strings in the colonial parliaments.

By contrast the aim of the councils, headmasters, housemasters and teachers of the independent schools such as Sydney Grammar and the King's School in New South Wales, Melbourne Grammar, Geelong Grammar and Scotch College in Victoria, Launceston Grammar and Hutchins School in Tasmania, St Peter's and Prince Alfred Colleges in South Australia, and Guildford Grammar in Western Australia was to fashion the sons of the well-to-do into Christian gentlemen and leaders of society.

The independent schools for girls were about to be awakened from the slumbers into which they had fallen as academies where gentlewomen's daughters were prepared to take their place in their walk of life. In February 1875 at the ceremony to mark the opening of 'The Ladies' College in connection with the Presbyterian Church of Victoria' the headmaster C. H. Pearson reminded his audience that the industrial revolution and radical ideas about equality were altering the conception of the role of women in society. They were no longer to be thought of solely as helpmeets to men, as persons under a divine command to obey husbands or to act as wives and mothers and as hirelings whose labour was exploited to the greater glory of men. Women must be educated to play a new and as yet undefined role in a future he could not describe. He could only sense its turbulence and excitement.

Charles Henry Pearson, who had been educated at Rugby School at a time when the Arnold vision had not yet grown dim or become formalized, and at King's College, London, was one of those clergymen's sons who tried the faith of the Enlightenment as a compensation for the loss of faith in the life of the world to come. In 1875 he began to teach, together with Andrew Harper and four women teachers. Sixty girls were enrolled in the first term, 120 in the second term and 165 by the end of the third term. They included a Miss Deakin whose brother Alfred was at Melbourne Grammar hearing from Dr Bromby bewildering intimations of a great tempest of doubt in the years to come. They also included Nellie Armstrong, a Lilydale gentleman's daughter, in whom the gods had planted both the gift of song and the madness of art.

In the classrooms, the playing fields, and the hall where they stood in prayer, these girls were called on to pick their way as best they could between the claims of Christ and the claims of Apollo. For there too the Judaeo-Christian view of the world was on a collision course with the Greek. During those times set apart for religious instruction they were told of their duty to renounce the pomps and vanities of this wicked world and all the sinful lusts of the flesh. To their bewilderment classes in divinity were often followed by a lecture from Professor Pearson in which the cultivation of the beauty of the body was held up as an ideal which, if pursued with that moderation and harmony counselled by the Greeks, would teach them to know ecstasy.

Pearson had his own great dilemma. He who on his own confession was a believer in social democracy was the headmaster of a school that drew its pupils and finances from the people in society who were the strongest defenders of the privileges he professed to abhor. He was a hireling of men whose values he despised; he was supping at tables groaning with luxuries purchased with what to him was sometimes ill-gotten wealth. In 1875, his first year at 'The Ladies' College', he published a series of articles on the land question in Victoria. In December 1876 he advocated publicly a progressive land tax to burst open the large estates in Victoria, it being unjust and undemocratic, he believed, for a few landowners to have a monopoly. The following year he joined a branch of the National Reform League and on 19 February 1877 he spoke from the same platform as Graham Berry at the Princess Theatre. This time the conservatives took action. Alarmed by the fall in numbers at the school, for such schools have the same interest in numbers as the parsons in the collection plate, and adjust their behaviour accordingly, the Reverend George Tait asked him to resign. Pearson complied. Within a year he sailed with Graham Berry, who was travelling to London to seek increased powers for his government—two liberals with the mistaken idea that the mother country would perform what they lacked the nerve to do for themselves. Soon after his return he accepted an offer to become the first professor of history at the new University of Adelaide, outwardly a victim of the bourgeois philistines of Melbourne but inwardly a man plagued by doubt about everything.

By then the canker of doubt was converting happy believers in the kingdom of heaven into disquieted members of the kingdom of nothingness. In 1871 the publication of *The Descent of Man* by Charles Darwin dealt the greatest blow to human pride since 1517 when Copernicus had shown that the sun, not the earth, was the centre of the solar system. 'Is there no one', asked Henrik Ibsen, 'no one in all the universe? No one in the Abyss—no one in Heaven?'. As Matthew Arnold put it in 'Dover Beach', all that men could hear of the 'Sea of Faith' was 'Its melancholy, long, withdrawing roar'.

The parsons and the priests responded to the rise of secular humanism with exuberant professions of their attachment to the old religion. The parsons took their stand on the Bible. 'I cannot for a moment entertain the idea of Science contradicting the Bible', the Anglican bishop Charles Perry told a huge audience at the Princess Theatre in 1869. He was just as sure, he told them, of the life, death and resurrection of his Lord and Saviour Jesus Christ as he was of the facts of geology. No one was going to convince him that 'all this beautiful and well-ordered universe was a "chance hit"'. For him the account of creation in the works of Lyell and Darwin was absurd. The Reverend George Mackie told his congregation in 1869 that he utterly rejected the proposition that man could trace his paternity back to the chimpanzee and the orang-outang. God, not a monkey, was the father of the first man. Animals and savages could not create a civilization.

Some within the churches, however, were deeply troubled. One of the anxious souls was John Edward Bromby, a doctor of divinity and headmaster of Melbourne Church of England Grammar School, an institution for all who professed and called themselves Christians. He was one of those men who had believed in his youth that religion and education helped to make the crooked straight. But ever since his undergraduate days at St John's College, Cambridge, God had presented him with nothing but riddles, and the agnostics with puzzles to which he knew he must find an answer if he was to retain any of the faith he had learned at his mother's knee. There had been those worrying words by Lyell in his work on geology in 1833; there had been German biblical criticism, which was up for discussion in England in the 1840s; there had been those challenging words by David Friedrich Strauss in his *Life of Jesus*, translated into English by George Eliot in 1846; there were those bothering questions put by Alfred Tennyson in the poem 'In Memoriam' in 1850; there was that beautiful prose poem by Ernest Renan on the life of Jesus, so full of love for man, so certain Christ was not the son of God; and there were those arguments by John Stuart Mill which portrayed Almighty God as an odious, caddish and loathsome bully. By 1869 he had developed the stoop of a man who seemed to be carrying some invisible burden around the world. He had developed the personal habits of the eccentric. He dug with a wild fury in his garden, as though he were searching for something with his spade. He muttered much to himself. When his family deciphered what was disturbing him, they found he was asking himself those questions most intellectuals were asking: whether God existed, who Christ was, what He said, and what the life of man in an age of unbelief was.

By the late 1860s he was ready to make his own contribution to the conversation of mankind and took the great risk of showing his view to the mockers of Melbourne. First he shocked the men in high places in the church by telling them he was in favour of higher education for women. Bishop Perry professed to be flabbergasted. Once again the lord bishop reminded his erring brother in Christ of the biblical authority for the proposition that men were different from women. Dr Bromby agreed that there were differences; even the eye of frail man was capable of seeing that. But he did not see why the bishop should advance these differences as a bar to the higher education of women. For his part he declared that it was the mark of a barbarian to maltreat women or place them in a position of permanent inferiority. All previous civilizations, such as the Hebrews and Britons, had a partnership between the sexes.

By then he knew that there were two questions to which he must give a public answer. First, was the account of creation in Genesis substantially correct? Second, what became of the great majority of souls when they died? To the first he replied in his lecture on prehistoric man on 9 August 1869 that after examining all the evidence he did not believe science had undermined the basics of religion. He could see no reason, he said, to doubt that the earliest created human beings sprang from a single pair. For him the account in the Bible was 'replete with religious truth'; it was not intended to be treated with 'prostration of mind amounting almost to superstition'. 'Let us bear in mind', he added, 'that the letter killeth, but the spirit it is which giveth life'. As for that other question of what became of the great majority of souls when they died, he believed Christians should be able to show that Jehovah was 'not an unrighteous and merciless despot'. He knew men had been greatly shocked by the Christian teaching that multitudes of souls went down the proud road to perdition, while very few entered in at that narrow gate which led unto life. He agreed that if such souls were to be tortured, as the church used and still seemed to teach, to all eternity, because they were not sufficiently gifted to be good Christians here, or because they had never heard the word of salvation, that would certainly be good ground for 'impugning the righteousness of God'.

The orthodox howled for his blood as a heretic, wanting at the very least to burn his words and shut him up, because in their civilized age it was no longer possible to burn his body. The clergy raised such a storm of protest that Dr Bromby said to a friend, 'If I had accidentally kicked over Aesop's proverbial hive of bees I could not have been in a less enviable predicament . . . '. Those for whom the prospect of annihilation and silence was unbearable noted that there was little for their comfort in the words of John Edward Bromby.

Charles Strong, the brilliant graduate of Glasgow University and minister of Scots Church in Melbourne since 1875, also wanted to strip away from Christian teaching any evidence that might sustain the charge that God's world entailed an infinitude of suffering and punishment for the immense mass of mankind. In the second half of 1880 he published an article in the *Victorian Review* on the doctrine of the Atonement, in which he argued that the Christian God was a God of love, not a bloodthirsty monster who exulted and gloated at human beings essaying tasks for which He Himself had pitifully equipped them. The pharisees and the letter-of-the law men in his church wanted to have him tried for heresy.

In 1883 Strong joined a society formed in Melbourne to agitate for the opening of the public library and the museum on a Sunday. Again other ministers accused him of opposing doctrines which he had sworn before God to assert, maintain and defend. Quite undaunted by all this sound and fury, Strong invited George Higinbotham to lecture in Scots Church on 1 August 1883 on 'Science and Religion', knowing that Higinbotham would present that milk-and-water God which was anathema to his opponents in the presbytery. Again his opponents gave notice of their intention to charge Strong with promulgating and publishing heretical and unsound doctrine. Having received assurance of support from those who regretted these outbursts by the philistines, Strong resigned, and looked for a church as a place of worship for all those who wanted Christ and not Frankenstein as their God. As he explained in one of his sermons, he was preaching not that cruel law of Moses, but the word of Christ.

The question was, what was man to put between himself and death, what was man to substitute for God and the life of the world to come? The poets were just as distinguished by variety and babble as the priests and parsons and the lay sermonizers and moralizers. Ada Cambridge, a vicar's wife, kept telling herself that there must be someone, somewhere who cared for what happened to mankind:

> And is the great cause lost beyond recall?
> Have all the hopes of ages come to naught?
> Is Life no more with noble meaning fraught?
> Is Life but Death, and Love its funeral pall?
> Maybe. And still on bended knees I fall,
> Filled with a faith no preacher ever taught.
> O God—*my* God, by no false prophet wrought,
> I believe still, in despite of it all!

Henry Kendall, driven to seek oblivion in alcohol because of colonial indifference to things of the spirit and colonial worship of the golden calf, felt that the spirit of place in Australia clashed with the dark, savage, elemental moral code preached by the men in black. Kendall was born on 18 April 1839 at Ulladulla in New South Wales, and after a varied life, including some years at sea on a whaling vessel, he essayed that Sisyphean task of earning his daily bread by literary labour in Australia; he faced for love's sake alone 'the life austere that waits upon the man of letters here'. After years of poorly rewarded labour, he came to the savage conclusion that Australia belonged to the 'clowns, liars and charlatans'. Behind the vast Australian gloom, behind that spiritual silence which had unnerved Harpur, he detected in nature in Australia the 'grounds for a finer hope' and 'the blind horizon for a larger faith'. He became aware of a benevolent God in the bush of Australia.

Adam Lindsay Gordon toyed with the idea of elevating the bushman's creed to the role of the bible for humanity in Australia. Gordon was one of those exiles from the mother country whose poetry was in part a melancholy elegy about the ache in his own heart and in part a threnody for the death of God. After a wild youth in England he was exiled by his parents for an offence he had probably not committed. His loves were idyllic in their chastity. He had loved a man, Charley Walker. He had loved a woman, Jane Bridges, with such purity that he could not bring himself to declare his love for her until it was too late. He sought relief in a wild life, which always led to agonies of remorse, self-lacerations, and vows of future continence which he could not possibly observe.

He arrived in South Australia in 1853 at the age of 20 and proved himself to be, in his own words, 'as game as a pebble', a man who could tame wild horses and confront danger with a courage that surrounded him with a hero's halo even in his lifetime. He had a great desire for things spiritual which was always coming into collision with descents into hell and wild debauches with drink and women. In October 1862, he married a woman beneath his class from the Caledonian Hotel, Margaret Park. She admired him as a horse-rider, but had no interest in Gordon's other quest to find someone who would tell him what it was all about, no interest in his struggle to reconcile the agnosticism of the head with the religious aspirations of the heart.

He put into verse the bushman's belief in boldness, courage, resource, and accepting all the ills that flesh is heir to without whining and without reaching for a crutch. In his poem 'Gone', which was published in 1867, Robert O'Hara Burke was a man who went 'to his doom with as bold a heart/As that dead man gone where we all must go'. Burke was a man who had 'fallen . . . stout and steady of soul'. Yet even Burke had not been able to escape annihilation or miss the void. What pained Gordon again in the bushman's creed was the thought that 'the bravest and fairest are earthworms'.

In 'Ye Wearie Wayfarer', he put forward the bushman's code as a guide for life:

> Question not, but live and labour
> Till yon goal be won,
> Helping every feeble neighbour,
> Seeking help from none;
> Life is mainly froth and bubble,
> Two things stand like stone:
> KINDNESS in another's trouble,
> COURAGE in your own.
>
> Courage, comrades, this is certain,
> All is for the best—
> There are lights behind the curtain—
> Gentles let us rest.
> As the smoke-rack veers to seaward
> From 'the ancient clay',
> With its moral drifting leeward,
> Ends the wanderer's lay.

He tried friendship with John Riddoch, the squire of Yallum Park. During his brief moments on that grand estate he was happy for a while. He wrote 'The Sick Stock Rider',which ended with a hope for something he believed ought to be true but never could be true now that man had entered into the kingdom of nothingness:

> Let me slumber in the hollow where the wattle blossoms wave,
> With never stone or rail to fence my bed;
> Should the sturdy station children pull the bush flowers on my grave,
> I may chance to hear them romping overhead.

By then the failure of his horse-training schemes at Ballarat, damage to the skull in falls from more reckless rides on horses, estrangement from his wife, and frequent attempts to achieve oblivion by drinking brandy had further soured him against life. After the death of his daughter Annie on 14 April 1868 his soul was seized with a dark melancholy from which he never recovered. He began to walk firmly towards the dark tower. On 23 June 1870, the day *Bush Ballads and Galloping Rhymes* was published in Melbourne, he had drinks with Henry Kendall, followed by more with yet another unhappy citizen in the kingdom of nothingness, Marcus Clarke, after which he made his way back to his home in Brighton, defeated, lonely, and puzzled that he, the day-dreamer, the man who had known ecstasy and madness, now yearned only for 'the long sleep'. At dawn the following morning he shot himself at Brighton Beach within sound of that sea which had once held out the promise of renewal and resurrection but now only murmured the vast indifference of nature in Australia to all man's strivings and sufferings.

Marcus Clarke had been putting the same questions to himself ever since his days at Swinton near Glenorchy in 1865. That summer, with the temperature standing at 110° in the shade, no rain for four months, and many squatters ruined, he found there was nothing left to do but drink Bass *ad libitum*, smoke *ad nauseam*, curse the climate, and join in those boring, never-ending conversations about 'Sheep, Sheep, Sheep, Plain, Plain, Plain, Sun, Sun, Sun, and Bush, Bush, Bush'. He pined for an English spring, felt cast out 'like a leper in the wilderness'. He believed himself banished from all society, from music, literature, and from all that makes life endurable.

In June of 1866 he moved to Ledcourt (a corruption of the Aboriginal word for a spear point), a sheep station at the very foot of the Grampians, a place of surpassing loveliness. There, with that curious feeling that overwhelms a man on the frontiers of civilization in Australia, he was aware of the magnificent country by which he was surrounded, but aware too that all beyond was a howling wilderness, which was elemental, savage and disturbing. The spirit of the place left him with a wild desire to spring up and shout, or run, or do something wild and extravagant. Sometimes when moonlight lit up the bush, a sudden exhilaration seized him; he felt very tender with man and beast and wanted to sing some hymn of praise to life.

But Clarke had begun to search for something to fill the space occupied by the Christian god. From the time of his return to Melbourne early in 1867 he determined to practise that one talent with which he was so handsomely endowed, the use of words to describe all the uproar in his heart, and the disquiet in his soul, in articles written for Melbourne newspapers and reviews. In March 1870 Clarke began to publish as a serial the novel which was to become known as *For the Term of His Natural Life*. In it he made a sustained contribution to the conversation of mankind on such universal human questions as the effect of a harsh environment on human behaviour, why there were men with hard hearts in the world, and men like the Reverend Mr North who lost their innocence and self-respect. Clarke had seen all the evil done in the world and had come to the same conclusion as Newman in *The Idea of a*

University: men might as well quarry the granite rock with razors, or moor a vessel with a thread of silk as employ 'such keen and delicate instruments as human knowledge and human reason to contend against those giants, the passion and the pride of man'.

When he wrote *His Natural Life* Clarke was like all those authors of stature who were aware of a problem to which they did not know the answer. What he did know by then was that religion could no longer be used to work the great marvel of taming the wild beast in a man. Men were already fast abandoning religious belief as a delusion. He put this explicitly in his last contribution to the great debate of his day, *Civilization without Delusion*. In this work he told his readers that the religion of the old time was insufficient for modern needs; that there had been an 'abandonment of belief in the Miraculous'. Science had succeeded in making mankind understand that the operations of nature were conducted upon certain first principles. The comforting but delusive theory that God interfered to aid those who venerated him, and punished those who venerated him not, had to be abandoned. Henceforth men must understand that no good deeds could avert misfortune, and no sins could call down the vengeance of heaven. There was no absolute certainty of any other life but this.

Clarke gave the same answer as Kirilov in Dostoevsky's *The Devils*, which was published in St Petersburg one year before Clarke addressed himself to the question of the life of man without God. Men, he argued, now had the chance to become as gods. 'Mankind', he wrote, 'freed from the terrors of future torments, and comprehending that by no amount of prayers can they secure eternal happiness for their souls, will bestow upon humanity the fervour which they have hitherto wasted in sighs and hymns'. The creed which teaches that the intellect should be distrusted would fade away. The interest now shown in churchmen's disputations would be transferred to discoveries of science. The progress of the world would be the sole care of its inhabitants, and the elevation of the race the only religion of mankind. It would be, he wrote (quoting a writer in the *North American Review*), 'a civilization without an active and general delusion'.

The history of European civilization in Australia had threatened to disqualify its inhabitants from becoming pioneers in the building of any brave new world for humanity. What had happened in the country since the invasion by the white man had made men not so much cynics as sceptics of the fruits of human endeavour. The experience of planting a civilization in an uncouth, barbaric land with only the labour of their hands, and all their subsequent history, had disposed them to be sympathetic with failure rather than to trust any promise of better things for mankind. As sections of humanity in other parts of the world prepared for the great leap forward the Australians remained the slaves of the spirit of the place and their own past. They were held back by their sardonic view of the world, by the absence of a large propertyless working class, and by the petty-bourgeois, private property-owning delusions of their workers. Clarke's own dissolution foreshadowed the shape of things to come, the power of the conservative, petty-bourgeois view of the world to render impotent all those who, like Clarke, dreamed a great dream, only to see it fade away before the stern facts of Australia's past.

Spurred on by the attempts to convey the spirit of the place in the works of Harpur, Kendall, Gordon and Clarke, a new school of landscape painters in the 1860s and 1870s began to see the country and its mantle no longer through the eyes of men for whom the oak, the elm, the poplar and the birch were the ideal of a tree, but through eyes which sensed a harmony between those 'weird scribblings of nature', the gum trees, and their setting. All previous landscape painters had done their wrist work with the images of European scenery still coming between them and the local scene. Johann Joseph Eugen von Guerard, who had arrived in Victoria at the end of 1852, superimposed the grandeur and darkness of the European Alps on to the rugged splendours of mountain scenery in New South Wales and Victoria. But the time was at hand for artists and writers to turn their attention to the appearance and behaviour of the 'ever restless European' in a new land. The time was at hand for the portrait of an Australian.

12

Uproar in the Bush

Ned Kelly was a wild ass of a man, snarling, roaring and frothing like a ferocious beast when the tamer entered the cage. Mad Ireland had fashioned a man who consumed his vast gifts in an insensate war on property and on all the props of bourgeois civilization—the police, the bankers, the squatters, the teachers, the preachers, the railway and the electric telegraph. His father, 'Red' Kelly, was a wild Tipperary man, sentenced to transportation to Van Diemen's Land in 1843 for stealing two pigs. The mother, Ellen Quinn, was an immigrant girl from Portadown. Edward Kelly was born at Beveridge in June 1855, at the foot of Pretty Sally on that plain bordered to the south by the Protestant-dominated, British philistine society of Melbourne, and to the north by the untamed country. Both parents taught their children that no Irishman could expect justice in an English lawcourt; both taught their children that the police were the paid hirelings of English landlords who had robbed Irishmen of their rightful inheritance on the land.

After the death of 'Red' Kelly at Avenel in 1866, the mother took her family of five daughters and three sons to settle on a small selection at Eleven Mile Creek between Greta and Glenrowan. She and her children took up land in one of those remote, inaccessible districts where the lack of religious and educational influences had produced a race of godless, lawless men and women—half bandits, half cattle stealers—who in the eyes of the defenders of property, law and order were wholly vicious. Ned grew to man's estate in a forcing house for crime. He lived in one of those tracts of country where the bonds of civilization had been so loosened that men threatened to become as savage as the region.

The Kellys became such notorious cattle and horse thieves that drovers were accustomed to go miles out of their way to avoid the Kelly farm at Greta, for fear of their stock being stolen. Policemen sent to inquire about the whereabouts of missing beasts were subjected to all sorts of indignities. Ned's favourite move with a policeman was to trip him and let him take a mouthful of dust, until the policeman, in Ned's words, was 'as helpless as a big guano after leaving a dead bullock or horse'. In 1870 when Constable Thomas Lonigan arrested Ned for receiving a mare knowing it to be stolen, Lonigan dragged Ned across the main street of Benalla by the private parts. From that time Ned vowed that one day he would give those police bastards 'something to talk about'.

On 15 April 1878 Constable Fitzpatrick arrived at the Kelly hut at Greta with a warrant to arrest Ned's younger brother for horse-stealing. Ellen Kelly rushed at him with a shovel. A shot was fired, the bullet lodging in Fitzpatrick's wrist. Ned was said to menace Fitzpatrick: 'Tell him', he said, 'if he ever does mention it, his life will be no good to him'. But Fitzpatrick, when he got back to civilization, did blab. A warrant was issued for the arrest of Ellen Kelly, and she was sentenced to three years in gaol by Sir Redmond Barry, who, with that rancour of the Irish Protestant towards the 'low Irish mob', lectured her on the duty of men to protect civiliza-tion against 'lawless persons'. Ned began to talk of himself, his family, and the Irish poor men in the district as a people who had been so wronged and persecuted that they could not be blamed for their violent feelings against the police and all agents of law and order. Driven to desperation, Ned and his younger brother Dan took to the Warby Ranges where they were joined by Joe Byrne and a bully named Steve Hart, a man with the dingo eyes of the bush barbarians. Together they searched for a life where a man could roam the bush as free as an eagle in the sky.

In October 1878 three Irishmen, Sergeant Michael Kennedy, Constables Thomas Lonigan and Michael Scanlon, and Constable McIntyre from Scotland set out from Mansfield to capture the gang. They camped at Stringybark Creek in one of those places of quiet majesty in the Australian forest. There on 26 October Ned shot Lonigan, Scanlon and Kennedy dead. McIntyre, after spending the night in a wombat's hole, galloped into Mansfield to raise the alarm.

The response of the public was just as mixed as the response to the outrages by other bushrangers. The *Argus*, speaking for bourgeois society, wrote about a gang of unscrupulous desperadoes who had insulted 'the majesty of the law' by murdering three constables in cold blood. The press in both Melbourne and the provinces published a story of how Ned, ignoring Sergeant Kennedy's pleas for mercy, had robbed him of his watch, and shot him a second time, the bullet entering that part of the anatomy calculated to humilate Kennedy in the most abominable manner. The government of Victoria declared the Kelly gang to be outlaws and offered a reward of £500 on the apprehension alive or dead of any one of them. By contrast, the songs of the bush portrayed Ned Kelly as a people's hero, a brave man, a daring horseman, a champion rifle shot, and a friend of the poor. 'He's as game as Ned Kelly' began to be the acme of praise in the Australian bush.

Success fed both the vices and the virtues of Ned Kelly. The delusions of grandeur and the pathological hatred of police, telegraph and railways grew to monstrous proportions: the deeds of kindness, the charisma with the bush people, the image of Ned as a latter-day Robin Hood also grew apace. Ned boasted of grandiose schemes of revenge against the police. Fitzpatrick would be the 'cause of as great slaughter to the rising generation as St Patrick was to the snakes and frogs in Ireland'. His conscience, he said, was 'as clear as the snow in Peru'.

On 8 February 1879 the four members of the gang rode into Jerilderie, a small country town 30 miles on the New South Wales side of the Murray River, captured the Post and Telegraph Office, cut the wires connecting the town with the outside world, captured three local police, rounded up the men of the town, and held them all in the parlour of the Royal Mail Hotel, which was also the office of the local branch of the Bank of New South Wales. There Ned indulged wantonly in the great passions of his life. He threatened to blow out the brains of a local squatter; he threatened to burn all the bank documents, all that evidence that men were slaving in the country to provide luxuries for bloated capitalists in the cities; he gave free drinks to all his captives in the parlour, treating everyone civilly. He dictated a letter of 7000 words to Living, the bank clerk, and ordered him to hand it over to people of influence in Melbourne. It was an apologia for all he had ever done, ending with a profession of a love for life that was to establish him as one of the few folk heroes of Australia. With one breath he talked of forcing the rich to give money to the 'widows and orphans and poor', so that he and they, liberated from their gaolers, might be free to live. With another breath he was weaving mad schemes for revenge against the police, threatening them that unless they obeyed him the consequences for them would be 'worse than the rust in the wheat in Victoria or the druth of a dry season to the grasshoppers in New South Wales'. He was a man with a grievance: 'I am', he said, 'a widow's son outlawed'. He was also by then a man suffering from a terrible delusion: 'My orders', he declared, 'must be obeyed'. Ned was beginning to walk into the night.

Before the gang's departure the local Methodist minister, the Reverend Mr Gribble, had the courage, possibly even the foolhardiness to request Ned to direct Steve Hart to hand back the watch he had stolen from him. Gribble was a man much troubled by the brutality meted out to the Aborigines by white landholders, a man who was soon to endure the wrath of his parishioners and his bishop for speaking the truth. Ned Kelly had no knowledge of Gribble at all, no idea that the man standing in front of him was moved by sympathy for those Aboriginal people whom Kelly despised. For a brief moment two brave men—two men at odds with authority—confronted each other in a dustbowl town on the Riverina before they went on their separate paths to the great ordeal of their lives. Ned ordered Steve to give the watch back. The Reverend Mr Gribble bowed to the bushranger and said, 'Good-bye to you, Ned Kelly'. To the accompaniment of cheers and hurrahs 'for the good old times of Morgan and Ben Hall', Ned and his gang rode off to their hiding place in the Warby Ranges. Gribble returned to his mission station at nearby Warangesda. From that day until he died he spoke with a slight stutter.

With the passage of time Ned the wit and Ned the wag gradually changed into Ned the murderer. In the winter of 1879 severe hardships in the ranges turned his mind to savagery as one possible relief for all his suffering. With their money gone, the friends and sympathizers began to fall off. The police, by then not short of a bob with which to buy informers, had infested the bush with spies and traitors. Rumours also reached the Kelly camp that the police were using black men as trackers. Dark thoughts again began to bubble in Ned's head. He began to entertain the idea of a raid in which 'traps' and black 'bastards' would be blown to smithereens and all traitors among the bush people shot, leaving him and his sympathizers to lead their lives free from police, railways, telegraphs and all those people who had told him what to do. By then he was boasting to his friends that the day was not far off when he would astonish not just the Australian colonies but the whole world. But until the beginning of June 1880 the details of such a plan of revenge and violent retribution had eluded him.

Sometime in the autumn of 1880 Joe Byrne learnt that the man he had loved in his boyhood, when the two had fished for yabbies in the local waterholes—one Aaron Sherritt—had been receiving his thirty pieces of silver for information on the whereabouts of the Kelly gang. Ned concocted a plan in which the death of Sherritt as the Judas of the Australian bush people would lure hundreds of police into the district in search of Ned, a search that Ned would turn into a bloody massacre. The police would arrive by train; the gang would tear up the rails at a place where the carriages would be certain to roll down the hillside. While the police were dying in hundreds, he and his merry men would join their supporters in a carousal in the hotel of Annie Jones at Glenrowan in the heart of Kelly country. The plan had everything: death to traitors, a massacre of traps and a drunken spree for Ned's friends among the bush people.

On the night of 27 June 1880 Joe Byrne shot Aaron Sherritt dead at the door of his hut at the woolshed on Reid Creek. He then called on the police inside to 'come out you buggers, and surrender'. When they did not stir, he threatened to set the hut alight and 'burn the buggers alive'. But time pressed and he and his mate galloped off to join the other members of the gang, who had in the meantime pulled up the rails in the cutting at Glenrowan. For a few hours on that frosty night there was wild revelry in the Glenrowan hotel. At its height Thomas Curnow, the local schoolteacher, asked permission to take his sick wife home, assuring Ned that he had no cause to fear him. 'I know it', Ned said, 'and I can see it . . . go quietly to bed and don't dream too loud'.

Between three and four o'clock in the morning excitement again swept the participants in the drunken spree at Glenrowan. The whistle of the train was heard. That 'sweet' moment of revenge was at hand. Suddenly the shouting and the singing stopped. The train had halted; something had gone wrong. A sound of rifle fire broke the silence of the night. Superintendent Hare, a gentleman on the field of battle, called out, 'Come on then boys'. Ned was heard to shout in the language of the bush, 'Fire away you bloody dogs'. Those police whom Ned had condemned to a horrible death, over whose mangled bodies he had been mentally gloating all through the night, were calling on him to surrender. Curnow the schoolteacher, one of those men who stood for civilization and order, had stopped the train and alerted Superintendent Hare to what was going on inside the hotel at Glenrowan.

All through the early hours of the morning indiscriminate firing continued. The blacks were particularly industrious in potting away at the premises. Joe Byrne was shot dead. Ned refused to raise the white flag. Sadleir, the officer in charge of the police (Hare by then being in a casualty room in Glenrowan Station with a bullet in the wrist), telegraphed for a big gun with which to blow up the hotel. Both sides were giving way to the bizarre and the extravagant.

As the first light of day uncovered the outlines of trees in the bush surrounding the hotel, Ned Kelly, his face and body covered with the armour hammered into shape for him by a bush sympathizer, walked out of the hotel and into the bush. His friends said later he was bravely trying to keep a rendezvous with his supporters, there being a prearranged plan for the discharge of a gun to herald the beginning of that new life for the 'fearless, the free and the bold'. Like so much else on that night, that too had gone wrong. His enemies said that Ned was making a desperate attempt to save his own skin, but was forced to seek again the shelter of the hotel from loss of blood. Whatever the cause, in the half light before that red disc appeared again on the eastern horizon as a sign of another cold frosty day, a tall figure, encased in armour, came out of the mists and wisps of frosty air whirling round the tree-trunks and made for the hotel. After the ordeal of the night, some thought it was a madman or a ghost; some thought it was the Devil, the whole atmosphere having stimulated in friend and foe alike a 'superstitious awe'. A savage exchange of shots occurred. The figure in the armour fell. The police surrounded him. Constable John Kelly pulled off the helmet, and said, 'By God, it is Ned'. Those who had some sympathy with Ned and his cause liked to believe that, in the hour of defeat, he found the words appropriate for the occasion: 'It's gone wrong', they say he said, 'it's all gone wrong'. Police sergeant Steele claimed Ned said, 'That is enough; I am done'. In the eyes of the police, Ned, despite all his talk about 'pluck and bounce', showed the white feather.

The police, some of them the intended victims of his murderous mind, carried Ned to the Glenrowan station. Sadleir gave orders for the hotel to be burnt to the ground, the proceedings of the police on that day being characterized by a hysteria similar to that which had swept through Ned during the days of suffering and hardships in the Warby Ranges. A Catholic priest had the courage to enter the burning building, hoping to succour the dying bushrangers with the comforts of their religion. He found the charred remains of Joe Byrne, Steve Hart and Dan Kelly. In the meantime Mrs Skillion, Ned's sister, kept up a never-ending dirge-like crying, the other relatives of the dead also weeping for those whom they had loved but now would see no more. As darkness came down over the bush another dirge was raised in Beechworth Gaol when Ellen Kelly, still locked up for her part in the Fitzpatrick episode, heard the police had roasted her son Dan alive and had Ned under lock and key in the same gaol.

In the central criminal court in Melbourne on 28 October 1880 the trial of Edward Kelly for the murder of Constable Thomas Lonigan began before His Honour Mr Justice Barry. Ned Kelly, the child of the Australian bush, the wild beast, was up for judgement by a pillar of the Protestant ascendancy. When the jury brought down a verdict of guilty, the judge asked the prisoner if he had anything to say. Ned said simply, 'I do not blame anybody'. His Honour accused him of the blasphemy of claiming God would not judge harshly a man who appeared to revel in having put men to death.

Ned replied that a day would come at a bigger court than this when they would see which was right and which was wrong. His Honour knew his duty. If civilization was to survive in the colonies, sympathizers must be shown that felons were as degraded as the wild beasts of the field. Ned Kelly must expiate his crimes: Ned Kelly must be hanged by the neck until he was dead. To which Ned replied, 'I will go a little further than that, and say I will see you there where I go'.

On the night of 5 November 4000 of Ned's sympathizers, together with the opponents of capital punishment and men of the under-world, packed into the Hippodrome, leaving an overflow of 2000 outside. They stamped their feet, whistled, and catcalled for Ned. Night after night Ned was glorified as a people's hero or treated as a victim of the hard-hearted Melbourne philistines. On the other side, the *Argus*, a mouthpiece for the forces of law, order, civilization and restraint, declared that those monster public meetings were attended by the dregs of the population, the criminal classes and the opponents of capital punishment who were combining to save the life of one of the greatest ruffians in the history of mankind.

Ned walked to his death in the Old Melbourne Gaol on the morning of 11 November 1880. His mother had urged him to die like a Kelly. Some said he looked frightened and morose and only managed to utter a lame 'Ah well, I suppose it has come to this'. Others said he summed it all up in that sardonic Australian remark 'Such is Life'. One young journalist, who watched the death throes, found to his consternation, gentle spirit that he was, that there was another person inside him who was a secret sharer of those gales of violence that had blown through Ned Kelly. His name was Alfred Deakin.

Ned lived on as a hero, as a man through whom Australians were helped to discover their national identity. He lived on as a man who had confronted the bourgeois calm-down with all the uproar of a magnificent Dionysian frenzy, a man who had taken down the mighty from their seat and driven the rich empty away. He lived on as a man who had savaged policemen in the old convict tradition, ranted against the blacks and denounced the brutal barbarism of those who clothed their sadism towards the common people in the panoply of the law. He lived on as a man who had been aware of the violence in the Australian tradition, a man who had sensed that the fist and the gun were the keys to power in a society that owed its very existence to an act of violence against the land and its original tenants. Ned had had 'gunfire in his eye'.

Ned Kelly was also like a man shouting into the wind. For the winds of a great change were blowing over all parts of the world dominated by European civilization. Wherever the railway went, some of what Australians understood by civilization was not slow to follow: hotels for refreshment, for lodging, for social intercourse; huge secular temples for human intercourse; fine general stores which stocked all articles required for life in the country; police stations, courthouses, lockups, metropolitan newspapers, and opportunities to purchase goods more quickly by mail orders to the capital cities.

The wheels of civilization ground very slowly. Neither the contribution made by the railway nor the effect of reforms of the land laws could banish overnight those pockets of white slavery in the Australian bush. To mitigate the financial difficulties of the selectors, especially their lack of capital, the colonial parliaments passed in the 1880s Closer Settlement Acts, in which the state advanced money loans on terms the settlers might be reasonably expected to meet, provided they were not visited by drought, or plagues of insects, or any of those other scourges which stood between a man and success on the land. Improvements in farming technique also held out a promise of relief from that cycle of birth, suffering and death. The stump-jump plough, the use of harvesting machines, the experiments in wheat-breeding by William Farrer at Lambrigg to produce strains of wheat that resisted rust and throve in dry areas, the refrigeration of meat for export to the United Kingdom, and the increase in overseas demand for foodstuffs due to rapid urbanization in North America and Europe all contributed to total prosperity.

In the decade from 1880 to 1890 the wheat fields flourished in the Wimmera, the Riverina, the Wellington Valley, the Clare and Naracoorte districts of South Australia. In the Grenfell district 'the wild unrest' and the 'barroom's noisy din' of the 'roaring days' of gold gave way in good seasons to the rustling of the wind in the green ears of wheat. Penola, where Adam Lindsay Gordon had been surrounded by a great sea of barbarism, was converted by drains taking the subterranean water away to the sea into a land of rich harvests of golden grain.

Tales of pockets of rural misery were still being told. Over at Gulgong Henry Lawson, who in the first fifteen years of his life had seen the last of the 'roaring days' on the western goldfields, spent some of his formative years tailing cows in that 'dreary old field' out Gulgong way. 'I grubbed, ring-barked, and ploughed', he recalled later,

in the scratchy sort of way common to many "native-born" selectors round there; helped fight pleuro and drought; and worked on

building contracts with "Dad", who was a carpenter. Saw selectors
slaving their lives away in dusty holes amongst the barren ridges;
saw one or two carried home, in the end, on a sheet of bark; the old
men worked till they died. Saw how the gaunt selectors' wives lived
and toiled. Saw elder sons stoop-shouldered old men at 30 . . . [and]
strong men who died like broken-down bullocks further out.

No wonder that by 1890 he sensed that 'There's trouble in the back
countree'.

Though there was no God in the outback, Lawson's bush people
still enacted the ritual of the faith of their fathers. In that country
which mocked all men's hopes, these men who never even seemed
to wonder whether there was any difference between the life of a
man and the life of a beast stood hushed and reverent while a priest
recited over a dead body those words about the resurrection of the
dead. Men passed round the hat to help not just those who were
temporarily down on their luck but to comfort and succour the
outcasts of society, the liars, the fornicators, the drunkards, the
prostitutes, the ones who knew they ought to stop but could not, all
those who, according to Saint Paul, would not enter the kingdom of
heaven. His bush people had kept alive the image of Christ in what
might otherwise have been a kingdom of nothingness, an emptiness
of mind appropriate for those plains of desolation west of the Great
Dividing Range.

Andrew Barton Paterson, who used the pen-name of 'The Banjo'
was a man who did not wear his heart on his sleeve. He was the
tough Australian, the one who believed a man should endure to the
end without wallowing in self-pity, without that sentimentality or
drunken debauchery which Rudd and Lawson placed between
themselves and death. What depressed Lawson, Paterson found
uplifting. Lawson had seen the plains of the western lands of
New South Wales very much as John Oxley, Thomas Mitchell and
Charles Sturt had seen them, namely as 'the plains of desolation'.
For him there was something off-putting, something repellent,
which made him recoil in fright and horror. In 'Clancy of the
Overflow', first published in the *Bulletin's* Christmas issue for 1889,
Paterson wrote with approval, indeed with enthusiasm, about the
life of man on those plains:

> And he sees the vision splendid of the sunlit plains extended,
> And at night the wondrous glory of the everlasting stars.

Paterson, who was born at Narrambla near Orange in New South
Wales on 17 February 1864 belonged by birth and temperament to
a very different section of humanity from Henry Lawson and Steele

Rudd. The education of Lawson and Rudd began and ended in the old bush school; Paterson's education was begun at Binalong, where he imbibed enough of the bush people's sympathy for the bushrangers to write for once with some enthusiasm for a folk hero who had gloried in barbarism and anarchy. His education was finished at Sydney Grammar School, where he imbibed those ideals of rank, of service and of heroism appropriate to those who were engaged in the task of subduing an ancient, uncouth continent, without the inhibitions of a fine conscience or the squeamishness of a man of Lawson's sensibilities. Lawson's eyes moistened at the sight of a giraffe of a man sending round the hat at Bourke on behalf of some Sydney tarts who were being drummed out of town by the Mother Grundys of the outback. Paterson's eyes noticed the strong men with approval, the men who performed heroic deeds, without sparing a thought for, possibly even feeling contempt for, those who were tortured by conscience.

Late in the summer of 1889-90 in that magical time of the year when the peaty soil 'up by Kosciusko side' was carpeted with alpine flowers, in one of those rare moments when a man can believe that a benevolent God created Australia, Paterson, having just turned 26, heard Jack Riley, a stockrider on a nearby cattle station, tell a yarn of a colt 'that had got away and been rounded up by a piece of fearless riding and superb horsemanship'. That gave him the raw material for 'The Man from Snowy River', a ballad which glorified the skill and courage of the Australian bushman. This was the Australian version of the horsemen on the walls of the Parthenon. The ballad ended with a celebration of Australia as a country with the 'torn and rugged battlements on high' where 'the rolling plains' were 'wide'. Paterson saw Australia as the appropriate setting for a race of heroes and of men who told tales of heroes like the Man from Snowy River:

> The Man from Snowy River is a household word to-day,
> And the stockmen tell the story of his ride.

The values of the God of battles became the values of the mature man. Unlike Lawson, Paterson was said to have a 'sort of cavalier swagger and swing and suggestion of the hard-riding hero who killed three horses under him and ate the third'. His was a view of the world and of human behaviour that would inspire Australians to find out the truth about life fighting for British causes far from home, just as the Man from Snowy River found the truth about life in a baptism of blood 'up by Kosciusko side'. The human family, like the animal world, was composed on the one hand of those who bore the 'badge of gameness' in their 'bright and fiery eye', those who faced danger and pain without flinching, and on the other of those who were 'curs'.

The 'curs' in the Australian bush were still the Chinese, but they were being joined by other 'coloureds' who threatened the popular dreams of prosperity in a white Australia. Between August 1869 and December 1870, 684 islanders or Kanakas were recruited for the sugar plantations of Queensland. The planters argued for coloured labour very much as the squatters had argued for convict labour in the period before the discovery of gold. They argued that Polynesian or some such description of cheap labour was essential to the successful working of sugar or other estates.

The bourgeoisie of Brisbane and Ipswich and the white workers argued very much as the anti-transportationists had argued, namely that coloured labour was slavery and that it would create a nation most thoroughly depraved in its vicious propensities. They argued that the idea of having servants over whom they had unlimited control—docile, industrious, cheerful—for wages so small that they were scarcely wages at all only served to gloss over the enormities of their recruitment, the desolation of homes, the ransacking and burning of villages to procure these men, and their being carried like cattle to the sugar ports of Queensland where they were sold like merchandise to the planters. Between 1868 and 1886 the bourgeois politicians in Brisbane, prodded by the working classes, passed a series of acts to regulate and control the introduction and treatment of Polynesian labourers. But still the supporters and opponents were not satisfied, the former arguing that the cultivation of sugar in the tropics was an unbearable occupation for white men, the pursuit of which would only reduce white workers to slavery. The abolitionists with equal vehemence and savagery warned white workers that those folks who had already made slaves of 'niggers' also wanted to 'make white slaves of you'. At the same time changes in the methods of sugar production, the introduction of machinery for clearing and ploughing the land, and for hoeing and transport of the crop, were gradually making it possible for the planters to use white labour, so rendering all the sound and fury of planter and moralizer as irrelevant as most arguments about what is good and fair and just.

At the same time nature was taking her own revenge against the white man for his crime of robbing and fleeing. The ancient, barbaric continent seemed to be drying up. Those engaged in agriculture and grazing reported in 1883 tales of distress. All over the country men held prayer meetings, at which they besought the Almighty to change the weather to meet their pressing necessities. But by then rational people had given up believing that the mysterious powers in charge of the universe either could or would suspend the laws of nature for the benefit of the graziers and farmers of Australia. The stations in the outback began to fall into the hands of the pastoral companies. Thomas Elder, co-partner with Barr Smith in Smith Elder and Co., took over stations on the Birdsville Track between Beltana and south-west Queensland. Goldsbrough-Mort took over stations in western Queensland and the Northern Territory. The one-time proud owners and lessees of thousands of square miles became managers on stations they had once at least nominally owned, or became hirelings for wages. A section of the old governing class was pressed down into the ranks of the working class. The attempt to put a class of smallholders between the large proprietors and the bush workers had largely failed. Henry Lawson wondered whether the coming clash between squatter and worker would develop into a revolution. But Australians as a people were too wedded to the petty-bourgeois ideal of the ownership of property to create the first Paris Commune in the New World.

13

The Earth Abideth For Ever

On Whit Sunday in June 1876 a congregation assembled in Scots Church, Melbourne, to render thanks to Almighty God for the great benefits they had received at His hands, and to ask for those things which were requisite and necessary as well for the body as for the soul. They were worshipping in a new building deemed to be worthy of a great city. The interior decoration was typical of their conception of the relation between man and his Creator. There was no 'dim religious light', no painted window, there were no statues of saints of doubtful virtue or doubtful authenticity to come between the worshipper and God. Everything was cold, severe and chaste, there being no embellishments to act as intermediaries or accessories to the exercise of human reason. The women, believing gorgeous display to be pleasing in the eyes of their God or, if not to Him, certainly in the eyes of their neighbours, attired themselves in costly dresses and wore a fortune in golden ornaments and precious stones. The men were clothed in that black serge which was the reigning symbol of virtue and respectability. They had incomes, it was said, which were reckoned by the thousands. There were squatters whose flocks and herds were greater than those of Abraham; there were merchants, bankers and lawyers. With one voice they sang hymns of praise to their God who had given them all such wondrous things. The Reverend Charles Strong comforted and reassured them that in a future heaven the poor, too, would receive their reward.

By the beginning of the 1880s alarming reports began to appear in the press of the capital cities. In Europe and North America, it was said, the very existence of civilization was threatened. London, Paris, New York and Boston might at any time be overwhelmed by an eruption of barbarians whom those cities had allowed to grow up in their midst. Millions of people were growing up in such cities prevented by their poverty from ever participating in the banquet of life. They were pushing and crushing each other in subterranean darkness, groping for a door at which to knock and seek for a way into the light of life, fearful that they might be smothered to death underground.

In the Australian cities there were already ominous signs. In January 1883 the Reverend S. Chapman of the Baptist Church in Collins Street, Melbourne, warned his congregation that within a stone's throw there were neighbourhoods whose dwellings would be a disgrace to the Ashantis and whose morals approximated to those of Sodom and Gomorrah. Those who 'cared' were visited by nightmares about a coming explosion in which everything would be brought to ruin, while the oppressors and exploiters prostrated themselves before the golden calf, shaking with terror as they waited for the barbarians.

Industrial civilization had already attracted huge numbers into the cities. The population of Sydney increased from 137 586 in 1871 to 224 939 in 1881; in the same decade the population of Melbourne increased from 206 780 to 282 947. Between 1870 and 1890 there had been a substantial growth of manufacturing in both Melbourne and Sydney, the principal activity being in clothing, printing, iron foundries, carriage-building, furniture manufacture, food-processing, brewing, tanning and leather-working. In both colonies approximately 10 per cent of the national output came from manufacturing.

The bourgeois press in Melbourne attributed this growth to the protection policies of successive Victorian governments, and thanked their God that they were so vastly superior to Sydney. The bourgeois press in Sydney attributed their astonishing growth to the free-trade policies of successive New South Wales governments, and thanked their God that they were so vastly superior to Melbourne. While the bourgeoisie in both cities were gloating over the causes of their superiority, the labouring men and women were being sweated in the factories, workshops and homes of both cities. To supplement the wages earned in the clothing factory, women were taking work home. This was reducing and degrading the comforts and conveniences of the domestic life of the working classes. Rumour had it that women were slaving for ninety hours a week to earn a mere pittance, often employing their daughters. In this way the tailoring business was staffed almost entirely by females who were paid less than men and were prepared to work fourteen to sixteen hours a day for a bare subsistence wage. In Carlton, Fitzroy, Collingwood and Richmond in Melbourne, and in Surry Hills, St Peters, and Redfern in Sydney women laboured in small, badly lit and ill-ventilated rooms, arguing that there was greater independence in the home, as well as freedom from the immoral conversation of the factory girls and, in the case of the Jewish tailoresses, immunity from being held up to ridicule and contempt as members of the Jewish race.

In neither Melbourne nor Sydney was there talk of some sub-terranean explosion, or of the human antheap in the working-class districts of the two cities erupting into violence or barbarizing the whole of society. Melbourne and Sydney had a social problem, but not a threat of proletarian revolution. While the metropolises of the Old World in Europe and the New World were besieged by terrorists, secret societies and revolutionaries who spoke of cleans-ing fires, uprooting, and baptisms in blood, the one bad festering sore in the social body of Melbourne and Sydney was the larrikin.

The one ambition of the Australian larrikin was to 'play buttress to a public house wall', and 'spit moral and material filth' at every respectable person who passed by him. Every Sunday morning in Sydney about a dozen hulking big fellows, devoid of coat or vest, in a half-intoxicated condition, leaned against the wall of a public house, smoking dirty black pipes, expectorating over the footpaths and insulting every respectable person who sought to walk in the public's pleasure-ground. No female could stroll in those gardens without 'encountering a volley of filthy invective and indecent observations'. No policeman could arrest a man in Sydney or Melbourne without running the risk of being set upon by a gang of larrikins. Larrikins went on board the late ferry boats in Sydney on Saturday and Sunday nights and molested the passengers. They burst open the doors of churches, smashed the windows, drank the communion wine and defaced all the sacred objects they could lay their hands on.

By the middle of the 1880s larrikins in both cities were wearing their own distinctive clothes. The men wore a soft felt hat dented in a way peculiar to their class and high-heeled shoes the toes of which were tapered to a sharp point. On the tips there were some-times affixed mirrors with which to observe those parts of women normally obscured by the full skirts of the day. Their coat was generally black, the shirt white, with a paper collar, and glass studs in front coloured to resemble rich rubies or precious diamonds. The female companions of the larrikins could be recognized by their draggle-feathered hats and their black eyes, often administered when the men were dancing on their prostrate bodies at the end of a wild fight. They were also recognized by their lairy walk, in which a wiggling of the bottom similar to that practised by South Sea islanders and a tossing of the head like an excited female cockatoo were the chief features.

By the end of the decade there were organized larrikin gangs called packs or 'pushes' in both cities. Banding together under such names as the Red Rose Pack, the Flying Angels, the Montague Dingoes, the Fitzroy Murderers, and the Richmond Dirty Dozen, they placed themselves under the king of the pack, to whom all the members swore absolute obedience. Like their spiritual ancestors in the convict era, they were quick to expel all those who strayed on to their 'pitch', whether it be a street, a park or a beach to which by long usage they believed they had proprietary rights. Like the members of the convict community they were the most noisy section of the working class of their day.

This was also the period which saw the rise of the *Bulletin*, which began publication on 31 January 1880. No one was quite sure what the paper stood for: it floundered in a mass of contradictions. It promised to rescue Australia from wowsers, yet to the disgust of the victims of the colonial Mrs Grundys, it denounced the morals of the larrikins with a fervour equal to that of the respectability-mongers of the suburbs. It called itself 'The National Australian Newspaper'; under the influence of the centenary fervours of 1888, it took as its motto 'Australia For the Australians'. It was proud of its circulation among the bush people and outside the narrow boundaries of New South Wales. Yet it fanned the flames of rivalry between New South Wales and Victoria with the same malice as the colonial politicians Henry Parkes and James Service.

It was Australian because it treated life as a cruel joke. Its mockery was Australian. Englishmen, Chinamen, Aborigines, Pacific islanders, and all the pretentious, all the pompous were held up to derision. The Prince of Wales was treated disrespectfully. The Pope was portrayed as that funny little man in Rome for whom the eating of a boiled egg was a great treat. It was wicked in its irreverence. It saw itself as a tearer-down, a remover of masks, a stripper-away of all those elaborate forms and ceremonies with which men had protected themselves against each other down the ages. The *Bulletin* was not so much the bushman's bible as the bible for the men who believed in and trafficked in the low-down view of life. It gloated over the weaknesses in a man's armour: its men were slaves to booze and boodle; its women were painted dolls, sirens or harridans. The *Bulletin* portrayed woman as a creature who hawked the body, a greedy animal between whom and man there was a never-ending war. The *Bulletin* knew nothing of that wonder of a man with a maid, or of that stroll down Lover's Lane for a 'walk with me, talk with me', or that heartache when the woman a man loved to distraction liked him but did not love him. For them a man in love was as much a figure of fun as a Jew out of his wits for money, or an Abo on the booze. They knew nothing of woman's love and sadness.

Their subject was Australia. It was a time when the native-born were chafing under the stigma of inferiority to which they were condemned by the Anglophiles in their community. The *Bulletin* encouraged Australians to believe in themselves, to like the way they talked, the way they walked, to like everything about their country, to believe that Australian English, both in its spoken and its written form, was a magnificent medium for the communication of what it was like to be a human being in Australia.

The *Bulletin* saw both the phenomenon of larrikinism and the severity of the punishments meted out to larrikins as legacies of convictism. Convictism, they argued, had bred in the working classes those traditions of antagonism to people in high places, that spitefulness against those who put on airs, and that devilish habit of deriving some base sensual satisfaction from inflicting pain and inspiring fear in the weak and defenceless. That was why, when a warm climate and an increase in the hours free from labour in Melbourne and Sydney gave the workers far more leisure in the open air, the larrikin section of the working class, not restrained by any teaching on the difference between right and wrong, and ignorant of all the canons and conventions of civilized behaviour, behaved like wild beasts.

At Clontarf on Boxing Day 1880 there had been such an orgy. Young men, young women and children, all dressed in the sartorial excesses of the larrikin class, crowded the dancing pavilion and jostled each other at the drinking bars. With their blood warmed by the dancing, and their passions inflamed by the strong drink, they began to behave in a way which the respectable bourgeoisie found hideous. The faces of these young Australians assumed the cunning, sensual and cruel appearance of people who derived satisfaction from wounding other human beings. Flushed, panting young girls clung in romping abandon to the bodies of young men. The drink and excitement soon led them to abandon the last restraints of modesty. A picnic at the seaside degenerated into a Bacchanalian orgy, as the women, incensed by competition for the men, flew like wild beasts at one another, boxed like men, and scratched and bit each other like cats. The men, encouraged by the sensual generosity of the women, made no pretence of preserving modesty. As the *Bulletin* put it, 'The devil had broken loose', as inflamed men and melting women continued their wild revel beside the blue waters of Sydney Harbour. Australia was not threatened with a social revolution; Australia was threatened with being barbarized by larrikins; Australians might become the Goths and Vandals of that civilization which had been transplanted to their continent when the British Government decided, in August 1786, to plant a colony of thieves at Botany Bay.

The *Bulletin* was not a lone voice, indeed the conversation about the nature and destiny of Australia was becoming increasingly complex and vigorous. In Melbourne there was Alfred Deakin, the brilliant orator, who had taken the oath of office as Commissioner of Public Works and Minister of Water Supply in the government of Graham Berry and James Service, a government committed to the prevailing liberal ethos of material progress as the vanguard of the moral progress and happiness of mankind. Deakin spurned this 'cheap and gaudy and facile display of worldly life'. He kept notebooks called 'Clues', in which he wrote down thoughts on the meaning of life. He read every author who had a clue to what it was all about: he devoured Shakespeare; he absorbed Wordsworth; later he was to read Dostoevsky's *The Brothers Karamazov*, much in fellow-feeling with Ivan Karamazov's great hope, 'I want to be there when everyone suddenly understands what it has all been for'. He believed the knowledge and love of God to be the fountain of all life and love and power. Apart from God, man's life was 'selfish mainly and sensual mainly—narrow, hard, harsh and discordant'.

Alfred Deakin was born on 3 August 1856 in Fitzroy, an inner suburb of Melbourne. Later Deakin recalled his schooldays at Melbourne Grammar as that time when a man with a fine con-science and exquisite sensibilities, Dr Bromby, was fated for a season to consume his substance teaching barbarians. Secretly Deakin joined in asking the question Dr Bromby had put to himself: what could a man of education any longer believe? Had science cheated humanity of its great comforter?

While at school and at the University of Melbourne, Deakin did all those things which enabled a man to climb the ladder of prefer-ment in bourgeois Melbourne, to cross that bridge separating working-class Fitzroy from bourgeois South Yarra. He was also a pilgrim who was always trying to find out the truth about life and about himself. On 25 April 1875 he had his phrenology chart drawn up; in November 1876 he had his astrological chart drawn up. On 19 February 1877, the year in which he turned 21, he sat in the stalls at the Princess Theatre in Melbourne while Graham Berry and Professor C. H. Pearson professed their faith in democracy, progress and material well-being for all. On 22 August 1877 he consulted a sibyl to find out which were his 'lucky days'. She asked him to tell her his deepest wish. He replied, 'To be wise'. In 1880 he was again consulting the phrenologists, fortune-tellers and sibyls, for this was an age when soothsayers, palmists, spiritualists and fortune-tellers were consulted by men in high places with the ardour and hopefulness of men who were disenchanted with the real world and were seeking refuge in things unseen and a world of fantasy. A Mrs Fielden prophesied in a trance that he would be called suddenly into public life and occupy an important position quite unexpectedly. That was very pleasing to hear, because salvation and success were the two master-mistresses of his passion.

At the same time he wanted someone to show him how he could rid his mind of a 'sense of the awfulness of nothingness'. The never-ending conflict between good and evil raged in Deakin's soul. In public he spoke the language of a bourgeois liberal, but in private he feared that generations to come would stray through 'an infinite nothingness'. In such an era he feared that the strong would bully all those who went on believing in the mystery at the heart of things.

By contrast Henry Parkes believed it was his destiny to lead humanity into an era of 'higher history' than any they had known hitherto. Greatness had become the master-mistress of his passion. He had taken up residence in a twenty-room house in Annandale which he called 'Kenilworth' after the manor house of that Lord Leigh who had evicted Parkes's father from his house in Stoneleigh. He had abandoned the youthful vows of vengeance against the enemies of his father. On 5 June 1877 he heard he had been created a Knight of the Order of St Michael and St George. He was specially pleased to take it in company with His Royal Highness the Prince of Wales who at the same time accepted the Grand Cross. He corresponded with the great: he dedicated a book of poems to Lord Tennyson, exchanged mind with John Stuart Mill and Thomas Carlyle. In England in April 1882 he was delighted when Lord and Lady Leigh asked him to do them the honour of paying a visit to their estate. So Parkes became an honoured guest in the ancestral house of the family which had destroyed his father. He began to feel more kindly towards a flunkeydom he had previously despised. He was now mixing on a footing of equality with those men in the laced coats and the silken breeches who had filled him in his youth with a wild despair.

In Sydney financial debt threatened him with ruin. Yet Parkes remained brimful of the 'vitalizing sap' of life. Like Danton he was 'a fiery furnace of a man', a man who lived on Faust's principle that all theory is grey, but green is the golden tree of life. In conversation with other men his language was Rabelaisian; in conversation with women it was inflammatory. Even in 1880, the year in which he turned 65, no woman was said to be safe in his presence. Rumour had it that he was 'balled like a bull'. He swallowed gargantuan quantities of food; he was generous to those who had despitefully used him.

He had once seen himself as the man who would open the batting for 'the innings of the people'. In 1850 he had wanted everyone to 'have a fair and equal race before them'. He had wanted every man in New South Wales to have the opportunity to become an owner of property. His failures in business on his own account, as an ivory-turner, a newspaper proprietor and an owner of property, had left him dependent on the spoils of office to support his family. This had caused a never-ending war between principle and expediency. By 1880 he had reached that stage in life when his rhetoric about the future greatness of Australia was greeted with derision. He had become a figure of fun, a man in whom the gap between profession and performance had become unbridgeable. The cartoonists mocked him as a one-time Chartist who had been corrupted by power.

Between 1883 and 1888 society in the Australian colonies was again disturbed by the same sort of fever which had swept over the inhabited parts of the country during the gold decade. All classes became possessed of a speculating mania begun by the discovery of silver, lead, gold and opal mines in those parts of Tasmania, New South Wales, Queensland and Western Australia hitherto judged unsuitable for the purposes of civilized man. Even the ranks of the clergy proved no exception to the rule. In Melbourne and Sydney some employees left their house of business to spend an hour or two at the stock exchange each day; others spent part of their dinner hour buying and selling mining scrip. In Adelaide, King William Street was crowded with people anxious for news from the mines, or the latest about land sales. Excitement rose so high that stand-up fights broke out between speculators and brokers. In Melbourne men who kept up an outward appearance of jollity and an affectation of virtue and respectability trembled at the touch of a strange finger on their shoulders, because of their terror that one day their skulduggery would be detected, that Mr Money Bags, he of the top hat and the striped trousers, would be charged as a common criminal. Brokers were making huge piles out of a confiding public. As with gold, the prophets foretold a day of reckoning: sooner or later, they predicted, there must be a downfall; the greedy must be punished for all this rash and blind speculation.

On 4 December 1871 James Smith, known to his acquaintances as 'Philosopher Smith', under the influence of his own experiences on the Victorian goldfields set out in search of gold in the rough

mountainous country south of Burnie in Tasmania. At Mount
Bischoff he discovered one of the richest tin mines in the world.
When the Mount Bischoff Tin Mining company was incorporated in
1873, the 'Philosopher' received 4400 shares, the remaining 7600
being sold to investors at £1 per share. In the ensuing 25 years
the original capital was repaid 200 times over. Miners lived in
barbarous conditions on the mountainside, while speculators
gambled on the share market in Launceston. The 'Philosopher' had
lifted Tasmania out of the backwater to which it had been condemned since the end of the convict era in August 1853. He entered
the Legislative Council in Hobart where he was sometimes seen to
smile but never to laugh.

Six years later, in February 1877, Owen Meredith pegged out an
area at Heemskerk in Tasmania for a tin-mine lease. The miners and
prospectors closed in, and Heemskerk became the centre of operations for the Great Western Company. The prospectors lived off
mouldy flour, soggy tea and putrid meat and kept the cold and the
damp at bay with copious doses of rum, driven on by hopes of a
lucky strike of gold, or silver or tin. While workers laboured in the
mines and were building a track from Heemskerk, Zeehan and Mt
Lyell to the coast, brokers and speculators won and lost fortunes in
Hobart and Launceston.

The mines of Tasmania were rushed from the activities of small-
time prospectors and speculators into a whirlpool of activity by the
intervention of interested parties on the mainland. In September
1883 Charles Rasp, a hand on Mount Gipps Station north-west of
the Darling from Menindie, went prospecting among the hard rock
on a hill not far from where William John Wills had shuddered in
horror at the malevolence of the land. At the place which came to be
called Broken Hill on 5 September 1883 he found specimens of
silver and lead. Rasp formed a syndicate with six other employees
of the Mount Gipps Station. In June 1885 they formed themselves
into the Broken Hill Proprietary Company Limited. When the
company declared a profit of £100 000 in November 1886, the fever
burst. A town of tents, houses, hotels, stores, humpies and sheds
increased in population in the two years between 1886 and 1888 to
6000 people.

By 1889 20 000 men were struggling for quick and easy money in
a great dust-heap at the foot of this iron range. Argent Street was a
road two chains wide crowded with men selling shares in mines. At
night, as an observer put it, 'the madness was intense' as the
'sudden glare of the molten metal plunging down the dump' lit up
'all those haggling eager faces with Rembrandt colour; lighted the
dust-laden air and the reeking horses of mail coaches and pros-

pectors' buggies and buck-boards', for day and night, everybody was in a hurry to go somewhere, and to do something immediately.

Reports of discoveries of new silver mines in the press fanned excitement white-hot. Transactions in silver shares became enormous. Men seemed prepared to take a punt on anything in the palmy days of the scrip mania. Shares changed hands for twenties, fifties and hundreds of pounds. Young men pegged out claims and sites for storekeepers, publicans, butchers and blacksmiths. For the boom in mining bred a special order of humanity: just as a muggy night brought out the mosquitoes, the boom brought out gentlemen who informed people in a sleazy confidential whisper that they had 'something good in silver' when everything about them, their clothes, their boots, their over-oiled hair, their eyes, and their mouth shouted that they had less of that precious metal about them than half a crown. As frauds became more and more the order of the day, the morals of public men and their good faith came up for discussion. Public men, it was said, had become shameless, as tricksters made hay in the shiny season. In Sydney in September 1887 the minister of mines was said to be 'up to his neck' in sales of the harbour frontage in Sydney.

In the cities the furore was intensified by a spree in the buying and selling of land. Brokers in land began to have a merry time. In the city of Melbourne, land which had fetched £40 an acre in the period before gold changed hands in 1888 for £3000 a foot. In Sydney syndicates bought land on beach fronts and resold them at huge profits. In the suburbs of Melbourne the 200 acres adjoining the railway line between Riversdale and Camberwell was sold in 1887 for £20 000, then for £32 000, then for £62 000 to the Real Estate Company, the directors of which were hopeful in March 1888 of clearing at least £50 000 from the deal, as it was just the class of investment that was sought after eagerly by speculators and capitalists. As one woman wrote, the boom made money smell rank in the nose. Those were the times when Melburnians and Sydneysiders gloried in being 'rich and dishonest and mercenary and vulgar'.

B. J. Fink, the king of the furniture trade of Melbourne, who had begun his career as a boy in a furniture shop, and later sold pianos as freely as other men retailed crayfish and peanuts, was said to be worth £250 000. He netted £20 000 a year from his business. C. H. James, a grocer of North Melbourne, made money selling pocket handkerchief allotments in the Fairfield–Ivanhoe districts. Sir M. Davies, the speaker of the Legislative Assembly in Victoria, was said to have £2 million profit on paper. J. Munro, J. Mirams and J. W. Hunt used the wealth they made to acquire the licences of the three largest hotels in Melbourne—the Grand (later the Windsor), the Victoria and the Federal—and convert them into coffee palaces, for the land-boomers were often renowned for their puritanical principles, their hatred of pleasure and their humourless faces.

By contrast Thomas Bent, who had laid the foundations of his material fortune by astute trafficking in land in the Brighton district adjacent to new railway lines, liked his gin and tonic 'strong and "fraquint"'. He was also said to have had such 'a rovin' eye for wimmen' that even in the days when he was Speaker of the Legislative Assembly he had left the Speaker's mace in a nearby whorehouse as a piece of buffoonery. Apart from elbow work and those 'other things', he was said to be 'as pure as the drivellin' snow'. As a good Australian male, he made sure that no coarse word passed his lips or those of his friends in the presence of his wife and daughter. They were kept under protection in Brighton when Thomas Bent took exercise with the other insects in Parliament to whom God had given sensual lust.

Bent had grown up in a hard school. He was born in Penrith in New South Wales on 17 December 1838 and moved to Melbourne in 1849 with his father who started a market-gardening business in Brighton, 'selling spuds and cabbages—Yes, my boy, jolly good cabbages they were, too'. By working up to eighteen hours a day Bent accumulated enough wealth to stand as a conservative for the electorate of Brighton against George Higinbotham in 1871 and beat him by thirty-two votes, for in Australia the upstart conservative, the mean man, often defeated the generous man and the visionary. By then he was bursting with vitality, a full-blooded, bull-necked man who rose at dawn and worked far into the night, always seeming to have plenty of time for conviviality, for jokes and bonhomie with the other vulgarians of his day. As he approached the treacherous middle years he was noted for the 'labouring roll of his corpulent body', his execrable songs and his Bentian jokes.

Yet in public life he was so ruthless in attacking the reputations of those who professed the hope of converting Victoria into a paradise for the working man that he was known as the 'whip'. He had played a major role in bringing down Berry's government. He fought all such men with the gloves off. He talked about managing the railways 'on business principles'. He believed there would be no rest for the wicked until they were lashed more frequently. He told the unemployed they were starving because they were too lazy to work. When one of them dared to argue with him, Bent scuffled with him and threw him out of the room.

The upper classes were going in for pleasure 'heels up'. The titillation of the senses became the order of the day. The Victorian

Parliament, which had proposed to spend £25 000 on improvements to the Exhibition Building for the silver jubilee of Queen
Victoria in 1887, ended up with a bill for £250 000 which was paid
without a demur, because in those giddy times no price was held to
be too high for 'a palace of pleasure'. Inside that building, society
women fanned their faces to hide their response to the sensuous
music of Wagner. Men fidgeted in their seats as a trumpet, bassoon
and big bass drum inflamed their senses. Men and women lolled on
soft cushions to enjoy the more the paintings lent by famous overseas galleries to honour 'marvellous Melbourne'. Children watched
the seals in the aquarium, and sucked lollies, the size and sugar
content of which said much about the spirit of the times. It was a
time when men who were strangers to that warning about giving
money upon usury, or taking rewards against the innocent, or
building memorials to the men their spiritual ancestors had slain,
occupied high places in public life. The money-changers had begun
to set the tone of public life in Australia.

The old round of pleasure continued as though the ruling class
were quite oblivious of and indifferent to the ferment of the time.
Everyone still seemed to have plenty of money and to spend it
freely on Garden Parties, At Homes, Balls and Government House
Dances. No one talked of any coming disaster. The members of the
squatting cousinhood were still intermarrying. On 27 January
1888 *Table Talk* in Melbourne announced the engagement of Miss
Chirnside (Muffy), daughter of Mr Chirnside, Werribee Park, to Mr
Claude Macdonald of Wantabadgery Station, New South Wales,
younger brother of Mr Falconer Macdonald, who lately married the
eldest daughter of Sir William Clarke, Bart. The squatters still held
dances in the ballrooms of their country estates or their Melbourne
mansions as though such things were from eternity and would
not change.

The pleasures of the working classes had changed in form but not
in content. In more barbarous times they had supplied the sound
and the fury at bull-baiting, cock-fighting and bare-knuckle fights
between men. That fierce thirst for blood which they had inherited
from their ancestors was now satisfied by the game of Australian
football. Modern civilization had found an answer to the human
craving for skill, excitement and cruelty. The footballer, it was said,
had murder in his heart. The spectators found both entertainment
and fulfilment of their wild lust for violence and their desire to
satisfy their baser passions in barracking the participants in the
new blood sport. They polluted the air with their oaths, their
obscenities, and their gift for anatomical wit, to the great scandal of
those who did not believe the playgrounds of Victoria should be

contaminated with anything unfit for the eyes and ears of their mothers and sisters.

On 13 September 1887 Henry Parkes was feeling very crushed. That day he had decided the only honest thing to do was to assign his estate for the benefit of his creditors. As he told the Legislative Assembly when tendering his resignation, he was then penniless: he was living in a breadless house, old, poor and friendless, not knowing how he could possibly pay his creditors the £20 715 18s 3d owing to them. He was so tired, he said, he could fall asleep any minute. He wept bitterly as he made his first public profession of his folly. It seemed to be the end, but his friends and supporters called a public meeting on 17 October 1887 at which they submitted the resolution, 'That this meeting is of the opinion that, as a national tribute to the long and distinguished public services of Sir Henry Parkes, a fund should be immediately created by his fellow-colonists to secure him from financial anxiety in the future'. Once again the bourgeoisie of Sydney restored to solvency a man who had broken all the rules, a man who had been 'boxing the political pecuniary compass' for years, borrowing money from friends and supporters well knowing that he was highly unlikely ever to pay it back.

The parsons and the priests pointed to greed, frauds, cruelty and lack of compassion in the community. In Sydney the Anglican bishop, Alfred Barry, denounced the sensuality of the 'dissipated wealthy', produced by a fine climate, outdoor life, more leisure and a fuller diet. Larrikinism, he believed, was on the increase with the increase in leisure and freedom. Some denounced Australians as a 'nation of drunkards'. Others prophesied that, with the triumph of democracy, the day of the elegant would give way to the day of the upstarts, and the fashionable suburbs would become 'mere gas-lighted wildernesses', or they blamed 'insolent infidelity' as the cause of the 'irreverence for all things holy'.

Another generation was coming to birth, no longer in terror of eternal punishment, or seduced and enticed by promises of walks through the Garden of Paradise. Jehovah the punisher, Jehovah the lawgiver was disappearing from the consciousness of mankind. Men were becoming this-sided, secular, pleasure-seeking, laying up for themselves treasures on earth.

Adam Lindsay Gordon had died in 1870 and Marcus Clarke in 1881. Henry Kendall died on 1 August 1882. Like Charles Harpur, Clarke and the legions to follow, Kendall's life had borne witness to the odd truth that drunkards have made the illuminating remarks about the Australian scene. He saw himself as a man who was saturated with the peculiar spirit of Australian scenery. Like Clarke, he believed the weird scribblings of nature in Australia were fashioning a new race of men. But unlike so many English-born men of letters, he had not seen the land as cursed or left incomplete by some bored or exhausted Creator. In rock and flower and tree, and moss and shining runnel, in the 'grave winds' of Australia and in the liturgy of her 'singing waters' he had found 'the broad foundations of a finer hope', the 'blessed horizon for a larger faith':

> . . . On thy awful brow
> Is Deity; and in that voice of thine
> There is the great imperial utterance
> Of God for ever; and thy feet are set
> Where evermore, through all the days and years
> There rolls the grand hymn of the deathless wave.

Old Australia was finished: the age of clowns, liars and charlatans had begun. But Kendall had moved on, hoping that past the darkness of the grave the soul would become omniscient. He was buried in Waverley Cemetery. There in 1886 Louisa Lawson, the mother of Henry Lawson, erected a monument in stone over his grave 'in grateful and lasting remembrance of his genius'.

Three years earlier Louisa Lawson had leased out the selection at Sapling Gully and moved to Marrickville in Sydney. Within five years of her separation from her husband, the bush wife and mother had blossomed into a feminist of the Australian suburbs. On 15 May 1888 she published the first issue of *Dawn*. For her the great hope for the future was the elevation of women as the only remaining influence capable of raising mankind to a wiser, happier and nobler level. She wanted women to be 'tall and strong', not to look 'weak and helpless'. What angered her was that in her society a woman could not bear a child without it being received into the hands of a male doctor, after which it was baptized by a 'fat male parson'. A girl, she argued, went through life obeying laws made by men. If she broke them, a male magistrate sent her to gaol where a male warder handled her and locked her in a cell at night. If she got so far as to be hanged, a male hangman put the rope round her neck. She was buried by a male grave-digger and she went to a heaven ruled over by a male God or a hell managed by a male Devil.

In *Dawn* on 23 May 1889 Lousia Lawson presented the argument for enfranchising women. The popular idea of an advocate for women's rights, she said, was an angular, hard-featured, withered creature with a shrill, harsh voice, no pretence to comeliness, spectacles on nose, and the repulsive title 'bluestocking' visible all over her, shaking her skinny fist at men and all their works. The only question was, who ordained that men only should make the laws to which men and women have to conform? 'If you want real practical wisdom', she contended, 'go to an old washerwoman patching clothes on the Rocks with a black eye, and you'll hear more true philosophy than a Parliament of men will talk in a twelvemonth'. She turned to Henry Parkes for support. That old fox, his antennae having told him the winds of a great change were about to blow over the civilized world, murmured agreement, for Parkes was always great of heart. It is possible too that women were the only ones with whom he could share his heart. By then, too, the great love of his later years, his daughter Annie, was his mentor on the woman question.

The radical press also lent their support. In Brisbane the *Boomerang*, edited by William Lane, advocated enlightening girls, throwing open to them the vast storehouses of knowledge, making them thinkers and wise women and not insipid dolls, fit only to talk with ignorant and untutored knights. In Sydney the *Republican* took up the same position.

In the professional middle classes isolated individuals had been arguing for years the wisdom and the justice of giving women the right to enter the professions. Down in Melbourne Dr John Edward Bromby, the headmaster of Melbourne Grammar, was another supporter of education for women. In February 1871 the doctor had hopes of persuading the council of the University of Melbourne to allow Miss Creed and Miss Bogle to sign the matriculation roll. Miss Bogle was the daughter of a woman at Sandhurst in Victoria who milked cows, churned butter, and taught her children. She scrubbed the washing with one hand while hearing her daughter grapple with her lessons in Latin, Greek and geometry. On 5 December 1871 the doctor wrote to the Registrar of the university to ask whether there was any cause or just impediment why Miss Creed should not enter the university in the next academic year. Council deliberated for an hour and decided the Registrar must not present a female for matriculation. But Dr Bromby did not despair: he had his supporters among the members of the professions in Melbourne and Sydney.

On Saturday 1 December 1883 the undergraduates of the University of Melbourne assembled in force to witness the admission of the first woman, Bella Guerin, to the degree of Bachelor of Arts. As an outward and visible sign of the absence of difference in intellectual achievement between male and female, Bella Guerin wore a cap and gown traditionally worn by men. The chancellor congratulated her on her achievement. The audience greeted her with tumultuous applause.

In the world at large the critics of such female activity had not been silenced. In Sydney the *Bulletin* argued that henceforth women would have to decide whether they wanted to be wives and mothers, or intellectuals. They could not be both. 'In short', they argued on 17 March 1888, 'if women are to cultivate the sciences they must remain celibates for life'. If they intend to fulfil their natural functions as wives and mothers they must stay as they are and be healthy animals. But humanity was on the march. In 1890 a college for women students was founded within the University of Sydney. 'If it is right and fitting', it was argued, 'that a man should be equipped for his lifework with all the auxiliaries likely to be of aid in his occupation, the same holds good with regard to women who from necessity or choice enter the working ranks'. No longer was it possible to assume that nature had endowed the feminine half of humanity with a 'scanty intellectual outfit'.

This revolution only touched a tiny proportion of the women in the Australian colonies. Those in domestic service still worked appallingly long hours, lived either in the basement or the attic, and received a pittance in return for their domestic servitude. The wives of the clergy were condemned to poverty and servitude, cloaked by gentility. Their husbands regarded them as intended for no other purpose than to wait upon the Lord's ministers. By strictly observing the customs and values of the day, pious men killed their wives by inches without even noticing they were doing so. The clergy's wives were expected to produce a child a year, keep house, do the parish work and take on other burdens.

Girls and women who worked in factories or shops were obsessed with problems of material rewards rather than with the dignity and status of their sex. Girls apprenticed to a trade for twelve or eighteen months received either nothing or 1s a week. If circumstances compelled them to live away from home, they had to cope as best they could with the problem of how to earn enough to live on without losing their respectability. Another problem was how such a girl could so improve her qualifications that she could rise from the ranks of the unskilled, ill-paid spheres of labour to higher, more interesting and more remunerative work. Such an effort, such an outlay might simply place her face to face with the highest wall of all to climb, the wall of competition with men. Those who deplored the dearth of domestic servants stressed the disadvantages and moral dangers in factory work pursued away from the restraining and edifying examples of the home. The well-to-do women looked down and despised their working sisters, but the stream was already too strong to be dammed, let alone reversed.

To help girls and working women resist temptation, the Young Women's Christian Association and the Girls' Friendly Society were there to exercise a beneficial influence on the female portion of the

rising generation. Impulsive and inexperienced girls who were
entering for the first time a life full of perils were surrounded with
a helping band of social workers who seemed to believe that the
Galilean had come, not that all mankind might have life and have
it more abundantly, but that girls entering factories in Sydney,
Melbourne and Adelaide might preserve their virginity. They
talked much to the girls about purity of heart, as though that too
were just something to do with the condition of the body, and about
modesty of conduct as 'the flower and crown of womanhood'.
The girls were reminded that whenever the storms of temptation
assailed them, or 'the deep waters of affliction' drowned their
consciences, the sympathizing hand of these societies was there
to support them. In this way working-class girls were being
bourgeoisified just as in previous decades the bourgeoisie had set
about the cultivation in the male working class of those qualities
which would qualify them to enter the kingdom of heaven rather
than of ideas which might delude them into hoping it was possible
to change substantially their lot in this world.

Women had more success in gaining admission to the professions than to membership of the skilled unions. The members of
professions which subscribed to Sir William Stawell's dictum that
'there must be an aristocracy of some kind in every country',
because there were some men in every community who would
always come to the front, opened their ranks to women. By 1890
women had been admitted to the bar, the practice of medicine and
the universities, but not to office in any of the branches of Christ's
Church. By contrast the members of the skilled unions who subscribed to equality, the brotherhood of man, and the end of all
distinctions based on race, sex or creed, still excluded women from
their ranks on the grounds of that great old Australian argument in
favour of male superiority, 'They wouldn't be really suitable,
would they?'.

Even as men rehearsed such arguments, society was confronted
with a more fundamental issue than the status of women. As the
Bulletin put it as early as May 1883, 'a frightful and catastrophic
contest between wealth and want, poverty and privilege' was about
to commence, a conflict in which both sides would use, 'without
ruth or hesitation', whatever weapons were available to them. The
police and standing armies would be used by one class for the
oppression of another. Throughout the whole civilized world the
labouring millions were in revolt against the organized army of
capitalists. Labour was becoming militant and aggressive; capital
was stolid and defiant. In Australia the struggle was complicated by
a legacy from the past. In Sydney and Melbourne an 'irruption of

barbarians' was threatening the very foundations of society. The old convict strain had inoculated the working classes with the virus of destruction. The question was whether civilization could find the right varnish with which to coat the underlying barbarism. The large towns on the coast ministered stimulants of all kinds to a people whose craving for excitement had been aggravated by the introduction of monotonous labour and long hours. Streetwalkers could see in shop windows the type of goods coveted and prized by society ladies. In the theatre, the lecture room, the bar and the brothel, men and women engaged in excitements to meet every taste and every capacity. In Victoria by 1883 40 per cent of the population were city-dwellers. The problem was to find in this ancient, barren land the roots that would clutch, branches that would grow out of the stony rubbish and prevent Australian society from degenerating into barbarism.

After the occupation on 26 January 1788 some Europeans found the landscape so alien they wondered whether the land itself was cursed. They were haunted by a fear that the spirit of the place and the primitive way of life would push the lower orders of society down into a barbaric way of life not unlike that of the original tenants of the land. One of Wentworth's nightmares had been the return of barbarism to the Australian wilderness, that a day might come when the white men had to abandon the land to the Aborigines and the sheep. Troops had stormed the barricades at Eureka in December 1854 to save the colony for civilization. The bush-rangers had raised again the bogy of barbarism. Now, in the 1880s, a new fear seized the heart of the bourgeoisie: there was barbarism in the Australian cities; there was a spiritual desert in the heart of suburbia.

To add to the fears, the grab for Africa had begun. Since 1883 British arms had been engaged in an activity intelligible to Australians: they were fighting for the cause of civilization against heathen savages in the Sudan. News of the death of General Gordon in Khartoum reached Melbourne and Sydney in February 1885; he had been clubbed to death in a most brutal manner, and his body subjected to unspeakable indignities by half-naked savages chanting blood-curdling music. People went mad in the streets and ran hot with their cries for revenge.

William Bede Dalley announced on 12 February 1885 that New South Wales was prepared to send a contingent of troops to the Sudan 'to testify to the readiness of the Australian colonies to give instant and practical help to the Empire'. Australians, Dalley said, must serve under 'the English flag'. A somewhat surprised British Government accepted the offer. On the day of departure of the troops, 3 March 1885, a public holiday was proclaimed in Sydney. Thousands packed the streets over which banners proclaimed the slogan 'For England, Home and Gordon'. Members of the crowd shouted 'Godspeed' or 'Give it to the Mahdi'. Some even called out 'Advance Australia', for that too was part of the response, though most accepted Dalley's point that 'The Queen's enemies are ours wherever they are'.

For Victoria, James Service offered to do likewise, only to be snubbed by the haughty Whitehall men. Nothing daunted, the Victorians proceeded to translate Gordon, the man with a passionate if somewhat reckless heart, into the hero of Khartoum. James Service thanked New South Wales for precipitating Australia from a geographical expression into a nation. He added that so long as Victoria had a man, a shop or a shilling, England would never lack assistance. In Melbourne prizes of £3, £2 and £1 were offered to schoolchildren who wrote the best essays on the subject of 'General Gordon as a Hero'. A demonstration on behalf of the Gordon Memorial Committee was held in the Exhibition Building, Melbourne on 27 September 1885, at which a vast audience applauded a programme of patriotic performances including a choir of 5000 schoolchildren which sang 'Unfurl the Flag'. As a more lasting memorial, the committee used the money raised by such efforts, as well as by subscriptions and generous donations from the admirers of the Empire, to put up a memorial to Gordon outside Parliament House in Melbourne. Australia, as one man pointed out, must have heroes, but they should be English heroes, heroes of whom Australians could be proud. Loyalty to the throne and the Empire were the answers to Australia's barbaric past, and the stuff to fill the void in the kingdom of nothingness created by the decay of the old faiths.

In June 1887 the colonials celebrated the silver jubilee of Queen Victoria with pyrotechnics and loyal jubilation. In Sydney the displays of Empire loyalty and celebration of the Sovereign's jubilee were met with a serious challenge. As soon as the doors of the Town Hall were thrown open for a jubilee meeting on 10 June, the mob swept in in a mass. Upright Empire loyalists such as Sir Alfred Stephen were caught in the centre of a turbulent mob and almost crushed. On the platform were all the leading citizens of Sydney, including members of both Houses of Parliament, men like Henry Parkes and Sir William Manning, the Chief Justice, aldermen, clergymen, magistrates, barristers and merchants—everyone who was anyone. On the floor of the hall were representatives of the Trades and Labor Council, leaders of the Secular Association, known supporters of republicanism and men who had rejected bourgeois values. Some of the latter rushed the table at which the gentlemen of the press were sitting and drove the latter away with sticks, umbrellas and fists. The leaders were said to be recent British immigrant labourers touched with socialistic doctrines; the mob was composed of followers of the old 'convict leaven'. In the infrequent lulls between groans and bursts of applause Mayor Riley called for 'Three cheers for the Queen'. The republican group countered with a resounding 'Three cheers for liberty', as free fights broke out between the contending groups. When some semblance of order was established Sir Frederick Darley, Chief Justice, Lieutenant-Governor, member by birth of the Protestant ascendancy in both Ireland and Australia, called on all loyal members of the community, all gentlemen in the room to agree that 'moved by feelings of indignation at the riotous conduct of a disloyal minority, they would unite and band together for the maintenance of order and the vindication of the loyal attachment of the people to the laws, institutions and throne of the British Empire'.

Sir William Manning said he was inclined to think Australians were elevating a band of ruffians into heroes. It was high time, he said, that society rose to put down an evil that might grow to they knew not what. He hoped their declaration of loyalty would be signed by not only tens of thousands but hundreds of thousands. Sir Henry Parkes told them he believed their opponents were opposed not only to limited monarchy but to the forms and conditions of settled government. Republicans wanted anarchy. For his part, in a peroration characterized by his fatal tendency to overtreat and overstate every subject he touched on, he urged them to take that night, and again tomorrow, and again the following day the necessary steps until there was 'a wholesome, genuine and unmistakable expression of the loyal sentiments of this country throughout the land'. That remark brought him what he loved almost as much as drinking champagne: loud and prolonged applause. But not even the magic of Parkes could still the madness of the people, the whole proceedings being characterized by an absolute chaos of uproar, confusion, faction-fighting and ruffianism of the most disgraceful character. After the close of the formal proceedings, one of the loyalists was said to have exclaimed, 'Thank God, there is an English fleet in the harbour'.

All those who repudiated 'free-thinkers' and 'democratic principles' decided to hold another meeting on 15 June at which rowdies, ruffians and republicans would not be admitted. The meeting was held in the Exhibition Building in Sydney. Admission was by tickets. Squads of police lined the walls waiting to pounce on any dissident and throw him out, to the roars of applause of the barrackers for the red, white and blue. The meeting was enormous, enthusiastic, and wellnigh unanimous. An army of loyal, order-loving people assembled there to hear speaker after speaker declare their attachment to and affection for the Queen, and repudiate and condemn everything disloyal. Every stage and every rank of life were there—men in the prime of life, grey and feeble men, Cabinet ministers, humble artisans. The crowd was impelled to sing over and over again 'God Save the Queen' and 'Rule Britannia'. Wild and enthusiastic cheers celebrated the passing of the resolution expressing their devoted loyalty to Her Majesty the Queen and their allegiance to the laws and institutions of the British Empire. Parkes and Manning spoke of her in language little short of idolatry. The evening ended with the huge crowd rising to their feet and singing with fervour 'God Save Our Queen'. Thanks to the co-operation of the Naval Brigade, the Volunteer Naval Artillery, the Lancers, the Newtown Reserves, the undergraduates of Sydney University, the Loyal Orange Institution, the Primrose League and several football clubs, no one dared to raise so much as a whisper against order and loyalty. The supporters of loyalty had used footballers, larrikin undergraduates and prize-fighters to silence the people of New South Wales. They had rounded up 'the dumb driven cattle' of the Orange Lodges to persuade the people into an expression of loyalty to the Queen.

On 4 July 1887, the anniversary of the declaration of independence by the Republic of the United States of America, the first issue of the *Republican* monthly newspaper was published in Sydney. Under banner headlines of 'Liberty, Fraternity, Equality' it declared as its objective to keep steadily in view their coming national independence, to express no more in grovelling language the adulation of the people to the throne and aristocracy of England, because this loyalty of the lip had imparted a species of rank which was the nearest approach to bogus peerage that ribbons and meaningless letters could give. It swore not to weary until Australia was ruled by Australians.

Incensed by the loud-mouthed exhibitions of loyalty to Her Majesty by the Orangemen of the colony, and by the sycophancy of Parkes, over 200 men gathered in the Temperance Hall in Sydney on the night of 4 July 1887 to found the Australian Republican Union. The venue was symbolical because like their predecessors in popular movements in Australia many republicans were characterized by a craven servitude to wowsers, puritans and prudes. These reformers had retained all those parts of the Judaeo-Christian view of the world which instructed men on how to behave, but not those parts which were pessimistic about the fruits of human endeavour. They were good Samaritan men. In general they were not advocates of Dionysian frenzy or of Apollonian restraint and discipline, but dry souls, who took a naive, simplistic view of the sources of human misery, and the chances of their disappearance. J. D. Fitzgerald was a prime mover. He had none of the characteristics of a Promethean figure, but many of those of an Old Testament moralizer and prophet. By contrast the young George Black was searching for a society in which love of woman would be even more pleasing to the senses than in a capitalist society. Annie Besant was also one of their teachers. She wanted to bring art, beauty, refinement, and a fair and gracious life within the reach of all.

Another one of those men who summed up in his person both the breadth and the narrowness of vision of those who professed faith in man's power in Australia to steal fire from heaven was William Lane. On 19 November 1887 he published the first edition of the *Boomerang* in Brisbane. He was born in Bristol of Protestant Irish parents, brought up a prisoner of that narrow creed, and lost his faith but not his morality. Lane's remedy for all the misery of mankind was not a change in the material foundations of society, but a change in men's hearts. Men must be sober ('Drink makes a man an empty braggart or a contented fool'), virtuous, and must trust each other. He was both an evangelist and a rationalist—a moralizer and a naive believer in human perfectibility. For him socialism was just being mates, and being mates was sharing one purse. Socialism was Paradise Regained.

He was also an Australian nationalist. His principles, he said, were easy to declare: 'They are Australian. Whatever will benefit Australia, that we are for'. He was no advocate of expeditionary forces to the Sudan, or of fighting for British imperialist causes on foreign soil. It was here in Australia that the battle against nature's brutal laws would be fought out. It was here in Australia that human society would develop itself and that the yet unanswered riddles of the sphinx would be finally solved. 'We are for this Australia,' he wrote in the first number, 'for the nationality that is coming to being, for the progressive people that is just plucking aside the curtain that veils its fate'. Australia was a fresh beginning. 'We want no monarchical institutions here with their accompaniments of licentious castes and grovelling masses. We want no aristocracy . . . We want no militaryism (*sic*) . . . We want to be left alone and here in Australia to work out a new civilization.' It was an Australia in which justice would triumph and where want and shame and misery and oppression would be no more. That was his millennium. It was what Australians were destined to achieve.

Despite his protestations of universal love, three groups were excluded from his paradise. Like the Apostle Paul he excluded all liars, fornicators and drunkards. He excluded the Aborigine as just another marsupial which was being wiped out of existence, and he would have none of the 'infamy' and 'insidious vices' of the Chinese hoards.

Another man who was enraged by the Sudan expedition and the loyalty-mongers at the meeting in the Exhibition Building on 15 June was the young Henry Lawson. He had come down to the great city of Sydney from the mighty bush in response to his mother's call to join her in Marrickville. There he had fallen among the thieves of Bohemia, those men who, to his undying pain, offered the vision splendid at the bottom of the winecup. He, the man who desperately needed a comforter, found he could use his precious gift with words to tell his people he had had a dream of a new heaven and a new earth. His bush people, those men and women who had slaved to earn a living in a hard country, were going to be there on the day when the rainbow lit up the whole earth.

Angered by the use of footballers, larrikin undergraduates, and prize-fighters to subdue the people of Sydney at the meeting of 15 June 1887, he wrote a poem, 'A Song of the Republic', in which he sketched a vision of the world clean different from the vision that sustained Sir Henry Parkes, Sir William Manning, and all those leading citizens who clapped their hands sore and shouted their throats hoarse in that great demonstration of loyalty. Lawson spoke for the people. The ones whom Sir William Manning called ruffians were about to arise and build a new world:

> Sons of the South, aroused at last!
> Sons of the South are few!
> But your ranks grow longer and deeper fast,
> And ye shall swell to an army vast,
> And free from the wrongs of the North and Past
> The land that belongs to you.

In 'The Flag of the Southern Cross', written in 1887, he prophesied that a day would come sooner or later when Australians would have to battle for their country against the yellow men who lusted after her. Australians should stand like the gallant Eureka men against Englishmen, plunderers, sneerers, and those who were sucking the life-blood out of her. Against all the loyalty-mongers who were storing up shame for them, Australians should stand by the 'Bonny bright flag of the Southern Cross'.

While Lawson was chewing over what Australians would substitute for those 'old-world errors and wrongs and lies', a young painter, Tom Roberts, had pitched camp in the bush at Beaumaris on Port Phillip Bay and at Eaglemont on the Yarra, where he was trying, as he put it, to get Australia down on his canvas 'as truly as we could'. Roberts had returned to Australia from Europe in 1885 with the ambition of founding a great Australian school of painting. At Beaumaris and Eaglemont he had joined up with Arthur Streeton, Frederick McCubbin, and Charles Conder, all of whom wanted to put on canvas Australia as seen through Australian eyes in the bright light of the sun. But what they were, and of what was inside them, they were not quite sure. In Melbourne Roberts wore a top hat; in the bush he wore corks hanging from his hat-brim. In Melbourne he inscribed his name in the visitors' book at Government House; at the same time he lived in a tent on the banks of the Yarra, cooked his nightly chop over the campfire, and swung his billy full of tea in the Australian way before squatting down for his evening meal with the sky as his roof. Like Lawson he was collecting atmosphere, getting ready for the time when he found he had something to say. The lessons learnt from the impressionists in France, the uniqueness of the Australian landscape which was their new material, and their own genius gave both him and Streeton a chance to put on canvas a vision of the world to which no Australian writers of prose or verse could aspire, prisoners as they were of colonial backwardness.

Henry Parkes knew what he wanted to say about life. For him Australia was 'the mistress of the Southern Seas'. For him England's name was 'the magic still'. For him, as for the other bourgeois public men, England was still 'Fatherland, our Fatherland'.

On 28 June 1887, in the afterglow of the Queen's jubilee, he laid before Parliament his proposals for the celebration of the centenary of the foundation of New South Wales. He suggested the conversion of the Lachlan Swamp in Sydney into a Centennial Park, in which would stand a pantheon to house the mortal remains of Australia's mighty men of renown. The time had come to wean the people away from false gods, false heroes such as bold Jack Donahoe, Ben Hall, Ned Kelly; the time had come to rid the minds of the people of the legacy of convictism, bush barbarism, male supremacy and brutality. This proposal was mocked at so savagely as a stunt for the glorification of 'St 'Enery' that he was obliged to drop the idea of the pantheon, while keeping Centennial Park. Undismayed he came back with the idea that New South Wales should be renamed Australia. This plunged Victoria into a state of 'muttering irritation'.

The day of the opening of Centennial Park in January 1888 was one of those halcyon days in Sydney when the radiance in the air was matched by the benevolence in the hearts of its citizens. The dazzling light of a brilliant sun shone down on a forest of masts of ships. Bunting flapped in the streets. Fifty thousand people gathered for the ceremony. The military band played martial airs, all those tunes which reminded some of those listening that the Lord was their defence, that in some inscrutable way the British had become like those hosts in the Old Testament who scattered their enemies and crushed them. The huge crowd cheered to the echo the arrival of that English peer—Lord Carrington, the Governor of New South Wales, whose carriage was preceded by a troop of Lancers. The cheering crowd believed that being British was the source of their present strength and their future greatness. They applauded as a British ceremony inaugurated the first people's park in Australia.

Henry Lawson angrily pointed out in the *Republican* in April 1888 that not one in every ten schoolchildren attending the national schools knew a single fact about the history of Australia. They could glibly recite the names of the English sovereigns from William the Conqueror to Victoria, name the rivers, mountains and towns of Europe, but asked where Port Phillip was, or what the events in the Black War in Tasmania were, the pupils became bashfully silent. It was quite time, he argued, for the children to be taught a little about their own country. 'Are they', he asked, 'always to be "Colonials" and not "Australians"?'. He wanted them to learn to love the blue flag with the white cross, that bonny 'flag of the Southern Cross', which rose only once to mark the brightest spot in Australian history. He wanted them to acquire a preference for some national and patriotic song of their own homes rather than 'stand in a row and squeal', in obedience to custom and command, 'God Save Our Gracious Queen'. He wanted them to believe in Australia for the Australians. Behind the music and the sounds of revelry and all the hollow noises in that centenary year, behind the nobles with their lineage so old, behind their women radiant in jewelled robes, he had heard the 'Tramp! tramp! tramp!' of 'the Army of the Rear', who wanted what God had given them, who wanted their portion here:

The wealthy care not for our wants, nor for the pangs we feel;
Our hands have clutched in vain for bread, and now they clutch for steel!
Come, men of rags and hunger, come! There's work for heroes here!
There's room still in the vanguard of the Army of the Rear!
Tramp! tramp! tramp!
O men of want and care!
There's glory in the vanguard of the Army of the Rear!

At the same time the ancient barbaric continent was taking another revenge against the men who wantonly robbed it of its wealth, or dreamed dreams of human splendours. All through January 1888 the weather continued very hot and dry. The shortage of water in the country districts gave cause for alarm. Down at Yass the river stopped running; creeks and springs which had not been dry for a decade or more ceased to run; ugly cracks in the earth opened up on the banks of creek beds; up Kosciusko way water in the Murrumbidgee dropped so low that sheep were walking across it; sheep were dying from lack of water and want of feed. Stories came down to Sydney of men out on the Barcoo doing a perisher for lack of water, and of men killing themselves rather than face the horrors of dying of thirst. Men were leaving their homesteads and making for the city. Out on the Maranoa, at Longreach and Cloncurry, round the horizon in the late spring and early summer of 1888 there hung a grubby collar of dust, and in the foreground particles of dust swirled in the heat haze. Each night the sun went down like a purple disc over the rim of the earth. Grass fires swept through many districts. Station-owners and managers trembled at the prospect of a visit by the man from Dalgety's, or the man from Goldsbrough-Mort's, or the man from Smith Elder's. One man out in Roma said that in comparison with a 'great dry' a Chinese invasion was insignificant. It was possible to fight their own species, it being taken for granted that Australians could take on all comers, but a drought was beyond human control. The farther west a man went in 1888, the less belief he found in anything, the less hope for anything. The ancient continent was becoming as dry as the deserts in the hearts of its human inhabitants.

BOOK FIVE

The People Make Laws
1888–1915

A new desmesne for Mammon to infest?
Or lurks millennial Eden 'neath your face?

Bernard O'Dowd, 'Australia'

So Ginger Mick 'e's mizzled to the war;
Joy in 'is 'eart, an' wild dreams in 'is brain.

C. J. Dennis, 'The Call of Stoush'

1

The Birth of Labor

In March 1891 the news from up-country in Queensland was alarming. Bush workers burned down woolsheds at Mangroo and Lorne. The shearers were again on strike. They set fire to grass on many stations on the Condamine and uttered abominable insults and obscenities to non-union labour. The landed gentry and the bourgeoisie trembled in their shoes. The Queensland Government dispatched troops to the areas of disaffection.

Late summer rains turned the camps of both soldiers and bush workers into quagmires and impeded attempts to track down unionists on the black soil plains of Maranoa. As the steam rose from that boggy ground on which the men had pitched their camp at Barcaldine, union leaders warned the men of property that if the bush workers could not get what they wanted by constitutional means they must get their tucker somehow. There on 21 March one of their leaders, Martin, roused them to fever pitch as he told them that 10 000 bushmen behind 10 000 steel blades were the only effective remedy for the unionists' grievances. There the men had held a mock trial of the Queensland Premier, Sir Samuel Griffith, and the local member. After the court condemned them to death as tyrants and traitors the men saturated the effigies with kerosene and set them alight, belabouring them with sticks and howling like fiends until the flames subsided.

Ever since the 1880s itinerant workers had felt threatened by changes in the techniques of production of wool. The extensive use of fencing, together with the introduction of barbed wire, had dispensed with shepherds. This had reduced the numbers in the work force in the pastoral districts. Over the same period machine shearing gradually supplanted shearing by hand. By 1890 a shearing machine invented by Frederick Wolseley, a woolgrower from the Riverina, had taken over in most of the sheds of eastern

Australia, increasing the tally of the individual shearer, and so reducing the numbers required to shear a shed in the allotted time. The improvements in production together with the increased demand for wool to feed English woollen mills increased the numbers of sheep in Australia from 21 million in 1861 to 107 million in 1891.

The bush workers believed it was just and right that they should enjoy some share in these riches. But the pastoralists had their own reasons for resisting such demands. Crippled by losses during the great dry of the 1880s they were anxious not to add to their costs by paying out more for shearing. On 5 January 1891 a delegate of the Shearers' Union called out 200 shearers and rouseabouts from the Logan Downs woolshed until such time as the pastoralists dropped the demand for freedom of contract. The men on strike formed a strike camp at Clermont. Within a few weeks similar camps were formed at Sandy Creek, Capella and Barcaldine.

From all these camps delegates rode round the district with armed bands calling on shearers to drop their blades, kidnapping any opponents and the faint of heart. They threatened free workers with a bullet in the backside if they did not clear the district by sundown. They burned the grass of any squatter who dared to enforce the principle of freedom of contract in his shed. They also burned down woolsheds. A policy of terrorism had been devised to coerce employers into accepting the terms of the delegates of the Shearers' Union. Faced with such lawlessness, and the danger of such anarchy spreading into the cities, the law-and-order men demanded that government take preventive measures against the strikers.

Trade unions were becoming a force in colonial life, organizing campaigns to improve wages and working conditions, particularly in mining, rural work and shipping. The strikes which resulted were bitter and sometimes bloody. In 1890 ships' officers established a union which affiliated with the Melbourne Trades Hall Council. This liaison so outraged the shipowners that they refused to negotiate with the officers until they severed their union ties. The employers said that 'freedom of contract' was a moral absolute. The unionists said that the freedom of a single employee to negotiate with a company was no freedom at all. The conflict erupted into a bitter maritime strike, which, like the other great strikes of the period, was defeated by the employers' use of lockouts, court action and strike-breakers. But the unions continued to grow.

It was a giddy time. An anonymous ballad-writer in the *Bulletin* held out the hope that the people of Australia were about to rise and 'catch Promethean fire':

The Psalm of Labour

Down with the old world race-dissentions,
Truth and justice lead the van;
Creed and Caste are hell's inventions:
Trust the brotherhood of man.

Direct action was not the only means by which labour sought to
achieve its objectives. The time had come for the workers to prowl
like lions in the corridors of political power. To win their rights, to
win what they were fighting for, the workers must win a majority
in Parliament. Early aspirants to a seat in a colonial parliament in
the cause of labour often indulged in a rhetoric which conservatives
confounded with revolutionary intentions. On nomination day for
the electorate of West Sydney on 22 October 1890 the Labour
candidate, Adolphus George Taylor, assured a turbulent multitude
that he cared deeply for the blood and bone of the country from
which he had risen, that he sprang from the working classes, and he
honoured the working classes, that as a working man he would see
that the sons of the working man had the same chance as the sons
of the rich man in the civil service. The time was at hand when 'the
hands of labour would pursue their vengeful purpose on the
throats of capital and traitors!' At the same time, Labour mobs
challenged the conventions of civilized behaviour by disrupting
conservative political meetings by showering the participants with
flour, rotten eggs and fruit.

The *Sydney Morning Herald* dismissed all this rhetoric and postur-
ing as the wild passions of the hour. When the Trades and Labour
Council finally accepted a Labour platform on 27 October 1890 the
influence of the wild visionaries had disappeared. Gone were the
references to the brotherhood of man, and how it was pretty near
time to lift the flag of Eureka again. Instead of faith in a new society
there was an anaemic commitment 'to any measure that will secure
for the wage earner a fair and equitable return for his or her labour'.
What they stood for came not from the pages of Bellamy, or William
Morris, or John Ruskin or any of the Utopians. There was no talk of
the day when blood would stain the wattle. They proposed to
squeeze a few material benefits out of capitalist society. Their
concern was with the amendment of unjust laws, not with the
making of a new society.

Labor (spelt thus officially from 1891) had come on to the stage
of public life as a party pledged to 'peaceful and constitutional
methods of procedure', in sharp contrast to those hotheads and
irresponsibles who were still uttering threats of burning pastoral

properties. In 1891, the parliamentary committee of the Trades and Labour Council recommended the formation of a Labor Electoral League. The sixteen planks of its first platform in New South Wales reflected the variety of influences within the party: there were demands for reforms to assist workers such as legislation for an eight-hour day, repeal of the Masters and Servants Acts, proposals for a complete democracy, and a proposal, which came straight from the American writer Henry George, that government revenue be raised by a tax on land. There was another utopian reference to the ownership of land—'the natural and inalienable rights of the whole community to the land', and a plank which summed up aspirations on rewards for labour: the wage-earner, they said, should 'get a fair return for his labour'.

In Queensland the heady talk of William Lane in the *Boomerang* and the *Worker* was translated by the hard-headed men who formed the Australian Labour Federation into a platform whose planks consisted of demands for specific reforms such as the abolition of the Legislative Council, state-aided village settlements, a state bank, factory acts, mines acts—a hotchpotch of what unionists had been demanding over the preceding decade. In the other colonies political Labor entered on the stage of political life as a party of reform. In general the hints of radicalism in the New South Wales and Queensland movements came in part from the presence of coloured labour, and in part from the legacy of the strikes. In the other colonies Labor was more conservative and less successful in attracting popular support, because there bourgeois liberals argued that the Australian dream could be achieved within the existing society.

Writing and talking as though the love of all mankind distinguished them from all previous political groups, articulate Labor spokesmen inflamed their followers with hatred against the Chinese, the Jews, the English, the Pacific islanders, indeed almost all strangers in their midst. Mouthing the platitudes of the Utopians about a new society in which all hatred would cease, and God's destroying angels would disappear off the face of the earth, their candidates for election to the colonial parliaments represented themselves to be reformers rather than revolutionaries, preservers rather than destroyers. As Frank Cotton declared when he opened his campaign for East Sydney on 6 April 1891, Labor was committed to 'a slow process of evolution'. Labor wanted 'practical legislation for present needs'. They were all 'common-sense men'.

There was still the rough and tumble. During the elections in Sydney in June 1891 howling mobs gesticulated, shook their fists and shrieked insults at the conservatives. Genial Daniel O'Connor, the Postmaster-General in Sir Henry Parkes's government, was pelted with eggs and flour balls, until he looked more like a pudding than a human being. But moderation attracted votes. At the elections for the Legislative Assembly of New South Wales held between 17 June and 3 July 1891 there were forty-eight Labor candidates. Thirty-six of these were elected, a result the idealists within the movement hailed as the fulfilment of the promise of a 'higher humanity and a stronger manhood and womanhood'. The *Australian Workman* believed they were 'at the dawn of a new and happier era for the workers of New South Wales'.

Up in Brisbane William Lane waxed lyrical about the result. The ballot-box, he claimed, could lift humanity into a higher plane of being. The goodness of the people in New South Wales had triumphed over the evils of a capitalist government. In future, he continued, Gatling guns would not so readily be turned against wage-earners. Henry Lawson thought there was about to be a social revolution. The time was coming when the lordly would no longer rule the land and build their mansions high, and ladies would no longer flaunt their jewelled plumes. The day of deeds, he declared, was nigh. The workers' new religion was about to hurl vice and Mammon from their pinnacles. The triumph of the people would be, he declared, 'the victory of God'—the victory of 'love' over the 'Monarch and the Rod'.

The label of Utopian could not be pinned on the breasts of the Labor men who took their seats in the Legislative Assembly of New South Wales. They behaved like men whose goal was the capture of political power. They appointed a Credentials Committee to decide who was and who was not a genuine Labor man. They appointed a managerial committee rather than a leader, for leadership, like the comforts of Parliament House, was a potential corrupter. They pledged to vote in the House in accordance with the position agreed upon by the majority of their number meeting in Caucus. The eight protectionists feared this might commit them to vote against their conviction. One suggested that they should hedge the issue: Labor would call for a people's referendum on the tariff question. Solidarity was stronger than principle, and expediency strongest of all.

George Black spoke to members of the Legislative Assembly on 15 July 1891. Black was an ardent socialist. He was subeditor of the *Bulletin*, a passionate man, a lover of wine, women, and life, but he was also the man who claimed he had invented the slogan 'support in return for concessions'. So after making the rafters ring with a resounding call, 'We have come into this House to make and unmake social conditions', he went on to announce that Labor's vote was up for sale to the highest bidder. Sir Henry Parkes, avid for popular approval, and desperately clinging to office, needing office both to satisfy his vanity and for the pay, shrewdly made the highest bid. Labor settled for an understanding with a man who had also once dreamed a great dream that in Australia mortals would learn to love each other with brotherly love and gentle hearts.

Political Labor was gaining strength in New South Wales and Queensland. In Victoria the capitalist class had no immediate reason to dread the use of the ballot-box by the members of these Labor Leagues. New South Wales had begun with a convict working class, Victoria with an immigrant working class. Melbourne had a broader spread of middle-class affluence. It had no need of the Labor dream. It was the same in South Australia. Tasmania was still that stricken society, haunted by ghosts of the original convict working class, possibly by the memory of the great act of evil against the original inhabitants of the island, still dominated by the country gentry, with no tradition of liberal criticism of society. Western Australia was still a tiny society of Europeans and Aborigines, the former seeing no reason to shed the myth of British institutions and national progress, the latter too broken by the recent past to hold any ideas on the future of their own people, let alone humanity in general.

By contrast, in Queensland the defenders of bourgeois society believed the bush strike was bringing the colony to the edge of revolution: wild visionaries such as Lane and the slogans of that drunken young poet Henry Lawson had deluded the bush workers into staining the wattle with the blood of their oppressors. Lawson's vision of them was as noble bushmen who were fighting to ensure that the toilers, not the idlers, owned the wealth they created. 'Freedom's on the wallaby', sang Henry Lawson, 'She'll knock the tyrants silly':

> We'll make the tyrants feel the sting
> Of those that they would throttle;
> They needn't say the fault is ours
> If blood should stain the wattle.

Once again the rebel flag was flying in Australia; once again a rebel song was being sung; once again Australians were singing a 'rebel chorus'.

The lesson of the armed shearers' camp at Barcaldine had not been lost on the enlightened bourgeois politicians. There must be some middle ground between conservatism of a Henry Parkes, a James Service, a John Forrest, an Inglis Clark, a Samuel Griffith, a

Richard Baker and the flying of a rebel flag in a bushman's camp. The institutions of the bourgeois state could surely be used to ensure a minimum wage, to conciliate and arbitrate in industrial disputes, and to regulate the hours of labour. Change must come quickly, or those words of the young Lawson would no longer fall on stony ground. The time had come to stop the charade of division between free trade and protection. That was no longer the ground of division in society. A great debate had begun in the whole civilized world over who should own wealth and how it should be divided. Unless concessions were made, there might be a terrible explosion.

By October 1891 the Premier of New South Wales, Sir Henry Parkes, looked very 'careworn and tired'. A political crisis had blown up over the Coal Mines Regulation Bill. In the committee stage of the bill the men in the middle ground, with the help of the members of the Labor Leagues, added a clause fixing the hours of work. On principle Parkes opposed the amendment. He explained to the House that all through his public life he had endeavoured to lighten the burden of those who laboured. He looked forward to the time when in the progress of enlightenment the necessity for toil would be greatly reduced. But the state must not dictate to a man how he sold his labour. 'If that creature', he put it, 'endowed with divine capacity, a human being, who we are told on the highest authority was created in the image of God himself, has any right in the whole world, it is the right to dispose of the attributes of his own life so long as he injures no other human being'. Parkes and his government were defeated. Within a few days he had offered his resignation to the Governor. The stage was set for the believers in the middle ground to use the state to save bourgeois society from the men who had flown the rebel flag.

Ill and worried, Parkes also resigned as leader of his party. To his undying pain the members proceeded to elect his mortal enemy, George Reid, to fill the vacancy. The old man had to endure the humiliation as best he could. He spoke to his friends of the pleasures of being finally released from the 'slavery of power' and how much he was looking forward to the quiet, simple life. It did not occur to him or to the others who observed his going that his withdrawal from active public life coincided with a new age in the history of Australia. The middle-roaders now had their chance to prove that there could be equality of opportunity, liberty of the individual, and material well-being for all without any radical change in existing society. Australian liberals believed they had a chance to persuade the bushmen and the city workers to take down the rebel flag and stop their rebel chorus.

2

A Time of Tumult

In February 1892 a run started upon the Savings Bank of New South Wales. For two days a howling mob raged round the doors, climbing over each other in a frantic endeavour to get their money. Men shoved, jostled and elbowed each other, women screamed. All through the day the police were busy rescuing depositors who had been trampled under the feet of the crowd or fat women who had fallen down exhausted. In an endeavour to calm the hysteria the directors announced they would pay in gold, and extend closing time from 7.30 p.m. to 10.15 p.m. When that time came some of those who had not managed to squeeze through the doors sat down to weep in the gutter, and some stood gaping at the windows of a bank which held, they believed, the key to their future well-being. Some who managed to withdraw their savings went on their way rejoicing, recklessly boasting that they were now saved, only to have their pockets picked, and some, with good money in their hand, after a cry of 'thank God', rushed to invest again in a land bank, believing that there, for sure, their money would be safe.

In Melbourne the first signs of trouble in the business world had appeared two years earlier. In February 1890 the Premier Permanent Building Association suspended payment. Rumours were soon circulating that the savings of little people were in danger. Doubts about Baring's Bank in London in November 1890 marked the end of the wild spree. In March 1892 the directors of the Mercantile Bank of Australia also suspended payment. When the Australian Deposit and Mortgage Bank closed its doors that same month, mobs rioted in the streets of Melbourne as angry depositors threatened to smash shop windows and break down doors of the bank. The bourgeoisie were dismayed and bewildered.

When the Colonial Investment Company failed, small investors appealed to the directors in letters which evoked the pathos and agony of the occasion. They were like gamblers confessing their losses. 'If you only knew', the proprietress of a small fancy goods shop wrote, 'how hard I had worked to pay money into your society'. The suffering in such classes was widespread and terrible. They had believed that capital was safe. The men and women who had practised the bourgeois virtue of thrift found they had entrusted the savings of a lifetime to men who had diddled them with a lying balance sheet or fraudulent advertising. What they had believed to be a safe investment in the hands of a good, honourable and pious man turned out to be the plaything of an evil man.

The press published stories of bankrupt businessmen who had killed themselves rather than live through the disgrace of appearing in the bankruptcy court. Prominent men, directors of Land Credit Banks, committed suicide in what the *Age* described as 'the coolest and most deliberate manner'. Men who had been looked up to as pillars of bourgeois rectitude were indicted before the courts on criminal charges.

The crisis cast a dark shadow aslant the Australian dream. Borrowings from London for both public and private purposes virtually ceased. Public works and private building came to a halt. Unemployment in the building trades increased: the army of clerks, agents and unskilled workers who had been attracted to the cities by high wages were faced with a grim struggle for survival. The straiteners of humanity attributed the sufferings of the unemployed to their own folly, or their indolence, or both. In Sydney and Melbourne sections of the bourgeoisie clamoured for their removal from the cities as though their presence challenged bourgeois order. In Brisbane the unemployed roamed the streets, or demanded the resumption of public works. The radical press howled for more prosecutions and stiffer penalties. The Catholic Archbishop of Sydney warned the faithful of the terrible retribution for the worshippers of such false idols as Mammon or atheistic socialism. As Henry Parkes saw it, the bitter strikes of 1890, together with the alarming news about Baring's in London and the impending drying up of the cash flow, had shaken the 'whole fabric of commercial industry', compelling workers to squander their little hoards of thrift and reducing their families to destitution. The streets of Sydney were disturbed by petty conflicts as free workers clashed with unionists; drivers of drays were torn from their vehicles. Bourgeois society was like a city feeling the first effects of an earth tremor and fearful that the tremor might erupt into a destructive quake.

The charitable institutions could no longer cope with the great needs of the hungry and the homeless. As a last move the un-employed turned to the ministers of the Crown, beseeching them: 'Save us or we perish'. On 20 January 1892 a deputation waited

upon the Premier of Victoria, James Munro, to call his attention to
the acute distress existing among the labouring classes. But Munro,
warm-hearted, pleasure-loving man that he was, lectured them on
why government could do nothing for them: aid to the needy was
not a function of government; governments were not dispensers of
charity. The new Premier of New South Wales, George Dibbs, one
of the native-born who had risen to the top, told a similar delegation
that he did not want to hear any of their 'red-hot socialism'.
Government ministers could only wring their hands and say that
salvation of that kind was nothing appertaining to governments.
The unemployed must help themselves: government help would
only sap initiative; it was a violation of the liberty of the individual.

Up-country bitterness bred by the great strikes of 1890 had not
evaporated. Anarchy threatened to spread over the occupied parts
of the Australian bush. The end of the first wave of strikes in
November 1890, coinciding as that did with the anxious news about
the fate of Baring's, looked more like a truce than a permanent
settlement of the struggle for power in the country districts of
Australia. Men spoke as though the time had come for a final
showdown.

In Broken Hill, the conflict between unionized labour and the
Broken Hill Proprietary had been stewing since the great strike
of 1890. The company's continued attempts to break the union
resulted in another walkout in July 1892. Again, as in the shearers'
strikes of 1891, the employer imported free labourers. Again tumult
and shouting reverberated over the great dust heap. At the end of
September 1892, just as the days were growing hot, a contingent of
free labourers arrived by train from Adelaide. As they proceeded
from the station to the mines a crowd of some 200 hooted them,
shouting menacing words. When the free workers began to pitch
camp near the mine, unionists and their sympathizers in the town
quickly gathered to hoot, jeer and utter threats of what they would
do to any free labourer who went down the mine. Police were called
in. The uproar subsided as the unionists strolled to the pub for a
yarn, and the free labourers huddled in their tents, fearful of what
the night and the days ahead held in store for them.

By 8 November 1892 the resources of the Strikers' Defence
Committee were almost exhausted. The impoverishment of the men
and their families gave the employers the opportunity to dictate
harsh terms of settlement. There would be no conference: the men
must accept the owners' version of the rule of the mines. The
men accepted. Once again the unionists had engaged in a trial of
strength with the employers, and had had to acknowledge defeat.

Still the uproar continued, as the divisions and the bitternesses and the rancour of 1892 spilled over into 1893. That year the commercial depression deepened. More banks crashed; land companies went into insolvency; families starved. Despairing of finding temporal salvation in bourgeois philistine Australia, William Lane pushed ahead with his scheme to start a socialist utopia somewhere in the jungles of South America. The *Royal Tar*, bearing a crew of twenty-seven and 220 passengers, set out to three cheers for 'Lane' and 'Freedom' and the singing of 'Auld Lang Syne' on 16 July 1893, bound for a New Australia in Paraguay.

Three women novelists and short story writers had their flowering time during the decades of tumult and questioning. They were Rosa Praed, 'Tasma' (Jessie Catherine Couvreur) and Ada Cambridge. All three portrayed the men and women of property, and the intellectual servants of the propertied class. All three examined marriage as an institution which prostituted a woman to a man. In such novels as *Uncle Piper of Piper's Hill* (1889), 'Tasma' presented the reader with what was for her women's central problem in life: what were they to do when marriage entailed living in servitude to drunkards, bullies, gamblers and adulterers? How could women avoid the fate of becoming prostitutes to their husbands—not just sexual prostitutes, but prostitutes in everything? She did not know the answer: she was an artist; she presented a problem.

So did Ada Cambridge. She, too, was born in England, in 1844, and had married a curate whose head was stuffed with the quaint notion that Christ was an English country gentleman. The role of companion, secretary and housekeeper caused Ada Cambridge to be plagued by doubts. How could a woman fulfil herself if she was expected to devote all her talents, all her energies, all her time, to the service of the career of her husband and the upbringing of her children? By whose strange laws did it happen that in such a life of total surrender she was not even to know sexual satisfaction? Why should a woman be obliged to think of a man as a 'heaven-sent guide'? Why should she love, honour, respect and obey another human being who was often, though in public a professor of some ideal, a hypocrite or a weakling or an emotional cripple? She did not know the answer. She did not want to be known as a Mary or a Martha of the country parishes of Australia: she wanted to be known as a person.

> But, O my God, that madest me to feel!
> Forgive the anguish of the turning wheel.

While artists probed the great questions of life, political activists were seeking answers to the suffering they saw around them. Political labour had ideas on the role of the state as a mitigator of the lot of the forlorn. But thereby hung a problem for labour in all the colonies: how were they to obtain a majority at the ballot-box? The vote for Labor candidates was still small, and the movement was divided on certain fundamental issues. The argument between free traders and protectionists had not been resolved. Labor was also split over an issue which became known as 'the pledge'. On the one side were those who were looking for ways of preventing Labor members of Parliament from being corrupted by power and the luxury of life in what already had the reputation of being the best club in Sydney. They believed that Labor members ought to be required to take a pledge that they would vote according to the majority decision of Caucus. The anti-pledgers were led by Joseph Cook who argued that members should be free to follow their own consciences and that they were answerable not to the labour movement but to their own electorates.

One of the new Labor men who offered himself for preselection for the New South Wales elections of 1894 was William Morris Hughes. Hughes came on to the stage of public life a hater and a punisher, rather than a dreamer and visionary. A bitter experience of life drove him to make others suffer for all he had been through. He was born in Pimlico in London on 24 September 1862. His mother died when he was 7, and the boy was sent to the small Welsh village of Llandudno where he knew love and tenderness in the bosom of his aunt's family. Each Sunday in the chapel the very marrow in his bones froze as Welsh preachers depicted 'the eternal torments of hell to which sinners were doomed and from which neither faith nor works would save them'. When old enough to think, Hughes claimed he turned away from this 'stern and joyless creed'. Yet he continued to believe that as a man sowed so should he reap: like that Jehovah who had terrified him in his youth he judged men harshly.

He arrived in Moreton Bay, Brisbane, on 8 December 1884 and took his first job at Boulia shovelling and breaking stones to build the rail track from Mitchell to Charleville. There by day in nauseous heat with the flies crawling into his eyes, his mouth and his nose, he crushed and shovelled stones till every joint in his body cried out in agony. By night he and his fellow boarders at Boulia sat outside the pub. Some told tall yarns about the heat in the summer which caused the kangaroos to fall down dead. It was here that the young Hughes learned how to survive: he had acquired an undying hatred for the men or the society which condemned human beings to such a life. He was learning that the world belonged to the brave, to the tough, not to those who preached about love and forgiveness.

He moved to Sydney where he mixed with Australians who dreamed of a better world. He devoured the literature of some would-be improvers of mankind. He read Marx, Bellamy, William Morris, Grönlund, and indeed any work which purported to reveal the way forward for humanity. In his shop in Balmain he sold or lent the books which held out the promise of salvation by co-operation. He participated in the debates at Leigh House where speakers conferred on politics the atmosphere of a religious revival. But his feet remained on firm ground. For Hughes politics was a simple question of who had the cunning and the resources with which to come to the top.

Following the election of July 1894, George Reid was able to form a government with the support of the anti-pledge Laborites led by Joseph Cook. In many ways Reid and the Labor members were strange bedfellows. Reid was a man of limited horizons. Despite all the apparent extravagance of his public posturings, he applied the values and interests of the bookkeeper to the conduct of public affairs. For him political virtue lay in a balanced budget and the reduction of government expenditure. Retrenchment was his answer to most problems, even if that meant impoverishing the health and education of the inhabitants of New South Wales. A lawyer by training, he applied the yardstick of cost to every proposition before his government. His only genuine eccentricity was his physical appearance. In many ways he was a caricature of a man. By 1894, at 49, nature and appetite for food and strong drink had left him with what Alfred Deakin called an 'immense, unwieldy, jelly-like stomach, always threatening to break his waist-band', a thick neck and a 'many folded chin'. In Parliament he often slept and behaved like a man who was a slave to idleness and sloth rather than to the bourgeois ethic of work. In his waking moments he sucked sweets, or drank the waters of stupefaction as though indulgence in such pleasures was all he knew about happiness or ecstasy. He had no deep convictions about the future of Australia, no ideas on the future of society, except for some platitudes about British institutions and personal gain as the only incentive to which human beings ever responded.

Reid's liberal counterpart in Victoria, George Turner, was also said to have 'no horizon in his mind, no perspective in his politics, no proud surface of principle upon which he rested'. But where Reid often flirted with the Bohemian fringe in Sydney, to the scandal of the frowners in St Andrew's Cathedral, Turner was always a model of British bourgeois propriety. Balancing the books was his great passion in life. By his great industry, his zeal and his deep conviction he helped to raise that criterion into the standard by which politicians came to be judged in Australia.

The liberals wanted a compromise between the conservative insistence that property must enjoy special protection in any colonial federal constitution, and the labour call for one man one vote. They were prepared to abolish plural voting for the legislative assemblies in the various colonies, not out of any sympathy with labour or radical talk about political equality, but as a means of appeasing the radicals. Plural voting was abolished in New South Wales in 1893.

On the role of the state in economic life the liberals saw themselves as supporters of the traditional role of government in planting civilization in the Australian wilderness. Government had played the major role in the supply, distribution and control of labour in the convict period. Government had performed a similar role in the selection, transport and distribution of free immigrants. Government had developed a network of country and suburban railways not on any abstract principle of the role of government but because in Australian conditions private or free enterprise could not or would not embark on such activities. Liberals believed in a continuing partnership between the two.

The Mildura experiment in irrigation was a model of that harmony of interests which the liberals detected between government and free enterprise. Alfred Deakin had been greatly impressed by the irrigation schemes set up by George and William Chaffey in California when he visited there in 1885. In 1888 the government of Victoria gave the Chaffey brothers a grant of 250 000 acres of land and certain rights to the waters of the River Murray on condition that they developed irrigation farms in the area and spent at least £300 000 on improvements during the next twenty years. The government of South Australia interested them in a similar scheme at Renmark. In Los Angeles, the Chaffeys had developed their schemes under the American practice of free enterprise—that, in American experience, was what produced the greatest wealth, the greatest efficiency, the greatest service to the consumers and the highest material rewards to people of initiative, drive and unbounded energy. That was what generated a lively society, a society with a great pulse of life, a people who were magnificently alive, and not characterized by the dullness and mediocrity of people mollycoddled by governments, churches, charity organizations, or those self-appointed improvers of humanity who made decisions for people, thereby depriving them of the exercise of the right to decide for themselves, a necessary condition for the flowering of the personality. The Chaffeys built their model villages and adjoining irrigation farms at Mildura and Renmark to the background of angry exchanges between conservatives very voluble on the evils of government interference and radicals clamouring for more government control.

The liberals also set out to remedy the abuses and grave evils in colonial factories, where hours were long and working conditions were frequently dangerous and unsanitary. The conservatives took their usual stand: no government had a right to prescribe the conditions under which men or women or children sold their labour. That was their own indefeasible right. Labour and the radicals wanted the state to have factory acts which defined rigorously hours and conditions of labour, including safety regulations, health and sanitary arrangements. Labour also called for legislation to prescribe minimum wages for all workers in all industries. Again the liberals occupied the middle ground between the two extremes. Between 1873 and 1896 the parliaments of all colonies except Western Australia passed acts for the supervision and regulation of factories and workshops. On minimum wages the parliaments opted for the liberal compromise. They shied away from interfering directly with the laws of political economy to define what those wages should be, but were prepared to appoint Minimum Wages Boards in various industries, charged with the responsibility of examining the conditions in those industries and recommending minimum wages compatible with the capacity of industry to pay and the economic needs of workers.

In all the colonies the liberals found that the conservatives made effective use of the legislative councils as the bastion against all social reform. Reid was turning over in his mind the idea that a federation of the colonies on liberal terms might be a means of getting round this obstruction in the legislative councils of the Australian colonies. By 1894 it was a truism of politics in Australia that, for the bourgeoisie, federation was infinitely preferable to revolution, even if federation meant the loss of a measure of power for the colonial parliaments. In New South Wales Edmund Barton and other liberals or near liberals were pressing for the federal solution. Deakin and men of like mind were pushing hard in Victoria.

That magnificent advocate of the federal solution, Sir Henry Parkes, was nearing his end. The triumph of Reid, the younger man, had rubbed salt in his wounds. Cartoonists were still portraying him as a toady to the English titled nobility, or as a man who did not know how to withdraw with dignity from either public life or the marriage bed. In March 1896, being then almost 80, he had to face yet another 'financial difficulty'. To keep the wolf from the door he put his library of books under the hammer. When that did not raise enough he put his collection of chinaware up for auction. At one moment he pleaded piteously with his friends not to leave him in a breadless home, and the next he would take a carriage to some public place where he would tuck his arm around the waist of a pretty woman and boast with Rabelaisian relish that there was life in the old man yet.

At four in the morning of 27 April 1896 the great heart cracked. The government and people of New South Wales had the grace to recognize it as a 'great going'. On 29 April his body was carried to Faulconbridge at the foot of the Blue Mountains where ministers of the Anglican persuasion read solemnly the words which had been read over the remains of Wentworth: 'My heart was hot within me: and while I was thus musing, the fire kindled'. No words in the pulpit, in the press, in the Parliament, or in the watering holes of Sydney could do justice to either the grandeur or the folly. The *Sydney Morning Herald* wrote of him as a 'most imposing figure': the *Daily Telegraph* compared him with the American, Abe Lincoln. He had been a man of vision. He had dreamed a great dream of Australia as the mistress of the southern seas. He had dreamed an even greater dream of an Australia where enlightenment wrought the great miracle of bringing wisdom and understanding to all people. But nature had so fashioned him that the greatness he coveted remained for ever out of reach. The future lay with the very people who had brought such pain to him in his closing years. He was not to know that what he stood for—federation under the Crown—was destined to weigh for generations to come on the brains of the living.

3

'Federation or Revolution?'

Australians were becoming confident that they could paint their own world and sing their own songs. All the gusto of the Sydney-siders was in the poetry of A. B. ('Banjo') Paterson. In 1895 his collection of ballads, *The Man From Snowy River*, was published. Sydney and the bush went wild with enthusiasm, and so even did Melbourne. By the end of the year sales had exceeded the wildest hopes of author and publisher. Paterson used the Australian language as his medium, the Australian bush as his setting and Australians as his characters. Here was a portrait of Australian men, of the men who knew and loved the bushland, the men who were not curs or cowards, the men who knew how to endure to the end without whining or indulging in self-pity or reaching for a crutch, the men worthy to recite the bushman's creed about kindness in another's trouble and courage in their own.

Yet not all the flowering of Australian writing and painting in the 1890s could upset or seriously threaten the domination of the Australian reading public by English literature. There was still no sign that the centre of literary gravity had moved from London to Sydney. The columns of the *Bulletin*, which carried on its title page the slogan 'Australia for the Australians' and boasted of its role as midwife of national sentiment, were still more concerned with the discussion and publication of the latest from London than with the local product. To the undying pain of Henry Lawson the professors of English literature at the Australian universities still wrote with condescension of the work of local writers.

Nor had the historians so far challenged Wentworth's idea of Australia as a 'new Britannia in another world'. The historians of the centenary in 1888, such as F. M. Bladen and George Burnett Barton, did not question the myth which saw the history of Australia as a story of national growth fostered by British genius and enterprise after 'a melancholy and ignominious beginning'. The historians had not observed the dictum that the whole point of telling the truth about the past was to help people to dispense with the past. They had not essayed the task of writing the history of that Australia which was coming to be: they were ensuring that the British past would continue to weigh on the brain of the living, that the myth of the past would come between the people and the realization of their own powers.

The moves towards federation were the product neither of popular hunger for independence nor of any widespread determination that Australians should claim responsibility for making their own history. In fact, as Alfred Deakin observed, the prospect of federation had failed to rouse public enthusiasm. The federalists, he wrote, were striving against 'the inexhaustible inertia of our populace as a whole'.

From time to time since 1847, politicians and officials had suggested that some form of Australia-wide administration might be desirable. In 1889 Major-General James Bevan Edwards, who was visiting Sydney to investigate the defence of the Australian colonies, reported that the only way to prevent a Chinese invasion lay in a federation of the colonies. Sensing that here was a chance to show posterity that there had once been a man of stature in Australia, the aging Henry Parkes had begun to preach federation to the Australian people. He had begun to champion a constitution which was to tie his adopted country in the twentieth century to the chariot wheels of the past. In February 1890 he dominated a federal conference at which thirteen colonial delegates agreed to establish a convention which would consider a federal constitution under the British Crown.

In March 1891, delegates to the National Australasian Convention met in Sydney to debate a draft constitution which had been prepared chiefly by the Premier of Queensland, Samuel Griffith. Griffith was a lawyer who called himself a liberal, because he had first come into prominence as an opponent of the squatters. His presence was commanding, his intellect towering, and like most of the delegates he wanted to remain side by side with the dear old England they all loved so well. Presided over by Henry Parkes, 46 representatives of the Australasian colonies, including New Zealand, endorsed the basic elements of this constitution. They also identified the issues which were to divide them—liberals from conservatives, protectionists from free-traders—when the debate resumed later in the decade.

After the convention rose, the delegates returned to colonies preoccupied with the problems of the depression. Debate was not resumed in earnest until March 1897 when elected delegates assembled in Parliament House, Adelaide, just as the dry South Australian summer was drawing to a close. Queenslanders stayed away, and the New Zealanders had withdrawn from any further involvement. All were middle-of-the-road men drawn from the ranks of the conservatives and the liberals in their respective colonies. They were colonial pragmatists who eschewed the entrenched ground of political ideology: men who believed federation was preferable to revolution, who believed in loyalty to throne and empire. They were enlightened bourgeois politicians who believed the interests of the bourgeoisie would be best served by federal union under the Crown. The one man who could reasonably be called a Labor delegate, William Trenwith from Victoria, was about to give up the long, unequal struggle: he had already decided in his heart that it was better for him to be a door-keeper in the house of Mammon than to dwell in the tents of unionists and socialists.

The convention was unofficially led by Edmund Barton, a genial soul who was a Pontius Pilate type of liberal. He did not like to face up to big questions. He was a man of wit and wide-ranging sympathies, but no one ever knew whether his belief in compromise sprang from some private political creed or from a more cynical belief that compromise preserved the way of life he loved, that life of ease of the patricians of New South Wales. When the formal business of the convention began on the second day there was nothing new in Barton's summary of the type of federal constitution the convention should establish. He proposed a parliament consisting of a State Assembly or Senate, and a National Assembly or House of Representatives. The National Assembly would be elected by districts formed on a population basis and would possess the sole power of originating bills, appropriating revenue or imposing taxation. He proposed an Executive consisting of a governor-general appointed by the Queen, and of such persons as might be appointed as his advisers. There should be a Supreme Court which should also be the High Court of Appeal for each colony in the federation.

Richard Chaffey Baker, President of the Legislative Council of South Australia, assumed the task of explaining why conservatives would not entirely agree with the Barton resolutions. Baker was by birth and education a profound conservative. He had been born into a patrician family in Adelaide in 1842 and had been educated in England, at Eton and Trinity College, Cambridge. As a firm believer in British institutions he wanted a form of government with which the delegates were familiar. A constitution, he said in the language of a man making a Burkean point in basic English, should be of historical growth, and not be manufactured. There was the rub for a conservative. As a conservative he maintained that the Senate must enjoy equal powers with the Representatives, the people's house—or there would not be equality of power between the two parties to the federal contract. But he did not want to be dogmatic: he was a sound British pragmatist.

So the issue was joined. In general the conservatives believed in constitutional safeguards for the protection of minority interests, especially the interests of property and education. By contrast the liberals believed that complete political democracy—one man one vote (even possibly universal franchise), equal electoral districts, and the limitation of the powers of any second chamber to the role of a house of review—was the way to avoid a future explosion. For liberals, the ballot-box was, paradoxically, the preserver of the existing order of society. The conservatives wanted the Senate to possess equal powers with the People's House: the liberals argued that would allow the minority to impose their will on the majority. The conservatives advocated indirect election of senators: the liberals proposed that the whole State should be the electorate. The conservatives wanted to vest the reserve powers of the Crown in the Governor-General: the liberals were divided and uncertain about that issue, thinking that these reserve powers had long been dead and buried.

The real debate began when the convention discussed a detailed draft. At first it looked as though the liberals had had their way: the Senate was to be elected directly by the people in each State rather than by the State parliaments as earlier drafts had proposed. But on all other questions the conservatives—Baker's men as they were called—had prevailed. On the crucial question of the right of the Senate to amend money bills Sir John Forrest announced confidently that the small States—Tasmania, Western Australia and South Australia—had the numbers. George Reid, to the disgust of Deakin, played politics. He went for compromise. The Senate could have the right to reject a money bill, but not to amend it. That was carried by 25 votes to 23.

It had become clear that the liberals did not have the numbers with which to write their views into the constitution. The best they could hope for was compromise. The convention adjourned on 5 May and some of the delegates sailed to England for the celebrations to mark the sixtieth anniversary of Queen Victoria's accession to the throne. In the colonies Jubilee Day, 22 June 1897, was marked by outbursts of loyal affection, festivities and services of worship. The *Worker* in Brisbane dismissed these 'Tory grovellings'. It wanted Australians to sing from the bottom of their hearts, 'God save the people'. But the people's heart belonged to the Queen. She was a symbol of that peace and material progress which they valued. In the words of the Catholic Archbishop of Melbourne, Thomas Joseph Carr, anyone who advocated separation from Great Britain must be either a knave or a dotard.

The delegates to the Federal Convention assembled again in Parliament House, Sydney, on 2 September 1897 and the debates, the haggling, the compromising continued. The conservatives and delegates from the smaller colonies wanted each of the States, regardless of their population numbers, to be represented by the same number of senators. This, they said, would protect the interests in the smaller States against the tyranny of the majority. But, objected the liberals, if the Senate was not to represent the will of the majority of voters, then at very least it could not be allowed to veto government bills, especially money bills. Again and again, the debate came back to the central question: where did power reside, in the people or in some minority?

In the same way, the liberal suggestion that deadlocks between the two houses might be resolved by holding a popular referendum aroused the fears and suspicions of conservatives and delegates from less populous colonies. J. H. Gordon, a member of the Legislative Council of South Australia, asked why there should be a Senate at all if the will of the people was to prevail. Sir John Forrest added that for his part if he could not get what he wanted then he would abandon federation. He was not going to be a party to any decision which empowered the more populous colonies to coerce the less populous. Federation was in danger.

Alfred Deakin told the delegates they were faced with a difference between those who had faith in the wisdom of the people and those who believed in the right, perhaps the divine right, of the few to rule. The conservatives almost choked with indignation. Simon Fraser, a member of the best club for gentlemen in the whole of Australia, the Legislative Council of Victoria, declared tersely he was not a believer in the decision of the people, notorious as they were for being 'fickle'.

While the tempest raged, Edmund Barton held his peace. But on 15 September he told the convention that the time had come for the display of wisdom and patriotism. New South Wales and Victoria must allay the dread of the less populous States. These in their turn must not wreck federation by pressing too hard for the federal principle against the principle of responsible government. Both sides must make a sane decision for the settlement of disputes. While the wild men of the convention hung their heads, Barton presented the wisdom of the middle way, arguing that bombast must give way before the duty to save federation even if such compromises entailed a vagueness in drafting displeasing to constitutional lawyers.

Compromise it was to be. Enough delegates from the less populous States agreed that the Senate should have a power to suggest, but not to make, amendments to money bills. On the method of resolving deadlocks, both the States and the people were given a voice. The Governor-General was to be appointed by the Queen, and to have vested in him all the reserve powers of the Crown. They had succeeded in drafting a federal constitution without abandoning the British heritage of responsible government. They remained loyal to the throne. They ended as they had begun with a profession of their love for Her Gracious Majesty.

Early in 1898 they had a constitution which they were ready to submit to a referendum of voters in each of the colonies. Alfred Deakin went home to pray. Edmund Barton drained his glass as usual with melancholy in his eyes and despair on his drooping lips. George Reid was already back in Sydney, knowing, for how could anyone not know, that neither Barton, nor Deakin, nor Kingston, nor Forrest, really liked or trusted him. Sir John Forrest was on the high seas bound for Perth. He believed that with any luck the federal constitution would prevent the Australian colonies from jumping over to extreme socialism for a long time. But he must hurry: 'lick on the lug' men were stirring up trouble in the recently established goldfields of Western Australia.

Many Labor leaders mistrusted the proposed federation. In Melbourne the *Tocsin* declared that equal representation of the States in the Senate was far too high a price to pay for federation, because that put a Tory enclave in charge of Australia. Democracy must not be trapped in an 'unyielding and cruel Constitution Act'. William Morris Hughes and the Melbourne radical Bernard O'Dowd both warned that the constitution had entrenched the power of a reactionary minority. They warned that a constitution which was deaf to the democratic will was likely to provoke violent revolution. No one seemed to care, no one even wanted to ask, as O'Dowd believed it was important to ask, why at the decisive moments of their history Australians preferred the conservative solution. Why were Australians enslaved to the world of Mr Money Bags? Why did so many Australians drink pointless toasts, and sing a meaningless hymn about their feelings for a widow who lived over 12 000 miles away? Australians were about to make their own contribution to the history of human folly.

In Sydney as the referendum approached, George Reid once again performed as a Yes-No man, rather than as a father of federation. At a huge public meeting he presented brilliantly all the New South Wales arguments against the bill, clowned his way through a series of vulgar jokes about the Victorians, played on local loyalties, and then, with one of those disarming contradictions which endeared him to some and angered so many, he astonished his audience by telling them he proposed to vote for the bill. Barton was disgusted. On reading a report of the speech, Deakin decided more firmly than ever that the man was not to be trusted. Reid had widened the gap between himself and the men who would come to power in a federal Australia. But Reid believed he was fighting for New South Wales, and for the preservation of democracy in Australia.

The referendum was carried in Victoria, Tasmania and South Australia, but received insufficient support in New South Wales. The following January, the premiers agreed to modifications proposed by Reid to satisfy the objections of that state. A second referendum was held on 20 June 1899 at which there was a decisive 'Yes' vote in New South Wales. The referendums in Victoria, South Australia and Tasmania were formalities. On 2 October a referendum was held in Queensland; they too decided, by a narrow margin, to join the federation. In no colony did more than 46.63 per cent of qualified voters cast a yes vote. Federation was still dragging its feet in the popular mind: the inertia continued despite all the passion in the parliaments and the press.

In the West there was uproar over the federation question. The restless miners on the goldfields at Coolgardie and Kalgoorlie were seeing their independence threatened as large mining companies moved on to the fields. They were angry that the Forrest Government refused to protect them, for Sir John Forrest was the John Bull of the West, a man who boasted of his contempt for the Rights of Man, a man who regarded the diggers' talk of democracy and miners' rights as the bellowings of anarchists. Now they were pressing Forrest to submit the amended Federation Bill immediately to a referendum of electors. Forrest delayed: he wanted concessions. Among other things, he wanted the federal Parliament to undertake to build a railway from Kalgoorlie to Port Augusta and for the Parliament of Western Australia to retain the power to impose its own customs duties for five years after the adoption of the first federal tariff. But out on the goldfields the cry had gone up: 'federation now, or separation of the goldfields from Western Australia with federation'. Eventually Forrest submitted. In July 1900, a referendum of Western Australia voters adopted the constitution. The federation was complete.

By then the passions of the people had been roused by events in South Africa. All through the debate over the Federal Bill the press had been publishing reports of the abominations committed by Boers on British subjects. When Great Britain declared war on the

Boer Republics on 5 October 1899 all the Australian colonies offered to send troops. A patriotic fervour swept the country. The Australian colonies were about to show the world their racial solidarity with the British Empire.

Some were unconvinced. A clergyman in Sydney told his congregation the war had been undertaken by greedy men eager for land or gold. William Morris Hughes accused Great Britain of engaging in the contemptible and cowardly undertaking of bullying the Boers. Members of the Labor Opposition in the Queensland Legislative Assembly laughed raucously when the Premier, James Dickson, indulged in a sentimental harangue on the sufferings of the British. Labor was not going to be led astray by jingoistic fever or by any mad claim that the Lord had reserved large parts of the world for the British. Henry Lawson was angry: Australians were willing to cross the sea and shoot men whom they had never seen and whose quarrel they did not and could not understand. England was not fighting for England but for the interests of wealthy syndicates. Australians were going to help a big nation crush a little one. They were committing a great evil just to have a 'knock-round', just to have 'some fun!'

Between 28 October and 5 November 1200 men with horses and equipment were embarked for the Transvaal to the sound of cheering, patriotic music and prayers of clergymen. The members of the Australian horse contingent were mainly bushmen—shearers, station hands, farmers or squatters, and the officers were squatters or sons of squatters.

After they arrived in Cape Town a woman short of height, plump of figure, and noble of face, asked 'Banjo' Paterson, 'Why have you come?' Why had such fine fellows as the Australians come to fight against those fighting for their liberty and their country? Australians, she said, did not understand. This was a capitalist war! The British wanted to get control of the Rand and the mines. She was Olive Schreiner, the author of the book *The Story of an African Farm*. The British, like the Athenians of old, had been guilty of hubris, or overweening pride and arrogance. Like the Athenians they would be punished.

When a man was murdered by a gang of blood-drunk hoodlum 'patriots' for having the temerity to say he was not convinced of the justice of the British cause in South Africa, Professor Wood, the first Challis Professor of History in the University of Sydney, took the risk of sharing with the reading public in Sydney his inner agonies about what the British were doing. Patriots and jingoes threatened to bully him into silence. In Hobart a meeting addressed by W. A. Holman was broken up. In Australia the world belonged to the tough, to the descendants of those men and women who had robbed the Aborigines of their land, who had grown rich and powerful by defying the conventions of civilized behaviour. The Australians in South Africa were the first representatives to the world of this new race of men bred by the ancient continent and its rugged history. The treatment of dissent during the Boer War was a strong hint that this new race of men were strangers to the ideal of not putting on black looks when a neighbour behaved in a way which was displeasing. Conformism was basic to survival.

On 19 May London went delirious with delight when news spread that Mafeking had been relieved: Melbourne and other Australian cities held their celebrations on 23 May. In all the cities the day developed into what the *Age* called 'a mad orgie [*sic*] of popular fervour'. Melbourne, the city in which the Goddess of respectability normally had her most fervent worshippers, was caught up in a saturnalia. A huge crowd thronged into the city. There was merry laughter, there were hurrahs, there were crackers, there was much waving of flags and singing of anthems. No displays of dissent were tolerated. As the *Age* put it: 'Woe to the man who did not "doff his cady" while the national anthem was being chanted. Off it went for him in a twinkling. If he demurred the crowd roughed him up'.

The premiers sent a delegation to London for discussions with Chamberlain if need be during the passage of the Australian constitution through the British Parliament. On 21 May 1900 Joseph Chamberlain introduced the bill into the House of Commons. He assured his fellow members that in sanctioning the union of Australia they had not impaired or weakened the Empire. This was the consummation of a great achievement, a tribute to the wisdom and patriotism of their Australian kinsmen. When the delegates heard on 21 May that all was well with the bill, they seized each others' hands and danced hand in hand in a ring around the centre of the room to express their jubilation.

As the year ended, in Rome Rosendo Salvado, a monk who had striven for 44 years to plant the image of Christ in the heart of the Aborigines of New Holland, was dying. Observers noticed late in November that he seemed to be trying to recall the names of the Aborigines whom he had loved, but no intelligible words escaped his lips. The men who had performed the miracle of drafting a constitution for Australia had not so much as dropped a word about the original inhabitants of the ancient continent. Henry Lawson was again at odds with the world in which he was living. Federation would mean royal times in Sydney, he prophesied, for the 'cuff and collar push'. There would be 'lots of dreary drivel and clap-trap'. One thing was certain: '. . . the men who made the land will not be there'.

4

The Tablets of the Law

From early morning on 1 January 1901 trams, trains and ferry boats carried thousands of people into the city of Sydney for the greatest day in their history: the inauguration of the Commonwealth of Australia. It was to be a people's festival. Triumphal arches stretched across the streets along which the representatives of the trades marched. Gaily caparisoned horses drew fire-engines to roars of applause. The crowd cheered wildly for the Eight Hours Banner, for the men of the Shearers' Union, the Australian Workers' Union, for the noble bushmen from the backblocks, the men with a certain freedom of bearing, the men who breathed the spirit of the outback, silver-miners from Broken Hill, gold-miners, seamen, tin-miners, timber-gatherers, tailors and slaughtermen. The crowd clapped classically draped ladies, wearing helmets and in all other ways suitably costumed to represent what the day was all about—Britannia and Australia. The crowd murmured their approval for another car in the procession containing a bust of Sir Henry Parkes, the father of what it was all about. Its banner proudly bore one of the many slogans on which he had conferred a measure of immortality: 'One People, One Destiny'. The highest honour was paid to the imperial troops, who presented a magnificent appearance, fine upstanding men, straight-backed, astride their well-groomed horses. They were on their way to the swearing-in pavilion in Centennial Park where the inauguration ceremony was to take place.

After hymns and prayers the clerk, E. G. Blackmore, read the Queen's Proclamation: 'We do hereby declare that on and after the First Day of January One Thousand nine hundred and one, the people of New South Wales, Victoria, South Australia, Queensland, Tasmania and Western Australia shall be united in a Federal Commonwealth of Australia'.

The Governor-General elect, Lord Hopetoun, was resplendent in black-and-gold full court dress, nature having endowed him with the height that impressed and a temperament to match his high position. He had all the graces of the nobleman and had taught himself to employ with colonials the non-stop bow, achieved by rocking backward and forward on the soles and heels of his feet. He possessed in abundance the 'tranquil consciousness of an effortless superiority'. On his face he wore the smile of the man whose very career depended on his public face, one of those smiles which those born to rule graciously bestowed on those born to serve.

Guns boomed; the band played the National Anthem. The bright helmets of the soldiers flashed in the sunlight, the feathers waved on the headgear of the guards, the rich uniforms of the Indian soldiers gave a warm glow of oriental opulence to the scene, as the last strains of the National Anthem roused the spirit of the crowd to fever pitch. The roars, the shouts, and the cooees rolled away over the grassy parkland towards the very vast sea on which their ancestors had ridden to glory or damnation on their way to plant British civilization in an inhospitable environment.

The Governor-General then asked Edmund Barton, Alfred Deakin, Sir George Turner, Sir William John Lyne, Charles Cameron Kingston, Sir James Dickson, Sir John Forrest, Richard Edward O'Connor and Elliott Lewis to be members of the Federal Executive Council of the Commonwealth of Australia.

To the *Bulletin* Inauguration Day was distinguished by its servility. It called on Australians to proclaim an Australia for the Australians, and turn their backs on 'Queen Victoria's nigger Empire'. Down at Shepparton in Victoria 'Tom Collins' (Joseph Furphy), the sage of the Riverine (*sic*), was revising those sections of *Such Is Life* in which he professed his attachment to the Australian idea of equality: 'It acknowledges no aristocracy, except one of service and self-sacrifice, in which he that is chief shall be servant, and he that is greatest of all, servant of all'. Australia now belonged to the firm of 'John Bull and Family'. But Mr Deakin and Edmund Barton could not see that there was anything amiss in what they had done, or understand why poets and visionaries should believe Australia had been betrayed or enslaved to Mammon. Mr Deakin was exhausted, but it was the exhaustion of a man who saw himself as one of the architects of a great federation under the Crown.

Almost immediately, the leaders began campaigning for the first federal election. Barton was still the Laodicean: he blew neither hot nor cold. He was neither a liberal nor a conservative: he was neither a free-trader nor a protectionist: he was neither British nor Australian, but a middle-of-the-road man, an Australian bourgeois politician. For Barton there was sober applause. George Reid clowned his way through the campaign, but it was the humour of a disappointed man. No one seemed to notice that by being trapped into using liberals such as Syme and Deakin as whipping boys Reid was coming perilously close to being the leader of political conservatism in Australia.

Mr Deakin explained to the electors the extent to which the state must interfere with individual freedom if Australia were to remain both white and progressive in things material. He was expounding a political philosophy for those who believed in the Australian dream. In a language intelligible to every man he explained how a judicious use of state assistance to economic activity could create a society in which there was both material well-being for all and equality of opportunity without the evil of servility or the vice of mediocrity. The task of Australian liberalism was to steer that middle course between the conservatives and Labor. There was no need to change society, because in Australia the Australian dream was being realized within the existing social order.

Labor was not sure where it stood. Some of its members subscribed to the slogans of millenarians and visionaries: they prophesied that a time would come when the sun would dance with joy over 'the renovated world of Labour Triumphant'. Some believed in the goal of a co-operative Commonwealth under a democracy of man as declared ages ago by 'the good revolutionist of Nazareth'. Others were as pragmatic as Barton. Some described themselves as believers in socialism without doctrines. John Christian Watson was such a man. Tall, handsome and gracious, he retained in his adulthood the vivacity of a clever boy. Apart from vague statements about approving any measure which would increase the material well-being of the worker, Watson was not committed to any ideology. He was fond of saying that Labor was the party of evolution rather than revolution, but neither he nor any of his colleagues in the New South Wales Parliament ever sketched what they were evolving towards.

They were politicians in an age sympathetic to reform within the existing system. In March of 1901 the Reverend Mr Edgar electrified his congregation by giving permission to the men during a Melbourne heatwave to remove their coats. He did not make so bold as to give women permission to remove their hats, because that would have transgressed St Paul's injunction to women to cover their heads in church. The supporters of the women's movement were working for the abolition of all those laws, conventions and social customs which condemned women to a position of inferiority. In September 1900 a newspaper to do battle for women appeared for the first time in Melbourne. It was called symbolically the *Australian Woman's Sphere* and was edited by Vida Goldstein. Vida Goldstein did not wear on her face, or put into words, any picture of men as the enemies of women. Taking as the epigraph for their paper that great standby of the secular humanists from the time of the Renaissance to the present, the words of Terence: 'I am a human being, and I believe nothing human is outside my sphere', these writers declared their aim to be 'the highest interests of women'.

Like Labor they were ballot-box democrats: they believed the victory of their cause would begin by winning votes for women. Believing the best way to discredit their opponents was to encourage them to reveal what was in their minds, they filled their columns with the speeches of men such as Sir John Madden, the Chief Justice of Victoria. He had warned in 1895 that women's suffrage would abolish soldiers, war, racing, hunting, football, cricket and all manly games. Sir John based his stand on the Bible: 'Thy desire shall be to thy husband, and he shall rule over thee'. 'Women suffragists', he believed, 'are the worst class of socialists. Their idea of freedom is polyandry, free love, lease marriages, and so on. Are those qualifications for the franchise? Are we going to allow women who would sap the very foundation of the nation to have votes?' The *Australian Woman's Sphere* replied with a list of the men who were not disqualified from voting: effeminate fops, drunkards, larrikins, drunken savages, opium-smoking Chinese, prize-fighters, 'Fat Man' politicians and wife-kickers.

Barton was the realist. As women already had the vote in South Australia it would be constitutionally impossible to exclude them in a Commonwealth Electoral Act. But he drew the line at women having the right to become members of either house of the Commonwealth Parliament. Labor continued to advocate one person one vote, but did nothing. George Reid clowned his way through the question of votes for women just as he had clowned his way through the argument about free trade and protection. There was a nothingness so deep in his mind on all great public questions that no one could fathom it.

At polling time on 29 and 30 March 1901, Barton and the supporters of the middle way obtained a working majority, provided the members of the Labor Party voted with them. Labor was prepared to keep the Barton Government in power in return for concessions to the Labor platform. Labor's main planks were declared to be: (1) White Australia; (2) adult suffrage; (3) old age pensions; (4) a citizen army; and (5) compulsory arbitration.

The aim of the Barton Government was to preserve the structure of society which existed in Australia. To ensure that, there was one principle from which they believed they should never make a concession: White Australia. That was to be the first principle by which the Commonwealth was to be administered and guided. The problem was how that was to be achieved. The Secretary of State for the Colonies, Joseph Chamberlain, had informed the premiers of the colonies in 1897 that any exclusion or discrimination based on a distinction of race or colour conflicted with the principle of equality before the law of all members of the British Empire. The British Government was also anxious not to offend Japan, on whose friendship and support the British were relying to contain the Russians in the Far East. For this reason the Barton Government accepted the suggestion that Australia should follow the precedent established in the province of Natal by applying the 'dictation test'.

Deakin told members that the national manhood, the national character, and the national future were at stake. Australians wanted to be one people, a united race inspired by the same ideas. Labor speakers stressed the threat of coloured labour to the workers' standard of living. That nice chap Chris Watson declared that the real question was whether Australians would want their brothers or their sisters to be married to any of these people. King O'Malley, a picturesque mountebank from North America, wanted Australia for the white race. Hughes declared that the 'leprous curse' would make Australia a country no longer fit for the white man. Jim Page, a Labor member from Queensland, pictured the horrors of 'plague leprosy', of the 'docile Hindoo' and 'full-blooded bucks' from Bombay being let loose among white women.

Outside Parliament the radical press whipped up the hysteria. The *Worker* in Brisbane asked whether Queenslanders wanted their state to be known as 'Mongrelia' or 'Kanakaland', or 'Leperland', or as a 'suburb of Asia'. Australian interests must not be sacrificed on the altar of Britain's eastern policy. The *Bulletin* put it quite bluntly: white Anglo-Saxons could not intermarry with niggers without lowering the national type: the Anglo-Saxon must be preserved in his pure state if he was to retain position as 'the best and strongest and most intellectual on this earth'. On 23 December 1901 Lord Hopetoun gave the royal assent to an Act to place certain restrictions on immigration. Among those who could be denied entry was any person who was unable to complete a dictation test in any European language, when asked to do so by an immigration officer. A tablet of the law of Australia had been cut.

The second tablet in the law of Australia was cut soon after. It was the Pacific Islands Labourers Act which was aimed at ending the use of coloured labour in the sugar industry in Queensland. The use of labour-saving devices, Barton assured the House of Representatives in October 1901, had made the South Sea islanders (the Kanakas) a declining factor in the industry. The question, as he saw it, was whether they could arbitrarily dispense with the remaining black workers without harming the sugar industry, which, he conceded, stood between Queensland and bankruptcy, or whether this development should be left to the slow evolution of ages. The answer was clear. Under the Act, Pacific islanders were banned from entering Australia after 31 March 1904. Any remaining after 31 December 1906 would be deported. The concerns of the cane growers were met by the government providing tariff protection to the industry. White Australia was now a tablet of the law. The third tablet of the law declared that no coloured labour was to be employed in the carriage of mails within the limits of the Commonwealth.

Until the passage of this racial legislation the Australian colonies had enjoyed a reputation in the United States and Europe as a paradise for the working man, where minimum wages, factory acts, conciliation, arbitration and trade unions had introduced the workers to a measure of middle-class affluence. Now the *New York Times*, the London *Times* and papers in India and Japan were saying that Australians had descended from their lofty eminence as a society of peace and goodwill. Australia had suddenly acquired notoriety in the civilized world as a centre of human barbarism. But Australians pushed on, untouched by guilt or anxiety, with the defence of their own standards of living and purity of race. White Australia, as Australians saw it, would make Australia a Working Man's Paradise.

It was to be a paradise in which Australians did not have responsibility for the defence of their own garden. Defence was an issue on which they were deeply divided. The members of the government and the Reid group were quite content to leave decisions on defence in the hands of the Imperial Government. Forrest professed he was content to have 'one of the most distinguished officers in His Majesty's Army' as commanding officer. Watson interjected that there were plenty of Australians who filled that bill. Reid insisted that control of the forces in Australia by 'an imported military man' would be infinitely better than the 'uncontrolled power of a civilian and a colonial'. Barton insisted that to maintain the imperial connection Australian forces must be placed under British control. Australia was not a nation; it had no national flag or national anthem; it had no national emblems on its postage stamps; its children swore allegiance overseas. The Australian colonies had not agreed to form a nation: they had agreed to unite 'in one indissoluble Federal Commonwealth under the Crown of the United Kingdom of Great Britain and Ireland'. That was the fourth tablet of the law.

Barton, Deakin, Kingston and Turner agreed that to advance Australian industry and production the government must protect Australian manufactures against outside competition. There would be a minimum standard of living below which the government would not allow any member of society to sink. The talented and the industrious would be rewarded with great wealth. That was the Australian dream. That sort of protection of local industry was the fifth tablet of the law of the Commonwealth.

While British civilization was being set in stone in Australia, the veneer of civilization was vanishing fast on the plains of South Africa: terrible things were happening. In attempting to restore law and order after victory in battle, British soldiers were descending to the level of the beasts of the field. Near Pretoria in February 1902 three Australians, Lieutenant Henry 'Breaker' Morant, Peter Handcock and George Witton were tried before a British military court for shooting prisoners of war. For using ruthless methods to fight a brutal war, Morant and Handcock were executed by firing squad. Morant behaved with the courage which had characterized his whole life. To the delight of his supporters, he wrote a last ballad in which he summed up the whole episode in the line: `Butchered to make a Dutchman's holiday'. No one saw the lives of Morant and Handcock as part of the price Australians paid for the imperial connection.

On 14 January 1902 Henry Bournes Higgins, the Member for North Melbourne, told the House of Representatives that the war had spattered shame and degradation on the fair name of England. The English, he said, were glorying in their evil intention to kill every Boer who did not submit to their tyranny. But the crowds remained patriotic. In synagogues and churches rabbis, priests and parsons promised divine rewards for those who volunteered for the war. Dissenters were vilified as unpatriotic. In New South Wales the Minister of Education instituted inquiries into all teachers suspected of making disloyal utterances.

On 12 February the Prime Minister of Australia, Edmund Barton, went down to Circular Quay in Sydney to say farewell to the first federal contingent to serve in South Africa. Neither wind nor rain could chill or damp the enthusiasm of soldiers and onlookers. For the first time in its history it was Australia, not any State or colony, that was going to war. At the same time the campaign against the war intensified. The Irish, most members of the Labor Party in New South Wales, the shearers, the rouseabouts, the members of the Australian Workers' Union—the most nationalistically Australian section of Australia—wanted an immediate end to the war on the basis of amnesty, compensation and immediate self-government.

In Australia the news of the Boer surrender on 31 May 1902 was greeted with an outburst of wild rejoicing. Church bells rang. Ships hooted on Sydney Harbour, Port Phillip and the Derwent. Crackers exploded. Men and women danced in the streets. Their God had not let them down. The British had brought salvation to both victor and vanquished. The Boers had recognized the lawful sovereignty of Edward VII, and accepted a gift of £3 million for the rebuilding of their farms and countryside. The cost had been light. It represented the cost of only two weeks' fighting in Africa. Of the 16 175 officers and men sent from Australia at either State or federal expense, or at imperial expense, 251 had died of wounds, 267 of disease, or 518 all told. The labour press grieved. The British Empire had spent £250 million on the war and all the Empire had got out of it was 'a monstrous pyramid of skulls and two Dutch islands in the Dark Continent'. The way was now clear for the 'capitalist cowards and animals to seize and enjoy the loot for which they instigated the war'.

The members of the Barton Government had other things on their minds. They were busy cutting the tablets of two more fundamental laws of the Commonwealth of Australia. The liberals and Labor agreed that as women were entering the work force in industry and professions they should not be deprived of the privilege to vote. William Lyne had confidence in the capacity of women. It was, he believed, anomalous that anyone should hesitate to extend the franchise to women when people in Australia and elsewhere in the British Empire had been content to 'sit under the domination of Queens who ruled well and ably'. Australia, as on other questions, should set an example of advancement to the world. Sir Edward Braddon and other conservatives were not happy with the proposal. They believed women belonged in the home and not on the hustings. But liberals and Labor members stood firm: a country notorious for the excesses of male domination conferred on women equality at the ballot-box.

On the question of franchise for Aborigines no such passions were aroused. No one argued that the equality to be extended to women should also embrace the Aborigines. Chris Watson, advocate of the brotherhood of man, said he did not much care how it was done, as long as those savages and slaves in the northern and western portions of Australia were not allowed to run the electorates in which they resided. King O'Malley declared there was no scientific evidence that the Aborigine was a human being at all. Edward Braddon remarked that if anything tended to make the concession of female suffrage worse it would be giving it to any of the numerous gins of the blackfellows. The Electoral Act of 1902 set in place the next tablet of the law: that all electorates should contain more or less equal numbers of voters. A little elasticity was allowed by way of compromise to those rural interests who feared a tyranny of the cities over the country.

To the question of what Australia was to be Mr Deakin, Sir Edmund Barton, Sir John Forrest, Sir George Turner, Charles Cameron Kingston and other members of the Commonwealth Government did not pause to give an answer. So far they had chosen the part of compromisers. They were neither British nor Australian. Early in 1902 a book had reached Australia in which a bush girl had raised the question of the identity of, and the right of self-expression and self-fulfilment of, Australian women. She was Stella Miles Franklin. With bitter irony she called her work *My Brilliant Career*. She was one of those 'hot young hearts beating in strong breasts' in Australia, one of the legion of women who wanted to know how they could get out from under the large net in which they were trapped. The book was a cry of anguish against male domination in Australia, a girl who wanted to decide for herself what was true and what was false, and not have it decided for her by men. She dreamed that a day would come when a woman would no longer say of her life in Australia: 'My ineffective life will be trod out in the same round of toil—I am only one of yourselves, I am only an unnecessary little bush commoner, I am only a woman'.

Early in 1903 the *Bulletin* published Joseph Furphy's *Such Is Life*. Like Lawson, Furphy believed in calling no biped lord or sir, and touching his hat to no man. The temper of the work, he said, was democratic. Its bias was 'offensively Australian'. He knew the case against living in Australia. He knew that in the eyes of the unwise Australia was known as 'the last place God ever made'. But he found it lovely. He believed in a meritocracy, in which he that was greatest should be the servant of all. No drunken English gentleman could ever compete in Australia with 'an iron-sinewed miner on the goldfields, or with a hardy, nine-lifed bushman in the back country'. As an Australian nationalist Furphy came perilously close to using his great wit to encourage the descendants of the bush barbarians to glory in their own variety of British philistinism. The kingdom of heaven was not a myth: it was within each man and woman. Australians were not doomed to be citizens in a kingdom of nothingness. An enlightened humanity would create the kingdom of God in the here and now. Furphy was a believer.

While Australians failed to agree on what they were, or what they wanted to be, there were visionaries among them who prophesied that one day the desert at the centre of Australia would blossom like a rose. On 24 January 1903 Sir John Forrest turned the tap to bring water to the goldfields of Coolgardie, Kalgoorlie and Kanowna. Sir John boasted on a scorcher of a day in Kalgoorlie that British genius had succeeded in bringing water into the arid regions of Australia. Man was like God: he was turning the hard rock into a standing water. The engineer who showed how it could be done was Charles Yelverton O'Connor. On the morning of 10 March 1902, just when victory was in sight, he had finally despaired of ever winning protection from the misrepresentation, mockery and abuse to which he had been subjected in Australia, and had gone for a ride on the beach at Fremantle and shot himself.

Early in 1902 the government established the High Court, the 'keystone of the federal arch', and interpreter of the Constitution. The tablets of the laws of the Commonwealth of Australia had been well and truly handed down.

In 1903 Barton resigned from Parliament to sit as a judge of the High Court. Deakin was about to begin the flowering time of his life. The bourgeois press welcomed him to the office of Prime Minister as a man who would lead Australia forward down the path midway between radicalism and conservatism. He appointed what the *Bulletin* called 'a Ministry of colourless respectability', in which conservatives were well represented. Now the bourgeois political parties must ensure the salvation of bourgeois society. If Australian politics was to stabilize, then two of the three evenly balanced parties must unite.

5

Embourgeoisement

Mr Deakin was turning over in his mind the idea of a Court of Conciliation and Arbitration for industrial disputes extending beyond the border of a State. The need for such a court had been one of the most powerful reasons for the creation of the Commonwealth of Australia. The lesson for the labour movement of the great strikes had been the need to capture the state. The lesson for the bourgeois parties had been that strikes with all their attendant losses would not be effectively handled unless there was a central government and legislature with jurisdiction extending over the whole of Australia. During the last two decades of the nineteenth century, when class conflict was ever threatening to become violent, some suggested the state should act as an umpire in disputes between capital and labour, should prescribe minimum conditions of health and safety in workshops and factories, maximum hours of labour, and minimum wages of employees.

Yet the Australian colonies had been slow to make any moves. Middle-class affluence, the absence of a class on whom birth conferred legal and political privileges, the pervading influence of the petty-bourgeois aspirations of an immigrant community, and a working class with a modest stake in the institution of private property, had persuaded bourgeois politicians that it was possible to introduce political democracy without threatening the private ownership of property. The colonial politicians had delayed the passing of social legislation. They had told themselves that the relatively high wages of workers in the colonies, the beneficial climate, the existence of a well-fed, well-clothed and well-housed working class, had dispensed with the Old World need for such legislation prescribing working hours, wages, or resolving disputes between capital and labour. The great strikes of the 1890s had challenged that delusion. Capitalists wanted ways and means of preventing a repetition of such losses. Labor leaders wanted a means of preventing the institution of the state being exploited and used by their opponents.

All was not well in the factories and workshops of the capital cities. The average weekly wages of a clothing factory pieceworker declined from 25s 9d in 1894 to 15s 2d in 1898. There were similar falls in all the main trades and occupations in the capital cities. In some retail shops young girls worked ninety hours a week without any rest on Sunday, their wages sometimes being as low as a miserable penny or less per hour. Some waitresses in cafés and restaurants worked 100 hours a week. The plight of the tailoresses, and other women and children employed on piece-wages, beggared description. Sweating was rife in the factories, shops, hotels, cafés, restaurants and workplaces of all the capital cities.

The liberal conscience was shocked. The *Age* had published an article on sweating in Melbourne on 28 May 1890. 'Sweating—mean, frowsy, depraved and pitiful'—the article had declared, was carried on in Melbourne to a degree hardly less horrible than in London. The colonial parliaments had done little to end the human degradation in home and factory. In the 1890s liberals were persuaded that factory legislation, minimum wages, and conciliation and arbitration in industrial disputes should be listed along with immigration and education as exceptions to the great liberal principle which limited the functions of the state to the preservation of law and order.

In 1896 both New South Wales and Victoria passed Factories Acts which prescribed safety conditions in factories and workshops, laid it down that the regular day's work for both boys under 16 and girls under 18 should begin no earlier than 7 a.m. and end no later than 6 p.m. Sanitary matters and dangerous machinery were also attended to. Both States regulated the hours of labour in Chinese furniture shops and all other factories in which Chinese were employed. The novelty in the Victorian Act was the establishment of boards to set the minimum wage for persons employed in industries notorious for sweating: clothing, furniture- and bread-making, and the meat industry. By 1900 extravagant claims were being made for success: 'I venture to affirm', wrote the Chief Inspector of Factories in Victoria, 'that there is now no sweating in the clothing trade in the State of Victoria'.

That left industrial disputes as the disrupter of capitalist society. The idea of the state as an umpire for the settlement of industrial disputes was not new. After the bitter strikes of the 1890s increasing numbers of employers and union leaders were converted to the idea of conciliation and arbitration as distinct from direct action. But when compulsory arbitration was introduced in New South

Wales in December 1901 by the Attorney-General, Bernhard Wise, radical sections of the labour movement greeted the move with suspicion. The unions, having just recovered from the débâcles of 1890 and 1893–94, feared that compulsory arbitration was another legal device, like the federal Constitution, to shackle the working classes to the existing ownership and distribution of wealth. Some of the provisions of the Wise Act confirmed labour suspicions. Strikes and lockouts were prohibited during the reference of any dispute to arbitration. Persons who initiated a strike or a lockout after a dispute had arisen, before giving reasonable time for an application to be made to the court, were guilty of a misdemeanour. For the rest there was to be a judge, appointed by the government assisted by two assessors, one representing the associations of employers and the other the trade unionists. Any employer dismissing a worker for belonging to a trade union was liable to a fine of £20. Either side to a dispute could employ counsel. The rule of law was at last to apply to industrial relations in New South Wales.

Mr Deakin wanted the rule of law in industrial relations to prevail over the whole of Australia. He wanted the state to ensure that all white Australian working men were protected by a fair minimum wage rate. But the division of powers between the States and the Commonwealth presented his 1904 Conciliation and Arbitration Bill with difficulties. A disagreement over the application of arbitration to State public servants resulted in Mr Deakin's minority government losing its support in the House. In April 1904 Chris Watson was invited by the Governor-General to form the first Labor government. In August this government lost its numbers when Mr Deakin sided with the conservatives, allowing Reid to become Prime Minister. By June 1905, Mr Deakin was again leading the government with the support of Watson and the Labor Party. During this period of shifting alliances, the legislative programme of the Parliament changed little. Conciliation and arbitration, old age pensions, a foreign and defence policy which yielded to British authority—such were the principles which endured.

Civilization continued to make its relentless progress into the backblocks of Queensland, the Northern Territory, South Australia, New South Wales and Western Australia. On cattle-runs which had employed black workers as boundary riders and station hands large improvements were made in the collection and conservation of water. Windmill pumps were erected; fences were put up, enabling the cattlemen to dispense with black labour. In Western Australia, Dr Walter Edmund Roth conducted a Royal Commission into Aborigines which found that half-caste children born in Western Australia were condemned to a life of vagabondism and harlotry, that in the Norwest employers were not obliged to pay wages to their black indentured servants, that in bringing back black workers to stand trial for absconding unlawfully from their employers iron chains were fastened to their necks, that station-owners and managers did flog black workers, that there was no system for the prevention of venereal disease, that all the advantages in labour contracts were on the side of the employers, that in the pearl industry Aboriginal men bartered their women to the Malay and Japanese crews in return for gin, tobacco, flour and rice, that Aborigines, with iron chains round their necks, were forced to plead guilty to charges laid against them at the muzzle of a rifle, that squatters, drovers and teamsters took Aboriginal women so frequently that Kombo-ism and brutality against Aboriginal women had become rife in the tropics—the list went on and on. There were dark days in sunny Western Australia. Aborigines were being reduced to misery while Watson and his colleagues were promising to secure to all white workers a fair share of the product of their labour.

In April 1904 a woman wrote to *The Times* in London to defend the station-owners of the Norwest in Western Australia. She maintained that the planters might not be 'plaster saints' but they were 'human and did not wantonly ill-treat their natives'. Wagging a reproving finger at all the self-appointed improvers and nigger-lovers on that coast of iron, she whitewashed the behaviour of the white man. Her name was Daisy Bates. Her defence of the members of her own class was as bizarre and theatrical as her own behaviour. The masters, she said, fastened iron collars attached to chains around the necks of the blacks because if they were to tie them around their forearms or their legs they would slip off because their limbs were so pitifully thin.

In Perth Government House circles Mrs Daisy Bates was known as the woman who revered her umbrella because the royal hand of the Duke of York had touched it briefly during his visit to Perth in July 1901. Her presence with the Aborigines was a puzzle. She had not come as a missionary; she had not to come prepare them for a higher material civilization, or to woo them away from their barbarous behaviour to each other, or to confer on them the benefits of the white man's medicine. She was an exile from her own people, an exile seeking a land and a people where her will would be sovereign. In 1905 she set up her tent with them at Cannington just south of Perth, not believing she would make their living better, but hoping perhaps she could make their dying easier.

The white man's civilization had its own challenges to meet. Mr Deakin had always argued that an Australian iron and steel industry could be developed only behind a protective tariff wall. In March 1906 he explained his vision to an audience of protectionists and manufacturers: the development of an Australian secondary industry would create more jobs for the working class. Under the umbrella of protection workers would be paid high wages. Enlightened capitalists and a skilled working class, encouraged to observe the bourgeois virtues of frugality, industry, sobriety and moral rectitude, would lead to social harmony. The *embourgeoisement* of the working classes would remove the threat of a social revolution. The skilled working class could be converted to bourgeois values and bourgeois culture. Material progress had made possible the appeasement of the proletariat. Economic nationalism would put an end to material backwardness. The Australian inferiority complex and the grovelling to the English would disappear. Alfred Deakin, a man who agreed with the Galilean that man did not live by bread alone, had become the servant of Mammon.

6

The 'Cooking' of Mr Deakin

In March 1907 a man walked down Pitt Street in Sydney without a hat on his head. Onlookers were astounded. Policemen, whose function it was in part to preserve the morals of the people, wondered whether he was mad or drunk. The gentleman was neither mad nor drunk: he was just demonstrating that the habit of wearing a hat on an autumn day in Sydney was absurd. The same month a woman rode a horse in the streets of Sydney 'in the manner of the alleged sterner sex'. She rode in bloomers. The same summer mixed bathing became common on the beaches of Sydney. Bishop Kelly thought such a commingling on the sand or in the surf was 'offensive to propriety'. He believed that every time a woman appeared in public in 'immodest circumstances' the respect for her was diminished. 'For a woman to be exposed to public view', as she was when surf bathing, was 'utterly destructive of that modesty', which was 'one of the pillars of our nationhood'. The bishop was especially disturbed by the practice of men gaping at the half-naked bodies of women on the surf beaches of Sydney. The practice of mixed bathing was there to stay. A new era was about to begin. Men and women were about to be liberated from their moral gaolers. Sections of the bourgeoisie clung all the more desperately to the old morality, because that had always so beautifully served their material interests.

On 7 February 1907 the *Bulletin* announced its intention to wipe off the Australian slate the last smudges of colonialism. It would publish a monthly magazine to be called the *Lone Hand*. It would prove that Australians were now 'adult enough to have their own literary and artistic organ'. It was a time when some Australians dared to say they preferred the appearance of their own country to England's green and pleasant land. Isobel Marion Dorothea Mackellar belonged by birth to the patricians and Anglophiles of Rose Bay in Sydney, one of the centres of the *haute bourgeoisie*. After education at independent schools in Sydney she travelled to England where she was expected to experience the 'love of field and coppice', the love of 'green and shaded lanes'. She knew that, but found to her surprise she could not share it. Her love was elsewhere. In the poem, *My Country*, first published in the London *Spectator* in 1908, she uncovered the love of her life:

> I love a sunburnt country,
>   A land of sweeping plains,
> Of ragged mountain ranges,
>   Of droughts and flooding rains,
> I love her far horizons
>   I love her jewel-sea,
> Her beauty and her terror—
>   The wide brown land for me!

Mr Deakin also believed that Australians were mature enough to enjoy a greater measure of political independence. The Labor members and some of the members of his government wanted to introduce a graduated land tax to provide money to build a transcontinental railway, to break up the large estates, and to provide land for immigrants, who would increase national wealth and provide a welcome increase to fighting manpower. Led by John Forrest, the conservatives in Deakin's government counselled delay. At the same time Watson was warning Deakin to go slow on immigration lest he provoke the wrath of organized labour in the eastern States. The *Sydney Morning Herald* thought Australian politics was worthy of treatment by Gilbert and Sullivan.

All through July exhaustion, giddiness, bouts of depression, stomach upsets, and nervous headaches assailed Mr Deakin. The faraway look on his face was more noticeable as his opponents taunted him in the House. The trouble was that he did not know the answer to the problems confronting his government. John Forrest had had enough of the shilly-shallying. He feared Australia was 'on the road to Destruction'. In his eyes there were only two parties in Australia—the Labor Party and the 'rest of us'. On 30 July Forrest resigned from the government.

Unseemly rows between Labor members and conservatives erupted in the House of Representatives. In October 1907 Watson resigned the leadership of the Labor Party. Like Deakin, Watson was not well. Over twenty years in public life had left him exhausted. To the chagrin of Hughes the members of Caucus chose Andrew Fisher. Hughes was elected deputy leader.

Fisher, it was said, was 'brilliant in nothing but his splendid integrity'. His closest friends were clergymen, especially those of the evangelical, puritanical Protestant denominations. He shared Deakin's conviction that the state should intervene in human affairs to stimulate Australian manufacturing, to share the fruits of prosperity and to liberate workers from exploitation. By November 1907 their scheme was well advanced: the working classes were about to enjoy the benefits of the policy which had become known as New Protection. The idea was simple. Manufacturers who paid their employees 'a fair and reasonable wage' would receive tariff protection. The first measure of this New Protection was introduced in October 1906, when manufacturers of agricultural machinery were made subject to an excise duty which was refundable to those firms which paid their employees fair wages. The Act left it to the Court of Conciliation and Arbitration to determine 'a fair and reasonable' wage level. Designed to rear a society of 'prosperous workers in a prosperous factory', the New Protection created such a prosperous working class that it became one of the grave-diggers of the dream of a better society. New Protection de-fanged radicalism in Australia. The 'Workingman's Paradise' was to be a bourgeois and conservative Australia. Yet the 1905 Conference of Employers opposed it; in 1907 the Associated Chamber of Manufacturers in Sydney came out against it. Those with the strongest material interest in preserving the existing order of society resisted the policy with all the forces at their disposal.

In 1907 the largest manufacturer of harvesters and other agricultural machinery in Australia, H. V. McKay, applied to the Conciliation and Arbitration Court for exemption from paying the excise on harvesting machinery manufactured in his plant at Sunshine near Melbourne on the grounds that he was paying 'fair and reasonable' wages. The so-called Harvester case established the principles by which future hearings would determine what constituted a fair and reasonable wage. Mr Justice Higgins said that he assumed that Parliament did not mean by 'fair and reasonable' what the workers could get by 'the ordinary system of individual bargaining with employers'. In that case, as he put it, the 'remuneration could safely have been left to the usual, but unequal, contest', the 'haggling of the market' for labour, with the pressure of bread on one side and benefits on the other. The standard of fair and reasonable must therefore be something else. He could not think of 'any other standard appropriate than the normal needs of the average employee, regarded as a human being living in a civilized community'. Fair and reasonable was a wage sufficient to ensure a workman and his family 'food, shelter, clothing, frugal comfort, provision for evil days, etc., as well as reward for special skill of an artisan if he is one'. Higgins also indicated that he would not accept any argument that the business could not stand paying its employees a fair and reasonable wage.

The enlightened bourgeoisie sensed the prospect of salvation from a revolution in a capitalist society prepared to share some of its affluence with the working classes, especially the skilled working classes. The *Age* hailed the judge's decision as setting a precedent which was 'manifestly sound and just'. The *Sydney Morning Herald* declared with less enthusiasm that no one could take 'serious exception to the definition of fair and reasonable wages as given by Mr Justice Higgins'. Labour and political leaders also welcomed the award. For the *Worker* in Sydney the Harvester award marked the beginning 'of a new epoch in human society . . . the inclusion of the last phase of human life outside the scope of law'. Labor, once it got control, would 'hit any and every sweating employer'. Labor became an even more fervent believer in capturing a majority in Parliament and becoming an instrument of social change. But the men in the Victorian Socialist Party, merged that July into the Socialist Federation of Australia, denounced the New Protection as one of those palliatives which obscured the workers' perception of the need for total emancipation from wage-slavery. The Australian worker was becoming hypnotized by the pleasures available to the opulent.

On 3 June 1908 the Attorney-General, Littleton Ernest Groom, introduced the second reading of a bill to provide for invalid and old age pensions. The bill provided for the payment of £26 per annum to be paid fortnightly. Men were to receive the old age pension at the age of 65: the Governor-General might declare by proclamation that the pension should be paid to women at the age of 60. Pensions were not to be paid to Asiatics (except those born in Australia) or aboriginal natives of Australia, Africa, the islands of the Pacific, or New Zealand. On 10 June 1908 the Act received the royal assent. Palliatives for white persons had become one of the tablets of the law in Australia.

Shortly afterwards, the government encountered a formidable obstacle. The judges of the High Court of Australia in Barger's case, by a majority of three to two, declared unconstitutional the law which rebated the duty on goods manufactured by workers receiving wages deemed by the Arbitration Court to be 'fair and reasonable'. The court had, in effect, ruled against New Protection. If the Commonwealth Government wanted to regulate industrial conditions in Australia then it needed to amend the Constitution. Mr Deakin was not prepared to take that step. Labor was. Its triennial federal conference, held in July 1908, called for an amendment to the Constitution to allow a future Labor government to reintroduce New Protection, arbitration and nationalization of monopolies. There was a mood of confidence in the Labor ranks, and an impatience with Mr Deakin's caution and the conservatism of some of his colleagues. The tide of public opinion seemed to be running with reform.

Mr Deakin decided to push ahead with his plan for an Australian defence force. Australian defences were a scandal. The 'defended' ports such as Adelaide, Port Phillip, Newcastle, Sydney and Thursday Island were in reality undefended. Like Labor, Deakin's ideal was 'a defence of the people, for the people, and by the people': a citizen soldiery. He wanted to remain both a Briton and an Australian, to sing both 'Rule Britannia' and 'Advance Australia Fair'. Even if he wanted privately to cut the painter the conservatives in his government would have prevented him.

Reports of mounting tension between the major powers in Europe were appearing in the Australian press. Europe was divided between two power blocks. The German General Staff had drawn up plans for the invasion of France. The question for Australia was: in the event of war in Europe, would an Australian expeditionary force fight under the command of British or Australian officers? Within the Labor Party opinion was divided. Some said military training was a device of the 'gorge and guzzle' class for the suppression of the working class. King O'Malley denounced militarism because it enabled 'gilt-spurred roosters' to blow a bugle and snatch sons of the working classes from their labours and send them to the slaughterhouse. Frank Tudor, a Labor member from Melbourne, doubted whether any army could be shorn of the 'gorgeous trappings' of class discrimination. By contrast, Hughes believed all able-bodied males should be trained to the use of arms and instructed in such military or naval drill as might be necessary for the purpose. Universal training would have a beneficent effect upon the morale, the physique, and the tone of the nation. Universal training was an instrument of national greatness. As a believer in the survival of the fittest, Hughes now accepted blood sacrifice as a rite in which men gained an insight into the meaning of life. At that time he was not a supporter of conscription: conscription bred the evils of militarism. He favoured universal training: for that would flower into a moral, industrious and contented citizenry.

Mr Deakin was not happy about compulsion, indeed about any measure which infringed liberty of conscience. But on 29 September 1908 the Minister for Defence, Thomas Ewing, moved the second reading of the Defence Bill which introduced compulsory military training. Like Mr Deakin and Hughes, Ewing stressed the benefits to the morals of the youth of Australia. There were to be no gorgeous uniforms. Mr Deakin was not a man to make a young Aussie look like an escapee from a Middle Eastern harem. Everyone was to be treated alike.

On 6 November Andrew Fisher told an eager House of Representatives that the Labor Party could no longer support the government. Mr Deakin acquiesced in this declaration with a resignation born of weariness. Fisher became Prime Minister. At last Mr Deakin had time to prune his trees and water his garden. He had more time for reading the recent writing on salvation.

While Deakin was seeking healing for his body and his spirit, a tempest was beginning to rumble across the shores of Sydney Harbour. In December 1908 rumours ran around Sydney town that Jack Johnson, the negro boxer from the United States of America, was not attending to his training. Johnson was in Sydney for a world heavyweight championship fight with Tommy Burns, a white man and a Canadian. Johnson, according to the rumours, had been flying about in a motor car with a cigar in his mouth, and calling from hotel to hotel. He had been seen far too often with a glass of liquid refreshment in his hand. He had been heard boasting of what he would do to the 'whitey' when he got him in the ring and of his prowess with the ladies. No one thought Johnson half so clever as he thought himself. Johnson, it was said, was training on champagne and female society. By contrast Burns and his wife had been seen leaving St Mary's Cathedral after attending mass.

On Saturday 26 December 17 000 people crowded into the Rushcutter's Bay Stadium in Sydney to watch the fight. Twice as many who were unable to gain admission gathered outside eagerly awaiting news passed out from inside. They were there to see the white man win. Johnson was larger and more brutish: Johnson grinned at Burns and the crowd from a mouthful of gold teeth which he seemed as anxious to show off as he was to display his animal strength. Johnson sneered and taunted Burns as a white man, and mocked him: 'I thought you were a great fighter, Tommy. Let's see what you can do, Tommy'. He asked the crowd: 'Ain't I clever, eh?' Johnson pummelled Burns so mercilessly that in the twelfth round the police stopped the fight. A black man, a champagne and female society man, had defeated a white man, a Britisher, and a man of bourgeois virtues. A black man was the heavyweight champion of the world. The black man, a self-confessed debauchee, had not crumpled up or behaved like a cur. An Australian crowd had wallowed in sensual cruelty, had come to the ringside to barrack for white supremacy, only to find it was a secret sharer of all the vulgar showing off and the animal pride of a man they had previously dismissed as a semi-civilized brute.

Three months later, on 30 March 1909, a crowd of 2000 jammed into the Olympic Hall in Gympie (Queensland) to hear a speech by Prime Minister Fisher. He was in a belligerent mood. He proposed to hold a referendum by which the people would be able to decide for themselves that Parliament should have the right to say what was a fair and reasonable wage to be paid to a white man. Labor would introduce Australian youth to military training, beginning at the age of 10. For defence and other purposes Labor would nationalize the iron industry. If they lacked the constitutional power he hoped the people would give them that power in a referendum. Labor would make Australians self-reliant. Labor, the nation-builder, had drafted the first truly national policy ever submitted to the Australian people.

On 31 May 1909 the *Sydney Morning Herald* argued that the time had come for Mr Deakin and the conservative leader, Joseph Cook, to compose their differences in the interests of what they understood by Australia. Bourgeois civilization was in danger: Labor's nationalist Australia was challenging the Australia of the Australian-Britons. But again Deakin agonized over what to do. In January he told Littleton Groom that Australia needed a government which was always liberal. He thought of Cook and his men as reactionaries, but perhaps it was possible for a liberal whose eye was single to spend time in the belly of the whale of Australian conservatism, and emerge with principles and faith intact. By reading the world's scriptures and mystics a deep peace had settled far inside him: now he felt a 'serenity at the core of my heart'. He wanted to know whether participation in the world's affairs would disturb that serenity.

On 25 May the three groups opposed to the Labor Government, the direct opposition led by Joseph Cook, the liberal protectionists led by Alfred Deakin, and the corner anti-socialist protectionist conservatives led by John Forrest, formally agreed to a 'fusion' of forces under Deakin. Every group had made concessions, but Deakin seemed to have given away most. He had thrown in the towel over New Protection. He had abandoned the graduated land tax and had thrown away the whole of the welfare programme which had made his party indistinguishable in social policy from the Labor Party.

For the next two days the Parliament was in uproar. The new alliance had the numbers to bring down the Labor Government. Billy Hughes rose to his feet and said that he heard some mention of Judas. 'I do not agree with that', he declared. 'It is not fair to

Judas, for whom there is this to be said, that he did not gag the man whom he betrayed, nor did he fail to hang himself afterwards.' George Reid's huge frame shook with laughter and his eyes danced with glee. When the heads were counted, the brief prime minister-ship of Andrew Fisher was ended. Mr Deakin believed he had won a great victory.

The *Bulletin*, the *Age* and the Labor press were dismayed and angered at what they saw as a sell-out. Mr Deakin, the patriot and democrat, had had his belly rubbed by the most odious foes of democracy such as John Forrest, William Irvine and Joseph Cook. Given the choice between the dreamer of great dreams and the representatives of 'Monopoly and Reaction', said the *Bulletin*, Mr Deakin had chosen the latter. Mr Deakin had been 'Cooked'.

Undismayed, Mr Deakin believed that the men of goodwill had won a victory against the forces of reaction and radicalism. They had preserved the most sacred liberty of all, the liberty of con-science. On 2 August he was guest speaker at a women's meeting in the house of Lady Best in Caulfield. After the music Lady Best asked the Prime Minister whether he would honour them with a few words. He stood there, with his hands clasped in front of his stomach and prophesied that the time was coming when the world would belong to women and the working classes. Here the Australian dream had been fulfilled. A man could rise in one generation from the poor to the wealthy classes, or descend from the wealthy to the lower classes. There should be no division or antagonism between the classes in Australia. When capital and labour pulled together no one could resist the combination. Mr Deakin had the gift to make the ladies feel that in the heartland of Australia suburbia all went well.

Outwardly it was the flowering time of his life and of all he stood for. Under him and liberalism Australia would fulfil the Wentworth prophecy of a 'new Britannia in another world'. The days of the Lib–Lab alliance were over. The bourgeois politicians were thinking and acting as a class. For Mr Deakin it had been a 'most eventful and critical year'. The strain had been so great that he had been 'winged'. He had no premonition that the liberalism to which he had devoted his whole public career had also been 'winged'. He had no inkling then that he was both an architect and a grave-digger of the liberal dream. At year's end he was aware of a strange paradox: in public he had known glory; in private, as he noted in his diary on 31 December, he was 'empty'.

7

The Era of the Common Man

In the caves of Arnhem Land where Aborigines had painted on the rocks their pictures of the creation, of the meaning of life, of all the beauty in the world, a new figure appeared on the rocks. It was the white man firing a gun from his shoulder. The *Bulletin* seemed to enjoy believing that the Aborigines were a dying race, but it was irritated with the parsons, the priests, and the do-gooders, who seemed reluctant to accept the inevitable. In November 1909 the *Bulletin* ridiculed the Australian Church Congress for uttering lamentations about the obvious passing away of 'our black brother Binghi'. What maddened the *Bulletin* was the tears from the advocates of the universal embrace. The bishops, the clergy, and all the other creeps had never been brave enough to say they wanted more Binghis in the world. To be born Binghi meant being black and often naked, to be a person who had an incurable tendency to lead a squalid life in a gunyah. Binghis, said the *Bulletin*, added nothing to the world's stock of knowledge.

In 1901 a group of Pallotine Fathers began to minister to Aborigines in the reserve around Beagle Bay on the north-west coast of Western Australia. By 1904 they had come to the melancholy conclusion reached by so many of their predecessors that the Aborigines were incapable of being civilized, that they would remain a Stone Age people. They were not more wicked than other people: they were just more simple, more unpretentious; in a word they were children.

Missionaries bequeathed this idea of the Aborigines to a more secular age. Baldwin Spencer, the Special Commissioner and Chief Protector of Aborigines in the Northern Territory for the Commonwealth of Australia, detected in the Aborigines that fondness for fun which distinguished children from adults, and was often a charming attribute of members of the brute creation. Baldwin Spencer was elected to the Chair of Biology at the University of

Melbourne in 1887; he typified the concern for the Aborigines of the men of science. He was not motivated by compassion for the least of the little ones: as a man of science he neither praised nor blamed. As he saw it, he recorded the facts.

The policies of the State and Commonwealth governments reflected these same notions. In December 1905, Western Australia created an Aborigines Department charged with promoting the welfare of the Aborigines, providing them with food, clothing, medicine and medical attendance, providing for the education of Aboriginal children, and generally assisting in the preservation and well-being of the Aborigines. A Chief Protector, not the Aboriginal father, was to be the legal guardian of every Aboriginal and half-caste child until such children attained the age of 16. Protectors were given the power to decide whether any Aboriginal should leave his district, or whether any white man should be permitted to enter an Aboriginal reserve. Protectors were also empowered to prevent Asiatic employers from exploiting Aborigines or half-castes. In all the acts, ordinances and regulations of State and Commonwealth parliaments the same paternalism prevailed.

If white Australians had difficulty understanding the Aborigines, they were also unsure about their own collective identity. When the Deakin Government passed the Coinage Act of 1909, it shunned decimal currency and mimicked the coinage of England. When the first new coins—the florin, shilling, sixpence and threepence—were minted they had a map of Australia on one side, and the King's head on the reverse side. With the flag the same dual loyalty was affirmed. In 1901 the Barton Government announced a prize of £75 for a design for the emblem of the Commonwealth. Some 30 000 designs were submitted. Four naval officers acted as judges. They chose one submitted by five contenders for the prize— a Union Jack on a blue or a red ground, a six-pointed star representing the six federated States of Australia, and the Southern Cross in the fly as a symbol of Australian national sentiment. This was forwarded to the Secretary of State for the Colonies, who submitted it to the King who, in turn, was graciously pleased to approve the design.

In the world of entertainment entrepreneurs found it was not to their material advantage to try any experiments in Australia. Even the popular success of the dramatized version of Steele Rudd's *On Our Selection* in 1910 did not persuade J. C. Williamson to abandon his conviction that only a repertoire of musical comedy favourites pleased the Australian public. Louis Esson had ideas on a national theatre for Australia, the writing and staging of Australian plays which would teach Australians the truth about their bourgeois

politicians, about the hopeless addiction of Labor leaders to out-
moded bourgeois values and the foolhardiness of depending on the
British. The entrepreneurs rebuffed him with a vast indifference.
The theatre-going public put that bland Aussie question to all
disturbers of bourgeois complacency: what's wrong with what
we've got? The theatre-goers of Australian cities, J. C. Williamson
had discovered, would go again and again to see what pleased
them. In 1911 the musical comedy 'Our Miss Gibbs' enjoyed an
eight-month revival in Sydney. 'Floradora' ran for 106 nights in
Melbourne. Williamson was prepared to risk an American play,
even a continental play, after a successful run in London: he
avoided local works like the plague.

Australia had no national song, no national heroes, no national
literature, and no national days of commemoration. Melbourne had
Melbourne Cup Day. On the first Tuesday in November each year
the Flemington race track was 'the Mecca of Australia'. Melbourne
also had Grand Final day, when two teams played off for the
premiership of the Victorian Football League. The Labor leader, Mr
Fisher, became a staunch patron of Australian Rules football. He
attended a match every Saturday afternoon. True to his democratic
principles Mr Fisher eschewed the exclusiveness of the grandstand
patrons and the private members' reserve. He paid his sixpence at
the turnstile, and stood with his fellow Australians in the 'outer'. He
did not utter the coarse language of his fellow barrackers, let alone
exhibit that superb wit of the Australian when addressing his fellow
countrymen at a football game. His face expressed excitement as the
changing fortunes of the game provided the occasions for fury,
ecstasy, terror and togetherness. The people in the 'outer' were the
'mob' in action, those masses whom some feared as the barbarians
who would destroy higher civilization, the ones who were as fickle
in their political opinions as in their ever-changing attitude to
players and umpires. Some saw them as 'loud-mouthed yahoos'
who encouraged the players to perpetrate brutalities on each other
by fostering an atmosphere of excitement. Some maintained that the
yahoo was degrading a game of skill into a blood sport. Some
wondered whether men of such passions could ever entertain for
long a vision of higher things. Australians had not created a Paris
Commune or fashioned a God in their own image. They had created
Australian Rules football in their own image.

Australians had also created Test cricket in their own image. The
bourgeoisie sat in the stand: the working classes stood in the 'outer'.
Ladies were 'as few among the outside [the 'outer'] crowd as daisies
on a well trimmed lawn'. Most carried their lunches with them
either in handbags, kit bags, or brown paper parcels, the men

preferring a leather grip bag, as that concealed from sight the container of 'cold tea' (whisky or brandy and water) which got them quicker to where they wanted to be. The boys carried their lunches in neat packages made up by adoring mothers or serving sisters who stayed at home to await the return of husbands, excited sons and brothers. Newsboys called: 'Here y'are. The best London Literatoor by the greatest living writers. Only a penny each'. The recent immigrants barracked for the 'Poms', the native-born for the good old Aussies.

The Anglophiles saw themselves as models of correct behaviour, displaying both in their clothing and their demeanour their origins in an aristocratic society: the English players wore cream trousers and flannel shirts. By contrast, the Australians affected on the field the demeanour of men nurtured in an egalitarian society: they wore 'whites', and a gawkish cap pulled down slightly askew. They lacked the discipline, the *'comme il faut'* standards of behaviour, a code of what was and what was not permissible on and off the field. The Australians gloried in their own irreverence.

In 1911 there was yet another revolution in the requirements of fashion. Once a small waist was the desirable feature for a woman: the hips and shoulders could be as wide as nature wanted them to be. To achieve that shape a tight-fitting corset supported by much elastic and whalebone had been an essential garment in a lady's wardrobe. Now in the age moving towards the idea that everything was allowable, women were no longer being corseted into something small: the stays on the corsets were being loosened. Woman began to decorate their ears, their necks, their forearms, their bosoms, their wrists and their fingers with jewellery which was not genuine. Decorative value, not monetary worth, had become the criterion. The age of the artificial was beginning. Fashions in hairdressing for young women also underwent change. The age of the 'flapper' was heralded by a change in hair styles. The wedding-cake coiffures of a more leisurely age were discarded for the centre parting, the girlish fringe, and the two bobtails fastened with black bows.

At the same time the material foundations of 'Old Australia' were crumbling. The mighty bush, the cradle of the noble bushman, of mateship and equality, of the prestige of the male virtues of pluck, resource and physical strength, the cradle of the ugly Australian, of male domination and of the belief in the 'stoush', was coming under the influence of industrial civilization. The iron rail, the telegraph, the telephone, the city newspaper, and the glamour of city life were slowly eroding the old ways. The large estates were breaking up and the contents of the great homesteads were up for auction at city sales. Male members of the squatting cousinhood were taking 'billets' in the big pastoral companies in the cities: the female members were moving to the cities, or becoming governesses on estates on which their ancestors had dreamed of pursuing a way of life similar to that of the landed aristocrats of the United Kingdom. The picturesque rural types of yesteryear—the itinerant workmen, shepherds, swagmen and hawkers—were fast disappearing as the age of conformity and the common man seeped into the Australian bush.

In the chaos and confusion of the coming of a new way of life, some people seemed to lose their way: politicians were bewildered. City barbarians replaced the bush barbarians as objects of terror for the bourgeoisie: the larrikin took the place of the bushranger; the city radical replaced the bush worker. Labor believed that these threats would be removed by palliatives for clear and present evils. Labor had won the federal election of 13 April 1910 under the leadership of Andrew Fisher. Labor members had many opinions on what could be done to de-fang the radicals and the agitators. King O'Malley wanted a people's bank. In November 1911 the government introduced legislation establishing the state-owned Commonwealth Bank.

The new society was the theme of the Victorian Socialist Party founded in 1905 by labour radicals. The party was committed to the capture of political power to enable it to get rid of the bourgeois state. It argued consistently that the institutions of the bourgeois state had been designed for the oppression of one class by another. By 1909 some of its members had abandoned hope of the Australian Labor Party ever becoming a socialist party. In the eyes of Tom Mann, a British theoretician on an extended visit to Australia, the Labor members of Parliament were in no way 'superior to capitalist members'. Labor, in his eyes, was the party of the middle class, which opposed monopolies to curry favour with petty-bourgeois small businessmen, rather than a party of believers in a socialist policy of nationalization.

In 1910 the Victorian Socialist Party and socialist parties in other states agreed to unite to form an Australian Socialist Party. Their objective was the common ownership of the means of production, distribution and exchange. They rejected Parliament as a bourgeois institution which must be smashed along with all the other institutions of the bourgeois state. Militant industrial action was the key to the overthrow of the bourgeois state and the creation of a workers' state. The party members did not ask how a bourgeoisified working class could be persuaded or cajoled into destroying bourgeois society.

The Australian Socialist Party had broken with the British tradition of reform by moral suasion and constitutional methods. The repudiation of constitutional means was the main point in the position taken up by the Industrial Workers of the World. Founded in Chicago in 1905, they had adopted a revolutionary preamble: 'The working class and the employing class have nothing in common. There can be no peace as long as hunger and want are found among millions of working people, and the few who make up the employing class have all the good things in life'. The workers of the world must organize as a class, take possession of the earth and of the machinery of production and abolish the wage system. By organizing industrially the workers would form the structure of the new society within the shell of the old. At a meeting in Adelaide on 6 May 1911 members of the Socialist Federation of Australia resolved to found branches of the IWW in Australia. So fourteen muddle-headed, prejudiced and ignorant pseudo-socialists founded the first significant revolutionary movement in Australia, committed to the destruction of capitalist society and the creation of a new society by militant industrialization rather than by the use of existing political institutions.

The emergence of an organized radical working-class movement presented the ALP with a dilemma. Driven by conservative criticism to disown the revolutionary aims and methods of the Australian Socialist Party, they used the language and tactics which substantiated the verdict that they were a bourgeois party tossing sops and palliatives to the workers. Labor had by no means exhausted its repertoire of palliatives. One of these was the creation of state enterprises. The High Court's decision in Barger's case had made it clear that under the federal Constitution the Commonwealth could not pass legislation to create a state enterprise except for purposes of defence.

So in April 1911 the Fisher government held a referendum in which it asked the people to approve two changes to the Constitution: one to extend the Commonwealth's powers to legislate on such matters as trade, wages, working conditions, and arbitration; the other to give power to the Commonwealth to nationalize any industry declared by both houses of Parliament to be a monopoly. Less than 40 per cent of voters participated. The proposals were defeated. This left such reforms to the States.

In Western Australia, the Labor government led by John Scaddon established a state shipping service, state sawmills, state brickworks and other enterprises, not as a first step on the road to socialism, but to protect the interest of a group in the community on whose votes Labor depended for success in the next State election. Similar moves were made by the government of 'Honest Jim' McGowen in New South Wales. State enterprises, Labor argued, would make capitalist society more efficient. They were what Labor meant when it spoke of its hope to promote 'the common good'. That followed on quite naturally from accepting the myth that British institutions were the means of achieving material well-being, liberty, law and order, and that decency, that veneer of respectability, which contained the madness in men's hearts.

Out of the depths of his drunken despair, Henry Lawson uttered the cryptic warning:

> Australia! your trial is coming

For him life had degenerated into a fearful muddle:

> I don't care if the cause be wrong,
> Or if the cause be right—
> I've had my day and sung my song,
> And fought the bitter fight.
> In truth at times I can't tell what
> The men are driving at,
> But I've been Union thirty years,
> And I'm too old to rat.

Bourgeois society in Australia was like the house built on rock: it promised to remain standing during the storms and tempests to come. Woe to those who challenged or questioned any of the taboos or sacred laws of the tribe, such as the family, or the institution of private property, or any of the moral laws and conventions deemed essential to preserve those institutions. In 1912 William Chidley conducted a campaign in speech and writing to persuade Australians to change their sexual behaviour. Like most reformers who dared to suggest that men and women should enjoy their sex life, Chidley affected eccentricities of dress guaranteed to goad the conformists of Melbourne and Sydney into retaliation. Sobriety did not come naturally to Chidley. He also offended by breaking another of the taboos of the bourgeoisie: he discussed the physiology of sexual intercourse in front of women. This roused the hounds into full cry. To prevent mischief, to stop Chidley corrupting the minds of the weak and the vicious, this crazy man complete with his fantastic garb must be kept out of harm's way in a place where he could not corrupt or deprave the morals of Australians. So Chidley was charged with offensive behaviour in August 1912, found guilty and incarcerated in Callan Park Mental Hospital. Released on 1 October he was again judged insane in December 1913.

The straiteners who silenced Chidley were equally dismayed that more and more women were displaying their forms on the beaches for the admiration and delight of men. Those who believed the beauty of the human body worthy of universal esteem applauded the tendency. Australia was a land for heroes, for Wagnerian supermen. It was fitting that such godlings should frolic with goddesses on Australian beaches. The clergy grieved: 'Woe betide Australia', pronounced Archibishop Kelly, 'if she is going to encourage immodesty in her women'. The municipal councils controlling the foreshores passed regulations to enforce modesty. In a St Kilda magistrate's court in March 1913 a number of male bathers were fined ten shillings each because they did not forthwith resume ordinary clothing on leaving the water. But no human forces could hold back the march of humanity down the path of pleasure.

In December 1913 an entrepreneur who had guessed correctly the direction of the winds of change, announced that he had built a Palais de Danse at St Kilda and the management announced that the tango would be introduced in Melbourne. The Argus warned its readers that dancing the tango was a prelude to sexual licence and depravity. On the night the Palais de Danse threw open its doors to let a breath of air from the healing waters of Port Phillip blow over the people of Melbourne who had been taught by parsons and priests to think of the body as evil, the Reverend Mr McNab ground on to an overflow meeting of nearly 1000 who had gathered to hear the warning that two human bodies moving in harmony over a polished floor could only lead to 'chambering and wantonness'. Despite all such prophecies, crowds flocked to the Palais. There in the dim light a searchlight swept the dancers, accentuating the beautiful curves the men wanted to draw near. There after the wild ecstasy of the tango drew them closer, man to woman and woman to man, partners drew even closer as the saxophones of the Palais dance band played on. Seeing the radiance in the eyes of the dancers, some asked: who would want to keep those bodies apart? Why did such pleasures make some people very angry?

The cinema was another means of escape. The production of films in Australia began with the shooting of the life story of the redeemer of mankind in 1899. At that time hopes were entertained that the screen would lead humanity from darkness into light. Between 1910 and 1912 Raymond Hollis Longford educated Australians in their own history with films such as *The Romance of Margaret Catchpole*. In 1913 he filmed *Australia Calls*, a story of a future Japanese invasion of Australia, in which with astonishing prescience he showed aeroplanes being used in squadrons with which to keep the navy of the Japanese away from Australian shores. In 1913 he made *On Our Selection*. But just when critics were praising him for having done for the Australian cinema what Henry Lawson had done for the short story and the revolutionary ballad, Nellie Melba for singing and Joseph Furphy for the novel, Longford and the Australian film industry were gobbled up by the Americans. By 1913 the cinema houses, like their predecessors the vaudeville theatres, had become fun palaces in which the masses gaped at luxuries they would never enjoy, sensual passions they were too shy to acknowledge to themselves, and a superficial optimism about the chances of happiness.

The spirit of the ancient continent and its harsh past have made Australians sceptical about the fruits of human endeavour. The environment and the past have bequeathed to them stern lessons on the conditions of existence. Australians have become sceptical of all comforters except those which provide a pleasing escape from reality. The beaches, the fun parlours (Luna Park was 'Just for Fun'), the sportsgrounds, the bars and the bright light of the sun have become their temples and their gods.

Young men were receiving military training. Articles appearing in the press predicted that in a war aeroplanes could lay waste whole cities by bombardment. There was talk of war in Europe. The Kaiser of the German Empire was again talking of the historic mission of the German people. In Australia there was a change of government. In April 1913 the Fisher Labor government was voted out of office. In city cafés pleasure-seekers enjoyed a tango tea. Henry Lawson was remembering the unutterable loneliness of the bush—the sectarianism, the sullenness, the uncouthness, bush ignorance and bush-buried rattiness. Alfred Deakin was glorying in his God and Saviour. Away in Zurich a Doctor of Medicine, who with some success was practising the new field of medicine called psychoanalysis, one Carl Gustav Jung, dreamed that rivers of blood were flowing over the whole world. When asked to comment on what the dream meant he replied, 'Look at it well: it will be so'. Down at the Palais de Danse in St Kilda the searchlight moved round the ballroom as the band played 'If you were the only girl in the world, and I were the only boy'.

8

On the Rim of a Maelstrom

On 28 June 1914 in Sarajevo, the capital of the province of Bosnia-Herzegovina, Gavrilo Prinzip, an 18-year-old whose heart was on fire with a desire to avenge the wrongs committed against his people by the Austrians, shot dead the Archduke Franz Ferdinand and his wife, formerly the Countess Sophia Chotek. Intense grief and horror were expressed in Austria-Hungary, where the Archduke was greatly loved. When told the news the old Emperor, Franz Joseph, who suffered much, became deathly pale and murmured: 'I am spared nothing'. The Emperor of Germany, Kaiser Wilhelm the Second, stood gravely silent when he heard the news. The Pope was deeply shocked. In Australia there was widespread sympathy with the Habsburg family. The Archduke had endeared himself to Australians during his visit to Sydney in 1893.

On the day the assassination was announced to the Australian public, the *Age* published an article on the 'Moloch of Militarism'. Writing with that moral passion which had always lent an air of distinction to its pages, the *Age* demanded that the Prime Minister honour his election promises to reduce the amount of money squandered on defence. Those jealousies which had turned faraway Europe into an armed camp need not inspire Australians with a similar insanity. There might be a war in their part of the world in the distant future in which Australia might have to defend itself against an 'Asiatic swashbuckler'. But they could forget about Europe: they certainly must not allow Europe to menace them with financial beggary.

The assassination at Sarajevo was like a smell which would not go away. In mid-July public men in Vienna called for punitive action against the Serbs. They talked of an eye for an eye and a tooth for a tooth. In St Petersburg and Moscow men in high places said that if Austria did not stop being haughty to the Slavs of Bosnia-Herzegovina then Holy Russia would protect her Slav brothers.

Some feared that the days of the *belle époque* were drawing to a close. Europe reminded observers of the point made by Gloucester in King Lear: 'We have seen the best of our time'. The know-alls of human affairs predicted that the dispute would not be confined to Austria and Serbia. Russia would come to the aid of her Slav brothers. Germany would be a knight in shining armour at the side of Austria. France was bound by treaty to declare war on any power which attacked Russia: Great Britain had a moral obligation to come to the aid of France if she were attacked.

By 31 July 1914 the soldiers of the Austrian army were pitching their tents in the streets of Belgrade: Russia mobilized; Germany mobilized; France mobilized. At the same time, Australians were in the midst of a campaign for a federal election. In June the previous year, the Cook Liberal government had won office with a majority of one in the House of Representatives and a Labor majority in the Senate. Cook's attempt to pass anti-union legislation had caused a deadlock between the two houses, and the Governor-General had agreed to Cook's request for a fresh election. As the drums of war grew louder, Fisher addressed an election meeting at Colac at which he urged all Australians to entertain the kindest feelings towards the mother country. 'Should the worst happen' after everything had been done that honour would permit, Australians would 'stand beside our own to help and defend her to our last man and our last shilling'. A Labor leader had borrowed the words first used by the conservative George 'Bon Ton' Turner during the Boer War. At Horsham Cook told the people who gathered to hear him that when the Empire was at war Australia was at war. All the resources of Australia were in the Empire, for the preservation and security of the Empire. Henry Lawson's great dream of an Australia where Old World errors and wrongs and lies were banished was dying. A roll had begun on a distant drum. William Holman, speaking for those who believed in Australian sentiment, protested that Australians could not be plunged into calamities merely at the bidding of some irresponsible ruler. Australia had self-government. But he was a voice shouting into a gale.

As the forces of war were marshalled, wild expressions of loyalty broke out in the streets of the capital cities. In Melbourne public servants, motor cyclists, dentists and ancient mariners professed their readiness to stand by the British. Billy Hughes declared this was 'a time when none shall be for the party, but all be for the State'. The *Labor Call* warned workers that they had nothing to gain but all to lose from the coming slaughter. 'Let us hope', it wrote, 'that this mad rush at one another's throats may yet be confined to as narrow an area as possible'.

At 1.30 p.m. on Wednesday 5 August special editions of the *Age* and *Argus* were published. Copies were devoured and the contents passed on. The inevitable had happened: Great Britain had declared war on Germany and Austria-Hungary. That afternoon the electric telegraph and the bush telegraph carried over the ancient continent the news that as the British had declared war, Australia was therefore also at war. That night in Melbourne a mob attacked the German Club. Crowds spilled over the streets, singing patriotic songs. In one café the band struck up 'Rule Britannia' to thunderous applause from the audience. A mob raided the Chinese quarters in Little Bourke Street, smashing shop windows, looting property and terrorizing the inoffensive Chinese inhabitants of the area. The 'hoodlum' had taken over the streets of Melbourne.

The dreams of visionaries melted away like the snow-drift. Henry Lawson announced that his heart was with England, France and Russia. The bugles of England were calling to the manhood of Australia. The *Labor Call* agreed that a great European war was 'a thing of appalling importance' but insisted that it was in reality of far less significance to Australians than the great electoral campaign in September. At a meeting of the members of the Australian Miners' Association at Broken Hill those present carried the following resolution: 'That this meeting views with sorrow and regret the armed hostilities between the nations of Europe, and we regard the present war as a display of civilized savagery and reversion to barbarism engineered by the financial interests of Europe to suit their own ends'.

Deakin went to bed early the night the mobs went on the rampage in the streets of Melbourne. He felt 'very composed'. A woman standing on Burwood station (Sydney) was so startled by the news of war that she went home to pray that God would remove the child from her womb, as she did not want to rear children for barbarism and frightfulness. Two nights later she asked God to forgive her for doubting His wisdom: she was comforted by William Cowper's words.

> God is His own interpreter
> And He will make it plain.

The Governor-General thought the spirit of the Australian people was excellent. His only concern was that because of the double dissolution there was no federal Parliament in existence to grant supply.

At an enthusiastic public meeting of women in Melbourne Town Hall on 7 August, women proudly pledged themselves to do their bit by providing clothing and other comforts for the gallant boys who volunteered to lay down their lives. The women were steeling themselves to face death in the family. Those who had never lifted a hand in their lives vowed that in the time of the Empire's great need they were prepared to learn to cook and nurse. The women sang 'God Save the King' with the same fervour as the mixed audience on the preceding night. At such public meetings there was a total lack of any critical or carping spirit. On 7 August Deakin scribbled a cryptic remark in his diary: 'Confused these days'.

In Berlin at the same time young Germans were leaving behind lecture theatres, school desks and work benches. In the short weeks of training they were already fusing into one great enthusiastic body. Like the Australians, those young Germans had grown up in an age of security, and were filled with a longing for high danger. The war took hold of them like wine. 'We had set off in a shower of flowers', one wrote later, 'intoxicated by roses and blood. For the war must bring us what was great, powerful and solemn. To us it wore the aspect of a cheerful shooting match on flowery meadows bedewed with blood'.

Cook announced his decision to place the ships of the Australian navy under the command of Admiral Patey. On 15 August the *Commonwealth Gazette* announced the appointment of Brigadier-General William Throsby Bridges as General Officer in command of the Australian contingent. The life of Bridges had prepared him to be a soldier of the Empire rather than of Australia. He was born into a service family in Scotland on 18 February 1861: his mother was a Throsby, a member of the ancient nobility of New South Wales. Bridges was educated for the army at the Royal Military College, Kingston, Canada, and served with the British army during the Boer War.

On his appointment as Inspector-General of the Australian armed forces in August 1914 his first recommendation was that the 20 000 troops under his command should be called the Australian Imperial Force. Few men loved him; many went in awe of him. This imperial officer was to be the commander of men who were believers in 'tramping in mateship side by side' and in democratic friendliness. As second-in-command the Cook Government appointed Cyril Brudenell Bingham White, another member of the country gentry, with feet deep in Australian soil and eyes for the contents of Debrett's Peerage. He was at once charming, aristocratic and aloof. What he liked most about Australians was their 'remarkably strong vein of Imperialism'.

On 10 August the government of the Commonwealth of Australia called for volunteers to serve in the Australian Imperial Force. They were calling for 20 000 Australians to volunteer for what the

Sydney Morning Herald called 'war as a baptism', for a secular age borrowed its literary images from the religion it rejected. On 11 August a vast crowd of men waited outside the barracks in Sydney for the doors to be opened. One was attracted by 'brilliant uniforms, marching soldiers, music, drums and glory'; one was 'itching to git a dig at a few Germans'; one wanted to 'do his bit to wipe out such an infamous nation'; one was there because if he had not been there he would never be able to look any decent girl in the face again; one was there because he would not be able to 'look men in the face again'; and another was there so that he would not have to look his wife in the face again for quite a while. Some were attracted by the pay, 4s a day in Australia, 1s deferred pay and 1s extra for service overseas, with allowances for wives and families—the equivalent of the wage of an average Australian worker. By 20 August over 10 000 men had enlisted in Sydney. By the second half of August the men from the bush began to pour into Sydney, Melbourne, Brisbane, Adelaide, Perth and Hobart. The sons of Dad and Mother Rudd, of Mrs Spicer, Mrs Baker and Brighten's sister-in-law were giving their 'particulars' to the recruiting sergeants.

British orders to the Australian Government to dispatch forces to take over German colonial possessions in the South-West Pacific were promptly and successfully carried out. On 12 August an Australian squadron raided Rabaul. An Australian and New Zealand Military Expedition Force dismantled German wireless stations in the surrounding islands which could be used to send signals to the German Pacific squadron. On 12 September the German officers at Rabaul surrendered. The next day the natives heard a new voice of command: 'All boys belongina one place, you savvy big master he come now, he new feller master . . . he look good you feller. Now he look out good you feller alonga him . . . No more "Um Kaiser". God Save "Um King".' On 21 September Germans and natives formally laid down arms.

By mid-September a change came over the mood of the people. Deakin wrote in his diary that the war news was 'sickening'. In western Europe the army of von Kluck had carried all before it. The gallant French army, out-gunned and out-generalled, was retreating towards Paris. The Kingdom of Belgium had been occupied, and there were reports of unspeakable German atrocities. The Russian 'steam-roller' had come to a halt on the plains of East Prussia. Von Kluck's army swung south-west towards Paris, hoping before the coming of the winter rains to know glory, dreaming of a *Te Deum* in Notre Dame and revelry on Montmartre.

While the fate of the war in western Europe hung by such a slender thread numbers of 'our boys', in the King's uniform, staggered about the streets of Sydney and Melbourne under the influence of liquor. As the sober and the unsteady paraded in the streets of capital cities, bystanders, idlers—the other army in Australia, the army of mockers and rowdies who roved about in search of targets for their wit—chiacked soldiers in uniform as 'six-bob-a-day tourists'. Publicans did not care how much shame was heaped on the King's uniform as long as their pockets were filled with most of that six bob a day. Recruiting slackened from a *presto* to a *rallentando*. The days of the idealists and the men of fine conscience were giving way to the cunning and the tough, those who totted up how well they would do on six bob a day, and those who knew what was what in the human scene.

On 5 September the Labor Party won a victory at the polls, gaining substantial majorities in both the House of Representatives and the Senate. When the ministry was announced, there were no surprises. Frank Anstey, who believed the people were held back from the paths of progress by prejudice and timidity and by the Tory cry of 'dragons and disasters', was not among the names of the ministers: nor was King O'Malley, with his somewhat windy rhetoric about 'roosters' and 'brotherhood'. Fisher, Hughes, Pearce, Tudor, Arthur, Archibald and Spence were pragmatists, men who wanted to walk on the earth, rather than soar in the air.

The top places in the Australian army were still held by a coterie from the country gentry: Labor did not challenge the alliance between militarism and squatterdom. Hungry for a note of recognition from the men of clubland, Labor ministers co-operated closely with Major-General Bridges and his advisers on how to win the war. On 26 September 1914, the government introduced censorship of the press and the mails.

The victory of the Brandenburgers would be a disaster for civilization. Norman Lindsay cartooned Kaiser Wilhelm II as a chief skull-gatherer, a man of such arrogance that he would be capable of issuing an ultimatum to heaven. In the state schools of New South Wales the schoolchildren were urged to sing such patriotic songs as:

Our Flag! Hurrah! My Flag! Hurrah!
Our Southern Stars our Southern home declaring,
England's cross and Ireland's cross and Scotland's faithful blue,
Home and Empire, Faith and Freedom, Home and Empire, Faith
    and Freedom sharing.

In the beginning there had been proud descriptions of the men in Australian uniform 'marching shoulder to shoulder with a fine easy swing'. By late September the behaviour of soldiers on leave in big cities had tempered this affection and admiration. On Friday 9 October soldiers in the camp at Broadmeadows had indulged in wild sexual orgies with a girl of 18. When copies of the newspaper reporting the incident reached the camp, soldiers seized them and tore them to pieces. Two days later an ugly riot occurred between the police and the soldiers in Melbourne during which excited soldiers rushed towards the offices of the newspaper which had published the offending article, shouting their intentions to 'destroy the bloody joint'.

In the meantime the troops and troopships for the expeditionary force were assembling in King George Sound, that magnificent sheet of water where the first European travellers had mused over the desolation of the land. On 1 November 1914 the first convoy set sail for the Old World. The relentless sea was the first intimation to the men that they were the playthings in a sport over which they had little control. On the morning of 9 November off the Cocos Islands, the cruiser *Sydney* engaged a German light cruiser, the *Emden*. When the gunfire ceased, the German ship had been beached and wrecked. The faces of the men on the troopships shone on receiving this first intimation of glory. The chaplains called on them to join together in rendering thanks to Almighty God for the great benefit they had received at His hands.

For the First Lord of the Admiralty, Winston Churchill, who was ruminating in London, the Australian soldiers held out promise as instruments of a grand design brewing in his teeming brain. Australians, aided by the gallant New Zealanders and guided by more experienced British and French forces, could be deployed in a manoeuvre which would bring much-needed relief to the Russians, knock the Turks out of the war at one blow, frustrate the German hopes of an uninterrupted line of communication between Berlin and Baghdad, and open up a theatre of war which might give the Western Allies the chance to end the war without the bloodbaths required to win the war in the West. He was like a man possessed by a wild demon. He flew into the execution of the idea without exposing it to the judgement of the measurers of Whitehall: the British navy would force the Dardanelles; Allied armies would land on the beaches both at Cape Gallipoli and at the southern entrance to the passage leading to the prize of Constantinople. Australian bushmen and London cockneys would knock Johnny Turk out of the war. Russia would be relieved: the English and the French could then roll back the German army to where it belonged, east of the Rhine.

The men on the convoy who were longing for a chance to 'get at 'em' learnt that their sacrificial blood would not hallow green fields in England, nor would the fallen lie beneath the roses of Picardy. The British had decided to send them to a training camp near Cairo. They were destined for a country not unlike their own, an arid country where the creeks ran dry, and sea and sky presented a vast indifference to all human striving, a site just to the north of another ghastly haggard country like their own, which had cradled a 'ghastly theology' about the punishing bully Jehovah. They were moving towards those deserts where a miracle-worker had been asked whether even He could command the stones to be made into bread. They were moving towards one part of the past which had made them what they were.

In the meantime a contingent of 10 500 Australian troops and 2000 New Zealanders left Australia to join their comrades. Their commander was Colonel John Monash. In October 1914 he had been made Commander of the 4th Infantry Brigade of the AIF. Monash was born in West Melbourne on 27 June 1865, the son of Jewish parents who had migrated to a British colony in the hope of acquiring a fortune in a country free from religious persecution. Educated at Scotch College and the University of Melbourne where he graduated Bachelor of Arts in 1887, Bachelor of Civil Engineering in 1890 and Bachelor of Laws in 1895, Monash quickly rose to the top as an engineer. Fate had played him strange tricks. Although born with the gifts to win distinction in both the Citizen Defence Force and in his chosen career, his birth excluded him from membership of the Melbourne Club. As a member of the Jewish community he could be the servant of the Most High, but never be fully accepted in such circles.

He sat in his cabin on the troopship detached, businesslike, viewing the movement of the ships in squadron like an exercise on an engineer's drawing board. Life had prepared him for the role the war would confer on him. With him was Colonel Granville Ryrie, the owner of Michelago Station on the Monaro, a bluff, hearty, tough man who had won notoriety as a conservative member of the House of Representatives by offering to knock out the champion boxer of Captain's Flat if the miners promised to vote for him. The men of courage, the men of talent and the men who stood firm when the world rocked, were coming to the top.

On arriving in the canal zone Monash learned that the members of the AIF were to be placed under the command of Major-General William Riddell Birdwood. An English gentleman soldier was to be the Supreme Commander of the Australian and New Zealand forces in Europe. The Labor leaders in Australia did not demur.

Birdwood behaved in ways which might have offended the rank and file, who saw themselves as being of 'temper democratic' and of a bias 'offensively Australian'. His voice had the bleat which suggested effeminacy to Australians. But nature had given him the gifts with which to win the affection and undying devotion of the men committed to his charge. He had a mysterious charisma, a bubbling warmth which appealed both to the boys from the bush and the men from the suburbs. To their surprise they found they adored him. Birdwood was an actor *manqué*. He could spin his monocle in the air and catch it between the right eyebrow and cheek on the way down. That trick had the troops on parade in hysterics of delight. Birdwood also had in abundance what Australians call the 'gift of the gab'. They loved him. After inspecting the Brigade commanded by Colonel Monash 'Birdie' told him that his men were the finest brigade in Egypt. Monash puffed out his chest like a pigeon.

The members of the AIF soon decided that Egypt was 'a land of sin, sand, shit and syphilis'. The Egyptians were 'filthy beasts!', or as a one-time sheep farmer from Tasmania put it: 'I was a sure believer in White Australia before I left home, but now I am a perfervid and rabid "White Australian"'. Stories went the rounds of all the tents of Mena camp of how the 'F——— Gyppoes' freshened up the grapes they sold to Australian soldiers at exorbitant prices by dipping them in urine, or washed tomatoes in pans of piss and shit. The Australians bargained with pedlars not with words but with sticks. 'The stick and plenty of it', was the language the Gyppo understood. Those who took their leave in Cairo first had their 'horizontal refreshment' with the girls, followed by that other sport which Australians seemed to love—tormenting the defenceless, the weak and all the creatures whom God seemed to have forgotten. Wherever Australians moved they quickly transformed the place into a 'vaudeville of devils'. While this human uproar raged in Cairo and at Mena camp the men in black in London were assigning a very special role to the troops from the New World: the frequenters of the brothels of Cairo were to become the saviours of the Empire: the men who had displayed such a taste for the lower depths were to show they could also climb the loftiest pinnacle of human achievement.

9

Ideals Cast to the Winds

On New Year's Day 1915 a bizarre event occurred at Broken Hill. Two men, who had concealed themselves near the railway line between the Hill and Silverton, fired on a picnic train, killing four passengers and wounding seven. In an ensuing shoot-out between the police and the assailants one man was wounded and the other was riddled with bullets and died later in hospital. These two men, identified as Turks, had begun their own war against the people of the British Empire. That night a furious crowd burned down the German Club in Broken Hill. Next day all the rowdies cheered wildly as 'a venturesome young man' yanked his way up the flagpole and hoisted the Australian flag on top of it.

In France Allied and German soldiers waded in blood. George V informed the Governor-General of Australia how very sorry he was to hear there had been a good deal of venereal disease and drunkenness in the Australian battalions since their arrival in Cairo. His Majesty was struck by the excessively high rates of pay for Australians, but assumed that was in conformity with the current rate of wages in the country. The autumn racing carnival in Sydney in March 1915 lured crowds of 30 000 a day: Melbourne racing officials at the same time rubbed their hands with glee at the prospects of a bumper winter season. The New South Wales Football League asked Maoriland to send over a team in June. Theatres were full. Young men pored over betting lists in newspapers, the results of the recent prize-fights, the cricket scores, or anything that represented or portrayed the froth of life.

To counter this complacency, press, politicians, parsons, priests and professors painted terrifying pictures of what would happen to Australians if they did not snap out of their indifference: Huns would overrun the country; barbarians would perpetrate here the same horrors they had practised on the women and children of little Belgium. Recruiters, known as 'urgers', visited the country towns to attract volunteers for the AIF. Enthusiasts organized 'cooee' marches and 'kangaroo' marches from country to city to swell the number of recruits. The 'urgers' accused eligibles who did not volunteer of 'hanging back'. The spiritual bullies posted a white feather to such eligibles. Women provided sandwiches and 'smokes' for the men as they boarded the train for the long journey to the recruiting centre in a capital city. Public men spoke of their pride that their town or their district was well represented in the 'great army of the Empire'. Others urged the 'cold footed' not to hang back. But by year's end recruiting figures showed that the bushmen were no more patriotic or imperial-minded than city-dwellers. The *Labor Call* claimed that 95 per cent of the volunteers came from the working classes. Unemployed men gathered outside Victoria Barracks in Melbourne eager to enlist to obtain food, shelter and clothing for their families, while Mr Fat Man rolled past Victoria Barracks in his motor car. Mr Fat Man was getting richer: the poor, poorer.

Australians were not makers of their own history. In London the men in black made a decision: on 18 March British naval ships, under the command of Admiral Roebeck, tried to force a passage by bombarding Turkish gun emplacements and destroying minefields in the straits of the Dardanelles. They were driven back by the Turks; Roebeck withdrew and informed Churchill that the navy could not force a passage without troops. That meant convincing Kitchener and General Ian Hamilton of the wisdom of a combined operation. Churchill fumed and raged. Delay increased the hazards of such an expedition. Warned by the unsuccessful naval attack, the German General Liman von Sanders began to reinforce the harsh inhospitable cliffs of the Bosporus. In the season when the cheep of sparrows at dawn conveyed the news that the days were about to grow hot in Babylon the British generals drew up their plans for a combined attack, never suspecting for one moment what their leisurely lunches beneath the green willows might add to the sum of human suffering. An English Army Service Corps man suggested they be known as A.N.Z.A.C. A legend was being born.

On 1 April an order was posted at the camp at Mena: 'All leave stopped'. On that morning soldiers from both Australia and New Zealand set out for the brothel district (the Wozzer) to settle scores for past humiliations before leaving for some unknown destination. With the energy of men who believed they might be close to their last days on earth they piled in a heap furniture and clothing and any items treasured by the despised 'Gyppoes'. To a chorus of drunken yells and encouraged by their mates to teach the bastards a lesson they would not forget in a hurry, they set the pile alight.

With a singular lack of discretion someone summoned the British military police, all police being anathema to a predominantly working-class Australian mob. A riot exploded into deeds of savagery as the Australians and New Zealanders incited each other to tear everything down and finish the bastards off. The appearance of the Lancashire Territorials outside Shepheard's Hotel quietened the soldiers: the Bacchanalian orgy collapsed as quickly as it had erupted. Drunken rioters resumed the mantle of solemnity and high seriousness.

At long last the men in high places had agreed on a plan of attack. The Mediterranean Expeditionary Force, under the command of General Ian Hamilton, was to land at two places on the Gallipoli Peninsula. Believing that untried colonial troops would need stiffening, British as well as Australian and New Zealand troops were to land on several beaches between the cliffs of Cape Helles and Sedd-el-Bahr. Under the command of General Birdwood the Australians and New Zealanders were to land at a beach 13 miles north of the British landing, near the promontory of Gaba Tepe. The armed might of a people committed to a democratic egalitarian army was about to go into action on a foreign shore under the leadership of two English generals who were devotees of class and caste. To the dismay of Churchill there was to be no attempt by the ships of the Royal Navy to force a passage through the Dardanelles. This time the army would go it alone at a place where over 500 years earlier the Turks had gathered for the fall of Constantinople.

In mid-April the Australian infantry, artillery, engineers, ambulance men and chaplains embarked at Alexandria in troop-ships for the rendezvous with the other participants in the enterprise in Mudros Harbour on the island of Lemnos, 60 miles from the Dardanelles. They were anchored opposite Troy, the battlefield of those Homeric heroes whose exploits had helped to shape their civilization. With the moonlight dancing in silver streaks over the waters, so reminiscent of Homer's 'wine-dark sea', the transports slipped out of Mudros Harbour on 24 April. At 3.30 a.m. steamboats towed landing craft towards the beach. It was Sunday 25 April—another 'sad Sabbath morn'. Unknown to the men on the landing barges, the current drifted towards a shore where the cliffs were less forbidding than the site chosen by the decision-makers. On what was going on in the hearts and minds of the men posterity was not to glean a rich harvest. They were Australians. No one so far had put down on paper or taught them what Australia was all about. No one had said why a man should die either for the haggard continent or what it stood for. In the majesty of the moment the minds of the men did not turn to their 'sun-burnt country', or 'the vision splendid of the sunlit plains extended'. Their thoughts turned to those they loved. For them kindness was the only comforter against the menace of nature and the malice of man. One soldier, G. Mitchell, who had an eye for the significance of the moment, wrote: 'We had come from the New World for the conquest of the Old'. 'All we thought of', wrote another, 'was to get at them'.

With the barges 40 yards from the beach, a single shot rang out. Machine-gun bullets from the shore and shrapnel ripped into human flesh. A voice cried out, 'They've got me'. Men fingered their bayonets, or what they called their 'pen-knives', to make sure everything was in order, before leaping into the sea to wade for the beach and scramble up that 'bloody cliff' and finish off the bastards at the top. One man was glad the blood had begun to flow: 'The ——s', he wrote in a letter, 'will give us a go after all'. A boat returned to a ship offshore carrying a young midshipman, waving his hand cheerfully with a shot through his stomach. On shore the first to land rushed a Turkish trench, gave them the 'pen-knife treatment' and drove the others away.

Then they began to climb the cliff. Colonials being practical above all else went about it in a practical way. By the time the sun had risen the first Australians had reached the ridge, where they dug trenches to prepare for the fall of the modern Constantinople. All morning the murderous fight went on. By afternoon the Turks were spraying the beach from Gaba Tepe with two field-guns, causing heavy casualties among the soldiers on the beach and those still attempting to land. The wounded were carried on stretchers back to the landing boats. No one had ever before witnessed such an astonishing response to pain and danger. The wounded cheered the crew of the ship to which they returned. The dying cracked jokes. Australian voices echoed over the still waters of Gaba Tepe.

They were no longer the voices of men whose only thought was 'to get at them'. They were surrounded by the bodies of their fallen comrades, and the voices of the wounded and the dying. Between them and Constantinople stood a brave and formidable foe. Gone was the boasting and the devil-may-care of the previous day. Though the ordeal had conferred a mantle of lasting glory on them, war, as one private had discovered, was 'simply terrible'. He had seen his pals shot down beside him. The roar of the 15-inch guns and the rattle of rifle fire were enough to drive a fellow mad. One man who had volunteered gladly for death or glory decided that night that all men were fools. He wanted to know where his thirteen mates were. He also wanted to know whether he too would soon join the acres of dead men rotting on the cliff, or on the beaches, or floating face down in the ever restless sea. That night General Birdwood, who had landed on the beach in the afternoon, congratulated the Australians and New Zealanders on their achievements and urged them to stand firm until sufficient reinforcements arrived to enable them to drive the Turks off the Gallipoli Peninsula.

While the survivors on the ridge were feverishly digging trenches in the rocky soil, and company commanders were coaxing men drunk with fatigue to make up a party to strengthen threatened sections of the line, the 16th Battalion of the Fourth Australian Infantry Brigade waded ashore under the command of Colonel John Monash. Like the heroes in the first landing these men began their task in a light-hearted mood. They whistled, they sang, they cracked jokes, they indulged in all sorts of Australian horse-play and fun. By nightfall on the 26th the survivors of that landing had an inkling that they had taken part in an event which would bring eternal glory to all who had participated in it. Monash was proud of the 'physique and sublime courage of his men'. He found them docile, patient, obedient and manageable as children. Despite their losses they were still laughing and joking and singing. When they were called on to attack the Turkish line they assured him they were 'ready for another go'. They sang 'Tipperary' and 'Australia will be There'. He loved it. His men were true Australian-Britons. They were true sons of the Empire.

At the same time Nellie Melba was cheerfully lending her voice to entice more men into the army, and to persuade all and sundry to give generously to the comfort funds. A brilliant audience gathered in the Melbourne Town Hall on the night of 27 April to hear Australia's Queen of Song. The Dives of this world provided substantial proof of their sympathy for a 'noble cause'. The most luxurious limousines glittering with plate glass and silver plating stopped under the portico of the Town Hall to deposit ladies in their gorgeous silks, and the men in their traditional sombre black. The people arrived on foot, or in rickety four-wheelers. Nellie turned her silvery trills into sovereigns for the relief of those stricken by the war. She auctioned the national flags of the Allies. A Russian naval ensign went for 24 guineas, the flag of Poland for £200. Two Australian flags went for £60 and £40, Nellie expressing her displeasure with a stamp of the foot and an indignant 'Forty pounds for Australia'. Slowly, very solemnly she unfolded the Belgian flag and told the audience in a hushed voice: 'This flag I hold in the deepest reverence'. She told them the flag would be hung in the Town Hall as a memento. Under it would be the names of those Melburnians who contributed £100. They took £6100 that night. The evening ended with the Governor-General calling for three cheers for Madame Melba.

To honour the living and the dead General Birdwood recommended on 29 April that the bay on which they had landed on 25 April be known from that time on as Anzac Cove. Their immortality began just as their own responses changed from recklessness and a lust for blood sport into the sardonic humour which had comforted and strengthened their ancestors when they became aware of the conditions of human existence in Australia. Like their ancestors they fell back on the sentimental:

> It's a long way to Riverina,
> It's a long way to go:
> It's a long way to Riverina,
> And the sweet bush girl I know.
> Goodbye, Wagga Wagga; farewell dear old Hay,
> It's a long, long way to Riverina,
> But we'll come back—some day.

By the end of April they were resigned to the simple fact that any further advance against the Turk was like their hopes of going home: it would happen some day. Despite the horror, the stench and the hardships their extraordinary cheerfulness remained. 'So long chaps', a wounded man would say, 'see you later. I'm off for a holiday'. A mortally wounded man asked for a pencil. His mates thought he wanted to send a message to his 'mum' or his 'sheila' back in Aussie, but he scribbled, 'Are we downhearted?' and died. In the trenches where they were so close to the Turks that they could hear the bastards (a word often used with great affection for a worthy foe) sending up their cries of anguish to Allah, their one expressed aim was not to be perforated like a sieve by snipers, or filled 'like a plum pudding with shrapnel pellets'. On the beaches daredevil Australian soldiers swam naked, not seeming to care twopence what happened. The saying went: 'If a shell comes the Englishman runs for shelter: the Indian calls on Allah: but the Australian merely looks around and says: 'Where the hell did that come from?''

While the blowflies buzzed over the corpses of dead Australians on the cliffs, back home on 8 May the press informed the Australian people of the landing at Gallipoli. They wrote in banner headlines of a 'Glorious Entry into War', of a 'Historic Charge', and a 'Brilliant Feat at Gaba Tepe'. They quoted General Birdwood: he could not sufficiently praise the courage, endurance and soldierly qualities of the colonials. Ignoring the implied condescension, the conservative press gloried in Australia's reputation for providing gallant soldiers of the Empire. The war brought death to Australians. By 30 April 61 officers and 799 other ranks were said to be lying dead on the heights of Anzac Cove, on the cliffs and on the beaches; 110 officers and 2641 other ranks were wounded. The true figures were probably much greater—probably 7000 to 7500 all told.

The publication of the casualty lists stunned some members of the labour movement. They brought the horrors of war home to the common people. The members of the working classes had been sacrificed again in the interests of Money Power. The conservatives screamed for more recruits: when a Briton fell another Briton must take his place. Sections of the labour movement wanted to stop the madness. A crack was becoming visible in Australian society.

In the meantime the Anzacs were carrying out the command of General Birdwood to 'Dig in and fight it out'. The war had developed into a stalemate. With water short, rations short and no diversions from the boredom of life in the trenches, the glory and the devil-may-care mood changed into sullen resignation. They still laughed and joked, but they knew that any advance party would be cut down like hay before the mower. As sickness, dysentery, boredom and discomfort assailed their spirits they saw the fighting less and less as an opportunity to win glory, and more and more as something which threatened to take away from them the most precious gift of all—their lives. They longed for rescue. The men who made their history had decided that no such rescue would take place.

William Throsby Bridges stuck to the task at hand. The welfare of his men, and not his own salvation, was always his prime concern. On 15 May while inspecting his troops in Shrapnel Gully he was warned by a medical officer, Clive Thompson, of the dangers in moving from one sandbag barrier to another. But, brave as ever, he told Thompson: 'I suppose I must run for it again'. Half-way across the gap he was seen to fall. When they dragged him to cover he knew and they knew he 'was for it'. Bridges breathed his last at 5.45 a.m. on 18 May on the hospital ship *Gascon*. Australia had lost one of the finest flowers of the Australian-British tradition.

On 18 May the men on Gallipoli launched a furious assault on the Turkish lines. Huge casualties were inflicted on the Turks, who lost between 7000 and 8000 men at a cost of 500 colonial casualties. The stalemate returned. Colonel Monash took a philosophic view. The men began to chafe and yearn for a decision.

At home the slowdown in recruitment began to lay bare the class differences in Australian society. According to the Labor press, the wealthy classes were very meagrely represented in the ranks because, unless he could get a commission, 'Gussie from Toorak does not care to take on soldiering'. Australia had a democratic people's army. Well-to-do young men should give up fat billets, quit comfortable homes, enlist in the ranks and take their chance of earning a commission by merit. When Holman, the Labor Premier of New South Wales, and Wade, the leader of the conservative party in that State, attended the Sydney Stadium together to make recruiting speeches early in August 1915, they were counted out by the noisier members of the working classes in Sydney, a city whose first working class had had no reason for sentiments of gratitude or affection to the British ruling classes. The two speakers had to throw in the towel and get out of the ring.

The hostility to Germans resident in Australia intensified. Miners and railway workers refused to work with Germans: factory workers told their bosses they would go out on strike unless all German employees were dismissed. Letters appeared in the press calling on all employers of labour—manual, clerical and professional—to get rid of enemy aliens. In his capacity as Attorney-General, Hughes enforced rigidly the section of the new War Precautions Act which empowered the government to suspend all publications in the German language. Only the *Review of Reviews* and one provincial paper protested against such fanaticism.

The war speeded the emancipation of women from domestic service and their enslavement to the new industrial juggernaut. In Sydney and Melbourne women were engaged as clerks, in railway offices and as bus and tram conductors. Women entered more and more professions and women were being employed in ammunition factories. As the army lowered its standards for recruits the openings for women increased. Women became part of the industrial army. Conservative women saw their role as organizers and leaders of drives to provide comforts for the troops. They pledged themselves to give up all luxuries. They patronized drives to help the soldiers and gave generously to comforts funds. They resolved to learn the rudiments of cooking so that their servants might work in clothing or munitions factories. They volunteered to serve at the Rest Home for Wounded Soldiers; they offered beds in their homes to soldiers to tide them over the time between discharge from hospital and taking a job.

On 2 June 1915 the Governor-Governor of the Commonwealth of Australia, Sir Ronald Munro-Ferguson, unveiled a brass plate and declared open the new steelworks erected by BHP at Newcastle. All previous attempts to begin an iron and steel industry in Australia had foundered because of competition with steel products imported from Germany, the United States and Britain. The Act of 1914 prohibiting trade with the enemy temporarily ended German competition and the British steel mills were at full stretch to meet the demands of war. Partly for military reasons, the Labor Government undertook to finish the transcontinental railway line between Port Augusta and Kalgoorlie. The war came like a good fairy to the aid of the directors and shareholders of BHP. The foundries of Newcastle would achieve what no amount of rhetoric and poetry had been able to accomplish: the material foundations for political and cultural independence.

General Hamilton had a plan for a renewed assault on the Dardanelles. On 2 August the British troops landed at Suvla Bay. On the evening of 6 August advanced Australian units made their first feint against the Turkish troops entrenched on the ridge at Lone Pine. Once again the Australians were descending into hell in an imperial cause. The Turks stood firm. The slaughter was unrelenting. In the fierce heat, the stench of rotting bodies filled the lungs of the living. Within a few days the dead on both sides were lying four or five deep along the trenches. As one Australian put it, Lone Pine was not a stoush: it was like being 'in a cage with a few playful lions and tigers for a year or two'.

The survivors from the ordeal no longer talked of glory: they talked of murder. They believed they had been let down, that, as in the charge of the Light Brigade, someone had blundered. The soldiers felt that few if any understood their plight. As they squatted on top of the dead bodies of their mates, news came from home of the welcome their wounded mates had received when they got back to Aussie. Men whose eyes had been shot away had sat all night in an unheated train between Melbourne and Sydney. The people of Sydney greeted them with a brass band playing 'Home Sweet Home'. The following day society ladies smiled with compassion on the men bedridden in a military hospital and gave the walking wounded tickets to attend houses of entertainment, picture shows and vaudeville where they could have a good laugh. Those who read were given copies of Nellie Melba's *Gift Book*, in which there were stories extolling the military virtues of courage, coolness and daring. But what they had gone through had rendered irrelevant the language of chivalry. Nellie Melba hailed them as heroes who had displayed the greatest of all the arts: to love nobly and die for liberty. Roderic Quinn praised them for scaling the heights of glory. Henry Lawson was proud that the sons of the bush people were now fighting for 'England's name'.

In September, Frank Anstey reminded the readers of the *Labor Call* that Money Power was doing nicely out of the war. Evil men were reaping vast profits from the 'mad slaughter'. In her book, *Put up the Sword*, Adela Pankhurst argued that the Germans had not

committed atrocities in Belgium and that Germans were forced to
torpedo British and neutral ships because the British had used their
naval power for the purposes of piracy. The *Bulletin* wanted her
book and the activities of her group, The Women's Peace Army, to
be submitted to the Australian censor. A plea for peace and sanity
had become an act of treason.

In the midst of all the uproar a very Australian writer put into
words his vision of what life was all about. C. J. Dennis saw himself
as a people's poet. His collection of poems, *The Songs of a Sentimental
Bloke*, was published in 1915. It told the life story of a larrikin, the
Bloke, and his girl, Doreen, from Spadger's Lane, Melbourne.
The Bloke entertained no hopes for the future of Australians. He
decided to 'take the 'ole mad world as 'arf a joke'. He confronted life
as a sardonic cynic and mocker, having in his bones the wisdom of
his Australian ancestors not to expect much from life. Like Henry
Lawson, Dennis was a divided man. He shared the sentiments he
placed in the mouths of his protagonists, and at the same time took
revenge against Australians for all that he as a sensitive man had
suffered from the Philistines of the suburbs and the barbarians of
the bush. Dennis was selling sentimentality to the bourgeoisie for
the 1915 equivalent of thirty pieces of silver.

Australians greeted the work with enthusiasm. Fifty thousand
copies were sold within a year. There had been nothing like it since
the publication of 'Banjo' Paterson's *The Man From Snowy River*.
Dennis followed it with a work which put into memorable words
the reasons why people of Australia found themselves participants
in the carnage at Gallipoli. It was the adventures of Ginger Mick,
another Melbourne larrikin, a city Ned Kelly—a people's hero in a
society whose centre of gravity had shifted from the bush to the
suburbs. On the streets, 'stoushin' some coot' eased ' 'is swellin'
'eart'. The Bloke believed in 'livin' an' lovin' '. Ginger Mick, a brain-
child of the war, added something to the Bloke's philosophy. War
transfigured Ginger from an Australian larrikin into a noble hero.
During his trial in the fiery furnace he discovered a truth about life:

> An' each man is the clean, straight man 'is Maker meant 'im for,
> An' each man knows 'is brother man at last.
> Shy strangers, till a bugle blast preached 'oly brother'ood;
> But mateship they 'ave found at last; An' they 'ave found it good.

As Henry Lawson had put it twenty years earlier, the better part of
a people's life came uppermost in a storm: the creed of the larrikin
was 'chivalry-upside down'.

The Australians at Gallipoli were in the mood to receive such a
message. In their misery they saw themselves as men who knew

that some things were worth fighting and dying for, as men who had fought with some of the finest mates that ever existed. They joked bitterly about the food, the water, the flies and the lice. They looked at each other as men who were not as other men, not dreamers of a new heaven and a new earth, but men whose experiences had wrought in them the miracle of a secular transfiguration.

While deep in this mood of both bitterness and exaltation they were visited in September by Keith Murdoch, a promising Australian journalist who had access to men in high places in both Melbourne and London. Murdoch came to the conclusion that something must be done to save the poor fellows on Gallipoli. He was impressed by the affection of the fine young Australian soldiers for each other and for their homeland: Australianism had become among them a more powerful sentiment than before. The men had proved their fighting qualities, and that special capacity of Australians to endure hardship. The men had a wonderfully generous view of life. They discussed death quite fearlessly: 'It is no disgrace', they said, 'for an Australian to die beside good pals in Anzac, where his best pals are under the dust'.

On one point the morale of the troops was low. They were thoroughly dispirited by their military prospects. The men had great faith in some of their leaders—in Birdwood, and some of their officers—but for Hamilton they had nothing but contempt. He was the absentee general who lived at Imbros. The French called him the general who lived on an island. The men were also convinced that appointments to the General Staff were made from 'motives of friendship and social influence'. Australians on Gallipoli loathed and detested any Englishman 'wearing red'—the military emblem of those distinctions of social class they despised. The Australians believed men had died because of the incompetence of Sir James Porter, the Englishman in charge of the medical services. He too came from the English upper class: he lived on a luxurious yacht in Mudros Harbour. Murdoch concluded that there would be catastrophe unless Hamilton were replaced and the troops withdrawn. In September he presented his case to the Australian Prime Minister in a long letter and in the same month he had interviews with Asquith and other ministers in London.

Back in Australia Andrew Fisher had grown weary of the world of politics. The radical wing of the Labor Party had been pestering him to use the defence power under the Constitution to implement a radical social and economic policy. The radical Frank Anstey collected facts and figures with which to embarrass Fisher during discussions at party meetings. Fisher had had enough: he had reached that point when he was not prepared to put up with any more of the supercilious political virtue and omniscience practised by the dreamers and the visionaries. He was astounded that a tormented and divided man like Anstey should have the effrontery to flaunt political virtue in his face. They could all go to hell. Fisher decided to resign.

On 26 October the Labor Caucus elected William Morris Hughes as leader of the Australian Labor Party. In his moment of triumph Hughes resembled a famous description by the poet Pope: he was that tortured, tortuous being who carried the force of genius in his tiny frame, a fate which neither fame, not achievement, love nor friendship, but only deceit and chicanery, betrayal and revenge, could sweeten or alleviate. Hughes seemed to have been left with only a public face. He could rant, roar and rage but not be conscience-stricken by the pain and suffering inflicted on others as the price of the victory of the forces which he so passionately served. He had come to believe that the future welfare of the Australian people depended on the victory of the Allies in the war. No price was too high to pay for that victory.

In mid-October the British Government took the decision to save those 'poor fellows on Gallipoli'. On 14 October they appointed General Sir Charles Munro to replace Sir Ian Hamilton as Commander of the forces in the eastern Mediterranean. Munro belonged to the school of thought which believed that only a decisive victory against the Germans on the Western Front could end the war. He arrived on the peninsula on 28 October; on 31 October he dispatched a telegram to Kitchener recommending a total evacuation. Kitchener was shattered. It was not until 12 December, after many somersaults of opinion, that Kitchener and the British Government finally resolved on evacuation. The energy and conviction which might have commanded victory were now concentrated upon flight.

At dusk on 18 December the withdrawal from the front-line trenches began. On the night of 19–20 December troops were marched to the beaches in parties of 400, where they embarked on troop carriers for the voyage to Mudros on Lemnos Island. By dawn on 20 December the hills and the valleys returned to a silence and a solitude like the solitude of the deserts of Australia. As they slipped through the darkness one man said: 'Let us move quietly when we pass our mates' graves, so that they will not know we are deserting them'. Others gripped their mates by the hand and managed to say through tears, 'See you later'. On one battleship the men celebrated the end of their long ordeal with a meal of porridge. At Mudros the privates had their taste of luxury, while their senior officers savoured again the delights of social privilege. Cards from home handed out to them when they disembarked at Mudros portrayed a kangaroo swishing a Turk off the peninsula with his tail. That hurt. Within a week they were back in Cairo, the officers in their soft beds in Shepheard's Hotel and the men at Mena camp. Soon the heroes of Gallipoli were once again the ockers of Cairo.

Between 25 April and 20 December 1915, 7818 died in the Dardanelles campaign. At a social gathering of the Returned Soldiers Association in the Melbourne Town Hall on 22 December Major-General I. G. McKay expanded on the meaning of their sacrifices. No historian of the future, he thought, could criticize Australian units because they had failed. The winter rains would fall again on Gallipoli: they might leave Australian graves indistinguishable from other graves. That was not the point:

> The memory was alive, and though none of them would ever see the Anzac beach again, the first great sacred spot in the history of Australia was the Anzac beach and the heights above it . . . There were 20,000 of us on a 380 acre selection for several months, under fire all the time. Small as it was, that bit of Gallipoli would forever be part of Australia.

Those present greeted his words with tumultuous applause. The Major-General wept, as men should weep on an occasion of tragic grandeur. Some Australians were abandoning their hopes of creating a society free of the evils of the Old World, a society where there was equality of opportunity without servility, mediocrity, conformity or greyness of spirit. For some Australians the void left by loss of belief in God and the life of the world to come had been filled by worship of a site and heroic deeds which held out no hopes for the future. Australians had acquired a sacred site. The Anzacs were transfigured into folk heroes. From that time on there was one day in the year when Australians who believed in calling no biped lord or sir, and touching their hat to no man, found themselves saying, through tears, the words of the Bloke: 'I dips me lid'. In Europe the killing went on.

BOOK SIX

'The Old Dead Tree
and the Young Tree Green'
1916–1935

Sons of the South, make the choice between
(Sons of the South, choose true)
The Land of Morn and the Land of E'en,
The Old Dead Tree and the Young Tree Green,
The Land that belongs to the lord and Queen,
And the Land that belongs to you.

Henry Lawson, 'A Song of the Republic'

The great idea of immortality would have vanished, and they would
have to fill its place; and all the wealth of love lavished of old upon
Him, who was immortal, would be turned upon the whole of nature,
on the world, on men, on every blade of grass . . . everyone would
tremble for the life and happiness of each; they would grow tender
to one another . . . and would be as caressing as children. Meeting,
they would look at one another with deep and thoughtful eyes, and
in their eyes would be love and sorrow . . .

F. M. Dostoevsky, *A Raw Youth*

1

Two Australias

On 1 July 1916 the British offensive began on the Somme. On that morning the English historian R. H. Tawney took communion to strengthen him for the ordeal, believing that a man should meet death 'brimful with Christ'. He heard the beautiful words of the communion service above the rattling of rifle-bolts, the bursts of song and occasional laughter from his comrades. He heard a priest of the Church of England invite all those who intended to lead a new life following the commandments of God to draw near with faith and take this holy sacrament to their comfort, meekly kneeling upon their knees. As he and his comrades climbed out of the trench he suddenly understood a passage in Bunyan's *Pilgrim's Progress*: 'Then I saw that there was a way to Hell'. By the end of the day he was lying face down with a bullet wound in his chest. When they attacked they were 820 strong: at nightfall 370 were left, and two days later 54 were left. Within a week the fields around the Somme were littered with bodies. All the trees had been cut off by shells. Raymond Asquith, the son of the British Prime Minister Herbert Asquith, saw 'craters swimming in blood and rotting and swelling bodies and rats like shadows fattened for the market moving cunningly and liquourishly among them, limbs and bowels nesting in the hedges and over all the most supernaturally shocking scent of death and corruption that ever breathed o'er Eden'. He thought the horror of it might 'almost be held to prove the existence of God. Who else', he asked, 'could have thought of it?'

Then the Australians moved into the battle. Haig has decided to use the Australian soldiers to capture the village of Pozières to give the 4th British Army a chance to push eastwards and punch a hole in the German line. To prepare the way for the Australians, British artillery softened up the German lines. On the night of 19 July the Australian First Division marched past the part-ruined cathedral at Albert where a golden statue of the Virgin swayed precariously from the steeple. On 23 July two of the Australian divisions began the attack to capture Pozières. Later that day they had captured the village, where they behaved as Australians always did after an ordeal: they smoked cigars, wore German helmets, and carried on as though they were men of the people satirizing their elders and their betters—a situation which always gave Australians great satisfaction. The real agony was about to begin.

By mid-August around Pozières and the British sector of the Somme the road and the trenches were strewn with the dead. The shrapnel left human bodies 'mere lumps of flesh'. A lieutenant cried like a little child. Some struggled and called out for their mothers, while others blabbered sentences no one could make out. The moans of the wounded and the dying were heard above the din of battle. One Australian soldier wrote to his parents: 'Don't forget to pray for me, as it's absolute hell here. Anyhow I have had the honour of being in the biggest battle in history. I expect to get a decoration out of it'. The soldiers had moved into a 'perfect Hell'. The men from the bush were blown into smithereens. Henry Farmer had roamed the bush in east Gippsland shooting wallabies and possums for skins, fossicking for gold, and snigging logs out of the forest. When he volunteered he decided not to let the banks have his money while he was away. He buried his gold sovereigns under a tree, and, cunning old bugger that he was, he decided to tell no one where it was. He was killed in the capture of Pozières. No one found his sovereigns. William E. Perry, teacher in the school at Combienbar, where Henry Farmer had worked, was much loved despite his frequent use of the strap, especially on days after lights had been seen in the bar at the local hotel. No trace of him remained after Pozières. On his gravestone the words were cut: 'Known Unto God'.

'The men', C. E. W. Bean wrote in his diary,

> are simply turned in there as into some ghastly giant mincing machine. The[y] have to stay there while shell after shell descends with a shriek close beside them—each one an acute mental torture— each shrieking tearing crash bringing a promise to each man— instantaneous—I will tear you into ghastly wounds—I will rend your flesh and pulp an arm or a leg—fling you half a gaping, quivering man like others that you see smashed around you, one by one, to lie there rottening and blackening.

During several days of heavy bombardment, wrote Bean,

> men were driven stark staring mad & more than one of them rushed out over the trench towards the Germans, any amount of them could be seen crying and sobbing like children their nerves completely gone . . . we were nearly all in a state of silliness & half dazed, but still the Australians refused to give ground.

Dear, kind Charlie Bean could not understand why a benevolent God would permit such things to happen. But, as he thought later, perhaps it was not for human beings to scan the mind of God: *'Non nobis Domine'*. It was not for us to say.

By the time the Australians were withdrawn from Pozières on 5 September and replaced by the Canadians there were 22 826 Australian casualties. The survivors never forgot the experience. For them the illusions of heroism and sacrifice and all the ideals of warfare were shattered. The 'bloody British top brass' had done it again, just as the same inhuman bastards had done it to their cobbers at The Nek and Lone Pine on the Gallipoli peninsula. After the fighting died down observers walked over the battlefield. The English poet John Masefield was one of them. 'Can you imagine', he asked his 'dear heart', 'a landscape in the moon, made of filth instead of beauty?' He wrote:

> There was a cat eating a man's brain, & such a wreck of war as I never did see, & the wounded coming by, dripping blood on the track, & one walked on blood or rotten flesh, & saw bags of men being carried to the grave. They were shovelling parts of men into blankets.

He had seen in a hospital the men suffering from burns.

> There were people with the tops of their heads burnt off & stinking like frizzled meat, & the top all red and dripping with pus, & their faces all gone, & their arms just covered with a kind of gauntlet of raw meat, & perhaps their whole bodies, from their knees to their shoulders, without any semblance of skin.

But despite all these horrors the gentle John Masefield believed the British should continue to fight until victory was attained. Theirs was a righteous cause—they were working with Providence towards 'a kind of justice'.

One man whose soul was not troubled was the GSO1 of the Australian First Division, Thomas Blamey. Before the assault on Pozières Blamey asked God for one thing: 'a clear brain to plan and think for it'. Blamey was a martinet of the parade ground. He read widely. Kipling's 'If' was his creed for what a man should be. He had a contempt for those who broke down under pressure. Under him he believed were 'the finest fighting men in all the world'. He would train them in 'military virtue'. There must be no weakness. The 7000 Australians killed at Pozières must not die in vain. Their brothers must fight on. Theirs was a noble cause. This was no time for the men with tender consciences. The world belongs to the brave.

Billy Hughes agreed. On 31 July, as the earth swayed and rocked at Pozières, Hughes spoke to the people at Fremantle of the

Empire's great task. The peoples of the British race scattered wide over the earth held essentially the same ideals wherever they were settled. They were 'animated by the same resolute determination to uphold them, come what may'. The crowd cheered. Hughes believed the people were behind him. He has just returned from Europe where he delighted the English, the Scots and Welsh with his rousing talks, where Lloyd George joined in the chorus of praise for the tough little Australian Prime Minister. In June he met with Haig and Joffre and he addressed the diggers, whose cheers rang out in the open air of France. Hughes was the leader of Australian heroes. He has come home knowing that the voluntary system of recruiting might not supply the men Haig needs. He is like a man possessed. He has won the admiration of the King, the dukes, the lords and others in high places in England, Scotland and Wales. In France he has sealed an everlasting bond with the diggers: now he was forging a bond with the Australian people. The Australian people, he believed, would overcome the storm and stress of this dreadful war.

But stories have got back to Australia about what had happened at Pozières. Country people have heard of how their mates were blown to pieces. Men they had known all their lives were no more. Wives and mothers were afraid of a knock on the door from the clergyman or the priest bringing news of the death of their loved ones. Patriots wanted the war to go on. But the number of the doubters increased. They were not so vocal. They feared being hounded as disloyal. Hughes was returning to a divided Australia.

Prominent liberals now threw their arms around a Labor leader, kissed and hugged him, and told him he was the most lovable man they had ever known. The *Worker* in Sydney and the *Labor Call* in Melbourne suspected the Liberals were after a coalition government. The Liberals wanted Hughes to commit himself to conscription, and so precipitate a split in the Labor Party. The Labor press was doing what the capitalist press traditionally did: criticizing a Labor leader. Hughes was not dismayed. His mind was made up. Winning the war must take priority over the platform of the ALP.

The recruitment drives went on. Alfred Deakin, the shell of the man he had once been, wanted Australians to be 'true to Australia and to our great Empire'. So did another young man who believed one day he would wear the mantle of Alfred Deakin: Robert Gordon Menzies. His parents gave him the name Gordon in memory of the hero and martyr of Khartoum, not foreseeing that a day would come when their illustrious son would say with pride to his fellow Australians: 'I am—like you—dyed in the wool British'. He was himself a country boy, who had been down to the great city of

Melbourne where he had fallen among thieves. Born at Jeparit on 20 December 1894, the son of a country storekeeper, by his ability and industry he won his way to Wesley College and the University of Melbourne, where he distinguished himself in Arts and Law, and by his performances as a public speaker. He heard war's 'wild, barbaric drum'. But for him this war was something more than 'mere insensate slaughter'. To fight for 'King, Country and Empire' was to display 'valour for the right'. It was 'the gleam of truth and righteousness'. He said to all who volunteered to fight for the British cause: 'go with God's glory on your face'.

But he had not volunteered himself. The mockers at the University of Melbourne accused him of hypocrisy and humbug. 'The promising military career of Robert Gordon Menzies', one student wrote, 'was cut short by the outbreak of war'. He will have his moment of glory, but that taunt will dog him down the years.

Cables arrived from London. Reinforcements were needed. The British were putting the pressure on. Hughes was determined to introduce conscription, but any such proposal aroused furious opposition within the Labor Party. By the narrowest of margins, both Cabinet and Caucus eventually agreed to a compromise: the government would apply compulsion only to fill any deficit in the numbers suggested by the Army Council in London, and there would be exemptions. Sure that the proposal had broad popular support, Hughes announced that the government would hold a referendum. 'Our national existence, our liberties, are at stake'. On 13 September Hughes revealed the words of the question to be submitted to the electors on 28 October:

> Are you in favour of the Government having, in this grave emergency, the same compulsory powers over citizens in regard to requiring their military service, for the term of this war, outside the Commonwealth as it now has in regard to military service within the Commonwealth?

That day Frank Tudor resigned from the government. The opponents of the proposal within the Labor Party came into the open. Frank Brennan predicted the Hughes Government would crumble.

It was clear there was not going to be a debate on the government's proposals: there were going to be just over eight weeks of hysteria. On 6 September Dr Alexander Leeper, fine flower of the Protestant ascendancy in Ireland, now warden of Trinity College in the University of Melbourne, moved in the Anglican Synod in Melbourne: 'That this Synod is so convinced that the forces of the Allies are being used by God to vindicate the rights of the weak and to maintain the moral order of the world that it gives its strong support to the principle of universal service . . .'. Archdeacon

Hindley seconded the motion, which was carried without discussion. The National Anthem was sung.

On 16 September Dr Mannix, the Catholic Archbishop of Melbourne, replied to Dr Leeper and other Protestant conscriptionists. He said, of course he wanted an honourable peace, but he believed that peace could be secured without conscription in Australia. Conscription was a hateful thing and always brought evil in its train. The crowd sang 'God Save Ireland'. Three days later Dr Mannix launched an appeal for the relief of the victims of the Easter Rising in Ireland which had been put down by the British with such brutality earlier in the year. Some Protestants accused him of treason. The cry went up: deport him, throw the traitor out of the country. Conscription has revived the old hatreds and the old suspicions.

Daniel Mannix was many things, and he spoke with many voices. He was the mystic who saw in the face of the Irish peasant the image of Christ. He was the Irish patriot nursing a grudge against those guilty of that ancient wrong against the Irish people. He was the priest who believed he had a divine mission to save souls from damnation. He said memorable things, using words and phrases which lived on because he spoke about things that mattered, and things that moved the human heart. A man out of sympathy with the temper of his age, a man who believed God alone could save human beings from all their folly, became for a brief moment an ally of the future-of-humanity men.

To the imperialists of 'Yarraside', Mannix was 'the Rasputin of Australia', the man whose treasonable speeches were preparing Australia for social revolution. Hughes agreed. He opened the 'Yes' campaign in the Sydney Town Hall on 18 September by reminding Australians they were only free as long as Australia remained part and parcel of the British Empire and Britain was unconquered. The Labor Premier of New South Wales, W. A. Holman, announced his support for conscription and was beginning to talk of the need for an all-party government.

Hughes and Holman were fighting for their political lives. On 15 September the central executive of the Political Labor Leagues of New South Wales expelled W. M. Hughes, the Prime Minister, from the Labor movement. They also withdrew the endorsement of Holman for the next State election. They reaffirmed the principle that Labor would oppose by all means conscription of human life for military service abroad.

Hughes took up the fight with a fiendish pleasure. He hissed and spat at his opponents like a cat defending its own territory against an intruder. Convinced his proposals were essential for victory, his government has prosecuted men and women for making speeches or publishing material prejudicial to recruiting. The Prime Minister of the 'freest country in the world', the man who in 1907 had written *The Case for Labor*, now suppressed issues of the *Socialist* which had opposed conscription. His opponents promptly seized on this as evidence for their argument: conscription would endanger the liberties of the people.

Hughes also believed he was fighting for the liberties of the people. On the day after he was expelled from the Labor Party he issued a Manifesto to the Women of Australia:

> Women of Australia, mothers, wives, sisters of free men, what is your answer to the boys at the front? Are you going to leave them to die? What is your answer to Britain, to whom we owe so much; to France, to Belgium? Are you going to cover with shame and dishonour the country for which our soldiers are fighting and dying?
> Now is your hour of trial and opportunity. Will you be the proud mothers of a nation of heroes, or stand dishonoured as the mothers of a race of degenerates?
> Prove that you are worthy to be the mothers and wives of free men.

In the country districts Shire Councils have passed resolutions in favour of conscription; local papers have supported it. The bush was the cradle of the bush culture, and the virtues of courage, resource, initiative and compassion which conferred a mantle of glory on the digger. It took courage to stand up to the tyranny of opinion in the country. Opponents of conscription were tarred and feathered. By contrast in Catholic districts such as Koroit in Victoria and Yass in New South Wales boys and girls whose parents supported conscription were tormented by the other school-children. A war of pamphlets and posters broke out. John Curtin, secretary of the Anti-Conscription League, authorized a poster telling the women of Australia a vote for 'Yes' was 'The Blood Vote':

> "Why is your face so white, Mother?
> Why do you choke for breath?"
> "Oh I have dreamt in the night, my son,
> That I doomed a man to death."

The Universal Service League countered with 'A Mother's Lament':

> Should this fair land be blighted,
> Should Australia meet her doom—
> Befouled, outraged, like Belgium
> In the shadow, in the gloom?
> Through all the years before me,
> As in solemn file they go,
> Burnt in my brain will be the stain:
> My God! I voted 'No'.

Within the Protestant community some clergymen were confident that if Christ were to appear in the 'wide brown land' he would favour conscription. Other parsons said Christ would have been 'exceedingly sorrowful' with these men in clerical garb who were 'dragging unwilling sacrifices to the altar of the Moloch of War'. Within the Catholic Church there was also division. Dr Mannix thought Australians had already done enough, and that conscription was a 'hateful thing' which was 'certain to bring evil in its train'. Archbishop Kelly in Sydney thought conscription would aid the British in their fight for right against might. Families were divided; friends of a lifetime found they were on opposite sides.

Hughes accused the anti-conscriptionists of being the tools of the Sinn Feiners and the Industrial Workers of the World. To prove his point, on 10 October twelve members of the IWW were charged in Sydney with organizing rebellion against the King, conspiring to burn down buildings and shops in Sydney, and attempting to intimidate or overawe Parliament. The press stressed that all of the twelve save one were not Australians, and some were associates of a notorious German who had escaped from an internment camp. One of them, Donald Grant, had said on 2 April that he was a rebel, and knew no King, and sabotage was the only effective weapon by which the workers could combat the master class.

On 24 September Adela Pankhurst presented the mission of the Australian people. The time had come, she said, when Australia and other countries must protect themselves against not only Militarism but also Capitalism. Australians must unite with the other peoples of the world to establish a social system in which goods would be produced for use and not for profit. The time had come to form a new political party in Australia which would embody those ideals and secure the people's full and free internal and external development. The people must answer Hughes, the imperial conscriptionist, with a demand for the complete independence and neutrality of Australia. A new vision of Australia was being born during all the sound and fury.

The vote at the referendum on 28 October was to be the beginning of a legend about Australia. By 30 October it was clear there would be a majority against conscription. By 11 December the figures were: Yes: 1 087 332; No: 1 151 881—a 64 549 majority for No. The anti-conscriptionists hailed the results as the beginning of a new era in the history of Australia. For Labor it was a moment of hope.

After the referendum Hughes mooched around his house in Kew, dressed in the clothes he always wore in his moods of despair. His opponents chanted: resign, resign, resign. On 14 November sixty-four members of the Labor Party held a special meeting in Parliament House in Melbourne to discuss the leadership. After heated debate Hughes asked those who supported him to follow him out of the room. Twenty-four followed him. The meeting then adjourned until 11 a.m. the following day. On that day the remnant elected Frank Tudor as their leader and Albert Gardiner as his deputy. Labor has paid an irreparable price for its stiff-necked adherence to principle and virtue. They have lost able men such as W. M. Hughes, J. C. Watson, the first Labor Prime Minister, W. A. Holman, the Labor Premier of New South Wales, W. G. Spence, the founder of the Australian Workers' Union, and G. F. Pearce, the efficient Minister for Defence. Labor has chosen mediocrities to replace a mighty spirit. Frank Tudor was a nice chap. He played his life and his cricket with a straight bat. But the times called for something more than correct behaviour: they called for a man of vision. The *Argus* summed up the Labor rump in a sentence that would live on: 'When the Caucus party expelled the most intelligent, most enlightened, and most capable of its members it blew out its brains . . . The weak limbs said to the brains, "We have no need of you."'

On the afternoon of 14 November Hughes had an interview with the Governor-General who commissioned him to form a new government. Negotiations began between Hughes and the Liberals over the exact form the new 'win the war' fusion party would take. By 18 February 1917 the deal had been struck. Hughes accepted five portfolios for his `National Labor' group and six for the Liberals: conservatives had a majority in the Australian Government. The new party became known as the Nationalists.

On the Western Front the Australian soldiers were ankle deep and sometimes knee deep in mud. Snow was falling. The men suffered from 'trench feet'. Their spirits were revived after the horrors of the Somme and Pozières and Ypres by Tommy Cookers (tins of solidified alcohol) for the drinkers, mugs of coffee and cocoa, a digger newspaper 'The Rising Sun', a small cinema show, and other comforts from the Comforts Fund, all the socks, and gloves and Balaclavas knitted by the girls 'back home'.

2

Victory of the Comfortable Classes

On 28 January 1917 Dr Mannix dropped one of his memorable remarks as he opened a new Catholic school in working-class Brunswick. It was high summer in Melbourne, and Mannix was clad in the finery of a bishop of the Church of Rome. The war had nothing to do with the rights of smaller nations, he told his flock. It was 'simply a sordid trade war'. Britain and Germany were engaged in a slaughter over markets.

At the same time John Curtin, who had spent five days in gaol for failing to enlist, was starting a new life in Perth. Curtin had grown up in a working-class suburb and had learnt his politics from Ruskin's *Unto This Last*, Bellamy's *Looking Backward*, the novels of Dickens, the speeches of Tom Mann, talks with Frank Anstey, and the *Tocsin*. He was well known in Labor circles as a passionate and eloquent speaker. He renewed his promise—made many times— to Elsie Needham, the woman he wanted to marry, to give up drinking. He had been offered and accepted the position of editor of the *Westralian Worker*. On 21 April 1917 he married Elsie and they went to live at Cottesloe, Perth. There a new man was born. The socialist became a pragmatist, a man who set out to prove that a pragmatist need not become an opportunist or a careerist concerned only with the capture of political power. From that time Curtin preached the gospel of work. He was never again to say that there could be no satisfactory system of government without social revolution.

Hughes looked for scapegoats on whom to pour his rage and his hurts. He blamed the Germans in Australia and the radicals in the Labor movement for the humiliations of October and November 1916. Under the sweeping powers of the War Precautions Act he had interned Germans resident in Australia, and deported others. There was talk of prohibiting the use of the German language on the telephone. Hughes also invoked the War Precautions Act to silence his critics. Anyone suspected of being wobbly on loyalty or patriotism was liable to prosecution. The revolution in Russia in March has alarmed the comfortable classes in Australia. Labor might revive its republican spirit; it might try to bring the war to an end. Hughes and his government were now fighting two wars: the war in Europe and the Middle East, and the class war in Australia.

In France Douglas Haig wanted action: punch a hole in the German line before they launch an offensive. The Fourth Australian Division would attack the German line at Bullecourt. Haig was confident. The tanks would cut through the barbed-wire entanglements, knock over the concrete machine-gun pillboxes, and prepare the way for the foot-sloggers to advance and finish off what the tanks and the land and air bombardment had softened up. The attack began on 11 April 1917. There were 10 000 casualties. The awful horrors were enough to drive men mad. Australians paid a terrible price for fighting under British officers. 'Birdie', who had travelled with the Anzacs to France, wept. But it was not over yet. On 3 May the Australians were again ordered to take Bullecourt. Another 7482 were killed.

'Birdie' has sent off letters to the Defence Department in Australia, and to the Governor-General, Sir Ronald Munro-Ferguson, asking for more volunteers to fill up the thinning ranks. Sir Ronald was not hopeful. The countryside was already drained of men. Australia was now an urban society composed of 'irresponsible, selfish and self-complacent men'. Conscription, he believed, was the answer, but Hughes has rashly promised the electors his government would not introduce conscription for overseas service without again seeking their approval in a referendum.

In the first week of May, as recruiting drives up and down the country attempted to whip up enthusiasm for the glorious cause of Empire, the people of Australia went to the polls. The new Hughes Nationalist Government won a decisive victory. Once again in the history of Australia, despite the talk about mateship, equality and the democratic traditions of the Australian people, Australians had voted conservative—to be chained to their past, rather than take the way forward. The members of the Labor Party were dismayed. The socialists blamed them for the defeat. Labor, they wrote in the finger-wagging way of men who knew all the answers to the human situation, has once again been punished for its 'betrayal of principles'. Now was the time for the 'regeneration and salvation' of the Labor movement.

At the front the Australian diggers were proud of the differences between themselves and the men in other armies. They were the egalitarians of the New World. Even in adversity and defeat they were never downhearted. They had a cheeky confidence in their own abilities. 'You give me the bloody battalion', one digger said on the Somme, 'I'll take the bloody place right now'. They believed the English had let them down, and said so. They wanted an Australian as their supreme commander. They enjoyed shocking refined Englishmen by asking them whether they would like to learn how to spit. They were proud to smell 'like a rum-vat' when not in the trenches. They were uneasy with all the English ways of expressing respect for those in authority—saluting, addressing officers as 'Sir', or speaking only when spoken to. In March 1917, on the eve of the Bullecourt bloodbath a British staff captain ticked off an Australian soldier for not saluting. The Australian patted him on the shoulder and said, 'Young man, when you go home, you tell your mother that to-day you've seen a real bloody soldier'. They were proud of their reputation for not keeping a civil tongue in their heads. They were egalitarians, dinky-di democrats, not grovellers.

But like their fellow Australians at home, they were also conservative. They would cheerfully push overboard or bully and stand over anyone who offended against their own code or lore, but they had no interest in any move to create a society in which domination ceased to be. The French army was in a state of mutiny for six weeks in the middle of 1917, an event which shook it to its foundations. The Australians were mutinous in their language and casual in their dress, but dismissed mutineers contemptuously as 'f—— no-hopers', 'fellers who ought to have their heads read', 'bloody fools who had gone clean off their rockers'. Their past had not fashioned them into participants in any Boston Tea Party or creators of a Paris Commune. Ignorant of their own history, they were doomed to go on repeating the past. They were rebels against authority, but not revolutionaries.

On 6 April 1917 America entered the war on the side of the Allies. Agitation against the war was growing. In England the poet Siegfried Sassoon, who had served in France and won the Military Cross, declared he believed the war was being deliberately prolonged by those who had the power to end it: 'I can no longer be a party to prolong these sufferings for ends which I believe to be evil and unjust'. He wanted to help to 'destroy the callous complacence with which a majority of those at home regard the continuance of agonies which they do not share'.

As though to confirm Hughes's deepest suspicion about a Labor conspiracy against the war, on 2 August a strike began in the Randwick State Workshops in Sydney. The workers ceased work to protest against the introduction of a time-card system to monitor the amount of work done by each employee. By the end of August

95 000 workers in the railways, the tramways and coalmines were
out on strike. Some were calling it a 'general strike'. The *Socialist*
wondered whether it was the prelude to revolution in Australia.
Hughes accused the strikers of preferring social revolution to
victory in France. The war must be won quickly before the maggots
of revolution ate too deeply into the foundations of capitalist
society. On 10 September the men accepted the terms offered to
them by the railway commissioners. The crushing of the strike
increased the bitterness within the Labor movement against the
comfortable classes.

Early in November the exhausted Australians were still fighting.
British forces, mainly Canadians and New Zealanders, captured
what remained of the village of Passchendaele on 10 November.
The British had gained a ridge, but had probably lost 100 000 men.
Since July 38 093 Australians had become casualties. That was 60
per cent of the AIF in France. But General Haig was still cheerful,
still in command. The German losses would be decisive. American
troops and reinforcements from the Dominions would give the
Allies the superiority in numbers they needed.

The news from Russia was grave. On 7 November the Bolsheviks
stormed the Winter Palace in Petrograd. On that night V. I. Lenin
announced the birth of a new era in the history of humanity. Lenin
spoke of peace, of bread and land, for the people: Hughes spoke of
war. On the morning of 8 November just as Lenin was electrifying
his followers in Petrograd, the Australian press published the
decision of the government. Hughes was going to hold a second
conscription referendum. He was behaving more and more like an
animal at bay. Enemies were everywhere. The Bolshies have joined
the Hughes list of villains. They were like Sinn Fein, the socialists,
Dr Mannix and the IWW. They were the enemies of liberty, White
Australia and the British Empire. He instructed the men in intelligence to establish the connection between Dr Mannix and these
enemies of the Empire. A vote against conscription, he told his
audiences, was a vote for the enemies of Australia. Loyal Australians would vote 'Yes', he declared. People cheered and waved
their hats, stamped their feet, clapped and whistled. Together they
would save the Empire. By contrast, the leader of the ALP, Frank
Tudor, spoke with dignity and restraint. Life, he said, was sacred,
and no government had a right to deal with it. He suggested
Australia's role should be to concentrate on providing foodstuffs
for Britain instead of conscripting men for slaughter.

This second conscription campaign had all the features of a comic
opera. All the stars of the first campaign sang again: Mannix,
Hughes, 'Iceberg' Irvine, Adela Pankhurst all mounted the plat-

form. But the result was unchanged. By midnight on referendum day, a smile of victory was on the face of Frank Tudor and a look of triumph on the face of Frank Anstey. The morning newspapers on 21 December announced a majority for 'No'. By then the vote was 718 465 for 'No' and 568 670 for 'Yes': majority for 'No', 149 795. The soldiers' vote, which had not been counted, could not affect the result. When the votes from the front came in they held little joy for the supporters of conscription. Nearly half the men who knew the horrors of war were unwilling to force their experiences on their fellow men. 'Birdie' was disappointed with the result; the Governor-General was surprised. Even at Hamilton, the capital of Australia Felix, the district which was expected to remain English for thousands of years, there was a majority for 'No'. In their euphoria socialist men and women spoke of their own hopes for the future.

The war news from the Middle East was promising. The Australian Light Horse, under the command of Harry Chauvel, were prevailing against the Turkish forces in Palestine and Syria. In December 1917 the women of Jerusalem strewed palm leaves in front of the victorious Australians as they entered the ancient city. One wit said he was so hungry he could eat Christ's shin-bones. Others wept as the monks sang, *Kyrie Eleison, Christe Eleison* at midnight Mass to celebrate the birth of Christ.

In Europe the bloody business dragged on through another brutal year. Place names of France were being written into the history of a distant and ancient continent: Ypres, Pozières, Villers-Bretonneux, Verdun, Passchendaele, the Somme—every battle a saga of terror and bravery and waste. In May 1918, Haig appointed John Monash to the command of the Australian Army Corps in France, and by August he was sensing victory. There were signs that the Germans were ready to talk about peace.

3

What Shall We Believe?

At the front the weather was awful. A light drizzle of rain was falling as a bugler sounded 'Attention' at 11 a.m. on 11 November 1918. The men at the front made no demonstration: they stopped firing. There was no cheering, no fraternizing with the enemy: there was an eerie calm. When one private in the Australian army was told it was all over he thought his informants were pulling his leg: 'Garn, yer silly bastards', he said incredulously. Another wanted to know why his dearest pals had fallen and he was still alive.

In London Robert Garran ascended from a basement barber's shop where he had been having his hair cut, and was greeted by the sight of flags fluttering from windows in the Strand. Soon the Strand was packed with a cheering, singing crowd. Robert Garran danced a two-step with a burly Anzac, his kazoo swelling the chorus of the victory songs. At nightfall an overflow audience in St Paul's Cathedral heard a tenor sing the aria: 'Comfort ye, comfort ye, my people'. Siegfried Sassoon was comfortless: for him the armistice was 'a loathsome ending to the loathsome tragedy'. The singing and the dancing went on for three days and nights.

At nightfall in Melbourne on 11 November, at the end of a blousy early summer day when a hot north wind made all human aspirations seem quite out of reach, the magic words 'Armistice signed!' were flashed outside the newspaper offices. Crowds quickly gathered. Cheer after cheer went up into the night. Voices broke out into song. Hundreds of flags were hastily flown, including the Union Jack and some bearing the Australian symbol of the Southern Cross. The words, 'Rule Britannia! Britannia rules the waves. Britons never, never, never shall be slaves' came in a mighty roar. Crowds of hysterical men and women lifted trams: others commandeered trams and drove them at dangerous speeds. It was long after midnight before the last cracker was heard, and the last cheer went up into the vast sky.

In 1918 and 1919 some observers of the human scene believed that the age of ruins had arrived. In Munich in 1918 Thomas Mann was asking the question: 'what shall we believe?' In 1918 Oswald Spengler published the first volume of *The Decline of the West*. The following year, in France, Paul Valéry, mindful of the terrible blood-letting in Flanders and Picardy, recorded the 'extraordinary shudder' that had shaken the marrow of Europe. T. S. Eliot was aware, as he put it, that 'The rats are underneath the piles'. How could anyone believe a benevolent God would permit the brutalities committed during the war? How could any serious person have faith in the capacity of human beings for 'better things'? With the gift of a drunkard to sum up the spirit of the times, Henry Lawson wrote to a friend: ' . . . it's all over . . . things are rotten all round'.

As a fitting backdrop to that black mood it was another dry year in Australia: grass was as scarce as feathers on a frog. The appearance of some soldiers who had returned from the war strengthened this sombre, melancholy mood. Human beings whose minds had been damaged by what they had seen and suffered appeared in the city streets: men with mutilated faces, limbless men, the lame, the halt and the blind. Who among those who passed them had eyes to see? The Christians sang the hymns of resignation and acceptance; they besought their God: 'Help of the helpless, Lord, abide with me'.

The *Socialist* was apocalyptic: 'The Long Night of Darkness' was passing, it declared. The horrors of war have removed the blinkers of religion from men and women's eyes. Human beings had a question for God: 'Father, what did You do in the Great War?' God was now on the list of missing persons. Socialism was the new religion of humanity. The death-knell of the capitalist system was being tolled. The socialists were setting the world on fire with the new gospel of the Brotherhood of Man. They had a noble duty to 'keep the Red Flag flying here'. With their comrade, Bernard O'Dowd, they sang of their love for Australia:

> We love our fair Australia,
> The gullies' noonday hush
> The wild things of the ranges,
> The magic of "the bush",
> The spring that breathes of wattle,
> The royal summer's blue—
> We love her, we her children,
> And Freedom, we love you.

On 16 January 1919 the Peace Conference held its first session in Paris. The victors had gathered to plan the post-war world and to argue over the price they wished to exact from Germany. The delegates were united in their wish to preserve bourgeois civilization, but divided on how that could be achieved. For France, Georges Clemenceau wanted revenge: in the streets of Paris almost every third woman was dressed in the black of mourning. The British Prime Minister, David Lloyd George, was at the height of his powers. A *bon viveur* and a generous man, he was an advocate for a magnanimous peace.

Hughes had no time for the American President Woodrow Wilson. The man was a dreamer. His great League of Nations would make no difference to the actual circumstances of mankind. Hughes had a stratagem: 'Give him a League of Nations, and he will give us the rest'. Hughes was determined to impress on the power-brokers at the conference the fact that the former German possessions—Nauru, the Solomons and German New Guinea—'encompassed Australia like fortresses'. Australia's dead, he told the delegates, entitled them to guarantees for her security. The territorial integrity of Australia could only be secured either by granting Australia control of the islands to her north or by their being placed in the hands of some other friendly nation. Hughes was prepared to let the President dream provided the delegates did not concede the Open Door in New Guinea. Wilson was unimpressed. In his ideal future there was no room for annexations. But the English had their eye on former German colonies in Africa. Backed by Lloyd George, Hughes eventually got what he wanted. The Little Digger strutted the world stage as the saviour of White Australia, little guessing that just over twenty-three years later, units of the Japanese Army would be advancing towards Port Moresby.

Meanwhile the New South Wales Government was taking measures to prevent the spread of Spanish influenza. The epidemic caused terrible misery. On 27 January 1919 theatres, picture shows, and places of indoor public resort in New South Wales were closed until further notice. The whole State was declared to be a quarantine area. Schools were not to reopen. Patrols were sent on house-to-house visits distributing advice about the disease. People were advised to wear masks over their faces in public places. Religious services were permitted, provided the clergyman stood at least 6 feet from members of the congregation. In Adelaide, where no cases had been reported, the chairman of the Central Board of Health recommended people not to 'go talking, coughing and sneezing in each other's faces, or shaking hands, or kissing'.

Other restrictions imposed under the odious War Precautions Act have not been lifted. The socialists and the militants within the Australian Labor movement have embarrassed the government by saying: well, if the war was a victory for believers in freedom, then prove it by rescinding all the regulations infringing individual liberty. Maurice Blackburn, Vida Goldstein and others, all high-minded, virtuous men and women, asked the Acting Prime Minister, Willie Watt, to prove that the power of the people to govern themselves was not an illusion. But Willie Watt was heart and soul a 'Yarraside' man. He was not going to let the 'Bolshies' and 'red raggers' exploit freedom to bring his civilization to ruin.

All over Australia the supporters of the King and the Empire clashed with the supporters of the Bolsheviks. In Brisbane on Sunday 23 March 1919 the 'red raggers' held a procession through the streets. Banners were held high; red flags were displayed in defiance of wartime regulations banning them; revolutionary songs were sung. Some onlookers cheered: some expressed their disgust. The following day the supporters of King and Empire replied with a demonstration of loyalty. Seven to eight thousand people gathered at the North Quay to hear returned soldiers call on those present to deal with 'this mob of Russians who let us down on the Eastern front'. To roars of applause one speaker declared: 'We are going to put them right out of Australia, and their sympathisers are going with them'. This display of Bolshevik disloyalty by a cowardly foreign element, who have come from a country that betrayed the Allies, would not be allowed to continue. The following night between 15 000 and 20 000 people gathered in Edward Street to hear speakers on how to root out the 'monster of Bolshevism'. They marched to the offices of the *Standard*. There they sang the National Anthem. One man did not take off his hat and join in with the others. Two men lifted him on to the roof of a car, as the mob shouted 'Sing it'. The man then sang it.

Turbulence and rioting were also spreading in Europe. The delegates must hurry. Hughes, Clemenceau and others demanded Germany should pay for the cost of the war. Wilson disagreed: Wilson said: 'No indemnities'. Lloyd George and his advisers worked on a British-style compromise. Clemenceau, Hughes and others did not want justice or righteousness: they wanted revenge. Germany must be bled white. Hughes's thirst for vengeance appalled one of his advisers, the reflective Deakinite liberal, Frederic Eggleston. Eggleston resigned from the delegation in disgust. 'Of all the criminal lunatics in the world', he wrote to his wife, 'Hughes is the worst. He is unbridled blood lust'. Advisers whispered to Lloyd George that the reparations demanded were beyond Germany's capacity to pay. Maynard Keynes warned Lloyd George that they would be reducing Germany to poverty at the risk of revolution. But Lloyd George's hands were tied: he had just won a 'khaki election' on the platform of 'Full reparations and hang the Kaiser'.

Troopships continued to arrive in Australia, carrying demobilized servicemen home from England. Albert Facey, before the war an itinerant worker in the country districts of Western Australia, was greeted in the streets of Perth by larrikins who sneered at him for going to the war. He silenced them with a straight left to the chin, and a right below the belt. Martin Boyd, a member of the British Expeditionary Force, and later an officer in the Royal Flying Corps, was called a 'pommy' soon after he disembarked. He felt he had been repudiated by his own country from the moment of his return. He did not like being in Australia. Bill Harney, a bushman from north Queensland and the Northern Territory, decided he had had enough of humanity. He chose 'the beaches and the quiet places that surround me'. He went back 'to sit on me beaches out from Darwin. Listen to the sea coming in and get the crabs and the fish and me mates come in and we talk and everybody's happy'. All over the country young boys and girls saw ex-diggers break down and cry when they met each other, and only manage to say to each other the words of consolation: 'I know, Charl., I know'. Children came suddenly on grown-up men in distress and were told: 'He's . . . crying. Can't stop . . . don't be frightened'.

No one knew how to handle these 'broken comrades', these men whose lives have been shattered by the war. Soldiers suffering from shock were observed to act in their sleep as though they were engaged in battle, and went through the pantomime of fighting with bombs, bayonet, machine-gun and rifle. Some suffered from what their contemporaries called 'loathsome diseases'. Numbers had consumption. Hospitals must be built. But where? No suburb wanted a hospital housing 'incurable consumptives'. In August 1919 Dr Cumpston, Federal Director of Quarantine, had published a statement that 55 000 Australian soldiers had suffered from venereal disease during the war. The president of the New South Wales Branch of the Returned Soldiers' and Sailors' League of Australia, Roy Teece, had replied that this was 'slanderous and misleading'. But the facts could not be overcome by abuse or self-righteousness. Soldiers, it was said, were a menace to health and morals. Some said there were 'bad eggs' among the soldiers; some were drinking themselves silly in public houses, reeling round the cities, suburbs or country towns, brawling and making lewd gestures to women. Soldiers were involved in serious riots in Melbourne in July 1919; shots were fired; the holy quiet of St Kilda Road was disturbed by drunken hooligans. They were angry men: thousands of poor devils who had offered their lives for their country and human liberty did not know where their next meal was coming from.

While heroes of the war were walking from house to house selling matches and trinkets to frightened housewives, memorials were being erected to the dead. Wealthy parents endowed prizes or scholarships at schools and universities in memory of the sons who had lost their lives. The public schools erected memorials in their honour—honour rolls in the chapel and stands to carry regimental flags. Bean persuaded Hughes to provide funds for a war memorial in Canberra, to be a tribute to the mighty dead and a building inside which Australians and others might learn what the war had been all about—a building to 'hold the sacred memories of the A.I.F.'. He entertained the shy hope that the spirits of the dead might hover over it. But on what the war meant he was not sure: as he put it in his version of the Psalm, it was not for us to say what it was all about—'Non nobis, Domine'. In cities, country towns and out in the bush, people erected memorials to the soldiers. On most of the memorials the one feature which was unmistakably Australian was the statue of the digger, with the left brim of the hat tucked up and pinned to the crown with the medal of the rising sun. Words about Australia were not carved on any monument. The people borrowed words from the Old World. They used Rudyard Kipling's 'Lest We Forget'; words from the Apocrypha, 'Their Name Liveth For Evermore'; the biblical words, 'Greater love hath no man than this'; a line by the poet Laurence Binyon, 'We will remember them'; or 'To our glorious dead'. There was no profession of love for 'a sunburnt country', nothing about the ones who 'bore the badge of gameness', no mention of mateship or equality: nothing of what Australians stood for. The war has not liberated Australians from their colonial past. With few exceptions, such as the crucifix on the memorial at Berridale in the Snowy Mountains, there were no religious emblems. God was rarely mentioned, Christ almost never. The past has bequeathed to Australians a long list of unmentionable words.

The voice of 'Yarraside' and all the comfortable classes wanted Anzac Day to be from that time 'first in the Australian heart'. For them it was a day of honour. Speakers and writers agreed that on that first sad Anzac morn the deeds of the Anzacs had apotheosized a blunder into an epiphany. The soldiers had overcome man's last enemy, death. Anzac Day has become what the poet David McKee Wright called a 'march through the hearts of men'. It has become a solemn occasion which turned the minds of Australians towards the things that mattered in life, an occasion 'not of little gains and little losses', but an occasion to 'hear the trumpet call' to a nobler life. Anzac Day was beginning to be the 'one day of the year', the central event in an Australian secular religion for one section of society.

Labor did not share this vision. The ALP decided at its Conference in March 1919 to eliminate from the School Papers (issued by the State education departments) all articles relating to or extolling wars, battles or heroes of past wars. That was on the eve of the fourth Anzac Day. The *Australian Worker* rebuked the bourgeois press and their readers for saying that Australia got a 'world-wide advertisement out of the bloody business'. Capitalism, they continued, considered the 'advertisement' of more importance than the lives of the men who were sacrificed.

For Labor the class war was the central fact of life. On 22 April 1919, 2000 men gathered on the wharf in Fremantle to prevent 'scab' workers getting on to the *Dimboola*. John Curtin had much to say about the evils of the presence of the police on the wharves, the brazen indifference of the Shipping Ring and the government of Western Australia, and their wicked attempts to 'govern by starvation'. The workers and the employers were spoiling for a fight. This time, John Curtin believed, capitalism would not win by forcing hunger to 'gnaw at the vitals of the men, women and children'. To ensure victory, to ensure there was no capitulation because of starvation, the Labor movement must make arrangements to feed the wharf lumpers and their families. In this 'happy country' 59 per cent of the people owned less than £200 each and 0.7 per cent owned more than £2000. Something must be done. The time had come for a redistribution of wealth.

Harry (Hal) Colebatch, the Premier of Western Australia, equipped and trained a squad of police as a military raiding party, complete with rifles, bayonets, ball cartridges, revolvers and other military tools to drive union workers off the wharves. On Sunday 4 May Colebatch attended in person to help his volunteers erect barricades on the wharves. Enraged by this act of provocation, the lumpers smashed the 'pick-up' bureau and threw the 'scabs' into the Swan River. The Riot Act was read. A crowd of 2000, composed of men and women armed with pieces of coal and stones, surged towards the police. Women, more desperate, it was said, than the men, insisted on being in the front row of the advancing army. The order was given for the police to charge: the mounted men galloped their horses towards the union crowd. One union man received a bayonet wound in the thigh. The police dispersed the crowd. There were thirty-three casualties. That evening Colebatch declared that the whole point at issue was whether or not law and order and constituted authority were to be maintained. Lawlessness, he said, could not serve the interests of the workers. John Curtin reminded

Colebatch that the Czar of Russia had called on law and order to perpetrate a Bloody Sunday, and look what had happened to him. The returned soldiers had rallied to the defence of unionism: blacklegs had been clearly shown they must not return to the waterfront. Negotiations were opened between the government and the lumpers. An agreement was in sight and peace returned to the waterfront. In Australia riots did not burgeon into revolution.

In Paris, the iron men have had their satisfaction. On 28 June Germany signed 'the disgraceful dictation of Versailles'. The next day Hughes returned to London where he had an enthusiastic reception from 500 soldiers at Victoria Station. The soldiers hoisted him on their shoulders. His hat fell off and a soldier jammed his own wide-brimmed Digger hat on to the head of Billy Hughes. The soldiers welcomed him with loud shouts of the words which brought tears to his eyes: 'Good on you, you little Digger', and that other phrase of Australian approval, 'You'll do me'. It was his high tide, his moment as the Little Digger, the Diggers' Friend, the Empire statesman. Before daylight on that same day a militant section of the meatworkers in Townsville raided the railway truck-ing yards, and dispersed 500 cattle over the surrounding country. The class war went on, as the war between the nations formally ended.

4

A Divided Australia

This was the age of the rootless man, the age of the kingdom of nothingness. The myths which have sustained human beings for hundreds of years have lost their relevance. The words of the priests and the parsons no longer fed the hungers of the human heart. A turbulent emptiness was replacing the time when there were 'certain certainties'. Old Australia was becoming a museum piece. The values of 'The Man From Snowy River' and the quest of the Sentimental Bloke for salvation in the country from the city's muck belonged to history. Australians must find out who they are, and what they might be. The Nationalists and the Country Party had no image of the Australian. Billy Hughes has said that Australia was as much a part of England as Middlesex. The young conservative politician, Bob Menzies, has said he was proud of being 'British to the bootstraps'. Labor was the nationalist party. Labor has professed since 1905 to stand for the 'cultivation of Australian national sentiment'.

But Labor was in disarray. In January 1920, the socialist Frederick Sinclaire regretted that Australians of all political persuasions were looking abroad for their ideas. Even the political radicals in Australia displayed a 'lamentable want of independence'. Australian radicals boasted they were not British, but instead of talking about being Australians, they borrowed their ideas from the Sinn Feiners, the IWW or the Bolsheviks. The time had come for Australians to think for themselves and make an effort to work out their own destiny. In the early days of the Russian revolution the Labor movement hailed the revolution as the dawn of a new era in the world. But for most, the infatuation is short-lived. In 1920 Robert Ross, the editor of the *Socialist*, returned to Melbourne after a visit to Moscow. He warned against the Russian method of 'creating the Kingdom of Heaven by violence'. The dictatorship of the proletariat was not the Australian way. Australians believed in the ballot-box, in freedom of expression, thought and association, not in the bullying methods of the Bolsheviks.

Laborites who rejected parliamentary reform and who believed in change by industrial action supported the One Big Union movement. The idea has been around for at least a decade. On 6 August 1918 a Trades Union Congress in Sydney passed resolutions to create the One Big Union, whose aim was to abolish capitalism though 'revolutionary industrial and political action'. The most charismatic official of the One Big Union was Jock Garden, a mesmerizer, a minister of the Church of Christ, a teacher with a message about love and justice and the universal embrace, a man with the reputation of being 'an unmitigated liar'. Soon after the Russian revolution of November 1917 he added the teachings of Marx and Lenin to the Sermon on the Mount. At the Labor Party Conference of 1919 the pragmatists moved successfully for the expulsion of Jock Garden and men of like mind from the Labor Party. Labor was interested in the capture of political power.

The divided party degenerated into a 'seething mass of vendettas, dogfights and double-crossings with a Kilkenny cat flavour scattered over the *tout ensemble*'. Especially in New South Wales, Labor politics became a mixture of innocence and corruption. Stories of vote-rigging and stand-over tactics were rife. The large Australian Workers' Union was convulsed by brawling and shady deals. In the thick of this volatile mixture of idealism and sharp practices was John Thomas Lang. Like Billy Hughes, Jack Lang learned in childhood all about the jungle of life. He was born in Sydney on 21 December 1876. His mother was a Catholic, his father a pre-marriage convert. Young Jack supplemented the family income by selling newspapers in the streets. There he learned that to survive a boy had to 'resist the invasion of his pitch with his fists'. His adult life was a fight to keep his place on the pitch—first as an accountant then as a real estate agent. In that profession he amassed a small fortune. On 14 March 1896 he married Hilda Amelia Bredt, the sister of Henry Lawson's wife.

Lang had a charisma for the little people, and a power to attract men and women to his service. There was about him the air of a 'big fella'. He was tall in height, massive in frame, and vast in ambition. The man of compassion, the man who wanted to do something for 'the least of the little ones', Lang kicked back if anyone kicked him. When he became Treasurer in the Storey Labor Government in 1920 the Communist press judged him to be 'not a Labor man at all, but . . . a mere Liberal, a middle-class politician'. His face was generally expressionless, a mask for the man within. It was only when he was helping the needy and the hungry or when he was savaging an

opponent that his face portrayed animation. Lang enjoyed ridiculing 'do-gooders' and sneering at Jock Garden as the 'parson in
politics' and 'the man with the perpetual smile'.

On 30 October 1920, the most militant organisations assembled to
form themselves into a Communist Party with the aim of achieving
'the complete overthrow of the Capitalist system'. By the beginning
of 1921 there were two Communist parties, both adopting the same
name and the same principles, both claiming to be 'correct' disciples
of the teaching of Marx and Lenin, both more concerned with
sullying the reputation of their rival, or exposing the bourgeois
character of the Labor Party than with building a new society.
Radical Labor was bogged down in a 'petty, paltry, pitiful squabble'.

On 1 May 1921 a crowd of 2000 or 3000 marched through the
streets of Sydney singing lustily 'The Red Flag', 'Solidarity Forever'
and other well-known IWW songs. At the Sydney Domain
members of the crowd hoisted a Union Jack on a pole and burned
it, tore the remains to shreds and trampled on them. Speakers
inflamed the listeners into 'the fever of sedition'. The *Sydney
Morning Herald* was worried. Even if the demonstrations and the
disgraceful scenes in the Domain were only 'impudent challenges
from a mean minority to a determined, even if slow-moving vast
majority', they must be stopped. There was danger in 'allowing
such public flaunting of rebellious sentiments'. The Returned
Sailors' and Soldiers' League agreed. They invited all who wanted
to 'keep the Union Jack on top' to rally round the flag in Sydney
Domain on Sunday 8 May. At least 100 000 people assembled in the
Domain to avenge the insult of 1 May. Amid wild scenes of patriotic
fervour those present unanimously agreed that the Union Jack was
the flag for Australia, and that the Red Flag or any other emblem of
revolution should not again be exhibited in the State.

Loyalty to King and Empire has become the secular religion of
Australian conservatism: Australians must conform. Labor must
find a counter-mythology. In June 1921 hundreds of prominent
trade unionists assembled in Melbourne for a great congress of
unions summoned by the ALP. They accepted almost unanimously
the motion: 'The socialisation of industry, production, distribution
and exchange to be the objective of the Labor Party'. Labor was
moving towards a mythology, a creed to set against the loyalty to
King-and-Empire men.

In October this recommendation was considered by the Commonwealth Conference of the Labor Party. Ted Theodore, the Labor
Premier of Queensland, was not happy. No socialist Labor Party, he
said, would ever gain power in a State or the Commonwealth, a
socialist programme being electoral suicide. The compromise men

had another victory. The Conference adopted a motion put by Maurice Blackburn:

> That this Conference declares:
>
> (a)   That the Australian Labor Party proposes collective owner-ship for the purpose of preventing exploitation, and to whatever extent may be necessary for that purpose.
>
> (b)   That wherever private ownership is a means of exploitation it is opposed by the Party, but
>
> (c)   That the Party does not seek to abolish private ownership of the instruments of production where such instrument is utilised by its owner in a socially useful manner and without exploitation.

The Communists cited the decision as further evidence that the ALP was what Lenin had said it was, namely, a 'liberal bourgeois party'. The conservative press was delighted. The lion's skin of revolution, as the *Daily Telegraph* put it, had fallen from Labor to reveal something 'quite harmless'. Communism has fallen over the horizon. Labor did not intend to deprive 'a man of his horse and buggy or his motor car'. Labor has chosen the Australian way. Hughes was not fooled. His Intelligence men warned him that revolutionaries were still gnawing and boring away like termites at the pillars of society.

While the labour movement debated and divided over the way in which the lot of the working-class Australian might be improved, governments have responded to the clamour of the soldiers for action. Ex-servicemen were taking up the blocks of land allotted to them by the Soldier Settlement schemes. Insufficient care was taken to inquire into the capital resources or the previous training of the prospective settlers, or into the adequacy of their farms. In the middle of the summer of 1920 one soldier settler arrived at Yenda, in New South Wales, to find that all the stuff he had read about being supplied with a tent and a stretcher on arrival was 'hot air'. He and his wife and his two children spent the night under the shelter of a big tree. For weeks he and his family had to depend on the hospitality of the ex-diggers for shelter. 'And thank God, the Digger Spirit is very alive here.' With the aid of his fellow diggers he put up a humpy. He had already spent his war gratuity getting started. He was hoping for the 'silver lining'. The *Soldier* reported that many diggers who had gone on the land were in 'straitened circumstances' and 'on the borders of starvation'.

By contrast, over in Western Australia the tough and resourceful Albert Facey was overcoming the difficulties of a soldier settler just as he had met the other challenges of his life. In 1922 he took up approximately 12 000 acres of land in the Narrogin district. Mr

Heuby in the Soldier Settlement Board was a 'very nice, understanding man'. Facey said he had 'a very fair deal from the Board'. Neither he nor his wife knew much about wheat and sheep farming, but they worked hard fencing and clearing the land, sowed wheat, grazed sheep, and made, as he put it, 'quite a lot of money dealing in the buying and selling of sheep'. In Australia the world belonged to the Albert Faceys, the industrious, the sober, and the ones handy with their fists. Again 'knuckle men' became 'cocks of the roost'.

Some soldiers were saying that the time had come to find ways of controlling elected governments, which were subject to the passions and prejudices of the mob. At least, there had to be a defence mounted of Empire values. Socialists in Australia were now like greyhounds on a leash, straining to get away. But the King-and-Empire men were determined those greyhounds would never even run on to the course. Distinguished army officers, prominent conservative politicians and men whose social life provided gossip to the 'social set', invited all loyal people in Sydney to the Town Hall on the night of 18 July 1920. Scenes of extraordinary enthusiasm marked the overflow meeting. General Sir Charles Rosenthal was in the chair. On the platform were 150 people: high dignitaries of the Church of England, many ex-army officers such as Brigadier-General Edmund Herring, colonels, majors, captains and lieutenants, the brave men back from France and Flanders. There were only three women. They sang the National Anthem with patriotic gusto. They raised the roof with 'Rule Britannia'. They decided to form the King and Empire Alliance to counteract the influence of disloyalty, and to build up and maintain a strong national pride of race and Empire. The men wanted the women to help them, knowing as they did what women could do for the King and Empire. They were creating, Sir Charles Rosenthal declared, 'an offensive alliance against all sorts and conditions of disloyalty'. All the disloyalists should either leave the country or be strung up. There was tremendous enthusiasm for that. The audience rose to its feet and sang again the National Anthem.

During a brief stay in Sydney during 1922, D. H. Lawrence had first-hand experience of this group. He realised that beneath the 'rather fascinating indifference to . . . soul or spirit' there was a body of ex-diggers who were looking for a leader. Under the surface indifference and the pursuit of independence, there were men who could be savage and monstrous to all who challenged their secular religion. With the help of the ex-diggers, General Rosenthal, Major Scott and men of like mind proposed to stop 'ant-men and ant-women' swarming over Australia. Australia was a country where eagles flew in the sky, and the tomtits, sparrows and willy wagtails of 'coziness' and 'convenience' would have to 'shut their traps'.

In Sydney a group of these eagles formed the Old Guard. It included businessmen like Philip Goldfinch, a descendant of Governor Philip Gidley King and now general manager of the Colonial Sugar Refining Company, R. W. Gillespie, a director of the Bank of New South Wales, Sir Samuel Hordern of the retail firm of Anthony Hordern, William McIlwraith, the largest grocer in New South Wales; ex-army officers such as Major-General Sir Charles Rosenthal, Major W. J. Scott and, at the outset, Lieutenant-Colonel Eric Campbell from Young; and members of the old landed gentry such as Brigadier General George Macarthur Onslow of Camden Park, Lieutenant-Colonel Frederic Hinton of Canowindra, and Lieutenant-Colonel Donald Cameron of Scone. They pledged themselves to maintain law and order: they were ready to co-operate in upholding what they called 'constitutional government': they would rid Australia of the foreign element, and put an end once and for all to any attempt to establish in Australia a 'black, brown and brindle autocracy'. They believed in free enterprise, in individualism, not the loss of identity in Fascist or Communist movements. They stood for the Digger tradition, the virtues of Old Australia, for courage, bravery, independence and resource. Australians should beware of 'rule by the multitude'. By the end of 1922 they had 25 000 members in the city and 5000 in the country. In the course of the next nine years similar groups would emerge in other States.

A man who had dreamed of a very different kind of Australia had nothing more to say. In August 1922 Vance Palmer stood in awe before the ruins of what had once been the wondrous Henry Lawson. There was a 'look of misery graven deep into his thin hollowed face'. On 2 September he was found dead in a house in Abbotsford, Sydney. As with the place and circumstances of his birth, the stories of his death varied. Vance Palmer told a friend later that when the body was found, inside his mouth, which was wide open, a blowfly was buzzing. In the presence of death the respectable people made their somersaults. The widow who had been in his lifetime both his victim and his accuser played the role of chief mourner. Billy Hughes, who had tickled the ribs of the *claqueurs* of Melbourne with stories at Lawson's expense, ordered a state funeral. On 4 September the members of the respectable classes gathered in St Andrew's Cathedral for a memorial service. The bush people he had loved were not there. The Reverend D'Arcy Irvine, Anglican Archdeacon of Sydney, preached about God's forgiveness: God, he said, would judge Lawson as Lawson himself had once said God would forgive the drunkard of the Australian bush:

> They'll take the golden sliprails down and let poor Corney in.

Out in George Street a crowd of possibly 100 000 people assembled to pay their last tribute. A brass band played the 'Dead March' from *Saul* as the coffin was placed reverently on the hearse, and the procession started on the last journey. At Waverley Cemetery a clergyman of the Church of England recited over the coffin the words which had been spoken over the mortal remains of another of Australia's great native sons just over fifty years before—William Charles Wentworth:

> The days of men are but as grass: for he flourisheth as a flower of the field.
> For as soon as the wind goeth over it, it is gone: and the place thereof shall know it no more.

He was buried in the same cemetery as J. R. Gribble, 'The Blackfellow's Friend', and Henry Kendall, 'Poet of Australia'. The greatest of his dreams had been about the destiny of Australia: 'We are Australians—we know no other land'.

5

'Can't We Do Anything Ourselves?'

Stanley Melbourne Bruce was everything Labor despised and mistrusted. He was an Australian who spoke and dressed like an Englishman. He was born in St Kilda, Melbourne, in 1883 and was educated at Melbourne Grammar School and Trinity Hall, Cambridge. He had played in the first teams and was captain of his school. At Cambridge he was given a rowing blue and coached their crew to victory on the eve of the war. Everything he did was done with great distinction. He enlisted in the British army on the outbreak of war. At Suvla Bay he won the Military Cross for bravery. After being invalided out of the army he won a by-election for the seat of Flinders in April 1917. He stood again in the federal election of December 1922 while his leader, Billy Hughes, strutted the platforms of Australia confident of victory. Contesting this election was a new political party on whom Hughes could sharpen his wit, the Country Party, led by Dr Earle Page. Hughes, the international statesman, dismissed them as 'hayseeds'; he mocked Dr Page as a lightweight who knew nothing about politics. When the votes were counted, Billy Hughes's Nationalists and the Labor Party had won thirty seats each. The 'hayseeds' held the balance of power with fourteen seats; Page refused to work with Hughes and agreed to support Bruce. There was to be a 'Bruce-Page' Government. 'Yarraside' again had one of its own as Prime Minister.

Labor ridiculed the wealthy young businessman with the la-di-da voice as a quasi-Englishman. But Bruce had always had the capacity to grow, the precious gift of moving with the great river of life. Unlike Billy Hughes he was neither a mocker nor a hater. Yet he always spoke from on high to those below. The members of his government, he insisted, were not Tories. They were progressive men of sanity, men who stuck to the field of the possible. They were realists: men who held it to be self-evident that the future prosperity of Australia and the key to its defence lay with the Empire.

Facing Bruce across the table in the House of Representatives was Matthew Charlton, the quiet and honourable man who led the Labor Party. On the same side of the chamber was a man of destiny, James Scullin. As a Labor man of the Irish Catholic variety, Scullin was ill at ease with Bruce's desire to strengthen Australia's bonds with the mother country. But Scullin was too timid a man to advocate an Australian Boston Tea Party. All he was prepared to say on 1 March 1923 was that Labor stood for the common man and Bruce for the gentleman.

Jimmy Scullin was born at Trawalla, Victoria, on 18 September 1876, and educated at Trawalla State School. He was a gentle spirit who had worn the hobnailed boots and the bowyangs of the Australian bush worker. He had the soul of a John Shaw Neilson, and the oratorical gifts of a Daniel O'Connell. A man with the image of Christ in his heart became the Labor member for Corangamite in April 1910. In the House of Representatives he was soon known as the 'hurricane orator', and the man whose heart was on fire over the wrongs of Ireland and the poor.

They were politicians in an Australia no longer isolated by time and distance. Radio, the telegraph, the steamship were drawing Australia ever closer to Europe. The new heroes of the 1920s were aviators: Charles Kingsford Smith, Charles Ulm, Hudson Fysh, Keith and Ross Smith, Bert Hinkler, and, at the end of the decade, the Englishwoman, Amy Johnson. They flew the Pacific. They were killed in crashes, disappeared without trace or survived to fly again. Whatever their story, the newsreels made heroes of them. The people could not get enough. On 16 November 1920 the Queensland and Northern Territory Aerial Services Limited—QANTAS—was registered in Brisbane for passenger and postal services at the Top End.

For the captains of industry it was a time of promise, a time of hope. Electrification and harnessing of water power would 'free Australia from the hampering traditions of the past' and launch Australia on a 'rising tide of progress'. That was the Bruce-Page vision: that was their answer to the gloom and doom men of the Left. A new era was about to begin. The 'vital spark' of electricity was working a silent revolution in transport, communications, the factory and the home.

In May 1921 the Victorian railway commissioners published their plan to electrify the Melbourne suburban railways by 1923. The Railways Department in Sydney had a similar plan. The States had plans to supply cheap electric power for street-lighting, factories, and private houses. In the forests of Australia trees were felled to make poles to carry wires transmitting electricity from power station to consumer. Pylons like miniature Eiffel Towers appeared in the countryside, to the anger of some and the delight of others. Electric power promised to be a remedy for that 'welter of discontent'. It restored the 'dignity of useful work' by reducing drudgery. Electric power expanded the class of skilled workers, the class which owed its privileged position to the expansion of capitalist society. Electric power speeded up the bourgeoisification of the worker.

Electric gadgets promised the Australian housewife relief from drudgery. There was the electric iron, the electric kettle, the electric stove and the electric toaster; there were hot-water services, radiators and refrigerators. Electric appliances did not liberate women from the home: but they did provide women with more leisure. Even ironing and pegging out clothes lost some of their burden. Humanity, or rather middle-class humanity, was marching towards a cleaner way of life.

People moved from the country to the city to benefit from the higher wages, the better facilities and the higher standard of living. In 1911 38.03 per cent of the population lived in the seven capital cities; in 1921 it was 43.01 per cent. The 1920s witnessed another suburban sprawl, 'a litter of bungalows . . . scattered for miles and miles'. The front lawn, the car in a garage, the wireless aerial, the front entrance to the house became measuring rods of status and respectability. For the bourgeoisie it was the age of 'jazz style', the age of the gramophone, the ebony elephant and the cocktail cabinet. For the working classes it was the age of the weatherboard villa, the interior decoration of which lacked the conspicuous waste and display of the bourgeoisie.

Between November 1923 and June 1924 the Government licensed four broadcasting companies: two in Sydney, one in Melbourne and one in Perth. On 23 November 1921, Station 2SB broadcast the first Australian wireless programme from a room in the *Smith's Weekly* building in Sydney.

The dance halls were the pleasure palaces for the masses, the cabaret for the comfortable classes. At the cabarets of Sydney and Melbourne everyone who appointed themselves to be 'anyone' or attached importance to being seen, and later in the evening to being heard, was there. One-time scholarship boys, and aspirants to social and public preferment, were seen 'rubbing elbows with the rich, with those millionaires'. The curious and the pryers received information on who was dancing cheek to cheek with whom in Melbourne and Sydney town. The moralizers likened the entrances to the cabaret and the dance palace to the 'doors of Hell', and named the time after midnight the 'danger hour', when the back seats of taxis and hansom cabs became 'brothels on wheels'.

The priests and the parsons deplored that God had been shouldered out of Australian life and replaced by paganism. Australians, said Dr James Duhig, the Catholic Archbishop of Brisbane, have become addicts to materialism: they have preserved the cult of 'outward respectability', alongside 'religious incredulity'. They preferred the exciting pleasures of the picture show, the dance hall, the racecourse, the football ground and the beaches to the adoration of the Blessed Sacrament. The sun, as Arthur Adams had said in *The Australians*, had defeated religion in Australia.

The new fashions associated with the flappers were positively shameful. Archbishop Kelly published in January 1922 a pastoral letter on women's dress. Clothing, he wrote, was given 'for our necessities, not for vanities'. God gave human beings clothing 'to hide the shameful members'. Catholic women, the *Advocate* wrote in January, 'with Mary Mother of God most holy always before them as their Model, should lead the van against everything that tends to lower a high standard of womanly purity'. Catholic fathers, sons and brothers should 'expostulate with flighty daughters, wives or sisters and refuse to escort them thus half dressed anywhere'.

Some blamed the new-fangled cinema for this decline into fleshly indulgence. The *Methodist* detected a connection between the erotic nature of some of the films and the erotic dances in the dance halls of the cities. The *Presbyterian Messenger* made the same point: the films were glamorizing and condoning marital infidelity. Plans were announced for bigger and more gaudy palaces expressive of the extravagance characteristic of the age. For adults the American films offered what *Table Talk* called a 'mad stampede of the emotions'. Early in the new year of 1922 patrons of the Globe picture theatre in Sydney saw on the silver screen an English woman disdain the advances of a demon lover of the deserts of Africa.

It was a time of change, outrageousness, optimism and madness—a post-war world in which people were giddy with life and drunk with despair. The churches were not alone in pining for lost certitudes. In the public schools, university colleges, the Royal Military College at Duntroon, Canberra, and the Naval College at Flinders initiations gave the members of those communities an early lesson in the duty to conform, and the expectations of their elders that they would be loyal to the prevailing virtues. In the state schools, the School Papers and the teachers introduced the children to English heroes such as Lord Nelson and the Duke of Wellington, and to their good fortune in belonging to an Empire on which the sun never set. Each Monday morning in term time the children were lined up around a flag pole, asked to place their right hand on their left breast and recite with the teacher a promise to obey their parents and their teachers, and to be loyal to their King and their Empire. To honour the Anzacs and the Empire, verses were added to some school songs. At Melbourne Grammar School verses were added which included the lines:

> Praise ye these who stood for Britain,
> These by foreign marksmen smitten;
> Praise them for their names are written
> High in storied fame.

It was nevertheless an age of doubt about everything: even the role given to women by God was open to challenge. Jessie MacDonald asked whether a woman was to have the individual right and liberty to control her own body, or was she to be a 'super-rabbit' to breed as long as she was physically capable. She and others advocated education in the use of contraceptives. By 1922 information about contraceptives was available to Australians in Marie Stopes's *Married Love*. The Australian Government had banned the book soon after it was published in London in 1918—after all, the woman said she wanted to teach men 'the sex tide in women'; she mentioned the role of the clitoris in sexual fulfilment. 'Yarraside' was offended. When the book was at last released in Australia, the churches called it an appeal to 'the licentiousness and the beast in man'.

Others were more excited by the contest between bat and ball. The people have found on the sporting field heroes who seemed to defy even the laws of gravity. In 1921 in England Warwick Armstrong, the captain of the Australian cricket team, wore shirts with extra-long sleeves to conceal the spin his fingers were imparting to the ball. The people worshipped him: they called him affectionately 'Warwick', the giant of the cricket field who stood well over 6 feet in his socks, and weighed well over 20 stone. The English believed gentlemen always defeated 'cads': this time the cads from 'Down Under' won easily. On the football field the heroes of the people also defied the laws of gravity. Roy Cazaly habitually took such a prodigious leap for a mark that as soon as he began his run the crowd would chant: 'Up there, Cazaly!' or, more affectionately, 'Up there, Cazza boy!'

While people at large were being nourished on a diet of pleasure, the intellectuals were discussing the decline of the West or searching for the 'roots that clutch' and the branches that 'grow out of this stony rubbish'. The serious-minded men and women of letters still looked to the literature of the Old World for wisdom and understanding, as though to say: 'I am Australian, but my ideas come from Shakespeare, from Milton, from Dostoevsky, from

Tolstoy. No Australian writer has taught me how to think or how to live'. Such would-be promoters of high 'culture' held little joy for the writer Vance Palmer. For years he has rebuked the 'Cultured Philistines' for insisting that nothing in art, literature, music or life was important unless it originated in England, Europe, or classical antiquity. In 1920 he told his readers that Europe was doomed: Europe is weighed down by its past. There 'dreams of dead men underground/Trouble the heavy air'. He was aware of what had happened in Europe: he was aware of 'the dark Somme flowing'. Australia does not need the dead hand of the past, said Palmer, Australia needs a vital and creative culture of her own. Her artists, writers and musicians must uncover her uniqueness and the uniqueness of her people to other Australians— the way they spoke, the way they lived, and above all what they lived by.

Vance Palmer was a boy from the bush. He was born at Bundaberg, Queensland, in 1885, and was educated at state school and at Ipswich Grammar School. For him, as for Lawson, the bush had been the nursery of Australian character and culture. But so far, said Palmer, the cities have not developed a culture of their own: now they have been swamped by the new commercial entertainment; the cinema, jazz, and the stacks of 'cheap and nasty' American magazines.

Hilda Esson asked Vance Palmer and his talented, long-suffering wife, Nettie, 'Can't we do anything ourselves as Australians?' When the film of *The Sentimental Bloke*, directed by Raymond Longford, was screened in Sydney in October 1919 the *Daily Telegraph* was delighted. It was, it wrote, 'Australian right through'. But the Palmers, the Essons and their circle did not share this delight. Louis Esson, the playwright, did not want Australians to take their entertainment from the sentimentalities of C. J. Dennis. Dennis was an anachronism, a man preaching that those who had wallowed in the city muck would find salvation in the bush. Esson agreed with Vance Palmer: Australia needed a culture for the suburbs.

Composers had plans to capture this new spirit of Australia in music. Henry Tate told Nettie Palmer that in his new composition, 'Australian Dawn', he would express in sound and words 'the dawn of Australia's Being as we know it'. The work would begin with bird calls, and then develop the theme of Australia as a country where the people were 'hanging nebulously between earth and heaven'. The composers would lift up the hearts of Australians, give them the confidence to believe that in their own country they could go for a walk 'in the Paradise Gardens'.

In May 1922 the Essons, the Palmers, Stewart Macky and others, with the support of Bernard O'Dowd, Frank Wilmot and Katharine Prichard, launched the Pioneer Players, who put on Louis Esson's comedy, *The Battler*, at the Playhouse in Melbourne. The first-night audience was large and enthusiastic. But then the problems began. The *Age* and the *Argus* were patronizing, the *Age* dismissing the play as 'too slight to make a whole evening's amusement'. Robert Ross was enthusiastic in *Ross's Monthly*. The play stood, he said, 'for the appreciation of our picturesque hills, gulleys [sic] and waterfalls'. The audiences dwindled; they patronized other theatres and the moving pictures. Australians, Robert Ross concluded, preferred 'legs and tinkling music' to the cultivation of Australian sentiment. Within a few weeks Frank Wilmot was telling Louis Esson the Pioneer Players had no need of a chucker-out at the Playhouse: what they needed was a 'chucker-in'. When Stewart Macky's play, *John Blake*, was performed in August the press boycotted it. Sometimes members of the Palmers' circle found that they did not like Australians. 'I don't care for its people', Louis Esson once wrote to Vance Palmer. He did not like Melbourne either. It was 'a wowser, bourgeois town, without an idea of any kind'.

The prominent painters also had a love–hate relationship with the country and its people. Arthur Streeton, the innocent who had created *Purple Noon's Transparent Might*, was now selling his paintings for huge sums at exhibitions in Melbourne and Sydney. Commercialism and money values have blunted his sensibilities. Tom Roberts returned to Melbourne in February 1923 and settled down in the Sherbrooke Forest near Sassafras, painting the majestic mountain ash. He still wanted to convince himself and Australians that the gum tree was not 'an uninteresting excrescence on the face of the earth'. But he still did not know where he belonged—to the top hat and white tie Government House society, or to the bush people, the wearers of bowyangs and moleskins.

The sense of uncertainty, which was so common in those years immediately after the war, was felt even among the men and women of 'Yarraside'. They had regained control of government, and yet it seemed to many that society was running out of control. The Labor Party was speaking as though capitalism itself was unjust. Communists were preaching revolution. The material expectations of working people were rising and they were starting to indulge in those new entertainments which seemed so vulgar and disruptive. On the first weekend in November 1923, the worst fears of 'Yarraside' were realized when a strike of disgruntled police officers opened the way to chaos; vast crowds indulged in two nights of rioting and looting in the heart of Melbourne. Amid the pandemonium, volunteer police took to the streets under the command of the old AIF network. 'Fascisti', in the words of the *Workers' Weekly*, were driving round the streets of Melbourne guarding the property of the bourgeoisie: the motor car has become a weapon in the class war. There was talk, too, that a secret volunteer 'White Army' had been set up to protect the interests of 'Yarraside' and bourgeois Melbourne from the revolutionary mob.

As the life of Bob Menzies showed, there was a good deal to protect. He had a weekend house at Macedon next to Staniforth Ricketson, stock-broker of Melbourne and future power-broker of Australian politics. Menzies was climbing to the top. He became a director in the firm of J. B. Were and Son, the Australian Foundation Investment Company, and the National Reliance Investment Company. Success in the world has not mellowed him. Despite the warning that anyone who said of another 'Thou fool' would be in danger of hell-fire, Menzies still enjoyed ridiculing men of weak intellects for presenting arguments in the form of 'tripe'.

On the other side of the continent, John Curtin was going for solitary walks on the beach at Cottesloe looking for answers to questions which concerned him as a Labor man. For him Labor was still the 'great cause'. He has not forsworn the hope, or become cynical. There was a man within, whom those privileged to know never forgot. He had a power to make people worship and idolize him.

In China Mao Tse-Tung was asking: Who rules over man's destiny?—and dreaming of setting the people of China afire with words of revolution, and teaching the people to count 'the mighty no more than muck'. In the Rhineland D. H. Lawrence, with the eye of the prophet to see into the heart of the matter, predicted that the Ruhr occupation and English nullity would drive Germany back to 'the destructive vortex of Tartary', that the 'heroes of humanity' were hatching a brood of 'dangerous, lurking barbarians' in Germany. In Australia men and women were singing around the pianola:

> Oh I wish I had someone to love me,
> I'm tired of living alone.

6

The Great Imperial Firm of Wealth, Progress and Opportunities Unlimited

Australia needed 'all the British blood she could get'. The United Kingdom had a surplus population; Australia had the empty spaces. All the people in high places agreed that migration from the British Isles would promote what they all wanted: 'The Great Imperial Firm of Wealth, Progress, and Opportunities Unlimited'. 'Men, money and markets' became the slogan of the Bruce-Page Government.

Yeomen from Devon would create another Devon in the Australian wilderness: the men of Somerset, where the cider apples grow, would plant another England in the land of sunshine and freedom. The government of Western Australia agreed to take 75 000 British migrants. They agreed to provide three days of hospitality for them, place them in suitable employment during a probationary period, and then help them to begin farming on their blocks. Migration literature read like an invitation to a walk in the Paradise Gardens.

One migrant from Devon found to his dismay that he and his family were housed in tin sheds near their blocks until they built a house of their own. They had expected a stone cottage with vine leaves covering the walls. When his wife saw their future house was a tin shed, her 'heart was up in her mouth straight away'. She told her husband she had come to the end of her days.

Another woman in England read greedily the literature in Australia House about the group settlements in Western Australia. She persuaded her husband to sell all they possessed, including her engagement and wedding rings, 'make a break' and start a new and better life near Albany. There in the bush there were no lavatories, no roads, no doctors, no hospital, no beds, no milk, no fruit. She and the children slept on the bare earth, sometimes in a tent, sometimes in a tin shack, while her husband slept under the sky. She missed the familiar sights, smells and sounds of civilized life—the pubs, church bells, factory sirens, the roar of a football crowd, and the uproar of the music hall. Instead she had to endure the silence of the Australian bush, and the pitiless Australian sun. As compensation she had what the migrant literature had called 'the freedom to roam wherever the spirit moved her'. But the questions were: where? and: how and when would they be rescued from the hell they were enduring? To add to her misery, by day she was plagued by flies, and by night by mosquitoes: by day and night both, there were fleas.

Within a year her burdens were eased. Cows were in milk, pigs slaughtered for meat, vegetables grew, crops were sown, schools and churches were built. The government planned to build a railway line, and to build roads and bridges to allow motor cars to come into the district. The wireless reduced the isolation and the loneliness, while feeding the restlessness. But many are not able to make a go of it. By April 1924 32 per cent of the immigrant group settlers and 42 per cent of Australian-born 'groupies' have walked off their blocks. But the promises continued. Sir Joseph Cook, the High Commissioner in London, told prospective migrants that Australia was 'the land of the better chance'. There was 'sunshine and laughter' in Australia.

Bruce believed that his government was setting 'the foundations of a great democracy . . . [to] populate and develop our great empty spaces, and realise the full destiny that lies before Australia'. While the government encouraged immigration, it also sought markets for Australian products. Bruce was determined that the government should render assistance to exporters. That was one of the tablets of the law in Australia. He did not propose to challenge it, even though he knew protection would probably increase the costs of production and so make Australian goods uncompetitive. Much has to be done. Marketing systems must be devised. The discussions on imperial preference begun at the London Conference of October 1923 must be continued. Bruce was moving inexorably towards binding Australia in an imperial vice.

Australia also needed money. The little old lady of Threadneedle Street must be their saviour. The British must invest their capital. In return prosperous Australians would buy British goods: Australia and New Zealand must revive 'the sick man of Europe'. But one day borrowers must repay the bondholders. It never occurred to Bruce, the Cambridge Blue, the captain in the Royal Fusiliers, that the little old lady of Threadneedle Street might turn into a tyrant.

A Labor win in the New South Wales State election on 30 May 1925 alarmed the conservatives. Lang was a demagogue, a man who roused the passions of the people by posing as their saviour.

The people had a hero. He had ideas on social reform. That, too, had its dangers. Social welfare—widows' pensions, sickness payments, unemployment benefits—could only be paid for by increased taxation. Lang would not be prudent: Lang would be prodigal, a spendthrift. Lang must be watched.

The Communists branded Lang as a capitalist politician masquerading as a Labor man. But they are optimistic: the workers will move further to the left. They will abandon Lang and embrace their revolutionary destiny. Bruce must save Australian bourgeois society from those Bolsheviks and wreckers, who were stirring up trouble on the waterfront, in the coalmines, and in transport. Ever since 1917 there has been industrial conflict on the waterfront. In the beginning of 1925 the waterside workers demanded changes to the system of 'picking-up' crews, which had many of the features of a slave market. They demanded that the 'pick-up' places should be the union offices on the wharves: the shipowners suggested the Mercantile Marine Offices. The union said no. All interstate shipping was held up pending the settlement of the dispute. On 29 January the Commonwealth Court of Conciliation and Arbitration gave a final warning to the union. The union accepted the award. The strike was over, but the atmosphere of unrest and confrontation remained.

Bruce decided to divide the moderates from the militants on the waterfront. He branded two leaders of the Seamen's Union, Tom Walsh and Jacob Johannsen, as alien agitators, and passed a law giving the government power to deport such people. Dr H. V. Evatt represented Walsh and Johannsen in the High Court and argued that the pair were not aliens—they had lived in Australia too long. On 11 December 1925 the High Court handed down its judgment; the majority agreed with Evatt. The appellants, Walsh and Johannsen, were released and toasts were drunk to their Honours in the pubs of Woolloomooloo and Port Melbourne. Encomiums were lavished upon them in the Trades and Labor Councils and the editorial offices of the Labor press.

The Jeremiahs have prophesied about a day of reckoning for a society obsessed with 'Men, Money and Markets'—a society in love with 'Wealth, Progress and Opportunities Unlimited'. In his book *Money Power*, published in 1921, Frank Anstey warned Australians there would one day be a terrible retribution because the money men in Australia were piling debts to British financiers higher and higher. Australians, he said, would one day pay a high price for the Bruce policy of borrowing in London for development. The money men have not heeded the warning. They have recklessly borrowed more, laughing at the Jeremiahs. Above the uproar in the stock exchanges of Sydney and Melbourne, Anstey heard the 'drum beat of the Armies of Revolution'. He prophesied they would beat louder and louder. No nation would escape the catastrophe. But Australians sat on Bondi Beach, or went to Luna Park: Just for Fun.

Bruce continued to speak of Australia as the country where capitalism would provide opportunities for all those with talent, industry and moral fibre. To aid the primary and secondary industries of Australia he created the Council of Scientific and Industrial Research in 1926. Science, he said, could better the conditions of the workers and bring greater prosperity to the Australian people. The CSIR would encourage that capacity for invention which had made Australia a pioneer in the fields of agricultural machinery, goldmining, wheat breeding and dry farming. It was headed by men who were concerned to tackle such problems as the prickly pear, diseases in sheep and cattle, dry farming. The engineers and the scientists would be the servants of bourgeois society.

Bruce also had plans to take the sting out of the socialist condemnation of capitalist society as the cause of the moral infamies of exploitation, poverty and unemployment. Early in 1926 he gave serious consideration to establishing a scheme of national insurance covering casual sickness, permanent invalidity, old age and unemployment, and providing maternity allowances and pensions for the destitute.

The Labor Party had no effective response. It was rent by factional bitterness and conflicting idealisms. All Communists have been expelled from the Party. But Jock Garden has let the cat out of the bag: he boasted that the shadow of Communism was over the Labor movement. Bruce, Page, and the Attorney-General, John Latham, were determined to smash atheistic Communism and to bring the unions to heel. The government increased its powers under the Crimes Act to supress the Communist Party and its publications. Bruce embarked on a campaign to smash the unions: the cause became a conservative crusade. At the same time, some in the Communist Party are bewildered. The party still has not become a mass movement. As Nettie Palmer's brother, Esmonde Higgins, put it in March 1925, the Communist Party was only 'a few little cliques', with no chance of organizing 'any left-wing opposition let alone a revolution'.

The Parliament House in Canberra, overlooking the lovely meadow of the Molonglo River and St John's Church, was opened on 9 May 1927. It was one of those days when the air was 'clear as crystal'. To the disgust of those who believed Australia was different from the Old World there was much 'bowing and scraping' as men in cocked hats and plumes arrived at Parliament House, where representatives of the 'cuff and collar push' greeted them. During the ceremony, Mr Bruce handed the Duke of York a golden key and invited him to open the doors of the building. As he did so, cheer after cheer broke out, flags were waved, as a surge of 'heartfelt emotion' swept like a tide over the assembled multitude. A solitary Aborigine sat watching on the lawn. In Australian public ceremonies nothing has changed.

Over in Belgium, on 24 July 1927, at the Menin Gate of the city of Ypres, another distinguished gathering, including King Albert of the Belgians, watched Lord Plumer unveil the memorial to the thousands of the Empire's sons buried in nameless graves around Ypres. The governments of every nation in the British Commonwealth had contributed to the memorial. Lord Plumer said relatives of loved ones whose bodies had never been found could now say to themselves: 'He is not missing. He is here'. Around Ypres the inscription on every tombstone spoke of somebody's loss, somebody's grief, somebody's hope. Some died 'that we might live'; some were unmistakably Australian, saying simply, 'From Mum and Dad'.

In Canberra another drama began. On 29 March 1928 Matthew Charlton, the leader of the ALP, informed the House of Representatives that due to failing health, he was resigning from the office of leader of the party. Everyone liked him. Members on both sides of the House praised him for his years in office. For Charlton was a most honourable man, a most virtuous man. He had won the loyalty and esteem of his colleagues. But no one could remember what he had done, or what he had stood for. Jimmy Scullin, the high-minded man and believer in the 'cause', took over the leadership of that pack of dreamers, battlers and pragmatists. In the same year, Bob Menzies decided to stand for election to the Legislative Council of Victoria.

Bruce continued his attempts to crush the unions. The Labor movement was being represented as the instrument of foreign subversives at the very time that Labor was dominated by men of moderation. He represented every industrial dispute as a manifestation of disloyalty to Australia and the Empire. On 22 June he proclaimed the 'bludgeon act', an amendment to the Conciliation and Arbitration Act which gave the authorities increased powers to enforce arbitration rulings.

On 21 August 1928 Judge Beeby brought down an award on working conditions on the waterfront designed to 'lay a new foundation for better relationships on the waterfront'. George Stephenson Beeby entered public life as an advocate of the cause of moderation in the Labor movement. He found the militancy of the Waterside Workers' Federation quite distasteful. He wanted the employers to stop their 'litigious spirit'. In the interests of industrial peace he was prepared to make what he called 'most generous concessions' to the waterside workers. He conceded the central pick-up system which the men had been demanding ever since 1917. He awarded two 'smoke-ohs' to men working 'bulk' or shovelling cargoes. He awarded double time to the men on the night shift.

The Waterside Workers' Federation was not impressed by all this 'blah blah' about harmony and reconciliation. Bruce's 'bludgeon act' must be repealed. The obnoxious clauses in the Beeby award—the provision for two pick-ups a day—must be changed. The days of the slave market on the waterfront must be brought to an end. The Beeby award means slavery: there must be no servile peace, no capitulation to the shipowners: class solidarity would break the bosses' attack. On 10 September the men on the Sydney waterfront boycotted the afternoon pick-up. The shipping companies threatened to employ 'free labour' if the members of the federation continued to boycott the afternoon pick-up. The federation stood firm.

Bruce, Latham and Page appealed to the people of Australia to defend White Australia against the Reds. Scullin and the Labor Party did not know what to do. An election was due at the end of the year. Scullin offered to use his influence with the men in the interests of industrial peace if Bruce used his influence with the employers. He wanted industrial harmony for Australia—and before the elections.

On 16 September the *Sydney Morning Herald* jubilantly announced the strike had been declared off: the men had capitulated. Two days later they announced that the owners had tried to use free labour. At Brisbane and Adelaide all work on ships was declared 'black' until such time as that pernicious clause in the Beeby award was struck out. Scullin once again offered to serve as an agent of peace. The militants disowned him. The *Workers' Weekly* called on the men to stand firm: victory was not far off. The moderates with political aspirations wanted industrial peace quickly. The militants, they said, were putting a trump card in Bruce's hand. Bruce threatened to invoke the Crimes Act against the union leaders. The election was drawing nearer, with Labor putting on yet another Kilkenny cat brawl.

With men still out on the Brisbane, Adelaide and Melbourne waterfronts, Bruce attacked again. In the last week of September he rushed an Act through Parliament which gave the government power to license transport workers. Any transport worker not approved by the government would be unable to obtain work. The workers called it the 'dog-collar' Act. Scullin was horrified by this 'proclamation of industrial martial law'. The government was deliberately throwing the 'apple of discord into the industrial arena'. But, with the native cunning of his people, he sensed that Bruce's extremism would antagonize middle Australia, that there were possible electoral gains for Labor in tempting Bruce into further onslaughts on the trade unions.

The unions decided to 'fight the Act to the last ditch'. Plans were laid to extend the strike on the waterfront. Bruce at last, in a conciliatory gesture, promised that licensing of workers would not be enforced at any port where the workers accepted the clauses of the Beeby award. The prevailing unemployment gave the employers plenty of labour ('free labour') to work the ships in port. Clashes occurred between unionists and non-unionists on the Melbourne and Adelaide waterfronts. By the beginning of October there were rumours that the South Australian Government had issued rifles and bayonets to a volunteer body of 500 men. In Melbourne the homes of a couple of stevedores who had helped to work some of the ships were damaged by bombs.

With tides of industrial violence sweeping the waterfront, the Bruce-Page Government was returned with a comfortable majority in both Houses in the November election. Labor added to its ranks the men of destiny: John Curtin won Fremantle by a narrow majority; Joseph Benedict Chifley, a 'light on the hill' man, won Macquarie from the Nationalists; Rowland ('Rowley') James replaced Matthew Charlton in Hunter; J. A. Beasley, who had learnt his politics in the Sydney Trades and Labor Council, won West Sydney. The actors in the drama to come were moving on to the stage.

7

The Imperial Firm Goes Bung

The economy, like the morals of the people, was sick. Revenue from all state-owned projects such as railways, tramways, irrigation, soldier settlement, and closer settlement was falling. Export prices were down. The States and the Commonwealth were in serious debt. Debt led to increases in taxation and the cost of living. Unemployment rose from 7 per cent in 1927 to 10.8 per cent at the beginning of 1928. Beggars were becoming common in the streets. It was the age of jazz, the age of the flapper. Jazz ages are like the grasses of the field. They have their moment before they are thrown into the cleansing fire and consumed. They live on in the record books of human folly.

The export of coal from New South Wales was declining, because the production cost was too high to compete in foreign markets. The Premier of New South Wales, Tom Bavin, and the coal-owners met in Sydney in January 1929, to discuss a scheme to reduce costs. Like Bruce they believed that the standard of living in Australia must be reduced if Australian products were to compete in overseas markets. But the miners would not listen to the proposals. To them this was proof that capitalist governments were plotting an assault on the living standards of Australian workers, and on the trade unions. The New South Wales Government asked the men to accept a small reduction in pay. The men said no wage cuts would be permitted. Owners and managers foretold 'grave industrial trouble'. Militants in the labour movement called on workers to stand firm.

There was more trouble on the waterfront. At the start of 1929 there was rioting on the docks of Port Adelaide as police and strike-breakers exchanged blows and gunfire with striking workers. A month later, timber workers were engaged in a strike which also became violent: Judge Lukin had cut their wages and restored the 48-hour week. Soon workers in Australia in the key industries of power and transport were on strike. Even in the National and Country Party rooms there were whispers of dissent. Old enmities were rising to the surface. Bruce's tough stand on industrial relations, his talk about root and branch reform of the arbitration system, were not universally supported. The light came back into the eyes of William Morris Hughes. The opportunity to take revenge for the wounds of 1923 was not far away.

The militants believed the decisive hour was approaching. At Yallourn on 7 May Jock Garden struck terror into the hearts of the bourgeoisie by speaking of a night of pillage. 'One night of darkness in Melbourne', he said, 'and there would be a few new suits in the city. The workers would have a few gold watches, too. One night of darkness would be more than enough, and that would be all we require of you'. Was it coming to that? Was property no longer safe? Must the law-abiding tremble in their beds, fearful lest they not survive the night? At the northern coalmines of New South Wales the militants were talking of using force to compel the bosses to open the mines on existing wages and withdraw the lockout notices.

Bruce remained confident. The upper-class habit of lecturing the lower orders on the error of their ways was ingrained in him. On 17 May 1929 he issued a statement on the errors of the strikers. The recent timber workers' strike, he said, like the waterside workers' strike, was against an award of the Arbitration Court. 'I would ask unionists', he continued, 'to consider the full significance of their action'. It was the Melbourne Grammar headmaster's argument to the non-conformists: 'You know you are doing wrong: why do you do it?' Why indeed? To save them from their own folly and madness, his government might be forced to deprive them of the boon of arbitration. Bruce would save the workers from destruction. Bruce needed to be saved from himself. All the warning signs were there. The eyes of Billy Hughes were shining: Bruce, he sensed, had dug his own grave. Labor was bubbling over with confidence. They sensed that their moment had come.

On Anzac Day 1929 Bruce opened the new War Memorial which his government had built at the foot of Mt Ainslie in Canberra. Once again there were to be no religious emblems on the Memorial, not because of sectarian differences or any reluctance to offend those groups which did not accept the divinity of Christ, but because most soldiers did not believe in the resurrection of the dead. Once again Australians borrowed voices from abroad—Rupert Brooke, the Apocrypha, Pericles, Laurence Binyon—to express their deepest feelings.

But this time there was a difference. Bruce did not dwell on the glories or benefits of belonging to the Empire. Speaking with unwonted passion, he told the audience that he was there to inaugurate the memorial of the Australian people as a nation. They were there to commemorate the sacrifices and sufferings of those who had created this Australian nationhood. There was still a gun salute for an English Governor-General. But Australians were beginning to talk on public occasions of what they stood for. Anzac has made Australians more aware of themselves. Bruce has discovered Australia, but not how to make Australia free.

As the slide towards economic depression continued, Bruce announced that his government had decided that the duplication and overlapping of the industrial powers of the Commonwealth and the States were retarding national progress and preventing industrial peace. They had therefore decided to repeal the federal arbitration legislation, retaining for the Commonwealth control only over shipping and the waterfront industries. He was determined to teach the militants a lesson. He would smash the unions. The tactic, he hoped, would divide labour. But Bruce lacked the art to read the signs of the times. In Parliament, on 10 September, Hughes moved an amendment against one of Bruce's industrial bills. After the amendment was carried, Bruce called an election. The people would support him: he ran on his record.

As the uproar on the coalfields continued, Scullin campaigned on a platform of 'sane finance' and sober administration. To stand for anything more would mean banishment to the political wilderness. On 9 October, three days before the election, Bob Menzies told the diners at an Old Trinity Grammarians' luncheon that what was wanted in Australia was 'the maintenance of the public school spirit'. But it was too late. Australia has left that world behind. When counting of votes ceased at midnight on Saturday 12 October it was clear there had been a massive swing to Labor. Curtin and Chifley increased their majorities. Bruce lost his seat by 305 votes to E. J. Holloway, a Melbourne trade unionist. Labor made huge gains in the country electorates at the expense of the Country Party.

Out in the Never-Never things were still the same as ever. A vast sky, and an inhospitable environment, spoke not of any new eras in the history of the ancient continent, but of all those things which were from eternity and would not change.

8

An Australian in the Palace of the King-Emperor

On the day the triumphant Scullin government was sworn in, hectic scenes occurred on the floor of the New York Stock Exchange. Brokers were frantic. The entire fabric of capitalist society threatened to come down. On 27 and 28 October there was again frenzied selling on the New York stock market. Panic spread quickly. Three days later the *Sydney Morning Herald* reported that the 'insensate optimism' of the decade had been replaced by a 'dire pessimism'.

Already there were victims of the financial crisis. According to Australian tradition, it was the churches and the benevolent societies that ministered to the needs of those who were in any way afflicted or distressed in mind, body or estate. These bodies now redoubled their efforts. Dr Mannix distributed charity to the inhabitants of the 'lower depths'. As he passed through Collingwood on his daily walk from 'Raheen' in Kew to St Patrick's Cathedral, the hungry went down on their knees and begged him for the love of Christ to spare a coin for themselves and their starving families. The archbishop blessed them and gave them a coin. Dr Dale, the Melbourne City Health Officer, published a daily diet which was cheap and would sustain life. Charity was not enough. Australians wanted their traditional diet of bread, soup, meat, vegetables, pudding and tea. All over the country charity workers strained every nerve to relieve suffering and hunger. Australians wanted not charity, but work. They did not want to sink into despair.

The government must do something for those out of work. But no one had a clear idea on the duty of government towards the workless. No one wanted to condemn the unemployed to 'the torments of dire poverty'. But the Australian bourgeoisie has inherited a tradition contrary to any 'wasteful expenditure' and believed in self-help. Government handouts were both wasteful and degrading. Labor was not a team of spendthrifts. Jimmy Scullin told the press 'this was no time for luxuries'. He would set an example. He and his wife would take rooms in the Hotel Canberra, instead of living in luxury in the Prime Minister's Lodge in Canberra.

Labor will be cautious. In opposition, Labor speakers such as Frank Anstey and Maurice Blackburn had called on the Bruce–Page government to modify the censorship of books, pamphlets and films. Lenin's *Imperialism* and Stalin's *Theory and Practice of Leninism* were both banned, as was James Joyce's *Ulysses*. Now J. E. Fenton, the Minister for Customs, said there would be no wholesale lifting of the ban, but cases would be considered on their merits. Books advocating extreme revolution and bloodshed would certainly not be admitted. Nettle Palmer and her circle were disappointed. The *Workers' Weekly* said Labor was an imperialist government seeking to blind Australian workers to world developments and in particular to the danger of an imperialist war.

The government must also try to resolve the bitterness which has caused the recent disputes between capital and labour. In November Scullin attempted to mediate between representatives of the mining unions and the mineowners. All to no avail. Neither side would budge. The coal workers left the conference angry that the new Labor government appeared to be backing away from its promise that there would be no reductions in wages. On the very day the conference broke up, 14 November, the New South Wales Premier, Bavin, announced that his government would take over three of the collieries and run them, if necessary, with non-union labour. The government was not going to be 'dominated by a mob of miners'.

Tension mounted. Unemployment rose from 9.3 per cent in the first quarter of 1929 to 12.1 per cent in the third quarter. The Federal Government's answer was a palliative. Scullin decided to provide £1 million for relief work. That would be the government's Christmas gift to the workless. Jimmy Scullin was still able to laugh. At a Party function on 1 December he was gracious and generous to Jack Lang, the leader of the Labor Party in New South Wales: he said New South Wales was the backbone of the Labor Party and had saved Australia from conscription. Lang beamed.

Every day in Sydney thousands of what the *Labor Daily* called 'ill-dressed, sad-eyed and gaunt-faced men' gathered outside the Government Labour Bureau in Sydney to collect their ration order. With their tickets they moved to the grocery department where they filled their suitcases or sugar-bags with supplies. It was the same in all the other cities. All sorts of solutions to unemployment were advanced. The *Daily Telegraph*, the self-appointed watchdog over the taxpayers' money, wanted the unemployed to be taught 'a deeper sense of individual responsibility, a stronger resolve to stand on [their] own feet'. All the conservatives said 'Amen' to that.

The unemployed members of the trade unions discussed their plight with Tom Bavin on 5 December. For Bavin, life was a 'high adventure', the goal of which was virtue, not happiness or pleasure. He believed that people must make their own opportunities, that there was nothing to prevent a man in Australia earning as much as he wanted to. He was full of understanding and compassion. He knew, he told them, that the unemployed were having 'a very rough spin'. But they must understand that the government did not have a 'bottomless purse'.

On 9 and 10 December Jock Garden exhorted the miners at Cessnock to stand firm, and to set up rank and file committees to take over control of the dispute from the union. Garden was advocating the Moscow policy of white-anting the Miners' Federation as a step towards creating Soviets in Australia. Bavin sent in nonunion labour to work the mine under police guard. On Monday 16 December there was a pitched battle when armed police attempted to break up a picket of several thousand miners. Nine miners and seven police were wounded. One miner, Norman Brown, was shot dead by police. He became a hero of the Australian working class.

> Oh Norman Brown, oh Norman Brown,
> the murdering coppers they shot you down,
> They shot you down in Rothbury town,
> to live forever, Norman Brown.

At the Strand Theatre in Cessnock on Sunday 12 January 1930 the oaths of membership of a 'Labor Defence Army' were solemnly administered to a number of men. That evening they provided a bodyguard for the miners' wives as they marched down the main street of Cessnock bearing banners calling for the intensification of the struggle against the rotten system of capitalism. The violence continued, bringing all work at the mines to a standstill, and Bavin resolved to starve the miners into submission. The Communists declared that the dawn of revolution had arrived, but the past, the vast sky, and the spirit of the place whispered 'Not now . . . not yet . . . Maybe, never'.

Warnings of further catastrophe were coming from all sides. In the third week of February Judge Beeby delivered a homily to the representatives of the metal trades. Beeby's sympathies were known to be with the 'underdog', but he told organized Labor it was disastrously wrong. Labor, he said, must grasp a few fundamental facts. The slump in the prices of wool and wheat was not seasonal, but, with slight variations, it was likely to remain.

Australian credit on the money markets was exhausted. Unionists must co-operate with employers to reduce the cost of production, or a huge reduction in wages would occur. Under existing conditions the closing down of public works was inevitable, because they were dependent upon non-existent loan money. To avoid these consequences members of the trade union movement must agree to a change of methods, or a reduction in wages was inevitable. The unions must accept progress. For these words of good sense Beeby's name was added to the long list of villains and traitors in the Labor version of Australian society. Fence-sitters, Pontius Pilates, social scientists, economists and lawyers were all villains if they did not toe the Labor or union line. This was no time for one of those wise men who understood everything and forgave everything.

The *Labor Daily* said the slogan of the hundreds of thousands who wandered hopeless around the dreary streets of Sydney was: We Want Work. Scullin was offering them the stone of financial respectability, of winning the approval of Labor's traditional villain, Mr Money Man in London. The situation was 'ghastly, simply ghastly'. In all the cities scarcely a week passed without a procession of the unemployed. During the marches they shouted and sang songs, and held aloft banners drawing attention to their plight. Scuffles with the police were common, accompanied by cries from forgotten and embittered men and women such as 'Why not take the lot of us?' (i.e., to gaol).

The *Australian Worker* was confident it knew the cure: 'An extensive programme of public works, backed by a nation-wide scheme of Unemployment Insurance'. But loans could not be raised unless governments reduced their expenditure and increased their revenue. Scullin decided that Australian industry needed protection against foreign competition. On 3 April 1930 he announced that there was to be a total prohibition on the import of some articles, and an additional 50 per cent import duty on a huge range of others. He had protected Australian industrial practices and Australian wages at the cost of removing incentives to experiment and improvement.

Six days later, on 8 April, Bavin swung the axe. He announced that his government would reintroduce the 48-hour week in New South Wales, or payment for time actually worked if the 44-hour week was maintained. He introduced a system of payment by results and bonuses for speed workers, a levy on wages, salaries and earnings of all kinds to provide funds to carry out works of a reproductive character, and the appointment of a committee representing employers and employees to ensure that such funds were administered in the most economic manner. He was dismantling many of the schemes introduced by the previous Lang Labor government to cottonwool the workers against capitalist greed and oppression.

At the end of March another source of conflict was added to Australian politics when Cabinet decided to recommend the appointment of Sir Isaac Isaacs, the Chief Justice of the High Court, as the next Governor-General. The son of a tailor from Beechworth in Victoria, Isaacs had risen to one of the highest offices in the land. His exclusion from 'Yarraside' and clubland (his faith debarred him from ever becoming a member of the Melbourne Club) was one of the many qualities which commended him to a Labor government. Scullin forwarded the name of Isaac Isaacs to the King. The King was not amused. Through his private secretary he wanted to know who Isaac Isaacs was. He wanted a list of names from which he would make the final choice. Ramsay Macdonald asked Scullin to wait until he arrived in London for the Imperial Conference. But Jimmy Scullin would not bow to all this pressure. The man who has grovelled to Mr Money Man would not grovel to the titular head of the British governing classes.

He was just as firm with the King-and-Empire men in Australia. Henry Gullett asked in the House of Representatives if it was true the government intended to appoint an Australian. John Latham, the leader of the Federal Opposition, thought the time was not quite right for such a change. Imperial organizations bristled; the whole thing smelt of republicanism. But Scullin did not apologize or cringe. 'I have yet to learn', he said, 'that it has been laid down that an Australian may not be recommended for the position'. The tradition which laid it down that Government House should be occupied by amiable men from the British aristocracy was coming to an end.

On economic questions Scullin continued timid and unadventurous. Australian economists had ideas for the solution of the government's problems. On 28 April a newly appointed professor of economics at the University of Melbourne, L. F. Giblin, addressed himself to the question: 'How are we going to pay our way?' He was an eccentric: his coat had no lapels, his shirt-sleeves were cut off at the elbow; his boots were massive, his pipe equally so. He shared the view of J. M. Keynes that the role of economists was to shield bourgeois society against revolution. He warned his audience that unless wages were reduced in Australia the unemployment figures would rise steeply. There would be famine, bloodshed and class hatred in the land. It would be the end of the Australian dream of a society in which equality of opportunity did not impinge on the liberties of the individual. He believed capitalist society could be patched up. He and Douglas Copland, another economist at the University of Melbourne, were already writing to Joe Lyons, a prominent Labor member from Tasmania, to tell him what ought to be done.

Something had indeed to be done. Men and women, mad with hunger, were ferreting about in gutters and garbage bins in Sydney for scraps of food. To collect the dole, they stood for hours in chilly, draughty places herded like wild beasts. Government officers mocked them; the unkind branded them as the 'sussos'. One unemployed ex-digger handed back the medal he had received from a 'grateful country' for his service in the war. Albert Jacka, a winner of the Victoria Cross, was knocking on suburban doors, and pleading with housewives to buy his soap. Every day in Sydney scuffles between the unemployed and the police broke out in the streets; punches were thrown, and men were bundled into the police wagons for a night in Darlinghurst Gaol. The moralizers lectured destitute girls on the consequences of not resisting the temptation to 'hawk the bod' in the streets of Sydney. A ragged army of human beings tramped country roads of Australia. They were called the 'Soldiers of Despair'.

The plight of the striking miners and their families on the northern coalfields had become desperate. They were close to starvation. On 22 May the exhausted men agreed to return to work under the terms and conditions of the 1929 award. The capitalist press was jubilant. The *Workers' Weekly* said the capitalist class had forced the comrades of the workers to 'bow to the slave terms'. Communists declared that the struggle against capitalism would go forward. Forward to victory!

Jimmy Scullin and his Treasurer, Ted Theodore, believed Australia's financial position required the use of the best brains the nation could bring to its solution. To the dismay of many Labor supporters, they sought answers in London. On the recommendation of British Treasury, they invited Sir Otto Niemeyer, a director of the Bank of England, to come to Australia to report on what should be done. Latham said the news of the appointment had 'created a good impression in the city'. The Labor press was apprehensive. The *Labor Daily* said the Scullin Government was 'being bluffed, well and truly, into handing over our present and our future into the clutch of the foreign Jews'. Don't let the English capitalists reduce the wages of the Australian workers to the level of the lowest Hindu or coolie Chinese. The *Australian Worker* was angry: 'Our workers spilt their blood to save England's war lords. Now they must go hungry to fatten England's money lords'.

Before Niemeyer arrived, the Scullin government suffered the temporary loss of one its most able minds. In July 1930 a judicial inquiry in Queensland found that Theodore had fraudulently obtained advantage during his term as Premier of Queensland (1919–25) when his government purchased the Mungana Mines company, a company in which Theodore himself had held a substantial undisclosed interest. Theodore insisted that the inquiry was a political stunt by the current conservative government of Queensland. He had strong support from Scullin and within the Cabinet, but he immediately resigned, declaring that he was confident a trial would acquit him. Scullin announced that he would act as Treasurer himself.

In July 1930 Niemeyer arrived in Australia. While hungry men and women tramped through the wintry streets of Melbourne, Sir Otto dined at the Melbourne Club with Richard Penrose Franklin, the headmaster of Melbourne Grammar School. That afternoon he had had talks on the Victorian budget with J. M. Niall of Goldsbrough, Mort and Co., and with E. R. Pitt, the Under-Treasurer of Victoria. The next day he saw the heads of the Commercial Bank of Australia, the English, Scottish and Australian Bank, the National Bank and the Bank of Australasia. In the next few days he spoke to senior officials, played golf at the Metropolitan Club, talked again with J. M. Niall, met Maie Casey, the wife of that promising young man Dick Casey, went to the races at Flemington, dined with Clive Baillieu, and went for a drive to Ferntree Gully and Sassafras, the retreat in the hills for the patricians of Melbourne.

On 21 August Niemeyer addressed a conference of the Prime Minister, the Premiers and Treasurers in Melbourne. His speech made a deep impression on those present. He warned them they were faced with a serious problem, the practical solution of which was not rendered any easier by the natural optimism of the Australian. Australians must learn there was not an unlimited market abroad for Australian goods; they must be stripped of the delusion that something would turn up. Australians were living beyond their means. Living standards were too high. Wages must be reduced. Governments must cut spending and stop borrowing.

Those present were penitent. They had sinned against the laws of political economy through their 'own most grievous fault'. They swore to try, with Sir Otto's help, and the help of the Bank of England, not to sin again. They would balance their budgets. The Loan Council would raise no more loans overseas until after the short-run indebtedness had been completely dealt with. They would not give approval to the undertaking of new public works which were not capable of paying for themselves.

Scullin believed that what they had done was for the good of Australia. By the end of August 1930, sick and exhausted, he was travelling on the *Orama* to London for the Imperial Conference. He has asked two men of like mind to his own to occupy key positions during his absence. J. E. Fenton was to be Acting Prime Minister and J. A. Lyons to be Acting Treasurer. A serious split in the Labor Party was threatened. There was opposition to the agreement reached at the Melbourne conference. Jack Lang was making wild statements about repudiating the London debts.

In the election campaign in New South Wales in September 1930, Lang announced his stand against the Niemeyer proposals. He would save the Australian standard of living. That was more important than paying money to the English bond-holders. Lang knew what he was doing. He was appealing to Australian mythology: Australia was the chosen home of a free people, who prided themselves on being liberated from Old World poverty; Australians had a destiny of their own, and Labor was the conscience of Australia.

Middle-class Australia took fright. In Sydney 1000 ex-public school boys were drilling secretly in preparation for an armed defence of bourgeois society. In Canberra Jack Beasley and Frank Anstey were openly supporting Lang's opposition to the Niemeyer proposals. Federal Cabinet decided to recommend to Caucus the reduction of Commonwealth expenditure by £4 million and a reduction in the salary of politicians and public servants. Caucus was to discuss the proposals on 27 October 1930.

On 25 October Labor swept to victory in New South Wales. Lang said it was a victory for Australian ideals, a victory for those determined not to allow the British to whittle down the Australian standard of living. Strengthened by the victory, at the Caucus meeting on 27 October Jack Beasley moved a motion, seconded by Dr Maloney, that 'this party disagrees with the tariff and industrial policy enunciated by Sir Otto Niemeyer . . . and affirms that the tariff and industrial policy of Australia are domestic matters to be determined by the people of Australia'. It was carried unanimously. Fenton, Crouch and the Acting Treasurer, Joe Lyons, did not vote. By accepting Niemeyer Scullin had given a Labor government's approval to an enemy of Labor. The following day, 28 October, there were angry exchanges in Caucus between Fenton and Theodore. Theodore wanted the government to have control over the Commonwealth Bank: Lyons and Fenton did not. Lyons and Fenton had started to see themselves as fighting a battle for moral responsibility.

Lyons received a large fan mail from people thanking him for the stand he had taken against the Labor extremists. Letter-writers planted in his mind the idea that he had a role to play as the saviour of Australia from moral and economic disgrace. A Toorak matron told him her prayer: 'God give us men a time like this demands'. Others praised his courageous stand against the repudiationists. Australia, one said, had 'found a real man'. Joe Lyons was finding new friends and admirers, not sensing, as his wife did from that time on, that both of them 'never again would . . . know peace'. Lyons said he would have to consider his position: he said he might resign: federal Labor was cracking up.

While the factions were destroying the party he loved, Scullin was pleading the case for an Australian Governor-General at the Court of the King-Emperor in London. On 11 November he met Lord Stamfordham, the King's Private Secretary. Stamfordham was brusque and condescending. The Australian Prime Minister, he complained, had pointed a pistol at the head of His Majesty. Gentlemen, he implied, did not do that sort of thing. When Stamfordham said of an appointment to South Africa that at least he was an Englishman, Scullin replied firmly: 'your real objection . . . is that Sir Isaac Isaacs is an Australian'. Jimmy Scullin would not budge. He told Stamfordham he would hold an election on the issue if the King did not agree. Jimmy Scullin must see the King-Emperor.

First he went to Ireland where he met relatives and found the strength to stand by the faith of his fathers. He met the King at Buckingham Palace on 29 November, only hours after he had bidden an emotional farewell to his relatives in the village of Ballyscullin. The King said he wanted to say something to the Australian Prime Minister: '. . . we have sent many Governors, Commonwealth and State, and I hope they have not all been failures'. Scullin said 'No', they had not all been failures. He then unfolded the reasons why they had nominated an Australian. It was fourteen years since Billy Hughes, another Labor Prime Minister, had been a guest at Buckingham Palace. But this time no Labor man need have any qualms about treachery or betrayal. After explaining to Mr Scullin that the last thing he wanted as King was to be the centre of a public controversy, the King said: 'I have been for 20 years a monarch, and I hope I have always been a constitutional one, and being a constitutional monarch I must, Mr Scullin, accept your advice which, I take it, you will tender me formally by letter'. An Australian was to be Governor-General. Australian conservatives did not like it, but Jimmy Scullin has spoken for the Australia that was coming to be.

On 3 December Scullin left England for a visit to the Australian battlefields in France. That night he heard a bugler sound 'The Last Post' at the Menin Gate. The following day he went to the fields near Pozières where, with the larks ascending, he stood on that mound of earth where boys from the Australian bush had known 'Hell itself' in 1916. There he heard French schoolchildren sing in French 'Australia will be there'. He was so moved he could not speak.

He did not know, as he stood there in that moment of tragic grandeur, that back in Australia 'Yarraside' was laying its plans. They had been watching the performance of Joe Lyons.

9

An Irish Catholic to the Rescue

When Scullin arrived in Fremantle on 6 January 1931 disturbances were breaking out all over Australia. Some conservatives were forming private armies: the Old Guard was recruiting in Sydney and rural New South Wales, the White Army was spreading through Victoria. The Communists were calling the workers to join the Labor Defence Army, to drill and prepare for a showdown.

Adelaide had the worst riot in its history on 9 January 1931, when 1000 unemployed marched into Victoria Square to protest against the withdrawal of beef from the ration issue. They stormed the Treasury building. The police drew their batons; the unemployed used iron bars and sticks. Several bodies fell to the ground with blood streaming from wounds; hats, coats and placards were strewn all over the footpath and the road. The riot lasted for an hour.

On 26 January Scullin recommended that Theodore be reappointed Treasurer even though he had not yet been cleared of the Mungana charges—Scullin had never believed the allegations. Caucus agreed by twenty-four votes to nineteen. Lyons was scandalized. Other members talked of resigning from the party. Theodore threw down the gauntlet. He told a meeting in Ashfield he had been advised there was a power vested in the banks to control credit: by extending credit he hoped to 'stem the tide of adversity'. He has already said that 'Australia to-day needs not £20 000 000 but £120 000 000 extra credit'. Latham warned that Theodore would do grave injury to the reputation of Australia. Sir Robert Gibson warned that the banks, particularly the central Commonwealth Bank, might not co-operate. 'Well,' Theodore said, 'the Government will take control over the banks'. Lyons and Fenton agreed with Latham. On 29 January they resigned from the government.

Lyons was 'at his wit's end to know where to turn and which course to follow'. The decision was taken out of his hands. He was approached by Staniforth Ricketson, a director of the Melbourne stockbroking firm of J. B. Were and Co. Ricketson had already talked with other members of the 'Yarraside' establishment, including Robert Gordon Menzies. Known as the 'Group', they resolved to persuade Lyons to leave the Labor Party, and Latham to hand over the leadership of any future conservative party to Lyons. Latham, they decided, was not capable of leading the party to victory and government. He had neither the magnetism that was required nor a real grasp of affairs. The Group would create a public image of Lyons as 'Honest Joe', the man who left the Labor Party because of Theodore's shabby finances and shabby public behaviour. Early in February 1931 Lyons indicated that he was interested. Before long Keith Murdoch, another member of the Group, was promoting 'Honest Joe' in the Melbourne *Herald* as the bulwark of dependability and sanity in a political scene overrun with madmen.

In the Federal Government there was strong support for Theodore's plan of using a note issue to fund government spending in order to stimulate the depressed economy. But there was also vocal opposition to Theodore's plan by the supporters of Jack Lang. Lang was still advocating that the governments of Australia should pay no further interest to British bondholders until Britain agreed to more lenient repayments. He also advocated that Australia should break away from the gold standard of currency, and set up in its place a currency based on the wealth of Australia. This meant, Lang claimed, there would be an immediate release in Australia of millions of pounds. Conservatives opposed both policies. Theodore's plan was based on a view of economics which was to become common in years to come, but in 1931 his proposals were seen by the righteous gatekeepers of economic orthodoxy as a chaotic formula for wild inflation. As for Lang, his was a policy dreamed up by madmen and thieves, and perhaps even by Communists. It was 'repudiation'. Lang must be stopped. Lyons must play the man of destiny, the saviour of Australia.

Leagues and organizations advocating political purity and 'sound finance' were mushrooming all over the country. The most influential of these were the All for Australia Leagues, two parallel organizations founded in Sydney and Melbourne in February. Similar to leagues in other States, the All for Australia was a populist conservative movement which spoke of a politics which transcended political parties—a politics of citizenry. Their meetings were full of fervour for a united Australia, in which there was co-operation between class and class, in which government finances were above suspicion and politics were pure.

Other conservatives were taking a more militant stand. On 18 February Colonel Eric Campbell, Major W. J. Scott and six other ex-officers of the AIF met in the Imperial Service Club in Sydney and decided to break away from the secretive Old Guard and form a more visible New Guard under Campbell's leadership. Their aim was not to revive the digger spirit in a time of crisis, but rather to protect what they understood by Old Australia. They wanted to stop British-Christian Australia from being destroyed by Langism, Bolshevism, the corruption and the immorality of those who believed everything was allowable. Campbell, a lawyer by profession, proposed to recruit men mainly from the suburbs into a private army. In his mind Labor and the Communists threatened the most precious thing in life—the individual human soul. They wanted the human ant-heap: Campbell wanted the free individual, the Ned Kelly life of the 'fearless, the free and the bold', without Ned Kelly's murderous criminality. He had the same values as Latham, Bavin, Stevens, Menzies, and Hughes; he differed on how to preserve the Australia they believed in.

Events moved swiftly. Wild rumours were abroad. In the Wimmera and the Mallee the word passed from farm to farm that the Communists had seized Sydney. There was another story that Communists from Mildura were marching on Melbourne. The know-alls dismissed such talk as 'childish and absurd rumour', but the members of the secret armies were drilling just in case. The conservative politicians believed they did not need the services of the secret armies. Australia had no tradition of that sort of thing, no record of military coups, or of the people being deluded by demagogues or political mountebanks. The conservatives had other methods: they made bargains with disgruntled Labor leaders. It had worked in 1917. The Group would make it work again. Lyons was agonizing over whether he should resign and throw in his lot with the power men of 'Yarraside'.

Lyons's old Labor colleagues appealed to him: 'Don't do it, Joe. Don't do it'. But Joe Lyons was wrestling with his conscience. It was because he had been a Labor man all his life, he said, that he desired to protect the workers from the misery and destitution that would befall them if Theodore or Lang had their way. Lyons resigned. For the rest of their lives, Joe and Enid Lyons were shunned as pariahs by Labor men and women. They had joined the list of traitors to be treated with undying hostility.

Labor was tearing itself asunder. Lyons and his supporters had quit. Soon afterwards the New South Wales branch of the Labor Party expelled Theodore, and began to discuss whether the other New South Wales federal members who had followed the Theodore policy should also be expelled. The Federal Conference of the Labor Party retaliated by expelling the New South Wales Executive, the supporters of the Lang plan, for having refused to acknowledge and accept the federal platform and constitution.

The next blow came from the militants. To the alarm of all right-minded people the New South Wales branch of the ALP at its Easter Conference passed resolutions which committed the State government to a Soviet-style five-year plan of socializations. Lang and Garden voted against the scheme, but the radicals persuaded delegates that reformism and capitalism had failed the workers. The time had come to change society fundamentally. What was more, the Education Committee of Conference recommended that Empire Day be no longer observed in New South Wales schools, and that the weekly ceremony of saluting the flag be discontinued. No one put in a plea for the teaching of Australian history or Australian literature.

As Labor fragmented, a formidable coalition of conservative forces was taking shape. They saw themselves as a 'great moral force', fighting the cancer of repudiation which was the brain-child of those disrupters, the Communists. They would drive the Communists out of the country. On 19 April the big decision was made in Melbourne. Representatives of the Group, Lyons, and officials from the National Union, the Citizens' League of South Australia, and the All For Australia Leagues, met in Melbourne. They decided to form a United Australia Party by an amalgamation of the Nationalists and the other organizations present at the meeting. Latham was persuaded to stand aside as leader of the Nationalists. Joe Lyons had become leader of the conservative forces of Australia.

Lyons had a huge following among the Australian people. His wife Enid, a woman of homely charm, was a great asset. In Adelaide she said the women of Australia had to save Australia today. Women had equal rights with men, and the responsibility for Australia's position was equally theirs. They should get behind her husband. Honest Joe Lyons has launched a successful crusade for the salvation of Australia.

Rumours were floating about in Sydney of heavy withdrawals from the Government Savings Bank of New South Wales. On 22 April the president of the bank announced that the bank would cease operations as from the morning of 23 April, and would remain closed until further notice. The *Sydney Morning Herald* called for Lang's resignation.

Scullin pleaded with his federal colleagues to show the people that federal Labor was just as honourable as the money-changers of

Melbourne, or the members of the Melbourne Club. The Prime Minister and his loyal Treasurer, Ted Theodore, met the premiers in a momentous conference which opened in Melbourne on 25 May. They had before them the report of a special subcommittee of the Loan Council on what should be done. The banks have informed governments they could not carry them any longer. It was not a time for Labor to 'make and unmake social conditions'. It was a time for sacrifice. At the end of days of torrents of rain, and with news of violent Communist riots in Sydney hitting the headlines in the press, Scullin announced the decisions of the conference. The premiers and the Federal Government had agreed to swallow the bitter medicine prescribed by Niemeyer. All governments would cut spending on wages, salaries, pensions and social services by 20 per cent compared with expenditure for the year ended 30 June 1930. Bondholders would be required to accept a 22 ½ per cent cut in interest. There would be a public debt conversion, the details of which had not been worked out, but which would certainly require legislative action. Theodore's expansionary Fiduciary Notes Bill was to be dropped.

Some members of the Labor movement were stunned. Scullin, the leader of a Labor government, has sentenced all those in the community on miserable pittances, helpless widows, the blind and the maimed, to 'slow but certain death'. Thousands of unemployed would be deprived of their means of support. Angry words were spoken when Scullin introduced the Premiers' Plan to members of Caucus in Canberra on 11 June. Some members wanted to exempt old age pensions, invalid and war pensions from the economy measures. Scullin ruled there could be no amendment to the plan. The following day, 12 June, the vote was taken: Caucus approved the Premiers' Plan by 26 votes to 13. John Curtin voted against it. A lone voice called out as the vote was taken: 'The most pitiful sight I ever knew in the history of the Labor Party'.

Two days later, on 14 June 1931, Ted Holloway resigned from the government. Labor was losing the confidence and faith of the visionaries and the missionaries. Riots of the unemployed assumed a note of desperation. Four hundred rushed the side gate to Parliament House in Sydney on 11 June. On 17 June forty policemen fought a pitched battle with sixteen men defending a barricaded house at Bankstown. Anti-eviction riots erupted in all the cities.

Frank Anstey was disillusioned. Scullin, in his eyes, has betrayed Labor and formed an alliance with the Nationalists and the Country Party. On 8 July he delivered an emotional attack on Scullin in the House: 'What would Christ have thought as He hung on the cross if the nails that pierced His hands and feet had been hammered in by His friends; if the sponge of vinegar had been held to His lips by His friends'. Today a Labor government was crucifying the very people who had raised its members from obscurity and placed them in power. He was appalled that a Labor man should even contemplate doing such a contemptible thing.

On 24 August the jury in the Mungana case found in favour of Theodore. Scullin sent him a telegram of congratulation. Now they must work together for the salvation of Australia. But the party is in ruins. In the House of Representatives on 25 November the Lang group voted with the Opposition to bring on an election. Let the people decide.

In the election campaign, Scullin's voice was scarcely noticed. The shell was still there, battered and reduced: but the light was no longer in the eye of Jimmy Scullin. He spoke like a man who had been betrayed, like a sacrificial victim. He spoke of his own ache, but the people had no interest in private aches. They wanted bread. Lang was a demagogue, but at least he gave the little men and women hope. So did Honest Joe Lyons—and 'Yarraside' was behind him.

Lyons told the people that the old ways were the best. 'Follow the example of Britain', he said to thunderous applause. 'Do not be tempted or seduced by financial tricks and devices'. Honest Joe, the one-time Labor man from Tasmania, now believed the only way for Australia was the way of the businessman. Private enterprise, production on the land, and measures to deal with the Communist Party were the only way. He would keep Australians loyal to the faith of their fathers; he would bind Australians to their past. Do as Britain did: vote for a truly national government. That was 'the grand example'.

In the election on 19 December the ALP received a crushing defeat. Twenty-two federal members and three Lang Labor men were defeated. Five ministers—including Ted Theodore and Ben Chifley—lost their seats. Eddie Ward was defeated in East Sydney and John Curtin in Fremantle. Curtin did not lose heart. He went back to his work on the *Westralian Worker*. His task, he said, was to 'rally the fainthearts', and continue the fight for the Federal Labor Party against Lang and his intriguers. The workers needed a leader, someone to give them hope and guidance. He walked again on Cottesloe Beach. His destiny was ahead. No movement, he knew, could rally without a leader—a Christ, a Mahomet, a Washington, a Robespierre, a Lenin. His time would come. He must win a victory over the 'strange infirmity'.

When Enid Lyons heard of the great victory she spoke to the press with tears of joy streaming down her face. There were celebra-

tions in Devonport and in Melbourne. She saw something again of
Bob Menzies. With a woman's gift to sense the shape of things to
come she had intimations of some future pain, of a time when she
would weep tears of sorrow. A time would come, too, when Bob
Menzies would weep, for he would pay a terrible price for marching behind the slogan, 'Follow Britain'.

10

'Tune in with Britain'

On 2 February 1932 the new Lyons Government announced it would seek a writ to force New South Wales to pay the £958 763 due to the overseas bondholders. Lang replied he would negotiate direct with the overseas bondholders to arrange a moratorium. The Commonwealth said if Lang did not meet his overseas commitments they would withhold from the government of New South Wales that portion of the loan money allocation to which it would otherwise have been entitled. The Commonwealth would dictate the policy and behaviour of a State. Lang declared he would fight for the right of the people to be fed.

On 10 February Lyons announced that Bruce would be stationed in London as resident minister to carry out financial negotiations on behalf of the Commonwealth Government. Bruce, the imperialist, would try to checkmate the attempts of A. C. Willis, the New South Wales Agent-General, to achieve a moratorium in London. The conservatives were using the Shylocks of the Empire to defeat a people's hero.

Colonel Campbell also took a stand. He said that if governments would not move against Lang, disloyalists and extremists, then he and the members of the New Guard would give the 'Commos' a hiding. Already, members of the New Guard and Communists were brawling with each other at public meetings. But this was Australia. Here there were only preliminary skirmishes: a show-down would never begin. Rumours flew around Sydney that the Colonel had a plan to kidnap Lang and hold him in captivity until someone 'respectable' opened the new Harbour Bridge.

Through the skill and courage of Australian workers, the iron span linking the city of Sydney with the north shore has been finished. In the eyes of Labor the Bridge was the quintessence of Australian democracy: it knew no class distinctions, no social barriers. The Bridge was a 'sacrificial offering' laid upon the altar of

Australian 'manhood, womanhood and childhood'. The opening celebration was to be a people's occasion. This time the Governor-General was an Australian, and the Premier of New South Wales was an apologist for the men and women who made Australia.

A great crowd gathered for the ceremony on 19 March 1932. Jack Lang made a speech in which he declared the Bridge open to traffic. He spoke of the achievement by all concerned in building a bridge spanning the world's most beautiful harbour and linking two sections of the greatest city in the southern hemisphere. Lang knew Australians would be tickled by a good old boast. The Bridge would unite people with similar aims and ideals. It was a happy example of the blending of English and Australian resources. The engineering brains and the finance had come from the centre of the Empire: the skill, the labour and the determination had come from the Australian people. The Bridge was therefore, he said, both an adornment to a beautiful Australian city, and a source of pride to the whole British Empire. Now Australians would build another bridge: the bridge of common understanding to serve all the Australian people. He declared the Bridge open to traffic, and pressed a button which unveiled a tablet recording the fact.

The crowd applauded, and clapped and whistled. The people's man then stood before the ribbon stretched across the width of the Bridge. The scissors were placed in his hand. Suddenly there was a commotion. A rider on a horse, dressed in the uniform of an officer of the King, advanced towards the ribbon. The horse, borrowed for the occasion, stood still. The man's sword would not reach to the ribbon. Frantic, he spurred the horse on as the police closed in on him. He slashed, but the blade of his sword fell short. He slashed again, and stood up triumphant in his stirrup irons and cried out: 'On behalf of the decent and loyal citizens of New South Wales I now declare this bridge open'. Like Eilert Løvborg in Ibsen's *Hedda Gabler* the rider has not done the deed 'beautifully'. The police dragged the man from the horse and took him into captivity, as an Australian voice cried out, 'Take him away'. The man on the horse said: 'You can't take me. I'm a Commonwealth officer'. A policeman replied: 'So am I'. A fresh ribbon was stretched across the Bridge. Lang cut it. The people's man had opened the Bridge.

The man on the horse told the police his name was Francis De Groot. He claimed he had been an officer in His Majesty's Hussars. As he was driven away in a police car sections of the crowd booed him. He became an object of hatred for Labor men and women. But other Australians turned the whole episode into a joke. Tooheys, the brewers of beer, coined a new slogan: 'I'd sooner open a bottle of Toohey's Pilsener any day'.

On 6 April the divided nation was united by the death of a horse. The mighty Phar Lap, winner of the Melbourne Cup, the performer of miracles on the race track comparable with Don Bradman's performances with the cricket bat and Nellie Melba's with the human voice, died that day in a stable in California. The veterinary surgeon reported that he died from a surfeit of fresh lucerne. But that was no hero's death. The popular imagination was soon busy at myth-making: Phar Lap suffered 'murder most foul' at the hands of envious Americans. Phar Lap was poisoned, just as another hero of the people, Ben Hall, was 'butchered by cowards in his sleep' out on the Lachlan plain, and Les Darcy, the boxer, was murdered by envious Americans. Australians would remember for generations when Phar Lap won the Cup. His body was brought reverently back to Melbourne, stuffed by a taxidermist, and placed in a glass case in the Victorian Museum for future generations to observe and revere, just as the skull of Ned Kelly was on display in the Institute of Anatomy in the nation's capital.

There were bizarre scenes each night outside Lang's house in Auburn. The police were taking special precautions to prevent New Guard members kidnapping him. Suspicious characters hid in shop doorways. Down-and-outs lay drunk in nearby gutters. Police patrolled the streets to keep an eye on the movements of any loiterers. It was said in Melbourne that the Melbourne University Rifles would deal with Lang if he went too far. It was a strange time in the affairs of humanity in Australia. More reliable rumour had it that the wild man of Australian politics was plotting the assassination of Lang. Australia had a long tradition of violence. There had been the violence against the land, violence against its original inhabitants, and against the convicts. Now class struggles were threatening to explode into violence. Lyons must act before the violence spread. The Governor of New South Wales must do his duty. Thousands of middle-class Australians were ready to follow a leader. But Campbell was a braggart, a strutter and a limelighter. The setting required a mob orator, but Campbell was no mob orator, no Mark Antony. He was something of an Australian Hamlet, a man with the cue for revenge, but not the single-mindedness.

On 7 April the Lyons Government published a regulation requiring the New South Wales Government to pay most of its income tax money to the Commonwealth, effectively depriving Lang of the funds to govern. In defiance of the Commonwealth regulation, Lang ordered the State police to barricade the State Tax Office and issued an instruction that payment of State public servants was to continue as normal. On May Day the new leader of the Communist Party, Lance Sharkey, denounced Lang for engaging in a sham fight with Lyons. The whole thing was a smokescreen, he said, to hide Labor's great betrayal of the workers. On 12 May the Governor, Sir Philip Game, presented Lang with an ultimatum. He gave him three options: to demonstrate the legality of his instruction to continue business as normal; to withdraw the instruction; or to resign. Lang refused. Late on the afternoon of 13 May, the Governor sent Mr Lang a letter: 'I feel it is my bounden duty to inform you that I cannot retain my present Ministers in office, and that I am seeking other advisers, I must ask you to regard this as final'.

When Lang read the letter he let slip how he was feeling in his comments to the gentlemen of the press. 'Well, I am sacked. I am dismissed from office. I am no longer a Premier, but a free man'. The conservatives were delighted.

There was better to come. The new leader of the conservatives was Bertram Stevens, a ruthless man with the heart of a bookkeeper. He fought a law-and-order campaign and won a crushing victory on 11 June. More than thirty followers of Lang lost their seats. Lang accepted defeat with the dignity which characterized him on great occasions, but he has paid a terrible price for indulging in the 'insane folly of faction fighting', which has killed the soul of Labor.

There was similar news from Victoria where on 14 May the Labor government had been decisively beaten at the polls. Queensland was a ray of hope for Federal Labor. On the same day as Lang Labor was routed in New South Wales, the ALP won the election for the Legislative Assembly of Queensland by a majority of two. As a bonus the two Lang Labor candidates secured only 559 votes between them. Labor owed its success in part to its leader William Forgan Smith. He had none of the arts of the demagogue, or the hungers of the megalomaniac. He held out no promise of better things for humanity and never promised with a tremble in the voice to make 'the rough places plain'. He spoke of public works. Forgan Smith was to prove by a record term in office that pragmatism was one way for Labor to win a majority. He presented Labor as an alternative committee to administer the affairs of the bourgeois state. There was about him none of the tragic grandeur of a Tom Ryan or a Ted Theodore. The age of the tragic heroes was over: after the giants the levelling flood has swept the country.

But there was still a patch of turf where Australian heroes walked. On 19 November a crowd of 53 916 entered the Melbourne Cricket Ground to see one of Australia's gifted sons, Don Bradman, face Harold Larwood, the Notts bowler reputed to be as fast as 'greased lightning'. Bradman came to the crease when the Australian score was 1 for 84. Like Betsey Bandicoot of old, he was the daredevil. Bradman square cut the first ball he received from Larwood for four. The crowd bubbled over with delight. The second ball from Larwood flew high over Bradman's head. He ducked. The crowd simmered, like a crowd at a prize-fight. The third ball was hooked by Bradman for four. The crowd went wild with excitement. The boy from the bush was making a monkey of these clever men from the British Isles. But when he reached 36 Larwood trapped him 'Leg Before Wicket'. The contest has been indecisive. That day the English captain, Douglas Jardine, was fishing for trout on the Kiewa River in Victoria. He had a plan. He believed that under the stress of physical danger the Australian cricketers would crack because they were 'yellow': there had been no sign of how the Don would respond to bowling aimed directly at his body. That day there was no need to test Jardine's plan. The Australians got themselves out to a man who bowled with great speed. Both the Don and Harold Larwood were at the height of their powers. In the second Australian innings Larwood bowled Bradman for thirteen. The English believed Larwood's demon speed had solved the Bradman problem: the Don, they said, disliked 'supercharged fast bowling'.

In the city streets, the dole riots continued. The Lyons Government prosecuted Communists. But for the moment all eyes and ears were on the cricket. On the eve of the first Test there was a sensation when the announcers on the evening news informed their listeners that Bradman was in such a seriously run-down condition he would not play in the first Test on the Sydney Cricket Ground beginning on Friday 2 December. There was consternation on the first day. Larwood and Voce rocked their deliveries in at high speed. The batsmen ducked, but often they were too slow. The short, rising balls struck the batsmen on the body. Jardine placed six fieldsmen close to the batsman on the leg side. The crowd on the hill let the Englishmen know what they thought of such tactics. When Jardine swatted the flies on his face one wit on the Sydney Hill called out: 'Leave our flies alone, Jardine'. Jardine took no notice. That was what he expected from Australians: when they were down they whinged and whined like ill-bred curs, or made jokes at the expense of their superiors. With 4 wickets down for 87 runs Australia was in a desperate situation. There was no boy from Bowral to rescue them.

That was the task of the boy from Grenfell, Stan McCabe, and the buccaneer from Adelaide, Victor Richardson. The latter made 49 before falling to Larwood in the leg trap. He was also limping from a blow on the leg from a ball by Larwood. But Richardson did not put on black looks, or scowl at the Notts genius. That night McCabe was 127 not out. The following day a packed ground rang to 'an ever-increasing crescendo' as their hero Stan McCabe despatched both fast and slow bowlers to all parts of the boundary. English leg-theory had no terrors for him. Like another boy from Grenfell, Henry Lawson, he was savouring that majestic moment 'when the world was wide'. He drove, cut, hooked, glanced and pulled the ball with the authority and skill of a veteran. The crowd was in a state of 'delirious joy'. He was 187 not out when the innings closed. His performance passed into the folklore of Australian sport. For generations it would be a mark of distinction to have been there when Stan McCabe hooked Harold Larwood for four on the Sydney Cricket Ground. Despite a beautiful six by Stan McCabe off Bill Voce in the second innings Australia was defeated easily.

The Australians did not like it. A letter writer to the *Sydney Morning Herald* accused the English bowlers of deliberately bowling at the batsman. If this went on, he said, then all the beautiful strokes of cricket would be eliminated, and the game would come to resemble baseball with players wearing padding and helmets. In a cable to London one journalist shortened the phrase 'on the line of the body' to 'bodyline'. The term stuck. Australians now had a word with which to communicate their reactions to the English tactics. Jardine put on an air of innocence. At Launceston he told reporters leg-theory (he was careful not to use the Australian term 'bodyline' which implied condemnation) had had its birth in Australian newspapers. 'We know nothing about it . . . The practice is nothing new, and there is nothing dangerous about it. I hope it goes on being successful.'

On Friday 30 December 1932 a world record crowd of 63 993 for a cricket match assembled inside the Melbourne Cricket Ground for the second Test match. A gasp was heard all around the ground as the names of the English bowlers were placed one by one on the score board—Larwood, Voce, Allen, Bowes—all fast bowlers. It seemed that the English were up to their tricks again. But the game passed without serious incident, memorable for a magnificent spell from the Australian leg spinner 'Tiger' Bill O'Reilly and for Bradman's second innings score of 103 not out.

It was in Adelaide, the setting for the third Test, that a national legend was forged. The ball-by-ball description of play kept every-one in the city and all round Australia in touch with what was going on. In hotel bars men drank their ice-cold beer as they listened to the scores, and the feats performed by their heroes under a hot sun beating down out of a brassy sky. After lunch on Saturday the Australian batsmen again faced the music, when Woodfull and Fingleton walked together into the bright light of the Adelaide sun. Larwood began his run. Woodfull was struck over the heart by a rising ball. As he collapsed to the ground Jardine was heard to say, 'Well bowled, Harold'. He clapped his hands. Six fieldsmen crouched close to the batsmen on the leg side. Larwood was to bowl 'bodyline' to a wounded batsman. That was in the eyes of the Australian players 'a dreadful display of heartlessness'. As Larwood began his majestic run-up to the wicket the crowd counted 'one, two, three, four, five . . .', reaching ten in a deafening crescendo. Jardine's face remained expressionless, though perhaps the man within was pleased to see Australians behaving as he had predicted they would: they were squealing. Disasters followed for the Australian batsmen. Allen bowled Woodfull, having previously had Jack Fingleton caught behind for a duck. There was worse to come. Larwood had Bradman and McCabe caught in the leg trap for low scores. Only Bill Ponsford and Vic Richardson defied the onslaughts of ball on bat and body. Both were bruised.

Hearing that Woodfull was in a 'distressed condition', the manager of the English team, 'Plum' Warner, breezed into the Australian dressing room, hoping for one of those heart-warming exchanges so dear to 'sporting chaps'. Woodfull, who was known to his friends as a 'steadfast man', said:

> I don't want to speak to you, Mr Warner. Of two teams out there, one is playing cricket, the other is making no effort to play the game of cricket. It is too great a game to spoil by the tactics you are adopting. I don't approve of them and never will. If they are persevered in it may be better if I do not play the game. The matter is in your hands. I have nothing further to say. Good afternoon.

'Plum' Warner went back to the English changing room, slumped into a chair, and said: 'He would not speak to me'. To fuel the rising anger among the Australian journalists and spectators on the Monday morning when the game was resumed, Bert Oldfield, the Australian wicket-keeper, a prince of good fellows, was struck on the forehead when he tried to hook a rising ball from Larwood. One more sacred convention of the game has been flouted by the Englishmen: it was not 'done' for a fast bowler to deliver a bouncer to a tail-ender. Oldfield was helped from the field. To his credit he blamed himself, saying he, not Larwood, was to blame for his injury. 'I made a mistake', he said. He retired hurt for 41: soon after Australia was all out for 222.

The shufflers, or slow movers, in the Australian team called for a ban on bodyline. Those who believed in drawing yet closer the links between Australia and the Empire wanted cricket to be 'saved'. Arthur Mailey, one-time Australian leg-break bowler, and now a cartoonist in the daily press, was shocked. Bob Menzies wanted something to be done. The English popular press mocked at the Australians. The *News Chronicle* had some advice: Australia should find quickly some batsmen quick enough to handle the English onslaught. The *Daily Herald* was disgusted by the 'undignified snivelling' of the Australians because the English bowling tactics had beaten their best batsmen. That, the English believed, was the point: the English had won, and the Australians did not like it. The Australians demanded an end to bodyline bowling. Believing the Australian sporting public was behind them, on 18 January 1933 the Australian Board of Control sent a cable of protest to the Marylebone Cricket Club. 'Body Bowling', they said, was menacing 'the best interests of the game and causing intensely bitter relations between players as well as injury'. Body bowling was 'unsportsmanlike'. They concluded: 'unless stopped at once, [it] is likely to upset friendly relations existing between England and Australia'.

Cricket was casting a shadow over the relations between Australia and England. The times were too serious to allow a sporting contest to jeopardize Australia's relations with the Empire. The Labor press had been critical of British imperialism in Australia, declaring the interests of Australian industry to be irreconcilable with the interests of British industry. It was most vocal of all in the denunciation of the English tactics as 'unsportsmanlike'. The Labor press has spoken up for Australia against the 'sneers and jibes' of the English press against Australia's champion, Don Bradman. Labor was again assuming the role of champion of Australian nationalism. At a meeting in the Sydney Town Hall on 30 January 1932 to protest against the suspension by the New South Wales Director of Education of a teacher because she had given a public address on conditions in Russia, a huge crowd sang 'The Internationale'. Labor was regaining its soul. Conservatives were putting blinkers on the eyes of the Australian people, not wanting them even to see the conditions of life in a socialist country.

On 30 January 1933 President Hindenburg invited Adolf Hitler, the leader of the German National Socialist Workers' Party, to form a Cabinet. Hindenburg has accepted the inevitable: the alternative was civil war. The Socialists and the Communists in Germany announced they would offer decisive resistance to any attempt to create a dictatorship hostile to the workers. Australian reaction was cautious. The conservatives hoped Germany was about to achieve political stability. The Labor press was not alarmed. There would be a rude awakening.

The cricketers must be reconciled. Cricket must be like a Charles Dickens Christmas, full of the spirit of forgiving and forgetting. 'Plum' Warner offered the hand of forgiveness to Bill Woodfull, and all was well between them. Bill Woodfull was received back into the world of 'chaps'. The Australian Board of Control offered the olive branch to the Marylebone Cricket Club, saying, of course it did not want to cancel the series. The Marylebone Cricket Club was delighted. More cables were exchanged. Both sides agreed the tour should go on. Messages were exchanged between the British and Australian governments. There was to be no Boston Tea Party. For Australians any extremism was like heaven or hell: Australians did not believe in either place. The English continued to bowl bodyline. The crowd in Brisbane was restrained. In Sydney during the fifth and final Test, between 23 and 28 February 1933, which the English won, the crowd rose to its feet to cheer Harold Larwood as he walked off the ground after making 98. Australians had the generosity and the magnaminity to recognize genius and grace on the sporting field.

The Australian Broadcasting Commission was established in May that year: broadcasters imitated English accents and disseminated the ideas and opinions of those Australians who were 'dyed in the wool British'. Under conservative leadership Australians have been committed to 'Tune in with Britain'. On 26 March Sir Charles Kingsford Smith flew across the Tasman from Thirty Mile Beach in New Zealand to Mascot Aerodrome in Sydney. 'Smithy' was again a hero. Women fought with each other to touch his garments. The way to get anywhere, he told them, was to fly. Australians were playing a role in bringing the parts of the Empire closer together. This was a British achievement.

England was still being presented to Australians as the 'Land of Hope and Glory', still the 'mother of the free'. In the School Papers published by the Education Departments of the States the children, as they learned to read, were indoctrinated in the double loyalty. They were enjoined to devote their energies to strengthening the bonds of the Empire. They were told to count being British as a great blessing. They were given curly questions to discuss with their teachers, such as: who was sorry when the Prodigal Son returned? what kind of fruit did Noah take into the Ark? should a woman get a man's wages? should you go to church with a cough? They were also encouraged to notice and enjoy the beauty of Australia, to savour the stately redgums near the banks of the Murray River, down-river from Albury, and enjoy the flight of the bronzewing pigeon. They were told to buy Australian goods: they were told Australian goods were as good as any they would find elsewhere in the world. So: 'Every day in every way—Australian raisins'. Support all those industries, all those farms, 'carried on by Australians for Australians'.

On 9 April 1933 the Chancellor of Germany issued a number of decrees which history was to know as the April Laws. Administrators with dictatorial powers were appointed in all the German states. Books deemed seditious or depraved were burned. Trade unions were abolished and replaced by State-controlled unions. Jews were no longer eligible for positions in the civil service, the army, the schools or the universities. Communists, Socialists and Jews were incarcerated in concentration camps. Strident voices were heard. Germans were singing with exuberance and fervour of a day when comrades would march together with ranks closed, and smash Bolshevism, liberalism, and the shameful Treaty of Versailles. *Kameraden* (comrades, or in the Australian language, 'mates') looked at each other with laughter in their eyes as they marched together in this 'revolution of nothingness'. Australians were alarmed. All shades of political opinion denounced the attack on the Jews. Germany was menacing the peace of the world.

The conservatives were in a dilemma. A barbarian was threatening the very foundations of society, but the barbarian might have his uses. He was offering to wipe Bolshevism off the map of the world: he was already destroying trade union power: in a most brutal and barbarous fashion he was rooting out decadence in Germany. The barbarian has talked of the German need for *Lebensraum* (living space): perhaps he could find it during his crusade against Bolshevism. Hitler could be used and then dropped—monsters had their uses.

Labor now had a formidable enemy. In its dying phases, as they saw it, capitalism was employing hoodlums to protect itself against the challenge from the workers. Capitalist governments, both in Australia and overseas, were demonstrating their inability to find answers to the problems of poverty and unemployment. Their inability to do so, their impotence before the great problems of the day and their moral bankruptcy drove the worst elements in the capitalist class, and their political lackeys, to support Fascism, Nazism, and New Guardism. Labor needed all the strength it could muster to meet the new challenge. Labor must stop faction-fighting, must regain its soul. The Communists were already responding to the challenge. They had the right sense of urgency. The *Workers' Weekly* said not a moment must be lost. The masses must be won over to revolutionary activity to save society from Fascism and Nazism.

That left the Labor Party. Visionaries were already working for a recovery after the débâcle of December 1931. John Curtin believed his destiny lay ahead. He must use his talents to 'mobilise the masses'. The key to the success of Labor at the ballot-box lay in an alliance between the workers and the producers. For Curtin agitation was the 'breath of life'. He was getting ready again to 'ride a storm'. The electorate was still volatile and unpredictable. In South Australia on 8 May 1933 the Labor Party was crushingly defeated in a State election. On the same day Labor defeated the Nationalists and the Country Party decisively in Western Australia, and in a referendum an overwhelming majority voted 'Yes' in favour of the secession of Western Australia from the Commonwealth of Australia.

For the unemployed, the ordeal dragged on. Jocka Burns and his unemployed mate used half their dole coupons at Yarraville (Sydney) to pay the rent. They relied on their persuasive powers to bite the butcher and the grocer for some meat and bread during their weekly attack of the 'shorts'. Stan Moran sang songs about the unemployed to audiences in the Sydney Domain on Sunday afternoons:

Oh those beans, bacon and gravy, they nearly drive me crazy,
I eat them till I see them in my dreams, in my dreams,
But I wake up in the morning, another day is dawning,
And I know I'll have another plate of beans.

On one occasion Stan Moran was speaking to those who had marched to the Botanical Gardens behind the banner of the Unemployed Workers' Union. He climbed on to the statue of Shakespeare, just as Jack Kidd had addressed the poor and hungry in Shakespeare's *Henry VI*. A policeman dragged him off the statue and bashed him with his baton.

Conflict between the unemployed and the police occurred in most cities. Eviction riots still occurred in working-class suburbs. In Sydney, members of the New Guard protected police who were engaged in the task of throwing people out of their landlord's property because they could no longer pay the rent. In Melbourne the Chief Commissioner of Police, Major-General T. A. Blamey, instructed the police to break up meetings addressed by Communists. In Sydney Road, Brunswick, mounted troopers drove men, women and children off the footpath, and into the path of the oncoming traffic on Friday nights. Citizens were being knocked down and injured. General Blamey has boasted to his cronies in clubland that when his police went into battle against a workers' demonstration he put his telescope to his blind eye. At the same time in the Northern Territory, north Queensland and the north of Western Australia police were driving Aborigines in chains over hundreds of miles on foot, to police stations where they were charged under laws they had never made and never accepted.

Joe Lyons told the people to be of good cheer. Australia was no longer 'sliding to financial ruin'. The pastoral industry was out of the woods: wool prices were 50 per cent above those in 1932. The architects of the plan to invite Lyons to 'come over and help us' were now full of gratitude. 'What a generous person you are Joe', Staniforth Ricketson told Lyons in a letter on 16 August, 'and how attractive it is that you have preserved that early asset of yours— real genuine humility. Your friends are very proud of you'. Ricketson was concerned to see Lyons looking so tired: 'You are', he added, 'very essential to the continuance of well-being to this whole community'. Stanley Bruce was also full of praise: 'you have the satisfaction of knowing that you have done for Australia what no other man could have done'.

The following year, the Commonwealth opposed the Western Australian request for secession. In a fit of provincial pique some Western Australians burned effigies of Prime Minister Lyons, and the Minister for Defence, Sir George Pearce, a sandgroper himself from way back. The Western Australians decided to petition the British Parliament to pass an Act granting them secession. But all this was a cunning move to squeeze more out of the teats of the Canberra cow. The *Bulletin* cynically commented that the Premier of Western Australia could not resist the temptation of a free visit to Buckingham Palace, Madame Tussaud's, and Lord's Cricket Ground. Cricket, after all, was destined to survive.

On 22 September 1933 the Australian Board of Control asked the Marylebone Cricket Club whether the latter now conceded that a direct attack by the bowler on the batsman was against the spirit of the game. The English governing classes had their motto: never apologize, never explain. They were not going to ask forgiveness, nor confess that it was all their own 'most grievous fault'. But a form of bowling which was obviously an attack by the bowler on the batsman was, they agreed, an offence against the spirit of the game. The Australians could come to England knowing the game would be played in the same spirit as in years past. They added they were glad the Australians proposed to take the question of barracking into consideration. There would be a warm welcome for the Australians in 1934: every effort would be made to see that their visit was enjoyable.

11

'The Old Dead Tree' or 'The Young Tree Green'?

For Sir Harold and Lady Luxton, for Bob Menzies, for all those who believed in 'Grammar and that sort of thing', and for all those who believed in the King and the Empire, the high summer of 1934 held out the promise of a good year. Unemployment was falling steadily. The roar of social protest was dropping to a whisper. Prince Harry was coming to Australia to be the guest of honour at the Centenary celebrations in Victoria.

From the lower depths there were still occasional upheavals. On 30 and 31 January 1934 there were nights of terror at Boulder on the Kalgoorlie goldfields of Western Australia. The miners of British descent met in the town to discuss what should be done about those 'bloody foreigners' who were easing them out of their jobs in the mines, and competing unfairly with British Australians in the business and shopkeeping world. While the meeting was in progress, and hotheads were swearing in the dinkum Aussie way of what they would do to the foreign elements on the fields, explosions were heard. The bloody foreigners were attacking Australians in their own country. Tempers flared: volunteers were called for. A mob armed with sticks, stones and rifles stormed over the railway bridge and advanced towards the camps where the foreigners were housed. Bullets flew. The police arrived. The Australians rushed forward to set fire to the camp of the foreigners, creating a flare which could be seen for miles. Two men, a Montenegrin and an Australian, were killed. Six Australians were wounded. As the Australian mob walked back to Kalgoorlie they set fire to every camp of foreigners they came across. The following day there were scenes of desolation at these campsites. The summer air still reeked with the odour of burning tents, huts, furniture, clothing and other household goods. Foreigners huddled in groups, petrified.

Four months later, the white man's justice was being dispensed to some of the original inhabitants of the soil. On 30 May 1934

'Tiger' and seven other Aborigines were found guilty in the Supreme Court of the Northern Territory, of the murder of Albert Koch and Stephen Arinski, two white prospectors, at Fitzmaurice River on or about 12 November 1932. The judge had the power to impose a less severe penalty than death. The lawyer for the accused urged him to do so, as seven of the accused knew nothing of civilization. Judge Wells explained to the court why he did not propose to use that power. Retributive justice, he said, was all that a savage could understand. It was a treacherous and cold-blooded murder. If the courts permitted Aborigines to murder white men in any circumstances without fear of the extreme penalty, Aborigines would consider that white men placed a low value on life. The judge then asked whether there was anyone in the Court who had anything to say in favour of the Aborigines. There was no reply. The judge sentenced them to death.

The Australian Board of Missions, philanthropists and humanitarians asked that the lives of the eight Aborigines be spared. Vain hope. The white man has not questioned his right to be there, nor heeded the words of the Psalmist: 'I am a sojourner here'. In the years of doubt about everything else, that doubt has not troubled the white man.

God has disappeared. Australians showed little interest in replacing the Christian heaven with a heaven on earth. Their history, the spirit of the place, and the creeds to which they have attached themselves—the dream of getting on, the ideal of owning a home and a block of land, and the digger ideals of sacrifice, courage, resource and endurance—have made them wary of any promise about future harmony. D. H. Lawrence had noticed in Australian suburbs the ugliness, the fly-blown shops with corrugated iron roofs, the endless stretches of 'cottages' with corrugated iron roofs, and the house-agents' booths plastered with 'For Sale' and 'To Let' signs. The inhabitants of suburbia had told him: 'You feel free in Australia'. Here, they said, there was a relief from tension. But by the mid-1930s the inhabitants of suburbia have become slaves to their own respectability, to their own rites. Display and conspicuous consumption were their answers to emptiness and despair. Popular songs helped to fill the sense of emptiness and futility with the promise of love:

> All I do, the whole night through,
> Is dream of you

On 4 July 1934 Lyons announced that there was to be an election on 15 September. The following day Latham announced he was retiring from politics, as he put it, for 'private reasons'. Frank Anstey has also decided to give up politics. Everything was sour in his mouth. He has decided the difference between Labor and the conservatives was the difference between Tweedledum and Tweedledee.

But there were others to keep the faith. Joseph Benedict Chifley was a 'light on the hill man', a man who shared John Curtin's view that Labor was dedicated to a 'holy crusade'. Chifley came from the working classes: he belonged to that generation of self-taught Labor men who believed that the workers had 'mighty work' to perform—they must set to it night and day. 'We work for humanity', he said, 'when we fight for better conditions'. He was born in Bathurst, close to the railway yards, on 22 September 1885, the year in which John Curtin was born. His father and mother were Irish. In childhood Ben Chifley had the innocence of the bush boy: in manhood he learned that the hearts of some men were filled with evil. Starting as a shop-boy in the locomotive shed of the New South Wales railways at Bathurst, he had such an abundance of natural ability that he quickly rose to be an engine-driver.

The war taught him much about the divisions in Australian society. The harsh and oppressive treatment of the railway strikers in 1917 planted in his mind the need to do something to protect the working man against the 'boss'. Years of experience in the trade union movement, the Labor Party and the Trades and Labor Council of New South Wales changed him from a utopian socialist to a pragmatist, just as the same years in the 'fiery furnace' of 1916–17 in Australia converted John Curtin from socialism to pragmatism. By the 1920s those who knew Ben Chifley found him a wondrous person, a Labor man with a mantle of tragic grandeur. He had the charisma to draw all manner of men, women and children unto him. He had a generosity and a magnanimity which suggested to those who knew him that if Ben Chifley were God he would forgive everyone. He believed in the light on the hill until the day he died.

When he spoke to the electors over the commercial broadcasting stations on the night of 9 August 1934 he spoke in part as a one-time utopian socialist. 'Scores of thousands of Australian men and women', he told the listeners, 'are hardly getting enough to keep body and soul together'. Something must be done because that would be an investment, as he put it, 'not only in material welfare but in the moral and physical well-being of the nation'. He wanted Australians to face up to 'the afflictions of many thousands of our people'. But Ben Chifley, like John Curtin and many others of those fashioned by 1916–17, was also a pragmatist—a vote-winner for the Labor Party. The pragmatist spoke of what Labor would do. While Chifley was campaigning in New South Wales Curtin was saying the same sort of thing in Fremantle. The leader of the Labor Party, Jimmy Scullin, was tired. He had little to offer. He did not rouse his people to sing a rebel chorus, let alone raise a rebel flag. At a rally on election eve, his audience sang 'For he's a jolly good fellow.'

Lyons campaigned on his record. By Monday 17 September it was obvious that the UAP and the Country Party had won a clear victory. Curtin won the seat of Fremantle by a majority of 1028 after the distribution of preferences. Menzies won the seat of Kooyong by an overwhelming majority. Two men who believed it was their destiny to be Prime Minister of Australia now faced each other across the table in the House of Representatives. Menzies, it was said, would be a welcome change to a party 'so ill-furnished with political brains', and, in the words of the *Bulletin*, so 'ordinary'. Bob Menzies would be the man to replace that 'tired, dull old man', Joe Lyons.

The matrons of Toorak, South Yarra, Vaucluse, Wahroonga, and other parts of Australia where the inhabitants saw themselves as being a bit above the ordinary, were busy at their dressmakers. Prince Henry, Duke of Gloucester, was coming to preside over the celebrations organized to commemorate the founding of the first British settlement in Melbourne in 1834. Wives extracted promises from their husbands to pay for new dresses for all the royal occasions. Daughters were measured for 'fetching fittings', the Duke being known in advance as a man who always asked the prettiest woman in the room for at least two dances. There would be a State Ball in Melbourne, a State Ball in King's Hall, Canberra, and a State Ball in Sydney. They would be the most brilliant functions ever to be held in Australia. Mothers who wished their daughters to be introduced to Prince Charming were advised to communicate with his military and official secretary who would forward full instructions to them. Prince Charming would also dedicate the Shrine of Remembrance in Melbourne and the Anzac Memorial in Sydney. There was to be gaiety; there was to be solemnity. There would be fun and games; there would also be moments when the people would worship at their shrine.

To the delight of the conservatives and those of like mind the Duke quickly endeared himself to the Australian people. The people of Perth experienced a wild ecstasy at the very sight of him. On the transcontinental journey from Perth to Adelaide the Duke showed he had some of the qualities of the Australian bushman. At Ooldea the original tenants of the deserts of Australia have given proof of their loyalty and affection. The Duke was seen earnestly talking to Daisy Bates. Now it was Adelaide's turn, and then Melbourne's turn. He was showered in adoration. At ceremonies of great pomp and sadness, he opened the Shrine of Remembrance in Melbourne and the Anzac Memorial in Hyde Park, Sydney. God save the King.

The Centenary Air Race from England to Melbourne was further evidence of the advantages in being British. Sir Macpherson Robertson gave the prize money. The Prince of Wales was at the Mildenhall aerodrome to watch the planes take off in the first light of dawn on 20 October. On 23 October C. W. A. Scott and Captain Campbell Black crossed the finishing line in Melbourne. The Dutch and the Germans have been defeated. The British have triumphed. The Fairy Prince told the two winners of the Centenary Air Race theirs was 'a wonderful achievement in a British machine'. England was now only three days away from Australia.

Beware, Australians, of what the British were up to. To counter the show to be put on by 'Yarraside' and their hangers-on, the Communists and the Militant Minority were holding an All-Australian Congress against War and Fascism, which began in Melbourne on 10 November. The Duke and the men in high places might glorify war at the Shrine in Melbourne but they would preach the gospel of peace. Theirs was the righteous cause. On 6 November the P & O liner *Strathaird* docked in Fremantle as a small crowd of militants waited expectantly on the wharf. On deck was a passenger who clenched his right fist, raised his right arm to the faithful and said: '*Rotfront*' (Red Front). He was Egon Kisch, the guest of the All-Australian Congress against War and Fascism. Commonwealth officers went on board to tell Kisch his entry into Australia was forbidden. The Commonwealth Government had information from the British Government about Kisch and had declared him to be 'undesirable as an inhabitant of, or visitor to, the Commonwealth'.

Kisch was Czech by birth, German by speech, and cosmopolitan by inclination. His newspaper articles and books have already won him the distinction of being known as 'a journalist of the highest order'. The titles of his books were a guide to his political convictions: *Zaren, Popen, Bolschewiken, Asien Gründlich Verändert* and *Paradies Amerika*. Kisch was an exuberant man, a man who would at one moment kiss a woman fair and square on the mouth, and the next clench the fist, and greet comrades with an enthusiastic 'Red Front'. The Congress against War and Fascism has made a brilliant choice for one of their guests: Kisch was a brilliant mass speaker. He loved the applause of a crowd. He had a long experience in not telling people in power things they wanted to know.

The legal wrangling over the government's attempts to deport him continued for a month, during which time Kisch addressed

huge anti-war rallies in Melbourne and Sydney. Kisch told them
how Germany was a great armed camp, that German children were
being taught to use hand-grenades and gas-masks, and how from
the age of 15 German boys wore military uniforms and carried
swords. Germany was rebuilding her military might. Don't let
Britain make a bargain with the Australian militarists for your
bodies. Don't be fooled by the honour and praise the ruling class
now bestowed on the bodies of dead Anzacs or the chauvinism
generated by the Duke. Join the movement against War and
Fascism. They cheered and stamped and hugged each other, and
pledged themselves to the cause.

The determination of the Attorney-General, Robert Menzies, to
silence Kisch aroused passionate opposition between those who
wished to silence revolutionary talk and those who upheld notions
of free speech and the right of Australians to hear ideas critical of
the society in which they lived. Menzies ordered that Kisch be
deported as an 'illegal immigrant'. But Robert Menzies was foiled
by Herbert Vere Evatt, when Mr Justice Evatt held in the High
Court that the deportation order was invalid under the Act. A new
hero of the people had walked on to the stage of public life. But
Menzies was determined. He ordered that Kisch be required to
submit to a dictation test as provided for in the Immigration Act,
a test he could not pass. This presented problems. Kisch was a
linguist. The advisers had the answer: Kisch could not pass a test in
Gaelic. The test was administered. An Australian police officer read
the passage. Kisch failed. A new order for his deportation was
drafted. But that order was also overturned when the High Court
found that Scottish Gaelic was not a 'European language' of the
class comprehended by section 3a of the Immigration Act. Kisch
could stay in Australia.

While the radicals made great sport of hiding Kisch from the
police and spiriting him in and out of public meetings, some Labor
members of Parliament, some university professors, some writers
and clergymen formed committees to protest against his exclusion.
Dear, kind Professor Walter Murdoch, friend and biographer of Mr
Deakin, no spouter of revolutionary slogans he, said the exclusion
of an author of international repute who was visiting Australia as a
guest of the anti-militarists was a disgrace to Australia. Bishop E. H.
Burgmann of Goulburn said a political system which feared public
criticism had no healthy future.

As conservatives called for Kisch to be imprisoned, the Labor
Party began to distance itself from him and his radical supporters.
After all, there were elections to be won. In any case, Kisch wanted
to return to Europe. On 11 March he boarded the *Oxford* at
Fremantle. When he saw Katharine Prichard on the wharf, he

rushed down the gangplank to farewell her, then he rushed back on to the ship, stood on the deck and gave the Red Front salute, and sang the song of hope: *Die Strasse frei: Rot Front!* Kisch was returning to the struggle for the liberation of humanity.

On the same ocean, Bob Menzies was being strengthened in convictions he had held ever since his student days. Menzies and his wife, along with Joe Lyons and others, were to attend the celebrations for the silver jubilee of George V in London, and an Imperial Conference. Menzies was about to begin the great love affair of his life. On the ship, the *Otranto*, he loved everything that was British. The young Englishmen on board had the 'usual attributes of cleanness, good manners, interest in Test Matches and the championship at Wimbledon'. 'Westward Ho!' for Bob Menzies. He was going to meet the loved one, while back in Australia the press was announcing that Australia would soon export pig iron to Japan, and John Curtin was still wondering about the future of Australia.

On 21 March he saw the white cliffs of Dover. For him the 'journey to Mecca has ended'. England was one delight after another—the green fields, leafless hedges and quietly grazing sheep, and the 'grey bulk of Buckingham Palace', the Mall and the Strand, followed by the Savoy. He was so excited that while his wife unpacked, 'I sneak out and look at Trafalgar Square and one of the Wren churches by starlight, and so to bed'. For him, this was possibly the only way he could savour and enjoy what meant so much to him. That was the trouble: he could only tell it to his diary. He was so happy, he could almost cry for joy. Englishmen in high places listened to him with respect. He sat in the Cabinet Room at Number 10 Downing Street, and pondered over the portrait of Robert Walpole, England's longest serving Prime Minister. Perhaps it was his destiny to hold the equivalent record in Australia. He travelled around the countryside, always seeking out the places associated with the two great passions of his life—literature and politics.

He saw John Gielgud as Hamlet and Jessica Tandy as Ophelia. They were both 'wonderful'. He was troubled by the behaviour of Hitler, who has just torn up one of the clauses of the Treaty of Versailles. He was not certain whether Hitler was a patriot who had found his country suffering from a feeling of 'inferiority and servitude and was determined to restore her self-respect, and recapture political power as a means to that end'; or a 'swashbuckler who [was] preparing actually for an aggressive war?' Much, he noted in his diary on 8 April, turned 'on the faith of this one man'.

England in the spring soon banished such dark thoughts from his mind. He loved the English countryside with its 'green and flowering things—a beauty no new country town in Victoria could ever possess'. He had found the homeland of his imagination. The English flattered him. There were meetings at the Foreign Office, meetings with royalty and persons of noble birth. He saw the guardsmen on parade, walked the streets and parks of London and danced in black knee breeches and silk stockings at a Palace Ball. He was in love. He knew the glory of adulation after he made a speech in Westminster Hall, possibly, he believed, 'the first Dominion Minister ever to speak in this spot'.

He and Pattie went to tea with the Duke and Duchess of York and the little Princesses Elizabeth and Margaret Rose on 11 July. He and Pattie watched the Princesses having a dancing lesson. He distinctly heard Princess Margaret bullying Princess Elizabeth who, he noted with his usual flair for such things, had 'a perfectly comical capacity for acting'. He was delighted. 'This is a real family', he decided. 'We leave walking on air.' The great passion of his life has begun—a veneration for and worship of the royal family. Menzies was moving away from the people. He has dined with the wealthy and the great. How different it all was from Australia, the country where the 'yahoos' expected to be treated as the equals of the *gens superieurs*. Here in England and Scotland 'I am made to feel that an Australian Robert Menzies who is Attorney-General is a person of consequence'.

On 6 September 1935 Bob Menzies returned to Sydney. He had a message for the Australian people. The English had much to teach Australians—much about freedom, tolerance and good nature in controversy. The Labor press treated him as a figure of fun and pinned abusive labels on him, calling him 'Bob Super Ming' and 'Ming the Merciless'.

The following day, 1 October, Caucus met in Canberra to elect a new leader of the ALP. Early in August Scullin had collapsed at mass in a church in North Richmond. At a special meeting of the Labor members of Parliament in Canberra on 23 September he announced his resignation. Labor needed a leader with something to say, a man who had an alternative to 'Yarraside', and Menzies' idea of Australia as a New Britannia in another world.

Ted Holloway believed there was such a man. Labor, he believed, needed a man of vision who had not supported the anti-working-class Premiers' Plan, a man who could heal the divisions within the party. He believed John Curtin was that man, and approached him. 'The chaps want me', he said to him, 'to guarantee that you would remain sober'. John Curtin replied: 'Of course, I would. Each Labor leader during his term of office has been a total abstainer, and I will not break that wonderful record'. He was to keep his word. In the fulfilment of what he had always believed to be his destiny he found the strength to succeed where previously all else had failed.

On 1 October 1935 the Labor Caucus in Canberra elected John Curtin leader of the ALP by one vote. Scullin was astonished. 'It can't be right', he said when told the result. The *Age* called the decision 'one of the greatest surprises in Federal political circles during recent years'. Curtin spoke with the dignity befitting the solemn occasion. 'My aim', he said, 'is to revive the spiritual unity of the Labor movement, to renew and vitalize its sobriety and commonsense so that it may once more serve the needs of Australia in an era in which the portents of evil are grave and ominous'.

The fruits of those walks on the beach at Cottlesloe were about to be given to Australians. He would teach Labor that it was possible to be pragmatic without being opportunist, that the inspired ideal-ism of their founders need not disappear in the pursuit of political power. He would teach Labor to work for a 'new social order', and stop fighting about whether the carter of bread should be in the bread carters' union or in the carters' and drivers' union. Labor must not degenerate into a band of machine men and women. The Henry Lawson vision lived on in him. Australians should and could banish from under their 'bonny skies'

> Those old-world errors and wrongs and lies
> Making a Hell in a Paradise
> That belongs to your sons and you.

Australians must make the choice:

> Sons of the South, make choice between
> (Sons of the South, choose true)
> The Land of Morn and the Land of E'en,
> The Old Dead Tree and the Young Tree Green,
> The Land that belongs to the lord and Queen,
> And the Land that belongs to you.

He would teach Australians that it was possible to have equality of opportunity without infringing individual liberty and without mediocrity, conformism or spiritual popery. He would teach Australians that the days of relying on the British navy for defence were over. The aeroplane has superseded the battleship.

It was a bleak time for a man who believed in the capacity of human beings for better things. Mussolini's pilots were bombing Abyssinian towns and villages, murdering men, women and children. The Communists were urging the workers not to let the war in Abyssinia spread to other parts of the world, and become the prelude to a new world slaughter. Prophets were talking of a relapse into barbarism. The consequences of nihilism were spreading to the masses. Political principles and faiths were now nothing but play-acting. There was an aura of the mediocrity and meanness of spirit Nietzsche had predicted would come in the century after human beings had killed their God.

The time was coming when an Australian voice would be heard in the age when men and women lived without faith either in God or in the capacity of human beings for better things. The time was coming when an Australian voice would be heard in the great debate on what it has all been for, telling the story of who Australians were and what they might be. A new discovery of Australia was about to begin. Australians must decide for themselves whether this was the land of the dreaming, the land of the Holy Spirit, the New Britannia, the Millennial Eden, or the new demesne for Mammon to infest.

Epilogue

In the years after 1935 some of the people in this history drew prizes and some drew blanks in the human lottery. Bob Menzies drew the prize he had coveted so passionately. In April 1939 he succeeded Joe Lyons as Prime Minister. He told the people not to believe what his enemies said of him. He was neither aloof nor supercilious. 'I am', he said, 'a singularly plain Australian'. But two years later he paid a terrible price for his arrogance and his allegiance to the 'Old Dead Tree'. On the night of 28 August 1941 his colleagues suggested he should resign. He walked from the Cabinet room to the Prime Minister's room in Parliament House, Canberra, fell into the arms of his secretary, Cecil Looker, and cried out in anguish: 'Looker, I'm all in'.

In the summer of 1941–42 the world Bob Menzies believed in threatened to collapse in ruins. The Japanese sank two British battleships off the east coast of Malaya on 10 December 1941. On 15 February 1942 the Japanese occupied the naval base of Singapore. Prime Minister Curtin turned to America as the keystone of the defence of Australia. As ever, life was not as tidy as art. In art, Bob Menzies should have been destroyed. In life, he had the strength and the courage to rise from the politically dead. In 1943 he delivered his message to middle-class Australia. He professed again his passionate belief in free enterprise, the liberty of the individual, justice, toleration, and being 'dyed in the wool British'. He no longer spoke with disdain of the common people as 'yahoos'. Over a chat and a chuckle with friends and admirers his eyes still lit up when he dismissed his critics as 'squirts'.

Menzies was about to enjoy the flowering time of his life. Prime Minister of Australia from 1949 to 1966, he retired full of honours and unvanquished. Almost two decades of Australian history were known as the Menzies era. It was the era of university expansion, the era of the growth of Canberra into a city worthy of being the nation's capital. In return for his devoted services to the British in Australia and to the royal family, the cities and universities of the United Kingdom showered him with honours and gifts. The boy from Jeparit became the darling of the British governing classes.

The first time he exercised power men judged him harshly. Now he was haunted by the fear that history might punish him as cruelly as had his colleagues on 28 August 1941. He knew his *Hamlet*: 'Use every man after his desert, and who shall 'scape whipping?'. The historians of Australia might wield the whip with the same relish as his political colleagues had done on that night of 28 August. His life was the tragedy writ large of the scholarship boy in Australia. It was not so much the tragedy of a man of vast gifts who yet lacked the one precious gift of reading the direction of the river of life. He knew the direction of that river: he knew what was inside him. But so clamorous were his passions for good food, good wine, the approval of the high and mighty and the honours the British conferred on their gifted loyal subjects in Australia, that his judgement was warped and his conscience stifled. To follow the path of reason and conscience meant shedding all the pleasure which was the stuff of life for him. So the boy from Jeparit, the 'singularly plain Australian', one of Australia's most gifted sons, served alien gods, and may have tasted deep damnation as the fruit of all his disquiet. History, he hoped, would view him with the eye of pity, and extend to him the love which had eluded him in life. He died on 15 May 1978 at the age of 83.

John Curtin also drew the prize he coveted. He became a Labor Prime Minister of Australia on 3 October 1941. He was greatly loved. His political opponents praised him as the 'best and fairest' man in Australian public life, the charismatic leader, with an abundance of wisdom and understanding. Just over a month after he became Prime Minister the national song, 'Advance Australia Fair', was sung at the official opening of the War Memorial in Canberra on Armistice Day, 1941. He had had a great dream. He had dreamed that here in the South Pacific Australians would rear a nation that would be an example to all others. He never gave up that dream. But he believed Australians should postpone the fulfilment of the dream until after victory in the war. Death cheated him of the glory of teaching Australians how to cultivate 'The Young Tree Green'. He died in Canberra on 5 July 1945, at the age of 60. He had always been an enigma. No one knew then or later why a man with such a lofty vision of Australia always wore a sad look on his face. Other human beings, what came up from inside him, and the spirit of the place have ravaged the face of the young man who had dedicated his life to a 'holy crusade' for Labor.

Ben Chifley drew two great prizes. He was loved. He was Prime Minister of a government which put on the statute book much of what Labor had preached, but had never been able to practise. He gave capitalism a human face, he encouraged excellence in things Australian by creating the Australian National University, and he promoted material well-being for all, being faithful to the Labor belief that creature comforts are the *sine qua non* of human well-being and happiness. But the Australian past was even stronger than the mighty spirit of Joseph Benedict Chifley. On 10 December 1949 his Labor Government was swept out of office in an electoral landslide to the conservatives. As on 5 May 1917 and 19 December 1931, a society of immigrants and their descendants, a society with a working class entranced by petty-bourgeois ideas of private ownership of property, and a society distinguished by the wide extent of middle-class affluence, uncovered the strength of conservatism in Australia. Electors were to do the same in December 1975 when they feared that another man of vision, Edward Gough Whitlam, was enticing Labor to liberate Australians from the dead hand of the past. Australia was still evidence for the prophecy by Alexander Herzen that petty-bourgeoisiedom is the final word of any civilization based on the unconditional rule of property. Australia has not been liberated from its past. So Chifley died on 13 June 1951 with the light on the hill as far off as ever. He was then 65.

Bert Evatt drew the prize of being elected, in October 1947, President of the General Assembly of the United Nations for 1948. But the office of Prime Minister eluded him. Under his leadership there was a split in the Labor Party which contributed to those 23 years in the political wilderness. The man who had the image of Christ in his heart and the teaching of the Enlightenment in his mind had to endure as best he could the humiliation of being the whipping boy of Bob Menzies for his frailties. The man who believed Labor was the Magic Flute leading Australians from ignorance and superstition up into the light, walked into a very dark night. He died on 2 November 1965, at the age of 71.

The intimations of Enid Lyons on the fate of her husband proved to be correct. The man who persuaded her beloved Joe to abandon the Labor Party and rescue bourgeois Australia cast a shadow over the last years of his life. Labor colleagues had warned him: 'Don't do it, Joe; don't do it'. But he did, and they never forgave him, and they never forgot. He died on 7 April 1939 at the age of 59.

Labor men and women never forgave Billy Hughes for the treachery of 1916. For 36 years he hoped for the gesture of forgiveness and reconciliation. But the gesture was never made. In March 1951 he attended the ceremony on Capitol Hill in Canberra to commemorate the choice of Canberra as the site for the capital city. It was 40 years since he and his Labor brothers had dreamed of the day when the gross inequalities between the rich and the poor would disappear, and Australians learn to spurn the luxuries coveted by the worshippers of Mammon. Life had robbed Hughes of all these visions. Ever since those decisive days in 1916 he had dismissed all such hopes as 'empty vapourings', just as Bob Menzies had ridiculed all the improvers of humanity as spouters of 'twaddle'. Australia, he said on that day, was not a place for weaklings. On that day in Canberra Hughes stood alone under the vast sky, still the man with the indomitable spirit encased in the tiny frame. He died on 28 October 1952 at the age of 90.

During his years of retirement Jimmy Scullin enjoyed the prize that human beings award to those endowed with goodness. Men on both sides of politics looked on him with reverence and awe. But he was haunted by the ghosts of 1929–31, the never-ending pain of knowing that it had all gone wrong. He died on 28 January 1953, at the age of 76. At the requiem mass in St Patrick's Cathedral, Melbourne, on 30 January, many wept, for Jimmy Scullin had been much loved. He had been the champion of the poor. For him Christ and Labor were one.

When his political career ended Ted Theodore pursued the other love of his life, the quest for the 'spangles of gold'. He had that satisfaction. But about his role in Mungana he spoke to no one. On one lovely day in autumn not long before he died, when the sun was painting golden fireballs on the waters of Sydney Harbour, an old friend, Alec Chisholm, a naturalist and editor, asked him: 'Tell me, Ted, what was the truth about Mungana?'. Ted Theodore replied: 'Alec, of all the lovely things in life there is nothing more lovely than Sydney Harbour on a day in autumn'. He walked away. He died in 1950 at the age of 65.

The Big Fella, Jack Lang, outlived them all—except Menzies. His quarrel was not with God or the conservatives. His quarrel was with the Australian Labor Party. The two passions of his life never left him—money and domination. Time did not soften him. But time conferred a mantle of majesty on Labor's great trouble-maker. He wanted to be remembered as the champion of the people. He died on 27 September 1975 at the age of 99. The huge crowd lining the streets of Sydney along which his funeral procession passed showed the people remembered that the Big Fella, the demagogue of Sydney Town, also had a capacious heart.

Stanley Bruce accepted with dignity the verdict of the Australian people that he could never again be the leader of a political party. In the autumn of his life he became the loyal and distinguished servant of both conservative and Labor governments. The man who spoke with passion about the birth of an Australian nation at the ceremony to inaugurate the Australian War Memorial on Anzac Day 1929 accepted a British viscountcy in 1947. But he chose to be known as Viscount Bruce of Melbourne, and before he died he directed that his ashes be scattered over Canberra. He was the noblest Australian-Briton of them all. He died on 25 August 1967 at the age of 84.

Nettie Palmer fought to the end for the development of an Australian culture. But what mattered most to her in life was never to be. She never heard or read the words she wanted to hear or read. She died on 19 October 1964 at the age of 79. Katharine Prichard drew the prize of literary fame, but had the mortification of seeing her hopes for a Communist Australia vanish into the great Australian silence. She was the 'child of the hurricane', but no social hurricane ever blew in Australia during her lifetime. She died on 2 October 1969 at the age of 85. Things went hardly for them both: for both, things were not 'lastly as firstly well'. They deserve our pity: they deserve our love.

In the second half of the twentieth century Australians lived in a country where neither the historians, the prophets, the poets nor the priests had drawn the maps. Revolutions in transport and communications finally ended the material backwardness and the isolation. Immigrants from Europe and Asia helped to deliver a mortal wound to the Giant of British philistinism. Grovelling to the British almost disappeared. Intellectuals and artists no longer agonized over whether to be second-rate Europeans in their own country, or live abroad. Australians no longer apologized for the way they talked, the way they walked, or the way they behaved. They no longer confessed they had erred and strayed from British canons of behaviour, and that they would try not to err again. The domination of class over class, of white man over Aborigine, of man over woman, of teacher over student, and parent over child was challenged. Women wanted both equality and the right to control their own lives, especially the life of their bodies. Aborigines wanted to decide for themselves their way of life. Students wanted to decide how and what they should be taught. Women wrote their own history. Aborigines wrote their history, maintaining that their ancestors were not immigrants, but were always here, and that white man's history was a catalogue of 'white lies'. The New Left wrote their history. Accounts of the past became part of the struggle for power in Australia. In an age of doubt about everything, even the past lost its authority. There was no final court of appeal on the human questions.

Australians gradually ceased to look to Europe as 'the land of holy wonders', but rather as a museum of past glories, a 'precious graveyard' of the origins of the Europeans and their descendants in the haggard continent of Australia. Painters such as Arthur Boyd, novelists such as Patrick White, Eleanor Dark and David Malouf, poets such as Judith Wright, Kenneth Slessor, Alec Hope, David Campbell and James McAuley provided food for the hungers of the human heart, and ministered to the desire of the human mind to be there when everyone suddenly understands what it has all been for.

Restraints on human behaviour were thrown aside. Nothing was sacred, nothing escaped examination. Men and women walked naked on the beaches, the stage and the screen and they were not ashamed. Men and women no longer conceded to politicians, priests, parsons, professors, or presidents of the Returned Services' League the right to draw up codes of behaviour, or prescribe what could or could not be read. The people broke the Tablets of the Law. The people killed their gods. The people turned to the worship of the Golden Calf.

The survivors from earlier generations were bewildered and dismayed. In an age distinguished by an abundance of consumer goods, gadgets and creature comforts, an age which confounded greed and titillation with pleasure and well-being, Colin Cartwright, a fictional character created by Barry Humphries, but very representative of the mood of the new age, said: 'I've come to the conclusion you can give kids too much'. An age which put a man into space, and saw a man walk on the moon was, paradoxically, characterized by doubt about everything. The two wars, the atomic bomb, the holocaust of the Jewish people, the mass murders for political purposes, shook humanity's belief in a benevolent, loving God, and in their own capacity for better things. It was 40 000 years and possibly more since the Aborigines composed their stories of creation. On 13 May 1987 it was 200 years since the First Fleet left the abode of a civilized people and sailed to a land they believed to be inhabited by savages. Of all the dreams of those Europeans of what Australia might be—the south land of the Holy Spirit, or the land where the great dream of the Enlightenment would be fulfilled, or the land where blood would never stain the wattle, or a New Britannia in another world—all that seemed to survive was the idea of Australia as a place of 'uncommonly large profit'. History has blurred the vision of Eden, allowing Mammon to infest the land. A turbulent emptiness seized the people as they moved into a post-Christian, post-Enlightenment era. No one any longer knew the direction of the river of life. No one had anything to say.

This generation has a chance to be wiser than previous

generations. They can make their own history. With the end of the domination by the straiteners, the enlargers of life now have their chance. They have the chance to lavish on each other the love the previous generations had given to God, and to bestow on the here and now the hopes and dreams they had once entertained for some future human harmony. It is the task of the historian and the myth-maker to tell the story of how the world came to be as it is. It is the task of the prophet to tell the story of what might be. The historian presents the choice: history is a book of wisdom for those making that choice.

CODA

by
Michael Cathcart

Democratic nations care but little for what has been, but they are haunted by visions of what will be.

Alexis de Tocqueville, *Democracy in America*

I take it, too, you all agree that history like poetry, music, painting, sculpture and dancing—is one of the great comforters which men have put between themselves and death—to make their living and their dying more bearable.

Manning Clark, 'The Writing of History' (1962)

Coda

As the night-train swayed into Bonn station, a young Australian peered through the icy window of his railway carriage. He was relieved to be away from Oxford and his thesis, and delighted to see his fiancée waving to him from the platform. Together, the two students made their way to the stairs and emerged into the light of a European morning. The young man would never forget that moment. Up and down the street, shops and businesses were in ruins. Some had been gutted by fire. The road and footpath were covered with a sea of shattered glass, and merchandise was strewn about like wreckage from a storm. Everywhere he saw the Star of David and slogans such as 'Death to the Jews' scrawled across walls and doorways. On the far side of the street, a squad of self-satisfied Nazis kept watch from the back of a truck. They had pistols strapped to their hips. In the midst of so much hatred, the young man asked himself, where was the Anglican God of his fathers; where was the God of Israel?

This was Germany in November 1938. In a government-backed night of terror, stormtroopers and their supporters had rampaged through the streets of German cities, destroying synagogues and burning or ransacking Jewish stores. So common was the sight of broken glass that that evening became known as *Kristallnacht*—the night of crystal. At the age of 23, Manning Clark had seen the face of evil.

Six months later, Bob Menzies—as Clark would one day put it—drew the prize he coveted so passionately: in April 1939 he succeeded Joe Lyons as Prime Minister, still speaking as if it were his destiny to preside over an Australia which was British, prosperous and peaceful. Like the British Prime Minister, Neville Chamberlain, Menzies believed that the fascists could be appeased. He admired them as patriots and had pointed to them as a role model for Australian youth. In Cabinet only the querulous

Billy Hughes was prepared to speak out against the fascists. Now Menzies' avuncular voice flowed out of wireless sets into homes throughout Australia. There was hope, he reassured the voters, that Mussolini and Hitler would turn back from the brink. Australians should remain calm. Everything that could be done was being done: Australians could continue their daily lives with confidence.

But talk was vain. The fascists had armed their regiments. To the north of Australia, the forces of Japan were also on the move; in 1931 they had overrun Manchuria. Yet for the past decade, Australian governments had spent little on defence. The conservatives had their faith. The British navy, bound by ties of blood and trade, would defend this little outpost of Empire against any threat from the yellow hordes of Asia.

When war finally broke out in Europe, there was neither panic nor euphoria in Australia. Menzies' broadcast to the nation on 3 September was subdued. 'It is my melancholy duty to inform you officially,' he told the people, 'that, in consequence of the persistence by Germany in her invasion of Poland, Great Britain has declared war upon her, and that, as a result, Australia is also at war.' The negotiations had failed. Now the Dominions, as a great family of nations, were involved in a struggle which they must at all costs win.

But the European war was far away. Australians were at last enjoying full employment. The shops were busy, the climate was mild, and life was better than most people could remember. A few Australians were apprehensive about Japan, but when black-out or air-raid drills were held, almost nobody treated them seriously. On the first Tuesday in November, 95 000 spectators packed into the Flemington Race Course for a much more important event, the running of a horse-race, the Melbourne Cup. As the new year unfurled in a blaze of summer glory, thousands of Australians crowded on to the golden beaches of Bondi, St Kilda, Glenelg or Fremantle. As they basked in the sun or swam and surfed in the clear blue ocean, it was difficult for them to believe that war was once again bloodying the sands of Egypt and the wintry fields of France.

Nevertheless, there was no shortage of young men who, through poverty, bravado or patriotism, volunteered to fight in the new European war. On 9 January 1940 the first contingent of Australian troops sailed from Sydney Harbour, many of them aboard towering ocean-liners from the North Atlantic run never before seen in Australian waters. Once again the native-born assembled on the shores of Sydney Harbour, waving flags and cheering as Australian sons sailed away to the battlefields of the Old World.

Over the next five years, the pilots among them defended Britain in the air. Australian sailors and soldiers fought in the Mediterranean, and in North Africa, Syria, Greece, Crete and Egypt. When the Italians and Germans drove the Allies out of Libya, a besieged Allied garrison—two-thirds of them Australian—held the port of Tobruk. They are known to this day as 'the Rats of Tobruk'. The Australian navy fought in the pivotal Battle of Cape Matapan which inflicted a serious defeat on the Italian navy and gave the British navy the upper hand in the Mediterranean.

At home, Menzies proposed a government of national unity, and was even prepared to concede the prime ministership to the Labor leader, John Curtin. But the Labor Party did not trust Menzies. They would bide their time. Late in 1940, Menzies once again embarked on a visit to the heart of the Empire. As he charmed his way about Whitehall and Fleet Street, he became alarmed at the way Churchill was conducting the war. The British Prime Minister's bulldoggish determination to wage total war against Germany was putting the entire Empire at risk: without the Empire, Menzies believed, Australia was finished. He was not alone in his misgivings about Churchill's bellicosity: to Menzies' delight there was talk in the newspapers that the Australian Prime Minister should enter the Mother of Parliaments at Westminster, that he was the man to lead the Empire in its darkest hour. At very least, the flatterers said, he should be appointed a permanent member of the War Cabinet. Though his political friends in Canberra urged him to return, Menzies tarried in London, infatuated with the prospect that the class-conscious British might look to a mere colonial to lead them through the conflict. In Canberra, the stolid, straight-talking Arthur Fadden had been acting-Prime Minister and had won increasing respect among his government colleagues. When Menzies at last returned on 24 May 1941, he found that his support in his own party and among the people had withered. On 28 August 1941, he resigned as Prime Minister, still hopeful that a greater destiny awaited him 'at home'. But to his dismay the call from England never came. To some who looked on that day, it seemed that Robert Gordon Menzies had fallen victim to his own vanity and had made his departure from the stage of public life.

Artie Fadden was appointed in Menzies' place, and piloted the ship of state for forty days and forty nights. In the House of Representatives on 3 October 1941 during the Budget debate, Curtin moved a vote of no confidence. The conservatives lost their slender majority when two independent members—a farmer and a retail magnate—voted with the Labor Party. John Curtin, the dreamer of Cottesloe Beach, had become Prime Minister of Australia. The slightly-built trade unionist gazed at the House through his round spectacles. After the well-upholstered and grandiloquent Menzies, Curtin looked an unlikely leader. But Australians had found a Prime Minister whose patience, tolerance and resolve united and inspired the nation just as the thunder of war grew terrifyingly close. The new Cabinet included two compassionate and intelligent men, Ben Chifley, who became Treasurer, and Bert Evatt. A decade earlier this reforming High Court judge had resigned from the bench to stand for Parliament, and now was appointed Attorney-General and Minister for External Affairs.

On 7 December 1941, the Japanese air force bombed the American Pacific Fleet at Pearl Harbor. The war had come to the Pacific. Over the next eight weeks Hong Kong, Borneo, Rabaul, Guam, the Netherlands East Indies, Burma and the entire Malay Peninsula fell to the Japanese. On 15 February 1942, the unthinkable happened. The British commander in Singapore surrendered in the face of the irresistible Japanese advance and led 85 000 Allied troops, including 15 000 Australians, into captivity. The fortress of Singapore, the symbol of British supremacy in the 'Far East', had fallen.

Four days later, over 200 Japanese planes swept out of the northern skies and bombed the Australian city of Darwin, sinking eight ships and killing 243 people. Public nerve broke. Bombed buildings were ransacked by looters while the mass of the population, soldiers included, panicked and fled. The *Sydney Morning Herald* called for toughness and sacrifice and for the surrender of every private interest to the national need.

As Australians braced themselves for an invasion, Churchill issued a summons to the Dominions. Burma had fallen; India was threatened: Australian troops in the Middle East would be diverted to defend the Indian sub-continent. But John Curtin's loyalty was to Australia. He realized that the British navy was abandoning the Pacific just as the Japanese were penetrating further and further south: Australian troops were needed to defend their increasingly vulnerable homeland. At the same time, Australia needed to find a new ally. In December 1941, Curtin announced that the government was determined that Australia would not fall to the Japanese and that 'free of any pangs as to our traditional links or kinship with the United Kingdom', he was calling on the United States to come to Australia's aid. The government would exert all its energies towards shaping a plan with the United States which would give the country some confidence of being able to hold out until the tide of battle swung against the enemy. In London Churchill fumed. From the opposite benches, Menzies thundered that the Prime Minister had made 'a grave blunder'. But Curtin stood firm; Australia's Sixth and Seventh Divisions were withdrawn from the Middle East to defend the islands of Sumatra and Java to the north of Australia.

Curtin's call was heeded by the Americans, who had lost their base in the Philippines. The lofty, austere General Douglas MacArthur established himself in Melbourne and later in Brisbane as Supreme Commander of the Allied forces in the South-West Pacific. The Australian navy and air force were placed under his direct control, while the army was under the command of the senior Australian general, the squat, smart and vengeful Sir Thomas Blamey. Soon the streets of Australian cities were filled with the American servicemen who, for the most part, were greeted with relief, gratitude and affection. American manners and speech habits, which Australians had seen glamorized in the picture palaces, were now all around them. Australian families took American servicemen into their own homes and entertained them. Australian girls took them to their hearts.

To further the war effort, opinion makers began to say that a woman's place did, after all, lie outside the home. In late 1941 women were admitted into non-combat positions in the armed services. The following year, civilian women were recruited to work in factories and foundries, in transport, communications, commerce and on the farms. Middle-class women, who in peacetime had regarded wage labour as unladylike and vulgar, were now manufacturing bullets, collecting train fares, harvesting wheat or working as nurses in military hospitals. Although such women were usually enthusiastic about their new roles, there were problems. Women were almost always paid less than men who were doing the same work (though the gap narrowed during the war); and there were many male trade unionists who warned that this cheap female labour would rob men of their rightful jobs once the war was ended.

For the most part, however, old conflicts were laid aside. On the left, the Communist Party and Labor radicals gave their wholehearted support to the war against fascism and Japanese militarism. On the right, Essington Lewis, the profit-driven, union-hating manager of the great mining and steel company Broken Hill Proprietary, was appointed Director-General of Munitions by the government. Under his management, the government took control of the nation's industries. Australian workers began manufacturing guns, aeroplanes, precision optical equipment as well as many necessary goods previously imported. In 1942 the government extended Manpower Regulations already established by Menzies, conscripting labour to build airfields and shipping facilities and to carry out other tasks officially classified as 'essential'. For the first time in their history, white Australians were feeling the effects of war in their daily lives. Tobacco and liquor were scarce. Severe petrol rationing, introduced by Menzies, continued in force. Even items which Australia produced in huge quantities, such as butter, eggs, meat and woollen cloth, were rationed: the troops had to be fed, and few Australians doubted that produce should be sent to Britain where food shortages were severe. The government minister with the un-popular job of overseeing rationing was a dour Scot named John Dedman. In a moment of folly, Dedman tried to reduce demand at Christmas by banning the use of Father Christmas in advertising, earning himself the title of the 'man who killed Santa Claus'.

When Curtin introduced conscription for military service in Australia's region of the Pacific, there was scarcely a murmur of dissent. The threat was too obvious. With terrifying speed, the Japanese had overrun many of the Solomon Islands and had landed in northern New Guinea, the large island to Australia's immediate north, where a handful of ill-equipped patrols of Australian and native troops operated in terrible isolation. Soon the Japanese were fighting and hacking their way across the rugged and fever-sodden Kokoda Trail and over the Owen Stanley Range until they threatened Port Moresby on the south coast. If Moresby fell, then an invasion of northern Australia seemed inevitable. The Australian authorities prepared secret plans for a withdrawal to the south-eastern quarter of the continent, defend-ing a line drawn from Brisbane to Adelaide.

But the speed of the Japanese advance caused the invaders to stumble. Japanese supply-lines were over-extended and within six months their drive began to falter. What was more, the attack on Pearl Harbor, far from crippling US naval power, had inflamed American resolve. In May 1942, the planes and carriers of a combined American and Australian fleet repelled the Japanese navy in the Battle of the Coral Sea off the south-eastern coast of New Guinea. The resulting stand-off was not only a psychological victory for the Allies, it also gave them time to gather their forces. The following month, the US Navy established its dominance of the Pacific when it overpowered the Japanese navy at the great Battle of Midway. In the meantime, the iron-willed Tom Blamey ordered more units of Australian infantry into tropical New Guinea. In the malaria-infested jungles and in the bleak mountain ranges, Australian and local soldiers, wearied by illness, gangrene and hunger, engaged in hand-to-hand slaughter with Japanese who were themselves ravaged by starvation and disease. By September the Japanese had been forced back to the northern side of the Owen Stanley Range, only to find that American troops were attacking them from the west and the north.

Most Australian service personnel felt no grudging respect for this yellow-skinned enemy as they did for Rommel or as they had shown the Turks in 1915. When a force of diggers finally wore down the enemy's last defences at Gona on the north coast of New Guinea in January 1943, even the war-hardened among them were sickened by what they found. The Japanese had been fighting in trenches putrid with blood and shit and rotting bodies. The soldiers had been firing from fortifications which were reinforced with corpses. Pervading everything, recalled Ian Morrison, was the stink of putrescent flesh. Morrison and many of his mates felt only disgust for human beings who were prepared to live and sleep like rats in such filth and stench. Germans and Italians, they said, would have preferred honourable surrender.

Likewise, the Japanese despised the values of the Allies. In the Japanese military code, a captured soldier honourably committed suicide rather than submit to the ignominy of imprisonment. So fundamental was this ideal, that throughout Asia Japanese treated their prisoners as sub-human filth. In Changi prison and in the death-gangs forced to build the Burma Railway, the Japanese captors brutalized near-naked Australian and other Allied prisoners of war until their bodies were racked by illness, starvation and torture. Thousands of men died, the rest were reduced to frail, living skeletons. In a country where forgiveness often comes easily, a generation of Australians never forgot the stories of Japanese barbarism which a few of the survivors found the strength to tell on their return.

In the Old World, as in Asia, the war was turning. The Australian Ninth Division was prominent in a decisive victory over the Germans and Italians in North Africa at El Alamein in October 1942. By the start of February 1943 the Germans had been decimated in the murderous Battle of Stalingrad and were in retreat from Russia. The Allies were sniffing victory.

With cautious confidence, in December 1942 the Australian Government set up a radical new department, with Ben Chifley as Minister, to plan the demobilization of servicemen and to shape postwar society. The powerhouse of this new Ministry of Postwar

Reconstruction was an optimistic team of young, well-educated public servants. Their leader was a shrewd, intelligent and profoundly compassionate man, Dr H. C. Coombs, who became known far and wide in Australia as 'Nugget' Coombs.

As the new Ministry turned its mind to the challenges of demobilization, the slaughter in Asia and the Pacific dragged on. For two and a half weary years, the battered Japanese forces continued to fight on land, on sea and in the air. In Japanese POW camps, Allied prisoners were dying by the hour. As 1945 opened, the Americans prepared for a full-scale invasion of Japan. The carnage on both sides would be terrible. On 21 July 1945, the intelligence officer of the US Fifth Air Force declared that 'the entire population of Japan is a proper military target. There are no civilians in Japan.' An awful decision had been taken. On 6 August an American pilot dropped an atomic bomb on the Japanese city of Hiroshima killing some 140 000 people. Three days later, Nagasaki was also bombed. On 14 August Japan surrendered. On ships, on airfields, in barracks, in hospitals, in trenches and foxholes, Allied servicemen and women cried and cheered with relief. In the cities of Australia men and women cavorted in the streets. The Pacific war was over. The troops were coming home.

Amid the cheers of victory, one voice was silent: one month earlier John Curtin had died, a man loved—as few leaders are loved—for his courage, modesty and compassion. He was succeeded by his gravel-voiced Treasurer, the pipe-smoking Ben Chifley. Like many in the Labor Party, Chifley had never forgotten the bitter days of the Great Depression when bankers and men of privilege had tolerated poverty and violence in the streets, while they themselves grew rich. Ben Chifley had the steady eye of the pragmatist and the builder, but his face never ceased to be lit by the glow of 'the light on the hill'. Under his leadership, Labor was determined to build a peace in which there was prosperity for all.

When the government introduced free university places for ex-servicemen and servicewomen with the necessary entrance qualifications, a generation of young men and women who had known the extremes of war surged into the universities. They brought an urgency and excitement to university life which challenged the old undergraduate order of conservatism and privilege. For the first time, an articulate, optimistic radicalism dominated campus debate. At Melbourne a radical young lecturer in history and politics, Mr Manning Clark, was encouraging his students to read Dostoevsky, T. S. Eliot, the Gospels, Euripides, Carlyle and Marx—to dive anywhere into the great works of European civilization in search of inspiration and revelation. His favourite quotation was from Dostoevsky: 'I want to be there when everyone suddenly understands what it has all been for.' He was collecting documents in Australian history which were shortly to be published as a book, and he set his students to studying them. His lectures were like secular sermons. The travails and tragedy of men, the struggle against evil in human affairs, and the coming of European civilization to Australia were his great themes. He was coming to believe that it might be possible for him to write a book in which he endowed Australians with the great and tragic stories of how they came to be. Unlike the history books written by his predecessors, it would not celebrate Australia as an offshoot of the British Empire. His heroes would be the Australian people themselves. He had glimpsed the outlines of *A History of Australia*.

Roosevelt's New Deal and the economic theories of J. M. Keynes inspired the government to believe that the individualist vigour of free enterprise could be combined with socialism's broad commitment to social justice. Even before the war had ended, the government began to lay the foundations of a mixed economy underpinned by a strong social welfare system. Child endowment, maternity allowances, and invalid and old age pensions were improved. Generous unemployment, sickness and hospital benefits were introduced. The government's plans for a comprehensive national health scheme, however, were thwarted by opposition from the conservative medical profession, whose representative body still bore the imperial title, the *British* Medical Association. The government also overhauled the Commonwealth Bank, making it responsible for overseeing the private banks and charging it with maintaining three ideals: a stable currency, national prosperity and, most radically, full employment.

The classes of women who had donned overalls and taken up spanners to help the war effort were now encouraged to return to their homes. As young couples married and started families, the building industry was faced with an insatiable demand for new houses. But the frustrations were many: skilled tradesmen and building materials were in short supply. Despite such shortages, Australian factories bought new machinery and increased their work-forces to satisfy the postwar clamour for wirelesses, cars, refrigerators and stoves. The American automotive firms, Chrysler, International Harvester and Ford all increased their operations in Australia, not least because the Labor government used public money to build huge plants for General Motors which produced GM's Australian car, the Holden. The cars made their way into Australian hearts. The profits went home to America. To the frustration of Australian motorists, the government continued to ration petrol, not because it was hard to obtain, but because it was an import which had to be paid for in American dollars. On the other hand, exports began to rise: shortages in Europe increased demand for Australian wool, wheat, meat, dairy produce, canned fruit and dried fruits. A long period of economic boom was unfolding.

In 1949 the government commenced the titanic Snowy Mountains Scheme, the largest public works project ever undertaken in Australia. By building great reservoirs and driving tunnels through the hearts of mountains, the Scheme's engineers planned to harness the wild waters of the Snowy River in southern New South Wales. Water plunging into underground power-stations would drive electricity generators, and then would be forced beneath the mountains and into the Murray and Murrumbidgee rivers where it would swell the supplies for irrigation.

The Scheme had almost universal support, for a great certainty had swept the land. The eyes of Asia, people said, would gaze greedily at Australia as long as vast acres languished unused. The deserts must be irrigated, farmed, civilized and claimed. Cities must rise in the wilderness. The forests must be turned to productive use. Idle nature must be put to work. Only then would the white man truly possess Australia.

But none of this was possible unless Australians increased their own numbers. The nation must 'populate or perish'. The Minister for Immigration, Arthur Calwell, announced that Australia would accept refugees, 'displaced persons' (DPs), from Eastern Europe on the condition that, for two years after their arrival, they work on projects designated by the government. Between 1942 and 1952, around 170 000 DPs were shipped off to somewhere called 'Australia'. At the outset, most Australians saw this as an isolated act of charity. They believed that their principal source of immigrants would continue to be Britain. Young British men and women were offered their chance to escape the Old World: for only £10 they could set sail for a prosperous new life in a blessed new land.

But Britain too was embarked on a process of postwar reconstruction, and young British workers had more reason than ever before to plan a future in their own country. Although the principal source of Australia's migrants continued to be Britain, the Mother Country could no longer fully satisfy the young nation's hunger for population. So Calwell, determined to keep the 'land-hungry Asians' at bay, led a drive to open Australia to workers from mainland Europe, particularly from Holland, Italy, Greece and Yugoslavia. By June 1959, such Europeans would comprise almost half the number of migrants to have arrived in Australia since June 1947. The terms of the White Australia policy where shifting, just a little. But no one foresaw that in the decades to come, these newcomers would work great changes on the culture and society of their adopted home.

Not only was Australia beginning to open itself to the rest of the world, it was also becoming involved in the affairs of its own region. The volatile Minister for External Affairs, Dr Evatt, campaigned at home and abroad for human rights and self-determination. He supported the right of the newly independent India to remain a member of the British Commonwealth. He supported the Indonesians in their struggle for independence from the Dutch. In so doing he helped to dismantle Australia's image in Asia as a pawn of British imperialism. So determined was he that Australia should develop independent and outward-looking defence and foreign policies, that in 1944 he established the ANZAC agreement with a half-hearted New Zealand. The two neighbours agreed that they would defend each other in time of war, that they would collaborate on regional affairs, and that they would oppose any attempt by the USA to claim sovereignty over the countries it had helped defend. In 1948, Evatt's stature in foreign affairs was recognized by his appointment as President of the General Assembly of the United Nations. In that post he treated cold-war warriors with contempt, enraging the Americans with his refusal to support their cold-war strategies for militarizing Europe, and ridiculing any suggestion that Soviet Russia had either the will or the resources to launch a full-scale war against the west. Throughout his public life, the Doc was intellectual, headstrong, brave and reckless. Manning Clark would one day write of him as a visionary who wanted men to have life and have it more abundantly.

As Evatt was all too aware, Australia's relations with the government of its larger neighbour, China, were poor. But in 1948 Mao Zedong drove the corrupt regime of Chiang Kai-shek into exile and established the Communist Party as the all-powerful government of mainland China. The Americans feared that Mao would incite revolution throughout the region, and refused to recognize the new government. Evatt was not a man to be bullied by the US State Department. Senior officers in his own Department of Foreign Affairs urged him to establish diplomatic relations with the new regime. But, for once, Evatt hesitated: the government was facing a federal election. The newly-formed Liberal Party was attempting to tar Labor with the Communist brush. Best delay the decision until after the election. That delay was to last for nearly a quarter of a century.

Labor entered the 1949 campaign exhausted by eight sleepless years in government and by deepening animosities between its own increasingly radical left wing and the powerful Catholic right wing. It had also shackled itself to a new and unpopular policy. Frustrated by a decision of the High Court to disallow a section of his new banking laws, Chifley had announced that the government would nationalize all the private banks. The policy was a godsend for the Leader of the Opposition who now confronted the government on the hustings. Bob Menzies had survived his fall from office and had grown in stature as the leader of the new Liberal Party which he had helped found. He told the people he would lower taxes. He would end petrol rationing. He would abolish Labor's centralized controls on the economy and its attempts to control the banks. The electorate paid heed. Labor's 'socialism' was starting to look old-fashioned. The Liberals were swept into power. But, once in office, Menzies cheerfully adopted many of Labor's initiatives. He kept most of its social welfare policies, its Snowy Mountains Scheme, its immigration policies, and its restructured Commonwealth Bank: he even retained the bank's new Governor, Nugget Coombs. Indeed, there was a broad consensus in postwar Australia that the state had a deep responsibility for relieving hardship and ensuing fair-dealing between people. Even Menzies himself had declared, 'Our social and industrial obligations will be increased. There will be more law, not less; more control, not less.'

The Liberals were a youthful, aristocratic and moderate free-enterprise party. While Menzies beguiled the electorate with his silver tongue, his twinkling eyes and his love of old England, able government ministers such as the punctilious Paul Hasluck, the formal and aristocratic R. G. Casey, the handsome and likeable Harold Holt and the cultivated Percy Spender carried on the work of government. Alarmed at the spread of communism in Asia, the government strengthened its ties with the non-communist regimes of Asia and the Pacific. By 1950, Australia had become involved in financing development schemes throughout the region and in providing training for engineers, doctors, economists and other young professionals who could assist their countries to develop and prosper in ways sympathetic to the West.

When friction between the Soviet-dominated government of North Korea and the capitalist government of South Korea erupted into war in June 1950, the cold-war warriors seemed vindicated. Australia joined an American-dominated United Nations force which unsuccessfully attempted to destroy the Kim Il-Sung government and reunify Korea. Australia's involvement was small, but it was a sign that the Australians were active in the affairs of their own part of the world. It was also a sign that they were determined to keep faith with the USA.

This display of loyalty was soon rewarded. In 1951, Australia, New Zealand and the United States signed the ANZUS security pact under which they agreed to act together if any one of them was attacked. In effect, Evatt's ANZAC treaty had been set aside. Many Australians heaved a sigh of relief; they had secured the protection of a great and powerful friend. ANZUS was a compact which was to dominate Australian foreign and defence policy for more than 40 years, but it was a contract for which the Australians were to pay a Faustian price.

As the chill of the cold war deepened, the Liberals won election after election through the 1950s and 1960s by raising the spectre of communist influence within the ALP and the trade unions. The intelligence services placed artists, writers and activists under surveillance, supplying Liberal government ministers with information which might be used to slur their political opponents. Manning Clark was monitored as a suspected fellow-traveller. In 1949 the intelligence service watched him as he travelled inland to take up the Chair of History at the small Canberra University College. The majority of his students were diplomatic cadets to whom he taught Australian History for the Department of External Affairs. At the end of 1953, intelligence got its way. A man for whom teaching was a reason for living found that he had been deprived of most of his students.

By the mid-1950s, the Australian economy was booming. Migrants from Britain, from the Mediterranean and other parts of Europe continued to arrive by the boatload. Often a young man would arrive alone, find a job, find a place to live and earn enough money to bring out his wife or fiancée to the new land. Throughout the 1950s and early 1960s, few Anglo-Australians appreciated the hardships and the isolation which the newcomers endured. Southern and Eastern European migrants were too often thought of as having escaped from backward, peasant societies—primitive villages in which there was no culture—just poverty and superstition: Australia was obviously a much better place to be. The migrants would be grateful for the jobs they were given, however menial. Some people ridiculed the newcomers as 'wogs' or 'Balts' or 'reffos'. Others welcomed them, with well-meaning condescension, as 'New Australians'. Either way, the newcomers were expected to fit in—or, as the policy-makers put it, to 'assimilate', to abandon their old languages and customs and to embrace a new ideal which had become known as 'the Australian way of life'.

What this 'way of life' was, no one really knew. One thing was certain: it had nothing to do with the bush nationalism of the nineteenth century. The 1950s 'Australian way of life' was concerned with homes and families. Its breeding ground was the great Australian suburbia, where a new pattern of life was coming to be accepted as decent and normal. Young men and women would leave school, find a job, become engaged, marry, negotiate a loan and buy a house, have children, and work to provide them with material goods. Suburban Australians were immersed in a culture which delighted in its own clichés: the 'typical Australian family' would own a Holden motor car, have a Hills hoist—an Australian-made rotary clothes-line—and a barbecue in the back-yard. Dad would mow the lawn with a Victa motor-mower. Mum would do the weekly shopping at one of the new 'self-service' supermarkets which had begun to replace the old, family operated shops. Cut off from regular contact with any other country, Anglo-Australians were becoming well-pleased with their own mediocrity. They didn't want to be exhilarated, or troubled, or impassioned. They wanted security, happiness and four weeks' annual leave. To some it was utopia: the English philosopher Bertrand Russell declared, after a visit to Australia in 1950, that Australians were pointing the way to a happier destiny for man throughout centuries to come. Others were less impressed: legend has it that the American actress Ava Gardner said that Melbourne was the ideal place to make a movie about the end of the world (which, as it happens, was the very reason she had come there). The ascendancy of the Liberals was based on their idealization of the suburban family. Menzies' most loyal support came from this rising middle class whom he extolled as 'the forgotten people': the class of hard-working tax-payers; they were the guardians of the moral, spiritual and economic foundation of the nation—the middle-class home. Unlike the Labor Party, which spoke primarily to working-class men, the Liberals championed the role of the Australian woman as mother, home-maker and guardian of the family. The government won broad support from women with policies such as extended child endowment payments, the provision of free tuberculosis screening, immunization programmes for babies and the supply of free milk for school children.

In this suburban view of what it meant to be 'Australian', communism, homosexuality, deviance of any kind, were met with hostility. Intellectuals were too clever by half. Modern art was the subject of ridicule and mistrust. Books and films were prudishly censored. To many thoughtful men and women in the 1950s, the boundless suburbs were a spiritual wasteland. It was common for artists and writers to flee Australia, to seek intellectual and cultural nourishment in Europe or the United States. But Manning Clark was one of those who stayed. He was determined to write a history of his own people, to show them the richness of their own past, to tell the stories of the land and of the people he loved.

In 1951, Chifley died, and Evatt succeeded him as leader of the Opposition. But it was not 'Doc' Evatt's destiny to bring the heat of his idealism and intellect to the Prime Ministership of Australia. He was about to be frozen out of public life by the stony-eyed servants of the cold war. In 1954, the curtain rose on a political melodrama: a Russian diplomat, Vladimir Petrov and his wife Evdokia, defected. As a federal election approached, the rumour-mongers were sharing their asides with the electorate: Petrov had made revelations: members of Evatt's own staff had been consorting with Russian agents. Menzies remained aloof from the scuttlebutt, but, off-stage, his hearty laughter rang through the dining room of his Melbourne club: his victory at the polls was assured. After the election, Menzies announced the final act. There was to be a Royal Commission into the whole affair. Evatt refused to distance himself from the action. He personally defended his staff before the Commission. But fear and mistrust were all around him. He began to accuse his accusers. Documents had been forged, he declared. A conspiracy was being waged against him. Perhaps, the whisperers said, the Doc was a communist after all; or perhaps he was no longer in full control of his mind.

Evatt was not alone in his suffering. The bitterness of the cold war reached deep into the Labor Party itself. Secretive factions schemed and plotted against each other until, in 1955, the Party was torn apart, the Catholic right forming a new ultra-conservative party, the Democratic Labor Party. The Labor rump languished in confusion, racked by animosity, and unable to make 'socialism' appeal to an increasingly settled and prosperous electorate. When, in 1956, Russian tanks rolled into Hungary, Labor's torment increased as the left was plunged deep into a crisis of self-doubt. Perhaps, after all, Stalin's Russia had not been the ideal new society. Evatt contacted Prime Minister Nehru of India. He urged him to prevail on the Russians to commute many of the death sentences they had imposed on Hungarians. While Evatt worked to save lives, Menzies thundered about the 'Red Terror', implying, all over again, that Dr Evatt was a tool of Moscow.

That same year, 1956, television came to Australia in time to broadcast the opening of the Olympic Games in Melbourne. One October day, as the preparations for the Games were nearing completion, Aborigines living in the desert near Maralinga in

South Australia watched in horror as an evil black mist came rolling through the mulga. With Menzies' secret approval, the British government had tested a nuclear bomb in the Australian desert. During the 1950s, there were seven major nuclear tests at Maralinga and five others elsewhere. The authorities' indifference to the welfare of the Aborigines was matched by their treatment of their own servicemen. While the scientists wore proper protective clothing, Australian soldiers were required to view the 1956 explosion from as close as eight kilometres, dressed in cotton shorts and shirts. As the Olympic torch was carried into the Melbourne Cricket Ground on 22 November, the great international crowd applauded and cheered. None of them knew that in the deserts near Maralinga old Aboriginal people were dying of radiation poisoning. Younger people were gripped by fevers and vomiting. Some people's eyes began to ache and a few were going blind. When the last of the tests were over, the British ploughed their radioactive waste into the desert sands and went home, leaving the land once more to the local Aborigines.

Life for most Aboriginal people in Australia continued to be difficult. Some were left alone on remote traditional lands. Others languished in reserves and missions. A few tribes shared their lands with large-station owners, the men employed as stockmen, some of the women working as domestics and the children sometimes receiving a little whitefella schooling. The old ways were not completely destroyed: away from the white man's sight and sites, many of these tribes continued the rituals of caring for the land, singing its stories and preserving its sacred places. But everywhere Aboriginal health was declining, as poor Western diet, alcohol and tobacco took their toll. Aborigines were still outsiders in their own country, robbed of their lands, unable to vote in the white man's elections and ignored by the urban majority of white Australia.

In 1962 the ANZUS pact began to claim its due. The United States supplied military advisers and equipment to the government of South Vietnam which was involved in a complex civil war with the communist North Vietnam. Australia immediately backed the Americans by sending thirty 'army advisers' of its own. Two years later, the US President, Lyndon B. Johnson, was facing an election. Johnson was a New Dealer who dreamt of 'the Great Society' in which social justice was the right of every US citizen. When his opponents said he was soft on communism, Johnson decided to show the voters that he was no red. Using an unverified report of an attack on a US warship as a pretext, he ordered the US Air Force to bomb North Vietnam.

A great tragedy began to unfold. In November that same year,

Menzies introduced conscription for military service: all 20-year-old men were required to register; conscripts were selected by ballot. Five months later, Menzies committed an Australian battalion to fight alongside the Americans. By 1967 there were 6300 Australians fighting in Vietnam; 40 per cent of them were conscripts.

The relentless brutality of the war was televised into Australian homes, and by 1968 the sounds of protest resounded through the suburbs. Songs of love, dissent and independence recorded in Los Angeles or London were being played on Australian radio. In coffee shops, dance halls and the open air, young men and women played guitars and sang gentle ballads about peace, love and 'alternative reality'. Young people danced with joyous abandon to the rhythm of bands which belted out their celebrations of sex and drugs and rock 'n' roll. A generation was in revolt—against the war, their parents, the system, the suburbs, Uncle Sam, the whole damn mess.

It was the age of the shaman and the charlatan, when the contraceptive pill liberated sexuality, and marijuana was the key to enlightenment. Conservative organizations, including the Liberals, the Democratic Labor Party and the RSL, warned that the countries of South-East Asia would fall like dominoes before the onslaught of communism, and that Australia itself was threatened. In many schools, principals with short hair looked out their office windows in dismay at a rebellious generation of boys who grew their hair long and of girls who wore their dresses short. University student newspapers, filled with radical articles and explicit sexual language, were seized by grim-faced police. Student unions provided sanctuary to 'draft dodgers', young men who were hiding to escape conscription. A generation seemed to be casting aside the values of security, the home, decency, hygiene, sexual morality and respect. For every father who abused the communists and the radicals and the filthy long-haired hippies, there was a son who imagined himself forced to napalm a Vietnamese village, and who knew that it was wrong. In the minds of the young, it was the Age of Aquarius: nothing would ever be the same again.

In 1970 a series of great anti-war rallies, 'the Moratoriums', was held in Australian cities. As typists, clerks and managers gazed down from their office windows, the city streets of Melbourne were packed with chanting protesters—block after block of noisy people and coloured banners. When they came to a halt they were addressed by speakers including Dr Jim Cairns, a senior Labor Member of the House of Representatives. The people, he declared, had a right to defy those immoral laws which prevented them from marching in the streets and handing out political leaflets on the footpath. He told the people that the killing and the maiming in Vietnam must end. The people's voice was ringing in the streets, and resounding across the world. The old order was trembling.

The questions multiplied. In 1971, the South African rugby team, the Springboks, toured Australia. They were the heroes of the white supremacists. Everywhere they played the Springboks were met by the roar of demonstrators. In Melbourne protesters who ran on to the pitch were seized by the hair and dragged screaming from the ground by mounted police. From the grand-stands, the rugby fans hooted with delight. They believed that protests against South Africa's system of apartheid had no place at a football match. At the same time, demonstrators standing in the 'outer' chanted with rage and disbelief. Some hurled bottles, cans and firecrackers, attempting to injure the police patrolling the ground.

In Sydney, a powerful building workers' union took direct action of a more peaceful kind. Under the leadership of their secretary, Jack Mundey, the workers placed so-called 'green bans' on certain construction projects whose design would destroy historical sites, parkland or bush. Throughout Australia, concern for the environment was beginning to temper the national enthusiasm for development.

Women, too, were on the move. In 1969, the Women's Liberation Movement was launched in Adelaide. The following year, an expatriate academic, Germaine Greer, published *The Female Eunuch*, which demanded new freedom for women who were sick of powdering their noses and putting up with domineering men. By 1970, women's organizations and trade unions were demanding that the Arbitration Court award women equal pay with men. At the same time the Women's Electoral Lobby gave women a voice in Australian politics, publishing surveys which enabled voters to see where individual candidates stood on the rights and concerns of women.

Throughout the 1960s Aborigines had begun to find a stronger voice in white Australia through community leaders such as Charles Perkins and the poet Kath Walker (later known as Oodgeroo Noonuccal). In 1967, a national referendum was passed by a massive majority of white Australians declaring that Aborigines were full citizens of Australia. The will for change was clear. But, despite the government's expressions of goodwill towards them, thousands of Aborigines continued to languish in poverty. In the mid-1960s, they comprised only 3 per cent of the population of Western Australia, but they occupied 30 per cent of the gaol cells. In January 1972, Aboriginal protesters erected tents on the wide stretch of European lawn in front of Parliament House in Canberra. They declared themselves to be an embassy representing the Aboriginal nation and demanded the return of their lands. The demand for land rights was about to become a pre-eminent issue in Australia.

The tide of idealism had turned against the Liberals. After Menzies retired in 1966 to live out his days in the leafy groves of 'Yarraside', the government was led by a succession of men, some of them spirited individualists, but none of them able to free the Party from its frightened elitism, and all of them bogged down in the bloody quagmire of Vietnam. It was time for change. The struggle against the war had transformed the Labor Party. So too had the changing composition of the work-force: for the first time white-collar jobs outnumbered blue-collar. The old working-class activists were joined by middle-class, university-educated re-formers like Dr Cairns. The party held its working-class appeal, but it now spoke to the progressive elements in the bourgeoisie as well. The spirit of liberalism had abandoned the Liberal Party and had once more joined hands with the Left.

At last, the Labor Party was united behind a new leader, a giant of a man who was articulate, cultivated and inspirational. The conservatives loathed him. One Sunday, as the decisive federal election of December 1972 drew near, Gough Whitlam stepped to the microphone in a hall in the city of Queanbeyan, near Canberra. As he spoke, he held a crowd of men and women from all walks of life in rapt attention. Seated among them was a professor from the Australian National University; he was Australia's best-known historian, Manning Clark. That night tears came to his eyes as he rose to his feet with his fellow Australians and clapped and stamped and cheered when Whitlam told them that, when he became Prime Minister of Australia, the last vestiges of colonialism would disappear. The years of shame in Vietnam, the mistreat-ment of the Aborigines would come to an end. To Manning Clark, it seemed in that moment that the years of unleavened bread were over. At long last Australians had a teacher who might lead them out of the darkness into the light, always provided they did not cut him down, that they spared him a little before he went from hence and was no more seen.

When the votes were counted on election night, it was found that a safe majority of the people had declared an end to 23 years of conservative rule. The Whitlam era had begun. Among conserva-tives, there was panic. Some predicted that communism, feminism and free love would sweep the nation. The military agencies of the United States were appalled: Whitlam was some sort of socialist patriot who threatened to undo the deep security relationship between the two countries, and whose supporters were clamouring for the removal of US military bases from Australian soil. Once again, men in grey suits met behind closed doors and planned what might be done to rescue democracy from itself.

In its first four weeks, the new government abolished conscription and released the conscientious objectors from gaol. It recognized three communist countries, Vietnam, East Germany and Australia's largest buyer of wheat, China. It announced plans for education reform, it spoke of justice for Aborigines and unveiled its free medical scheme for all Australians. The hunting of endangered crocodiles, and the export of crocodile and kangaroo skins were banned. The great symbol of 1960s liberation, the contraceptive pill, was placed on the pharmaceutical benefits list. For the first time, the Labor Party spoke out on women's issues: old ways die hard, but feminism was at last becoming part of the Labor agenda.

Early in the New Year, the imposing figure of Lionel Murphy, Labor's gracious and reformist Attorney-General, presented his passport at Heathrow. He had come to London to negotiate the end of Britain's remaining legislative powers over its former colonies, and to end legal appeals to the supreme court of the old Empire, the Privy Council. Henceforth, Australia's own High Court would be the final court of appeal. The system of British imperial honours—knighthoods and the like—was abolished in favour of a new Order of Australia. The Liberals clung to their colonial traditions, and blustered with indignation.

Over the next three years the confident ministers of the Whitlam government set out to transform Australian society. They cut import tariffs by 25 per cent to increase the efficiency of industries which had grown lazy with excessive protection. With Government support, the Arbitration Commission introduced the principle of equal pay for women. A new Family Law Act simplified divorce. An elected Council of Aborigines was set up to advise the minister of Aboriginal Affairs, and spending on Aboriginal welfare was increased. Whitlam – a lover of art, scholarship and good books – doubled expenditure on education, abolished university fees and introduced grants for tertiary students in financial need. Money was lavished on the arts; creative people involved in literature, theatre, painting, film, music and dance revelled in an endless summer of creative nationalism.

Many urban Australians had begun to delight in their own ethnic diversity. In Melbourne and Sydney particularly, immigrant Greeks, Italians, Serbs, Croats, Maltese—any number of national groups—had established churches and clubs and shops. In the Barossa Valley in South Australia, Germans had established a flourishing wine industry; the macho Australian idea that wine was a pansy's drink was breaking down. In the rich Murrumbidgee Irrigation Area, Italians, Spaniards and South Americans joined the many others who had raised farms, orchards and towns from the wilderness.

The new spirit of tolerance was far from universal: there were still Australian-born men and women who resisted this diversification: employers who discriminated against workers of Mediterranean origin: factories where migrant women were forced to work in sweat-shops under conditions no Anglo women would tolerate: thugs who would thump any wog bastard who dared spout his lingo in the street. There were migrant groups, too, who attempted to revive Old World animosities against other ethnic groups. Labor's Minister for Immigration, Al Grassby, was a colourful, gregarious politician. The son of Spanish and Irish parents, he ridiculed the orthodoxy which said that migrants should be expected to assimilate to some imaginary, ideal Australian culture. The new government would celebrate and encourage the ethnic diversity of Australia. This new ethos was proclaimed as 'multiculturalism'. The government established multilingual radio and television stations. Many native-born Australians were frightened by these developments. In the next election Grassby lost his seat. But the conservatives were too late. The idea that all Australian citizens should conform to a single culture was officially dead. No subsequent government has sought to revive it.

The reforms of the Whitlam government made many enemies. Business, long used to the idea of centralized wage-fixing, was outraged when the government sought to regulate prices. There were those who said that Whitlam might even try to nationalize foreign-owned companies. Since the 1960s, the mining industry had been booming, but Labor was questioning the cost of subsidizing foreign mining companies, which expatriated their profits. If more of the income from mining went to the Australian government, then Australia's minerals could become a source of enormous public wealth. Whitlam was a dangerous man.

At an election on 18 May 1974, the Whitlam government again won a safe majority in the House of Representatives, the chamber where the government is formed. In the Senate, the chamber which represents not the people but the individual states, the numbers were evenly poised. The new term began badly. The engines of Western capitalism were being throttled by a crisis in the supply of oil from the Middle East. Everywhere, inflation was rising. In Australia, the unions, basking in the luxury of the first

Labor government for a generation, were campaigning for higher and higher wages. The spiral seemed to be out of control. The government was rich in critiques of capitalism, but less well endowed with expertise for making it work. The situation was not improved by the appointment of Dr Cairns as Treasurer. The gentle man, who had inspired multitudes when he spoke about peace, civil disobedience and human dignity, reassured few that he could manage an economy. A philosopher of the decade of love, he candidly expressed the affection he shared with his private secretary, Junie Morosi. The warmth of their relationship stirred the gutter instincts of the newspapers as the press barons became determined to bring the government down.

But the Party's supporters kept the faith. There was much to do. Rex Connor was an old-fashioned Labor patriot, with a big belly and generous dreams. He believed that the oil crisis need not trouble Australians. Inspired by the success of the Snowy Mountains Scheme, Connor planned a great pipeline carrying natural gas from the rich oil fields of Western Australia across the continent to the homes and factories of the eastern states. He had schemes to convert coal to motor fuel, and uranium to yellow cake. He would develop the coal fields and the ports, and electrify the interstate rail system. He would reclaim Australia's resources from the American and Japanese multi-national companies, and would enrich Australians for generations to come. Labor was going to 'buy back the farm'.

The sober men in Treasury and the Commonwealth Bank were unlikely to co-operate. They bleated about inflation. The country could never service the necessary loan. But Labor would not be defeated by small-minded bureaucrats who—anyway—had risen to power during the long grey years of conservative rule. Connor contacted a Pakistani middle-man, Tirath Khemlani, who claimed he could raise US$4000 million in the Middle East. The loan was approved at a meeting of the Executive Council at Whitlam's official residence, the Lodge in Canberra, on the second Friday in December 1974. It was Friday the thirteenth.

On Christmas Day two weeks later, tropical cyclone Tracy descended on the defenceless city of Darwin, flattening hundreds of houses. A few days later, a ship crashed into Hobart's principal bridge, bringing road traffic between the two sides of the harbour to a standstill. The times were out of joint. Whitlam was not at home when he was needed: he was overseas, playing statesman on the world stage. To some, his absence looked like arrogant indifference. It was to be Whitlam's last Christmas in power.

In the course of the next six months, Labor lost two of its

senators. In defiance of convention, conservatives contrived to replace them by appointing one independent and one obscure Labor renegade who had vowed to bring down Gough Whitlam. Without a single vote being cast, the government had lost control of the Senate. Politics blazed from the front-pages of the newspapers as the government forged on in chaotic splendour. When the disorganized Dr Cairns inadvertently misled Parliament, Whitlam sacked him. There were other resignations, other Cabinet reshuffles. In October came the most damaging scandal of all. The press revealed that Rex Connor had lied to Whitlam, to the Cabinet and to the Parliament. Determined to pursue his vision, Connor had continued to negotiate with Khemlani, even though his authority to do so had been withdrawn. The press seized on these secret loan negotiations, promoting them as 'the Loans Affair'. Khemlani was flown into Australia and paraded before the television cameras, so that people could see the oily little man who had been grafting for the government. Connor resigned, a broken-hearted man. But the conservatives wanted more: there were calls for an election. Whitlam travelled the land. He was still magnificent. The waverers wanted to be reassured.

In Canberra, Malcolm Foster, the stoic Leader of the Opposition and squire of Australia Felix, felt his destiny stir within him. This rabble of trade unionists, pinkos, feminists and star-gazers had shown themselves unfit for government. The country was being ravaged by industrial unrest and inflation. Fraser had been raised as the son of squatters and educated by the schoolmasters of 'Yarraside'. He knew it was the function of his class to rule, and he believed, as a matter of honour, that it was their responsibility to rule in the interests of all. The majority which the conservatives had achieved in the Senate would be his weapon to undo the follies of democracy.

In October 1975, the government introduced its Budget for the coming year. All eyes were on the Senate. Would Fraser use his majority in the Senate to starve the elected government of funds? Labor experts on the Constitution said that such an action would breach the fundamental convention that the government is formed in the lower house. But Fraser was not interested in constitutional niceties; the government had to be stopped. The Senate blocked the Budget. The government ran out of money. It could no longer pay public servants. The press gave the impression that the country was days away from bankruptcy, that the secret loan negotiations had been the government's shady attempt to forestall the inevitable crisis. An opinion poll showed that about half the electorate believed that the issues should be resolved by a general election.

Whitlam was defiant. He would advise the Governor-General, Sir John Kerr, to call an election for half the Senate. The people would back the visionaries and restore Labor's majority in the Upper House. And the Governor-General would do his duty: he would observe constitutional convention and follow the advice of his Prime Minister. But Whitlam had misjudged his man. Sir John had become absorbed with the principle that his office placed him above politics. The letter of the Constitution endowed him with sweeping powers which most legal commentators believed could be exercised only on government advice. But Kerr sought other counsel. He consulted the ultra-conservative Chief Justice, Sir Garfield Barwick. Barwick gave him an extraordinary opinion: the Governor-General need not accept the advice of his Prime Minister. Unlike its British counterpart, the Australian government held office only at the pleasure of the Crown. The Governor-General could dissolve Parliament, and call a general election on his own initiative.

The army was placed on stand-by. Formidable forces of the state and capital were massing against the government. On the morning of 11 November 1975, Kerr took upon himself the full and terrible authority of an autocratic colonial governor. When Whitlam arrived at Government House to recommend an election for half the Senate, Kerr refused to hear his advice. He handed him a letter of dismissal. Fraser, who was waiting in a nearby room, was appointed caretaker Prime Minister on the understanding that a general election would be held as soon as possible. When the news broke that Whitlam had been sacked, prices on the stock exchanges soared as stockbrokers cheered with relief and joy. Champagne flowed in the Melbourne Club where the lights burned late into the night.

By 5 o'clock, Australian cities were surging with stunned Labor demonstrators. There had been a 'constitutional coup'. Whitlam's eloquence brought tears of devotion and rage to the eyes of the faithful. If he had sounded the clarion of revolution, thousands would have manned the barricades. But Whitlam was a Fabian and a man of reason. He believed that parliamentary democracy had the power to transform a nation. His own eloquence would convince the voters to restore the rightful government of Australia to power. The President of the Australian Council of Trade Unions, Bob Hawke, told unionists to avoid direct action. Labor's best chance was a peaceful election campaign. One radical trade union leader, John Halfpenny, had the words of a revolutionary song by Henry Lawson pinned to his office wall. It was a song which had often stirred the blood of Manning Clark:

We'll make the tyrants feel the sting
Of those that they would throttle
They needn't say the fault is ours
If blood should stain the wattle.

Was that the ethos the unions would adopt? No, Halfpenny told a newspaper reporter: political violence in Australia was always instigated by the Establishment; never by the forces challenging the Establishment. Labor would regain office by constitutional means.

Each leader was vilified by the supporters of the other as a dictator, a megalomaniac, and an enemy of decency. The papers maintained their campaign against Labor. As the election approached, the Melbourne *Age* published a photograph on its front page of Malcolm Fraser petting his favourite dog. On page five was a blurred photograph of Gough Whitlam, wearing a skull cap at a Jewish festival. At the election on 13 December, Fraser won by the biggest landslide in Australian history. The Liberals and the Governor-General declared themselves vindicated. The people had decided. But the rage in Labor ranks would not die down: Fraser had seized power by perverting the Constitution. In their eyes, his administration was never the legitimate government of Australia.

Manning Clark viewed the election from the remoteness of Derby in England. For him, it was a day of tragedy and shame, a day when the Australian electors, bombarded for months by stories of incompetence, bungling and corruption, had returned to government a group of men who had the moral values of a troop of boy scouts and the economic values and social values of a right-wing junta. In the following year, Clark became a familiar figure on Australian television, with his broad hat, his flowing white hair and white beard. He had become a prophet, proclaiming to the foolish people whom he loved that they had cut down a giant, that they had turned from the path of life and richness and independence, that they had abandoned the Kingdom of the Spirit and returned to the Kingdom of Nothingness. 'The dreams of humanity,' he later wrote, 'had ended in an age of ruins.'

Inflation was running at 16.9 per cent. Nearly 300 000 Australians were unemployed. Fraser was grim: the cure would be austere. Government spending would be slashed. Wages would have to fall. 'Life,' he warned, 'wasn't meant to be easy.' It seemed to Labor supporters that the cold mantle of conservatism had once more settled over Australia.

Once in power, however, Fraser's severity was tempered by a patrician sense of duty towards the poor and the disadvantaged.

Despite his autocratic pronouncements, he retained most of the reforms introduced by the Whitlam government. He advanced Whitlam's Aboriginal policies by passing a law which recognized Aboriginal land rights in the Northern Territory. To the dismay of some of his supporters, Fraser was an immovable advocate of sanctions against racist South Africa. To the bewilderment of monarchists, he held a referendum to choose a national anthem to replace the imperial 'God Save the Queen'. But to the satisfaction of the conservative medical profession, he abolished Labor's universal health benefits scheme.

By the early 1980s, with Fraser's support, 'multiculturalism' had become a new orthodoxy in Australia. Cultural diversity had transformed the appearances of Sydney and Melbourne: old Australians were growing accustomed to the sight of Orthodox and Italianate churches, shop-signs in foreign languages and houses painted in exuberant Mediterranean colours. While new languages percolated through the hubbub of the streets, tantalizing smells wafted from the new food shops and restaurants which were transforming Australia's dull, traditional cuisine. But multiculturalism had its opponents, especially among conservatives and country people. As Australia opened its gates to thousands of refugees from Vietnam and other parts of South-East Asia, there were some commentators who predicted that Australia was about to fragment into a nation of tribes.

The era conservative Anglo-Australians longed for, the era of Mr Menzies and the 'Australian way of life', was gone forever. Most people were now on first-name terms with each other. Respectable women no longer wore gloves in the street. The grey felt hat, a symbol of male conformity, had all but disappeared. Divorce rates were climbing. Homosexuality was becoming more open. It was seen as acceptable, even sensible, for young couples to live together before they married. Australia was awakening to a pluralism and informality which 'the straiteners' could do little to resist.

Also gone was the old sense of suburban prosperity and well-being. The economic problems ran deep. The gap between rich and poor had begun to widen. Increasingly, the waste and misery of unemployment was breaking the hearts of breadwinners aged over 50 and of the young. Suburban moralists reviled them as 'dole bludgers', and many conservative parliamentarians seemed to share this view. A Royal Commission showed that the social welfare system itself had become a poverty trap for a new class of outcasts and unemployed. Rural production, for so long the basis of Australian wealth, was in crisis. Not only had it become impossible for most Australian farmers to sell inside the European Economic Community, but they were being undercut by Europeans dumping subsidized produce around the world. Huge American suppliers of subsidized wheat were competing in Australia's markets. Commodity prices tumbled. Manufacturers, especially in the clothing industry, were unable to compete with cheap goods made in Asia. The car industry was inefficient. Mining, however, remained productive for the time being, buoyed up by the smelters and manufacturers of the dynamic East Asian economies. The corporate sector began talking of a resources boom. Perhaps Australia could quarry its way back to prosperity.

In the midst of this tumult, Fraser appeared to be an increasingly lonely leader. His apparent disdain divided and embittered the nation which he had sought to rescue from itself. He spoke of stimulating investment and introduced a regime of tariffs, subsidies and tax concessions to encourage local and foreign capital. At the same time he lectured ordinary wage-earners about 'sacrifice' and railed against inflation, idleness and union power. Soon after he took office, he froze wages: the working person's pay would rise to keep pace with the cost of living, but no further. It was a policy which could have been presented in moderate terms. But to Fraser, moderation was a sign of weakness. His message was curt. Self-advancement, it seemed, was only for the rich. When he relented, and allowed wages to be fixed by 'collective bargaining' between workers and employers, the new policy created the conditions for a wages explosion in the early 1980s.

During the 7 years and 4 months that Fraser remained in office, the opposition Labor Party transformed itself. Whitlam resigned in December 1977 to be replaced by the decent, good-natured Bill Hayden. By 1981, the television cameras were focused over Hayden's shoulder, on the charismatic leader of the trade union movement, Bob Hawke. Hawke was a larrikin, a legendary drinker and a populist with a flair for resolving disputes. He made no secret of his ambition. His father, a preacher, had told him that one day he would be Prime Minister.

The transition was swift. In a matter of months, Hawke had entered Parliament, dislodged Hayden and, on election night in March 1983, set the usually self-possessed Malcolm Fraser trembling with tears. Labor was back in power. To Manning Clark it seemed that the politics of fear had been defeated by Hawke's politics of hope: 'Women wept when they heard him, old men began again to dream dreams, and the young, if not to see visions, then at least to entertain hope again.'

Clark himself was now a revered public figure. Despite the fact that he was a jeremiah who proclaimed spiritual truths to this most secular of peoples, no other academic was held in such high popular esteem and affection. To the Labor Party he had become a seer, his great *History* seeming to entrust Labor with the torch of Australian nationalism which would light the way towards the proud and independent republic which Australia must soon become.

Like governments around the world, the new Labor administration found that, in economic matters, it was little more than a committee of management in the midst of a global economy. The old Keynesian theories had faltered. The protectionist consensus of postwar Australia was crumbling. Scarcely anyone in the Labor Party spoke of socialism any more. Hawke saw himself as a healer, as a man whose destiny it was to forge a new consensus between labour and capital. Under his leadership, with his savvy Treasurer Paul Keating at his side, unions, big business and government set about 'restructuring the economy': their agenda was to reduce labour costs, transform the wage-fixing process, increase 'flexibility' of work practices, and open the economy to competition. The dollar was floated. Foreign banks were welcomed. An 'Accord' was struck between the new government and the trade unions. The unions agreed to exercise wage-restraint and to co-operate in the much-needed restructuring of inefficient industries. In return, the government undertook to maintain the so-called social wage by upholding the welfare system and restoring the national health benefits scheme. Some Labor cynics said that Hawke and Keating were implementing policies more conservative than those of Fraser. Certainly, deregulation had its costs. Control of the exchange rate passed to 'screen jockeys' of the international currency market; unemployment remained around 10 per cent. The division between rich and poor continued to widen. But Marx was dead; Menzies was dead: the majority of voters saw no alternative. As the Liberals moved further to the laissez-faire right, Labor maintained its control over the federal Parliament. In the years which followed, Hawke was destined to be usurped by his Treasurer, the republican Paul Keating. Under his leadership, new challenges replaced the old. New acts of courage, treachery and folly were added to the store of Australian folklore.

The principal events which stirred Manning Clark as he wrote the six volumes of his mighty work had now been played out. In a history book there can be no conclusion. Nothing is ever quite resolved. But on 26 January 1988 there was a conclusion of a sort. As a massive crowd gathered on the sun-drenched shores of

Sydney Cove, a magnificent fleet of sailing ships broke on to the clear, blue waters of the Harbour, to be greeted by flotillas of colourful boats and yachts. At the height of a glorious Australian summer's day, white Australians on the cliffs and beaches shouted and cheered and waved flags. They were celebrating the bicentenary of the First Fleet. On a headland high above the water, a group of Aborigines assembled beneath the Aboriginal Flag, declaring that, for them, there was nothing to celebrate. In protest they threw a history of Australia, published to coincide with the Bicentenary, into the sea. Amid the laughter, the pageantry and the colour, the Aborigines' patient vigil stirred the conscience of White Australia. Many whites knew at last that, in this most blessed among nations, there was a great and lingering wrong which needed to be put right. As the tall ships dropped anchor and a costumed Governor Phillip stepped ashore, the promise of a new beginning hung in the air above Sydney Cove. It hangs there still.

This brief account of the years following 1935 is written from secondary sources, including: **General histories:** Geoffrey Bolton, *The Middle Way 1942–1988*, volume 5 of *The Oxford History of Australia* (1990); F. Crowley, *A New History of Australia* (1974); Russel Ward, *Concise History of Australia* (1992); F. G. Clarke, *Australia: a concise political and social history* (1992); W. F. Mandle, *Going it Alone* (1977).

Additional sources include: **1939–45 War:** Tom Frame, *Pacific Partners: A History of Australian-American Naval Relations*, (1991); Ian Morrison, *This War Against Japan*, (1943); M. McKernan, *Australians in Wartime* (1980); P. Ryan, *Fear Drive My Feet* (1959); **Chifley government:** L. F. Crisp, *Ben Chifley* (1961); Allan Dalziel, *Evatt the Enigma* (1967); **Menzies:** Cameron Hazlehurst, *Menzies Observed* (1979); David Day, *Menzies and Churchill at War* (1986); I. M. Cumpston, *Lord Bruce of Melbourne* (1989); Judith Brett, *The Forgotten People* (1992); **post-war society:** Richard White, *Inventing Australia* (1981); John Rickard, *Australia: A Cultural History* (1988); **Manning Clark's life and ideas:** Manning Clark, *A Short History of Australia*, first published in 1963 and last updated in 1986; the second volume of Clark's autobiography, *The Quest for Grace* (1991); his *Occasional Writings and Speeches* (1980); also Stephen Holt, *Manning Clark and Australian History* (1982); Fiona Capp, *Writers Defiled: Security Surveillance of Australian Authors and Intellectuals, 1920–1960* (1993).

My sincere thanks to Dymphna Clark, Sebastian Clark, Dr Axel Clark, Dr David Goodman and Professor Stuart Macintyre, each of whom read and suggested corrections and improvements to drafts of this chapter.

Index